Handbook of Energy Law in the Low-Carbon Transition

De Gruyter Handbuch

Handbook of Energy Law in the Low-Carbon Transition

Edited by
Giuseppe Bellantuono, Lee Godden, Hanri Mostert,
Hannah Wiseman and Hao Zhang

DE GRUYTER

ISBN 978-3-11-075233-5
e-ISBN (PDF) 978-3-11-075240-3
e-ISBN (EPUB) 978-3-11-075245-8

Library of Congress Control Number: 2022949431

Bibliographic information published by the Deutsche Nationalbibliothek
The Deutsche Nationalbibliothek lists this publication in the Deutsche Nationalbibliografie; detailed bibliographic data are available on the Internet at http://dnb.dnb.de.

Typesetting: WMTP GmbH, Birkenau
Printing and binding: CPI books GmbH, Leck
Cover image: Gettyimages/alexsl

www.degruyter.com

Tracy-Lynn Field

Preface

This magisterial work on energy law in the low-carbon transition aims to define and explore the variety of legal pathways that developed and developing jurisdictions have set upon or charted to deal with the climate crisis. The notion of a legal pathway, initially formulated by Gerrard and Dernbach, provides an organizing conceptual frame for the book's comparative, multi-layered approach which aims to discern similarities, differences and connections across regional, national and local scales.

The volume highlights the significance of institutional contexts, with a view to better informing the legal feasibility of low-carbon transition scenarios. As the editors point out in the Introduction, feasibility analyses of low-carbon transition scenario modelling that rely on indicators obscure the reality of context-dependent and geographically differentiated legal pathways. As a result, institutional feasibility concerns are significantly greater than technological or economic feasibility concerns.

A context-sensitive approach is required, one that examines the texture of the institutional landscape shaping legal pathways, i. e. the specific allocation of competences across institutional levels, including the degree of centralisation or decentralisation of energy mandates; the relative balance between legislative, executive, judicial and regulatory powers, which determines which tools and decision-making procedures become available for low-carbon transition reforms; the manner in which climate institutions and rules interact with other parts of the legal system; the plurality of legal orders; and the dominant legal interpretive practices. By emphasising the significance of institutional context, the volume therefore pitches for a contribution to multi-, inter- and transdisciplinary studies on the feasibility of low-carbon transition scenarios.

The Handbook is largely successful in these twin aims and its coverage of institutional contexts is impressive. In particular, developing country experiences come to the fore in a variety of ways.

The section on energy markets, for example, includes Chisanga's analysis of trade-offs around nuclear energy in the context of Kenya and Zambia's recent moves to set up institutions, planning frameworks and environmental assessment procedures for nuclear power, while Chege argues that South Africa and Kenya already possess the appropriate institutional infrastructure to take advantage of green hydrogen for production and export. Mitkidis' contribution on greening global value chains (GVCs) in this section is particularly helpful because she tackles a central fault-line in greenhouse gas accounting: National greenhouse gas inventories fail to address the scope 3

Tracy-Lynn Field is Professor in the Wits School of Law, University of the Witwatersrand, Johannesburg, South Africa.

https://doi.org/10.1515/9783110752403-002

emissions that are predominantly produced in developing countries. Her argument for taking GVCs as a basic unit of analysis is well taken, and her analysis of the procurement, reporting, and market-based measures that can be used to decarbonize GVCs is a seminal contribution (albeit that arguments relating to the moral and legal right of developing countries to prosper from scope 3 emissions is not a central focus of this chapter, although explored in another work).

A number of contributions articulate the decarbonisation challenge of the Global South. As Addaney points out in the section on regional experiences, in Africa policy- and decision-makers not only contend with the global imperative of decarbonisation, but also with the critical need to address poverty, famine, and gender inequality. This is not a national or even regional concern, but a global one. As Bhullar points out in her valuable contribution on the diverse meanings of energy justice in the low-carbon transition, in the coming decades developing countries will account for over two-thirds of the world's energy demand. National accounts of legal pathways toward decarbonisation in Brazil, India, Indonesia, and Mexico illustrate some of the difficulties developing countries are facing as they try to balance competing policy demands. Although there is no express treatment of the topic, one should add that these difficult balancing acts occur in a context where developed countries have failed to honour their $100 billion per annum commitment to climate finance, which is likely to be one of the most contentious issues on the COP27 agenda. Accounts of the regional experience in Africa and South America nevertheless highlight the further critical importance of investment frameworks.

The volume's focus on energy law is justified on the basis that a low-carbon transition depends on technological and economic transformations in energy generation, transport and use. And while this is especially true of contexts where high-carbon energy generation, transport, and use are already well-entrenched, it bears repeating that large swathes of the developing world are already "low carbon". The transition work in these contexts is profoundly different from developed nations, and the focus should arguably fall on upscaling the institutions necessary to deal with energy access, droughts, and floods, or how well energy transitions address the nexus of energy, water, food and sanitation. Du Plessis and Moyo, in their contribution on the role of cities in the low-carbon transition, point to the scholarly work that needs to be done in this area. But much work remains to be done. The recent floods inundating a third of Pakistan which UN Secretary-General António Guterres described as the worst climate carnage he had ever seen, the floods that caused billions of rand's worth of damage in South Africa's Kwa-Zulu Natal province, and even Europe's current worst-in-500-year drought underscore the urgency of the work needed on the water and nature transitions that must unfold alongside a low-carbon transition in the coming decades.

The editors and authors of the Handbook must nevertheless be congratulated on a timely and valuable comparative contribution on energy law in the low-carbon transition that illuminates the diversity of legal pathways to a low-carbon future. It amply illustrates the variety of institutional contexts in which legal decision-making must take place and will serve students, policy makers, and legal decision-makers the world over.

Leigh Hancher
Preface

As the introduction to this volume explains, a better understanding of the variety of low-carbon transitions is the primary motivation behind this Handbook. Authors from nineteen countries discuss the legal underpinnings of climate policies in six continents – testifying to this volume's ambitious goals. It aims at identifying similarities, differences and connections across regional, national, and local experience. Importantly, it develops the concept of legal pathways of decarbonization 'to systematically present the components of the institutional contexts directly affecting the pace and direction of the low-carbon transition'.

Undoubtedly, this approach to legal knowledge can improve the interdisciplinary understanding of different decarbonization scenarios. Several chapters expand and develop the concept of legal pathways, inter alia to identify the institutional factors able to influence the low-carbon transition in different jurisdictions. A comparative assessment of this nature allows for a broader assessment of the multiple linkages between energy law, climate law, and the specific institutional contexts in which they are designed and implemented. This is not only of great practical importance, but it will help new scholars tailor a methodology for further research.

The institutional context is rightly understood as both a source of opportunities and constraints for technological, economic, and social changes – and hence as a means to explore legal feasibility of different options towards decarbonisation. This Handbook is an invaluable mapping exercise. It provides the information on which the links between legal feasibility and legal pathways can be identified in most continents, including Europe. Indeed, European energy law and policy features in all five parts of the handbook. This is hardly a surprising result. As Penttinen rightly observes in her chapter, for decades the European Union (EU) has been considered one of the forerunners in deploying a toolbox of various successful policies to stimulate the transition towards a low-carbon energy future and achieve reductions in greenhouse gas emissions, including the launch of the world's first emissions trading scheme (under Directive 2003/87/EC, the 'ETS Directive 2003').

To meet concerns over the pace of climate change and in the light of its commitments under the Paris Agreement, the EU has more recently committed to the adoption of more ambitious goals, culminating in the agreement on the European Green Deal in late 2019, the launch of the 'Fit for 55' exercise in July 2021, and subsequently, a Decarbonisation Package in December 2021. The adoption of Regulation (EU) 2021/1119 (the 'Climate Law') incorporates the goal of climate neutrality in binding EU

Leigh Hancher is Professor of European Law at the University of Tilburg, The Netherlands and part-time Professor at the Florence School of Regulation within the European University Institute, Italy.

https://doi.org/10.1515/9783110752403-003

legislation at the latest by 2050, thus reducing emissions to net zero by that date. These various initiatives include extensive legislative provisions – mostly in the form of regulations, but also secondary legislation, as well as a variety of soft law instruments. Importantly, the Commission updated its guidelines on state aid for climate, energy, and environmental support in January 2022 (the CEEAG).

With the outbreak of the tragic war in the Ukraine and the enormous if unanticipated impact that this is having on the EU's security of gas supply, it remains to be seen whether these ambitions are likely to be realized by 2050. Following the reduction of Russian natural gas flows, massive investments are now being made in securing alternative gas supply – threatening to crowd out available funds for renewable energy projects and even to prolong the EU's dependence on fossil fuels. Even in the absence of these latest events, the achievement of the increasingly ambitious targets adopted during the past few decades has been and still is hampered by limited competences at EU level. Article 194 of the Treaty on the Functioning of the European Union (TFEU) sets out the EU's competences on energy matters. These are shared competences. The common EU energy policy objectives defined at Treaty level include the establishment of an EU wide energy market, security of supply, promotion of energy efficiency and renewable energy as well as interconnection of energy networks in the EU. However, Member States retain competence to determine their own 'energy mix' and to determine the make-up of their own national energy portfolio. How to reconcile the need for common action with individual energy and climate policy goals?

This theme resonates throughout the book's chapters on all matters European. First, the chapters on governance models, policy instruments, and implementation and enforcement mechanisms identify the major legal dimensions of climate policies in the EU and other continents. Second, as the chapter by Wu explains, renewable energy integration into the market is one of the most obvious aspects of energy transition in response to climate change. But decarbonising the electricity sector to achieve carbon emission goals cannot afford to lose robust legal support. Wholesale electricity markets themselves are not sufficient for incentivising renewable energy integration, which necessitates the adoption of legal and regulatory instruments to achieve the goal of decarbonising the electricity sector. The interaction between legal and regulatory instruments promoting renewable energy integration and the wholesale electricity market reform measures pursuing fair prices cannot be ignored because their effectiveness depends on this interdependency.

The third part of the book focusses on regional experiences and includes chapters on cross-border initiatives in the EU. The goal of the contributions to this part three is to assess strengths and weaknesses of regional governance for the low-carbon transition. The EU's approach to decarbonization policies had traditionally focused on sector-specific measures. The so-called '20-20-20' targets might have even contributed to the 'silos' thinking that has dominated the implementation of the various EU legislative tools each designed to further the realization of its sector-specific target by the deadline of 2020.

The fourth part devotes several chapters to national experiences, including three developed countries facing serious implementation problems for their domestic climate policies, including one of the largest Member States, Poland, as well as countries striving to reconcile sustainable development and investment-friendly regulatory frameworks.

The fifth and final part turns to local experiences, the institutional level where expectations for change and fossil fuel use reduction are high, but where many legal barriers to project feasibility remain. This is especially so with reference to energy communities and peer-to-peer energy trading in the EU, concepts which have become more prominent following the adoption of the consumer-focused Clean Energy Package of 2019. As explained, the mainstreaming of community energy requires significant structural adjustment to governance and regulatory systems built around large-scale energy production and distribution.

EU energy law, EU climate law, and the EU energy market and energy policy governance are therefore prominent themes throughout this highly useful Handbook. The various chapters in the five different parts allow for comparative evaluation of the legal and policy instruments as well as for a deeper understanding of the very real legal and political tensions between the national, regional, and wider European levels.

This raises an important question: has the EU (and its member states) performed better in realizing their climate ambitions than other countries? Equally, have recent reforms introduced at EU level galvanized performance within the Union compared to the past? It is interesting to reflect on the results of research into the 2012 EU Energy Efficiency Directive (EED). Differentiated implementation will usually occur when member states makes use of the discretion given to them by EU legislation. The EED indeed offers broad discretion to member states in choosing and specifying targets and measures related to energy efficiency. If differentiated implementation does indeed occur, what does this mean for the effectiveness and legitimacy of the directive in question?

Earlier research has confirmed the importance of path dependency in this respect too. Member states have invariably used the discretion to retain domestic measures that were already in place. This pattern is driven by a combination of inertia and the wish not to disrupt well-working approaches. Overall, the pattern of differentiated implementation that resulted has arguably had a positive effect on goal-achievement as well as domestic acceptance of the EED. At the same time, the EED's impact on domestic policies and approaches has been limited.[1] The EED is now subject to further revision as art of the 'Fit for 55' package mentioned above and as initiated by

1 S. Princen et al., Flexible implementation and the energy efficiency directive, Working Paper, EUI RSC, 2022/31.

the adoption of the new EU Climate Law. It will be recalled that Article 2(1) of the new European Climate Law of 2021 establishes a binding objective of climate neutrality in the EU by 2050, and its Article 4(1) sets a binding EU target of a net domestic reduction in GHG emissions of at least 55% compared to 1990 levels by 2030.

To meet these objectives and targets, the Climate Law requires Member States and EU institutions (including the Commission) to 'prioritise swift and predictable emission reductions' (Art. 4(1)) and to 'take the necessary measures ... taking into account the importance of promoting both fairness and solidarity among Member States and cost-effectiveness in achieving this objective.' (Art. 2(2)). Does this new measure introduce an important step-change to path dependency? Importantly the Commission must now assess the consistency of any draft measure or legislative proposal with the EU's climate targets and objectives before adoption and include that assessment in any impact assessment accompanying these measures or proposals and make the result of that assessment publicly available at the time of adoption (Art. 6(4)). The Commission must also 'endeavour to align' its draft measures and legislative proposals 'with the objectives' of the Climate Law and 'provide the reasons' for any non-alignment. This should eliminate the risk of a 'silo-based' approach.

The new Climate Law only entered into force in July 2021, and at a time when the EU's economy was just beginning to emerge from the national lock downs imposed in response to the COVID pandemic. If economic life was showing signs of returning to normality, that has proved to be a shorted lived intermission. By October 2021 gas and electricity prices were at all-time highs and by February 2022 a full-blown energy security crisis had caused the European Council, the Commission, and the EU member states to turn their attention to dealing with energy shortages over the coming winters.

To borrow from the title of Swora's chapter on the 'Polish Pathway to Just Transition', EU energy law may risk being trapped 'Between Sustainability and Security of Supply'. It is therefore of key importance to all actors concerned, public and private, producers and consumers, traders and network operators, local energy communities, and multinational investors, that there is a clear route to avoid that trap – or at very least – to find a legally feasible way out of it.

This Handbook offers timely guidance – and not just for the EU – but for every jurisdiction that must urgently confront similar challenges.

Table of contents

Part II: **Energy Markets**

Part III: **Regional Experiences**

Part V: **Local Experiences**

Notes on contributors

Giuseppe Bellantuono is Professor of Comparative Law at the University of Trento, Faculty of Law, Italy.

Lee Godden formerly was Professor at the Centre for Resources, Energy and Environmental Law, Melbourne Law School, The University of Melbourne, Australia.

Hanri Mostert is the DST/NRF SARChI Research Chair for Mineral Law in Africa and Professor of Law at the University of Cape Town, South Africa.

Hannah J. Wiseman is a Professor of Law, Professor and Wilson Faculty Fellow in the College of Earth and Mineral Sciences, and Institutes of Energy and the Environment Co-funded Faculty Member, PennState Law, United States.

Hao Zhang is Associate Professor at the Faculty of Law, The Chinese University of Hong Kong.

Leigh Hancher is Professor of European Law at the University of Tilburg, The Netherlands and part-time Professor at the Florence School of Regulation within the European University Institute, Italy.

Tracy-Lynn Field is Professor in the Wits School of Law, University of the Witwatersrand, Johannesburg, South Africa.

Giulia Sonetti is Transdisciplinary Researcher at CENSE – Center for Environmental and Sustainability Research & CHANGE – Global Change and Sustainability Institute, NOVA School of Science and Technology, NOVA University Lisbon, Portugal.

Osman Arrobbio is Researcher at the University of Parma, Department of Humanities, Social Sciences and Cultural Industries, Italy.

Lovleen Bhullar is Assistant Professor at the University of Birmingham, United Kingdom.

Kenneth Richards holds appointments at the O'Neill School, the IU Maurer School of Law, and the Ostrom Workshop in Political Theory and Policy Analysis, Indiana University, United States.

Lisa Benjamin is an Associate Professor at Lewis & Clark Law School in Portland, Oregon, United States.

Kathryn McCallum is Attorney at Keller Rohrback, LLP, Seattle, United States.

Lan Wu is a PhD student at the Faculty of Law, The Chinese University of Hong Kong.

Shaimerden Chikanayev is a PhD Student at the Faculty of Law, The Chinese University of Hong Kong.

Kangwa-Musole George Chisanga is Lecturer, National Institute of Public Administration, Lusaka, Zambia.

John Wiseman is a Senior Research Fellow with Melbourne Climate Futures and an Adjunct Professor at the Melbourne School of Population and Global Health, University of Melbourne, Australia.

Anne Kallies is a Senior Lecturer at the RMIT Graduate School of Business & Law, Melbourne, Australia.

Kennedy Chege is a Researcher and PhD candidate at the DST/NRF SARChI: Mineral Law in Africa (MLiA) Research Chair at the University of Cape Town, South Africa.

Liebrich M. Hiemstra is Researcher at the University of Tilburg, School of Law, The Netherlands and Senior Legal Counsel at Vattenfall, Amsterdam, The Netherlands.

Katerina Mitdikis is Associate Professor at the Department of Law, School of Business and Social Sciences, Aarhus University, Denmark.

Michael Addaney is a Lecturer in environmental policy and sustainability planning at the University of Energy and Natural Resources, Ghana, an Earth System Governance Fellow and Research Associate of the Centre for Public Management and Governance of the University of Johannesburg, South Africa.

Bernard Kengni is Postdoctoral Research Fellow, NRF/DST SARChI Research Chair: Mineral Law in Africa, Department of Private Law, University of Cape Town, South Africa.

Sirja-Leena M. Penttinen is Assistant Director of the Tulane Center for Energy Law, Tulane University, United States.

James W. Coleman is Professor of Law, Southern Methodist University, Dedman School of Law.

Isabella Bellera Landa is an Associate at White & Case LLP, Washington, D.C., United States.

Blair Trahan is an Associate at White & Case LLP, Washington, D.C., United States.

https://doi.org/10.1515/9783110752403-005

Ashley O. Nemeth is an Associate at White & Case LLP, Washington, D.C., United States.
Guilherme Junqueira de Sousa Leal is Partner at Graça Couto Advogados. LL.M in Energy Law from the University College London, UK, and in Environmental Law from the George Washington University, USA.
Mariana Fernandes Miranda is a Lawyer at Graça Couto Advogados. Master in Energy from the Energy and Environment Institute of the São Paulo University, Brazil.
Claire Nan Guo is Associate Professor, Faculty of Law, Jiangnan University, China.
Uday Shankar is Registrar & Professor of Law at Hidayatullah National Law University, India.
Arindam Basu is Assistant Professor at the Indian Institute of Technology Kharagpur, Department of Rajiv Gandhi School of Intellectual Property Law, India.
Satoshi Kurokawa is Professor at the Faculty of Social Sciences, School of Social Sciences, Waseda University, Japan.
Jose Maria Valenzuela Robles Linares is Research Fellow at the Institute for Science, Innovation and Society, University of Oxford, United Kingdom.
Marisol Anglés Hernández is Researcher at the Institute for Legal Research, National Autonomous University of Mexico (UNAM), Mexico.
Mariusz Swora is Senior Partner at the Law Office of Mariusz Swora, Poland and former full member of the EU ACER Board of Appeal.
Uma Outka is William R. Scott Law Professor at the University of Kansas, School of Law, United States.
Annalisa Savaresi is Associate Professor at the Centre for Climate Change, Energy and Environmental Law, University of Eastern Finland.
Saskia Lavrijssen is Full Professor of Economic Regulation and Market Governance of Network Industries at the Law School of Tilburg University, The Netherlands and director of the Tilburg Institute of Law, Technology and Society (TILT).
Leonie Reins is Professor of Public Law and Sustainability at Erasmus School of Law, The Netherlands.
Thijs ten Caten is Student Assistant at Tilburg Institute for Law, Technology, and Society (TILT), Tilburg University, The Netherlands.
Alexandra B. Klass is the James G. Degnan Professor of Law at the University of Michigan Law School.
Christopher Cerny is an Attorney at Winthrop & Weinstine, Minneapolis, United States.
Anél du Plessis is Professor of Law and the South African Research Chair in Cities, Law and Environmental Sustainability, North-West University, South Africa.
Chantelle Moyo is PhD candidate at the South African Research Chair in Cities, Law and Environmental Sustainability, North-West University, South Africa.

Abbreviations

ACER	Agency for the cooperation of energy regulators
AU	African Union
ASEAN	Association of Southeast Asian Nations
COP	Conference of the Parties to the UN Framework Convention on Climate Change
EC	European Commission
ECT	Energy Charter Treaty
EPA	US Environmental Protection Agency
ETS	Emission trading system
EU	European Union
EV	Electric vehicle
FDI	Foreign Direct Investment
FERC	Federal Energy Regulatory Commission
FIP	Feed-in Premium
FIT	Feed-in Tariff
GHG	Greenhouse gas emission
GVC	Global value chain
IAM	Integrated assessment model
IDB	Inter-American Development Bank
IEA	International Energy Agency
IPCC	Intergovernmental Panel on Climate Change
IRENA	International Renewable Energy Agency
NDC	Nationally Determined Contribution
RES	Renewable energy sources
RPS	Renewable Portfolio Standard
UNFCCC	United Nations Framework Convention on Climate Change
USA	United States of America
WTO	World Trade Organisation

https://doi.org/10.1515/9783110752403-006

Giuseppe Bellantuono, Lee Godden, Hanri Mostert, Hannah Wiseman, Hao Zhang

Introduction: Comparing Low-Carbon Transitions

Abstract: The introductory chapter sets out the goals of the Handbook. A large literature has explored the multiple facets of the transition. The Handbook adds to this scientific debate a thoroughly comparative perspective on the legal underpinnings of the transformations taking place in energy systems worldwide. The concept of legal pathways of decarbonisation is proposed as a heuristic device to analyse the institutional contexts influencing the policy choices in each country or region. From an explanatory point of view, the concept of legal pathways draws on comparative legal methodologies to identify the role played by each component of the legal system. From a normative point of view, legal pathways should be integrated into theories of the low-carbon transition and decarbonisation scenarios policymakers rely on. Such integration is needed both to foster the interdisciplinary dialogue and ensure the transition proceeds at the right pace and in the right direction. The chapter concludes with an overview of the five parts of the Handbook.

1 Goals of the Handbook

With the publishing market flooded every year by books and articles related to climate change, a new book on the low-carbon transition calls for a strong justification. When we embarked on this project a few years ago, we thought each of us knew a lot about a little. The 'little', in this case, is the unfolding of the low-carbon transition in the continent where each of us usually works. Our acquaintance with energy and climate law scholars from many countries tells us this is a widespread condition: we all have an in-depth knowledge of the regulatory frameworks closer to us, but only a

Giuseppe Bellantuono is Professor of Comparative Law at the University of Trento, Faculty of Law, Italy.
Lee Godden formerly was Professor at the Centre for Resources, Energy and Environmental Law, Melbourne Law School, The University of Melbourne, Australia.
Hanri Mostert is the DST/NRF SARChI Research Chair for Mineral Law in Africa and Professor of Law at the University of Cape Town, South Africa.
Hannah J. Wiseman is a Professor of Law, Professor and Wilson Faculty Fellow in the College of Earth and Mineral Sciences, and Institutes of Energy and the Environment Co-funded Faculty Member, Penn-State Law, United States.
Hao Zhang is Associate Professor at the Faculty of Law, The Chinese University of Hong Kong.

https://doi.org/10.1515/9783110752403-007

bare understanding of the regulatory frameworks governing the low-carbon transition in other countries and regions. The problem is not the availability of information: climate policies in any place can be easily identified. The crucial issue is how to connect such information to the multiple impacts of the transition. The latter fundamentally transforms traditional legal concepts and the relationships among legal branches. It also presses legal scholars to find new ways to engage in interdisciplinary research and explore the interplay between legal and non-legal dimensions.

A better understanding of the variety of low-carbon transitions is the primary motivation behind this Handbook. Previous legal work focused on climate policies in representative regions and countries (e.g., Hunter et al., 2020; Oyewunmi et al., 2020; Roggenkamp et al. 2021; Reins and Verschuuren, 2022). We expand the reach, with authors from nineteen countries discussing the legal underpinnings of climate policies in six continents. Each chapter can be an entry point to a much larger body of literature. Beyond providing updated information, we aim at identifying similarities, differences, and connections across regional, national and local experiences. We start from the premise that such an approach helps make sense of the transformations taking place on a scale never seen before.

Furthermore, the legal dimensions analyzed in this Handbook should ease the search for the myriad links with non-legal disciplines. In the energy and climate fields, interdisciplinary dialogues are thriving, but face theoretical, practical, and institutional barriers (Sonetti and Arrobbio, in this volume). To a large extent, they are the same barriers any interdisciplinary research involving legal disciplines faces. Though, with regard to climate change, interdisciplinarity is often said to represent the only approach capable of driving the transition in the right direction. We share the view that interdisciplinarity is desperately needed, but we do not subscribe to the position that a single approach should be pursued. Methodological pluralism is better equipped to deal with different problems and the variety of contexts the transition has to face. We propose to rely on the concept of legal pathways of decarbonization to systematically present the components of the institutional contexts directly affecting the pace and direction of the low-carbon transition. We argue that this kind of legal knowledge should be drawn upon to improve the interdisciplinary understanding of decarbonization scenarios.

Which readership do we have in mind? The intended audience includes researchers, policymakers, undergraduate and graduate students. We expect that the wide geographic coverage of the Handbook and its comparative approach will find wide appeal among readers in different roles. Our chief intention is for the Handbook to become the reference point for readers, scholars and practitioners alike, without previous acquaintance with energy law. We also want the Handbook to be a scholarly resource for more experienced readers interested in learning about developments in jurisdictions other than their own. Parts of the Handbook can usefully complement traditional textbooks in courses on energy and climate law taught worldwide. We share the view that finding a place for these topics in the law school curriculum is much more than a professional duty (Ireland-Piper and James, 2021). This Handbook is how we take charge of such a task.

In the balance of this chapter, we first define legal pathways and explain how they relate to the existing literature on the institutional dimensions of the low-carbon transition (sec. 2). We then explain how legal knowledge could be integrated into low-carbon scenarios and transition theories (sec. 3). An overview of the five parts of the Handbook is provided in sec. 4.

2 Finding legal pathways of decarbonisation

The first in-depth treatment of legal pathways was provided by Gerrard and Dernbach (2019). Drawing on the results of the Deep Decarbonization Pathways Project, the book assembled more than 1000 proposals to decarbonize the US economy. The pathways identified by the Project relied on a backcasting approach: assuming that a specific climate target must be achieved by a specified date, the required technological and economic changes are singled out. Gerrard and Dernbach (2019) collected the legal options available in the public and private sectors to support such changes, no matter how politically realistic they might be.

For this Handbook, we expand on legal pathways in several respects. First, we use the concept to identify the institutional factors influencing the low-carbon transition in different jurisdictions. In Gerrard and Dernbach (2019), the focus on a single legal system meant that many factors were left in the background. The shift to a comparative assessment requires instead a broader assessment of the multiple linkages between energy law, climate law, and the specific institutional contexts in which they are designed and implemented. Second, we are interested in understanding the 'legal feasibility' of the low-carbon transition. Each institutional context is hence understood as both a source of opportunities and constraints for technological, economic and social changes. More on this in sec. 3. Third, the interplay between legal pathways and decarbonisation scenarios requires further reflection. In Gerrard and Dernbach (2019), the prevailing approach is instrumental: given a set of technological and economic decarbonisation imperatives, public and private law should pave the way for their accomplishment. The broader geographical scope of the contributions in this Handbook suggests alternative readings. What someone perceives as a barrier could instead be viewed as a preference for a different decarbonisation pathway. Moreover, how the impact of climate policies on different groups is mediated by law directly shapes choices about pathways. Hence, the concept of legal pathways could be useful to refine transition theories proposed in the social sciences and the assumptions underlying climate models.

Moving from the premises mentioned above, we propose the following definition:

> Legal pathways of decarbonisation represent the set of (formal and informal, public and private) institutions, (formal and informal, public and private) legal tools, and interpretative practices available in a specific legal system to pursue decarbonisation goals. Legal pathways interact with political, economic, technological, and social drivers of decarbonization and influence the design and effects of climate policies.

This definition casts the net wide. The breadth and depth of the transformations required by the low-carbon transition suggest that almost no components of each institutional context will be left untouched. The public and the private sectors, as well as formal and informal rules, are expected to be equally relevant. The catchy slogan 'We are all climate lawyers now' (Young, 2021) aptly summarizes the plurality of ramifications, although simply describing them is not enough. The concept of legal pathway becomes useful for analytic purposes if it provides guidance on where to look: which legal dimensions are most relevant? Which institutions? How do the different institutional components interact? A detailed answer to these questions is beyond the scope of this introduction. However, we can guide the reader through the myriad of legal details each jurisdiction displays and aggregate them in a few legal dimensions. We identify such dimensions through studies that analyse variation in the unfolding of low-carbon transitions across regions and countries. Our working hypothesis is that each legal pathway is a peculiar combination of institutions and legal tools. Variation can be expected not only in how institutions and tools are combined but also in how each is shaped by the broader legal context in which it is embedded. In line with what was observed above about interdisciplinarity, we take into account the comparative studies of climate policies proposed in other disciplines, for example comparative environmental politics and comparative institutional economics. Although they often rely on streamlined views of institutions that legal scholars find difficult to accept, they alert us to the mutual interactions between legal and non-legal dimensions. Furthermore, they can highlight factors influencing the shape of legal pathways a purely legal analysis would overlook.

It is useful to distinguish the broader institutional context and the set of climate institutions and policies. They are schematically represented in Figure 1. Understandably, the literature on the low-carbon transition tends to focus on climate institutions and tools. However, it would be a mistake to forget the influence of the broader context. Several components can shape climate institutions and tools. In the environmental law literature, it has been proposed to consider the influence of the main branches of a legal system, from public law to private law to criminal law (Viñuales, 2019, p. 28). As explained below, we place more emphasis on the broader institutional context. The double-sided arrow in Figure 1 signals that climate policies can also influence the latter. For example, the literature on climate constitutionalism shows that climate policies can be reflected at the highest levels in the hierarchy of sources of law (e.g., Ghaleigh et al., 2022).

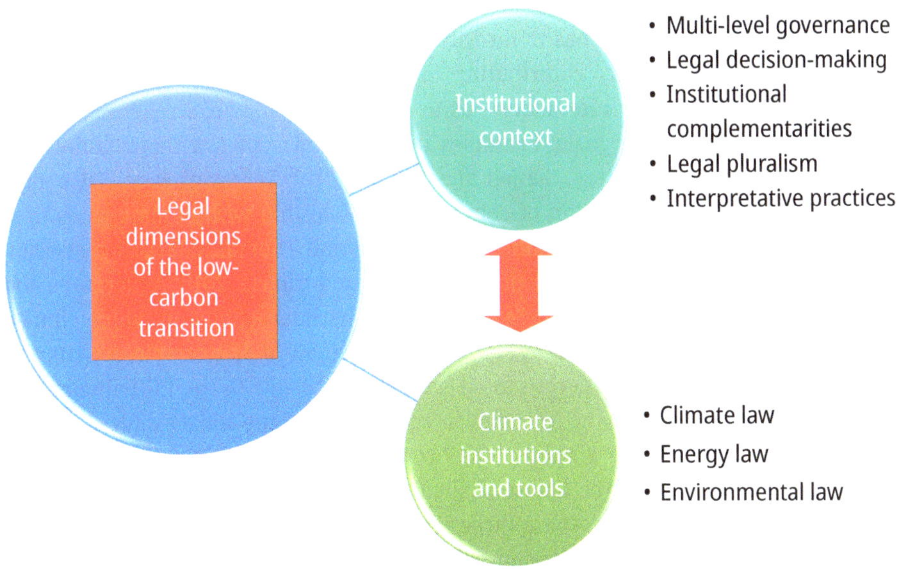

Figure 1: The components of legal pathways.

How should the relationships between the two domains be explored? For this preliminary inquiry, five legal dimensions with a significant impact on climate policies can be singled out:

1. The allocation of competencies across institutional levels directly affects climate policies. Any degree of centralization or decentralization in multi-level systems could foster or hamper the low-carbon transition, depending on interactions with several other factors that affect horizontal and vertical coordination across institutional levels (Balthazar et al., 2020; Sauer and Monast, 2021; Wiseman, in this volume). Many such factors have to do with constitutional architectures and the legal doctrines developed over decades, if not centuries, to give them stable meanings.
2. The role played by the legislative, executive, judicial, and regulatory powers determines which tools and decision-making procedures become available. Each branch has its preferred means of intervention and its strengths and weaknesses. Which options are deployed may affect levels of greenhouse gas (GHG) emissions or clean technologies adoption. For example, it makes a lot of difference to enact climate legislation that entrenches policy goals in the national rulebook and exploits the legitimizing effect of state authority (Scotford and Minas, 2019: p. 73 f.), rely on regulatory authorities that have to stretch the boundaries of their statu-

tory mandates to address climate issues (Spence, 2022), or put in place dedicated bodies with the required expertise and powers to manage the transition (Abraham-Dukuma et al., 2020; Dubash, 2021; Jacobs, 2021).

3. Climate institutions and tools interact with other branches of the legal system. One possible interaction has to do with measures (e.g., on air pollution or waste management) indirectly contributing to climate policies (Scotford and Minas, 2019: p. 77 f.). Another interaction has to do with existing legal regimes that can be adapted to climate goals. Examples include a turn toward sustainability for corporate governance (e.g., Sjåfjell and Bruner, 2020; Ferrarini et al., 2021; Bruner, 2022), the interpretation of competition law in line with climate goals (e.g., Holmes et al., 2021; Malinauskaite, 2022; Inderst and Thomas, 2022), or a revision of traditional private law concepts (e.g., Mattei and Quarta, 2018; Akkermans and van Dijk, 2020; Demeyere and Sagaert, 2020). The interactions on which climate measures depend to be effective are no less relevant. For example, no support schemes for renewable energy would have been possible in the EU without a favourable interpretation of free movement law and State aid law (de Sadeleer, 2014; Penttinen, 2020). Similarly, the constraints imposed by the Supremacy Clause and the Commerce Clause shaped state support schemes in the US (Mormann, 2017; Ferrey, 2021). These three interactions can foster new complementarities or preserve existing ones. But frictions between climate policies and existing legal regimes are by no means rare. Ignoring the interactions between the two domains usually leads to implementing climate measures with limited effectiveness (Bogojevic, 2019; van Zeben, 2020; Boyd, 2021; Richards, in this volume).
4. The plurality of legal orders shall be acknowledged. It is a permanent feature of both developed and developing countries' legal systems (Tamanaha, 2021; Bussani and Infantino, 2022). Simply assuming that state official rules drive the low-carbon transition will likely lead to disappointing results. The specificity of each legal order, including informal ones, has to be carefully assessed to identify its potential contribution to climate policies. Legal research on the interplay between indigenous and non-Western views on environmental resources and energy policies clearly shows that legal pathways of decarbonization have to embrace legal pluralism (e.g., Godden and O'Neill, 2016; Atapattu et al., 2021; Macpherson, 2021; Huneeus, 2022)
5. Dominant patterns of legal thought and interpretative practices could influence both the meanings attributed to climate issues and the perceived legitimacy of each legal tool. Values enshrined in each legal system could offer different ways to balance conflicting interests involved in environmental protection, from individual economic rights to political rights to participation rights (Lees, 2019, p. 40–42). Most importantly, national legal cultures and the plurality of orders they host are likely to filter claims arising from energy justice concerns and selectively take on board those aspects that are understood to be compatible with existing legal structures. This means that legal pathways must consider the meaning of

energy justice emerging in each system (San Martín and Wood, 2022, Kashwan, 2022; Bhullar, in this volume).

As our definition of legal pathway suggests, the key issue is the interplay between the legal dimensions and the non-legal drivers of the low-carbon transition. While sec. 3 looks at ways of integrating legal pathways into transition theories and decarbonization scenarios, in the balance of this section, we assess the possibilities for interdisciplinary dialogue with comparative studies of climate policies in political science and economics. Two aspects are worth highlighting: first, the contextual factors non-legal studies point to should be understood as tightly linked to legal factors; second, quantitative analyses, which include institutional indicators, could become more useful if grounded on studies of legal pathways.

With comparative environmental politics as a point of departure, one can observe a focus on the determinants of political processes and outcomes, which is not very far removed from the goals of legal studies. Research aimed at testing theories, or developing new ones, about the causal relationships between mitigation and adaptation policies and political structures, coalitions of interests, bureaucratic incentives, or ideas about the state and the market offers a different perspective on the main components of the institutional context (Steinberg and VanDeveer, 2012; Cao et al., 2014; Purdon, 2015; Biesbroek et al., 2018; VanDeveer et al., 2022). For interdisciplinary studies, the interesting question is what kind of interaction between legal and political structures can be expected: are the former just the vehicles for the latter? Or do the former contribute to shaping the latter? Similar questions can be raised about social science research, which underlines the relevance of cultural factors for the low-carbon transition. From electric vehicles to solar home systems to house retrofitting to clean cookstoves, the adoption of clean technologies must be 'culturally compatible' (Sovacool and Griffiths, 2020; Stephenson et al., 2021). The question, then, is how such an outcome can be facilitated by legal interventions that draw on cultural studies to identify the barriers to be overcome and the solutions to increase public acceptance.

Turning now to quantitative analyses, three streams of literature exemplify the opportunities for interdisciplinary dialogue. The first stream exploits large datasets of climate laws and policies worldwide to identify the main trends in climate legislation (Eskander and Fankhauser, 2020; Lamb and Minx, 2020; Eskander et al., 2021; Nascimento et al., 2022). Besides documenting that measures compatible with the goals of the Paris Agreement have yet to be introduced, these studies also show a correlation between the adoption of climate laws and the quality of institutions, the latter being quantified through the World Bank Governance Indicators. Higher scores of institutional quality are associated with a stronger propensity to adopt climate laws and a larger reduction of GHG emissions intensity. This analysis calls for a more in-depth assessment of the institutional components directly related to implementing climate laws.

The second stream of quantitative analyses deals with the long-term determinants of institutional quality and the way they affect climate policies. The argument has been made that the accumulation of statehood experience across the centuries interacts with the legal heritage of the colonial empires. A large number of former colonies adopted the civil law or the common law tradition. Common law countries are expected to adopt weaker climate policies because of their anti-regulation stance. The persistent effects of this legal heritage are mediated by historical statehood: the stronger the governance capabilities accumulated, the larger the likelihood of a lasting influence of legal origins (Fredriksson and Wollscheid, 2015, 2018; Ang and Fredriksson, 2017, 2021).

Similarly, the pro-regulation stance of civil law countries is said to provide a more favourable institutional environment for investments in renewable sources (Liu et al., 2021). Using a different theoretical framework, studies of Comparative Capitalism suggest that coordinated market economies (usually associated with continental Europe countries) fare better than liberal market economies (usually associated with Anglo-Saxon countries) in promoting renewable energy (Benney, 2021; but see a broader discussion in Loewen, 2022). There are two problems with this approach. First, comparative legal studies have downplayed the common law-civil law dichotomy and, more generally, the taxonomy of legal families (Siems, 2022: pp. 51 ff., 82 ff.). Relying on such taxonomy for empirical analysis may be misleading. Each legal family is a model that does not correspond to the actual workings of a legal system in a specific historical period. Mixed and hybrid legal systems (Siems, 2022: pp. 99–108) and the plurality of legal orders mentioned above further compound the difficulties of legal taxonomies.

Interestingly, none of the chapters in this volume, nor more generally the legal literature on the low-carbon transition, mention legal families among the relevant legal dimensions. It seems that non-legal scholars are relying on institutional variables, which are easy to use in quantitative analyses but not very informative. Second, the theory that links economic performance to legal origins has been heavily criticised (Garoupa et al., 2017). There is no credible evidence that the persistence of past colonial heritages is one of the main drivers of current regulatory choices. Legal origins interact with a host of other legal factors. It is that interaction that ultimately determines the outcomes we observe today. Also, attributing a pro- or anti-regulation bias to each legal family does not provide an accurate description of the evolution of legal regimes.

The third stream of quantitative analyses explores the drivers of climate policies diffusion. The main research questions have to do with the channels through which diffusion takes place, the domestic and international conditions favouring it, and the impact it has on emissions reduction. Mechanisms like learning, economic competition, emulation, and coercion are usually discussed (Baldwin et al., 2019; Zhou et al., 2019; Bergero et al., 2021; Dolphin and Pollitt, 2021; Raghoo and Shah, 2022). There seems to be evidence that diffusion contributes to reducing emissions (Linsenmeier et al., 2022). This literature does not consider legal factors. Are they relevant in sparking diffusion? Can they be incorporated into the above-mentioned diffusion mechanisms? For example, it has been observed that the ambition of carbon pricing depends on trade interdependencies and the role of the state (Steinebach et al., 2021). This analysis would benefit from a more thorough understanding of the domestic decision-making procedures leading to the selection of specific design features for carbon pricing. Equally relevant is a discussion of how diffusion mechanisms interact with (are supported or hampered by) international trade law and carbon border adjustment mechanisms (Leal-Arcas, 2021; Delimatsis and Reins, 2021). More generally, comparative legal studies deal with the determinants and effects of legal transplants (Graziadei, 2019; Siems, 2022: pp. 288 ff.). A fruitful exchange could be expected if these more qualitative approaches were used for empirical testing. Even more importantly, quantitative analyses usually focus on binary questions (whether or not a climate policy was adopted). But there are additional questions about the design of climate policies and their stringency. For example, one of the few large-scale comparative studies on national renewable energy laws considers over one hundred countries and shows that they diverge significantly (Crossley 2018). Even in the EU, where pressures for harmonization are stronger, convergence toward common rules has been partial (a finding confirmed in the political science literature: see Boasson et al., 2021). Reasons for persistent divergence have to do with the use of renewable laws to address national problems (from economic growth to sustainability to network reliability to energy security), differences in how renewable technologies are defined, and the combination and structure of support schemes. In the face of these differences, observing whether diffusion occurs could be less relevant than establishing how climate policies are designed and implemented. The literature on policy evaluation (e.g., Jordan and Huitema, 2014) usually addresses the latter aspects, but legal dimensions are equally relevant for both diffusion and evaluation.

Criticisms of quantitative analyses are not meant to exclude their relevance. But they suggest that alternative research avenues shall be identified. Three possible directions can be mentioned. The first one is the design of quantitative analyses, which draw on concepts developed by legal theory (along the lines proposed by Dagan et al., 2018). Such analyses would better reflect the real workings of legal systems. The second is mixed methods research designs (see Hesse-Biber and Burke, 2015; Bazeley, 2018; Creswell and Plano, 2018). Quantitative analyses could either provide the starting point for a follow-up qualitative analysis of legal pathways or be employed to extend case studies that have previously identified legal pathways. The third one is to identify those domains in which no quantifiable legal variables can be found, and interpretative approaches appear more useful for exploring the relevant context (Barkin et al., 2021). This could be when open-ended legal concepts like the proportionality principle, respect for cultural diversity, or due diligence and good faith principles play a crucial role.

This section has dealt with the legal dimensions most relevant to the low-carbon transition. The next section moves towards normative analysis and asks how legal pathways should fit transition theories and decarbonization scenarios.

3 Legal pathways and climate science

If the legal pathways of decarbonization are context-dependent and geographically differentiated, how do we move from describing and explaining them to prescribing the legal reforms that should support the low-carbon transition? The answer to this question requires dealing with the nexus between law, policy, and climate science. In the last decades, a wealth of knowledge has been accumulated about the transformations of the major components of the climate system (atmosphere, land, oceans, biosphere and cryosphere, and the carbon, energy, and water cycles: see IPCC, 2021) and the processes regulating the stability and resilience of the Earth system (Steffen et al., 2015; French and Kotzé, 2021; Persson et al., 2022). Policymakers can draw on such knowledge to plan the transition toward a low-carbon society. However, climate science does not dictate decarbonization pathways. Even the looming risk of the planet becoming inhospitable by the end of the century cannot stop the debate about separating and integrating scientific assessments and policy choices. The high-profile climate litigation cases of the last decade made it clear that the interplay between scientific and judicial reasoning is far from settled (Peeters, 2021; Sulyok, 2021). Those cases are just the tip of the iceberg. The broader issue is how to make sure that climate models and decarbonization scenarios are not built on assumptions that are incompatible with the basic structures of legal systems. A sharp distinction between scientific objectivity and normative assessments is becoming increasingly blurred and contested. Hence, the credibility of climate science directly depends on how an assortment of analytic frameworks are taken into account. This section first reviews the processes that lead to identifying decarbonization scenarios, then discusses proposals to integrate the role of institutional contexts. It is on the latter aspect that the concept of legal pathways could prove useful.

The earliest attempts at developing models that could represent the interactions between the environment and the economy started in the 1970s (Farber, 2008, 2015; van Beek et al., 2020, 2022; Bosetti, 2021). From then on, mounting evidence of global warming drove the demand for comprehensive computer-assisted models embracing the climate, energy, and land systems. A large variety of integrated assessment models (IAMs) were developed, first within the IPCC and then by interconnected communities of climate modellers. IAMs proved to be flexible enough to gradually incorporate new data sets from many disciplines. Their role grew in parallel to the international climate change regime: if the first IPCC assessment report provided the scientific basis for the 1992 UNFCCC, later assessment reports (and the emission pathways they highlighted) shaped the negotiations for the 1997 Kyoto Protocol and the 2015 Paris Agreement. To be sure, models and policy needs constantly interact: what kind of models are developed partly depends on what policymakers require, or at least on what modellers perceive to be the most policy-relevant scientific contributions (Süsser et al., 2021; Silvast and Foulds, 2022).

Emission projections structured by IAMs led to the development of thousands of decarbonization scenarios. Generally speaking, scenarios are descriptions of alternative future developments. They do not predict what will happen, but suggest options and explore their implications. Possible courses of action and their associated emission levels are identified. The prominence of scenarios suggests that, after the Paris Agreement, climate science entered a new phase. The role of the IPCC turned from providing evidence about climate change to suggesting ways to address it (Livingston and Rummukainen, 2020; Hermansen et al., 2021; van Beek et al., 2022). Such a change creates tensions with the official image of the IPCC as a neutral body completely detached from policy tasks. Yet, policymakers increasingly demand assistance with interpreting complex decarbonization scenarios (Süsser et al., 2022; Pedersen et al., 2022a). This means that the IPCC and, more generally, the climate research community are under pressure to produce scientific results that match the needs of their users while at the same time defending their independence from political interests.

Straddling the line between these two goals is by no means easy. Consider the five Illustrative Mitigation Pathways proposed by the IPCC (2022: pp. 1–34 ff.) in the Sixth Assessment Report. They allow us to explore different ways to achieve the Paris Agreement targets: a gradual strengthening of current climate policies, extensive use of technologies for net negative emissions, a focus on renewables and low demand, or a phase-out of fossil fuels. Each pathway conveys information about the set of social, economic, and technological transformations required to achieve more or less ambitious emission targets and the timing of emission reductions. However, the IPCC's Illustrative Pathways leave out alternative, perhaps more radical, approaches to achieve the targets of the Paris Agreement. This means alternative ways could be weakened or precluded (McLaren and Markusson, 2020; Beck and Oomen, 2021). More significantly, for this Handbook, none of the IPCC scenarios tell policymakers what policies to implement. A recurrent criticism over the years has been that the scenarios lack the information policymakers need most (Pedersen et al., 2022b; Keppo et al., 2021). One of the built-in features of IAMs has traditionally been to only include carbon prices as a proxy for the effects of climate policies. There is no discussion about the implementation of real-world carbon pricing. The IPCC (2022: p. 3–14) admits that this is a 'rudimentary' representation of institutional factors. Starting with the Special Report on the 1.5° C target (IPCC, 2018), an additional analytic step was introduced to increase policy relevance: the scenarios undergo a 'feasibility' test, covering multiple dimensions. Two refer to the physical environment, and four to analytical frameworks: economic, socio-cultural, technological, and institutional/political (IPCC, 2022: pp. 1–55, 3–109). These analytic frameworks stem from transition theories and are used to link them to quantitative models. But what is the meaning of feasibility? And how does it consider legal factors?

Initially proposed in the field of political science (Majone, 1975; Jewell and Cherp, 2020) and developed by political philosophers (e.g., Gilabert, 2017; Kenehan and Katz, 2021a,b), a feasibility analysis is also employed in regulatory proceedings as an alternative to cost-benefit analysis to assess technologies and their costs (Driesen, 2022). It took on new meanings in the debate about the low-carbon transition. According to one interdisciplinary proposal, 'initiative feasibility' refers to the likelihood of adopting and implementing a specific climate measure, which is influenced by various factors (Nielsen et al., 2020; Gilligan and Vandenbergh, 2020; Stern et al., 2022). While this proposal remains open to relying only on qualitative data, other studies decidedly moved toward integrating feasibility within scenario models (Andrijevic et al., 2020; Brutschin et al., 2021). Indicators of institutional quality were used to connect the mitigation efforts in each scenario and the required institutional capacity. The latter was assumed to evolve together with economic and educational development. One important insight is that, except for developed countries, the lack of institutional capacity leads almost everywhere to a significant feasibility mismatch in most scenarios. Moreover, concerns about institutional feasibility are significantly greater than technological and economic feasibility concerns. In another study (Roelfsema et al., 2022), the realism of scenarios is amplified by using the impacts of climate policies to change the inputs for the IAMs.

The main problem with this approach is that it does not offer information on the institutional trajectories that should support the legal reforms required by the low-carbon transition. Admittedly, aggregated indicators cannot capture this kind of contextual information. But this observation suggests that other ways to employ contextual information should be found. As discussed in sec. 2, there are several possibilities to combine quantitative and qualitative analyses. The dimension of institutional feasibility should be linked to the definition of the legal pathway proposed in this introduction. Instead of assuming that indicators of institutional quality offer a faithful representation of national institutional contexts, a direct reference to the legal factors listed in sec. 2 could suggest which scenarios and decarbonization efforts are 'legally' feasible in each region and country. The analysis should start with contexts, not with indicators. Synthesizing such information with indicators should be the second step of the analysis, not the first one. The debate on the interplay between models and transition theories already offers indications of the range of strategies that could be deployed to integrate legal information. The degree of integration can vary and does not always require quantification (Hirt et al., 2020). Moving from global and regional scenarios to national scenarios in the IAMs community (Fujimori et al., 2021) opens up interesting opportunities to further develop this perspective. Common modelling protocols to assess emissions trajectories ease comparison among countries. Such protocols could include data relevant to the identification of legal feasibility concerns and be tailored to the needs of each country.

The chapters in this Handbook can be read as a first attempt to provide information on the links between legal feasibility and legal pathways in most continents. Of course, more detailed analyses are needed. The attention paid to the institutional dimensions of the low-carbon transition is a welcome improvement in climate science. But a simplified representation of legal contexts will not allow significant progress. The concluding chapter highlights the contributions that, for a selected number of topics, legal scholars could offer to the broader debate on accelerating and supporting the low-carbon transition.

4 Overview of the Handbook

The chapters in this Handbook are written by a group of junior and senior scholars. We strived for geographical variety, a larger number of contributions from less well-known regions and countries, and a good balance between academic seniority, gender, and ethnicity. Our focus on energy law can be justified on a number of grounds. First, the low-carbon transition depends on technological and economic transformations taking place in energy generation, transport, and use. Energy law is the primary body of rules that supports or hinders such transformations. Second, we do not assume that energy law is neatly separated from other branches (see discussion in Heffron et al., 2018). How boundaries are drawn depends on national and regional institutional contexts. As discussed in sec. 2, the complementaries and conflicts across legal regimes are one of the main institutional factors to consider. Hence, the chapters in this Handbook adopt an encompassing definition of energy law. Third, many climate policies depend on energy markets for their design and effectiveness. More generally, the argument can be made that the peculiar features of energy law in each legal system determine what climate policies are implemented. Therefore, our focus on energy law can be considered a necessary analytical step to explore the variety of legal pathways. Fourth, the energy sector has many interdependencies with other sectors. Although reciprocal influences cannot be excluded, we expect energy law to play a major role in managing such interdependencies. Some of them are addressed in dedicated chapters on transport systems (Klass and Cherny, in this volume) and city planning (Du Plessis and Moyo, in this volume).

The five parts of the Handbook move from analytical tools and apply them to specific legal contexts. The first part on methods and concepts lays the ground for assessing the variety of low-carbon transitions. The chapters on interdisciplinary research (Sonetti and Arrobbio) and energy justice (Bhullar) supply the theoretical frameworks that help locate the contributions of different disciplines and the normative goals to be pursued. The chapters on governance models (H. Wiseman), policy instruments (Richards), and implementation and enforcement mechanisms (Benjamin and McCallum) identify the major legal dimensions of climate policies. The second part on energy markets discusses both the fate of old generation technologies (J. Wiseman on coal, Chikanayev on natural gas, Chisanga on nuclear energy) and the transformations required to decarbonize the energy system (Wu on electricity markets, Kallies on the regulation of infrastructures, Chege on hydrogen systems). Specific attention is paid to the impact of the low-carbon transition on the financial architecture of energy markets (Hiemstra) and the organization of global supply chains (Mitdikis). The third part on regional experiences includes chapters that focus on cross-border initiatives in Africa (Addaney and Kengni), Asia and the Pacific (Zhang), the EU (Penttinen), North America (Coleman), and South America (Landa et al.). The goal is to assess the strengths and weaknesses of regional governance for the low-carbon transition. The fourth part devotes seven chapters to national experiences. The sample includes two major emitters (Guo on China, Shankar and Basu on India), three developed countries facing serious implementation challenges for their domestic climate policies (Godden on Australia, Kurokawa on Japan, Swora on Poland), and two countries striving to reconcile sustainable development and investment-friendly regulatory frameworks (Leal and Miranda). The fifth part turns to local experiences, the institutional level where much action has to take place and many barriers are found. Both new opportunities and the hurdles they face are discussed with reference to energy communities (Outka and Savaresi), peer-to-peer energy trading (Lavrijssen et al.), low-carbon mobility (Klass and Cherny), and urban transitions (Du Plessis and Moyo).

In the concluding chapter, the editors reflect on the relevance of the contributions to the Handbook for legal research on the low-carbon transition, interdisciplinary dialogue, and legal reform. The discussion is organized around six themes: significance of the distinction between developed and developing countries for the low-carbon transition, patterns of radical or incremental change, roles of different institutional levels, regulation of infrastructures, instruments selection, and energy justice.

This Handbook has been a wonderful intellectual journey. We wish to acknowledge the dedication of all the contributors. They have been willing to put their deep knowledge of energy law at the service of this collective effort to understand the dynamics of the low-carbon transition. They never complained when we organized online meetings at inconvenient times or asked them to meet strict deadlines. We learned a lot from them, and we trust readers will also benefit. There is still much we want to learn, but we hope the detailed analyses offered by this Handbook prove a source of inspiration for new legal and interdisciplinary research.

The contents of all chapters have been peer-reviewed by the editors. Warm thanks to the editorial staff at De Gruyter for linguistic revisions and proof-reading, as well as assistance throughout the publishing process.

References

Abraham-Dukuma, M.C., Dihoa, M.O., Bogado, N. et al., 2020. Multidisciplinary composition of climate change commissions: transnational trends and expert perspectives. *Sustainability*, 12, 10280.

Akkermans, B., and van Dijk, G., eds., 2020. *Sustainability and private law*. The Hague: Eleven International Publishing.

Andrijevic, M., Cuaresma, J.C., Muttarak, R. and Schleussner, C.-F., 2020. Governance in socioeconomic pathways and its role for future adaptive capacity. *Nature Sustainability*, 3, pp. 35–41.

Ang, J.B. and Fredriksson, P.G., 2017. Statehood experience, legal traditions, and climate change policies. *Economic Inquiry*, 55(3), 1511–1537.

Ang, J.B. and Fredriksson, P.G., 2021. Does an early start help or hurt? Statehood, institutions, and modern climate change policies. *Energy Economics*, 94, 105075.

Atapattu, S.A., Gonzalez, C.G. and Seck, S.L., eds., 2021. *The Cambridge handbook of environmental justice and sustainable development*. Cambridge: Cambridge University Press.

Baldwin, E., Carley, S. and Nicholson-Crotty, S., 2019. Why do countries emulate each others' policies? A global study of renewable energy policy diffusion. *World Development*, 120, pp. 29–45.

Barkin, J.S., Chase, V.M. and van Wees, S., 2021. Interpretive methodologies, quantitative methods, and comparative environmental politics. In: J. Sowers, S.D. VanDeveer and E. Weinthal, eds., 2021. *The Oxford handbook of comparative environmental politics*. Oxford: Oxford University Press.

Bazeley, P., 2018. *Integrating analyses in mixed methods research*. Thousand Oaks, CA: Sage.

Beck, S. and Oomen, J., 2021. Imagining the corridor of climate mitigation – what is at stake in IPCC's politics of anticipation? *Environmental Science and Policy*, 123, pp. 169–178.

Benney, T.M., 2021. Varieties of capitalism and renewable energy in emerging and developing economies. *Journal of Economic Policy Reform*, 24(4), pp. 413–38.

Bergero, C., Rich, M.J. and Saikawa, E., 2021. All roads lead to Paris: the eight pathways to renewable energy target adoption. *Energy Research & Social Science*, 80, 102215.

Biesbroek, R., Berrang-Ford, L., Ford, J.D. et al., 2018. Data, concepts and methods for large-n comparative climate change adaptation policy research: a systematic literature review. *WIREs Climate Change*, 9, e548.

Boasson, E.L., Leiren, M.D. and Wettestad, J., eds., 2021. *Comparative renewables policy: political, organizational and European fields*. London and New York, NY: Routledge.

Bogojević, S., 2019. Trading schemes. In: E. Lees and J.E. Viñuales, eds., 2019. *The Oxford handbook of comparative environmental law*. Oxford: Oxford University Press, pp. 926–948.

Bosetti, V., 2021. Integrated assessment models for climate change. In: *Oxford Research Encyclopedias, Economics and Finance*, published online 22 January 2021.

Boyd, W., 2021. The poverty of theory: public problems, instrument choice, and the climate emergency. *Columbia Journal of Environmental Law*, 46(2), pp. 399–487.

Bruner, C.M., 2022. *The corporation as technology: re-calibrating corporate governance for a sustainable future*. Oxford: Oxford University Press.

Brutschin, E., Pianta, S., Tavoni, M. et al., 2021. A multidimensional feasibility evaluation of low-carbon scenarios. *Environmental Research Letters*, 16, 064069.

Bussani, M., and Infantino, M., 2022. *Introduzione al diritto comparato*. Firenze: Le Monnier.

Cao, X., Milner, H.V., Prakash, A. and Ward, H., 2014. Research frontiers in comparative and international environmental politics: an introduction. *Comparative Political Studies*, 47(3), pp. 291–308.

Cresswell, J.W. and Plano, V.L., 2018. *Designing and conducting mixed methods research*. 3rd ed. Los Angeles, CA: Sage.

Dagan, H., Kreitner, R. and Kricheli-Katz, T., 2018. Legal theory for legal empiricists. Law & Social Inquiry, 43(2), pp. 292–318.

de Sadeleer, N., 2014. *EU environmental law and the internal market*. Oxford: Oxford University Press.

Delimatsis, P. and Reins, L., eds., 2021. *Trade and environmental law*. Cheltenham: Elgar Publishing.

Demeyere, S. and Sagaert, V., eds., 2020. *Contract and property with an environmental perspective*. Cambridge: Intersentia.

Dolphin, G.G. and Pollitt, M.G., 2021. The international diffusion of climate policy: theory and evidence. Resources for the Future Working Paper 21–23, August.

Driesen, D.M., 2022. Feasibility analysis and the climate crisis. *Yale Journal on Regulation*, 39, pp. 533–563.

Dubash, N.K., 2021. Varieties of climate governance: the emergence and functioning of climate institutions. Environmental Politics, 30(sup1), pp. 1–25.

Eskander, S.M.S.U., and Fankhauser, S., 2020. Reduction in greenhouse gas emissions from national climate legislation. *Nature Climate Change*, 10, pp. 750–756.

Eskander, S.M.S.U., Fankhauser, S. and Setzer, J., 2021. Global lessons from climate change legislation and litigation. *Environmental and Energy Policy and the Economy*, 2(1), pp. 44–82.

Farber, D.A., 2008. Modeling climate change and its impacts: law, policy, and science. *Texas Law Review*, 86, pp. 1655–1699.

Farber, D.A., 2015. Coping with uncertainty: cost-benefit analysis, the precautionary principle, and climate change. *Washington Law Review*, 90, pp. 1659–1725.

Ferrarini, G., Grünewald, S.N. and Busch, D., eds., 2021. *Sustainable finance in Europe: corporate governance, financial stability and financial markets*. Cham: Springer.

Ferrey, S., 2021. Null climate federalism: state frustration of federal renewable energy entitlements. *Virginia Environmental Law Journal*, 39(1), pp. 1–69.

Fredriksson, P.G. and Wollscheid, J.R., 2015. Legal origins and climate change policies in former colonies. *Environmental and Resource Economics*, 62, pp. 309–327.

Fredriksson, P.G. and Wollscheid, J.R., 2018. Legal origins and environmental policies: evidence from OECD and developing countries. *Letters in Spatial and Resource Sciences*, 11, pp. 369–375.

French, D. and Kotzé, L.J., eds., 2021. *Research handbook on law, governance and planetary boundaries*. Cheltenham: Elgar Publishing.

Fujimori, S., Krey, V., van Vuuren, D. et al., 2021. A framework for national scenarios with varying emission reductions. *Nature Climate Change*, 11, pp. 472–480.

Garoupa, N., Gómez Ligüerre, C. and Mélon, L., 2017. *Legal origins and the efficiency dilemma*. London and New York, NY: Routledge.

Gerrard, M.B. and Dernbach, J.C., eds., 2019. *Legal pathways to deep decarbonization in the United States*. Washington, D.C.: Environmental Law Institute.

Ghaleigh, N.S., Setzer, J. and Welikala, A., 2022. The complexities of comparative climate constitutionalism. *Journal of Environmental Law*, Advance Articles 23 July.

Gilabert, P., 2017. Justice and feasibility: a dynamic approach. In: M. Weber and K. Vallier, eds., 2017. *Political utopias: contemporary debates*. Oxford: Oxford University Press.

Gilligan, J.M. and Vandenbergh, M.P., 2020. Beyond wickedness: managing complex systems and climate change. *Vanderbilt Law Review*, 73(6), pp. 1777–1810.

Godden, L.C. and O'Neill, L., 2016. Agreements with indigenous communities: the Native Title Act in Australia. In: L. Barrera-Hernández, B. Barton, L. Godden et al., eds., 2016. *Sharing the costs and benefits of energy and resource activity: legal change and impact on communities*. Oxford: Oxford University Press, pp. 135–154.

Graziadei, M., 2019. Comparative law, transplants, and receptions. In: M. Reimann and R. Zimmermann, eds., 2019. *The Oxford handbook of comparative law*. 2nd ed. Oxford: Oxford University Press, pp. 442–473.

Heffron, R.J., Rønne, A., Tomain, J.P. et al., 2018. A treatise for energy law. *Journal of World Energy Law and Business*, 11, pp. 34–48.

Hermansen, E.A.T., Lahn, B., Sundqvist, G. and Øye, 2021. Post-Paris policy relevance: lessons from the IPCC SR15 process. *Climatic Change*, 169(7).

Hesse-Biber, S.N. and Burke, J.R., 2015. *The Oxford handbook of multimethod and mixed methods research Inquiry*. Oxford: Oxford University Press.

Hirt, L.F., Schell, G., Sahakyan, M. and Trutnevyte, E., 2020. A review of linking models and socio-technical transitions theories for energy and climate solutions. *Environmental Innovation and Societal Transitions*, 35, pp. 162–179.

Holmes, S., Middelschulte, D. and Snoep, M., eds., 2021. *Competition law, climate change & environmental sustainability*. New York, NY: Institute of Competition Law.

Huneeus, A., 2022. The legal struggle for rights of nature in the United States. *Wisconsin Law Review*, pp. 133–162.

Hunter, T., Herrera, I., Crossley, P. and Alvarez, G.M., eds., 2020. *Routledge handbook of energy Law*. London and New York, NY: Routledge.

Inderst, R. and Thomas, S., 2022. Sustainability agreements in the European Commission's draft horizontal guidelines. *Journal of European Competition Law and Practice*, Advance Articles 22 April 2022.

IPCC, 2018. *Global warming of 1.5°C – Special Report*.

IPCC, 2021. *Climate change 2021: the physical science basis. Contribution of Working Group I to the Sixth Assessment Report. Summary for policymakers*.

IPCC, 2022. *Climate change 2022: Mitigation of climate change. Contribution of Working Group III to the Sixth Assessment Report*.

Ireland-Piper, D. and James, N., 2021. The obligation of law schools to teach climate change law. *University of Queensland Law Journal*, 40(3), pp. 319–350.

Jacobs, S., 2021. Agency genesis and the energy transition. *Columbia Law Review*, 121, pp. 835–935.

Jewell, J. and Cherp, A., 2020. On the political feasibility of climate change mitigation pathways: is it too late to keep warming below 1.5°C? *WIREs Climate Change*, 11, e621.

Jordan, A. and Huitema, D., 2014. Innovations in climate policy: conclusions and new directions. *Environmental Politics*, 23(5), pp. 906–925.

Kashwan, P., 2022. Globalization of environmental justice: a framework for comparative research. In: J. Sowers, S.D. VanDeveer and E. Weinthal, eds., 2022. *The Oxford handbook of comparative environmental politics*, online publication May 2022.

Kenehan, S. and Katz, C., eds., 2021a. *Climate justice and feasibility: normative theorizing, feasibility constraints, and climate action*. Lanham: ML. Rowman & Littlefield.

Kenehan, S. and Katz, C., eds., 2021b. *Principles of justice and real-world climate politics*. Lanham: ML. Rowman & Littlefield.

Keppo, I., Butnar, I., Bauer, N. et al., 2021. Exploring the possibility space: taking stock of the diverse capabilities and gaps in integrated assessment models. *Environmental Research Letters*, 16, 053006.

Lamb, W.F. and Minx, J.C., 2020. The political economy of national climate policy: architectures of constraint and a typology of countries. *Energy Research & Social Science*, 64, 101429.

Leal-Arcas, R., 2021. *Climate clubs for a sustainable future: the role of international trade and investment law*. Alphen aan den Rijn: Kluwer Law International.

Lees, E., 2019. Value in comparative environmental law – 3D cartography and analytical description. In: E. Lees and J.E. Viñuales, eds., 2019. *The Oxford handbook of comparative environmental law*. Oxford: Oxford University Press, pp. 35–56.

Linsenmeier, M., Mohommad, M. and Schwerhoff, G., 2022. The international diffusion of policies for climate change mitigation. IMF Woking Papers 22/115, June.

Liu, J., Zhang, D., Cai, J. and Davenport, J., 2021. Legal systems, national governance and renewable energy investment: evidence from around the world. *British Journal of Management*, vol. 32, pp. 579–610.

Livingston, J.E. and Rummukainen, M., 2020. Taking science by surprise: the knowledge politics of the IPCC Special Report on 1.5 degrees. *Environmental Science and Policy*, 112, pp. 10–16.

Loewen, B., 2022. Revitalizing varieties of capitalism for sustainability transitions research: review, critique, and way forward. *Renewable and Sustainable Energy Reviews*, 162, 112432.

Macpherson, E., 2021. The (human) rights of nature: a comparative study of emerging legal rights for rivers and lakes in the United States of America and Mexico. *Duke Environmental Law & Policy Forum*, 31, pp. 327–377.

Majone, G., 1975. On the notion of political feasibility. *European Journal of Political Reseach*, 3, pp. 259–274.

Malinauskaite, J., 2022. Competition law and sustainability: EU and national perspectives. *Journal of European Competition Law and Practice*, 13, pp. 336-348.

Mattei, U. and Quarta, A., 2018. *The turning point in private law: ecology, technology and the commons*. Cheltenham: Elgar Publishing.

McLaren, D. and Markusson, N., 2020. The co-evolution of technological promises, modelling, policies and climate change targets. *Nature Climate Change*, 10, pp. 392–397.

Mormann, F., 2017. Constitutional challenges and regulatory opportunities for state climate policy innovation. *Harvard Environmental Law Review*, 41, pp. 189–242.

Nascimento, L., Kuramochi, T., Iacobuta, G. et al., 2022. Twenty years of climate policy: G20 coverage and gaps. *Climate Policy*, 22(2), pp. 158–174.

Nielsen, K.S., Stern, P.C., Dietz, T. et al., 2020. Improving climate change mitigation analysis: a framework for examining feasibility. *One Earth*, 3(3), pp. 325–336.

Oyewunmi, T., Crossley, P., Sourgens, F. and Talus, K., eds., 2020. *Decarbonisation and the energy industry: law, policy and regulation in low-carbon energy markets*. Oxford: Hart Publishing.

Pedersen, J.T.S., Gomes, C.M., Gupta, J. et al., 2022a. The policy-relevance of emissions scenarios: policymakers require simpler, relevant, and more communicative scenarios. Working paper Available at https://ssrn.com/abstract=4073175.

Pedersen, J.T.S., van Vuuren, D., Gupta, J. et al., 2022b. IPCC emission scenarios: how did critiques affect their quality and relevance 1990–2022? *Global Environmental Change*, 75, 102538.

Peeters, M., 2021. Climate science in the courts. In: V. Abazi, J. Andriaensen and T. Christiansen, eds., 2021. *The contestation of expertise in the European Union*. Cham: Palgrave Macmillan, pp. 145–172.

Penttinen, S.-L., 2020. *Free movement and the energy sector in the European Union: the role of the European Court of Justice*. London and New York, NY: Routledge.

Persson, L., Carney Almroth, B.M., Collins, C.D. et al., 2022. Outside of the safe operating space of the planetary boundary for novel entities. *Environmental Science & Technology*, 56, pp. 1510–1521.

Purdon, M., 2015. Advancing comparative climate change politics: theory and method. *Global Environmental Politics*, 15(3), pp. 1–26.

Raghoo, P. and Shah, K.U., 2022. A global empirical analysis on the diffusion & innovation of carbon pricing policies. *Journal of Cleaner Production*, 362, 132329.

Reins, L. and Verschuuren, J., eds., 2022. *Research handbook on climate change mitigation law*. 2nd ed. Cheltenham: Elgar Publishing.

Roelfsema, M., van Soest, H.L., den Elzen, M. et al., 2022. Developing scenarios in the context of the Paris Agreement and application in the integrated assessment model IMAGE: a framework for bridging the policy-modelling divide. *Environmental Science and Policy*, 135, pp. 104–116.

Roggenkamp, M.M., de Graaf, K.J., and Fleming, R.C., eds., 2021. *Energy law, climate change and the environment*. Cheltenham: Elgar Publishing.

San Martín, W. and Wood, N., 2022. Pluralising planetary justice beyond the North-South Divide: recentring procedural, epistemic, and recognition-based justice in earth-systems governance. *Environmental Science and Policy*, 128, pp. 256–263.

Sauer, J. and Monast, J., 2021. The law of energy transition in federal systems. *Transnational Environmental Law*, 10(2), pp. 205–2010.

Scotford, E. and Minas, S., 2019. Probing the hidden depths of climate law: analysing national climate change legislation. *Review of European Community and International Environmental Law*, 28, pp. 67–81.

Siems, M., 2022. *Comparative law*. 3rd ed. Cambridge: Cambridge University Press.

Silvast, A. and Foulds, C., 2022. *Sociology of interdisciplinarity: the dynamics of energy research*. Cham: Palgrave Macmillan.

Sjåfjell, B. and Bruner, C.M., eds., 2020. *The Cambridge handbook of corporate law, corporate governance and sustainability*. Cambridge: Cambridge University Press.

Sovacool, B.K. and Griffiths, S., 2020. The cultural barriers to a low-carbon future: a review of six mobility and energy transitions across 28 countries. *Renewable and Sustainable Energy Reviews*, 119, 109569.

Spence, D.B., 2022. Naïve administrative law: complexity, delegation and climate policy. *Yale Journal on Regulation*, 39, pp. 963–1010.

Steffen, W., Richardson, K., Rockström, J. et al., 2015. Planetary boundaries: guiding human development on a changing planet. *Science*, 347, 1259855.

Steinberg, P.F. and VanDeveer, S.D., eds., 2012. *Comparative environmental politics*. Cambridge, MA: The MIT Press.

Steinebach, Y., Fernández-i-Marín, X. and Aschenbrenner, C., 2021. Who puts a price on carbon, why and how? A global empirical analysis of carbon pricing policies. *Climate Policy*, 21(3), pp. 277–289.

Stephenson, J.R., Sovacool, B.K. and Indeberg, T.H.J., 2021. Energy cultures and national decarbonization pathways. *Renewable and Sustainable Energy Reviews*, 137, 110592.

Stern, P.C., Dietz, T. and Vandenbergh, M.P., 2022. The science of mitigation: closing the gap between potential and actual reduction of environmental threats. *Energy Research & Social Science*, 91, 102735.

Sulyok, K., 2021. *Science and judicial reasoning: the legitimacy of international environmental adjudication*. Cambridge: Cambridge University Press.

Süsser, D., Ceglarz, A., Gaschnig, A. et al., 2021. Model-based policymaking or policy-based modelling? How energy models and energy policy interact. *Energy Research & Social Science*, 75, 101984.

Süsser, D., Gaschnig, A., Ceglarz, A. et al., 2022. Better suited or just more complex? On the fit between user needs and modeller-driven improvements of energy system models. *Energy*, 239, 121909.

Tamanaha, B.Z., 2021. *Legal pluralism explained*. Oxford: Oxford University Press.

van Beek, L., Hajer, M., Pelzer, P. et al., 2020. Anticipating futures through models: the rise of Integrated Assessment Modelling in the climate science-policy interface since 1970. *Global Environmental Change*, 65, 102191.

van Beek, L., Oomen, J. and Hajer, M., 2022. Navigating the political: an analysis of political calibration of integrated assessment modelling in light of the 1.5°C goal. *Environmental Science and Policy*, 133, pp. 192–202.

van Zeben, J., 2020. Governmental environmental action: legal bases and restraints. In: K. Richards and J. van Zeben, eds., 2020. *Policy instruments in environmental law*. Cheltenham: Elgar Publishing, pp. 17–31.

VanDeveer, S.D., Steinberg, P.F., Sowers, J.L. and Weinthal, E., 2022. Comparative environmental politics: contributions from an emerging field. In: P.G. Harris, ed., 2022. *Routledge handbook of global environmental politics*. 2nd ed. London and New York, NY: Routledge, pp. 161–74.

Viñuales, J.E., 2019. Comparative environmental law: structuring the field. In: E. Lees and J.E. Viñuales, eds., 2019. *The Oxford handbook of comparative environmental law*. Oxford: Oxford University Press, pp. 3–34.

Young, M.A., 2021. Climate change and law: a global challenge for legal education. *University of Queensland Law Journal*, 40(3), pp. 351–370.

Zhou, S., Matisoff, D.C., Kingsley, G.A. and Brown, M.A., 2019. Understanding renewable energy policy adoption and evolution in Europe: the impact of coercion, normative emulation, competition, and learning. *Energy Research & Social Science*, 51, pp. 1–11.

Part I: **Methods and Concepts**

Editorial Introduction

The broad term "energy law" is difficult to encompass within one definition, and the methods of describing and researching energy law are quite varied. The chapters here introduce the ways in which policymakers, academics, and others conceptualize energy law, particularly as it applies to the global energy transition, and the methods that these groups follow to define, create, implement, and study energy law. In the context of the energy transition, these chapters define energy law or governance and its key facets; explore the means of enforcing and implementing energy transition mandates and goals; highlight the many disciplines (academic and beyond the academic sector) encompassed within the energy transition; and analyze how energy justice underlies all aspects of energy law and, in the view of some scholars, is a unifying principle for this unruly area.

Energy law or "governance," as defined in this portion of the book, is the set of private and public institutions – rules and organizations – that dictate and implement standards for the entire energy system, ranging from fuels and electricity generation to transmission, distribution, and energy consumption. Energy law centrally shapes the types of primary and secondary energy sources that power global society and thus plays a central role in the energy transition. Human behavior, informal norms, and economic factors are equally important, but these, too, are all shaped and influenced by governance, and vice versa. As the chapter on inter- and transdisciplinarity recognizes, while a simple vision of energy governance often involves a 'roadmap' toward larger percentages of low-carbon energy and coordinates stakeholders toward a common goal, a more comprehensive approach recognizes the many intertwined 'socio-technical' systems within which energy governance operates. These systems complicate a seemingly simple roadmap toward a zero-carbon or net-zero carbon world.

The forms of energy governance that shape the energy transition vary but also exhibit surprisingly common themes around the globe. All themes share the overarching descriptor of "silos" – separations among the levels of governing systems for energy, the types of governing systems in which energy transition objectives are addressed (e.g., courts versus private industry standards or legislatures), energy versus climate policy, substantive disciplines, and disparate energy impacts and energy access amongst individuals and communities. All of these silos can be quite difficult to understand, transcend, and coordinate.

The first common silo-based theme involves conflicts between different levels of government that set and enforce energy standards, such as taxes, subsidies, and command and control regulations. In the examples from nations such as Australia, China, and the United States explored in the following chapters, the division of authority among governance levels poses the challenge of "piecemeal" action and, in some cases, direct conflicts between standards at different levels. In China, despite a strong centralized approach to the production of renewable energy technologies, local gov-

https://doi.org/10.1515/9783110752403-008

ernance barriers to the integration of renewables onto the electric grid have at times impeded the transition to lower-carbon generation. In Australia, the federal government controls much of the electricity transmission system and wholesale energy markets, but states govern the electricity generation mix. After a large blackout in South Australia, the federal government blamed South Australia's heavy reliance on wind energy, whereas in actuality the federal government is responsible for reliability regulations. The jurisdictional division is similar in the United States, where federal policies – such as Federal Energy Regulatory Commission-approved rules for regional electricity generation capacity markets – sometimes impede state renewable energy initiatives. This has led some states threaten exit from the federal and regional markets. The sphere of international law – for which there is no public international energy treaty – adds an additional complicating layer, with WTO principles of non-discrimination and free trade often leading to the demise of national or state-based measures to support domestic low- and zero-carbon energy.

Jurisdictional silos that generate conflicting policies at local, state, federal, and regional levels, or inaction, can also cause stakeholders to seek energy transition solutions within different types of governing bodies. Private governance, in which shareholders drive change or firms set and enforce standards for low-carbon energy, has grown substantially in recent years. Additionally, parties increasingly seek solutions within courts at the federal and state levels, arguing for the inclusion of climate considerations within human rights, duties of care by governments and corporations, and other claims. In most nations discussed in this chapter – particularly China, where parties filing court cases must work within existing laws that do not directly address climate – environmental review acts are a key component. In the United States, China, and elsewhere, environmental NGOs increasingly argue that the climate impacts of government decisions must be addressed within environmental review.

Another common global energy governance theme that impacts the pace and shape of the energy transition is the existence of separate energy policy and climate policy silos in many nations. This is the case in both Australia and the United States, for example, where federal energy regulations formally address issues such as electricity reliability and rates, not climate. Piecemeal subsidies for zero-carbon energy at the federal and state levels are accordingly the primary drivers of the energy transition in these nations. Governments enact and end these subsidies in fits and spurts, and the zero-carbon energy enabled by these subsidies sometimes bumps up directly against energy regulations, such as those addressing the interconnection of new generation with the grid or reliability regulations.

A final silo-based theme within energy law is the existence of numerous disciplines that are inseparable from "standards" that mandate or incentivize changes in fuels, energy generation, or energy consumption. Energy policy is both shaped by and shapes physical and technological limitations and advances; socio-economic principles such as affordability of and access to energy; and psychological and cognitive factors such as the level of stakeholder trust in energy decisionmaking processes, among many other areas. Although these subjects are inherently intertwined, the terminology of each disciplinary silo is sometimes difficult to transfer to other disciplines, and respect for other disciplines is at times limited. Additionally, these many substantive aspects of energy reside within the academic sphere and beyond, thus requiring both interdisciplinary approaches to the energy transition (those that simultaneously incorporate numerous substantive disciplines) and transdisciplinarity – approaches that draw from knowledge within and outside of the academic sphere, including knowledge held by communities, industry, policymakers, and other groups.

Energy justice is a concept that can provide a unifying theme both for energy law and the many substantive areas that are inseparable from the law itself. Although energy justice has numerous definitions, nearly all definitions encompass many substantive areas – recognizing and addressing unequal distribution of energy development and energy access through socio-technical studies and policies; involving a variety of stakeholders within enhanced energy decisionmaking processes and trans-disciplinary research; giving rights to and enhancing academic study of those groups for which the harms of energy processes and access to energy are historically under-recognized; and restoring under-recognized groups to a more equal position through public and private standards, climate litigation, and other tools explored in the following chapters. The added pillar of "cosmopolitan justice" calls for an even greater expansion of inter- and transdiciplinarity research, which addresses the extraterritorial effects of enhanced reliance on batteries and energy minerals, for example, and calls for national and international policies that address these effects. A more comprehensive approach to energy justice would also draw non-anthropocentric, intersectional (race, class, and gender), intergenerational, and rights-based aspects of energy justice into both research and law.

The chapters that follow explore this complex, siloed space that we call "Energy Law" and the ways of thinking about, researching, and regulating this space – including with potentially unifying themes and approaches such as energy justice, interdisciplinarity, and transdisciplinarity.

Giulia Sonetti, Osman Arrobbio

Inter- and Trans-Disciplinary Research in the Energy Sector: an Overview

Abstract: Europe's energy transition – and that of the rest of the world – is a crucial challenge for our generations to meet. All past, current and future energy challenges are entwined with, and indeed co-produced with, society; energy has only ever been an issue because of society's apparent 'need' for it. Furthermore, because society's demand for energy is linked to laws and norms regulating people's professional and everyday lives, it is clear that achieving ambitious low-carbon aspirations will require a societal transition. Moreover, any low-carbon 'solutions' put forward will, however technological they seem on the surface, still be grounded in and depend upon specific social contexts. Research and action tackling these complex issues often need to have a high level of inter and transdisciplinarity. This chapter aims at getting to know what is needed to make different forms of collaborative research successful (i.e. multidisciplinary, interdisciplinary, cross-sectoral, transdisciplinary or even transformative ways of working). We briefly review existing academic literature around the need for and contribution to a better integration of SSH (Social Sciences and Humanities) in the energy field, including collaboration with other types of knowledge, to discuss what type of integration might be needed in different settings, and how to best organise these processes.

1 Introduction

Although interdisciplinarity in urban transition research is not new, the need to bring intentionality, excellence and legitimacy to the task of connecting moving parts of integrated projects is becoming increasingly important to address broad, interconnected problems and meet ambitious sustainability goals (Arrobbio and Sonetti, 2021). Whether dealing with medicine, energy, water supply, agricultural practices, climate change readiness, or environmental protection, iterative communication and coordinated parallel work are required to move forward in the urgent and synchronous sustainability transition (Fazey et al., 2020).

Giulia Sonetti is Transdisciplinary Researcher at CENSE – Center for Environmental and Sustainability Research & CHANGE – Global Change and Sustainability Institute, NOVA School of Science and Technology, NOVA University Lisbon, Portugal.
Osman Arrobbio is Researcher at the University of Parma, Department of Humanities, Social Sciences and Cultural Industries, Italy.

https://doi.org/10.1515/9783110752403-009

Our purpose with this initial chapter is to articulate and promote the need for an interdisciplinary research practice specifically for the energy field, and to improve readers' tools, best practices, success metrics, and modus operandi.

A first caveat must focus on the scientific legitimacy of these underutilized cooperative types of knowledge creation. Even though interdisciplinary collaboration, translation, and synthesis are critical to the success of complex scientific endeavours, these functions are frequently handled haphazardly or by people in 'alt-academic' careers with a much less established, valued, and visible path than the traditional tenure track (Sonetti et al., 2020). This results in sub-optimal research outputs, and it frequently fails to acknowledge the intellectual leadership and experience required to build linkages, enable cooperation, and synthesize ideas that are larger than their parts.

That is why there is still not a corpus in literature specifically dedicated to research methodologies for complex socio-technical domains such as the energy-related ones (Sovacool et al., 2015), and this is why one may find 'surfing' among the heterogeneous and sometimes heterodox sources we will cite along with the chapter. 'Multistakeholder interests' is a recurring theme in energy sector literature, and the purpose of this chapter is indeed to lay out the major disputes and conceptual shortcomings from which we might deduce research and policy consequences. We organised the flow as follows: first, an overview of the degree of interdisciplinarity in the energy sector literature. Then, an overview of related methodologies for researchers and action research. Lastly, recommendations and tips for fruitful collaboration among policymakers, citizens, private actors and academics for inter and transdisciplinary effort toward a fair and just energy transition.

2 Interdisciplinarity in the energy sector literature

The energy sector is influenced by a variety of technical and social processes. They all tackle specific problems from moment to moment, hour to hour, day to day, and over the medium and long term, but none of them is in charge of the entire energy complex (e.g., generation, transportation, distribution, storage, marketing, consumption, and so on) at the same time. Instead, a division of labour has been established to allow for a high degree of 'organised complexity', as all of those elements must work together to provide energy services. This division of labour is only conceivable if people, groups, or organizations who work primarily in one functional system of society (e.g., economy, politics, science, or law) are largely unburdened by the complex details of the other areas.

No societal agent is overseeing all energy-related actions because there is no all-purpose machine creating and distributing energy. This includes law as an agent: while energy supply is often seen as a public service, stakeholders from academia (experts), industry (power plant operators), and the general public (customers) all contribute to the operation of the energy system. Energy services are generally recognized to be maintained exclusively by the 'bounded rationality' of interest-driven actors.

Plus, around the world the energy transition governance substantially fluctuates alongside disruptive events (Saltelli et al., 2020; Sumpf et al., 2018). In 2011, for instance, prices soared as a result of the Libyan War, and oil production abruptly dropped off the market at a massive level. Alternatively, we had Hurricane Katrina and other major occurrences including, very recently, the Russia-Ukraine armed conflict, which similarly affected energy supply and prices. Worldwide we are not just in the midst of an energy crisis, but also in the midst of a pricing war about oil, natural gas, coal, metals, and power costs. On top of that, there is the post-COVID recovery and demand, as well as a variety of natural phenomena and weather-related causes, all so interconnected that a dry season in China or Brazil can mean a lack of hydropower, which means higher demand for natural gas, coal, and oil.

Regional collaboration on integrated power markets and investment in regional energy infrastructure integration are becoming more common to face these contextual issues (European Commission, 2016; Sarrica et al., 2018). This type of collaboration must be enhanced in numerous parts of the world. South-South cooperation may play an important role in this respect, particularly in the exchange of experiences and best practices. Many industries are already shifting, driven by economic considerations as well as a feeling of social and moral duty, referred to as 'social license to operate'. As technology advances and countries enforce stricter environmental rules, manufacturers around the world are ramping up manufacturing of electric vehicles. But energy actors who work alone risk enacting policies that stifle energy availability, limit economic growth, and ameliorate one environmental consequence while exacerbating another. As a result, broad stakeholder participation is critical (Robison et al., 2018).

'Multi-stakeholder interests' are a major subject in European energy transition discussions (Hafner and Raimondi, 2020; Robison et al., 2018). Multiple players are involved in carrying out the visions set forth by designers, industry, and politics (Nieße et al., 2012) to realize the lofty goals of "great changes" (Pérez et al., 2019; German Advisory Council on Global Change, 2011, p. 5). For example, "consumers" (p. 25), "industry" (p. 43), and "SMEs" (Small and Medium-sized Enterprises; p. 141) are mentioned as relevant actors in energy transitions to ensure coherence and complementarity of activities and leverage of knowledge and investment possibilities.

In the latest Horizon Europe EU's research funding programme, the partnership for energy transition is expected to foster close collaboration and synergies with other ongoing EU and nationally-funded R&I actions, the mission on 'Climate-neutral and Smart Cities' as well as other relevant Horizon Europe European Partnerships (e. g., Clean Energy Transitions; Built environment and construction; Rescuing biodiversity; Safe and Sustainable Food System; 2ZERO; Cooperative, Connected and Automated Mobility (CCAM); EIT Urban Mobility, and Water4All). Particularly in the Horizon Europe – Work Programme 2021–2022 Climate, Energy and Mobility, much importance is placed on developing an Interoperability Maturity Model (IMM) to indicate the level of maturity in organisations, and the further effort/actions needed to be made to reach higher levels of interoperability. To create a network of interested parties, and eventually, setting up a distributed European ecosystem of centres for the Interoperability testing of data-driven energy solutions, requires linking stakeholders at living labs, digital innovation hubs, JRCs Interoperability testing lab-related ERA-Net program calls and Clean Energy Transition Partnership.

In the same Horizon Europe, the Clean Energy Transition Partnership (CETP) also intends to accelerate the energy transition and contribute to the EU's objective of being the first climate-neutral continent by 2050 from a research and innovation standpoint. To attain this lofty aim, Europe must begin a transformational process including the energy system, its supporting technologies, and society as a whole. This change will require key enabling and disruptive technologies, as well as system innovation. The energy transition may be transformed into an opportunity for long-term prosperity and competitiveness by investing heavily in innovation and technology development, generating high-quality employment and leaving no one behind.

ETIPs, IWGs, and/or similar fora are encouraged to align and coordinate their activities, defining cross-cutting aspects for accelerating the clean energy transition and contributing to the development of a European Research Area in the energy field, taking into account the overarching goal of the clean energy transition. On the last note, the call "HORIZON-CL5-2021-D2-01-12: Fostering a just transition in Europe" (European Union, 2021) is dedicated to climate and environmental advantages to be combined with intra- and intergenerational justice, for example, through reducing poverty and inequality across different sectors of society, as well as within and across nations and regions. Proposals to be funded should look into the connections and combinations of climate-focused policies with social, fiscal, and employment policies, among other things. Recommendations on the most effective levers for an inclusive, just, and equitable ecological transition should be made, meaning that Europe now explicitly requires researchers to mobilize and build on knowledge from a wide range of social sciences (including behavioural science, political science, sociology, economics, law, gender studies) as well as the humanities, and to engage all members of the helix (governments, industry/SMEs, social partners, academia/research, citizens/civil society) in a meaningful transdisciplinary and cross-activity manner. This is all to be conducted in synergy with the HORIZON-CL5-2021-D2-01-15 subject on Transition Super-Labs, since equality and fairness issues will also be essential in that context. Of course, this cooperation is far from being 'physiological' when implemented in joint research projects.

While energy-related Social Sciences and Humanities (energy-SSH) research frequently focuses on conflicting interests, hidden motives, and lobbies in the energy sector who prevent change and have no interest in cooperation, in contrast to the political ideals of stakeholder cooperation to achieve a broader goal (see for example (Geels et al., 2016; Sovacool, 2014)), others, generally with a STEM background, argue in favour of so-called 'roadmaps' (overarching step-by-step plans) that only need to be prepared to coordinate multi-stakeholder cooperation for the development of society.

In general, SSH researchers consider energy systems to be a socio-technical system or a huge technical system (representing many others: Mayntz, 2009):

- Socio-technical systems include not only artificial and physical, chemical, and biological components, but also psychological, cognitive, and social factors that are recursively linked to form 'socio-technical' entities;
- They also pervade and span all aspects of modern society, linking not only infrastructure systems but also the functional domains of politics, economics, law, and science;
- They are required for the bulk of other technical systems to perform properly;
- Finally, socio-technical systems are supposed to provide a broad variety of services to the entire population. The population is included in the function and performance capability of largescale systems through a network-like interaction of specialized organizational systems, even though the people have been generally excluded from (infrastructure) decision-making processes.

As a result, we can identify the issues of operational safety, supply security (which includes data protection in smart grids), service affordability, and sustainability in the use of scarce resources and emissions reduction as overall goals of grand-scale energy systems. This normative system logic, which is founded on societal ideals (such as data privacy and sustainability), is not always in line with the aims and interests of the contributing social actors.

There is disagreement not just about how to attain these objectives, but also over how safe, secure, economical, or sustainable energy services may and should be (Sovacool et al., 2015). Multiple goals and values also conflict with one another, and pursuing competing objectives inevitably results in trade-offs. Examples include the fact that safety and security are costly, that everyone's affordability eats into earnings, and that sustainability entails passing up current opportunities in favour of future ones. As a result, in the SSH sector, the term 'stakeholder' has come to be used to indicate the pursuit of a single ('particularistic') interest. There is a clear inference that a social entity (e.g., an individual, group, or organization) pursues interests in the result of an operation, exercise, project, or process, in addition to the definition of 'actor'. We can see how each energy issue has many references to the appropriate functional domains when broken down to the energy field: every power plant operation has scientific, economic, legal, and political ramifications. Every power plant's development, implementation, operation, and, eventually, decommissioning, unites, combines, and consolidates multi-stakeholder interests until some usable output may be expected.

We refer to specific cross-cutting dimensions, which require ongoing attention to reproduce energy services, to structure the multi-stakeholder interest landscape:

1. 'Complexity and control', for instance, all those persons engaged in maintaining control over the delivery of energy services amid increasingly complex technological and social processes; in system operation (power plants and grids, for example); in the supervision of operations and market activities; and security of technical installations and cyber-infrastructures (Groth and Corijn, 2005);
2. 'Institutional change and learning', i.e. those maintaining stable orientations notwithstanding the requirement for testing and learning for the development and enhancement of the energy complex. For example, knowledge protection and exchange, legal rulings, norm establishing, economic investment programs, political financing schemes, stimulating innovation and dissemination, scaling up experiments, executing participatory exercises, and so on (Lyall, 2019);
3. 'Coping with uncertainty, risk, and danger', all the things necessary to absorb uncertainty despite rising non-transparency in socio-technical systems and institutions, to maintain action capability. For example, faith in top-down decision systems, education, active consumer engagement, etc. (Lotz-Sisitka et al., 2015).

Linking these three dimensions is the challenge of any inter and transdisciplinary approach to the low-carbon transition in the energy sector. To grasp the complexity of the interplay between these regimes, we invite you to refer to the beautiful paper of Geels and colleagues (Geels et al., 2004), in which they delve into the institution's black box, which should be utilized to explain more than mere inertia and stability of the energy system depicted 'just' as a map. Dynamics are essential to think about how actors and structures interact in real-time. Using concepts from sociology, institutional theory, and innovation studies, Geels and colleagues give a cohesive conceptual multi-level view of long-term dynamics, changes from one socio-technical system to another, and the co-evolution of technology and society. As a result, socio-technical problems are understood as distinct nuclei to which disciplinary perspectives are related and then unfold, possibly while maintaining theories and methods that are unique to respective disciplines. Sociotechnical problems (control, change, and action) are historically invariant, while their numerous methodologies for problem-solving are contingent and variable.

3 Methods for inter- and trans-disciplinary research in the energy sector

In energy research and policy, integration has been considered the 'gold standard' (Siedlok and Hibbert, 2014). However, given the difficulties of establishing functional collaborative processes aimed at integration, we must remain sceptical about the utility, need, and relevance of any kind of integration and/or collaboration in connection to the quality of the desired product. Differences across disciplines are frequently cited in the literature on interdisciplinarity as a major impediment to efficient multidisciplinary teamwork. The "discipline culture" is shaped by these epistemic disparities (Bonaccorsi, 2018). Each discipline, or even field, has its own definition of what makes knowledge and what constitutes dependable sources of legitimate knowledge claims. Even how such information may be utilized correctly varies by field (Tuana, 2013). Epistemological and ontological differences manifest geographically, effectively, and through uneven epistemological power relations (Callard et al., 2015), both in interdisciplinary and above all in transdisciplinary approaches.

At first glance, drawing a clear line between interdisciplinary and transdisciplinary research appears difficult, with "the boundaries between interdisciplinary and transdisciplinary projects [being...] diffuse and dependent more on a subjective judgment on the level of holism applied than on the presence of clear boundary markers" (Stock and Burton, 2011, p. 1102). Transdisciplinarity, in contrast to multidisciplinary work, necessitates collaboration outside academics, including a varied range of players from many sectors (e.g. policymakers, end users, practitioners, and communities) to take a holistic approach. Furthermore, transdisciplinary research design, as well as the definition of relevant knowledge and problem definition, involves a participatory process in which non-academic actors are invited to co-create and co-produce knowledge, such as through real-world laboratories (field labs, social labs, and living labs) in which experiments are conducted (De Boer et al., 2006). Transdisciplinarity deals with "problem fields in such a way that it can:

1. grasp the complexity of problems;
2. take into account the diversity of life-world and scientific perceptions of problems;
3. link abstract and case-specific knowledge, and;
4. develop knowledge and practices that promote what is perceived to be the common good" (Pohl and Hadorn, 2007, p. 20).

Qualitative social science methods like qualitative research, ethnomethodology, and action research are beneficial for accessing and exploring the knowledge of researchers and actors in the real world. Quantitative research methods are supplemented with qualitative research approaches (Creswell and Creswell, 1994; Gutscher et al., 1996). The symmetry principle that "enjoins us to seek the same type of explanations for both correct and wrong, rational and irrational beliefs [...]" should lead the analyst who employs such procedures (Bloor, 1991, p. 175).

On the other hand, STEM disciplines may give information about factors that have a role in the problem and aid in the development of an upgraded model of the problem in terms of how various parameters are associated with hard systems thinking. While an economist may offer information on economic factors that contribute to energy poverty, psychologists can look into the issue at the level of household use, and sociologists can look into the dynamics of global societal change. Their findings can be used in both qualitative and quantitative models.

Soft systems thinking recognizes that scientific discoveries are only significant in the context of a discipline's conceptual and methodological framework. In that case, it is disciplinary viewpoints, not data integration, that must be addressed. In addition, the viewpoints of players in the real world, which are framed by their roles, experiences and values, must be integrated with scientific ideas.

In both soft and hard thinking, the transdisciplinary approach in energy-related issues means that a linear model is replaced by a recursive model. The research process should be organized in such a manner that theory and techniques are regularly evaluated by putting them into practice, and underlying assumptions can be amended if they are proven to be unsuitable. This type of recursive design is a practical technique to keep a project from being stuck due to ambiguity or a lack of information.

Operational or operations research (van Raan and van Leeuwen, 2002), action research and policy sciences (Heidenreich et al., 2017) are disciplinary contributions to the topic of practical relevance in a real-world setting. Several participatory research methodologies are available in operational research and action research, such as issue structuring approaches (Schauppenlehner-Kloyber and Penker, 2015), soft-systems thinking (Checkland, 1994), and the strategic choice approach (Fleiter et al., 2018). These strategies are often applied in a highly pragmatic manner, with the primary purpose of contributing to solving issues in a real-world setting (Saltelli et al., 2020). According to Horlick-Jones and Rosenhead (2007, p. 595), issue structuring strategies are a "methodological bricolage". "Shall the practitioner stay on the high, hard terrain where he may practice rigorously [...]? Or shall he descend to the swamp where he can engage the most important and challenging problems [...]?" (Schön, 1987, p. 42). Theoretical and methodological contributions from ethics and political philosophy also apply to the conceptual analysis phase (Plant and Stone, 1991). Furthermore, political science provides participatory methods for deliberations such as hearings, advisory committees, panels, and juries, mediation, negotiated rulemaking, round tables, and consensus conferences (Renn, 1998), which can be useful in the research process as a means of knowledge production.

While meeting these methodological integration challenges is crucial to guarantee a collaboration between relevant institutions, technologies, and infrastructure that shape the energy system (Schuitema and Sintov, 2017), in an article written in 2021 (Arrobbio and Sonetti, 2021) we wanted to unveil the barriers for this integration to happen. Aligned with plenty of literature on this topic (see for instance Guimarães et al., (2019)), we found out that the cognitive, emotional, and interactional aspects have been found to varying degrees in all networks within and beyond academic contexts, and they relate to the necessity of alignment between people, organizations, and institutional objectives for effective cooperation. Although many scholars acknowledged that the borders between these domains are permeable, Tuana (2013) defines three basic categories: institutional obstacles, (ii) disciplinary barriers, and (iii) epistemic hurdles. Personal elements including beliefs, expectations, objectives, and experience; the physical surroundings; and bureaucratic and structural concerns are all antecedents.

So, to conclude on the methodological aspects, for a successful joint research endeavour we stress the importance of cultivating the characteristics of an inter-trans-disciplinary researcher, who shall possess:

- the ability to build bridges and networks, as well as develop good communication and listening skills (i.e., the capacity to engage in meaningful dialogue that suspends one's point of view) (Polk, 2014);
- the ability to absorb information (Fam and O'Rourke, 2020; Goldstein and Butler, 2010);
- the capacity to integrate knowledge, think in a complex and interconnected manner, and relate to the logic of complexity (Anzai et al., 2012; Napoli, 2018; Rau et al., 2018);
- the ability to find and use relevant information, compare and contrast different methods and approaches, clarify how differences and similarities relate to a specific task and create a synthesis, an integrative framework, or a more holistic understanding of a specific theme, question, or problem (Klein and Falk-Krzesinski, 2017);
- The ability to distinguish themselves for having a powerful social conscience and awareness (Klein, 2015); the capacity for disciplined self-reflexivity (Spreng, 2014);
- and finally, metacognitive skills that enable lifelong learning, such as critical thinking, learning on demand, and self-directed learning (Yanez et al., 2019).

Pohl and Hadorn (2007) emphasize the need to learn more about the range of viewpoints among participants, as well as investigate and explain their differences, to facilitate conversation and collaborative integration within a group or team. In inter- and trans-disciplinary projects, the overall goal is to encourage shared group learning and problem resolution. Mutual trust, personal chemistry, and a sense of security are all important factors in this form of research (Callard and Fitzgerald, 2015).

4 Conclusions

In general, the distinction between the complexity of the overall energy system (production, transportation, distribution, and consumption) and the interests of all connected stakeholders from business and industry, as well as politics and the general public, must be acknowledged. Stakeholder-specific agendas are the 'regular mode,' and they help to keep the system working within the status quo. However, the topic of how those restricted stakeholder interests, through their interplay, really form a coherent overall energy system that undeniably communicates output (e.g. electricity) may gain greater attention from a dedicated range of transdisciplinary researchers.

Both academic/industry researchers (via projects and platforms) and policymakers must be aware of the rising infrastructure convergence between analogue and digital energy technologies to manage complexity and control as a crucial feature of transitioning energy systems. This convergence (for instance in 'smart grids') results in the creation of hybrid knowledge combining engineering, computer science, and social sciences. A lack of reflection in this area might lead to omissions in realizing the potential of smart grids in particular: owing to communication barriers within disciplines, certain stakeholders not only strive to slow down this growth but also do not engage in collaboration.

This is of utmost importance for those coming from the law sector in terms of energy system governance since government initiatives often encourage and enforce the 'unbundling' of vertically integrated energy generation, transportation, and distribution networks. Better services, lower prices, and higher reliability are among the political expectations. Researchers in the energy-SSH community, however, question the usefulness of these aims in accomplishing them. The organization of energy supply was imposed in this context by system external regulation, which required vertically integrated enterprises to perform legal, operational, informational, and accounting unbundling. This is an instance of a structural rupture between technological installations and social organization, as experts (e.g. Künneke 2008) point out. This has the ability to degrade (and corrupt) the system's overall performance: "The electricity value chain seems to evolve towards unbundling and specialisation, whereas technology is based on integrated system planning" (Künneke, 2008, p. 239). Individual actors and their economic calculations of return on investment, on the one hand, and the overall system and the technical requirement of central control, on the other, can be deduced from this observation, which crystallizes in light of different rationalities. As a result, movements in the direction of power plant expansion may be observed, with economic incentives and stakes driving decisions rather than the overall demands and long-term stability of the system.

Energy-SSH research, in part, reveals a significant normative bias, not only in terms of comprehending transitions but also in terms of developing governance choices to promote the transition/transformation toward sustainability. Indeed, transformation research aims to contribute to goal-oriented transformation governance by analyzing these processes, as well as the impact of external variables and stakeholder configurations. Such study, on the other hand, rarely entails the formulation of explicit norms or principles for action and policy-making. We can state that energy-SSH research has created a rich corpus of insights into transformational dynamics due to its focus on change and accompanying bias for sustainability, innovation, and niche development. However, the balance required for stable orientations in extremely complex fields has been somewhat overlooked in energy systems. Instead, SSH inquiries into the acute problem of uncertainty, such as an investor or consumer uncertainty, might be useful here. All relevant parties must deal with uncertainty, which is different for decision-makers (e.g., politicians, utilities, start-ups) and those who are affected by decisions (consumers, population, enterprises). The latter may be hesitant or even hostile to engaging in large-scale energy transitions that are unavoidable trials, which is a compelling case for performing more uncertain research in the energy sector.

To conclude, there is a pressing need to develop and execute legislative and regulatory frameworks that allow for faster energy transitions throughout the world. The COVID-19 epidemic has demonstrated that governments can respond fast to difficulties and address concerns when they are faced with a pressing need to do so. Energy transitions, on the other hand, will not occur at the same rate in every country or location. They must take into consideration all stakeholder groups, including all levels of government, regulators, utilities, cities, and civil society, including youth, and must represent national needs, priorities, and abilities.

Engagement with the private sector is also essential, and public capital providers (such as multilateral and national development banks) play a key role in attracting private investments. The existing frameworks underpinning the electricity sector, for example, were originally designed for large-scale and technically complex conventional power-generation and transmission systems, designed and built primarily by regulated entities, resulting in high transaction costs and lengthy project development and finance timelines.

The deployment of modern decentralized solutions is hampered by these traditional systems. They will need to be altered by laws that can accommodate a variety of decentralized and variable energy sources, as well as the vaster number of customers who have assumed the role of prosumers. This entails short-term transformative change for economies and society while ensuring long-term sustainability.

Energy transformations (before energy transitions) will need policymakers to skilfully balance many technological, economic, and societal issues. Renewable energy prices are lowering, and fast innovation and information exchange have made this balance easier to achieve than in the past. Given the global economy's substantial reliance on fossil fuels, the issue of reconciling short-term requirements with long-term implications in an unpredictable global economic climate should not be overlooked. Labour and social-protection policies must be customized to the individual circumstances of each area and country in order to ensure a just transition. To facilitate the transition, a conversation between the government, employers, employees, and civil society must be developed. Short-term employment services, such as connecting positions with competent applicants, allowing on- and off-the-job training, and providing safety nets, are examples of labor-market interventions. Longer-term programs should work on the education system as a whole to guarantee that curriculum are aligned with society's future requirements. To fully tap into societal potential and guarantee that no one is left behind, social equity issues, particularly gender and youth components, must be included into policy and program design.

References

Anzai, T., Kusama, R., Kodama, H., and Sengoku, S., 2012. Holistic observation and monitoring of the impact of interdisciplinary academic research projects: An empirical assessment in Japan. *Technovation*. 32(6), pp. 345–357.

Arrobbio, O., and Sonetti, G., 2021. Cinderella lost? Barriers to the integration of energy Social Sciences and Humanities outside academia. *Energy Research & Social Science*, 73, 101929.

Bloor, D., 1991. *Knowledge and social imagery*. Chicago: University of Chicago Press.

Bonaccorsi, A., 2018. Towards an epistemic approach to evaluation in SSH. In: A. Bonaccorsi, ed., 2018. *The evaluation of research in social sciences and humanities*. Cham: Springer, pp. 1–29.

Callard, F., and Fitzgerald, D., 2015. *Rethinking interdisciplinarity across the social sciences and neurosciences*. Cham: Palgrave Macmillan.

Callard, F., Fitzgerald, D. and Woods, A., 2015. Interdisciplinary collaboration in action: tracking the signal, tracing the noise. *Palgrave Communications*, 1(1), 15019.

Checkland, P., 1994. Systems theory and management thinking. *American Behavioral Scientist*, 38(1), pp. 75–91.

Creswell, J.W. and Creswell, J.D., 1994. *Research design*. Thousand Oaks, CA: Sage.

De Boer, Y., De Gier, A., Verschuur, M., and De Wit, B., 2006. *Building bridges researchers on their experiences with interdisciplinary research in the Netherlands*. Den Haag: Advisory council for research on spatial planning, nature and the environment RMNO et al.

European Union, 2021. Cross-sectoral solutions for the climate transition (HORIZON-CL5-2021-D2-01). Retrieved from https://ec.europa.eu/info/funding-tenders.

European Commission, 2016. *Urban Agenda for the EU*. Pact of Amsterdam (May 30).

Fam, D., and O'Rourke, M., 2020. *Interdisciplinary and transdisciplinary failures: lessons learned from cautionary tales*. London and New York, NY: Routledge.

Fazey, I., Schäpke, N., Caniglia, G. et al., 2020. Transforming knowledge systems for life on Earth: visions of future systems and how to get there. *Energy Research & Social Science*, 70, 101724.

Fleiter, T., Rehfeldt, M., Herbst, A. et al., 2018. A methodology for bottom-up modelling of energy transitions in the industry sector: The FORECAST model. *Energy Strategy Reviews*, 22, pp. 237–254.

Geels, F., Berkhout, F., and Vuuren, D., 2016. Bridging analytical approaches for low-carbon transitions. *Nature Climate Change*, 6, pp. 576–583.

Geels, F. W., Elzen, B., and Green, K., 2004. General introduction: system innovation and transitions to sustainability. In: B. Elzen, F.W. Geels and K. Green, eds., 2004. *System Innovation and the Transition to Sustainability: Theory, Evidence and Policy*. Cheltenham: Edward Elgar Publishing, pp. 1–16.

German Advisory Council on Global Change, 2011. *Transforming Energy Systems. WBGU Factsheet No. 2*.

Goldstein, B.E. and Butler, W.H., 2010. Expanding the scope and impact of collaborative planning: combining multi-stakeholder collaboration and communities of practice in a learning network. *Journal of the American Planning Association*, 76(2), pp. 238–249.

Groth, J. and Corijn, E., 2005. Reclaiming urbanity: indeterminate spaces, informal actors and urban agenda setting. *Urban Studies*, 42(3), pp. 503–526.

Guimarães, M.H., Pohl, C., Bina, O., and Varanda, M., 2019. Who is doing inter-and transdisciplinary research, and why? An empirical study of motivations, attitudes, skills, and behaviours. *Futures*, 112, 102441.

Gutscher, M.-A., Kukowski, N., Malavieille, J., and Lallemand, S., 1996. Cyclical behavior of thrust wedges: insights from high basal friction sandbox experiments. *Geology*, 24(2), pp. 135–138.

Hafner, M., and Raimondi, P.P., 2020. Priorities and challenges of the EU energy transition: from the European Green Package to the new Green Deal. *Russian Journal of Economics*, 6, pp. 374–389.

Heidenreich, S., Throndsen, W., Sari, R. et al., 2017. *Competitive, secure, low-carbon energy supply – A social science and humanities annotated bibliography*. Cambridge: SHAPE ENERGY Project. Available at: https://shapeenergy.eu/wp-content/uploads/2017/07/SHAPE-ENERGY-Annotated-Bibliography_COMPETITIVE_SECURE_LOW-CARBON-ENERGY-SUPPLY.pdf. [Accessed 6 December 2022].

Horlick-Jones, T., and Rosenhead, J., 2007. The uses of observation: combining problem structuring methods and ethnography. *Journal of the Operational Research Society*, 58(5), pp. 588–601.

Klein, J.T., 2015. Reprint of "Discourses of transdisciplinarity: Looking back to the future". *Futures*, 65, pp. 10–16.

Klein, J.T. and Falk-Krzesinski, H.J., 2017. Interdisciplinary and collaborative work: framing promotion and tenure practices and policies. *Research Policy*, 46(6), pp. 1055–1061.

Künneke, R. W., 2008. Institutional reform and technological practice: the case of electricity. *Industrial and Corporate Change*, 17(2), pp. 233–265.

Lotz-Sisitka, H., Wals, A.E.J., Kronlid, D., and McGarry, D., 2015. Transformative, transgressive social learning: rethinking higher education pedagogy in times of systemic global dysfunction. *Current Opinion in Environmental Sustainability*, 16, pp. 73–80.

Lyall, C., 2019. Towards new logics of interdisciplinarity. In: C. Lyall, ed., 2019. *Being an interdisciplinary academic: how institutions shape university careers.* Cham: Springer International Publishing, pp. 91–109.

Mayntz, R., 2009. *Über Governance: Institutionen und Prozesse politischer Regelung*. Frankfurt a. M.: Campus Verlag.

Napoli, G., 2018. The complexity of value and the evaluation of complexity: social use value and multi-criteria analysis. In: G. Mondini, E. Fattinnanzi, A. Oppio et al., eds., 2018. *Integrated evaluation for the management of contemporary cities*. Cham: Springer International Publishing, pp. 187–198.

Nieße, A., Lehnhoff, S., Tröschel, M. et al., 2012. Market-based self-organized provision of active power and ancillary services: an agent-based approach for smart distribution grids. *Complexity in Engineering (COMPENG). Proceedings*. IEEE, pp. 1–5.

Pérez, M. de la E.M., Scholten, D., and Stegen, K.S., 2019. The multi-speed energy transition in Europe: opportunities and challenges for EU energy security. *Energy Strategy Reviews*, 26, 100415.

Plant, R.E., and Stone, N.D., 1991. *Knowledge-based systems in agriculture*. New York, NY: McGraw-Hill.

Pohl, C., and Hadorn, G.H., 2007. *Principles for designing transdisciplinary research*. Munich: oekom Verlag.

Polk, M., 2014. Achieving the promise of transdisciplinarity: a critical exploration of the relationship between transdisciplinary research and societal problem solving. *Sustainability Science*, 9(4), pp. 439–451.

Rau, H., Goggins, G., and Fahy, F., 2018. From invisibility to impact: recognising the scientific and societal relevance of interdisciplinary sustainability research. *Research Policy*, 47(1), pp. 266–276.

Renn, O., 1998. Three decades of risk research: accomplishments and new challenges. *Journal of Risk Research*, 1(1), pp. 49–71.

Robison, R., Dupas, S., Mourik, R. et al., 2018. Europe's local energy challenges: stories and research priorities from 17 multi-stakeholder city workshops. Cambridge: SHAPE ENERGY Project. Available at: https://shapeenergy.eu/wp-content/uploads/2018/12/Workshop-Key-Findings.pdf [Accessed 6 December 2022].

Saltelli, A., Benini, L., Funtowicz, S. et al., 2020. The technique is never neutral. How methodological choices condition the generation of narratives for sustainability. *Environmental Science & Policy*, 106, pp. 87–98.

Sarrica, M., Biddau, F., Brondi, S., Cottone, P., and Mazzara, B.M., 2018. A multi-scale examination of public discourse on energy sustainability in Italy: empirical evidence and policy implications. *Energy Policy*, 114, pp. 444–454.

Schauppenlehner-Kloyber, E., and Penker, M., 2015. Managing group processes in transdisciplinary future studies: how to facilitate social learning and capacity building for self-organised action towards sustainable urban development? *Futures*, 65, pp. 57–71.

Schön, D.A., 1987. *Educating the reflective practitioner: Toward a new design for teaching and learning in the professions.* San Francisco, CA: Jossey-Bass.

Schuitema, G. and Sintov, N.D., 2017. Should we quit our jobs? Challenges, barriers and recommendations for interdisciplinary energy research. *Energy Policy*, 101, pp. 246–250.

Siedlok, F., and Hibbert, P., 2014. The organization of interdisciplinary research: Modes, drivers and barriers. *International Journal of Management Reviews*, 16(2), pp. 194–210.

Sonetti, G., Arrobbio, O., Lombardi, P. et al., 2020. 'Only social scientists laughed': reflections on social sciences and humanities integration in European energy projects. *Energy Research & Social Science*, 61, 101342.

Sovacool, B.K., Ryan, S.E., Stern, P.C. et al., 2015. Integrating social science in energy research. *Energy Research & Social Science*, 6, pp. 95–99.

Sovacool, B.K., 2014. What are we doing here? Analyzing fifteen years of energy scholarship and proposing a social science research agenda. *Energy Research & Social Science*, 1, pp. 1–29.

Spreng, D., 2014. Transdisciplinary energy research – Reflecting the context. *Energy Research & Social Science*, 1, pp. 65–73.

Stock, P., and Burton, R.J.F., 2011. Defining terms for integrated (multi-inter-trans-disciplinary) sustainability research. *Sustainability*, 3(8), pp. 1090–1113.

Sumpf, P., Büscher, C., Claudot, P. et al., 2018. *Reflexive review of interdisciplinary working.* Cambridge: SHAPE ENERGY Project. Available at: https://shapeenergy.eu/wp-content/uploads/2019/03/SHAPE-ENERGY-D4.2-Reflexive-review-of-interdisciplinary-working.pdf. [Accessed 6 December 2022].

Tuana, N., 2013. Embedding philosophers in the practices of science: bringing humanities to the sciences. *Synthese*, 190, pp. 1955–1973.

van Raan, A.F. and van Leeuwen, T., 2002. Assessment of the scientific basis of interdisciplinary, applied research: Application of bibliometric methods in Nutrition and Food research. *Research Policy*, 31(4), pp. 611–632.

Yanez, G.A., Thumlert, K., de Castell, S., and Jenson, J., 2019. Pathways to sustainable futures: A "production pedagogy" model for STEM education. *Futures*, 108, pp. 27–36.

Hannah J. Wiseman

Energy Governance Models

Abstract: The shape and pace of the transition to low-carbon energy will differ around the globe due to variations in energy governance models. Energy governance, broadly defined, is the system of mandates and incentives that shapes the types of fuels and electricity generation infrastructure used within geopolitical boundaries. Two central features of energy governance involve the organization and structure of the institutions that regulate energy and the economic actors that provide fuels and electricity. With respect to institutions, some energy governance involves federalist-type systems, such as the United States or the European Union, in which a top-down actor issues directives for lower-level governments to implement, or top-down and lower-level actors operate in parallel. Energy governance also involves more centralized approaches and decentralized ones, in which governmental sub-units issue their own mandates and incentives – sometimes in coordination with each other, and sometimes not. With respect to the economic organization of energy actors, there are three basic models: government-owned and directed fuel extraction and electricity provision; competitive and partially deregulated industries; and hybrids, involving both government-led and private energy development. There are many organizational variations within these three primary economic models. For example, some systems primarily involve vertically-integrated firms that provide electricity generation, transmission, and distribution or fuel production and transport, whereas others are more restructured. All of these models pose opportunities and challenges in terms of transitioning rapidly to zero-carbon or net-zero carbon energy. For example, a strong, centralized government with a government-owned, vertically-integrated energy industry can quickly lower emissions, but any institutional disinclination to do so can stall the transition. A relatively decentralized approach involving numerous private, restructured actors can result in slower, more tepid or disorganized efforts to lower carbon but also allows for the development of innovative, aggressive carbon reduction strategies that might ultimately find broader support.

Hannah J. Wiseman is a Professor of Law, Professor and Wilson Faculty Fellow in the College of Earth and Mineral Sciences, and Institutes of Energy and the Environment Co-funded Faculty Member, Penn-State Law, United States.

https://doi.org/10.1515/9783110752403-010

1 Introduction

The global transition toward lower carbon energy resources is emerging within a highly varied set of energy governance structures, which control or influence individuals' and organizations' behavior and are, in turn, influenced by such behavior. Indeed, governance systems are the foundation of the energy transition: they drive the substance and pace of the transition. Two features of these governance systems that centrally shape the energy transition include institutions – rules, and organizations that write and enforce rules – and the actors subject to governance. In the context of the low-carbon energy transition, the actors subject to governance are numerous, ranging from residential and commercial energy consumers to large power plants, automobile manufacturers, and industrial operators. Increasingly, statutes and regulations require and incentivize the electrification of residential and commercial heating systems and vehicles, steer power generation toward renewable or nuclear sources, and mandate or fund movements toward industrial electrification or transitions to green fuels, such as hydrogen produced with zero-carbon energy.

There are two major types of institutions within energy governance systems. These include public organizations – traditional public institutions such as legislative bodies, executive leaders, and agencies or ministries – and the statutes and regulations that they promulgate. Secondly, private actors govern through consensus rules or standards or "environmental and social governance" (ESG principles). Through ESG approaches and similar corporate governance, corporations change their behaviors in response to shareholder or consumer demand, internal pressures, or influence from the communities in which they operate (Vandenbergh & Gilligan, 2017; Reali et al., 2018).[1] ESG is increasingly important in the transition to lower carbon energy resources, particularly for filling in public governance gaps or influencing public approaches to the transition. The urgency of the energy transition is pushing public and private energy institutions to be more flexible – testing the extent of their malleability.

In the context of public governance, several features affect the ability of institutions to adapt to energy transition needs and address the impacts of the transition in an equitable way. The features discussed here include the degree of centralization of public governance institutions; the level of public involvement in the ownership and control of governed energy resources; and, relatedly, the extent to which energy markets are regulated or restructured. Exploration of these public governance features and private governance tools in this chapter provides context for the detailed analyses of energy transitions throughout the book.

1 ESG typically refers to corporate behavior in relation to investors, whereas the terms corporate governance, "private environmental governance," and corporate social responsibility refer to a broader suite of voluntary corporate behaviors in the environmental space (ISO, 2010; Schanzenbach & Sitkoff, 2020; Vandenbergh, 2007; Vandenbergh, 2013).

2 Public Energy Governance

2.1 Degree of Centralization

Public governance regimes in energy and other policy areas differ along multiple lines, from the type of electoral and representative systems to the degree of democratic or authoritarian control. But a feature that centrally affects the flexibility of a governance system in response to energy transition demands is the extent to which the government relies on top-down, centralized control or more diffuse authority. In this regard, governance regimes rest at various points on the following spectrum: 1) highly centralized – involving top-down authority emanating from one or several national governing institutions, 2) highly decentralized, involving municipal governments, states, or provinces holding primary governmental authority, or 3) a hybrid, in which centralized and decentralized governments share authority. Indeed, the broader theoretical literature on the merits of hierarchical and polycentric governance informs analysis of governance in the energy sphere (Feeley & Rubin, 2008; Osofsky, 2016; Ostrom, 2012). Centralization, decentralization, and hybrid approaches can influence both the substance and pace of the energy transition in several ways. First, a top-down, centralized approach might tend to identify specific fuels or technologies to be phased out or implemented and direct all actors to follow these requirements. Alternatively, in decentralized systems, different states, provinces, or local governments are likely to implement varied approaches, some more flexible and successful than others. And in hybrid regimes, such as the United States, Europe, and China, both top-down and bottom-up forces drive or impede the energy transition.

Decentralized regimes offer potential advantages of innovative, relatively rapid approaches to the energy transition. Additionally, they serve as a buffer against national inaction. In a decentralized regime, when one state or province within a country refuses to act, others can potentially fill in the gaps. This type of regime can also address economic, political, climatic, and geographic differences that affect the ease and feasibility of the energy transition in specific regions. Decentralized approaches to the energy transition are not necessarily a natural governance fit, however, given the interconnected nature of the electricity grid (physical connections across sub-national and national lines) and the fact that the externalities of energy production and use also cross sub-national and national borders.

Centralized regimes address these physical and externality-based realities of the energy transition, allowing for a coordinated approach to an interconnected electricity grid and addressing some of the cross-border externalities of production. Additionally, if centralized actors choose to move forward with the energy transition, they can sometimes implement more ambitious and comprehensive transition measures. Centralized actors can also form and implement a coordinated transition regime, and they avoid potentially duplicative administrative overlap and conflicting sub-national requirements that could be costly for governance and governed actors. Conversely, if centralized actors move forward slowly with the transition and preempt subnational action, this decision might impede the energy transition more substantially than inaction by a few subnational actors. Furthermore, centralized approaches might fail to account for some of the sub-national economic, political, climatic, and geographic differences noted above and might not be as innovative or effective as those initiated at the sub-national level.

Hybrid regimes offer a potential balance between the benefits and costs of decentralized approaches. Sub-national governments with some independent authority can move forward with innovative measures above a nationally-established and relatively ambitious floor, such as a minimum percentage of renewable energy capacity consumption to be a achieved on a specific timeline (e.g., Saurer and Monast, 2021, p. 207; Balthasar et al., 2020, p. 6). With some implementation flexibility, sub-national governments can develop policy tools that address their unique economic, political, and other needs while achieving the national floor. The national floor also guards against inaction by sub-national actors, and although it risks being inadequately ambitious, it allows dedicated subnational actors to pursue their own, more ambitious efforts. A hybrid system also gives "policy entrepreneurs" more "access points" to energy decisions, potentially allowing for innovation in energy transition policy (Balthasar et al., 2020, pp. 5–6). But hybrid approaches, if not well coordinated, can create conflicts among governing actors, confusion for regulated parties, and even inaction (e.g., Saurer and Monast, 2021, p. 207). Indeed, federalist systems involving national, state, and local control create more "institutionalized blockage" points for "veto players" such as fossil fuel interests that might successfully prevent the formation of energy transition policies (Balthasar et al., 2020, p. 5). The following case studies explore the benefits and challenges of centralized, decentralized, and hybrid approaches.

Very few, if any, countries follow a wholly centralized or decentralized form of energy governance, but most lean toward one end of the spectrum. The EU and US provide helpful contrasts. Both of these regimes are hybrid models – a central authority does not make all of the energy or climate decisions. But the EU is more centralized and coordinated than the US in both energy and climate governance and has progressed farther in the energy transition – exhibiting more flexibility, drive, and innovation. This is not to say that centralization alone has hastened the transition. Political and cultural differences, among other factors, also play an important role. But this section explores the contribution of centralized approaches to Europe's energy transition and the challenges posed by the more decentralized US approach. For a discussion of Chinese energy governance see Chapters 7 and 22.

2.2 Europe's Efforts Toward an Integrated, Centralized Energy Policy

The European Union and its institutional arms have long prioritized centralization and integration of energy and climate policy while recognizing subsidiarity principles – the goal of leaving decisionmaking authority at the lowest possible governance level (Treaty on the European Union Article 5(3), 1997; Protocol on the Application of the Principles of Subsidiarity and Proportionality, 1992). In the energy context, the focus on centralization arises in part from concerns relating to member state dependence on Russian natural gas (Maltby, 2013 at 436). As early as 1968, the European Commission ("Commission") established a "Community Energy Policy" with goals of enhanced integration of member state policy and an EU energy action framework (Maltby, 2013, p. 437). Few of these goals took hold, however, until the 1990s, when the European Council and Parliament first issued directives for an internal market for natural gas, building from enabling measures in the 1986 Single European Act (Maltby, 2013 at 438. 2006 and 2008). Green papers and strategic energy reviews from the Energy Commission also emphasized the continued problem of member state-centric energy policy and recommended further integration (Maltby, 2013, p. 439). And in 2005, the EU – building from a 2000 Commission green paper – established the EU Emissions Trading System (ETS). The ETS enabled European-wide free trade in emissions allowances, a union-wide registry to track emissions allowance ownership (operative in 2012), and, in 2013, an EU-wide cap on greenhouse gas (GHG) emissions (European Commission, 2022h). The EU also made a more formal, broader move toward centralized and integrated energy governance in 2009 with the Lisbon Treaty, which identified energy as an area of shared EU-member state competence (Maltby, 2013, p. 440). In areas of shared competence, both Member States and the Union may legislate, but the states may legislate only if the Union has not acted (European Union 2022). This section explores recent, larger steps toward integration and centralization of policies for climate and energy production, energy infrastructure such as transmission lines and storage, and the socioeconomic effects of the energy transition.

2.3 Climate and Energy Policy

In 2009 and subsequent years, the EU has taken substantial steps toward integration and centralized leadership for energy transition policies. In 2009 the EU enacted legislation targeting a 20% EU-wide reduction in GHG emissions from 1990 levels (Dir. 2003/87 as amended), 20% of EU energy from renewable energy sources (Dir. 2009/28), and a 20% improvement in energy efficiency (Dir. 2012/27). Pre-pandemic numbers from 2019 showed a 24% European-wide reduction in 2019 as compared to 1990 levels (European Parliament, 2022). For energy sectors not covered by the EU-wide ETS and caps, including emissions from agriculture, waste, housing, and transportation, the Member States set binding annual national emission reduction targets through 2020 under Effort Sharing Regulation (Regulation (EU) 2018/842). Although the Effort Sharing Regulation is state centric, unlike the EU-level ETS with an EU-wide cap and monitoring, the title of the legislation highlights its collective nature. Binding targets are established based on Members States' relative wealth, thus involving a commitment by the wealthier states to take on a greater obligation for the collective whole. The Member States are currently in the 2021–2030 phase of this legislation (European Commission, 2022e).

The 2030 EU-wide targets for GHG emission reductions and removals are 40% below 1990 emissions levels, 32% of EU energy from renewable energy sources, and a 32.5% improvement in energy efficiency (Directive 2009/28/EC; Directive 2012/27/EU; European Commission, 2022c). These will be achieved through several measures, including the ETS, national binding emission reduction targets under Effort Sharing Legislation, and 2018 legislation on land use-based emissions (European Commission, 2022d). Perhaps the most ambitious efforts at integration and centralization of climate and energy to-date fall under the European Council's "Clean energy for all Europeans package," adopted in 2019, which consists of eight laws (European Commission, 2022f). The package aims to further integrate European electricity markets to enhance reliability and security and support renewable energy, including through strengthening the Agency for the Cooperation of Energy Regulators. One law within the package also requires Member States to adopt integrated national energy and climate plans (NECPs) and reporting; the Commission required all states to submit draft NECPs for comment by the Commission and final NECPs, and it issued an EU-wide assessment of the plans in addition to individualized assessments (European Commission, 2022f).

2.4 Energy Infrastructure Planning, Financing, and Siting

Another area of top-down integration and coordination in the EU involves the infrastructure necessary to support the energy transition, such as expanded transmission lines for renewable energy and storage projects to address intermittency and enhance reliability. The Trans-European Networks for Energy (TEN-E) regulation identifies three priority onshore electricity transmission corridors and five priority offshore areas for infrastructure development (Regulation (EU) 2022/869). To prioritize infrastructure development in these and other areas urgently in need of infrastructure expansion, the EU has created "Projects of Common Interest" (PCIs), which are shepherded forward by regional groups (see Chapter 11). These projects – approximately 61 of which were transmission projects in 2021 – receive streamlined planning and permitting within a national "one-stop-shop" that coordinates all permits (European Commission, 2018 at 16; European Commission, 2022k). The EU also provides financial assistance for PCIs (European Commission, 2018 at 16). Transmission challenges remain, however, as evidenced by Germany's drawn-out negotiations with Bavaria for the siting and ultimate undergrounding of transmission lines to carry wind power from the German north (Reuters, 2015).

2.5 Social Impacts of the Energy Transition

As Europe transitions toward zero-carbon sources of energy and reduces GHGs, the EU has taken substantial steps to centralize and coordinate policies to address the impacts of the transition on workers in the fossil fuel industry and communities that formerly hosted mining and drilling operations or fossil fuel-fired power plants. The Just Transition Mechanism provides approximately € 55 billion in 2021–2027 to the regions of Europe that are experiencing the greatest socio-economic impacts (European Commission, 2022l). The Mechanism supplies direct funding for investments, leverages private sector investments through the InvestEU "Just Transition" scheme, and offers loans from the European Investment Bank. Finally, the European Commission's Just Transition Platform provides a centralized knowledge database of transition tools in the areas of economic diversification and worker retraining, among other topics (European Commission, 2022l). The Platform centralizes and makes accessible information on funding opportunities and regulatory updates in addition to other knowledge that can assist member states endeavoring to support impacted workers and communities (European Commission, 2022l).

In another top-down effort to support regions experiencing socio-economic change due to the energy transition, the European Commission launched the Initiative for coal regions in transition in the Western Balkans and Ukraine in 2020, in partnership with the World Bank, Energy Community Secretariat, and other international collaborators (European Commission, 2022g). This initiative will provide an information-sharing platform for transition best practices and to support stakeholder dialogue, among other purposes, and will offer a Coal Regions Learning Academy to share effective tools for the transition (European Commission, 2022g).

2.6 US State-Led Energy and Climate Policy

With respect to the centralization of climate and energy policy, the US stands in marked contrast with the EU, which has Union-wide binding targets for industrial and electricity sector emissions reductions; coordinated state-specific limits for other GHG emissions and for the percentage of electricity produced from renewable energy resources; a centralized one-stop-shop for priority energy infrastructure projects; and a centralized fund and platform to address the socioeconomic impacts of the energy transition. The US has no binding national requirement for GHG emissions reductions; no national requirement for the level of renewable energy production that must be achieved by specific dates; limited national authority for planning for and siting electricity transmission infrastructure; and no dedicated national program to address the socio-economic impacts of the energy transition.

2.7 Climate and Energy Policy

In lieu of national GHG and renewable energy commitments to drive a US energy transition, many individual US states have voluntarily established "renewable portfolio standards," which require that a certain percentage of energy consumed within the state (or consumed from the state's major investor-owned utilities) come from renewable energy by a specific year. A growing subset of states use "clean energy standards," which are similar to RPS but in some cases cover zero-carbon resources beyond renewable energy, such as nuclear energy, and several also require energy storage installations. By August 2021, 30 states and the District of Columbia had binding renewable energy or clean energy standards, and 9 states had energy storage targets (National Conference of State Legislatures, 2021; DSIRE, 2021). Beyond requirements for zero-carbon energy, 24 states have greenhouse gas emissions targets, which aim to reduce GHGs below a specified baseline within a defined timeline (Center for Climate and Energy Solutions, 2022a). Some of these targets are carbon neutral or net-zero targets, thus allowing for emissions removal, among other emissions netting measures.

Some US climate action is even more localized. The Brookings Institute reports that 45 of the 100 most populous US cities have GHG emission reduction targets – with most tending to use the Paris Agreement goal of an 80 percent reduction of GHGs below 2005 levels by 2050 (Markolf, et al., 2020, p. 2). An additional 555 local governments in the United States have established similar targets, although many local governments – both large and small – are lagging behind their stated targets or have not completed emissions inventories that allow for effective measurement of progress (Markolf, et al., 2020, p. 2).

Finally, three US states have or are in the process of implementing GHG cap and trade programs. California has an established program, Washington State is in the process of implementing one, and Massachusetts – also a member of the 11-state Regional Greenhouse Gas Initiative for capping and trading carbon emissions – has its own cap and trade system for the electricity sector (Center for Climate and Energy Solutions, 2022).[2]

Beyond the state and local levels, regional actors have played an important role in US energy and climate governance. Two-thirds of the US population lives in areas

2 Pennsylvania would be the twelfth state to join RGGI, but the state's effort to join has been a politically-fraught process, with a deeply divided legislature attempting to block the measures necessary to finalize RGGI participation.

covered by “regional transmission organizations” (RTOs) or “independent system operators” (ISOs) (Federal Energy Regulatory Commission, 2022). RTOs and ISOs are non-governmental organizations that operate the physical electric grid and markets for energy (injection of electricity into the grid by generators), capacity (commitments to produce power in the future – these markets only operate within some RTOs and ISOs), and ancillary services (last-minute balancing of supply and demand). Several of these organizations have spearheaded efforts to plan for and finance new transmission lines to support renewable energy, although states ultimately have a say over where the transmission lines may be sited (Klass, 2017; Wiseman, 2022). Other RTOs have stymied state efforts to move toward 100 percent low-carbon energy by designing markets that disfavor renewable and nuclear energy, resulting in states threatening to exit the RTO (Welton, 2021).

Despite the bottom-up nature of most US climate and energy governance, there has also been some critical top-down leadership that has spurred portions of the US energy transition. The US Environmental Protection Agency (EPA) prepares an annual national GHG emissions inventory based on data collected from “individual facilities and suppliers of certain fossil fuels and industrial gases” under the Greenhouse Gas Reporting Program and data from experts (US Envtl, Protection Agency, 2021). Under the national Clean Air Act, the EPA also regulates GHG emissions from newly-constructed power plants; volatile organic compounds and methane from newly-drilled oil and gas wells; and, with the National Highway Traffic and Safety Administration, GHGs from transportation (primarily through fleetwide fuel economy standards). Much of this national action is the result of a lawsuit filed by several US cities, states, and nonprofit organizations, which argued that GHGs from the transportation sector are “air pollutants” that should be regulated under the Clean Air Act. In 2005, the US Supreme Court agreed that GHGs were air pollutants, which the EPA would be required to regulate if GHGs were deemed to endanger human health (Massachusetts v. EPA, 2005). The EPA subsequently made an “endangerment” finding for GHGs emitted from the transportation sector, which triggered regulation of GHGs for this sector (Envtl. Protection Agency, 2009). However, EPA efforts to regulate GHGs from existing sources of electricity generation – the second-largest source of US GHGs – have faltered politically and within the courts (West Virginia v. EPA, 2022).

FERC, which regulates interstate sales and transmission of natural gas and electricity in the US, has also taken some leadership on the climate issue, primarily through wholesale electricity market design. FERC has issued orders that somewhat ease the ability of renewable energy resources to interconnect with the grid through uniform standards, although long queues for interconnection remain. FERC has also made it easier for clean distributed energy resources and demand response resources to participate in wholesale markets (FERC, 2020; FERC, 2008, 2011, 2020). In some cases, though, the agency has impeded renewable energy within markets. For example, under the Trump administration, FERC required a price adder for state-subsidized resources such as renewable energy and nuclear power bidding into markets, thus making it less likely that these resources would clear the markets and be compensated (Welton, 2021).

The Biden administration has endeavored to take more climate action at the national level, including setting a Nationally Determined Contribution under the Paris Agreement for a net reduction of greenhouse gas emissions of 50 to 52% below 2005 levels by 2030, and preparing a 2021 Long-Term Strategy detailing how the United States can achieve net-zero GHG emissions by 2050. Additionally, Congress passed legislation in 2021 – the Infrastructure Investment and Jobs Act, also called the Bipartisan Infrastructure Bill – that devoted billions of dollars to enhancing the US transmission grid for renewable energy and reliability, retrofitting low-income homes for energy efficiency, and supporting clean hydrogen and battery development, among other low-carbon energy measures. Historically and through the present, congressionally-enacted tax credits have also played a major role in spurring US wind and solar energy development. These tax credits frequently expire and must be renewed, however, leading to uncertainty for developers and investors (Mormann, 2016). The Inflation Reduction Act of 2022 expands these credits and provides additional funding for zero-carbon energy and supporting infrastructure. More recently, a tax credit for carbon capture and sequestration (CCS) has begun to spur CCS investments, although CCS remains only the nascent stage within the US (Congressional Research Service, 2021).

Although national leadership on climate has emerged in fits and spurts within the United States – primarily when a Democrat sits in the executive office – states and local governments have led the US transition to lower-carbon energy. Some of this action has been coordinated, as evidenced by the 11-state carbon cap and trade initiative in the Northeastern United States and some action by RTOs and ISOs. But coordination and integration do not appear to nearly rise to the levels seen in the EU.

2.8 Energy Infrastructure Planning, Financing, and Siting

The lack of centralization of transmission policy again sets the US apart from the EU in terms of energy transition governance. Unlike the EU, the US lacks a national one-stop-shop for transmission line permitting, with individual states often blocking transmission lines that cross state borders. There is also no dedicated centralized fund to support transmission and other energy infrastructure projects, although federal legislation in 2021 dedicated approximately $65 billion to transmission infrastructure (Infrastructure Investment and Jobs Act, 2021). With respect to planning for new transmission lines needed to support renewable energy and a more reliable grid, FERC issued an order (FERC Order 1000) requiring regional and interregional planning for new transmission lines, but this order has met with limited success, aside from notable exceptions spearheaded by RTOs and ISOs (Wiseman, 2022).

Beyond planning and financing, the federal government has very little authority over the siting of electric transmission lines – even those that cross state lines. The only major exceptions are transmission lines developed by federal energy authorities or in partnership with them (Klass et al., 2022). Additionally, the federal Department of Energy can identify priority transmission corridors called National Interest Electric Transmission Corridors (NIETCs), and the Federal Energy Regulatory Commission can require the siting of transmission lines within these corridors if states deny the lines and refuse to act (Klass et al., 2022). Yet initial attempts to establish NIETCs met with successful legal challenges to the process for identifying the corridors, and no additional corridors have been established (Piedmont Envtl. Council v. F.E.R.C., 2009; California Wilderness Coalition v. US Department of Energy, 2011). The 2022 Inflation Reduction Act reverses the *Piedmont* decision, but it is unclear if NIETCs will be a meaningful path forward to national transmission siting. The 2021 Bipartisan Infrastructure Bill established a revolving loan fund process through which the Department of Energy can initially participate in a transmission project, building up to half of the capacity of the transmission line and then selling it to private entities (Infrastructure Investment and Jobs Act, 2021).

Beyond its differences from Europe, US electricity transmission policy also contrasts with countries such as South Africa and Turkey. These and other countries have identified areas for renewable energy development zones (or similarly-named zones) and transmission lines connecting these zones to customers (AA Energy, 2019; Republic of South Africa, 2022). Turkey has completed several successful auctions for renewable energy development within these zones (AA Energy, 2019). Texas successfully used a similar mechanism – identifying competitive renewable energy zones (CREZ) and mandating construction of transmission lines between these zones and load centers, but there is no parallel national tool (Cohn & Jankovska, 2020).

2.9 Social Impacts of the Energy Transition

Just as the United States has limited national involvement in transmission planning, financing, and siting, there has been little national action addressing the socioeconomic impacts of the energy transition. In contrast with Europe, there is no centralized platform to provide information on energy transition tools to the states, and there is no dedicated fund to support the areas that are hardest hit by the transition. (The 2022 Inflation Reduction Act begins to address this gap through green energy incentives in “Energy Communities.”) Despite some recent federal action, states and local governments have taken on the lion’s share of the work. In states such as Wyoming, local governments experiencing shuttered coal mines and dramatic drops in revenues are primarily relying on local economic redevelopment agencies to attempt to attract new industries (Baka et al., 2022). In Colorado, the state has created a Just Transition Office and has recommended the formation of State Action Teams to channel existing social funds toward areas hardest hit by the energy transition. This is still a nascent effort, however, and the Just Transition Office has limited funds and staff (Baka et al., 2022). New Mexico has made somewhat more progress, establishing an energy transition economic development fund to help diversify and promote economic development in communities losing fossil fuel industries (Baka et al., 2022).

The national contribution to addressing the socioeconomic impacts of the energy transition lies primarily within the 2021 Infrastructure Investment and Jobs Act. This Act provides $21 billion to help clean up and remediate abandoned minds and oil and gas wells as well as other polluted sites and $750 million in grants for "advanced energy technology manufacturing projects in coal communities," as described by the US Department of Energy. It also supports hydrogen hubs, several of which are proposed to be built in former coal regions (Infrastructure Investment and Jobs Act, 2021).

Relatively weak national coordination and integration of state policies in all areas, including climate and energy policy; infrastructure planning, finance, and siting; and socio-economic support for fossil fuel workers and communities may partially explain the slower progress in the US. The United States reduced *net* GHGs by 13.0 percent below 2005 levels as of 2019, as compared to Europe's 24 percent reduction in 2019 (US Envtl. Protection Agency, 2021; European Parliament, 2022). Table 1 compares the extent of centralization of US and European climate and energy policies.

Table 1: European and US Regulation of Climate, Energy Production, Energy Infrastructure, and Socio-Economic Impacts of the Energy Transition.

	Europe	United States
Emissions data: collection and reporting	**Hybrid**: EU inventories systems under Regulation on the Governance of the Energy Union and Climate Action; European Environment Agency prepares EU's greenhouse gas emissions inventory (compilation of inventories prepared by member states)	**Hybrid**: Environmental Protection Agency inventories national greenhouse gas emissions; some individual states and regions collect their own data for verifying compliance with emissions caps.
GHGs from power plants	**Centralized**: Emissions Trading System – centralized cap with trading beneath the cap	**Centralized** for new power plants: Clean Air Act regulation **Decentralized** for existing power plants; federal regulation attempted but challenged in court, withdrawn
GHGs from industrial sources	**Centralized**: Emissions Trading System – centralized cap with trading beneath the cap	**Decentralized**: limited state economy-wide greenhouse gas emissions reduction targets

Table 1: European and US Regulation of Climate, Energy Production, Energy Infrastructure, and Socio-Economic Impacts of the Energy Transition.

	Europe	United States
GHGs from transportation	**Hybrid**: Effort Sharing Legislation, binding national targets for member states dictated by relative wealth	**Centralized**: Environmental Protection Agency and National Highway Traffic and Safety Administration fuel efficiency standard; California has waiver to regulate more stringently
GHGs from agriculture, waste, housing	**Hybrid**: Effort Sharing Legislation, binding national targets for member states dictated by relative wealth	**Decentralized**: state and local building codes and gas appliance bans, some state subsidies for methane capture from agriculture (North Carolina)
Renewable energy targets	**Hybrid**: EU-wide target achieved through National Energy and Climate Plans	**Decentralized**: state renewable portfolio standards and clean energy standards
Planning for and siting transmission and storage infrastructure	**Hybrid**: EU Projects of Common Interest: one-stop permitting and EU finance support, but member state siting laws apply	**Hybrid**: regional and interregional planning required, but individual states must approve siting of the lines. 2021 federal legislation slightly expands federal siting authority for transmission lines.
Addressing labor and community impacts from the transition	**Hybrid**: EU-wide Initiative for coal regions in transition; EU Just Transition Mechanism; EU Just Transition Platform; individual member state approaches such as North-Rhine Westphalia, Germany	**Largely decentralized**: Aside from Bipartisan Infrastructure Bill and Inflation Reduction Act financial support, most efforts are currently housed within local or state governments.

3 Competitive and Regulated Electricity Markets

Beyond the centralized, decentralized, or hybrid nature of energy governance, an important defining feature of energy governance is the extent to which governance systems define the generation, transmission, and distribution of electricity as a regulated natural monopoly or a competitive enterprise. Competitive markets can enable innovation and potentially a faster transition to lower-carbon resources – particularly with government subsidization of low-carbon resources that compete within these markets. Regulated, less competitive approaches, which rely on state-owned enterprises or closely-regulated utilities to provide electricity, can tend to entrench more traditional, higher-carbon resources. Alternatively, regulators in less competitive markets can and sometimes do mandate a transition of state-regulated or state-owned utilities toward lower-carbon energy. This section explores the role of markets in the energy transition using case studies from Mexico and the US.

3.1 The US Path to Restructured Electricity Markets

Electricity in the US began as a competitive enterprise, quickly morphed into a highly-regulated regime, and underwent substantial restructuring in the 1990s and 2000s to emerge once again as a competitive (yet regulated) wholesale market (with some competitive state retail markets). It appears that competitive wholesale markets, in addition to declining capital costs, have spurred investments in renewable energy, with wind and solar energy now outcompeting natural gas-fired generation in some regional markets. But federal subsidies and state requirements for renewable energy have also played a large role in incentivizing renewable energy development.

US electric utilities were initially distributed and competitive, with numerous power plants serving localized areas. Over time, however, particularly as technological changes enabled the long-distance transport of electricity, large utilities began to serve broader geographic areas. As the reach of utility service areas expanded, large utility companies slowly persuaded all US states to follow a regulated natural monopoly model. Under this model, states treated generation, transmission, and distribution as an integrated activity to be provided by one business entity – an investor-owned utility, or IOU. States granted these utilities service territories in which they were the exclusive provider of electricity. In exchange for this monopoly – an economic gift to the utility company – the utility was obligated to provide service and rates established by the state. Through this "regulatory compact," each party was deemed to benefit. The utility faced no competition, and electric ratepayers were protected by regulated rates and service provisions such as a requirement that utilities offer electricity to all people within the service territory and follow specific procedures before disconnecting non-payers. To help keep retail electricity rates "just and reasonable," state regulators required utilities to obtain "certificates of need" or "certificates of convenience and necessity" proving the importance of new infrastructure before building new power plants or related infrastructure.

Wholesale electricity in the United States operated beneath a similar federal regulatory structure, beginning with the Federal Power Act of 1937. This act gave the Federal Power Commission – later FERC – the authority to regulate wholesale sales of electricity and transmission of electricity in interstate commerce. FERC regulated the rates charged for wholesale sales of electricity – sales from one utility to another for resale to customers – and the rates that utilities could charge for the use of their transmission lines. Under this model, utilities jealously guarded space in their transmission lines, often refusing to "wheel" electricity, meaning they refused to transport electricity on behalf of other utilities. Transmission lines therefore became bottlenecks.

Beginning in the 1970s, regulators and courts began to make small modifications to this wholly regulated natural monopoly model. Congress encouraged the construction of new small, competitive generation (including renewable generation) by guaranteeing minimum rates and interconnections for this generation – essentially a feed-in tariff (Public Utility Regulatory Policies Act, 1978). The US Supreme Court determined that electric utilities were subject to antitrust regulation and required one utility to wheel other utilities' electricity (Otter Tail Power Co. v. United States, 1973). FERC began to grant wheeling requests on a case-by-case basis and incentivize utilities to allow wheeling. The most substantial move away from the monopolistic wholesale electricity model came in 1996, when FERC required that transmission lines be "open access" to all generators on a first-come, first-served basis (Federal Energy Regulatory Commission, 1996). This opened up markets to competitive generators, allowing them to reach new customers.

Another important move toward competitive electricity markets in 1996 and again in 1999 was FERC's encouragement of the formation of regional organizations in the form of ISOs or RTOs (often generally referred to as RTOs) introduced above in Part I.A (Federal Energy Regulatory Commission Order, 1996; Federal Energy Regulatory Commission Order, 1999). Through RTOs, utilities that construct and own transmission lines voluntarily (or as required by the US state in which they operate) give up operational control over their transmission lines to a regional independent organization, the RTO. RTOs offer relatively uniform transmission rates throughout a large area. This allows generators to transport electricity over long distances without having to pay different transmission owners different rates – a costly practice called "rate pancaking." RTOs also schedule the flow of electricity over the wires through competitive markets for energy and ancillary services, and as noted above, several also operate capacity markets.

As FERC, the courts, and Congress pushed wholesale electricity markets toward a restructured, more competitive status, many states – which regulate retail electricity generation, transmission, and distribution – engaged in similar restructuring. In the most common model, states required electric utilities to unbundle their generation business from transmission and distribution and to allow customer choice, in which customers could choose their generator and the utility would be required to transmit and distribute electricity from the chosen generator to the customer. But many states did not restructure or pulled back from restructuring after some energy companies wreaked havoc in competitive electricity markets. Therefore, in some parts of the country, vertically-integrated state-regulated retail utilities operate within federally competitive wholesale markets, or within wholesale markets dominated by bilateral contracts. These utilities still operate within state-approved service territories, receive state-approved rates designed to allow them to recover costs, and must obtain approval before building new infrastructure. But in areas with competitive auctions for wholesale electricity, regulated utilities' options for procuring energy and capacity are much broader – and sometimes greener and less costly – than the options of regulated utilities operating in areas without competitive wholesale auctions (Cicala, 2017; Winegarden, 2021).

Competitive electricity markets in the United States – combined with state requirements for renewable energy and federal tax credits – have helped to spur the transition toward wind and solar resources (Rhodes et al., 2021; US Envtl. Protection Agency, 2022). These markets have allowed new generators to access a greater number of customers in a broader area, and as renewable energy prices have declined, renewable generators have enjoyed a growing advantage within these markets. Indeed, renewable energy resources and lower-carbon natural gas resources increasingly outbid coal-fired power plants and nuclear power plants in competitive wholesale markets, therefore pushing out one high-GHG source and another zero-carbon source (US Dept of Energy, 2020; US Energy Information Administration, 2021). This disadvantage for coal, in particular, led the Trump administration Department of Energy – citing to reliability concerns – to try to force the Federal Energy Regulatory Commission to essentially withdraw coal-fired power plants and other power plants with a stable, on-site fuel supply from competitive wholesale markets, giving these plants a government-established, guaranteed rate instead. The Commission refused, citing to the benefits and importance of competitive markets and the lack of evidence that natural gas, renewable energy, and other sources were unreliable (Federal Energy Regulatory Commission, 2018).

In contrast with competitive wholesale and retail markets, there are parts of the US where retail electricity markets are heavily regulated and wholesale energy is still procured through bilateral contracts rather than competitive auctions (Federal Energy Regulatory Commission, 2022). In these areas – particularly the Southeastern US – many utilities still must obtain legislative or regulatory permission before constructing a utility-scale renewable installation, and renewables are not always considered "least cost" or in the public interest. Indeed, in some regulated states, companies are not allowed to install solar panels on rooftops and sell solar electricity to the customer (a practice called "third-party solar," which has predominated in markets such as California). In these states, the third-party solar providers are viewed as impermissibly intruding within regulated electric utilities' territories.

Despite the tendency of regulated, relatively non-competitive US electricity markets to disfavor renewables, there are important exceptions. Many regulated states require utility-led integrated resource planning (IRP), in which utilities indicate how they will meet customer demand over a relatively long period, such as ten years. Increasingly, states require carbon-based considerations in the IRP process.

3.2 Mexico: The Push and Pull of Competition

Similar to the US, Mexico has experienced changes in the competitiveness of its electricity sector over time, although perhaps exhibiting even more dramatic shifts. (Both countries have also restructured their natural gas sectors, but electricity restructuring is more directly relevant to the energy transition; also see Chapter 26.)

Mexico historically relied on one state-owned enterprise – the Comision Federal de Electricidad (CFE) – to generate, transmit, and distribute all electricity within the country (Wood, 2018, pp. 1–2). In 2013, through laws effective in 2014, Mexico's Congress reformed the Constitution and enacted implementing legislation to introduce competition within the electricity sector. The reforms opened up the electricity market for investment by private generating companies through auctions; required unbundling of electric utilities (separation of generation from the transmission and distribution functions, thus increasing competition in the generation sector); and created an independent system operator for the transmission grid (Wood & Martin, 2018, pp. 32–33). This ISO – Centro Nacional de Control de Energía (CENACE) – ran auctions for energy, capacity, and ancillary services, among other commodities. CENACE markets ran on least-cost principles, meaning that the lowest-cost resources were called upon (dispatched) first into the market, followed by the resource with the next lowest cost, and so on, until all demand was fulfilled (Sanchez, 2018, pp. 48). As a result of renewable electricity procurement auctions, a large number of private companies built relatively low-cost renewable energy generation in Mexico. One 2017 bid from an Italian wind company represented an all-time low price for energy at that time (O'Sullivan, 2022).

The election of President López-Obrador suggested a potential new course away from competition in Mexico's electricity sector. The president cancelled a planned fourth CENACE-run auction for energy generation in 2019, and in 2021, Mexico's Congress enacted legislation that reinstated state control over the electricity market. Courts invalidated portions of this legislation, but President López-Obrador continued pushing for constitutional reform efforts in 2022 (O'Sullivan, 2022). These reforms failed to pass Mexico's lower house, but if successful, they would have limited private generators' participation in energy markets to 46 percent – leaving a 54 percent private share for CFE, changed the electricity dispatch regime (which currently dispatches lowest-cost resources first) to favor CFE in dispatch (Murray, 2022). The reforms also would have ended reliance on CENACE for electric grid control, among other measures. Analyses suggest that this proposed reform would have increased Mexico's GHGs because much of the private investment in the electricity sector took the form of renewable energy, whereas CFE predominantly owns and operates fossil fuel-fired plants (albeit with some hydroelectric and nuclear resources) (Bracho et al., 2022). Furthermore, the cost of procuring power to meet demand would have risen given the abandonment of least-cost dispatch (Bracho et al., 2022, p. 1). Although the 2022 reforms did not pass, the 2021 reforms give CFE priority dispatch, and CFE is not required to acquire electricity through a public bidding process (Herbert Smith Freehills, 2022; also see Coleman and Anglés-Hernàndez and Valenzuela, both in this volume).

In summary, given the increasingly competitive price of renewable energy resources, efforts in Mexico or the US to limit competition in the electricity sector tend to reduce renewable energy investments. Competitive markets, in contrast, support a more rapid transition, although they raise important equity and justice issues that must be addressed. For example, although new renewable energy resources are relatively inexpensive as compared to most other forms of generation, replacing a large amount of fossil fuel-fired infrastructure with a zero-carbon resources will require equally massive investments. If ratepayers must equally shoulder this burden, the bulk of the impacts will fall on low-income individuals for whom energy is a higher percentage of their annual income. Designers of competitive energy markets can and sometimes do account for these types of impacts to encourage relatively rapid growth of zero-carbon energy while addressing the inequities caused by markets. But a great deal more must be accomplished in this area for the energy transition to proceed in an equitable manner.

4 Private Governance

Governance of energy markets enabling and encouraging competition in the energy sector relies on some natural forces to hasten the energy transition in a lower-cost way. But in some cases, the private sector itself is pushing this transition forward, instituting its own mechanisms for change. Private sector efforts to reduce GHGs and increase investments in zero-carbon energy are often described under the umbrella of ESG – voluntary measures taken by corporations to mitigate their socioeconomic and environmental impacts, particularly in the sphere of climate.

As corporate governance experts Michael Vandenbergh and Jonathan Gilligan note, private sector actions on climate come in a variety of forms, including, inter alia, pressuring the public sector to act, both through leading by example and publicly lobbying for change; achieving private sector emissions reductions through carbon neutral commitments; placing an internal price on GHG emissions and measuring and publicly disclosing emissions; and addressing supply chain emissions (see Chapter 14). Some of these actions are initiated by corporate boards and CEOs, whereas others are shareholder-driven. And while legitimate questions remain about “greenwashing” – corporate claims designed to attract investors or consumers but not actually achieved – private governance mechanisms appear to be making a meaningful dent in GHG emissions if corporations follow through on their commitments. As Vandenbergh and Gilligan (2017) observe, Walmart has set a goal of reducing emissions from its global suppliers by an amount equal to the emissions of the entire US iron and steel industry. And shareholder pressures have induced corporations to reduce GHG emissions by an amount equal to Italy’s annual emissions. To achieve emissions reduction commitments, many large corporations are entering into long-term power purchase agreements with renewable energy generators or purchasing renewable energy credits, as well as modifying supply chain practices.

Beyond highly-publicized commitments to emissions reductions and renewable energy investments, corporations are taking a variety of steps to participate in the transition and keep pace with changing investment preferences. Some fossil fuel producers are investing in biofuels; renewable energy generation; green or blue hydrogen; and carbon capture, utilisation, and sequestration (CCUS) projects. In the United States, some utilities are also installing new dual fuel plants that can burn either natural gas or hydrogen, or a blend, in anticipation of a potentially changing fuel mix (US Energy Information Administration, 2022b; S&P Global, 2021).

In the sphere of socioeconomic impacts of the energy transition, some corporations are deeply involved in private governance. Electric utilities, which have long operated within service territories and have longstanding relationships with customers and power plant employees, sometimes lead economic redevelopment projects within the communities where they shutter fossil fuel-fired plants. Some coal mining unions in the US are also lobbying politicians for a package of miner-friendly transition tools, such as expanded tax credits for renewable energy supply chain manufacturing in coal country, and funding for mine reclamation (De Chant, 2021). The Biden administration has channeled $11.3 billion in funding to be distributed over fifteen years to coal mine reclamation (US Department of the Interior, 2022).

In addition to self-initiated and shareholder-driven ESG in the energy transition context, public governance systems increasingly pressure change in the private governance sphere. For example, in 2022, the US Securities and Exchange Commission proposed rules that would require registering corporations to disclose "any climate-related risks," which are "actual or potential negative impacts of climate-related conditions and events on a registrant's consolidated financial statements, business operations, or value chains, as a whole." These risks would include "physical risks" posed by short-term weather extremes and changing weather patterns, as well as transition risks such as declining demand for a registrant's carbon-intensive product, market impacts from changing consumer behavior, and the "devaluation or abandonment of assets," among other risks (Securities and Exchange Commission, 2022; on private governance see also the chapters by Richards, Benjamin and McCallum and Mitkidis, in this volume).

5 Conclusion

Governance of the energy transition involves several distinct policy areas including GHG emissions from all sectors of the economy, zero-carbon renewable energy generation, and the socio-economic impacts of a changing energy economy. This chapter has explored several key differentiating features of governance in these areas. Public and private governance systems both play a central role in these areas, with important distinguishing characteristics. More centralized public governance regimes such as Europe's, which leverage and coordinate member state expertise and resources while also issuing top-down directives – appear to play an important role in spurring a more rapid energy transition and addressing the impacts of this transition. Additionally, competitive markets for electricity generally support renewable energy resources, although zero-carbon resources such as nuclear energy have struggled in US competitive markets.

There is no single formula for success in effectively governing the energy transition. For example, some non-restructured retail electricity markets in the US, which operate within competitive wholesale markets, have achieved relatively high levels of renewable energy penetration and reductions in greenhouse gas emissions. These benchmarks have been achieved through a combination of a supportive state legislature – which approves or requires utility investment in the energy transition – and relatively affordable procurement of zero-carbon resources stemming in part from competitive wholesale markets. Yet competitive wholesale markets are not a panacea, and designing and governing a transition to competitive markets can be difficult, as exhibited by Mexico, Europe, and other jurisdictions discussed in this book. Full integration of markets can be difficult, as can the reduction of market power wielded by formerly dominant utilities – a challenge that arose in Mexico.

As public governance systems work to achieve GHG emission commitments that require a relatively rapid transition of the energy sector, private governance systems will continue to push public governments and make their own contributions to the transition. Increasingly, these contributions will move the economy toward lower-carbon energy resources, albeit not always in this direction.

References

AA Energy, Turkey finalizes second YEKA wind tenders, 30.05.2019, https://www.aa.com.tr/en/energy/wind/turkey-finalizes-second-yeka-wind-tenders/25643.

Baka, J., Blumsack, S., Vitti, C. and Wiseman, H., 2022. *The local social and economic context of energy transitions.* https://celp.psu.edu/wp-content/uploads/2022/04/CELP_EnergyTransitions_Apr2022.pdf.

Balthasar, A., Schreurs, M.A. and Varone, F., 2020. Energy transition in Europe and the United States: policy entrepreneurs and veto players in federalist systems. *J. Envt. & Development*, 29(1), pp. 3–25.

Bracho, R., Guerra Fernandez, O.J., Brancucci, C. et al., 2022. *National Renewable Energy Laboratory impacts analysis of amendments to Mexico's unit commitment and dispatch rules.* https://www.nrel.gov/docs/fy22osti/81350.pdf.

California Wilderness Coalition v. U.S. Dept. of Energy, 631 F.3d 1072 (9th Cir. 2011).

Center for Climate and Energy Solutions, U.S. State Greenhouse Gas Emissions Targets. https://www.c2es.org/document/greenhouse-gas-emissions-targets/.

Center for Climate and Energy Solutions, Market-Based State Policy. https://www.c2es.org/content/market-based-state-policy/.

Cohn, J. and Jankovska, O., 2020. Texas CREZ lines: how stakeholders shape major infrastructure projects. Research Paper, Baker Institute, Rice University's Institute for Public Policy (November 17). https://www.bakerinstitute.org/media/files/files/eb251d15/ces-pub-texascrez-111720.pdf.

Congressional Research Service, 2021. The tax credit for carbon sequestration (Section 45Q). https://sgp.fas.org/crs/misc/IF11455.pdf.

Database of State Incentives for Renewable Energy (DSIRE), *Energy Storage Targets* (2021), https://ncsolarcen-prod.s3.amazonaws.com/wp-content/uploads/2021/08/DSIRE_Storage_Targets_August2021.pdf.

De Chant, T., 2021. Coal miners' Union lobbies for jobs from renewable energy, *ARS Technica*, (Apr. 20). https://arstechnica.com/tech-policy/2021/04/coal-miners-union-lobbies-for-jobs-in-renewable-energy/.

Directive 2003/83/EC of the European Parliament and of the Council of 13 October 2003 establishing a system for greenhouse gas emission allowance trading within the Union and amending Council Directive 96/61/EC, OJ L275/32, 25.10.2003.

Directive 2009/28/EC of the European Parliament and of the Council of 23 April 2009 on the promotion of the use of energy from renewable sources and amending and subsequently repealing Directives 2001/77/EC and 2003/30/EC, OJ L140/16, 5.6.2009.

Directive 2012/27/EU of the European Parliament and of the Council of 25 October 2012 on energy efficiency, amending Directives 2009/125/EC and 2010/30/EU and repealing Directives 2004/8/EC and 2006/32/EC, OJ L315/1, 14.11.2012.

Envtl. Protection Agency, 2009. Endangerment and cause or contribute findings for greenhouse gases under section 202(a) of the Clean Air Act. Final Rule. https://www.epa.gov/sites/default/files/2021-05/documents/federal_register-epa-hq-oar-2009-0171-dec.15-09.pdf.

European Commission, 2022a. *Climate action, development of EU ETS (2005–2020)*. https://ec.europa.eu/clima/eu-action/eu-emissions-trading-system-eu-ets/development-eu-ets-2005-2020_en.

European Commission, 2022b. *Climate Action, 2020 Climate & Energy Package*. https://ec.europa.eu/clima/eu-action/climate-strategies-targets/2020-climate-energy-package_en.

European Commission, 2022c. *Climate Action, Union Registry*. https://ec.europa.eu/clima/eu-action/eu-emissions-trading-system-eu-ets/union-registry_en.

European Commission, 2022d. *Climate Action, 2030 Climate & Energy Framework*. https://ec.europa.eu/clima/eu-action/climate-strategies-targets/2030-climate-energy-framework_en.

European Commission, 2022e. *Effort sharing 2021–2030: targets and flexibilities*.

European Commission, 2022f. *Energy, Clean Energy for All Europeans Package*. https://energy.ec.europa.eu/topics/energy-strategy/clean-energy-all-europeans-package_en.

European Commission, 2022g. *Energy, Initiative for Coal Regions in Transition in the Western Balkans and Ukraine*. https://energy.ec.europa.eu/topics/oil-gas-and-coal/coal-regions-western-balkans-and-ukraine/initiative-coal-regions-transition-western-balkans-and-ukraine_en#:~:text=The%20Initiative%20for%20coal%20regions,that%20this%20transition%20is%20just.

European Commission, 2022h. *EU Emissions Trading System (ETS)*. https://ec.europa.eu/clima/eu-action/eu-emissions-trading-system-eu-ets_en.

European Commission, 2022i. *National Energy and Climate Plans*. https://ec.europa.eu/info/energy-climate-change-environment/implementation-eu-countries/energy-and-climate-governance-and-reporting/national-energy-and-climate-plans_en.

European Commission, 2022k. *Questions and Answers on the Fifth List of Energy Projects of Common Interest (PCIs)*. https://ec.europa.eu/commission/presscorner/detail/en/qanda_21_6093/.

European Commission, 2022k. *Regional Groups and their role*. https://energy.ec.europa.eu/topics/infrastructure/projects-common-interest/regional-groups-and-their-role_en.

European Commission, 2022l. *The Just Transition Mechanism: making sure no one is left behind*. https://ec.europa.eu/info/strategy/priorities-2019-2024/european-green-deal/finance-and-green-deal/just-transition-mechanism_en.

European Commission, 2018. *Guidance on Energy Transmission Infrastructure and EU Nature Legislation*.

European Parliament, 2022. *EU Progress Towards its 2020 Climate Change Goals*, updated Feb. 21. https://www.europarl.europa.eu/news/en/headlines/society/20180706STO07407/eu-progress-towards-2020-climate-change-goals-infographic.

Federal Energy Regulatory Commission, *Electric Power Markets* (last accessed 2022), https://www.ferc.gov/electric-power-markets.

Federal Energy Regulatory Commission (US), 2020. *Order No. 2222.*

Federal Energy Regulatory Commission (US), 2018. *Order Terminating Rulemaking Proceeding, Initiating New Proceeding, and Establishing Additional Procedures.* https://cms.ferc.gov/sites/default/files/2020-05/20180108161614-RM18-1-000_3.pdf.

Federal Energy Regulatory Commission (US), 2011. *Order No. 745.*

Federal Energy Regulatory Commission (US), 2008. *Order No. 719.*

Federal Energy Regulatory Commission (US), 1999. *Order No. 2000.*

Federal Energy Regulatory Commission (US), 1996. *Order No. 888.*

Feeley, M.M. and Rubin, E., 2008. *Federalism: political identify and tragic compromise.* Ann Arbor, MI: University of Michigan Press.

Herbert Smith Freehills, 2022. Mexico Energy Alert: Reform of Mexico's Electric Power Industry, (Apr. 19). https://hsfnotes.com/latamlaw/2022/04/19/mexico-energy-alert-reform-of-mexicos-electric-power-industry/.

Infrastructure Investment and Jobs Act, Public Law 117-58 (2021), https://www.congress.gov/117/plaws/publ58/PLAW-117publ58.pdf.

ISO 26000, Guidance on Social Responsibility, ISO (2010), https://www.iso.org/obp/ui/#iso:std:iso:26000:ed-1:v1:en.

Klass, A., 2017. Expanding the US electric transmission and distribution grid to meet deep decarbonization goals. *Envtl. L. Reporter*, 47, pp. 10749–10766.

Maltby, T., 2013. European Union energy policy integration: a case study of European Commission policy entrepreneurship and increasing supranationalism. *Energy Policy*, 55, pp. 435–444.

Markolf, S.A., Azevedo, I.M.L., Muro, M. and Victor, D.G., 2020. *Pledges and progress: steps toward greenhouse gas emissions reductions in the 100 largest cities across the United States.* Brookings Institute Report (October).

Massachusetts v. Envtl. Protection Agency, 549 US 497 (2005).

Mormann, F., 2016. Fading into the sunset: solar and wind energy get five more years of tax credits with a phase-down. *TRENDS* (May/June). https://www.americanbar.org/groups/environment_energy_resources/publications/trends/2015-2016/may-june-2016/fading_into_the_sunset/.

Murray, C., 2022. Mexican president's radical energy reform defeated in Congress, Financial Times (Apr. 18).

National Conference of State Legislatures, 2021. *State Renewable Portfolio Standards and Goals.* https://www.ncsl.org/research/energy/renewable-portfolio-standards.aspx.

O'Sullivan, M.L., 2022. *Mexico's energy reforms: a blow to realizing the most competitive and dynamic region in the world.* Brookings Institute. https://www.brookings.edu/blog/up-front/2022/02/28/mexicos-energy-reforms-a-blow-to-realizing-the-most-competitive-and-dynamic-region-in-the-world/.

Osofsky, H.M., 2016. Polycentrism and climate change. In: D.A. Farber and M. Peeters, eds., 2016. *Climate Change Law.* Cheltenham: Edward Elgar Publishing, pp. 324–336.

Ostrom, E., 2012. Nested externalities and polycentric institutions: must we wait for global solutions to climate change before taking action at other scales?. *Econ. Theory*, 49, pp. 353–369.

Otter Tail Power Company v. United States, 410 U.S. 366 (1973).

Piedmont Envtl. Council v. FERC, 558 F.3d 304 (4th Circuit 2009).

Public Utility Regulatory Policies Act, Public Law 95-617 (1978), https://www.govinfo.gov/content/pkg/STATUTE-92/pdf/STATUTE-92-Pg3117.pdf.

Protocol on the Application of the Principles of Subsidiarity and Proportionality, 119997D.PRO/07 (1997).

Regulation (EU) 2018/842 of the European Parliament and of the Council of 30 May 2018 on binding annual greenhouse gas emission reductions by Members States from 2021 to 2030 contributing to climate action to meet commitments under the Paris Agreement and amending Regulation (EU) No 525/2013, OJ L156/26, 19.6.2018.

Regulation (EU) 2022/869 on guidelines for trans-European energy infrastructure, amending Regulations (EC) No 715/2009, (EU) 2019/942 and (EU) 2019/943 and Directives 2009/73/EC and (EU) 2019/944, and repealing Regulation (EU) No 347/2013, OJ L152/45, 3.6.2022.

Reali, P., Grzech, J. and Garcia, A., 2021. ESG: investors increasingly seek accountability and outcomes. https://corpgov.law.harvard.edu/2021/04/25/esg-investors-increasingly-seek-accountability-and-outcomes/.

Republic of South Africa, Department of Forestry, Fisheries & The Environment, Renewable Energy Development Zones (REDZs) and Strategic Transmission Corridors, https://egis.environment.gov.za/redz (last visited 2022).

Reuters, 2015. German cabinet agrees to costly underground power lines (Oct. 7). https://www.reuters.com/article/germany-energy-power/german-cabinet-agrees-to-costly-underground-power-lines-idUSL8N12722320151007.

Rhodes, J.D., Kiesling, L.L., Davidson T. and Webber, M.E., 2021. Assessment of the emissions performance of wholesale electricity markets. Energy Choice Coalition (November 18).

S&P Global, 2021. First major US hydrogen-burning power plant nears completion in Ohio (Aug. 12). https://www.spglobal.com/commodityinsights/en/market-insights/latest-news/electric-power/081221-first-major-us-hydrogen-burning-power-plant-nears-completion-in-ohio.

Sanchez, G.J.G., 2018. The fine print of the Mexican energy reform. In: D. Wood, ed., 2018. *Mexico's new energy reform*. Washington, DC: Wilson Center Mexican Institute, pp. 36–52.

Saurer, J. and Monast, J., 2021. The law of energy transition in federal systems. *Transnational Envtl. L.*, 10(2), pp. 205–210.

Schanzenbach, M.M. and Sitkoff, R.H., 2020. Reconciling fiduciary duty and social conscience: the law and economics of ESG investing by a trustee. *Stanford Law Review*, 72, pp. 381–454.

Schreurs, M.H., 2011. Federalism and the climate: Canada and the European Union. *International Journal*, 66(1), pp. 91–108.

Securities and Exchange Commission, 2022. Proposed Rule: The Enhancement and Standardization of Climate-Related Disclosures for Investors, 17 *Code of Fed. Regs.* 210.

The United States of America, 2021. *Nationally Determined Contribution, Reducing Greenhouse Gases in the United States: A 2030 Emissions Target* (April 21).

US Department of Energy, 2021. DOE Fact Sheet: the bipartisan Infrastructure Deal will deliver for American workers, families and usher in the clean energy future (Nov. 9).

US Department of Energy, 2020. Restoring America's competitive nuclear advantage. https://www.energy.gov/sites/prod/files/2020/04/f74/Restoring%20America%27s%20Competitive%20Nuclear%20Advantage-Blue%20version%5B1%5D.pdf.

US Department of the Interior, 2022. Biden Administration announces nearly $725 million to create good-paying Union jobs, catalyze economic revitalization in coal communities. https://www.doi.gov/pressreleases/biden-administration-announces-nearly-725-million-create-good-paying-union-jobs.

US Energy Information Administration, 2022a. Five states updated or adopted new clean energy standards in 2021. https://www.eia.gov/todayinenergy/detail.php?id=51118.

US Energy Information Administration, 2022b. Hydrogen explained https://www.eia.gov/energyexplained/hydrogen/use-of-hydrogen.php.

US Energy Information Administration, 2021. https://www.eia.gov/todayinenergy/detail.php?id=48696.

US Envtl. Protection Agency, *U.S. Electricity Grid & Markets*, https://www.epa.gov/green-power-markets/us-electricity-grid-markets (last visited 2022).

US Envtl. Protection Agency, 2021. *Inventory of U.S. greenhouse gas emissions and sinks 1990–2019*. https://www.epa.gov/sites/default/files/2021-04/documents/us-ghg-inventory-2021-main-text.pdf.

Vandenbergh, M.P., 2007. The new Wal-Mart effect: the role of private contracting in global governance. *UCLA Law Review*, 54, pp. 913–970.

Vandenbergh, M.P., 2013. Private environmental governance. *Cornell Law Review*, 99, pp. 129–199.

Vandenburgh, M.P. and Gilligan, J.M., 2017. *Beyond politics: the private governance response to climate change*. Cambridge: Cambridge University Press.

Vogel, D., Toffel, M.W., Post, D. and Nazli, Z.U.A., 2012. Environmental federalism in the European Union and the United States. In: F. Wijen, K. Zoeteman, J. Pieters and P. van Seters, eds., 2012. *A handbook of globalization and environmental policy*. 2nd ed. Cheltenham: Edward Elgar Publishing, pp. 321–361.

Welton, S., 2021. Rethinking grid governance for the climate change era. *California L. Rev.*, 109, pp. 209–275.

West Virginia v. Environmental Protection Agency, 597 U.S. __ (2022).

Winegarden, W., 2021. *Affordable and reliable: creating competitive electricity markets to deliver consumers affordable, reliable, and low-emission electricity*. Pacific Research Institute. https://www.pacificresearch.org/wp-content/uploads/2021/09/ERR_EnergyCompetition_F.pdf.

Wiseman, H.J., 2022. Regional cooperative federalism and the U.S. electric grid. *George Washington L. Rev.*, 90, pp. 147–236.

Wood, D., 2018. Introduction: a reform years in the making. In: D. Wood, ed., 2018. *Mexico's new energy reform*. Washington, DC: Wilson Center Mexican Institute, pp. 1–4.

Wood, D. and Martin, J., 2018. Of paradigm shifts and political conflict: the history of Mexico's second energy revolution. In: D. Wood, ed., 2018. *Mexico's new energy reform*. Washington, DC: Wilson Center Mexican Institute, pp. 17–35.

Lovleen Bhullar

Meanings of Energy Justice in the Low-Carbon Transition

Abstract: This chapter will explore the meanings of energy justice in the specific context of the low-carbon transition. I start with the dominant three-tenets theoretical framework of procedural, distributional, and recognition justice. Then I examine the relationship between energy justice and other concepts of justice such as climate, environment, mobility, and planetary justice as well as 'just transitions'. Developing countries will account for over ⅔ of the world's energy demand in the coming decades but scholarship continues to view the concept of energy justice largely through a Western perspective. So, I analyse the extent to which scholarship relating to the low-carbon transition in developing countries considers 'universal' meanings of energy justice, develops context-specific versions of the concept, or relies on other concepts such as energy ethics, energy equity, energy poverty and equity sovereignty. I then turn to the relationship between energy justice and energy injustice. The conclusion reflects on some challenges facing the quest for meanings of energy justice and identifies some areas for future research.

1 Introduction

The low-carbon transition involves a gradual shift from fossil fuels towards low-carbon energy sources. This transition is not going to occur in a vacuum. It must address the injustices of the existing global energy system and prevent the emergence of new forms of energy injustice. In other words, the low-carbon transition must be a just transition. This chapter considers the plurality of meanings of energy justice in the low-carbon transition and invites readers to problematise some of them and to discover others in specific jurisdictional contexts.

The rest of the chapter is structured as follows: The first section provides an overview of the concept of energy justice and its links with environmental justice and energy justice as well as other energy concerns. The next section examines the tenets of energy justice as well as alternatives and highlights the need to adopt a context-specific non-Western approach in developing countries. The third section considers these tenets of energy justice in the context of the low-carbon transition and identifies certain key considerations going forward. This is followed by the conclusion.

Lovleen Bhullar is Assistant Professor at the University of Birmingham, United Kingdom.

https://doi.org/10.1515/9783110752403-011

2 Conceptualising energy justice

Scholars have engaged with several justice dimensions of energy for some time, without specifically labelling them as energy justice concerns (Jenkins et al., 2017, p. 631; Heffron and McCauley, 2017). The concept of 'energy justice' is of recent origin and it can be traced to a law journal article (Guruswamy, 2010). Heffron et al. (2018, p. 42) claim that this concept can provide a unifying normative underpinning to energy law, which has been lacking, and they propose energy justice as one of the seven core principles of energy law.

Even though there is an inextricable link between the concept of justice and law, most of the discussion of energy justice has occurred in the energy policy space where it is defined as 'a global energy system that fairly disseminates both the benefits and costs of energy services, and one that contributes to more representative and impartial energy decision-making' (Sovacool et al., 2016, p. 4). Energy justice offers a new way of balancing the familiar energy trilemma of security, affordability, and sustainability according to principles of justice and equity, rather than economic efficiency (Heffron et al., 2015, p. 169). Justice principles apply to all forms of energy, and across the entire energy lifecycle including mining of resources, production, transportation, transmission, distribution, consumption, and waste disposal. In addition, there are links between energy justice and energy law and policy, energy security, energy activism and climate change (see, e.g., Jenkins et al., 2016, p. 174).

Interestingly, scholars tend to contextualise discussions of energy justice with reference to energy injustice. Sovacool and Dworkin (2014, p. 377) highlight the extreme injustices and asymmetries within the global energy system, which can arise from having too much energy or from not having enough energy (Sovacool et al., 2016, p. 1). According to Jenkins et al. (2016, p. 175), energy justice 'evaluates (a) where injustices emerge, (b) which affected sections of society are ignored, (c) which processes exist for their remediation in order to (i) reveal, and (ii) reduce such injustices.' However, ensuring energy justice is not the same as preventing energy injustice. McCauley et al. (2019, p. 452) reframe the discussion of energy justice in terms of energy injustice at different scales and domains before engaging with movements for divestment of fossil fuels.

The concept of justice has been applied in relation to the environment, climate change, and energy. The environmental justice movement connects the environment with race, class, gender, and social justice issues (Taylor, 2000). Climate justice centres on the causes of climate change and the unequal distribution of the negative impacts of climate change between countries in the Global South and the Global North (Schlosberg and Collins, 2014). The environmental justice movement has influenced the development of energy justice (McCauley et al., 2013, p. 107; Rasch and Köhne, 2017), and the three tenets of energy justice discussed in section 2 below directly build on the threefold-tenet approach to global environmental justice (Schlosberg, 2004).

At the same time, energy justice is distinct from environmental and climate justice. First, energy justice '"provides a way of bounding" and separating out energy concerns from the wider range of topics addressed within both environmental and climate justice analysis campaigning' (Bickerstaff et al., 2013, p. 2). Second, it enables focus on consumption and access issues, in addition to environmental injustices arising from energy production and transportation (McHarg, 2020, p. 19). Third, it is a smaller scale and more strategically impactful concept than environmental and climate justice (Jenkins, 2018, p. 119). Finally, because energy justice has largely developed as an academic concept, this gives it greater conceptual rigour and clarity, which increases its likelihood of successfully influencing policy (ibid., pp. 119–120). As a result, energy justice is capable of practical application by decision-makers including the government, the private sector, and the public. However, unlike environmental justice, climate justice, and even just transition, the activism roots of energy justice are not always recognised (Heffron and McCauley, 2017).

Energy justice is also linked to energy vulnerability and energy/fuel poverty as well as energy sovereignty and energy security. Research on energy (in)justice highlights vulnerability of individuals and communities in terms of access to or affordability of energy services (Hernandez, 2015; Reames, 2016). Energy injustice may also be expressed in terms of energy poverty and fuel poverty. Energy poverty refers to a lack of access to affordable and sustainable modern energy services (Faiella and Lavecchia, 2015; Herington and Malakar, 2016). Fuel poverty refers to the inability of households to afford to heat their home to an adequate temperature. Further, a rights-based approach to energy justice highlights the importance of energy sovereignty. The latter refers to 'the right of people to access energy resources within ecological limits to have a dignified life' (Castán Broto, 2017). Energy security or insecurity can lead to energy justice or injustice respectively. Energy security assesses (a) the security of supply and production, and (b) emergent insecurities (such as availability and pricing) with a view to promoting the safeguarding of energy supply and 'indigenous' production capabilities (Ang, Choong and Ng, 2015). Hernández (2015) adopts a narrow understanding of energy insecurity as 'the everyday challenges in meeting basic household energy needs' while discussing energy justice.

3 The 'triumvirate of tenets' of energy justice and beyond

This section focuses on the meanings of energy justice with reference to the tenet-based justice framework as well as alternatives with reference to the non-Western context of developing countries. In this way, it endorses the need to shift from a universalistic to pluralistic understanding of energy justice.

3.1 Tenets of energy justice

As mentioned above, the environmental justice movement has influenced the development of the 'triumvirate of tenets' of energy justice, namely distributional justice, procedural justice, and recognition justice. Subsequently, restorative justice and cosmopolitan justice were added to this list.

3.1.1 Distributional justice

Distributional (or distributive) justice is concerned with the equal or unequal distribution of benefits and costs across society. It entails an assessment of 'where' energy injustices occur (McCauley et al., 2019, p. 917). In the context of the global energy system, distributional justice is concerned with the production and distribution of energy services. The former includes the siting of energy infrastructure in areas inhabited by certain sections of society. The latter includes energy poverty resulting from unequal distribution of modern energy services. In this context, Jenkins et al. (2016, p. 176) observe:

> The fuel poverty agenda has revealed the uneven distribution of burdens with regards to affordable access to energy services. In this regard, energy justice concerns both physical access to heating and electricity, and questions the extent of an individual's freedoms, i.e. the extent of choice a person has over his/her life.

Distributional justice can facilitate the development of 'energy systems in which costs are shared and participants benefit as equally as possible' (Sovacool et al., 2019, p. 588). However, there is an overwhelming emphasis on the spatial dimensions of energy justice and injustice. For McCauley and Heffron (2018, p. 2), distributional justice is more than proximity and they identify new distributional frameworks as well as recognition justice. Further, the environmental justice-based origin of distributional justice has translated into a considerable emphasis on the race dimension. Sovacool et al. (2017) express the absence of gender and class from the discourse in terms of insufficient attention to the question of intersectionality. Guruswamy (2020) discusses the specific impacts of energy poverty on women, and Govindan et al. (2020) highlight the predominantly 'gender-blind' approach of electricity policies in developing countries.

3.1.2 Procedural justice

The three pillars of the UNECE Convention on Access to Information, Public Participation in Decision-making and Access to Justice in Environmental Matters (the Aarhus Convention) aim to promote procedural justice. Availability of and access to information about decision-making processes and decisions improves transparency and accountability (Siciliano et al., 2018, p. 206). It can also promote access to and participation in all stages of the decision-making process concerning energy, as well as access to justice. However, access to and participation in decision-making is inadequate if forms of access and participation are not meaningful and becomes a box ticking exercise.

Jenkins et al. (2016) adopt a broad perspective in respect of inclusion in energy decision-making processes. They identify three mechanisms of inclusion: mobilisation of local knowledge held by indigenous peoples as well as scientists, full and impartial disclosure of information by public and private actors, and improved representation of different sections of society (e.g., gender, ethnic minorities) in institutions, which promotes intersectionality (ibid., p. 179). At the same time, procedural justice cannot be confined to inclusion in the decision-making process; there must be involvement in delivering a more equitable outcome (Jenkins et al., 2016, pp. 178–179; McCauley et al., 2019, p. 917). This leads to the question: does the energy law- and policy-making process promote or undermine procedural justice?

Procedural justice unites distributional justice (above) and recognition-based justice (below) through a combined demand for both formal and informal forms of involvement in decision-making (McCauley et al., 2019, p. 917). The former include access to law- and policymaking processes and the legal system. The latter include bottom-up community led initiatives for energy democracy and energy sovereignty (McCauley et al., 2019) as well as activism, resistance, and protest (Jenkins et al., 2016). Here, the definition and the role of the community is very important. Who gets access to information, decision-making processes, and justice mechanisms? Is the role of the community active or passive? In other words, are they involved in designing the intervention or are they involved at the end of the process to accept it? Legal issues relating to prior consent, notification, and redress become important in case of resettlement due to energy infrastructure projects. Finally, because energy justice scholarship focuses on energy systems, it is not enough to ensure justice for some within specific spatial and temporal frames (McCauley and Heffron, 2018, p. 4). Procedural justice must be reconceptualised as taking place in multiple locations (McCauley et al., 2013; Heffron and McCauley, 2014).

3.1.3 Recognition justice

Recognition justice identifies the victims of injustice in the global energy system (McCauley et al., 2013; Heffron and McCauley, 2017). It is also described as post-distributional justice (Bulkeley et al., 2014). The victims of energy injustice are individuals and communities including socially deprived or ethnic minorities who are adversely affected, for instance, by decisions concerning siting of energy infrastructure, disabled or less able and elderly people who face fuel/energy poverty, and students who resort to energy activism (McCauley et al., 2013, 2019; Welton, 2018). Recognition justice places emphasis on understanding differences (Sovacool et al., 2019, p. 589).

Like energy justice and injustice, misrecognition sets the stage for recognition justice. There are three main categories of misrecognition: cultural domination, non-recognition, and disrespect (Fraser, 1995). Cultural domination involves being subjected to patterns of interpretation and communication that are associated with another culture and are alien and/or hostile to one's own (ibid., p. 71). The specific needs of certain groups, for example, the elderly, the infirm and the chronically ill, may be invisibilised or not recognised in the debates concerning energy poverty and energy inefficiency. There may be disrespect for the concerns of certain groups, for example, local communities opposing the siting of energy infrastructure projects. Recognition justice is not confined to recognition of such individuals and communities; they must receive fair representation, freedom from physical threats, and complete and equal rights (Schlosberg, 2003).

3.1.4 Restorative justice

Restorative or corrective justice focuses on actions to mitigate or address energy injustices (Heffron and McCauley, 2017; McCauley and Heffron, 2018). It is based on the idea that if X's actions or inactions have caused harm to Y, X should desist or act and compensate Y. Restorative justice pre-dates distributional, procedural and recognition justice. Heffron and McCauley (2017) view restorative justice as a practical application of energy justice. *Ex ante* restorative justice may require, for example, an energy infrastructure developer to undertake these actions: 'realisation of Social and Environmental Impact Assessments (SEIA) before energy decisions are made, the use of social safeguards measures, monitoring and mitigations of the impacts post construction and operation' (Siciliano et al., 2018, pp. 200–201). *Post facto* restorative justice can be viewed as an application of the polluter pays principle, for instance, to address the issue of historical responsibility for climate change.

3.1.5 Cosmopolitan justice

Cosmopolitan justice adopts a universal approach and applies the above-mentioned justice principles to all human beings in all countries (McCauley et al., 2019, p. 917). There is a single global community of individual human beings based on a collective morality. All human beings have equal moral worth, and our responsibilities exist beyond national borders. Ethical responsibilities apply everywhere and to all moral agents capable of understanding and acting on them, not only to members of one community or another (Sovacool et al., 2016). Cosmopolitan justice is concerned with the protection of global human rights and accounting and mitigation of global negative externalities (Sovacool et al., 2019, p. 591). It is also strongly anthropocentric in nature (Sovacool et al., 2016, p. 4).

These tenets of energy justice do not apply in a particular order, although Jenkins et al. (2016) focus on distribution, recognition, and finally procedural justice. These tenets are not distinct either; they overlap. Recognition justice is an inherent precondition for distribution justice. A fair distribution of benefits and harms cannot happen without knowing who is affected, and in what ways (Schlosberg, 2004). Recognition justice is also an integral part of procedural justice. No one can participate without being recognised and respected (ibid.). Procedural justice could address inequitable distribution and ensure substantive participation for affected vulnerable groups (ibid). Procedural justice also includes elements of restorative justice. 'Meaningful engagement and inclusion of affected societies through procedural justice is designed to restore trust between the alleged perpetrator and affected communities' (McCauley and Heffron, 2018, p. 5).

3.2 Beyond the tenets of energy justice

The three-tenet approach to energy justice is not without limitations. Lee and Byrne (2019) point out that the driving forces of social injustice caused by economic and political structures are largely missing in energy justice research. Further, it focuses on identifying injustices, rather than solving them. Therefore, Healy and Barry (2017) make the case for explicitly politicising energy justice.

There are other ways of understanding the concept of energy justice. Sovacool et al. (2014) explain energy justice using affirmative and prohibitive principles. The affirmative principle asserts that 'if any of the basic goods to which people are justly entitled can only be secured using energy services, then, in that case, there is also a derivative entitlement to the energy services' (ibid., p. 3). The prohibitive principle states that 'energy systems must be designed and constructed in such a way that they do not unduly interfere with the ability of people to acquire those basic goods to which they are justly entitled' (id.). In other words, the affirmative principle emphasises individuals' positive right to basic energy, and it is relevant in the context of energy poverty. The prohibitive principle focuses on negative externalities of the energy sector. In addition, Sovacool and Dworkin (2015) developed eight principles of energy justice: availability, affordability, due process, good governance, prudence, intergenerational equity, intragenerational equity, and responsibility.

Another limitation of the above-mentioned energy justice framework is that it is based on Western notions of justice mostly derived by Western thinkers, and/or by researchers concentrated in the West. This is inadequate for examining issues of energy justice and injustice in developing countries, which are expected to account for two-third of the global energy demand. According to Damgaard et al. (2017, p. 12), the Western concept of energy justice is rooted in concerns over centralised, conventional energy systems and negative externalities/burdens, and builds on predominantly Western discourses of human rights. In contrast, the non-Western concept considers non-conventional energy systems, focusses on equality rather than justice, and emphasises poverty alleviation and equal development to a greater extent than the distribution of benefits and costs. In a similar vein, Castán Broto et al. (2018) observe that the Western concept of energy justice lacks a contextual understanding of the socio-spatial factors that shape people's energy needs in non-Western countries.

As an alternative to the Western concept of energy justice, Sovacool et al. (2017) highlight the concept of capability-centred justice developed by Sen (1992) and Nussbaum (2011). Sen (1992) defines capability as 'a person's freedom to pursue functionings that he/she has reason to value' (ibid., pp. 4–5). According to him, functionings constitute a person's being, including both well-being and agency (ibid., pp. 59–62). Further, Sen extends the concept of capability beyond a purely rights-based discourse of justice by highlighting the burdens/responsibilities associated with personal freedom. Damgaard et al. (2017, p. 2) apply this capability approach to energy justice and observe: 'a concern with equality of capabilities transcends questions of access to energy as a 'good' or a service, to include also a focus on individuals' freedoms and functioning in terms of agency.' In a departure from the Western, individual-based approach to energy justice, Guoyu et al. (2020) link energy justice to the construction of community with a shared future for mankind.

Non-Western religions can also contribute to developing context-specific meanings of energy justice (Sovacool et al., 2017, pp. 678–680). Sen (2009) grounds the temporal nature of policies and decisions in the teachings of the Hindu *Bhagvad Gita* that emphasises time-based notions of 'consequence-sensitive' and 'duty-focused'. Malakar et al. (2019) draw upon Sen's interpretation of the *Gita* to understand the temporal nature of energy decision-making.

The role of elites in creating or exacerbating energy injustice in developing countries also merits further attention (Lacey-Barnacle et al., 2020, p. 131). Issues include institutional instability and the lack of proper state governance infrastructure because of destabilising past conflicts (Lappe-Osthege and Andreas, 2017), widespread corruption (Kotikalapudi, 2016; Yenneti and Day, 2015, p. 672) or post-disaster situations (Herington and Malakar, 2016; Islar et al., 2017). Elite capture also draws attention to developed country (government or private sector) interest in energy projects in developing countries (Lacey-Barnacle, Robison and Foulds, 2020, p. 132). A multi-scalar approach to energy justice that incorporates the global energy system allows researchers and practitioners to examine the relationships between nations. This is also relevant from the perspective of cosmopolitan justice.

4 From a low-carbon transition to a 'just' low-carbon transition

The low-carbon transition is characterised by a shift from fossil fuel sources to renewable/sustainable energy sources (energy production), and the need to strike a balance between meeting the energy needs of individuals and communities on one hand and achieving energy efficiency on the other (energy consumption) (McCauley and Heffron, 2018, p. 1). Energy justice scholars point out that 'simply decarbonising the *status quo*...is not energy justice' (Healy and Barry, 2017, p. 457). Eisenberg (2019, p. 282) observes that 'a world with low carbon emissions does not somehow transform into a utopia. A shift to a clean-energy economy stands to perpetuate or exacerbate current patterns of inequity'. She argues that 'the shift to a low-carbon economy is an opportunity to rectify the injustices of the fossil fuel economy, and to not do so, or to allow inequities to worsen, would itself effectuate injustice' (ibid., p. 280). This means that the low-carbon transition must not reinforce energy injustices related to the existing, fossil fuel-intensive global energy system (e.g., Healy and Barry, 2017; Carley and Konisky, 2020). Further, one cannot assume that the low-carbon transition will automatically promote energy justice (Newell and Mulvaney, 2013; Welton and Eisen, 2019). The transition may itself become the source of energy injustices (Carley and Konisky, 2020, p. 571).

The concept of just transition is presented as 'a fair and equitable process of moving towards a post-carbon society' (McCauley and Heffron, 2018, p. 2). The concept originated in the 1980s US trade union movement in response to new regulations to prevent water and air pollution (McCauley et al., 2019, p. 454). Just transition has 'the potential for uniting climate, environment and energy (CEE) justice to provide a more comprehensive framework for analysing and ultimately promoting fairness and equity throughout the transition away from fossil fuels' (Heffron and McCauley, 2018, p. 1). There will be little or no support for the low-carbon transition if it exacerbates energy injustices of the energy system or leads to new forms of energy injustice. Scholars argue for integration of the concept of energy justice with just transition (Williams and Doyon, 2019). Healy and Barry (2017, p. 452) claim that this would facilitate theorisation of social benefits and changes beyond the energy sector, e.g., the extraction of resources to facilitate the low-carbon transition.

4.1 The tenets of energy justice and the low-carbon transition

The different meanings of energy justice are relevant for a just low-carbon transition. With a focus on energy law in the low-carbon transition, the chapters in this volume identify several issues and solutions that promote energy justice or exacerbate energy injustice. Justice remains a key concern even where it is not expressly mentioned.

Distributional justice: The low-carbon transition involves the development of new energy infrastructure. Therefore, proximity remains important from the perspective of distributional justice. Further, the low-carbon transition may not address or may even exacerbate energy poverty and energy insecurity (see section 1 above) where the cost of energy increases in the short- and medium-term to cover the cost of new energy infrastructure (Carley and Konisky, 2020, p. 571). Du Plessis and Moyo (in this volume) refer to energy poverty while focusing on the role of cities in the low-carbon transition. Further, some of the new technologies such as electric vehicles and smart devices may remain beyond the reach of large sections of the population.

Recognition justice: The benefits and costs of the low-carbon transition may not be equally shared among different sections of society. The losers include workers in and communities dependent upon fossil fuel industries. The workers often encounter difficulties in finding a new job because of a skills gap or are forced to make sacrifices such as substantial wage loss and long-distance commutes, along with compromises in culture, community identity, and sense of place. Fossil fuel industries play an important role in the local tax revenue base; the decline of the industry may adversely affect public services such as education, transportation, and waste management (Carley and Konisky, 2020). The social consequences of labour disruptions may also extend to other employment sectors within fossil fuel-based communities (ibid., p. 571). Further, the costs of decommissioning of fossil fuel infrastructure in the form of creation of wasteland and generation of waste will be disproportionately borne by individuals and communities in the vicinity.

The negative externalities of low-carbon energy infrastructure will be disproportionately experienced by communities in the vicinity (Welton and Eisen, 2019). These externalities include the negative social, health, and environmental impacts of renewable energy projects (del Guayo and Cuesta, 2022). Chisanga (in this volume) explores some of the potential risks of nuclear energy as a contributor to the low-carbon transition. However, communities in the vicinity of low-carbon energy infrastructure will neither receive its financial benefits nor be able to access energy from the grid. The low-carbon transition may also exacerbate inequitable access to clean energy and energy poverty (del Guayo and Cuesta, 2022), and worsen the vulnerability of certain sections of society such as the poor and the ill (who cannot pay high energy costs), and the unemployed (Sovacool et al., 2019, p. 589). Women, indigenous peoples, ethnic minorities, rural communities, and the poor may remain excluded from the benefits of the low-carbon transition such as new employment opportunities, involvement in decision-making processes, and access to technologies.

Procedural justice: Recent years have witnessed growing public interest in energy generally and energy decision-making more specifically. This is likely to translate into increasing demands for access to information, public participation in decision-making, and access to justice. Energy decentralisation at the community-level may enhance public participation in the decision-making process. The low-carbon transition can lead to a shift in the focus of procedural justice, from viewing protest as an integral component of the engagement process to a mechanism for ensuring the long-term acceptance of renewable/sustainable energy infrastructure projects in communities (Yenneti and Day, 2015; McCauley and Heffron, 2018). Smith and Scott (2020) investigate participation and empowerment of indigenous peoples in renewable energy generation in Canada. Savaresi and Outka (this volume) focus on communities that host energy infrastructure and develop energy resources.

Restorative justice: The transition may require rectification of an existing energy injustice reinforced by the transition or a new injustice resulting from the transition (Heffron and McCauley, 2017). A low-carbon just transition may create new jobs in low-carbon/green sectors to compensate for the loss of jobs in fossil fuel-based industries. These new jobs must provide decent working conditions, pay a living wage, and be accessible to people with a range of skills, while providing clear career progression and opportunities (Bird and Lawton, 2009). From the perspective of intersectionality, the distribution of new jobs and economic opportunities must also consider issues relating to race, class, and gender. However, restorative justice is not confined to job creation. Mitigation and compensation funds may be established for workers in fossil fuel industries and dependent communities (McKinnon et al., 2016, p. 43). McCauley and Heffron (2018, p. 5) capture the temporal dimension of energy justice while extending restorative justice to 'past damages, existing crimes against human beings, the environment and climate, and the unforeseen, future harms resulting from the transition'.

Cosmopolitan justice: The low-carbon transition involves a shift towards renewable/sustainable energy sources such as solar power and energy efficient technologies. Cosmopolitan justice requires us to consider the negative social and environmental impacts in other countries of extraction of critical minerals for the manufacture of components of such infrastructure or technologies (Heffron, 2020).

4.2 Expanding the meanings of energy justice

Going forward, certain aspects of energy justice merit greater attention generally and in the specific context of the low-carbon transition. These relate to accommodation of non-anthropocentric values, intersectionality, temporality, rights, and activism.

First, energy justice in the low-carbon transition must transcend its overwhelmingly anthropocentric understanding (Sovacool et al., 2016, p. 1). In the past, the jobs-focused framing of the just transition has resulted in a 'jobs versus environment or climate' binary. The low-carbon transition must recognise the co-dependence of human and environmental benefits and costs at the very least. Energy justice scholarship incorporates non-anthropocentric values, albeit to a limited extent. Heffron and McCauley (2017) note that restorative justice aims to repair the harm done to society as well as nature by energy decisions. Sovacool et al. (2017) identify non-anthropocentric theories and applications of energy justice. Further, non-Western justice perspectives, especially those rooted in religion and philosophy, are likely to incorporate non-anthropocentric views to a much greater extent than Western justice scholarship.

Second, there is little multi-scalar activism encompassing the intersectional concerns of income inequality, low carbon alternatives, and procedural and distributional equity (Fuller and McCauley, 2016). Issues of energy justice are intertwined with race, class, or power and the treatment of non-humans (Sovacool et al., 2017, p. 687). Sovacool and Dworkin (2016) expand their list of eight energy justice principles to include intersectionality. In Bangladesh, activists contest energy injustices from a range of scales – critiques of persistent energy poverty, rejection of the ecological costs of coal mining and processing, and climate change concerns (Bedi, 2018, p. 169). Gender represents another key consideration in intersectionality (Feenstra and Ozerol, 2021).

Third, the temporal dimension of energy justice plays a crucial role in ensuring inter-generational equity (Jenkins et al., 2017). The principle of inter-generational equity focuses on the moral responsibility of current generations to protect future ones (Weiss, 1987). Energy justice concentrates upon the current contestations and disputes over resources (Rasch and Köhne, 2017) between and within states. According to McCauley et al. (2019, p. 917), however, distributional justice considers temporal variations in impact and the risks to future generations. Similarly, Malakar et al. (2019) examine the tension between addressing energy poverty of the present generation and ensuring a low-carbon transition to safeguard the future generations.

Fourth, we need to consider the contribution of a rights-based approach to energy justice. Hernández (2015) proposes four basic rights to energy justice: right to healthy, sustainable energy production, right to best available infrastructure, right to affordable energy, and right to uninterrupted energy service. Sovacool et al. (2017, p. 3) draw a link between distributional justice and rights. Bedi (2018) explores the intersection of energy justice and rights inspired by activism in Bangladesh and concludes that the articulation of rights is fundamental to the framing of energy injustice. The invocation of a rights-based approach in the context of energy justice generally and specifically in the context of the low-carbon transition can accommodate individual and community interests. According to Bedi (2018, p. 170), '[t]he ideals of rights emerge in Bangladesh energy activism in quite a distinct form, not centred on the idea of individualism'. Further, the right to energy justice does not exist in isolation. There may be cases of synergy or contestation with other rights. Siciliano et al. (2018, p. 201) extend Sovacool and Dworkin's (2015) energy justice principles of availability and affordability from energy services to other natural resources for local populations affected by energy projects.

Finally, and related to the above point, the rights-based approach to energy justice provides the basis for activism and litigation, which can advance the conceptions of energy justice discussed in section 2 above. Jenkins et al. (2016, p. 180) contrast the activist origins of environmental and climate justice with the absence of activism from the energy justice movement. Sovacool et al. (2017, p. 687) add resistance or standing up to injustice to their list of eight energy justice principles. Resistance expressed as activism can play an important role in addressing energy injustices where the development of energy systems/infrastructure violates human rights, for instance, of marginalised communities.

5 Conclusion

This chapter examined the meanings of energy justice for the low-carbon transition. Over the years, the list of tenets of energy justice has expanded, and there are synergies and contestations among these tenets. Energy justice is inextricably connected with other energy concerns such as energy poverty, energy sovereignty, and energy security. The meanings of energy justice also reveal trade-offs among economic, social, and environmental objectives, and overlaps and contestations among different tenets that need to be reconciled while reducing injustices.

The meanings of energy justice highlight its multi-scalar nature. A lot of energy research focuses on global energy justice and systems but recognises that actions at the local level have national and international effects (McCauley and Heffron, 2019, p. 2). Another multi-level feature of energy justice is the focus on full life cycle analysis (Healy and Barry, 2017) and whole system approach (Jenkins et al., 2014). Of course, this needs to consider the capacity of existing weak and fragmented energy governance institutions. Energy justice also expands the field of governance to encompass different actors including democratic and non-democratic/authoritarian regimes (Wang and Lo, 2021), the private sector, non-governmental organisations, social and environmental movements, and labour unions, as well as consumers and other members of the public who are affected by the low-carbon transition.

It is imperative to examine the legal and regulatory context in which energy justices and injustices occur (Jenkins et al., 2017) in the low-carbon transition. The first issue is a tension between expediency and the pace of transition on one hand and the (often) gradual nature of law-making and implementation on the other. A second concern is the overwhelming influence of neoliberalism on law that may undermine social and environmental considerations. Third, the multi-level nature of laws (international, regional, national, and local laws) and the interplay between them must be considered. The relevant international and domestic laws may relate to energy, the environment, climate change, human rights, water, etc. Domestic constitutions and legislation relating to land ownership and tenure as well as financing of energy infrastructure and energy pricing are also relevant. Wiseman (this volume) refers to the impact of competitive markets on energy justice. Decentralised energy systems for the low-carbon transition require robust regulations and accountability and monitoring mechanisms.

A key consideration that is missing from this chapter is the influence of political economy factors including unequal relations of power, use, access to and ownership of energy. Governments play a central role in the design and implementation of suitable energy systems for the low-carbon transition. Whether or not these initiatives can promote energy justice may influence their acceptance (McHarg, 2020, p. 18).

Part of the appeal of the concept of energy justice is its potential practical application to law- and policymaking for the low-carbon transition. By incorporating energy justice, the low-carbon transition can strike a healthy balance between the regulatory objectives of efficiency, effectiveness and equity or fairness. No doubt, the shift from conceptualisation of energy justice to its practical application in the low-carbon transition in the real world presents an immense challenge. This chapter lays the foundation to make connections and to address gaps in our knowledge and understanding about energy justice in the low-carbon transition.

References

Ang, B., Choong, W. and Ng, T., 2015. Energy security: definitions, dimensions and indexes. *Renewable and Sustainable Energy Review*, 42, pp. 1077–1093.

Bedi, H.P., 2018. 'Our energy, our rights': national extraction legacies and contested energy justice futures in Bangladesh. *Energy Research & Social Science*, 41, pp. 168–175.

Bird, J., and Lawton, K., 2009. *The future's green: jobs and the UK low-carbon transition*. London: IPPR.

Bulkeley, H., Edwards, G.A.S. and Fuller, S., 2014. Contesting climate justice in the city: examining politics and practice in urban climate change experiments. *Global Environmental Change*, 25, pp. 31–40.

Carley, S. and Konisky, D.M., 2020. The justice and equity implications of the clean energy transition. *Nature Energy*, 5, pp. 569–577.

Castán Broto, V., 2017. Energy sovereignty and development planning: The case of Maputo, Mozambique. *International Development Planning Review*, 39(3), pp. 229–248.

Castán Broto, V. et al., 2018. Energy justice and sustainability transitions in Mozambique. *Applied Energy*, 228, pp. 645–655.

Damgaard, C., McCauley, D. and Long, J., 2017. Assessing the energy justice implications of bioenergy development in Nepal. *Energy, Sustainability & Society*, 7(8), 8.

del Guayo, Í and Cuesta, Á, 2022. Towards a just energy transition: a critical analysis of the existing policies and regulations in Europe. *Journal of World Energy Law and Business*, 22, pp. 212–222.

Eisenberg, A.M., 2019. Just transitions. *Southern California Law Review*, 92, pp. 273–330.

Faiella, I. and Lavecchia, L., 2015. Energy poverty in Italy. *Political Economy*, 31, pp. 27–76.

Feenstra, M. and Ozerol, G., 2021. Energy justice as a search light for gender-energy nexus: Towards a conceptual framework. *Renewable and Sustainable Energy Reviews*, 138, 110668.

Fraser, N., 1995. From redistribution to recognition? Dilemmas of justice in a "post-socialist" age. *New Left Review*, 212, pp. 68–93.

Fuller, S. and McCauley, D., 2016. Framing energy justice: perspectives from activism and advocacy. *Energy Research & Social Science*, 11, pp. 1–8.

Govindan, M. et al., 2020. Gender in electricity policymaking in India, Nepal and Kenya. In: G. Bombaerts et al. (eds.), *Energy justice across borders*. Cham: Springer Nature, pp. 111–135.

Guoyu, W., Guan, J. and Li, L., 2020. Energy justice and construction of community with a shared future for mankind. In: G. Bombaerts et al. (eds.), *Energy justice across borders*. Cham: Springer Nature, pp. 217–235.

Guruswamy, L., 2010. Energy justice and sustainable development. *Colorado Journal of International Environmental Law and Policy*, 21(2), pp. 231–276.

Guruswamy, L., 2020. Energy poverty, justice, and women. In: S. Atapattu, C.A. Gonzalez and S.L. Seck (eds.), *The Cambridge handbook of environmental justice and sustainable development*. Cambridge: Cambridge University Press, pp. 368–382.

Healy, N. and Barry, J., 2017. Politicizing energy justice and energy system transitions: Fossil fuel divestment and a "just transition". *Energy Policy*, 108, pp. 451–459.

Heffron, R.J., 2020. The role of justice in developing critical minerals. *The Extractive Industries and Society*, 7(3), pp. 850–863.

Heffron, R.J. and McCauley, D., 2014. Achieving sustainable supply chains through energy justice. *Applied Energy*, 123, pp. 435–437.

Heffron, R.J. and McCauley, D., 2017. The concept of energy justice across the disciplines. *Energy Policy*, 105, pp. 658–667.

Heffron, R.J. and McCauley, D., 2018. What is the 'Just Transition'? *Geoforum*, 88, pp. 74–77.

Heffron, R.J. et al., 2018. A treatise for energy law. *Journal of World Energy Law and Business*, 11, pp. 34–48.

Herington, M.J. and Malakar, Y., 2016. Who is energy poor? Revisiting energy (in)security in the case of Nepal. *Energy Research & Social Science*, 21, pp. 49–53.

Hernández, D., 2015. Sacrifice along the energy continuum: a call for energy justice. *Environmental Justice*, 8(4), pp. 151–156.

Islar, M., Brogaard, S. and Lemberg-Pedersen, M., 2017. Feasibility of energy justice: exploring national and local efforts for energy development in Nepal. *Energy Policy*, 105, pp. 668–676.

Jenkins, K., 2018. Setting energy justice apart from the crowd: Lessons from environmental and climate justice. *Energy Research & Social Science*, 39, pp. 117–121.

Jenkins, K. et al., 2014. Energy justice: a whole systems approach. *Queen's Political Review*, 2(2), pp. 74–87.

Jenkins, K. et al. 2016. Energy justice: A conceptual review. *Energy Research & Social Science*, 11, pp. 174–182.

Jenkins, K., McCauley, D. and Forman, A., 2017. Energy justice: a policy approach. *Energy Policy*, 105, pp. 631–634.

Kotikalapudi, C.K., 2016. Corruption, crony capitalism and conflict: Rethinking the political economy of coal in Bangladesh and beyond. *Energy Research & Social Science*, 17, pp. 160–164.

Lacey-Barnacle, M., Robison R. and Foulds, C., 2020. Energy justice in the developing world: A review of theoretical frameworks, key research themes and policy implications. *Energy for Sustainable Development*, 55, pp. 122–138.

Lappe-Osthege, T. and Andreas, J.-J., 2017. Energy justice and the legacy of conflict: assessing the Kosovo C thermal power plant project. *Energy Policy*, 107(C), pp. 600–606.

Lee, J. and Byrne, J., 2019. Expanding the conceptual and analytical basis of energy justice: Beyond the three-tenet framework. *Frontiers in Energy Research*, 7, pp. 1–10.

Malakar, Y., Herington, M.J. and Sharma, V., 2019. The temporalities of energy justice: Examining India's energy policy paradox using non-western philosophy. *Energy Research & Social Science*, 49, pp. 16–25.

McCauley, D. and Heffron, R., 2018. Just transition: integrating climate, energy and environmental justice. *Energy Policy*, 119, pp. 1–7.

McCauley, D.A. et al., 2013. Advancing energy justice: the triumvirate of tenets. *International Energy Law Review*, 32(3), pp. 107–110.

McCauley, D. et al., 2019. Energy justice in the transition to low carbon energy systems: Exploring key themes in interdisciplinary research. *Applied Energy*, 233-234, pp. 916–921.

McHarg, A., 2020. Energy Justice: Understanding the 'Ethical Turn' in Energy Law and Policy. In: Í. Del Guayo et al. (eds.), *Energy justice and energy law*. Oxford: Oxford University Press, pp. 15–30.

McKinnon, H. et al., 2016. *The sky's limit: why the Paris climate goals require a managed decline of fossil fuel production*. Washington: Oil Change International.

Newell, P. and Mulvaney, D., 2013. The political economy of the 'just transition'. *The Geographical Journal*, 179(2), pp. 132–140.

Nussbaum, M.C., 2011. *Creating capabilities: the human development approach*. Cambridge, MA: Harvard University Press.

Rasch, E.D. and Köhne, M., 2017. Practices and imaginations of energy justice in transition: A case study of the Noordoostpolder, the Netherlands. *Energy Policy*, 107, pp. 607–614.

Reames, T., 2016. Targeting energy justice: exploring spatial, racial/ethnic and socio-economic disparities in urban residential heating energy efficiency. *Energy Policy*, 97, pp. 549–558.

Schlosberg, D., 2003. The justice of environmental justice: reconciling equity, recognition, and participation in a political movement. In: A. Light and A. De-Shalit (eds), *Moral and political reasoning in environmental practice*. London: MIT Press, pp. 125–156.

Schlosberg, D., 2004. Reconceiving environmental justice: global movements and political theories. *Environmental Politics*, 13, pp. 517–540.

Schlosberg, D. and Collins, L.B., 2014. From environmental to climate justice: climate change and the discourse of environmental justice. *WIREs Climate Change*, 5, pp. 359–374.

Sen, A., 1992. *Inequality reexamined*. New York: Oxford University Press.

Sen, A., 2009. *The idea of justice*. New York: Penguin Books.

Siciliano, G. et al., 2021. Low-carbon energy, sustainable development, and justice: towards a just energy transition for the society and the environment. *Sustainable Development*, 29, pp. 1049–1061.

Smith, A.A. and Scott, D.N., 2020. Energy without injustice? Indigenous participation in renewable energy generation. In: S. Atapattu, C.A. Gonzalez and S.L. Seck (eds.), *The Cambridge handbook of environmental justice and sustainable development*. Cambridge: Cambridge University Press, pp. 383–397.

Sovacool, B.K. and Dworkin, M., 2014. *Global energy justice: Problems, principles, and practices*. Cambridge: Cambridge University Press.

Sovacool, B.K. and Dworkin, M.H., 2015. Energy justice: Conceptual insights and practical applications. *Applied Energy*, 142, pp. 435–444.

Sovacool, B.K. et al., 2016. Energy decisions reframed as justice and ethical concerns. *Nature Energy*, 1(5), Article Number 16024.

Sovacool, B.K. et al. 2017. New frontiers and conceptual frameworks for energy justice. *Energy Policy*, 105, pp. 677–691.

Sovacool, B.K. et al. 2019. Decarbonisation and its discontents: a critical energy justice perspective on four low-carbon transitions. *Climatic Change*, 155, pp. 581–619.

Sovacool, B.K., Sidorstov, R.V. and Jones, B.R., 2014. *Energy security, equality and justice*. Oxon, New York: Routledge.

Taylor, D.E., 2000. The rise of the environmental justice paradigm. *American Behavioural Scientist*, 43, pp. 508–580.

Tomain, J.P., 2022. Energy justice in a net-zero world. *Journal of World Energy Law & Business*, 22, pp. 173–182.

Wang, X. and Lo, K., 2021. Just transition: a conceptual review. *Energy Research & Social Science*, 82, 102291.

Weiss, E.B., 1987. Inter-Generational Equity in International Law. *American Society of International Law Proceedings*, 1, pp. 127–128.

Welton, S. and Eisen, J., 2019. Clean energy justice: charting an emerging agenda. *Harvard Environmental Law Review*, 43, pp. 307–371.

Williams, S. and Doyon, A., 2019. Justice in energy transitions. *Environmental Innovation and Societal Transitions*, 31, pp. 144–153.

Yenneti, K. and Day, R., 2015. Procedural (in)justice in the implementation of solar energy: the case of Charanaka solar park, Gujarat, India. *Energy Policy*, 86, pp. 664–673.

Kenneth Richards

Energy Policy Instruments for a Low-Carbon Energy Transition

Abstract: Definitions, taxonomies, and impact of policy instruments are heavily debated, both from a theoretical and empirical point of view. This chapter suggests that the usual dichotomy between command-and-control and market-based instruments is overly narrow. The relative merit of instruments depends highly on the specific applications and economic, institutional, and political context. The chapter lays out the basic structure of policy instruments, particularly highlighting three branches of instruments. It then discusses each of those three branches with examples of applications from a wide range of geographic locations. Hybrid instruments and other combinations of the basic instruments are briefly analysed.

1 Introduction

As an increasing number of countries make commitments to lower their greenhouse gas emissions broadly, and to reduce use of fossil fuels specifically, it is important to consider the policy instruments available to governments to move from policies and targets to implementation and action. The purpose of this chapter is to provide a systematic overview for considering the broad range of policy instruments available, their characteristics, and the circumstances under which each might be most appropriate. The overview will be illustrated with the examples from several different countries.

The task of enumerating and exploring the many policy instruments is challenging in several respects. First, there is some ambiguity concerning the definition of a policy instrument. For this discussion, we adopt the definition from (McDonnell and Elmore, 1987) that policy instruments are "mechanisms that translate substantive policy goals into concrete actions." Thus, instruments are the various tools such as taxes, regulations, information programs, and legal requirements, that induce changes that governments seek. They are not, as is often mistakenly suggested, the goals them-

Note: The author gratefully acknowledges the able research assistance of Evy Lou and the support of the Tobias Center for Innovation in International Development, Hamilton Lugar School of Global and International Studies, Indiana University.

Kenneth Richards holds appointments at the O'Neill School, the IU Maurer School of Law, and the Ostrom Workshop in Political Theory and Policy Analysis, Indiana University, United States.

https://doi.org/10.1515/9783110752403-012

selves (e.g., information diffusion, increased innovation, increased energy efficiency) or the technologies (e.g. wind power, cogeneration). Policy instruments are a means to an end.

The second factor that makes this exercise challenging is that the range of energy applications is broad. Governments will need to address energy use across many economic sectors – manufacturing, transportation, electricity supply, and buildings, to name a few. These applications can involve private or public investments, or both. Policies can be targeted at energy extraction (e.g., pumping oil), conversion (e.g., burning coal to produce electricity), or consumption (e.g., using natural gas to heat homes). In some cases, governments will seek to induce development and adoption of new technologies and in other applications they will work to change behaviors related to energy demand. For policies that implicate technology choice, particularly as relates to electricity production, governments may seek to slow fossil energy use or spur adoption of renewable energy. And in some cases, policies are intended to act throughout the entire economy (e.g., carbon pricing) and in others to be very focused (e.g., government provision of electric vehicle charging stations). Clearly, to support a transition to a low-carbon technology, governments will need to address a vast range of applications.

Third, while many analysts recognize a narrow range of policy instruments (e.g., Salzman, 2013; Pacheco-Vega, 2020), the fact is that there is a broad range from which governments can choose (e.g., US Department of Energy, 1989; Richards, 2000; Schmitt and Schulze, 2011). In fact, many policy instruments that are described as discreet actually lie on a continuum of instruments, which means that conceptually there are an infinite number of instruments from which to choose, complicating the process of characterization.

Finally, the relative merits of policy instruments are highly context specific, varying according to the application (e.g., energy conservation versus renewable energy diffusion) and the geopolitical environment (e.g., industrialized economy versus emerging economy). Further, the effectiveness and efficiency of policy instruments is highly sensitive to the political environmental, established institutions, and specific legal constraints.

It is not uncommon for authors to suggest that policy makers face a dichotomous decision in instrument choice – market-based or command-and-control instruments, and that virtually always the former is preferred (Stavins, 1991; Stanton, 2012). This chapter suggests that approach presents a false dichotomy that it is overly narrow in the range of instruments, and that the relative merit of instruments depends highly on the specific applications and economic, political, institutional, and political context. One size does not fit all.

The next section of this chapter lays out the basic structure of policy instruments, particularly highlighting three branches of instruments. The subsequent three sections discuss each of those three branches with examples of applications from a wide range of geographic locations. The discussion then turns briefly to hybrid instruments and other combinations of the basic instruments. The chapter finishes with brief conclusions.

2 Organizing the Policy Instruments

There are many approaches to categorizing and analyzing policy instruments. For example, the forthcoming report from the Intergovernmental Panel on Climate Change, Working Group III (2022) identifies three main categories of instruments – economic instruments, regulatory instruments, and other instruments (Dubash and Mitchell, 2022). While that approach has the advantage of simplicity, it primarily focuses on the dichotomy of market-based instruments versus regulatory strategies, emphasizing the superior cost-effectiveness of the former. While that distinction is important, a categorization based entirely on a single dimension risks leaving the reader with an overly narrow view of the range of both the instruments and the relation among them.

The approach applied in this chapter is rooted in the First Fundamental Theorem of Welfare Economics, and informed by New Institutional Economics, legal theory, political economy, public economics, and public finance. Developed for environmental policy, it recognizes three primary reasons that governments intervene in what are essentially market decisions.

First, when the choices of decision makers affect others who are not part of the decision, i.e., they create externalities (negative or positive), the government intervenes to adjust incentives. Second, when society does not understand a problem or does not have adequate options to address a problem, governments intervene to induce basic research and innovation. This is necessary, because the creation of knowledge is essentially providing a public good, which, if left to the private market, will be underproduced. Third, even when there is adequate knowledge of a problem and there are sufficient technical options to address the problem, the information may not be readily available to the decision makers who need that information. To address this "information imperfection," governments can adopt policies to disseminate the information and increase understanding of the energy issue and the options available to address it. To address each of these three market failures – externalities, public good nature of research and innovation, and imperfect information – there are three separate branches of policy instruments.[1]

The instruments in each of the three branches can be further categorized according to several dimensions, three of which will be considered in this chapter. First, the

1 In addition to these three types of market failures that underlie virtually all environmental problems, and to which virtually all environmental policy instrument can be tied, in the field of energy the government plays a significant role in addressing monopoly behavior and facilitating coordination among parties. This chapter will not address those issues or the associated policy instruments.

instruments can be distinguished according to the role of government, i.e., whether they rely on private ordering or public ordering. With private ordering instruments, the government assigns entitlements under property, liability, and contracting rules (Vandenbergh, 2013). The government also provides a set of support mechanisms to allow individuals to enforce their rights, including a judicial system and infrastructure. With the entitlements assigned, the government leaves the specific outcomes to individual exchange.

The hallmark of public ordering, in contrast, is that the government sets goals, establishes programs, and initiates enforcement of the rules. Within the public ordering approach on each of the three branches the instruments can be further distinguished according to how much of the economic burden they place on private actors and how much discretion they leave to private actors. Note that in contrast to the first two dimensions, these are both continuous, leading to a policy instrument space, as illustrated in Figure 2. These dimensions will be further explored in the subsequent discussions of the three branches.

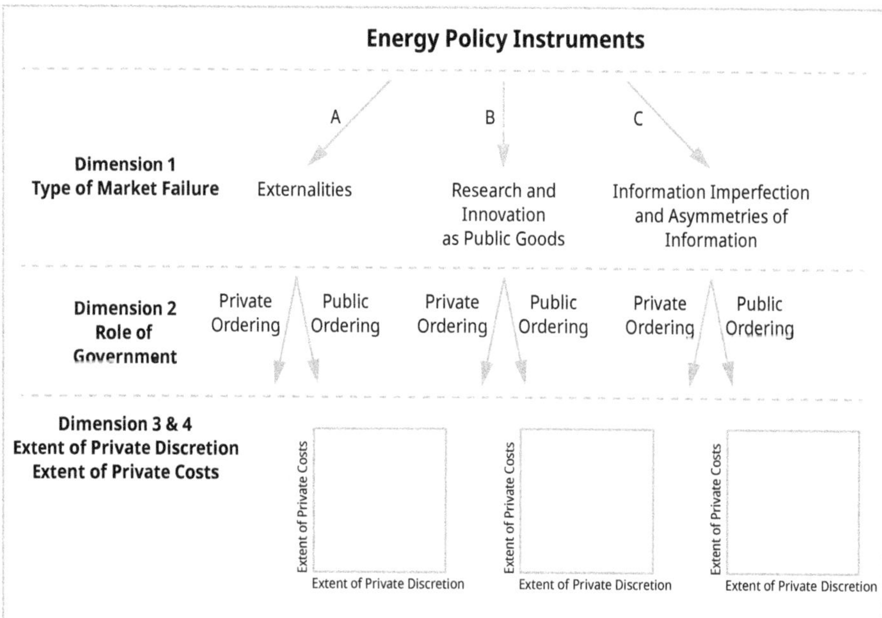

Figure 2 : Policy Instruments Classification.

The next three sections examine how "pure" instruments from each of the three branches have been deployed by governments around the world to support decarbonization of the energy sector. The subsequent section examines how the instruments are used to in combination or as hybrids within and across the branches. The discussion in those sections is intended to provide an overview of the full range of policy instruments and the relationship among them.

3 Branch A – Instruments to Address Externalities

Most discussions of policy instruments focus on the levers that governments use to adjust incentives and drive behavior change. In the field of energy policy, these are used to induce reductions in the use of fossil fuels, increase the adoption of renewable energy, promote energy efficiency and conservation, and reduce emissions of greenhouse gases associated with the extraction and transportation of coal, oil, and natural gas. These instruments, found on Branch A of Figure 2, take effect through either private or public ordering.

3.1 Branch A – Private Ordering in Externalities

To encourage the efficient use of energy resources, governments can clarify entitlements, including using property rights. For example, Bronin (2009) reports that at least 2000 years ago, "Romans protected the right to solar heat and light through prescriptive easements, government allocations and court decrees." In the United States, about two thirds of states have statutes recognizing easements that protect solar developments from having their sunlight blocked (Megaloudis, 2017) and over half of the states have solar access laws that limit the restrictions that homeowners associations' covenants can place on residential solar installations (Bowman, 2022).

In many cases, private parties have taken the initiative to promote the public interest through their private transactions. This is often described as private environmental governance (Vandenbergh 2013), and involves private parties exercising property, liability, and contracting rights to induce adaptations in business transactions. In some cases, firms work with their suppliers to decrease the energy intensity of production or to induce shifts to renewable energy. For example, as part of its *Guidelines for Sustainability in Supply Chain*, Nippon Telegraph and Telephone Corporation requires suppliers to "reduce energy consumption and greenhouse gas emissions" by improving energy efficiency and using renewable energy as much as possible. A broader discussion is provided in the chapter by Mitdikis.

Increasingly, independent organizations are providing standards and guidance that firms can incorporate in their supply chain contracts. For example, the International Standards Organization (ISO) 50001 standard provides guidance on energy management systems that can be incorporated by reference in supply contracts. The World Economic Forum (2021) has advised companies on how to incorporate contractual provisions to decarbonize their supply chains. Trade organizations have also provided mechanisms for private ordering of energy issues; e.g., the International

Chamber of Shipping (2021) has proposed a carbon tax on global shipping, with the funds to be paid to the United Nations' International Maritime Organization to promote zero-carbon fuels and related infrastructure.

3.2 Branch A – Public Ordering in Externalities

The efficacy of the private ordering approach is limited by the commitment of firms to improvements in energy systems and reductions in greenhouse gas emissions. Very often, to achieve large scale transitions, governments must intervene in decisions that are otherwise left to the market. This is the public ordering approach, in which governments set energy or environmental goals, initiate programs, and enforce compliance with the rules of the program.

To support this public ordering approach, governments can draw on a virtually infinite range of arrangements. Two of the most important dimensions for distinguishing among those instruments are the extent of private discretion they permit and the extent of private cost they impose. Table 2 provides several examples of public ordering instruments used to support the transition to a low-carbon energy economy.

Table 2: Branch A Policy Instruments for the Low-Carbon Transition.

Country	Program/ Policy Name	Instrument Type	Dates	Description	Extent of Private Discretion	Extent of Private Economic Burden
Costa Rica	Costa Rican Electricity Institute	Government provision	1949 – present	The state-owned electricity company promotes renewable energy.	Low	Low
India	Solar Energy Corporation of India (SECI)	Government procurement	2011 – present	Solar Energy Corporation of India (SECI) uses reverse auctions for solar energy	High	Low
South Africa	Renewable Energy Independent Power Producers Procurement Programme (REIPPPP)	Government Procurement	2010 – present	REIPPP is aimed at bringing additional megawatts onto the country's electricity system through private sector investment in wind, biomass and small hydro, among others.	High	Low

Table 2: Branch A Policy Instruments for the Low-Carbon Transition.

Country	Program/ Policy Name	Instrument Type	Dates	Description	Extent of Private Discretion	Extent of Private Economic Burden
China	Notice on Playing the Role of Price Leverage to Promote the Healthy Development of the Photovoltaic Industry	Subsidy	2013 – present	Chinese government provides a net-metering subsidy of 0.42 yuan (US$ 0.06) per kWh for distributed solar energy systems	High	Medium
South Africa	National carbon tax	Emissions tax	2019 – present	The South Africa carbon tax places the liability on emitters of greenhouse gas emissions	High	High
New Zealand	New Zealand Emissions Trading Scheme (NZETS)	Emissions trading system	2008 – present	The NZ ETS allocates allowances freely, and requires emitters to surrender their emissions to cover emissions.	High	Medium
United Kingdom	Energy efficiency standards for industrial plants	Command-and-control regulation	2016 –	Establishes minimum energy efficiency standards for industrial processes	Low	Medium
Vietnam	Regulations on Industrial Energy Efficiency	Command-and-control regulation	2014 –	Specifies parameters for energy efficiency in industrial processes, with a focus on the chemicals industry.	Low	Medium

In some cases, governments both fund and control the transitions they seek. For example, in Costa Rica the government owns the electric generation facilities, which the government operates through the Costa Rican Electricity Institute (ICE). Through this arrangement the system delivers electricity that is nearly 100 percent renewable, including hydropower and geothermal, supplemented with wind, solar, and biomass.

In contrast, the government could operate through the market to procure the energy services it seeks. The Solar Corporation of India (SECI), a state-owned operation under the administrative control of the Ministry of New and Renewable energy (MNRE), employs reverse auctions to procure development of solar power capacity. Under this procurement approach, companies submit bids that specify the capacity of their proposed project and the price at which they will supply electricity. Projects are selected from the lowest cost offers until the required capacity is reached. In 2020, SECI procured 2 GW of new solar power with the most competitive bid offering electricity at the lowest price (US$ 0.031/kWh) for solar-powered electricity in India's history. This is similar to the system used in Poland, where the regulatory authority awards contracts for supply of renewable energy through reverse auctions and in Mexico, where the Federal Electricity company purchased clean energy certificates for more than 30 percent of its electricity supply. South Africa has used a similar competitive bidding process to induce the private sector to invest in a broad range of renewable energy developments (Eberhard, Kolker, and Leigland 2014).

Notice that while the government (or its customers) are paying for the developments in both Costa Rica and India, the latter leverages high powered market incentives by giving private parties discretion regarding how they deliver on the government's goal of expanding renewable energy.

Subsidies are similar to procurement in the sense that they also provide government financial support while maintaining significant private discretion. They differ from government procurement, however, in terms of the structure of the offer to the private sector. In the case of procurement, the government sets a quantity goal, and accepts the lowest cost combination of offers that meet that goal. With pure subsidies, the government sets the price it is willing to pay, and essentially accepts all offers that meet the technical requirements. For example, as described by Kurokawa in this volume, Japan developed a feed-in tariff for small solar photovoltaic electricity systems that was set at a generous fixed price for ten years. The result has been an increase of more than 2000 percent in the generation of solar electricity between 2010 and 2019. In contrast, China has also offered subsidies for solar energy production, but there are several technical limits (particularly on solar cell efficiencies) that significantly reduce private discretion (Zou et al., 2017).

In contrast to the procurement, subsidy, and government provision approaches described above, the government can instead place the economic burden on private sector parties. When the government taxes carbon emissions or auctions emissions allowances, private parties incur two types of costs. First, they incur the costs of reducing their emissions. Second, they pay the price of their residual emissions, the unabated emissions, for which they have a tax liability or an allowance obligation.

These two instruments – marketable allowances and taxes – have a similar quantity versus price relationship to the procurement and subsidy instruments discussed above. With marketable allowances, the government chooses a quantity of emissions and allows the market to determine the price at which they will be sold. With emissions taxes, the government determines the price for emissions, and allows market responses to determine the quantity of total emissions.

In some cases, the government will reduce the burden on private sector parties by allocating the allowances to private parties freely, as in the case of the New Zealand Emissions Trading System (ETS). This means that emitters are responsible for the costs of reducing their emissions, but have much lower liabilities for their residual (unabated) emissions. The European Union ETS started off with freely allocated allowances in its early phase, and then transitioned to an auctioned approach in the subsequent phases.

Regardless of whether emitters bear the costs of allowances, the carbon tax and emissions trading systems provide substantial discretion to the parties regarding how they reduce emissions. Contrast that to the command-and-control approach, which provides relatively little discretion. For example, the United Kingdom has established energy efficiency standards that mandate the performance of industrial processes. Similarly, Vietnam has specified industrial energy efficiency parameters for a range of processes, including combustion, heat supply, cooling, and waste heat use. These two approaches constrain the range of options that parties can deploy to reduce their emissions.

In an interesting combination of command-and-control and market-based instruments, the province of British Columbia, Canada has developed a low-carbon fuel standard (BC-LCFS), under which the government sets a carbon intensity target for fuels (based on life cycle emissions). Fuel suppliers earn credits for producing fuels below the target carbon intensity, which they can sell to those suppliers that do not meet the target. In this sense, the standard provides an intermediate level of discretion to the regulated parties regarding how they reduce their emissions.

4 Branch B – Instruments to Induce Research and Innovation

Often governments' environmental and energy goals focus on advancing the state of knowledge, either better understanding the underlying science of the problem or developing better options to address the problem. This requires investment in research and development. But knowledge itself is a public good, and those who invest in creation of new knowledge may not be able to appropriate the full value of their investment. Consequently, the unregulated market tends to underprovide the creation of new knowledge relative to the social optimal. To induce increased investment in scientific research and innovation, the government can adopt either public or private ordering approaches.

4.1 Branch B – Private Ordering in Research and Innovation

Knowledge is a public good, meaning that there are incomplete property rights in its use and replication. Therefore, one solution is to create property rights in knowledge.

Many governments use patent systems to create rights in innovations, and renewable energy patents have been a major focus of activity. From 2002 to 2012 the number of new patents for renewable energy technologies published under the World Intellectual Property Organization grew more than five-fold, from 831 to 4,541, leading to an expected decline in the cost of renewable energy over the long-term (Nurton, 2020).

By creating property rights via patents, the government increases private incentives to invest in research and innovation. Having established the entitlement to use and license specific knowledge, the government leaves private parties to negotiate rights and payments for its use. There are, however, limits to the effectiveness of this policy tool. First, it is largely limited to new technologies. Patents do little to encourage investment in basic scientific research. Second, patents essentially create a monopoly in the new technologies. This means that once a technology is created, it will likely be underutilized relative to the socially optimal level.

4.2 Branch B – Public Ordering in Research and Innovation

To address the limitations of the patent system, governments can turn to public ordering in research and innovation. As with the Branch A instruments that address externalities, the range of public ordering instruments vary along two important dimensions – the degree of private discretion they provide and the extent to which the private sector bears the economic cost.

At one extreme, a government can conduct research within its own facilities, bearing all costs, and controlling all research decisions. For example, Australia's Commonwealth Scientific and Industrial Research Organisation (CSIRO) is a government corporate entity that engages in research and development that benefits the country broadly. CSIRO has been actively engaged in research and development related to direct removal of atmospheric carbon dioxide, carbon dioxide storage, and nature-based solutions as well as a broad range of basic climate science and greenhouse gas monitoring.

In contrast to the CSIRO system, the United States Department of Energy (USDOE) operates its national laboratory system through contracts with nongovernment operators.[2] Using the contracting policy instrument, the government pays for most of the research in the national laboratory system, but shares discretion in the conduct of

2 These are referred to as "government owned/contractor operated" (GOCO) laboratories. For example, the Pacific Northwest National Laboratory is currently operated by Battelle Memorial Institute on a cost-reimbursable basis under contract to the US Department of Energy. Argonne National Laboratory is operated by the University of Chicago and Sandia National Laboratories is manged by National Technology and Engineering Solutions of Sandia, LLC, which is a subsidiary of Honeywell International, Inc.

that research with private contractors. Through its national lab system USDOE has, for example, developed new roofing materials to reduce cooling costs in buildings, contributed to increased wind turbine efficiencies, developed high efficiency "smart windows," and made major contributions to new battery technologies to support renewable energy.

Similarly, to implement its New Sunshine Programme (see Kurokawa, in this volume), the Government of Japan relied on a combination of industrial, government and, university groups for its basic research on photovoltaic technologies (Hamakawa and Tohma, 1993).

Often governments further devolve control of research and innovation to businesses and institutions through research grants. In the process of applying for support, parties describe their research objectives and methods, and often negotiate specific details and products. The funding generally involves a contract, detailing the timing of the work, its general conduct, the amount of the funding, and the expected outputs. However, once the research grant is awarded, governments tend to be less involved in the conduct of the research than in the case of the United States national laboratories.

The government can further shift discretion to private parties through technology prizes. While there are many variations of this instrument, sometimes called an X-prize or inducement-prize, in concept the government defines a technological development, provides technical specifications of that development, and offers a reward to the first party that provides a design that meets the specifications. For example, after the United States Federal Government announced a ban on incandescent bulbs in 2007, the Department of Energy instituted an inducement prize for an affordable LED light bulb to replace 60-watt light bulbs. The prize was won by Phillips, although the retail price was originally expected to be approximately US$50 (Whoriskey, 2012).

In all the applications described above, the government is essentially bearing the economic cost of the research. However, under all those arrangements, the government can share the cost of research and innovation with private parties. For example, in 1993, the US Department of Commerce developed the Partnership for a New Generation of Vehicles, a public-private partnership with automobile manufactures to advance the design and manufacturing capacity for high efficiency vehicles

5 Branch C – Instruments to Disseminate Information

It is not enough that information exists on the nature of the climate change, the energy sector's contributions to it, and options for transitioning to a low-carbon economy. It is necessary for decision makers to have access to that information and to apply it. For example, when consumers do not understand the relative energy efficiency of appliances, they cannot evaluate the costs and benefits of alternatives, even if the social cost of carbon is fully reflected in the price of electricity. When manufacturers are not aware of advances in motor efficiency, they cannot evaluate the performance of their current productive capital or effectively make decisions regarding investment in improved energy efficiency.

Similarly, when consumers are choosing which companies and brands of goods to support through their market decisions, they cannot evaluate the sustainability performance of alternatives if they do not have access to data on individual firms' track records. And investors who want to support the transition to a low-carbon economy need reliable information on the relative performance of firms.

As described below, this need to put useful information in the hands of decision makers is addressed through both public and private ordering approaches.

5.1 Private Ordering to Disseminate Information

There are many ways that private, nongovernmental actors, operate to provide essential information to support the transition to a low-carbon future. One strategy is to provide information about options to lower emissions to consumers, producers and governments. For example, in Europe a consortium of 11 research and advocacy organizations formed Solutions to Tackle Energy Poverty (STEP) that facilitates the flow of information to energy-poor consumers, helping them save energy and improve their standard of living.[3] Trade associations often provide their members with guidance on best practices and strategies in energy and environmental management.[4] The World Resources Institute has provided guidance for municipal governments on approaches to promote energy efficiency in buildings.

Private organizations also provide information on companies' performance related to energy and GHG emissions. For example, the CDP[5] provides a platform for companies to report their emissions levels to promote transparency with investors, customers, and governments. In a more confrontational approach, organizations have developed sophisticated strategies to "name and shame" organizations for their (often very indirect) climate and environmental effects. For example, to draw atten-

3 https://www.stepenergy.eu/about-step/

4 See, e.g., the International Council of Chemical Associations' guidance on lifecycle analysis (https://icca-chem.org/wp-content/uploads/2020/05/How-to-Know-If-and-When-Its-Time-to-Commission-a-Life-Cycle-Assessment.pdf); the RE100 program sponsored by the Climate Group and CDP provides guidance for members to achieve and report progress toward embedding 100 percent renewable energy in their operations (RE110 2022). The International Air Transport Association (2021) has adopted a resolution encouraging its members to achieve net-zero carbon emissions by 2050.

5 Formerly, the Carbon Disclosure Project.

tion to practices in Artic oil exploration, Greenpeace carried out a prolonged public campaign of "brandalism" against Lego, drawing attention to its long-term contract with Shell Oil.

Although these are all examples of private ordering in support of information diffusion, note that the government still plays an essential role in facilitating the process by establishing systems and rules for the exchange of information. First, the government often provides the infrastructure that facilitates the private exchange of information – e.g., the Internet, government-owned newspapers, and telecommunications systems. In some cases, of course, governments impede the free flow of information by blocking access to resources on these systems. Second, in many cases the government provides tax incentives to support nonprofit organizations that advocate to the public for change or provide information sources. Finally, governments provide a legal framework for liability in information through laws on libel and slander, truth in advertising, and similar rules to promote veracity in communications. But once the government has provided the ground rules for information exchange generally, when the government acts through private ordering in information exchange, it does not determine the nature, rate, or responsibility for that exchange.

5.2 Public Ordering to Disseminate Information

Often, the government takes a more direct role in the dissemination of information to support its policy goals. As with private ordering, this can involve providing information about energy use effects, options for reducing energy use and emissions, or information about participants in the market. As with policy instruments on Branches A and B, the government's choice of policy instruments to provide information have implications for the extent of discretion left to private parties as well as the extent to which private parties bear the costs of providing information.

Often governments initiate public information campaigns, run and financed by the government itself. These are generally very broadly aimed to raise public awareness and understanding of an important issue. For example, the US Department of Energy provides a series of consumer guides and factsheets on energy efficiency.[6] In some cases, however, governments provide much more focused information, aimed at an industry or even a specific party. For example, the US Environmental Protection Agency's Heat Island Reduction Program provides a compendium of strategies to mitigate heat island effects as well as a series of podcasts, news updates, and related materials (US Environmental Protection Agency, 2008).[7]

6 See, https://www.energy.gov/energysaver/publications.
7 See, https://www.epa.gov/heatislands/what-epa-doing-reduce-heat-islands.

Alternatively, rather than delivering the public information or education initiative through its own resources and personnel, the government can engage nongovernment parties to carry out the program under contract or through cooperative programs, sharing discretion regarding the content and means for the information program. The US Government Accountability Office (2006) reported that in 2003 seven federal departments spent over US$162 billion on contacts with advertising agencies, media organizations, and public relations firms for a range of services, including to reach the public regarding government programs and to plan public awareness programs. Government efforts to engage private parties in public education and awareness programs can range from contractual to collaborative. The City of Santa Fe 2018 Sustainability Plan identified numerous partnerships to increase public awareness in support of the plan including with electric and gas utilities, nonprofits, federal agencies, and media partners.

Governments can also compel parties to report specific information. In some cases, for example, products are required to carry energy efficiency labels, as in the case of Singapore, which requires vendors of light vehicles to provide labels listing both carbon emissions and fuel consumption figures. Similarly, in the field of financial transactions, as described by Shankar and Basu in this volume, India is working to regulate the private green bond market to ensure that investors are not misled by unscrupulous fund managers who might misrepresent the sustainability benefits of their projects.

As the focus turns from products to companies themselves, governments have increasingly required publicly traded firms to report their emissions and sustainability initiatives as part of their financial reporting requirements.

As governments seek soft law that is nonetheless effective, they have increasingly turned to management-based regulation. Under this approach rather than direct firms to undertake specific actions or provide incentives to change behavior, the government requires firms to develop and publish a plan to address an environmental issue (Coglianese, 2010). This provides considerably more discretion to firms regarding the nature and extent of their energy conservation and emissions abatement activities.

6 Combinations and Hybrids of Policy Instruments

In many cases governments' energy policy goals face multiple market failures simultaneously – a combination of externalities, public goods, and imperfect information. In other cases, policy design and implementation encounter limitations imposed by politics, law, and limited capacity. In these cases, government often adopt combinations or hybrids of policy instruments. In many cases, these arrangements are so common that they are often treated as if they are policy instruments themselves, as in the case of carbon offsets, deposit-refund schemes, and voluntary programs.

It is very common, for example, for governments to combine their research initiatives with information dissemination programs, essentially coordinating instruments from Branches B and C.

Deposit-refund systems are essentially a tax on the initial acquisition of a good combined with a subsidy for its return – both Branch A tools. In China, for example, retailers pay a deposit on electric vehicle batteries, a portion of which is refunded when the battery is collected.

Many countries rely on offsets to supplement their carbon pricing instruments. From a policy instrument perspective, an offset system is

> ...an addition to a core regulatory program that allows entities that are regulated under the core program to meet a portion of their obligations through environmental improvements that take place outside of the core. The offset activity provides an environmental benefit of the same type and at least as large in value as the environmental damage caused by the relaxation in the core program. The offset activities can be carried out by the regulated party, another private party or a government entity (Hahn and Richards, 2013).

Ideally, the core regulation would cover all relevant sources of emissions, but for reasons of politics or legal constraints, governments have found it is difficult to fashion regulations that cover all significant emissions. To this end, they allow firms to demonstrate that they have decreased their emissions or increased their sinks outside the scope covered by the carbon tax or allowance program. Firms undertaking offsets are awarded with a subsidy (in the form of a tax credit) or an in-kind payment (under a marketable allowance program). For example, under the South Africa carbon tax, firms can reduce their tax liability by up to 10 percent by submitting certified offset credits. Similarly, under the EU emissions trading system emitters were able to use offset credits to meet their allowance requirements, although the system was adjusted in 2020.[8]

Voluntary programs gained considerable currency during the 1990's and have continued to find favor in government programs. While definitions of voluntary programs vary widely (Richards and Richards, 2020), when they are initiated by governments, they generally involve combinations of instruments from any of the three branches discussed above, with shared discretion between the government and nongovernment parties, often with weaker incentives (positive or negative) than would be expected under standalone programs.

8 https://ec.europa.eu/clima/eu-action/eu-emissions-trading-system-eu-ets/use-international-credits_en

7 Conclusions

As governments seek to facilitate the transition to a low-carbon energy future, they have a wide array of policy instruments from which to choose. Broadly, they can select instruments from three different branches, each designed to address a type of underlying problem (or market failure) – externalities, the public good nature of research and innovation, or imperfect information. It is important that governments match their choice of policy instrument to the conditions that require government intervention.

On each branch, the government also needs to decide the nature of its intervention – whether adopting an active, public ordering approach or a more passive, private ordering approach. When the government adopts the public ordering approach, it chooses from a range of instruments that vary significantly with respect to both the degree of private discretion they permit and the extent of the economic burden they place on the targeted party.

References

Bowman, S., 2022. New law protects Hoosier property rights, makes it harder for HOAs to say no to solar. *Indianapolis Star*, March 11. https://www.indystar.com/story/news/environment/2022/03/11/indiana-solar-panels-homeowners-association-hoa/6987099001/.

Bronin, S.C., 2009. Solar rights. *BUL Rev.*, 89, pp. 1217–1265.

City of Sante Fe. 2018. *Sustainable Sante Fe: 25-Year Plan: Appendix.* https://www.santafenm.gov/media/files/Sustainable_SF_Commission/Sustainable%20Santa%20Fe%20Appendices%20Oct%2010%20Final%20Draft.pdf.

Coglianese, C., 2010. Management-based regulation: implications for public policy. In: *Risk and regulatory policy: improving the governance of risk.* France: OECD Publishing.

Dubash, N.K. and Mitchell, C., eds., 2022. National and sub-national policies and institutions. In: Intergovermental Panel on Climate Change. *Mitigation of Climate Change*, Sixth Assessment Report, Working Group III.

Eberhard, A., Kolker, J. and Leigland, J., 2014. *South Africa's renewable energy IPP procurement program: success factors and lessons.* Washington, DC: World Bank Group. https://openknowledge.worldbank.org/handle/10986/20039.

Hahn, R.W. and Richards, K., 2013. Understanding the effectiveness of environmental offset policies. *Journal of Regulatory Economics*, 44(1), pp. 103–119.

Hamakawa, Y. and Tohma, K., 1993. New Sunshine Programme and recent advances in solar energy technology in Japan. World Solar Summit, High-Level Expert Meeting, UNESCO Headquarters, Paris, 30 June. http://specialcollections.nust.na:8080/greenstone3/library/sites/localsite/collect/unesco/index/assoc/HASH018c/2b14eee9.dir/New%20sunshine%20programme%20and%20recent%20advances%20in%20solar%20energy%20technology%20in%20Japan.pdf;jsessionid=C9CD87FD5B4091F7E69B3D0EA9D78E86.

International Air Transport Association, 2021. *Net-Zero carbon emissions by 2050* (4 October). https://www.iata.org/en/pressroom/2021-releases/2021-10-04-03/.

International Chamber of Shipping, 2021. *International Chamber of Shipping sets out plans for global carbon levy to expedite industry decarbonisation* (6 September). https://www.ics-shipping.org/press-release/international-chamber-of-shipping-sets-out-plans-for-global-carbon-levy/.

McDonnell, L.M. and Elmore, R.F., 1987. Getting the job done: alternative policy instruments. *Educational Evaluation and Policy Analysis*, 9(2), pp. 133–152.

Megaloudis, G., 2017. Solar easements and solar leases and what they mean for title insurance. *New England Real Estate Journal.* https://nerej.com/solar-easements-and-solar-leases-and-what-they-mean-for-title-insurance-by-george-megaloudis.

Nurton, J., 2020. Patenting trends in renewable energy. *WIPO Magazine*, pp. 50–56. https://www.wipo.int/export/sites/www/wipo_magazine/en/pdf/2020/wipo_pub_121_2020_01.pdf.

Pacheco-Vega, R., 2020. Environmental regulation, governance, and policy instruments, 20 years after the stick, carrot, and sermon typology. *Journal of Environmental Policy & Planning*, 22(5), pp. 1–16.

RE110, 2022. *RE100 Reporting Guidance 2022.*

Richards, K., 2000. Framing environmental policy instrument choice. *Duke Environmental Law & Policy Forum*, 10(2), pp. 221–285.

Richards, S., and K. Richards. 2020. Voluntary environmental agreements. In: K. Richards and J. van Zeben, eds., 2020. *Elgar Encyclopedia of environmental law.* Cheltenham: Edward Elgar Publishing Limited, pp. 363–376.

Salzman, J., 2013. Teaching policy instrument choice in environmental law: the five P's. *Duke Environmental Law & Policy Forum*, 23 (3), pp. 363–376.

Schmitt, S., and Schulze, K., 2011. Choosing environmental policy instruments: an assessment of the 'environmental dimension'of EU energy policy. *European integration online papers*, 15(1), Article 9.

Stanton, M.S., 2012. Payments for freshwater ecosystems services: a framework for analysis. *Hastings W.-Nw. J. Envt'l L. & Pol'y*, 18, pp. 189–290.

Stavins, R.N., 1991. Project 88–Round II, incentives for action: designing market-based environmental strategies. *Public policy study sponsored by Senators Timothy Wirth and John Heinz, Washington, DC, May.*

U.S. Department of Energy, 1989. *A compendium of options for government policy to encourage private sector responses to potential climate changes: methodological justification and generic policy instruments.* U.S. Department of Energy, Office of Environmental Analysis, Assistant Secretary for Environment, Safety and Health.

U.S. Environmental Protection Agency, 2008. Reducing urban heat islands: compendium of strategies. https://www.epa.gov/heatislands/heat-island-compendium.

U.S. Government Accountability Office, 2006. *Media contracts: activities and financial obligations for seven federal departments.* Washington D.C.

Vandenbergh, M.P., 2013. Private environmental governance. *Cornell L. Rev*, 99, pp. 129–199.

Whoriskey, P., 2012. Government-subsidized green light bulb carries costly price tag. *The Washington Post*, March 8. https://www.washingtonpost.com/business/economy/government-subsidized-green-light-bulb-carries-costly-price-tag/2012/03/07/gIQAFxOD0R_story.html.

World Economic Forum, 2021. *Net-Zero Challenge: the supply chain opportunity.* https://www3.weforum.org/docs/WEF_Net_Zero_Challenge_The_Supply_Chain_Opportunity_2021.pdf.

Zou, H., Du, H. Ren, J. et al., 2017. Market dynamics, innovation, and transition in China's solar photovoltaic (PV) industry: a critical review. *Renewable and Sustainable Energy Reviews*, 69, pp. 197–206.

Lisa Benjamin, Kate McCallum

Implementation and Enforcement Mechanisms in Energy Law

Abstract: This chapter will discuss the role of private and public enforcement in energy law, with some examples from international law and a selection of national jurisdictions, as well as a snapshot of climate litigation in these jurisdictions. There is no public international treaty on energy, so international enforcement mechanisms appear under a mixture of international law, primarily the Energy Charter Treaty and World Trade Organization dispute settlement mechanisms, as well as within domestic jurisdictions. Existing international institutions have a number of biases in their approaches to energy, particularly in favour of energy security and free trade. Apart from these public international structures, other energy systems are largely domestic in nature (with the exception of some EU countries). This chapter will assess a selection of national jurisdictions, including the United States, Australia, and China, looking at regulatory enforcement mechanisms at various levels of government across jurisdictions. In the United States, the fragmentation of energy law and regulations across different energy sources and different levels of government presents enforcement difficulties, notably in the fracking industry. With a comparable federalist system, Australia faces similar fragmentation issues, however, it also boasts a unique brand of co-operative federalism within the energy sector through the National Energy Market. In comparison, despite being a one-party state, China is not immune to federalism issues, with provincial and local governments given significant regulatory and spending powers, creating obstacles for the implementation of national energy policies. This chapter will conclude with a brief summary of climate litigation in these jurisdictions, and how this litigation interacts with existing energy enforcement structures.

1 Introduction

This chapter will discuss the role of private and public enforcement in energy law, with some examples from international law and a selection of national jurisdictions. It will also provide an overview of climate litigation brought against both private sector firms and government actors. This chapter will assess the low-carbon energy transition through the lens of institutional feasibility, with a focus on institutional biases at the international level, and illustrate some opportunities as well as constraints

Lisa Benjamin is an Associate Professor at Lewis & Clark Law School in Portland, Oregon, United States.
Kate McCallum is Attorney at Keller Rohrback, LLP, in Seattle, Washington, United States.

https://doi.org/10.1515/9783110752403-013

posed by the federalist model at the domestic level. The ability of enforcement mechanisms to serve as pathways to the low-carbon energy transition depends on the existing regulatory structures and institutional design of legal frameworks to which they are attached. At the international level, institutional feasibility for low-carbon energy transitions appears hindered by existing international architectures and negatively affected implementation. At the domestic level, federalist systems provide both opportunities for experimentation as well as constraints on implementation. This chapter focuses on judicial decisions and arbitration awards, and their enforcement impacts at both the international and domestic levels.

There is no public international treaty on energy, so international enforcement mechanisms appear under a mixture of existing international law treaties, primarily the World Trade Organization (WTO) dispute settlement mechanism, and the Energy Charter Treaty (ECT) arbitration system, as well as within domestic jurisdictions. Existing international institutions have a number of biases in their approaches to energy, particularly in favour of free trade in the context of the WTO, and energy and investment security in the context of the ECT. These institutional structures and biases have influenced how these institutions do or do not facilitate pathways for low-carbon energy transitions. Apart from these two international treaties, energy regulation and associated enforcement mechanisms are largely domestic in nature (with the exception of some EU countries).

This chapter will assess a selection of national jurisdictions, including the United States, Australia, and China, looking at regulatory enforcement mechanisms at various levels of government in these jurisdictions, with a focus on some of the opportunities and constraints the federalist model poses. By federalist model, we mean countries with a combination of self-rule and shared rule across two or more levels of government in the field of energy transitions (Saurer and Monast, 2021). These countries are some of the top emitters in the world, with the US and China leading the world in greenhouse gas emissions, and Australia being the primary global exporter of coal. Australia and the US have also experienced the largest number of climate litigation cases to date.

In the United States, the fragmentation of energy law and regulations across different energy sources and different levels of government presents enforcement difficulties. The Federal Energy Regulatory Commission (FERC) is the primary regulatory agency at the federal level, but only has responsibility for certain energy transactions, with states being responsible for regulating other energy transactions. With a comparable federalist system, Australia faces similar fragmentation issues. However, it also boasts a unique brand of co-operative federalism within the energy sector through the National Energy Market (Kallies, 2021). Despite being a one-party state, China is not immune to federalism issues, with provincial and local governments given significant regulatory and spending powers, creating obstacles for the implementation of national energy policies (Schreurs, 2017). This chapter will include a brief summary of climate litigation experienced to date in these three jurisdictions, and consider how this climate litigation movement provides further opportunities for low carbon energy transitions, or is itself grappling to overcome the constraints of federalism.

2 The World Trade Organization – trade biases in renewable energy disputes

The World Trade Organization (WTO) is an international treaty-based system, formally established in 1995, although its original agreements were agreed post-World War II. The WTO promotes principles of free trade and non-discrimination (through most favoured nation and national treatment principles), and disciplines domestic protectionism measures that are considered to impede free trade. It currently has 165 member states. Member states join the WTO as a 'single package', by ratifying a series of multilateral covered agreements. These agreements establish global trading rules on goods, services, agriculture, subsidies, countervailing measures and intellectual property, and other areas in discrete agreements, together referred to as 'covered agreements'. There is no agreement on energy at the WTO, and so treatment of energy is fragmented across a number of these covered agreements. For example, biofuels disputes might be affected by provisions in the General Agreement on Trade and Tariffs (GATT), Agreement on Agriculture (AoA) and the Subsidies and Countervailing Measures Agreement (SCM Agreement). Most of the WTO energy disputes to date involve the GATT and the SCM Agreement (Cottier, 2009). However, despite the high level of subsidies provided to the fossil fuel industry, fossil fuel subsidies have never been subject to dispute at the WTO (Meyer, 2018).

The WTO is the only truly international global trading regime, although a number of bilateral and regional trade arrangements have recently gained in popularity. Its covered agreements provide limited policy exceptions to countries under Article XX of the GATT. These exceptions allow countries to engage in discriminatory practices in order to protect domestic policy imperatives such as the protection of health and welfare of citizens or of the environment. These exceptions, however, are not unconditional, and a series of tests have been developed that condition and constrain States' ability to rely on these exceptions. These exceptions have been invoked in a series of renewable energy disputes at the WTO.

One of the covered agreements includes the Dispute Settlement Understanding (DSU), which all member states of the WTO accede to. The DSU is considered to be the "linchpin" of the entire trading system (Jackson, 1997, p. 35). It provides an enforcement mechanism that member states are required to adhere to in order to continue their membership in the organization. It provides any member state the right to have a panel process and panel decision initiated, as well as access to an appellate procedure through an Appellate Body of at least three judges. The Panel and Appellate Bodies also adjudicate the implementation of remedies following the outcome of a dispute. The dispute settlement body (or DSB) administers the entire process, and the WTO system eliminates the ability of parties to block adoption of panel or appellate body decisions. In addition, Appellate Body decisions follow a system of precedent, providing a level of certainty and stability of outcomes and implementation by States. This stability was undermined by the US blockage, under the Trump Administration, of appointment of judges to the Appellate Body of the DSB, lowering the number of judges to below the required minimum threshold of three, and therefore preventing the Appellate Body from functioning. This action has continued under the Biden Administration, and so the future of the DSB remains uncertain.

Part of the motivation of the US in blocking appointments to the Appellate Body is to delay or prevent the adjudication of ongoing trade conflicts around renewable energy, particularly with China and India. Countries, including the US, are using domestic protectionist measures in order to boost their own competitiveness in renewable energy manufacture and export, and these domestic policies potentially violate existing WTO trade rules. There is no international environmental or energy treaty, and so the disputes around renewable energy at the WTO provide one of the few international sources of adjudication of global energy disputes. The outcome of these disputes has been affected by the free trade impetus which underpins existing covered agreements at the WTO. The WTO is not an environmental or sustainable development organization – it promotes free trade, and therefore conditions and restricts domestic protectionist measures, even when those measures contribute to low-carbon energy transitions. This has become problematic in the renewable energy sphere, where countries have attached domestic conditions to the promotion and trade of renewable energy products and technology. These conditions have included linking subsidies to the inclusion of local content or domestic workers in the manufacture of wind turbines or solar panels, for example. These types of conditions are part of a 'green' industrial policy strategy of countries (Wu and Salzman, 2014). These local content requirements are popular with both developed and developing countries, but they have been subject to discipline under the DSU.

The two main "environmental" subcategories under Article XX of the GATT are XX (b) and XX(g). Article XX(b) provides an exception for measures "necessary to protect human, animal or plant life or health . . . ." and Article XX(g) provides an exception for measures "relating to conservation of exhaustible natural resources if such measures are made effective in conjunction with restrictions on domestic production or consumption. . . .". In addition to satisfying the subcategories under Article XX, countries must also satisfy the 'chapeau' of Article XX. This requires that any measures applied by a party are not applied in a manner that would constitute "a means of arbitrary or unjustifiable discrimination" or "a disguised restriction on international trade."

Article XX exceptions have been invoked by a number of countries defending their domestic policies around renewable energy, with little to no success. Renewable energy disputes started to take off in 2012, and have spanned disputes over biofuels to solar panels. Article XX defences in all cases in which they were invoked by countries failed to justify green industrial policies, largely due to those policies' protectionist elements. In addition, even where developing countries have found success in the biofuels disputes in law, their "successes" are being frustrated by developed countries through use of protectionist measures (Benjamin, 2021).

In only one of the renewable energy cases to date, The *Canada-Renewable Energy/FIT* dispute, has the Appellate Body expressly supported domestic policy making in support of domestic climate goals. In two subsequent cases, brought by the US against China and India respectively, domestic climate policies, which included local content requirements, were found to violate WTO trading rules. While Wu and Salzman (2014) consider these disputes to be unproblematic provided countries divorce their energy policies from protectionist measures, this is unlikely to happen anytime soon. The Biden Administration, for example, in the proposed Build Back Better Bill, expressly connected domestic subsidies to producers who manufacture renewable energy technology in the US, and with unionised workers. The substitute, modified bill enacted in place of Build Back Better, the Inflation Reduction Act, contains requirements for prevailing wages and apprenticeship labor in order for subsidies (tax credits) to be issued for renewable energy. It also adds bonuses for projects with domestic content. At least eight states, including Montana and Washington, have also connected state policies to in-state labor or content requirements. These policies were subject to a WTO dispute initiated by India, although the dispute's status at the Appellate Body remains uncertain, and means this dispute cannot proceed at this time. From a review of existing renewable energy disputes at the WTO, it is clear that Article XX is proving ineffective at salvaging domestic energy and climate policies that include domestic protectionist measures. This is due to the trade bias at the WTO, which disciplines any preferential treatment, even where the related policy has energy and climate benefits. Trade and climate objectives, therefore, are colliding through the WTO dispute resolution process. The judicial outcomes of this process are posing obstacles to low-carbon energy transition policies which include domestic preferences.

3 The Energy Charter Treaty – investor protection in arbitration awards

The Energy Charter Treaty (ECT) is the second example of an international treaty regime that focuses on energy. It came into force in 1998, and has 53 member states. The treaty was designed to protect energy investments made overseas. Energy resource investments are often long term, and therefore require a level of legal and policy stability in the host state (Banks, 2012). Resource-related investments are often deeply tied to issues of sovereignty over natural resources and international economic justice. Questions of national expropriation of private investments in the post-colonial era motivated investment-focused treaties such as the ECT. While the ECT is the major international investment treaty on energy, bilateral investment treaties and other multilateral treaties such as NAFTA (now USMCA) also contain provisions around energy investments. The ECT contains rules designed to protect investors in the territory of a contracting party (the host state). It provides rights, but not obligations, for investors. These rights are enforced through mandatory arbitration provisions, which both investors and the host state must abide by. By not imposing obligations on investors, the ECT has an investment bias built into its structure.

Article 10 of the ECT protects investors' use, enjoyment or disposal of their investments. Article 26 regulates investor-state disputes by providing a dispute resolution process which relies on arbitration mechanisms. Unlike the public dispute resolution process in the WTO, arbitration proceedings are mainly private, and so the ECT enforcement mechanisms are less transparent than WTO proceedings. After a three-month cooling off period, Article 26 provides investors with dispute resolution options, including submission to the courts of the host state, using any previously agreed dispute settlement process, or international arbitration.

Arbitration is to be decided in accordance with international law and the provisions of the ECT. The majority of renewable energy disputes have involved interpretation of the right for investors to be provided with fair and equitable treatment (FET) under Article 10(1) of the ECT. Unlike the WTO system, however, there is no formal precedent system in arbitration outcomes under the ECT, and so a number of disputes around renewable energy support have come to different outcomes. These differing outcomes have subjected the ECT, and its arbitration system, to significant criticism – that the ECT is skewed towards Western, neoliberal rules in energy trade (Tienhoara and Downie, 2018, p. 454).

Like the WTO, a significant number of disputes under the ECT have involved renewable energy, specifically around a reduction of support provided by host states for renewable energy. After the financial crisis in 2008, many ECT member states withdrew or reduced their financial support of renewable energy systems after the investment was made. They reduced support through domestic legislative changes, and a number of these changes were subjected to Article 26 proceedings. One of the first arbitration decisions in this vein was the decision in 2016 regarding the dispute brought against Spain by Charanne and Construction Investments. This dispute involved changes made by Spain, in 2010, to its legislation providing support for renewable energy projects. The investors claimed these changes led to loss of profitability and loss of value of the project, however the arbitration decision did not find these 2010 legislative changes violated the investors' FET rights.

The decision found that while FET had to take into account legitimate expectations of investors, interpretation of this provision had to follow the general principle of good faith. The arbitrators found that Spain had not given the investors specific commitments, so engendered no legitimate expectation that the laws would not be modified. In addition, investors had to do their due diligence – the original law clearly stated that the compensation model could be modified.

However, a later arbitration decision in 2016, regarding changes made by Spain in 2012 and 2014 to the original law, were held to violate the FET standard. In this dispute, Eiser Infrastructure Ltd. claimed that the removal of the feed in tariff structure, and its replacement with a different compensation scheme, destroyed their investment. Their claim was successful, and they were granted a euro 128 million award against Spain. The decision found that the legislative changes made in 2012 and 2014 were unreasonable. The decision found these changes undermined the value of the project for the Eiser investors, and such abrupt legislative changes did violate FET. Another arbitration decision in that same year, brought by a Belgian company, Blusun S.A. against Italy, was not successful. Changes made by Italy to its domestic laws were not held to violate FET, and the decision reiterated that a breach of FET is only likely where a host state implicitly or explicitly made specific commitments, assurances or promises to investors, on which investors relied.

Despite this positive outcome for Italy, Italy has withdrawn from the ECT, and several other EU countries, such as Germany, Spain and France, have also withdrawn. These three decisions illustrate the instability of interpretations around investor rights under FET. These differing outcomes are partly due to the lack of a formal precedent system under the ECT arbitration system. This interpretive instability means that renewable energy investors will be unsure whether legislative changes may be made by countries in which they invest. In addition, countries may be less willing to pass domestic legislation that provides comprehensive financial support for investors in renewable energy systems, particularly as the costs of renewable energy decrease rapidly. Any investor bias in arbitration outcomes could have a regulatory chilling effect for ECT member states (Dias Simoes, 2017, p. 304), thereby posing obstacles to the low-carbon energy transition. The ECT has engaged in a modernization process, launched in 2015. This process aims to expand the geographical reach of the ECT and led to the adoption of the International Energy Charter – a political declaration that highlights issues such as energy poverty and energy sustainability (Kustova, 2016, p. 359). An agreement in principle on the modernisation of the ECT was achieved in mid-2022, and should have been formalized in the Energy Charter Conference of November 2022, but the vote was delayed due to lack of consensus within the EU. The vote has been postponed until April 2023. It is claimed that the new ECT will be fully aligned with the goals of the Paris Agreement. Time will tell whether a revised ECT would better facilitate a low-carbon energy transition.

4 The United States – Federalism and FERC

The federalist model in the United States often preserves existing state regulatory authority, allowing for experimentation at the state level, treating states as 'laboratories of democracy' (Buzbee, 2017, p. 1049). This federalist model allows for opportunities to cater regulation and enforcement to local conditions and priorities of individual states. In fact some states, such as New York and California, have been leaders in the low-carbon energy transition. However, this approach can also lack uniformity of standards and therefore can heighten compliance costs and allow some states to lag behind others in clean energy standards (Buzbee, 2017, pp. 1091–1092).

The Biden Administration focused its clean energy and climate policies around the national electricity infrastructure, promising a 100% grid transition to clean energy by 2035. However, the history of electricity regulation segregates federal and state authority, applying them to different electricity transactions. Historically, all electric utilities in the US were vertically integrated, and therefore owned generation, transmission and distribution assets. They provided electricity to set service territories, which were small, and so often provided electricity intrastate. The passage of the Federal Power Act in 1935 (FPA) closed the 'Attleboro gap', and established the Federal Power Commission (now FERC). FERC is an independent agency, and operates through a bipartisan five-member Commission. It regulates most energy resources in the United States, including wholesale sale of electricity and its interstate transmission, as well as oil and natural gas transportation (although the Environmental Protection Agency is responsible for clean air standards and therefore has some regulatory authority for greenhouse gas emissions).

The FPA established a dual federalism or collaborative federalism model, which preserved existing state authority over retail sale and intrastate transmission (Killeen, 2020), but granted to FERC the authority to regulate the sale of electric energy at wholesale in interstate commerce and the transmission of electric energy in interstate commerce (Section 201, FPA). This division of regulatory authority between federal and state levels of governance in the FPA was often referred to as a 'bright line' (Christiansen and Macey, 2021, p. 1364). Since the 1930s, energy markets and providers have changed significantly with merchant generators, new generation resources, the introduction of new technologies such as batteries and other storage resources, distributed energy sources, and the growth of demand response, microgrids, and electric vehicles, as well as the rapid decline of the cost of such technologies. These advances have put pressure on the regulatory divisions contained in the FPA, and FERC has had to navigate these tensions.

FERC introduced new technologies into Independent System Operators and Regional Transmission Operators (ISOs and RTOs), which operate regional wholesale markets, and these technologies have arguably exceeded the traditional boundaries of its FPA-mandated jurisdiction (Killeen, 2020, p. 286). One example of this activity has been Order 745, issued by FERC in 2011, in order to promote demand response in electricity markets. Demand response is traditionally understood as actions to reduce electricity demand undertaken by end-consumers, and so would fall on the retail side of the FPA's bright line. However, Jacobs notes that FERC bypassed the FPA's statutory federalism boundaries by crafting Order 745 to apply to wholesale markets (2015, pp. 886–887). Some retail electricity programs allow middlemen to act as aggregators of demand response commitments from end customers, and sell those aggregated commitments in RTO and ISO wholesale markets (Jacobs, 2015, p. 980). FERC used Order 745 to overcome state intransigence in promoting demand response by ordering RTOs and ISOs to pay locational marginal prices for demand response operating in wholesale markets, thereby providing a lucrative wholesale market for these services (Jacobs, 2015, p. 913). As a federal agency, FERC is subject to the Administrative Procedure Act (APA), which allows for judicial review of agency action on the basis of several grounds, including that the agency action is arbitrary and capricious.

A group of generators, the Electric Power Supply Association (EPSA), challenged Order 745 under the APA standard of arbitrary and capricious. They claimed that FERC mandated payments for demand response programs were effectively regulating retail rates, which were within the regulatory purview of states, not FERC. This case made its way to the Supreme Court, illustrating how important the Court considered this jurisdictional issue to be. The Supreme Court disagreed with EPSA, holding that Order 745 remained within FERC's jurisdiction under the FPA, establishing a two-prong test (*FERC v. Electric Power Supply Ass'n*, 577 U.S. 260 (2016)). The first prong adopted a 'common sense' limitation – that FERC's jurisdiction extended only to matters that 'directly affected' wholesale rates. In that regard, Order 745 only applied to payments that would reduce wholesale rates. The second prong established that FERC could not enact a regulation that transgressed Section 201(b), and so could not directly target or aim at, for example, retail rates, even where those would have an effect on wholesale rates. FERC's regulation was aimed at wholesale markets, and so even though Order 745 affected retail rates, it did not violate the FPA. Combined with two other cases (*Oneok Inc v. Learjet Inc., 575 U.S. 373 (2015)* and *Hughes v. Talen Energy Marketing, LLC*, 578 U.S. 150 (2016)), the Supreme Court has established a deeply functionalist approach to the jurisdictional divides in the FPA (Christiansen, 2015, p. 101), allowing cross-jurisdictional effects. Jacobs notes that due to Congressional gridlock, ageing statutes and new exigencies, this agency bypassing of statutory federalism divides is likely to continue (2015, p. 938). This judicial approach has opened up opportunities to further low-carbon energy transitions by FERC. However, other approaches adopted by FERC can also be detrimental to state renewable energy policies (Killeen, 2020), and so this judicial approach can provide opportunities, but also obstacles, to the low-carbon energy transition.

5 Climate change litigation in the United States

In addition to some agency regulation, the US is also the jurisdiction that has experienced the highest number of climate litigation cases. This rise in climate litigation may be due to the relative regulatory void in the US of federal climate legislation. There are a number of definitions of climate litigation, but the definition inclusive of cases where climate change is at the core, and that generally raise climate-specific arguments or judicial analysis referring to climate change, is adopted here (Osofsky and Peel, 2015). Some of the original climate litigation cases in the US (the first wave), involving tort claims, failed due to problems establishing causation and the political question doctrine, but also judicial reluctance to take on the complexity of climate science. These cases also failed as a result of a clear judicial preference to defer the issue to legislative bodies based on, among other issues, federal displacement arguments. Litigation around federal action (or inaction) included a petition, submitted by the State of Massachusetts (and other plaintiffs), for rulemaking to the Environmental Protection Agency (EPA). The EPA had refused to regulate GHG under the Clean Air Act as an air pollutant. The EPA originally denied the petition on the basis that it had no authority under the Clean Air Act to address global emissions and a causal link between GHGs and increases in global surface air temperatures was not unequivocally established. The US Supreme Court remanded the issue back to the EPA, finding that GHGs could be regulated as an air pollutant under the Act.

Two other major cases in the first wave of litigation were *American Electric Power Co. v. Connecticut (AEP)* (2011) and *Native Village of Kivalina v. ExxonMobil Corp. (Kivalina)* (2012), both of which involved nuisance claims and which were dismissed by the courts. These cases illustrate judicial inadequacies when dealing with climate science, as well as a judicial reluctance to adjudicate such a systemic issue as climate change (Benjamin, 2020). *AEP* was a public nuisance suit brought by eight states and New York City against six electric and utility corporations. The plaintiffs argued that the emissions of these corporations interfered with public rights and asked the court to impose declining emission caps on these entities in order to reduce emissions. The Supreme Court rejected the claim, holding that the Clean Air Act "displaced" any federal nuisance action dealing with climate change, and closed the door to future federal nuisance common law claims.

A more recent, and second wave of climate litigation cases, initiated in 2017 and 2018, have attempted to circumvent federal displacement by grounding their claims more firmly in state legislation, such as consumer protection legislation. Many of these cases have been initiated by individual cities, counties and states against carbon major companies. These Plaintiffs have also been assisted by new scientific processes and developments, which have clearly attributed the majority of historical GHG emissions to carbon-major corporations, and judges have started to engage more confidently with this new climate science. For example, New York City claimed, in federal court, that the City had incurred, and would continue to incur, substantial costs due to climate change, and that the largest five fossil fuel companies should be responsible for these costs. This claim failed in 2018 due to federal displacement by the Clean Air Act. However, a number of cases may remain in state court. For example, a case brought by Baltimore against carbon major companies found its way to the Supreme Court on a narrow jurisdictional question. While the Supreme Court agreed with the defendants on the Federal Officer Removal Statute, it declined to decide the federal/state jurisdictional issues. Cases in California, Baltimore and Hawai'i have recently decided that the claims should remain in state courts. There is no guarantee that these cases will be successful on their merits, but if they are, state-based outcomes could supplement, or in some states, deter, existing state regulatory efforts in the low-carbon energy transition.

6 Australia – cooperative federalism and the National Energy Market

Like the United States, Australia has a dualist, cooperative federalist system of energy regulation, with responsibility for energy market regulation and climate change policy shared between federal and state governments. Both federal and state governments have adopted legislation to support the transition to renewable energy, however competing priorities at different levels of government in respect of energy security, together with a federal economic reliance on fossil fuel exports, has undermined enforcement efforts and shifted the responsibility of transitioning the national energy system to the states (Kallies, 2021, p. 234). It has also led to a geographically skewed distribution of renewable energy across the country (Godden, 2020, p. 178).

The shared responsibility for electricity regulation in Australia has come about from the creation of the National Energy Market (NEM) that established interconnections between state electricity systems in the eastern half of the country in the 1990s. The NEM covers around 80% of Australia's electricity demand, stretching across five states and the Australian Capital Territory, and covering over 40,000 km of transmission lines and cables. Prior to its creation, energy policy was the domain of state governments, which owned and operated vertically integrated monopoly electricity commissions (Rai and Nelson, 2020, p. 167). Along with the creation of the NEM came the creation of a federal regulatory scheme, and a decline in state government control with the privatisation and unbundling of public commissions (*Id.*, p. 165). In the early 2000s, national regulatory bodies were established for the NEM including the Australian Energy Market Commission (AEMC), responsible for rulemaking and energy market development; the Australian Energy Regulator (AER), responsible for the economic regulation of the wholesale market and networks; and the Australian Energy Market Operator (AEMO), responsible for overseeing and facilitating the wholesale electricity market and for transmission network planning (Kallies, 2021, p. 227). However, in addition to these federal institutions, each state retained its own statutory agencies responsible for licensing participants in the electricity industry within the state.

The NEM governance framework was set up to harmonize energy regulation across the states, however it was kept expressly separate from climate mitigation policies, including renewable energy targets. Rai and Nelson (2020) observe that this lack of integration between emissions and energy policies together with a reliance on production subsidies for low carbon technologies at both the federal and state level has created a disorderly transition towards low-carbon energy, upsetting the supply-demand balance and increasing wholesale electricity prices (pp. 173–174). It has also led to confusion about the respective responsibilities of the federal and state governments, particularly in respect of energy security.

A common example given of the conflict between different levels of governments over the transition to renewables is the public debate between the federal and South Australian governments that took place over the reliability of wind power following an extreme weather event in 2016 that destroyed power lines and triggered a state-wide power outage (see e.g. Kallies, 2021; Abbott and Cohen, 2019; McGreevy et al., 2021). While the Prime Minister and Federal Energy Minister at the time claimed that the state was responsible for the stability of its electricity system, and insinuated that the state's reliance on wind power was to blame for the black out, in actuality, federal institutions were responsible for the reliability of the national electric grid, and renewable energy policies at the federal level had been a key driver behind the growth of funding and investment in wind farms in the state, in particular the Renewable Energy Target (Kallies, 2021, p. 213).

With various renewable energy targets, tariffs and energy efficiency programs across the different states, Australia's regulatory framework for the low-carbon transition policies can be aptly described as piecemeal and aimed at encouraging the adoption of low-emission technologies through subsidies rather than taxing emissions-intensive ones (Nelson et al., 2019, p. 179). Although renewable energy investment continues to be supported by state policy and legislation, the lack of federal regulation supporting renewables has led to fragmentation and acts as a barrier to integrating state renewable energy policies within the NEM framework (Kallies, 2021, p. 236). Kallies notes that this situation calls for a re-evaluation of energy federalism in Australia, using the existing federal regulatory scheme for the NEM to integrate climate change policies and enforce the low-carbon transition (*Id.*, p. 237). The passing of new climate change legislation by the federal government in September 2022 has opened up the possibility for meaningful reform of Australia's energy market to align with Australia's emissions reduction targets. The *Climate Change Act 2022* (Cth) and the *Climate Change (Consequential Amendments) Act 2022* (Cth) codifies into law Australia's emissions reduction targets and provides a broad policy framework for how they will be achieved. These Acts do not impose new obligations on emissions-intensive sectors, but instead set the parameters for future sector-by-sector reform.

7 Climate change litigation in Australia

After the United States, Australia has the highest amount of climate change litigation (Setzer and Higham, 2021, p. 10). As in the United States, this large number of climate cases may be due to the gaps in regulatory enforcement of decarbonisation policies and targets.

Although Australia's small population means that its contribution to global greenhouse gas emissions is relatively minor, it is a key player in the global carbon economy due to its dominance in coal exports, and increasingly, LNG exports. This context explains the 'first generation' of climate litigation cases in Australia, which consisted of administrative challenges to coal and gas projects under state and federal environmental laws relating to a failure to take into account climate change impacts (Peel, Osofsky and Foerster, 2017, pp. 795–796; Wilensky, 2015, p. 156). These administrative law cases enjoyed some success, in part due to the specialist state environmental courts in which they were brought, impacting how each case was litigated, how climate science was received, and the regulatory impact of court opinions (Peel and Osofsky, 2015, p. 25).

The NSW Land and Environment Court in particular has developed a line of case law establishing precedent that climate change considerations should be included in environmental impact assessments for fossil fuel projects. In the Anvil Hill case, *Gray v Minister for Planning & Ors* (2006) 152 LGERA 258, the Court rejected an environmental impact assessment for a large coal mine on the grounds that it failed to take into account indirect "Scope 3" greenhouse gas emissions from burning the extracted coal. More recently, in the Rocky Hill case, *Gloucester Resources Limited v Minister for Planning* (2019) 234 LGERA 257, the Chief Justice of the Court upheld a planning decision to refuse consent to the construction of a coal mine in part because of the contributions of that mine to global greenhouse gas emissions and their impact on the temperature goals under the Paris Agreement (Lesley, 2019, p. 347). His Honour indicated approval for taking a scientific approach to determining the contribution of "scope 3" emissions from the burning of coal extracted from the mine once exported overseas (*Id.*).

Peel, Osofsky, and Foerster observe that in addition to mandating the meaningful consideration of climate change impacts in planning decisions, this first generation of cases played an important role in raising awareness of climate change as a key environmental issue in the public, private, and government sectors (2017, p. 796). Nevertheless, these cases have not led to widespread regulatory changes; nor did they recognise any legal duty on the part of the government to address climate change. This could change with the 'second generation' of climate cases, encompassing a broad range of claims, from shareholder class actions against both private companies and the government in respect of climate risks, to adaptation, rights-based and tort-based cases.

This second generation of climate cases includes novel claims seeking to establish a duty of care on the part of the government to protect citizens from the impacts of climate change. In *Sharma v Minister for the Environment*, the Federal Court of Australia handed down a preliminary judgment finding that the Minister of the Environment owed a duty of care to all children to protect against personal injury or death resulting from climate change when deciding to approve the extension of a coal mine

(*Sharma v Minister for the Environment (No 2)* [2021] FCA 774). This judgment was later overturned on appeal, concluding that framing such a duty of care implicates core policymaking and considerations unsuitable for resolution by the courts (*Minister for the Environment v Sharma* [2022] FCAFC 35). There is, however, another human rights case raising a duty of care argument pending before the Federal Court. This case was brought by First Nations leaders in the Torres Strait against the federal government as a whole asserting breach of a duty of care relating to lack of action taken to address climate change and sea-level rise (VID622/2021: Pabai Pabai & Anor v Commonwealth of Australia).

Another line of cases involves claims brought against governments and companies for failing to disclose climate-related financial risks in financial products such as bonds and pension funds (*O'Donnell v Commonwealth of Australia* [2021] FCA 1223; *McVeigh v Retail Employees Superannuation Pty Ltd* [2019] FCA 14). Finally, there is an emerging line of cases brought under state-based human rights statutes and international law, challenging the approval of fossil fuel projects and government involvement in the fossil fuel industry. In one case heard by the Queensland Land Court, plaintiffs (a youth environmental organisation) succeeded in challenging the approval of a coal mine on the grounds that it infringed on the plaintiffs' human rights due to its contribution to climate change (*Waratah Coal Pty Ltd v Youth Verdict Ltd & Ors (No 6)* [2022] QLC 21). In another case brought by Tiwi Islander Traditional Owners against Santos over an offshore drilling license for gas, the Federal Court overturned the approval, finding that the licensing body had failed to consult with the Tiwi Islanders, who have a direct and immediate interest in their traditional sea country (*Santos NA Barossa Pty Ltd v Tipakalippa* [2022] FCAFC 193).

This new generation of climate cases has raised litigation risks for both private companies and government in Australia and illustrates that climate litigation is becoming an important tool for compelling decarbonisation in the absence of effective government action.

8 China – Multi-level climate governance under "market-preserving federalism"

Despite being a unitary, one-party state, China's economic decentralisation in the 1980s opened up experimentation at the provincial and local levels of government as to the implementation of national policies (Schreurs, 2017, p. 169). Therefore, understanding China's energy and decarbonisation policies requires consideration of political actors from the central, provincial and local levels of government. While broad policy goals and direction are set at the national or "central" level, provincial and local governments are often given autonomy over how they are implemented in practice, and how financial resources will be spent to fulfil those goals (Schreurs, 2017,

p. 164). This multi-level governance has been labelled by Weingast as a type of "market-preserving" or "fiscal" federalism, used by provincial and local governments to create markets and pursue economic growth (Weingast, 1995, p. 22). The focus on economic growth at the local level, supported by decades of growth targets set by the national government that persist today, has led to a fragmented approach to implementation and regulatory enforcement of climate and environmental policies (Kostka and Nahm, 2017, p. 570).

Like the United States and Australia, China does not have a single government authority that governs renewable energy deployment. Instead, more than ten national regulations are in place, with several national agencies involved in their implementation, including the National Development and Reform Commission (NDRC); the State Electricity Regulatory Commission (SERC), responsible for regulating and overseeing China's electricity industry; and the National Energy Administration (NEA), which sits within the NDRC responsible for energy planning (Hua, Oliphant and Hu, 2016, p. 1046). Although the NDRC is responsible for setting the price for energy, including setting renewable energy feed-in tariffs, the Ministry of Finance is in charge of the provincial power markets, while the Ministry of Commerce oversees implementation of the national Renewable Energy Law, with a number of other ministries also involved in renewable energy policymaking (*Id.*). In addition to national regulations and policies, local governments have published detailed local regulations for implementing the Renewable Energy Law, adding further complexity to the regulatory system (Gang, 2019, p. 34).

Policies and subsidies designed to promote the development of renewable energy in China have succeeded in making China the world leader in producing, exporting, and installing solar panels, wind turbines, batteries and electric vehicles (Heggelund, 2021, p. 15). When it comes to integrating renewable energy into Chinese markets, however, the regulatory system is less effective at the enforcement stage, both due to the lack of punitive measures to penalise participants in markets who block grid access for renewables, and due to a lack of cohesion between the central government and local authorities when it comes to implementing policies at the local level (Gang, 2019, p. 35). Poor enforcement of renewable policies, together with the inability of the grid system in China to incorporate large quantities of intermittent renewable energy, has led China to having one of the highest curtailment rates for wind and solar power in the world, in 2017 reaching 13.6 percent and 15.5 percent, respectively (*Id.*, p. 54).

As both Heggelund and Gang observe, local governments particularly in coal-rich provinces like Inner Mongolia and Shaanxi may have a vested interest in trying to obstruct the integration of renewable energy in favour of existing or even newly constructed coal-fired power stations, perceived as the most reliable energy source (Heggelund, 2021, p. 15; Gang, 2019, p. 58). In an effort to address enforcement problems, in 2016 the NDRC and NEA issued a series of policy documents attempting to restrict coal-fired power development, and in 2020 issued notices dealing with excess capacity, in particular of renewable energy (Heggelund, 2021, pp. 14–15). Nevertheless,

China's energy structure has remained heavily reliant on coal, and China continues to build new coal-fired power plants as part of its post-pandemic economic recovery plan, installing three times as much new coal power capacity as the rest of the world combined in 2020 (Global Energy Monitor, 2021).

Improving enforcement of laws and policies governing renewable energy generation at the local level will be critical to the success of China's low-carbon transition. Recent trends in China's energy policy have shown, however, that the complex and fragmented regulatory system promoting renewable energy at the national level has failed to overcome issues of overcapacity, market and grid reform and tensions in central-local relations (Zhang et al., 2017, p. 642).

9 The emergence of climate change litigation in China

Unlike in the United States and Australia, climate change litigation in China is in a relatively early stage of development, receiving little academic attention. For example, as at December 2022, the Climate Change Litigation Database run by the Sabin Center for Climate Change Law records only a single case from China. That case, *The Friends of Nature Institute v. Gansu State Grid*, concerns a pending lawsuit brought against a state-owned power grid company relating to their failure to connect renewable energy to the grid in violation of the Renewable Energy Law. He (2021, p. 415) notes that this database is a limited resource for climate change cases in China because it only records cases where the outcome of a case would be different if the court had not referred to a fact or legal obligation related to climate change. In other words, the database is limited to cases that fit the general definition described by Peel and Osofsky as raising climate-specific arguments or resulting in judicial analysis referring to climate change.

Zhao et al. (2019, p. 361) take a broader approach to the framing of climate litigation in China, noting that Chinese cases do not meet the stereotypical features of climate litigation, and instead involve civil cases brought by and against private companies, backed up by government law and policies, with the courts acting as quasi-regulators. They give as an example an emerging line of tort-based cases relating to air pollution that are backed by government policies and emissions standards, where the plaintiffs are generally non-government organisations, using the expanded public interest standing introduced in China's 2015 revised Environmental Protection Law (Id., p. 366). The first of these cases was brought in 2015 by the NGO All-China Environment Federation against a producer of plate glass Jinghua Group Zhenhua Co. Ltd for the unlawful emission of air pollutants including sulphur dioxide and nitrogen oxide. After receiving a successful ruling in 2016, within a year 15 further civil cases were brought in relation to air pollution caused by excessive industrial emissions and vehicle emissions, primarily against petrochemical companies and motor vehicle manufacturers (Id., p. 366). Qin and Zhang observe that the progress made for environmental public litigation under the revised Environmental Protection Law, together with the development of specialised environmental courts throughout the country, are key conditions for the future potential of climate litigation in China (2021, p. 380–381).

He (2021, p. 417) takes a narrower approach to classifying Chinese cases as climate change litigation and argues that instead of focusing on tort-based litigation, administrative law cases brought against the government, especially involving environmental impact assessments, have greater potential as a pathway for climate litigation in China. The types of administrative cases He cites follow the likes of the first generation of climate cases in Australia involving challenges to environmental impact assessments for the failure to consider climate change impacts (He, 2021, p. 423). He notes that the key difference between climate litigation in the United States and Australia, compared to in China, is how cases are framed and treated by the courts (2021, pp. 418–419). In the United States and Australia, climate change litigation has been driven by both the absence of effective climate change policies and laws, and by the failure of government agencies to exercise their authority to regulate climate change issues. In contrast, in China plaintiffs must phrase their cases under existing law and with the support of existing government policies, due to the overarching authority and control of the government over the courts. He argues that a combination of both government policies in respect of greenhouse gas emissions together with existing obligations to consider reducing emissions under various statutes including the Environmental Impact Assessment Law can provide a basis for administrative climate change cases (*Id.*, pp. 430–431).

For both administrative and tort-based claims, public interest organisations face the same legal barriers of demonstrating standing and causation faced by plaintiffs in the US and Australia. Since the introduction of public interest standing for NGOs in environmental cases, China has seen a dramatic rise in environmental public interest cases, from 49 filed in 2015, to over 3,500 petitions heard by judges in 2020 (Liu and Kan, 2021). The introduction of public interest standing for civil cases, together with what He describes as a relaxation of standing requirements under China's Administrative Litigation Law, means that climate litigation brought by civil society groups has the potential to serve as an enforcement tool of existing climate and environmental regulation, as well as to raise awareness of climate change issues generally, contributing to the development of Chinese climate governance (He, 2021, p. 435).

10 Conclusion

The effectiveness of both public and private enforcement mechanisms to support the low-carbon energy transition depends on the regulatory structures and institutions in place within a jurisdiction, whether that be international or domestic. In the international context, the existing institutions governing the trade in energy under the WTO and ECT are creating roadblocks, rather than pathways, for the low-carbon transition. This is due to the institutional biases set in favour of free trade and investment security for the WTO and ECT, respectively, which often conflict with individual states' energy and climate policies. As a result, public enforcement through regulation on a domestic level, together with private enforcement through litigation, provide more efficient pathways to decarbonisation.

In geographically large and diverse countries, such as the United States, China and Australia, multi-level energy governance through a co-operative federalist system presents opportunities for a coordinated transition towards renewable energy. However, without clear agreements over the sharing of regulatory responsibilities between national and subnational actors, multi-level energy governance can also present challenges involving the fragmentation of laws and policies as well as conflicts between different levels of government. Where government regulation falls short, climate litigation is beginning to have a significant impact in raising awareness about climate change and creating financial risks for companies and governments that continue to invest in carbon-intensive industries. Some litigation efforts, particularly in the United States, have traditionally been stymied by the federalism model. But litigators have become creative, focusing on state-based legislation and torts in order to overcome the jurisdictional divide, although it is as yet unclear whether this approach will be successful. While the majority of climate change cases have been filed in the United States and Australia, they are becoming an important tool around the world for compelling governments and the private sector to decarbonise. Climate cases can take a variety of approaches, including administrative claims in China and are thus an important, alternative regulatory pathway for the implementation and enforcement of the low-carbon transition.

References

Abbott, M. and Cohen, B., 2019. Maintaining the security of supply in the Australian National Electricity Market with higher levels of renewable energy. *The Electricity Journal*, 32(9), pp. 1–21.

Australian Government, Department of Industry, Science, Energy and Resources, 2021. *2021 National Gas Infrastructure Plan*. Commonwealth of Australia. Available at: https://www.energy.gov.au/sites/default/files/Australian%20Energy%20Statistics%202021%20Energy%20Update%20Report.pdf (Accessed: 17 January 2022).

Banks, N., 2012. Decarbonising the economy and international investment law. *Journal of Energy and Natural Resources*, 30(4), pp. 497–510.

Benjamin, L., 2020. The road to Paris runs through Delaware: climate litigation and directors' duties. *Utah Law Review*, 2020(2), pp. 313–381.

Benjamin, L., 2021. Renewable energy and trade: meeting the Paris Agreement's goals through a two-step jurisprudential advance. *Minnesota Journal of Law, Science and Technology*, 22(1), pp. 1–82.

Buzbee, W., 2017. Federalism hedging, entrenchment and the climate challenge. *Wisconsin Law Review*, pp. 1037–1113.

Canada-Certain Measures Affecting the Renewable Energy Generation Sector (2013) ¶ 1.1, WTO Doc. WT/DS412/AB/R (adopted May 24, 2013). Available at: https://www.wto.org/english/tratop_e/dispu_e/412_426abr_a_e.pdf (Accessed: 17 January 2022).

Christiansen, M., 2015. *FERC v. EPSA*: functionalism and the electricity industry of the future. *Stanford Law Review Online*, 68, pp. 100–110.

Christiansen, M. and Macey, J., 2021. Long live the Federal Power Act's Bright Line. *Harvard Law Review*, 134, pp. 1360–1422.

Cottier, T. et al., 2009. *Energy in WTO Law and Policy* 8. NCCR Trade Regulation, Working Paper No. 2009/25, 2009. Available at: https://www.wto.org/english/res_e/publications_e/wtr10_forum_e/wtr10_7may10_e.pdf (Accessed: 17 January 2022).

Dias Simoes, F., 2017. *Blusun S.A. and others v Italy*: legal (in)stability and renewable energy investments. *Review of European, Comparative & International Environmental Law*, 26(3), pp. 298–304.

Gang, C., 2019. *Politics of renewable energy in China*. Cheltenham: Edward Elgar Publishing.

Global Energy Monitor, 2021. *China Dominates 2020 Coal Plant Development*. Centre for Research on Energy and Clean Air, February 2021. Available at: https://globalenergymonitor.org/wp-content/uploads/2021/02/China-Dominates-2020-Coal-Development.pdf (Accessed: 17 January 2022).

Godden, L., 2020. Energy justice and energy transition in Australia. In: I. del Guayo et al., eds., 2020. *Energy justice and energy law*. Oxford: Oxford University Press, pp. 178–199.

He, X., 2021. Mitigation and adaptation through environmental impact assessment litigation: rethinking the prospect of climate change litigation in China. *Transnational Environmental Law*, 10(3), pp. 413–439.

Heggelund, G., 2021. China's climate and energy policy: at a turning point?. *International Environmental Agreements: Politics, Law and Economics*, 21, pp. 9–23.

Hua, Y., Oliphant, M. and Hu, E., 2016. Development of renewable energy in Australia and China: A comparison of policies and status. *Renewable Energy*, 85, pp. 1044–1051.

Jackson, J., 1997. *The World trading system*. 2nd ed. Cambridge, MA: The MIT Press.

Jacobs, S., 2015. Bypassing federalism and the administrative law of negawatts. *Iowa Law Review*, 100, pp. 885–945.

Kallies, A., 2021. The Australian energy transition as a federalism challenge: (un)cooperative energy federalism?. *Transnational Environmental Law*, 10(2), pp. 211–235.

Killeen, P., 2020. FERC's tether tantrum: why suppressing state support for renewable energy violates the Federal Power Act and threatens U.S. climate leadership. *American University Law Review*, 70, pp. 271–307.

Kostka, G. and Nahm, J., 2017. Central–local relations: recentralization and environmental governance in China. *The China Quarterly*, 231, pp. 567–582.

Kustova, I., 2016. A treaty à la carte? Some reflections on the modernization of the Energy Charter Process. *Journal of World Energy Law and Business*, 9, pp. 357–369.

Lesley, H., 2019. The Rocky Hill decision: a watershed for climate change action. *Journal of Energy & Natural Resources Law*, 37(3), pp. 341–351.

Liu, J. and Kan, K., 2021. China wants more climate court cases, but only the right ones. *Bloomberg Green*, 19 June. Available at: https://www.bloomberg.com/news/articles/2021-06-19/climate-litigation-must-navigate-china-s-complex-legal-system (Accessed: 17 January 2022).

McGreevy, M. et al., 2021. Expediting a renewable energy transition in a privatised market via public policy: The case of South Australia 2004-18. *Energy Policy*, 148(A), pp. 1–14.

McNeill, S., 2021. As Australia's climate policy disappoints, hope is found in court. *The Age*. Available at: https://www.theage.com.au/national/as-australia-s-climate-policy-disappoints-hope-is-found-in-court-20210910-p58qmc.html (Accessed: 17 January 2022).

Meyer, T., 2018. Free trade, fair trade, and selective enforcement. *Columbia Law Review*, 118(2), pp. 491–566.

Nelson, T. et al., 2019. Efficient integration of climate and energy policy in Australia's National Electricity Market. *Economic Analysis and Policy*, 64, pp. 178–193.
Osofsky, H. M. and Peel, J., 2015. *Climate change litigation: regulatory pathways to cleaner energy*. Cambridge: Cambridge University Press.
Peel, J., Osofsky, H., and Foerster, A., 2017. Shaping the 'next generation' of climate change litigation in Australia. *Melbourne University Law Review*, 41(2), pp. 735–844.
Powers, M., 2019. Anticompetitive transmission development and the risks for decarbonization. *Environmental Law*, 49(4), pp. 885–929.
Qin, T. and Zhang, M., 2021. Climate change and the individual: a perspective of China. In: F. Sindico and M.M. Mbengue, eds. *Comparative climate change litigation: beyond the usual suspects*. Cham, Switzerland: Springer, pp. 369–385.
Rai, A. and Nelson, T. 2020. Australia's National Electricity Market after twenty years. *The Australian Economic Review*, 53(2), pp. 165–182.
Saurer, J. and Monast, J., 2021. The law of energy transition in federal systems. *Transnational Environmental Law*, 10(2), pp. 205–210.
Schreurs, M., 2017. Multi-level climate governance in China. *Environmental Policy and Governance*, 27, pp. 163–174.
Setzer, J. and Higham, C., 2021. *Global trends in climate change litigation: 2021 snapshot*. London: Grantham Research Institute on Climate Change and the Environment and Centre for Climate Change Economics and Policy, London School of Economics and Political Science.
Simões, F., 2018. Article 26: settlement of disputes between an investor and contracting party. In: R. Leal-Arcas, ed. 2018. *Commentary on the Energy Charter Treaty*. Cheltenham: Edward Elgar Publishing, pp. 338–358.
Tienhoara, K. and Downie, C., 2018. Risky business? The Energy Charter Treaty, renewable energy, and investor-state disputes. *Global Governance*, 24(3), pp. 451–471.
Weingast, B. R., 1995. The economic role of political institutions: market-preserving federalism and economic development. *Journal of Law, Economics and Organization*, 11(1), pp. 1–31.
Wilensky, M., 2015. *Climate change in the courts: an assessment of non-U.S. climate litigation. Duke Environmental Law & Policy Forum*, 26(1), pp. 131–179.
Wu, M. and Salzman, J., 2014. The next generation of trade and environmental conflicts: the rise of green industrial policy. *Northwestern University Law Review*, 108(2), pp. 401–474.
Zhang, L. et al., 2017. The dragon awakens: innovation, competition, and transition in the energy strategy of the People's Republic of China, 1949–2017. *Energy Policy*, 108, pp. 634–644.
Zhao, Y., Lyu, S. and Wang, Z., 2019. Prospects for climate change litigation in China. *Transnational Environmental Law*, 8(2), pp. 349–377.

Part II: **Energy Markets**

Editorial introduction

This part focuses on the impact of the low-carbon transition on energy markets. The eight chapters deal with two parallel developments. On one hand, existing trading arrangements have to adapt to the transformations brought by the transition. On the other hand, new commercial relationships and new marketplaces must be established. The chapters discuss the regulatory frameworks in five continents. Collectively, they suggest that no legal system can move forward with the transition without deciding how to use energy markets. At the same time, energy markets do not play the same role everywhere. Three areas where different ways to organize them become more visible can be identified.

The first area has to do with the leeway enjoyed by private autonomy. A large spectrum of solutions can be identified: at one extreme, the phase-out of fossil fuels plants is left to market decisions, financial contracts in energy markets are regulated lightly and the decarbonization of global chains depends on voluntary initiatives; at the other extreme, state interventions significantly constrain private autonomy and impose binding obligations. The crucial question is which legal systems are able to switch to more binding solutions when needed. Some legal systems are more likely than others to be stuck at the extreme where only voluntary initiatives and light regulation are feasible. Reasons why this could happen and why legal systems are located to one extreme are tightly linked to the interplay of the two domains discussed in the Introduction.

The second area has to do with support for renewable energy. Both the chapters in this part and in other parts of the Handbook suggest that state intervention is required in all phases of the innovation cycle. When some clean technologies have gained a foothold in energy markets, state intervention is needed for the next generation of clean technologies. This is not to say that the same type of state intervention shall be available or is recommended everywhere. In those institutional contexts where state capabilities are more limited, the goal is to harness resources from the private sector or local communities. Hence, energy markets differ from the point of view of the co-existence of different public and private financial channels for the development of renewable energy.

The third area has to do with the role of competition in energy markets. We know that textbooks models for the liberalization/restructuring of the energy sector have not been followed anywhere. Each country/region has made market design choices compatible with its own energy security and financial interests. Furthermore, the most advanced solutions for liberalized markets might have led to increased coordination costs along energy chains. At least in theory, more competition should foster technological innovation. But it is by no means clear that the low-carbon transition requires all countries to embrace the textbook model of energy liberalization. The controversies surrounding carbon markets, as well as the sheer variety of designs they display, caution against recommending a new wave of liberalization reforms. A

https://doi.org/10.1515/9783110752403-014

more useful approach is to explore the origins of the variety of hybrid market structures we observe and discuss the institutional conditions for a shift to a new (and probably still hybrid) market structure. It is highly likely that, in the low-carbon energy markets, the meaning of competition itself, as well as the standards to judge the legality of business practices, will undergo significant changes.

Lan Wu

Interaction between Renewable Energy Integration and Wholesale Electricity Markets: a Legal and Regulatory Perspective

Abstract: Electricity market design and regulation affect the extent to which energy transition policies can deliver their desired results. The economics and policy scholarship has identified varying taxonomies of electricity markets according to different classification criteria. From the perspective of openness of market structure and electricity sector management, electricity markets are liberalised or regulated. Carbon pricing is a crucial regulatory instrument facilitating energy transition. A fully liberalised and competitive electricity market may provide the ideal opportunity to achieve the goals of carbon pricing and energy transition policies. However, fully liberalised electricity markets are far from the norm worldwide. Instead, electricity markets are often subject to government regulation tailored to specific domestic conditions. Most often seen are interim status markets that deviate from strictly regulated ones but are still not fully liberalised with a certain degree of institutional interventions. In particular, the regulation of electricity prices in wholesale markets, which is at the core of the electricity market design, has the most significant effect on introducing regulatory tools of renewable energy integration and carbon pricing that facilitate the energy transition. This chapter discusses the interplay between the wholesale market and renewable energy integration; facilitators such as capacity remuneration mechanisms and carbon pricing are also considered. It focuses on the electricity markets architecture for later chapters to understand how different market design patterns, initially pursuing the liberalisation, carry different weights with carbon market options serving the purpose of decarbonisation and energy transition.

1 Introduction

The design and regulation of the electricity sector affect the extent to which renewable energy integration laws and policies can deliver the desired results. Historically, governments play an essential role in the electricity sector and actively shape the electricity market design in a 'top-down' manner (IEA *et al.*, 2016). When administrative management showed its limitations in efficiently allocating resources, liberalisa-

---

Lan Wu is a PhD student at the Faculty of Law, The Chinese University of Hong Kong.

https://doi.org/10.1515/9783110752403-015

tion of the electricity sector and market competition were advocated to overcome them. Therefore, the electricity industry in most jurisdictions witnessed a common trend of evolving from a heavily regulated sector to liberalised power markets. A variety of electricity market structures emerged, with different degrees of openness and diverse approaches to governance around the world.

Despite this liberalisation trend, fully liberalised electricity markets are far from universal rule worldwide (Sioshansi, 2013). Most often, electricity markets are still under construction and subject to regulations tailored to specific domestic circumstances. Reform processes and development of electricity markets vary from one jurisdiction to another, with a wide range of electricity market designs and regulatory patterns. The creation of a wholesale electricity market usually represents the step in establishing competitive markets for electricity at the upstream level. In contrast to the bulk trading of electricity in wholesale electricity markets, retail electricity markets usually involve more electricity end-users but lower volumes of electricity being traded.

Consequently, retail electricity market design and regulation incorporate distinct elements from the wholesale electricity markets. Since it is believed that effective retail electricity market competition is usually based on an efficient liberalised wholesale electricity market with effective spot prices (Hunt, 2002), well-established competitive retail markets are less common among jurisdictions (Rudnick and Velasquez, 2018). Legal provisions and the actual presence of competition in retail electricity markets mainly exist in developed countries that made more progress in wholesale electricity market reforms, such as the EU Member States and the US Additionally, reform programmes are adopted selectively and often stagnate in the electricity sector of the majority of developing countries, and this leads to the situation of an intermediate stage of reform with only some liberalised market elements (Huenteler *et al.*, 2020). The majority of developing countries' electricity sectors are only partially liberalised with a certain degree of institutional interventions, especially the regulation of electricity prices in wholesale markets. Due to the importance of pricing in electricity market design and regulation, regulators devote meticulous attention to electricity pricing issues.

In efforts to achieve the reduction of greenhouse gas (GHG) emissions and energy transition goals, support for renewable energy-sourced electricity (RES-E) became a prominent element in electricity market design and regulation. Integrating renewable energy requires additional legal and regulatory efforts in both partially and fully liberalised electricity wholesale markets. Beyond wholesale electricity markets, capacity compensation mechanisms and capacity markets can also facilitate RES-E integration. In addition, several legal and regulatory instruments have been adopted and subjected to experiments worldwide in order to reduce emissions from electricity sectors and facilitate the integration of RES-E into power systems, including the emission trading scheme (ETS) and Renewable Portfolio Standards (RPS). It is crucial to understand how these legal and regulatory instruments interact with wholesale market design and regulation from the perspective of wholesale pricing for decarbonising the electricity system.

Therefore, this chapter focuses on pricing issues in wholesale electricity markets. It zooms in on the wholesale electricity market architecture to explain how different market design patterns initially pursuing liberalisation goals carry different weights with support schemes for renewable energy integration. To achieve this, it draws on examples from different jurisdictions regarding electricity market design choices. This is followed by the analysis of capacity remuneration issues that are of great relevance to renewable energy integration. Then it provides an analysis of the interrelation between wholesale market pricing and carbon pricing, and the interplay with RPS is also analysed. It also utilises an analysis of the interaction between wholesale market pricing and renewable energy integration in the context of regulated power markets. The last section synthesises the discussions and concludes the chapter.

2 Wholesale electricity market pricing

Despite the diverse circumstances in jurisdictions worldwide, wholesale electricity market design models fall into two categories, as identified by engineering scholarship: centralised or decentralised electricity markets. This engineering taxonomy reflects the diversity of technical features of electricity dispatching systems worldwide. However, it fails to reflect the economic relationships, legal rights, and responsibilities between electricity market players, making it less attractive to legal and regulatory analysis. A more relevant taxonomy distinguishes between wholesale electricity markets according to the nature of the transaction relationship between market players. From this perspective, wholesale electricity markets are categorised into unilateral trading models (also called 'mandatory power pool') and bilateral trade models (or bi-directional trading), reflecting the different electricity trading arrangements in wholesale markets. Despite the specific circumstances and practices varying among jurisdictions, in essence, these two models represent the two options for wholesale electricity market design worldwide (Onaiwu, 2009). In addition to this classification of wholesale electricity markets from the perspective of electricity trading methods, the taxonomy based on the structure of the electricity sector is of greater relevance to the legal and regulatory analysis of electricity market design and regulation because it captures the different degrees of electricity market openness and management. It refers to the different ways in which electricity sector participants can interact (Cretì and Fontini, 2019). Following this taxonomy, power sector structures can be grouped into four major models, including the vertically integrated industry (or utility), the single buyer model, the wholesale competition model, and the retail competition model (Hunt, 2002). The introduction of competition and the liberalisation of electricity sectors usually starts by separating electricity generation functions from transmission and distribution ('unbundling'), representing the first method of electricity market reforms (Bradford, 2018). Then a Single Buyer model is usually adopted before the wholesale and retail markets are smoothly functioning and competitive. Within this single Buyer model, Power Purchase Agreements (PPAs) are concluded between the single buyer (usually the entity that performs the function of the system operator or dispatcher) and the Independent Power Producers (IPPs) separated from the vertically integrated utilities (Cretì and Fontini, 2019). These PPAs, in legal terms, are contracts that allow a certain degree of competition on the electricity generation side. To further create competitive wholesale markets (Wholesale Competition Model), the single buyer is further reorganised into several entities in charge of specific activities along the electricity supply chain, including one entity that manages the power grid and dispatching, and distribution companies that are responsible for activities of electricity distribution and retailing (Cretì and Fontini, 2019). With the gradual reforms towards a higher level of openness to competition in wholesale markets, it is possible to separate retailing activities from distribution companies and establish distinct entities, including distributors and suppliers, to replace the former distribution companies. The distributors and suppliers compete with each other to supply electricity to end consumers in each distribution network when retail electricity markets or fully liberalised electricity markets are created, and end consumers are entitled to free choice of their suppliers.

For different stages of development within each market structure model, electricity market design and regulation have to be adapted to different levels of openness and management. Although the power sector structure models are generalised concepts that do not cater for specific national circumstances, it is helpful to understand the electricity market reform goals at different stages. However, fully liberalised electricity markets that are effectively competitive at both wholesale and retail levels are far from being universal in the real world. The market reform measures are adopted selectively and are not packaged or sequenced in a logical way (Foster and Rana, 2019). As a result, electricity market reforms in most jurisdictions are at an intermediate stage without full competition in the retail market (Foster and Rana, 2019). Among the wholesale market elements, pricing is one of the most important ones at the core of market design and regulation debates. Based on the understanding of general wholesale market development stages and taxonomy, this chapter further analyses the intersection between the wholesale power market and RES-E integration from the perspective of pricing.

3 Legal and regulatory instruments facilitating renewable energy integration

Renewable energy integration is one of the most visible aspects of the energy transition in response to the climate crisis. The decarbonisation of the electricity sector to achieve carbon emission goals requires robust legal support. Wholesale electricity markets themselves are not sufficient for incentivising renewable energy integration, which necessitates the adoption of legal and regulatory instruments to achieve the goal of decarbonising the electricity sector. The interaction between legal and regulatory instruments promoting renewable energy integration and the wholesale electricity market reform measures pursuing fair competition cannot be ignored: their effectiveness depends on this interdependency. For example, subsidy policy (such as the Feed-in Tariff) for renewable electricity can lead to distortions of wholesale price signals, and it does not encourage direct price competition between different renewable energy projects (Nicolini and Tavoni, 2017; Kalkuhl *et al.*, 2013). Therefore, it is important to understand the interaction to achieve the goals of promoting renewable energy integration and avoiding the distortion of wholesale market competition in the meantime.

This interaction analysis focuses on four major aspects, including the legal and regulatory issues with the capacity compensation mechanism and capacity market, the impact of the Renewable Portfolio Standards (RPS) on wholesale market pricing, the interrelation between wholesale electricity pricing mechanisms and carbon pricing policies (especially emission trading scheme), and price regulation as an obstacle to RES-E integration.

The capacity compensation and market mechanisms are also of great relevance to the analysis of the interaction between the wholesale electricity market and renewable energy integration. Moreover, the adoption of RPS as a legal instrument for promoting renewable energy integration is closely interlinked with wholesale electricity market pricing. In addition, legal and regulatory instruments for carbon emission reduction also have the function of facilitating renewable energy integration. From this perspective, the analysis of legal and regulatory instruments for carbon emission reduction, such as carbon pricing mechanisms, cannot be neglected in the analysis of renewable energy integration into wholesale electricity markets.

At the opposite side of the electricity market reform spectrum, the regulated electricity sector with electricity prices determined not by market forces but by administrative decisions challenges RES-E integration. Therefore, this analysis also pays attention to the regulated electricity sector, where electricity pricing is not fully liberalised and interacts with the legal and regulatory instruments for RES-E integration in a different pattern.

4 Renewable energy integration and the potential solution by capacity remuneration mechanisms

4.1 Various designs of capacity remuneration mechanisms

There are different forms of regulatory instruments to ensure that electricity generation capacity can meet the load in a specific time to keep the system balanced. These regulatory instruments can help to achieve the goal of securing resource adequacy by creating revenue for capacity services in addition to the revenue that generators gain from selling energy itself. Capacity services refer to services of generators ready to generate power or services of the load being able to be shed (Cretì and Fontini, 2019). To create revenue for capacity services, various forms of capacity remuneration mechanisms have been designed and implemented in different jurisdictions, such as strategic reserve, tender for new capacity, central buyer, capacity obligation, and targeted or market-wide capacity payment. These different types of capacity remuneration mechanisms can be employed in the same jurisdiction. For example, France adopted the tender for new capacity, strategic reserve (interruptibility scheme), and de-central obligation (or guarantee). Ireland adopted the tender for new capacity, market-wide capacity payment, strategic reserve (interruptibility scheme), and central buyer mechanisms. Multiple capacity remuneration mechanisms of the same type can also be adopted in one jurisdiction, as is the case in Germany, Portugal, and Spain (European Commission, 2016; ACER/CEER, 2020; ACER/CEER, 2021). The categorisation of the capacity mechanisms in the EU is based on the taxonomy in the European Commission's Report (European Commission, 2016). Likewise, the PJM Interconnection represents one of the most critical power systems in the US, where a capacity market was established in 2007. A more recent example is the U.K., where there is a capacity market based on auctions introduced as part of the Electricity Market Reform by the Energy Act 2013.

Generally, these capacity remuneration mechanisms can be categorised into price-based or quantity-based, market-wide or targeted on certain groups of entities (European Commission, 2016; ACER, 2013; Pugl-Pichler *et al.*, 2020). Different capacity remuneration mechanisms have their adaptation to different development stages of wholesale electricity markets and the particularities of a jurisdiction. The common aim of these different capacity-supporting mechanisms is to ensure generation capacity adequacy, which is also closely related to renewable electricity generation. The capacity remuneration mechanisms may change with the development of the energy market, as well as the increase of RES-E shares in the electricity system. However, it remains unclear in many jurisdictions how to achieve the harmonisation of capacity mechanisms and renewable energy support mechanisms (Kozlova and Overland, 2021).

The smoothly functioning capacity market mechanism is not the norm in most jurisdictions worldwide (Bublitz *et al.*, 2019). Even in Europe, where electricity markets are considered liberalised and relatively mature, capacity market mechanisms have not been introduced universally, and there has been no standard form of capacity remuneration mechanisms for all. Up to 2021, twelve EU Member States were adopting different forms of capacity numeration mechanisms, and only seven of them have been approved by the European Commission for compliance with State Aid rules (ACER/CEER, 2021). The Clean Energy for all Europeans Package defines capacity remuneration mechanisms as a temporary measure to ensure the security of supply, and the introduction and implementation of capacity remuneration mechanisms are only allowed when it is essential for addressing the EU Member States' energy security concerns (Pugl-Pichler *et al.*, 2020). This is probably because of the ongoing debates about the necessity of introducing capacity renumeration mechanisms and the controversy of renewable electricity generators' participation in capacity renumeration mechanisms.

The capacity market mechanism features a combination of market-oriented elements and regulated aspects. Ideally, the capacity market price signal has the most desirable effect in incentivising investment in flexibility facilities that benefit renewable energy integration. It works best when the wholesale electricity markets can function well and deliver proper price signals. For example, capacity price signals depend to a large degree on the accuracy of load forecast and the calculation of revenue from wholesale electricity market trading, since the capacity market is designed to compensate for the deficiencies of cost recovery from energy markets. However, capacity markets are not the best option for an immature wholesale electricity market since the demand prediction in the capacity market is based on the performance of wholesale electricity markets. Moreover, well-functioning capacity markets require a high level of information disclosure, which can be found normally in well-established wholesale electricity markets rather than partially reformed ones.

Furthermore, the integration of RES-E also impacts the stability of wholesale electricity markets. It has the merit order effect of decreasing wholesale electricity prices due to the low marginal cost of wind and solar power generation. In the wholesale electricity market, the revenue of generators, to a large degree, depends on the power prices. The lower power price led by RES-E can potentially generate the risks of uncertain cost recovery of capacity investment. This risk is also exacerbated by the price volatility caused by the intermittent or variable output of wind and solar power. Price volatility harms investor's confidence, which causes difficulties in ensuring the generation capacity in the long term. Consequently, there will be negative impacts on system security and wholesale market stability. With well-designed capacity remuneration mechanisms tailored to wholesale market circumstances, the difficulties in ensuring adequate capacity can be eased and resolved.

4.2 Capacity remuneration mechanisms and RES-E integration

The integration of renewable energy, especially wind and solar power generation, produces grid reliability challenges due to their intermittent or variable output. This requires improving the existing energy markets or additional arrangements to ensure a reliable electricity supply. There are current debates about how to design such an arrangement and what are the optimal regulatory options for a particular jurisdiction or region. One of the arrangements is to introduce capacity market mechanisms operating alongside energy-only markets. Supporters of the introduction of the capacity market mechanism argue that it will compensate for the availability of the reserved capacity for generating power during a stated period in a more direct way than the energy-only markets, thus providing a more explicit assurance of the ability to meet the load. In addition to the argument for the electricity system's reliability, supporters of the capacity market also believe that it will improve the flexibility of electricity generation because it provides an additional price signal (and expectation for the revenue) for the reservation of generation capacity. The principal argument for a capacity market is to alleviate the 'missing money problem' (Cramton and Stoft, 2006; Joskow and Tirole, 2007; Joskow, 2008; Harvey *et al.*, 2013; Newbery, 2016; Léautier, 2019). It is believed that a well-designed capacity market can provide a compensation channel for the deficiency of energy-only markets in terms of the fixed-cost recovery of generators, as well as better incentives for investment in system security and adequacy. This is crucial to the electricity system with a higher penetration of RES-E, which requires a higher level of system flexibility, especially the ability of fast ramping-up and capacity reservation. With the increase in RES-E integration, the arguments for introducing capacity remuneration mechanisms become more solid. This is because with the higher penetration of RES-E, the system becomes less responsive at both the demand side and the supply side, and there will be higher impacts of the limits imposed by price caps. The introduction of capacity remuneration mechanisms is required to ensure the adequacy of resources (Henriot and Glachant, 2013). Along with the heated debates on the necessity of introducing capacity markets to achieve a RES-E-dominated electricity system, a further question is how to design the capacity market or payment (or compensation) mechanism and how to link it to the existing energy-only market to ensure the maximisation of the benefits it is expected to generate. There have been heated debates on the design of capacity remuneration mechanisms (Joskow, 2008; Batlle and Pérez-Arriaga, 2008; Cramton *et al.*, 2013; De Sisternes and Parsons, 2016; Lin and Vatani, 2017; Byers and Botterud, 2018; Perico *et al.*, 2018; Teirilä and Ritz, 2019; Shang *et al.*, 2021). These debates are particularly relevant to renewable energy integration.

A smoothly functioning capacity market arrangement can help to ensure the availability of reserved capacity when there is no wind or sun. It also has the potential to help in the cost recovery of flexible generation fleets and hence incentivises investment in such capacity or investment in the modification of existing installations to fit with the intermittence or variability of wind and solar power generation, where the energy-only market fails to provide price signals to do so effectively. As the key to RES-E integration, the flexibility of the electricity system is at the core of the clean energy transition solutions. It can be increased by options such as the reserved electricity generation capacity, energy storage facilities and demand-side response resources, and electric vehicles. Investment in these options becomes increasingly important with the higher shares of renewable energy in the electricity system. For this reason, the capacity market is desirable to encourage investment in these areas to increase system flexibility and contribute to the integration of renewables.

The debates over capacity markets are particularly relevant to the issue of renewable energy integration, at least for the following considerations. Poorly designed capacity markets hinder wholesale market electricity price signals by increasing the oversupply of production capacity. Distortive capacity market price signals can cause the oversupply of renewable energy generation capacity, resulting in difficulties in the consumption of the RES-E. Poorly designed capacity markets also run the risk of subsidising the polluting coal-fired generation capacity or delaying thermal retirement. Besides, ill-suited capacity markets may increase the risk of not providing sufficient flexibility for the system if the reserved or added capacity stems from inflexible generators. This will have a negative effect on coordinating the coal-fired power generation with RES-E production and slow the transition from a coal-based electricity system toward a renewables-dominated electricity market.

Finally, capacity market mechanisms can only deliver the desired results when capacity market players are under proper market regulation by competent authorities to avoid the abuse of market power and the activities disturbing market orders. This is only possible when the law provides robust market regulation support. Such legal support is crucial to deal with the potential capacity market introduction for the sake of the integration of renewables. The impact of RES-E integration seems to present a strong argument for the necessity of creating regulatory conditions supporting the introduction of capacity markets.

From these perspectives, the design and regulation of the capacity market are crucial, considering that defectively designed or poorly functioning capacity markets will interplay with the renewable generator adversely and exacerbate the difficulties of renewable energy integration.

Partially because of these risks, the electricity markets in many jurisdictions stick to the existing energy-only market framework. The commonly cited reasons include the benefit of administrative simplicity, a higher degree of certainty for investors, and better understanding and support by the industry and end consumers. It is not yet sufficiently clear how RES-E generators can play their role in capacity remuneration mechanisms in most jurisdictions. However, it is very likely that RES-E generators will be exposed to wholesale market signals with the advent of grid-parity. A hybrid energy-plus-capacity market arrangement can still be considered an option for providing additional price signals to RES-E generators and facilitating RES-E integration into markets.

5 Interrelation between wholesale electricity pricing mechanisms and carbon pricing

5.1 Mainstream carbon pricing mechanisms: carbon tax and Emission Trading Schemes

The legal aspects of renewable energy integration are closely interlinked with the institutions that promote carbon pricing, including two major mechanisms – emission trading schemes and carbon taxes. These carbon pricing mechanisms have taken shape in the form of setting emission standards and targets, sharing information and networking, operating pilot and demonstration projects, and financing (Skovgaard and Canavan, 2020). Both have significant impacts on the electricity market that cannot be neglected in the legal analysis of electricity market design and renewable energy integration.

There have been carbon pricing institutions since the 1990s, such as the carbon tax in Finland and Sweden. Later efforts include establishing the emissions trading systems such as the EU ETS, as well as hybrid systems implementing both the carbon tax and an emission trading scheme in jurisdictions such as the U.K., Japan, and France.

In general, the carbon tax is a 'price-based' policy instrument that regulates the price of emissions, while the carbon market is considered a 'quantity-based' one that regulates the number of emissions (Skovgaard and Canavan, 2020). The theory behind a carbon tax relies on the 'Pigouvian tax' (Pigou, 1920). Its central tenet is that the problems with market failure from pollution can be addressed by taxing the pollution on the basis of its social marginal damage because this would equate to private and social marginal costs (Metcalf, 2021). On the other hand, ETS is developed on the basis of the Coase Theorem (Coase, 1960), which provides a theoretical foundation for addressing the carbon emission problems through free market forces (Weber, 2017).

In practice, the former was mainly adopted in Europe in the 1990s, and the latter quickly became popular following the adoption of the Kyoto Protocol (Skovgaard and Canavan, 2020). Both serve the same aim of internalising the externalities of electricity generation and follow the "polluters pay" principle. However, they have different impacts on wholesale electricity markets from the perspective of pricing.

5.2 The influence of carbon tax on wholesale electricity pricing

The electricity sector is usually covered by carbon tax since it contributes a significant amount of GHG emissions. The payment of carbon taxes directly translates the environmental cost of electricity generation from fossil fuels into the business operation cost if carbon cost pass-through allows for higher electricity prices (Kim *et al.*, 2010; Sijm *et al.*, 2012; Neuhoff and Ritz, 2019). This carbon cost influences wholesale electricity pricing, depending on the design of a carbon tax and the cost pass-through mechanisms. The details of carbon tax design vary in different jurisdictions. In general, the impacts of the carbon tax on wholesale electricity pricing can be observed from the relationship between carbon taxes and wholesale electricity markets. There have been extensive discussions on this (Wong and Zhang, 2022; Maryniak *et al.*, 2019). Introducing a carbon tax is desirable for renewable energy integration: the competitiveness of coal-fired power plants will be reduced because they are usually included in the carbon tax base. Because wind and solar photovoltaic power generation emit almost no carbon, they can have relatively higher competitiveness in wholesale markets, considering their carbon cost is negligible. Overall, the influence of carbon tax on wholesale electricity pricing significantly depends on the design of carbon tax and the carbon cost pass-through mechanisms that determine how the tax payment can be reflected in higher electricity pricing. Therefore, this influence can vary drastically among different jurisdictions.

5.3 ETS interaction with wholesale market pricing

The emission trading mechanisms and wholesale electricity market design and regulation can align in terms of the common goal of transforming the electricity sectors into a clean system based on open markets allowing for competition.

In general, the ETS interacts with electricity markets through market elements, especially those subject to government regulation, including electricity prices, investment, and dispatch, which can act as regulatory barriers to the introduction of ETS (Acworth *et al.*, 2020).

Among these elements, pricing is at the core of the electricity market architecture and the core of analysis of the interaction between ETS and electricity markets since mature liberalised electricity markets allow for the internalisation of the carbon allowance costs into electricity prices and the pass-through to end consumers. This means that the carbon allowance price signals under ETS can induce changes in electricity prices to incentivise market players to meet the goal of reducing emissions.

The allowance price signals of good quality are expected to equal the marginal abatement cost of electricity generation (Ye *et al.*, 2012). Distortions occur when they are unequal and cause functional issues in the ETS and the wholesale electricity markets. The interaction between ETS and the electricity market is more evident at the wholesale level than in retail electricity markets. This is partly because the pricing issue normally traces its roots to the pricing mechanism in wholesale markets closer to the generation segments with significant emissions. This is also because the emergence of grid-connected renewable energy integration issues primarily stems from wholesale markets. Moreover, the great relevance also reflects that renewable energy policies affecting wholesale electricity prices have implications for the ETS allowance price signals (Koch *et al.*, 2014).

In addition to wholesale electricity pricing, the way ETS interacts with wholesale electricity pricing is closely intertwined with another market element – electricity dispatching, which is the sequence in which each power generation source is being called upon to meet demand (Stoft, 2002). The ETS can interact with electricity markets by changing the order of dispatching due to its influence on the marginal costs of power generation if the price of emission allowances under ETS is calculated into the power generation costs. The emission allowances will increase the cost of conventional fossil fuel power generation due to its high emissions features, while the price of ETS allowances has less impact on RES-E generation because of its low emissions attributes.

This interaction varies considerably among jurisdictions, depending on the different dispatching methodologies tailored to the particularities of wholesale electricity markets. Liberalised competitive electricity markets are often paired with the dispatch system based on economic operating costs (Keppler, 2010). This dispatching pattern is termed economic dispatch and uses the cheapest generation to minimise the total cost of power production by calling upon suitable generators in the right amounts at the appropriate times (Stoft, 2002). For example, when the power system mainly follows the economic dispatch in competitive electricity markets, such as the case in the EU, the ETS can exert its effect on changing the dispatching order, and this actually prioritises low-emission and low-marginal-cost RES-E.

However, as mentioned earlier, the fully liberalised electricity market with a pure economic dispatching pattern is not the rule in most jurisdictions. Even in the relatively mature electricity markets in the EU, before fully bringing the RES-E into competitive wholesale markets, priority was given by system operators to RES-E in being dispatched. In most jurisdictions with partially reformed electricity sectors, dispatching is still subject to diverse degrees of regulation by authorities. In planned power systems, dispatching can be organised based on other considerations such as environmental protection and pollution reduction. The considerations of environmental or climate policies such as ETS can be the basis for determining the dispatching order, including the consideration of the ETS allowances price in dispatching prioritisation (Acworth *et al.*, 2019). However, it is believed that the administratively planned dispatch system cannot really help in achieving the desired effect of ETS for changing the dispatching rank into a cleaner one since the dispatching order is determined by administrative instructions, and it cannot be altered by the prices of emission allowances (Acworth *et al.*, 2019).

Similar to the analysis of carbon tax, another critical aspect of the interaction between ETS and wholesale electricity pricing is carbon cost pass-through. The way the cost of ETS allowances can be passed through to electricity consumers is affected by key factors, including the design of carbon markets under ETS (especially the allocation method of ETS allowances) and the structure of electricity markets (Fabra and Reguant, 2014). There are two main ETS allowances allocation methods: free allocation (grandfathering and benchmarking) and paid allocation (auctioning). As the pioneer of ETS in the world, the EU has been in its fourth ETS implementation period since 2021. Experience from the previous periods shows that the compulsory auctioning of tradable allowances might trigger an increase in wholesale electricity prices, at least in the short run (Dagoumas and Polemis, 2020).

6 Wholesale pricing of RES-E and its interplay with Renewable Portfolio Standards

6.1 Renewable Portfolio Standards as a regulatory instrument facilitating RES-E integration

The Renewable Portfolio Standards (RPS), also referred to as the Renewable Obligation or Renewable Quota System, is one of the popular regulatory instruments that aim at renewable energy promotion (Dong, 2012; Du and Takeuchi, 2020; Cointe and Nadaï, 2018). It refers to mandating a certain market share of RES-E generation by legislation (Wang and Xu, 2016). This means that RPS is a quantity-based instrument distinct from the price-based subsidies for renewables such as feed-in tariffs (FITs).

In most cases, this mechanism is accompanied by the creation of tradable renewable energy certificates (RECs), also known as tradable green certificates, to facilitate the fulfilment of the quota requirement (Wang and Xu, 2016). RECs are a kind of certificate of renewable energy generation, which can be honoured as a currency (Zhang *et al.*, 2017). Traditional thermal power plants and electricity grid companies are demanders for RECs, and renewable electricity generators are RECs suppliers. RECs are used by obliged entities to demonstrate their compliance with mandated targets under the RPS mechanism, which is usually referred to as the compliance RECs. It is also an instrument used by voluntary purchasers to show compliance with the environmental attribute of electricity when voluntary RECs are traded. They represent the legal property rights to the 'renewables' of RES-E production, and the owner has the exclusive right to claim the usage of or 'being powered with' the RES-E associated with that particular REC. It is the currency of renewable energy markets that allows the circulation of the monetised 'renewables' in artificially created markets.

An RPS mechanism is considered a market-based instrument since the price of RECs is determined by market forces – the demand and supply in the RECs trading market, rather than the energy administrative authority. The regulated element is the government's control over the quantity of RES issued to market players. Moreover, the RPS mechanisms usually mandate specific technologies (such as wind power generation and solar power generation) to be used. It is a controlling mechanism aiming to achieve a specific quota of RES-E, especially wind and solar photovoltaic power.

Allowing the trading of RECs can increase economic efficiency (reducing the cost of meeting the target) and flexibility (allowing alternative channels to fulfil targets) to meet the quota requirement (Schuman and Lin, 2012). With the accompanying RECs trading mechanisms, electricity producers can fulfil the quota requirement by either producing electricity from renewable energy sources or by purchasing RECs from other renewable electricity generators (Zuo *et al.*, 2019). Consequently, there are two sources of revenue for RES-E generators under an RPS mechanism – the income from RES-E trading in electricity markets (especially the wholesale electricity market) and the bonus from the trading of RECs.

RPS is gaining increasing attention from regulators worldwide. There are RPS implemented in some states of the US and the Renewable Electricity Standard (RES) at the federal level. There are also mechanisms similar to RPS adopted in other jurisdictions, such as the Quota System in China, Renewables Obligations in the U.K., and Renewable Energy Targets in Australia (Heeter *et al.*, 2019).

RPS helps address renewable energy integration by improving the relative economic advantage of RES-E relative to fossil fuel-generated electricity (Cleveland and Morris, 2005). With an RPS, the government publishes the targets or quotas, and electricity companies are obliged to ensure that a particular market share of capacity or electricity generation is sourced from renewable energy (Dong 2012). It promotes RES-E generation by increasing the demand for renewable electricity.

6.2 Interaction between Renewable Portfolio Standards and wholesale pricing

The RPS actively interplays with the wholesale electricity market. This can be observed when the obliged utility under the RPS mechanism cannot fulfil the quota obligation by their generation installations or even when obliged utilities do not own generators: they need to purchase electricity from the wholesale electricity market to satisfy their end-user's demand (Liao, 2020). Considering that RPS is usually paired with RECs markets, RPS obliged entities can also fulfil the quota obligation by purchasing RECs. In a liberalised electricity wholesale market, the cost of purchasing RECs to comply with RPS policy can be calculated into the wholesale electricity prices when there are cost pass-through mechanisms. Therefore, with a cost pass-through mechanism embedded in the wholesale electricity market design, the increase in REC prices can trigger an increase in wholesale electricity prices.

After the initial issuance, the price of RECs in markets depends on the demand and supply at the time of the transaction, and it is subject to fluctuation. Pricing mechanisms are different for compliance RECs and voluntary RECs. The fluctuation of compliance RECs is usually limited to a certain scope. Most compliance seen is a price cap for RECs, determined by the particular calculation methods in a specific market situation and the rules for the RPS mechanism. For voluntary RECs, the price is largely determined by negotiations between REC sellers and buyers. Overall, the RECs' prices are often impacted by the policy and laws underlying the RPS mechanisms.

Economic studies show that the implementation of RPS can reduce electricity prices in the wholesale market (Barbose, 2016). Since the RECs are the representation and confirmation of the non-hydro RES-E generation and the proof of its consumption, power plants with RES-E generation capacity are motivated to increase their RES-E output level in order to profit from RECs trading. Apart from the profit driver, enterprises are also motivated by reputational advantages and corporate social responsibility.

The linkage between the electricity market and the RECs market can also be observed through the overlapping subjects participating in both markets. Electricity generators are market players that participate in both wholesale electricity markets and RECs markets. Their electricity generation decision-making will influence not only the electricity price but also the RECs' price. The grid companies participate in both the wholesale electricity market and the RECs market. On one hand, grid companies (or independent system operators) operate the system and adjust the amount of the on-grid RES-E according to the physical security and reliability constraints of the networks; on the other hand, they participate in the RECs market as obliged entities (often the utilities, or electricity suppliers) to fulfil the quota obligation under the RPS mechanism.

The RPS has the potential to enable the cost pass-through of RES-E integration to electricity consumers, depending on the design of RPS and RECs mechanisms. One of the debates on RPS and accompanying RECs mechanisms design is whether the REC is 'bundled' with the underlying RES-E, to be more specific, tied to a power purchase agreement (PPA) for the RES-E. The term 'bundled RECs' is used when the compliance of RPS has to be attributed to specific RES-E generation units, and the trading of RECs has to be attached to the actual consumption of RES-E in the same amount, while the 'unbundled RECs' mechanism allows for RECs trading without attachment to the underlying energy, which presents chances for creating a secondary market for RECs trading (Holt and Wiser, 2007). The basic difference lies in whether the energy value of RES-E and the environmental attribute of RES-E can be sold separately. It means a distinct requirement for methods to trace the source of the RES-E. Under the 'unbundled REC' system, the RES-E generator may sell the physical electricity and the unbundled REC associated with that amount of output separately. The policy choice between these two options is open to debate (Fang and Norman, 2006). Whether a bundled or unbundled RECs mechanism can have the optimal effect on promoting RES-E integration depends on the particularities of the electricity market of a jurisdiction. Established electricity markets can be more desirable for implementing the 'unbundled REC' system, but overall, it is still subject to heated debate. Besides, competition in the RECs market provides incentives for technology innovation of RES-E generators to pursue cost reduction and gain market shares. In addition, although RECs trading in some jurisdictions, such as China, is not mandatory, it has the potential to be more closely linked to the RPS mechanisms and to be developed into a mandatory RECs trading mechanism, which provides market-based solutions to RES-E integration in line with the general electricity market architecture.

7 Regulated wholesale prices as an obstacle to RES-E integration: the example of China

7.1 The lack of market price signals for RES-E integration

With the increase of RES-E penetration into electricity systems, the regulated wholesale electricity price has become more of a problem for renewable energy participation in the electricity market. This is because the lack of market price signals cannot accommodate the need for RES-E to participate in market trading. The low marginal cost of RES-E generation gives it a clear advantage in market transactions, even though the intermittence and uncertainty of wind and solar photovoltaic power generation pose challenges to power system reliability and stability that cause higher costs in power storage or ancillary services to ensure system operation. The forward electricity market or spot electricity market mechanism does not provide sufficient economic incentives for market players to integrate RES-E into power systems. Therefore, additional institutional arrangements are necessary to make the transition toward a cleaner power market happen.

This is more evident in jurisdictions where the power systems are still in the process of reforming towards a competitive market-based system. Since the regulation of the electricity sector and market reform progress varies drastically among jurisdictions, it is difficult to generalise the way of regulated wholesale pricing as an obstacle to RES-E integration. Therefore, this analysis takes China as an example in order to gain a better understanding.

7.2 An example of the previously regulated electricity sector in China

The electricity pricing mechanism in China was heavily regulated by public authorities before the market reform was initiated in the 1980s. There have been reform efforts to introduce competition on the generation side and gradually establish and fine-tune competitive wholesale power markets since 2002. Recent market reforms in 2015 followed the philosophy of 'liberalise the two ends, grasp the middle'. They aim at liberalising the generation and retail segments, which are potentially competitive, and regulate the networks segment. Despite these reform efforts, Chinese wholesale markets are not sufficiently well-established to accommodate high shares of RES-E in power systems. One of the critical hurdles is the wholesale market pricing mechanisms that are influenced by the regulated on-grid tariff approach that China adopted previously.

In the case of China, electricity market reforms are still not mature enough to provide desirable price signals to market players. China has been gradually liberalising the wholesale electricity market through provincial pilots and constantly making regulatory efforts to complete the electricity market architecture following the philosophy of 'a unified market, two-tier operation'. It refers to the goal of building up a national electricity market allowing for resource allocation in the whole country and, at the same time, operating power markets at both the intra-provincial and cross-provincial (and cross-regional) levels. Moreover, the electricity market architecture is designed on the basis of power trading at different time spans, including the primary forward power market and the spot market. The former plays a major role in arranging the medium-and-long-term contract-based electricity transactions; the latter is subject to experiment in selected provinces to gain experience and try out different market design models before establishing the nationwide wholesale electricity market.

Despite the regulatory efforts that China has made to complete its electricity market architecture, RES-E integration is still hindered by insufficient legal support for market mechanisms. This is evidenced by the high curtailment rate in the Northern, Western-North, and Eastern-North areas, where renewable energy resources are abundant but demand for electricity is relatively low due to limited development of the local economy. Although the curtailment problem has been alleviated in recent years, it does not mean that electricity market reforms in China will realise the transition toward a low-carbon power system in the future.

At the initial stage of the RES-E development, China adopted the feed-in tariff policy and the measures of guaranteed purchase of RES-E, representing an administrative approach to promoting renewable energy. This is suitable for the development level of renewable energy in China before the market mechanisms become effective. With the advancement of renewable energy technologies and the consequent cost reduction of RES-E generation, as well as the progress China made in establishing power markets, the feed-in tariffs have brought more problems than benefits, and the electricity price formation has been changed from fixed tariff regulation to market-based pricing. This requires legal support for the transition to deal with the electricity market liberalisation and the power system decarbonisation at the same time. The progress in market liberalisation in China is expected to facilitate RES-E integration: well-functioning power markets are conducive to RES-E fully exploiting its advantages of low marginal costs. However, the adoption of market pricing mechanisms in China encountered obstacles of historically regulated wholesale market prices that still prevent RES-E from being integrated into markets of a broader scope. This is especially clear from the slow rollout of spot market pilots, the stagnation in cancelling energy subsidies, and the problems with transmission and distribution network tariff reforms in China.

8 Conclusion

The wholesale electricity markets designed in liberalised markets or the regulation in partially reformed electricity sectors in different jurisdictions face diverse challenges of renewable energy integration in the energy transition towards a clean electricity system. Wholesale electricity pricing is at the core of understanding how market design and regulation, or regulatory instruments, interplay with the wholesale electricity markets. Along with the energy-only wholesale electricity markets, capacity remuneration mechanisms can be an option to facilitate renewable energy integration by increasing system flexibility. Carbon pricing mechanisms can deliver their desired effects of emissions reduction by internalising the externalities of power generation activities and sending additional price signals to wholesale market players. Cost pass-through is one of the critical issues that have to be carefully considered, given that carbon pricing mechanisms can trigger changes in wholesale electricity prices and the prices for end consumers. In the context of regulated power sectors, the lack of price signals hinders the delivery of desirable effects of renewable energy integration tools. Therefore, reforming wholesale electricity sectors and establishing well-designed power markets are crucial to RES-E integration in jurisdictions such as China.

References

ACER. 2013. *Capacity remuneration mechanisms and the internal market for electricity*. Available at: https://www.acer.europa.eu/Official_documents/Acts_of_the_Agency/Publication/CRMs%20and%20the%20IEM%20Report%20130730.pdf. [Accessed: 11 December 2022].

ACER/CEER, 2020. *Annual Reports on the results of monitoring the Internal Electricity and Natural Gas Markets In 2019 – Electricity wholesale markets volume*. Available at: https://documents.acer.europa.eu/Official_documents/Acts_of_the_Agency/Publication/ACER%20Market%20Monitoring%20Report%202019%20-%20Electricity%20Wholesale%20Markets%20Volume.pdf. [Accessed: 11 December 2022].

ACER/CEER, 2021. *Annual Reports on the results of monitoring the Internal Electricity and Natural Gas Markets in 2020 – Electricity wholesale markets volume*. Available at: https://documents.acer.europa.eu/en/Electricity/Market%20monitoring/Documents/MMR%202020%20Summary%20-%20Final.pdf [Accessed: 11 December 2022].

Acworth, W., de Oca, M.M., Boute, A. et al., 2020. Emissions trading in regulated electricity markets. *Climate Policy*, 20(1), pp. 60–70.

Acworth, W., Kuneman, E., La Hoz Theuer, S. et al., 2019. Influence of market structures and market regulation on the carbon market: interim report. German Emissions Trading Authority.

Barbose, G., Wiser, R., Heeter, J. et al., 2016. A retrospective analysis of benefits and impacts of U.S. renewable portfolio standards. *Energy Policy*, 96, pp. 645–660.

Batlle, C. and Pérez-Arriaga, I.J., 2008. Design criteria for implementing a capacity mechanism in deregulated electricity markets. *Utilities Policy*, 16(3), pp. 184–193.

Bradford, T. 2018. *The energy system: technology, economics, markets, and policy*. Cambridge, MA: The MIT Press.

Bublitz, A., Keles, D., Zimmermann, F. et al., 2019. A survey on electricity market design: Insights from theory and real-world implementations of capacity remuneration mechanisms. *Energy Economics*, 80, pp. 1059–1078.

Byers, C., Levin, T. and Botterud, A., 2018. Capacity market design and renewable energy: Performance incentives, qualifying capacity, and demand curves. *The Electricity Journal*, 31(1), pp. 65–74.

Cleveland, C.J. and Morris, C.G., 2005. *Dictionary of energy*. Amsterdam: Elsevier.

Coase, R.H., 1960. The problem of social cost. *The Journal of Law & Economics*, 3, pp. 1–44.

Cointe, B. and Nadaï, A., 2018. *Feed-in tariffs in the European Union: renewable energy policy, the internal electricity market and economic expertise*. Cham: Springer.

Cramton, P.C. and Stoft, S., 2006. The convergence of market designs for adequate generating capacity with special attention to the CAISO's resource adequacy problem. MIT-CEEPR Working Papers 2006–007.

Cramton, P., Ockenfels, A. and Stoft, S., 2013. Capacity market fundamentals. *Economics of Energy & Environmental Policy*, 2(2), pp. 27–46.

Cretì, A. and Fontini, F., 2019. *Economics of electricity: markets, competition and rules*. Cambridge: Cambridge University Press.

Dagoumas, A.S. and Polemis, M.L., 2020. Carbon pass-through in the electricity sector: an econometric analysis. *Energy Economics*, 86, 104621.

De Sisternes, F.J. and Parsons, J.E., 2016. The impact of uncertainty on the need and design of capacity remuneration mechanisms in low-carbon power systems. *MIT Center for Energy and Environmental Policy Research* (February).

Dong, C.G., 2012. Feed-in tariff vs. renewable portfolio standard: An empirical test of their relative effectiveness in promoting wind capacity development. *Energy Policy*, 42, pp. 476–485.

Du, Y. and Takeuchi, K., 2020. Does a small difference make a difference? Impact of feed-in tariff on renewable power generation in China. *Energy Economics*, 87, 104710.

European Commission, 2016. *Final Report on the Sector Inquiry on Capacity Mechanisms*. Available at: https://eur-lex.europa.eu/legal-content/EN/TXT/PDF/?uri=CELEX:52016SC0385&from=EN. [Accessed: 11 December 2022].

Fabra, N. and Reguant, M., 2014. Pass-through of emissions costs in electricity markets. *American Economic Review*, 104(9), pp. 2872–2899.

Fang, H. and Norman, P., 2006. To bundle or not to bundle. *The Rand Journal of Economics*, 37(4), pp. 946–963.

Foster, V. and Rana, A., 2019. *Rethinking power sector reform in the developing world.* World Bank Publications.

Harvey, S.M., Hogan, W.W. and Pope, S.L., 2013. *Evaluation of the New York capacity market.* FTI Consulting. Available at: http://lmpmarketdesign.com/papers/Final_New_York_Capacity_Report_03_13_2013.pdf. [Accessed: 11 December 2022].

Heeter, J., Speer, B. and Glick, M.B., 2019. International best practices for renewable portfolio standard (RPS) policies. National Renewable Energy Laboratory. Available at: https://www.nrel.gov/docs/fy19osti/72798.pdf. [Accessed: 11 December 2022].

Henriot, A. and Glachant, J.M., 2013. Melting-pots and salad bowls: the current debate on electricity market design for integration of intermittent RES. *Utilities Policy,* 27, pp. 57–64.

Holt, E.A. and Wiser, R.H., 2007. The treatment of renewable energy certificates, emissions allowances, and green power programs in state renewables portfolio standards. Lawrence Berkeley National Laboratory.

Huenteler, J.T., Hankinson, D.J., Rosenthal, N. et al., 2020. Cost recovery and financial viability of the power sector in developing countries: Insights from 15 case studies. *World Bank Policy Research Working Paper* (9136).

Hunt, S., 2002. *Making competition work in electricity*. New York: John Wiley & Sons.

IEA, RETD and TCP, 2016. *Electricity market design and RE deployment (RES-E-MARKETS).* Utrecht: IEA Renewable Energy Technology Deployment Technology Collaboration Programme.

Joskow, P.L., 2008. Capacity payments in imperfect electricity markets: need and design. *Utilities Policy,* 16(3), pp. 159–170.

Joskow, P. and Tirole, J., 2007. Reliability and competitive electricity markets. *The Rand Journal of Economics,* 38(1), pp. 60–84.

Kalkuhl, M., Edenhofer, O. and Lessmann, K. 2013. Renewable energy subsidies: second-best policy or fatal aberration for mitigation?. *Resource and Energy Economics,* 35(3), pp. 217–234.

Keppler, J.H., 2010. The interaction between the EU ETS and European electricity markets. In: A.D. Ellerman, F.J. Convery and C. de Perthuis, eds., 2010. *Pricing carbon: the European Union emissions trading scheme.* Cambridge: Cambridge University Press, pp. 293–328.

Kim, W., Chattopadhyay, D. and Park, J.B., 2010. Impact of carbon cost on wholesale electricity price: a note on price pass-through issues. *Energy, 35*(8), pp. 3441–3448.

Koch, N., Fuss, S., Grosjean, G. and Edenhofer, O., 2014. Causes of the EU ETS price drop: recession, CDM, renewable policies or a bit of everything? – new evidence. *Energy Policy,* 73, pp. 676–685.

Kozlova, M. and Overland, I., 2021. Combining capacity mechanisms and renewable energy support: A review of the international experience. *Renewable and Sustainable Energy Reviews*, p. 111878.

Léautier, T., 2019. *Imperfect markets and imperfect regulation: an introduction to the microeconomics and political economy of power markets.* Cambridge, MA: Mit Press.

Liao, S. 2020. Coping with the Renewable Portfolio Standards: A utility's perspective. *Operations Research Letters,* 48(4), pp. 393–396.

Lin, J. and Vatani, B., 2017. Impact of capacity market design on power system decarbonisation. *2017 14th International Conference on the European Energy Market (EEM)*IEEE.

Maryniak, P., Trück, S. and Weron, R., 2019. Carbon pricing and electricity markets – The case of the Australian Clean Energy Bill. *Energy Economics,* 79, pp. 45–58.

Metcalf, G.E., 2021. Carbon taxes in theory and practice. *Annual Review of Resource Economics, 13,* pp. 245–265.

Neuhoff, K. and Ritz, R., 2019. Carbon cost pass-through in industrial sectors. Energy Policy Research Group, University of Cambridge.

Newbery, D. 2016. Missing money and missing markets: Reliability, capacity auctions and interconnectors. *Energy Policy,* 94, pp. 401–410.

Nicolini, M. and Tavoni, M. 2017. Are renewable energy subsidies effective? Evidence from Europe. *Renewable and Sustainable Energy Reviews*, 74, pp. 412–423.

Onaiwu, E., 2009. How does bilateral trading differ from electricity pooling. *University of Dundee Report.*

Perico, G., Checchi, C. and Canazza, V., 2018. The Italian capacity market: an attractive design for market players?. *2018 15th International Conference on the European Energy Market (EEM)*IEEE.

Pigou, A.C., 1920. *The economics of welfare.* 4th ed. London: Macmillan.

Pugl-Pichler, C., Tyma, F., Süßenbacher, W. et al., 2020. Capacity remuneration mechanisms on European electricity markets – legal basis and actual implementation status. *The Journal of World Energy Law & Business,* 13(5–6), pp. 498–517.

Regulation 2019/943 of the European Parliament and of the Council – of 5 June 2019 – on the Internal Market for Electricity. [2019] OJ L158/54, 14.6.2019.

Rudnick, H. and Velasquez, C., 2018. Taking stock of wholesale power markets in developing countries: A literature review. *World Bank Policy Research Working Paper*, (8519).

Schuman, S. and Lin, A., 2012. China's Renewable Energy Law and its impact on renewable power in China: progress, challenges and recommendations for improving implementation. *Energy Policy,* 51, pp. 89–109.

Shang, N., Song, Y., Zhang, X. and Lin, Y., 2021. Capacity market mechanism design considering network optimisation and energy transition. *CSEE Journal of Power and Energy Systems,* Early Access, November 9.

Sijm, J., Chen, Y. and Hobbs, B.F., 2012. The impact of power market structure on CO_2 cost pass-through to electricity prices under quantity competition–A theoretical approach. *Energy Economics*, *34*(4), pp. 1143–1152.

Sioshansi, F.P. 2013, *Evolution of Global Electricity Markets: New paradigms, new challenges, new approaches.* Amsterdam: Academic Press.

Skovgaard, J. and Canavan, J., 2020. Carbon pricing: overlaps and formal collaboration. In: F. Zelli, K. Bäckstrand, N. Nasiritousi et al., eds., 2020. *Governing the climate-energy nexus: institutional complexity and its challenges to effectiveness and legitimacy*. Cambridge: Cambridge University Press, pp. 156–180.

Stoft, S., 2002. *Power system economics: designing markets for electricity*. New York, NY: IEEE press.

Teirilä, J. and Ritz, R.A., 2019. Strategic behaviour in a capacity market? The new Irish electricity market design. *The Energy Journal,* 40(1), pp. 105–126.

Wang, J. and Xu, W., 2016. Present situation and problems of large-scale wind power transmission and accommodation policy. In: N. Wang, C. Kang and D. Ren, eds., 2016. *Large-Scale Wind Power Grid Integration*. Amsterdam: Elsevier, pp. 257–276.

Weber, R.H., 2017. Emission trading schemes: a Coasean answer to climate change?. In: K. Mathis and B.R. Huber, eds., *Environmental law and economics*. Cham: Springer, pp. 355–377.

Wong, J.B. and Zhang, Q. 2022. Impact of carbon tax on electricity prices and behaviour. *Finance Research Letters,* 44, 102098.

Ye, B., Tang, J., Wang, D. and Lv, X., 2012. Pricing carbon allowance based on marginal abatement cost. *2012 2nd International Conference on Remote Sensing, Environment and Transportation Engineering*. IEEE.

Zhang, Y., Zhao, X., Zuo, Y. et al., 2017. The development of the renewable energy power industry under feed-in tariff and renewable portfolio standard: A case study of China's photovoltaic power industry. *Sustainability,* 9(4), 532.

Zuo, Y., Zhao, X., Zhang, Y. and Zhou, Y., 2019. From feed-in tariff to renewable portfolio standards: An evolutionary game theory perspective. *Journal of Cleaner Production*, 213, pp. 1274–1289.

Shaimerden Chikanayev

The Role of Natural Gas in the Energy Transition

Abstract: The chapter examines the role and prospects of natural gas as an energy source during the fourth energy transition, and also analyzes the conflict between the concepts of a "just energy transition" and "energy security", which have worsened due to the ongoing "gas war" between Europe and Russia. Attention is drawn to the importance of the role of natural gas as a "transitional fuel" and as a source of maneuverable energy in the development of renewable energy sources and the reduction of anthropogenic greenhouse gas emissions. Expected significant and at the same time different impact of the global energy crises caused by the war in Ukraine on the prospects of pipeline natural gas and liquified natural gas (LNG) in the energy balances of the countries of the European Union (EU) (one of the world's largest importers of natural gas) and the Eurasian Economic Union (EAEU) (one of the world's largest exporters of natural gas) is noted. In general, this chapter aims to analyze as a case study the contrasting legal pathways of the EU and EAEU to reform and design their gas markets and the effects of such reforms on the role of natural gas in the energy transition in the respective regions of the world, especially in the context of the global energy crisis of 2022 caused by the war in Ukraine. The author of this chapter also draws attention to the emerging trend of an increased role for the State and, accordingly, public law in regulation of gas markets in many countries of the world, in particular in regulating natural gas prices. For instance, as of September 2022 due to the unprecedented shortage of natural gas and rapid increase in gas prices, even the countries of the EU are now considering the introduction of an EU-wide gas price cap, which is obviously an obvious offset from the policy of liberalization of gas markets carried out in the EU so far, including the liberalization of gas prices.

1 Introduction

By February 2022, governments and experts in most countries of the world had already formed some understanding of how the energy transition would take place in their countries. Several important studies had been published on the role of natural gas in the energy transition (e.g. Olawuyi and Pereira (2022) and Cameron et al., 2020; IEA, 2019). Moreover, many countries of the world in their national energy strategies planned to use natural gas as a "transitional fuel", setting specific deadlines for its re-

Shaimerden Chikanayev is a PhD Student at the Faculty of Law, The Chinese University of Hong Kong.

https://doi.org/10.1515/9783110752403-016

placement with energy from renewable or alternative energy sources. However, in February 2022, the war unleashed by Russia in Ukraine turned everything upside down and led to a "the first truly global energy crisis in history" (IEA, 2022). In the "new reality", cardinal and urgent adjustments to the energy strategies and laws of many countries are obviously required, as well as a fundamental rethink of the role of natural gas in the global energy transition, including from the point of view of influencing the legal regulation of national and regional gas markets.

The urgent need to reevaluate the role of natural gas in the energy transition and ensuring energy security is especially urgent for the direct participants in the "gas war" unleashed by Russia: the European Union (EU) with its single gas market, which is the largest importer of Russian gas, on the one hand, and on the other hand Russia, which will have to solve the problem not only in an emergency mode redirection of gas flows from West to East, but also take into account the regulatory aspects of the common gas market to be created within the framework of the Eurasian Economic Union (EAEU), which is scheduled to be launched on 1 January 2025. The ongoing gas war between Europe and Russia will inevitably lead to tectonic changes in the global gas market, and it has already become obvious that ensuring energy security in the EU and the EAEU will take priority over managing the energy transition. At the same time, the next few years will see a real test of the strength of the "principle of energy solidarity" as a legally enforceable principle of EU law (Boute, 2020). It can be argued that there is a similar principle of solidarity in the law of the EAEU, since in accordance with Article 79 of the EAEU Treaty (2014), the EAEU member states have pledged to "conduct coordinated energy policy". Therefore, the axiom established in the academic literature that "energy transition is determined by technology and economics, but influenced by government policies" needs to be reformulated now that it has become clear that the energy transition also depends on geopolitics (Mu and Jena, 2020, p. 15). Geopolitics, namely the war in Ukraine, will have an even greater impact on the legal pathways of decarbonization and the role of the natural gas in the energy transition of the EU, as one of the biggest natural gas importers in the world and the EAEU, as one of the biggest gas exporters in the world.

2 Trends and evolution of the global natural gas market

Before Russia's invasion of Ukraine on February 24, 2022, it is fair to say that the development of the global natural gas market took place in a natural, evolutionary way. In particular, the following main trends in the global gas industry were noted in the literature:

1. Previously, natural gas was a purely local energy source, since its transportation, unlike oil, was possible only through pipelines and over fairly short distances.

Accordingly, there was no single global gas market, but only national and regional gas markets. Each region of the world had its own gas suppliers through pipelines, and natural gas prices differed significantly, since there was no competition among suppliers. For example, while in the past natural gas was much more expensive in East Asian markets than in European markets, a study of gas prices in 2020 found that they had nearly converged in Asia, Europe and the US (Aczel, 2022, p. 27). Today, an interconnected and global natural gas market has already appeared, and natural gas itself has become a global tradeable commodity, mainly due to advances in liquefied natural gas (LNG) technology (Olawuyi and Pereira, 2022, p. 1). The advantages of LNG over pipeline natural gas have been compared to those of a bus system over a tram system. Pipeline natural gas can only be sold to countries where the necessary rails (i.e. pipelines) have been laid, whereas LNG can be delivered anywhere in the world. For instance, floating LNG allows new and small markets to open. In the legal scholarship, LNG technology has been hailed as a "transportation revolution": LNG can be exported profitably by sea routes from North America to Asia or Europe, without the limitations and disadvantages of gas pipelines or reliance on regional suppliers (Aczel, 2022, p. 23).

2. Unlike other hydrocarbons (oil and coal), the level of production and consumption of natural gas has been constantly growing over the past three decades, partly because it has better green credential than does coal. At the same time, the main growth in gas production has taken place in the United States (US) due to the shale gas revolution, whereas the main growth in consumption has taken place in Asia (particularly China) and also in Africa.
3. LNG is a cyclical business, as there is a lag of around 5 years between the initial investment decision and the first gas deliveries. Therefore, each cycle of active investment in infrastructure for LNG production and an increase in LNG prices and, accordingly, an increase in LNG production lasts on average five years, followed by the next cycle caused by overproduction of LNG. This new cycle of low prices also lasts an average of five years and causes underinvestment in infrastructure for LNG production. The cycle usually ends when the demand for LNG exceeds the available market supply (Henderson, 2019).
4. There has been a decades-old "gas symbiosis" of mutually beneficial gas cooperation between the EU and Russia. The economies of European countries gained a competitive advantage due to cheap (compared to LNG) Russian pipeline gas, while in return Russia was able (a) to subsidize its population and industry through export earnings, providing them with gas at a price often below cost; (b) to buy technologies, including for the production of LNG; and (c) to actively gasify remote and sparsely populated areas of the country. This mutually beneficial gas symbiosis was so successful that as of 2021 nearly 45% of all imported gas to Europe came from Russia (IEA 10-Point Plan, 2022).

5. Gas pricing on exchanges (gas hubs), without reference to oil. However, even though global gas markets are becoming more interconnected, there is still no "global gas price" (IEA, 2019).

3 Prospects of natural gas as primary energy source and LNG as secondary energy source in the global energy mix

According to statistical studies conducted before Russia invaded Ukraine in February 2022, the prospects for natural gas were quite rosy. In particular, many researchers expected that the share of natural gas in primary energy demand would expand, and some even predicted that gas would become the second largest source of global energy by 2040 (Mu and Jena, 2020, p. 14). The Russian invasion has upended these calculations, and the outcome of the war remains difficult to assess. As military operations remain in flux, it has been difficult for researchers to assess both the medium-term impact of the Russian invasion on gas markets, and the longer-term impact of the unfolding energy crisis caused by the war in Ukraine and the "gas war" between Russia and the EU. In any case, for the forseeable future we should expect a higher degree of uncertainty regarding the prospects for natural gas, since natural gas as an energy source "is highly scenario dependent and consequently policy-driven" (Poudineh, 2022).

In the meantime, it can already be stated that the image of the "war enabler" acquired by pipeline natural gas as an energy resource in the eyes of the world community, and especially among Europeans, as well as Russia's use of natural gas for blackmail and influencing other states, has obviously "damaged the reputation of natural gas as a reliable and affordable energy source, casting uncertainty on its prospects, particularly in developing countries where it had been expected to play a growing role in meeting rising energy demand and energy transition goals" (IEA Gas Market Report Q3-2022, 2022).

At the same time, in the short and medium term, the role of natural gas will definitely grow all over the world, since it is not at present possible to replace natural gas with some other energy source. So, in all scenarios, both BP and McKinsey forecast that gas demand will grow, especially in Asia, underpinned by policies encouraging continued coal-to-gas switching, and will peak during the decade 2025–2035. However, the long-term prospects for natural gas, even without taking into account the impact of the war in Ukraine, are not so rosy, since, according to all forecasts, after this watershed period of 2025–2035 gas demand will likely be subject to larger uncertainties. The share of natural gas in primary energy demand is therefore expected to decline from current 23% to 15% by 2050 (McKinsey, 2022; BP, 2022).

At the same time, the prospects of pipeline gas as a primary energy source and LNG as a secondary energy source in the global energy mix in the medium and long term differ. Moreover, "the role of natural gas in the form of a LNG or a pipeline gas in the transition to low and/or zero-carbon energy systems is evolving and varies from region to region" (Pereira and Olawuyi, 2022, p. 25). Between 2020 and 2050, "natural gas traded as LNG is projected to decrease 60 per cent, and gas trade via pipeline is expected to fall by 65 per cent" (Sever, 2022, p. 109).

It is also reasonable to expect that natural gas will play a more prolonged role in emerging economies that are very carbon-intensive today, helping to push more polluting fuels out of the system (IEA, 2019). Indeed, many scholars believe that "natural gas will maintain a strong position as an important transition fuel, especially in energy-poor and developing countries" (Ladan et al., 2022, p. 587). For example, it is obvious that in the medium term, the EU will try to "get off" from Gazprom's "pipeline gas needle" at an accelerated pace, relying partly on LNG supplies from the United States, Qatar and elsewhere as substitute sources of supply. But the laws of supply and demand suggest that Gazprom will find other buyers for its unwanted gas, even if it has to sell at a lower price. China has already increased its pipeline gas supplies from Russia this year, most likely receiving a good discount from Gazprom, while reducing its imports of more expensive LNG (Robinson, 2022). The war in Ukraine should therefore result in a significant drop in imports from Russia of pipeline gas to Europe in the medium term, counterbalanced by a noticeable increase in imports of pipeline gas from Russia to China. Moreover, it should be expected that countries and regions with natural gas reserves, such as the EAEU (in particular Russia and Kazakhstan, as its main gas suppliers), will place more emphasis on domestic consumption of natural gas within the borders of the EAEU than on exports. Russia faces the challenges of increasing the competitiveness of its domestic industry, gasifying the country at the expense of cheap domestic gas, and "pivoting to Asia". It is now subject to substantial international sanctions, and faces the prospect of a complete embargo on oil and gas and, accordingly, the lack of windfall profits from gas exports to Europe. Overcoming these challenges will require the Russian economy and the Russian gas industry to be placed on a war footing.

It is obvious that due to the convenience of transportation and the absence of LNG, unlike pipeline natural gas, a "war enabler" plume and a "tool of geopolitics", natural gas supplies in the form of LNG will grow more actively in the world than gas supplies through pipelines. Accordingly, the prospects for LNG during the energy transition are definitely better than for pipeline gas. According to many researchers, therefore, "LNG will potentially be an important part of the energy transition as global energy demand grows" (Aczel, 2022, p. 33).

Interestingly, according to all forecasts, China's role as a demand-growth engine for natural gas is expected to be taken over by Southeast Asia after 2030 (McKinsey, 2022). Therefore, in the long term, Russia should count on demand for its gas not from China, but more from India, which means that it should think about building new gas pipelines not only to China, to diversify its risk, but also to India.

In general, it should be expected that the role of gas as a transitional fuel in developing countries, especially countries with own gas reserves, will increase and last for a longer period of time, since in the conditions of the impending economic crisis and the global food crisis, all countries will prioritize energy security over achieving carbon neutrality. In developed countries, on the contrary, the prospects for natural gas as a transitional fuel in the long term are worse, because the rich countries of the "Global North" will try their best to accelerate the energy transition to achieve the same goal of energy security (i.e. security of supply), namely to move away from dependence on gas supplies, which has proven to be too politicized as an energy source. For instance, in the wake of Russia's invasion of Ukraine, the European Commission officially announced that gas consumption in the EU would "reduce at a faster pace, limiting the role of gas as a transitional fuel" (CNBC, 2022).

4 The roles of natural gas in the global energy mix during the energy transition

As for the possible roles for the use of natural gas in the future, according to all forecasts, natural gas is still expected to play a key role throughout the energy transition with its wide range of applications. It is one of the few energy sources that can be used across all sectors of the global economy, and it emits between 45% and 55% lower greenhouse gas emissions than coal when used to generate electricity, according to IEA data.

For example, according to a BP study, "natural gas can potentially play two important roles as the world transitions to a low-carbon energy system: increasing the speed at which fast-growing emerging economies reduce their dependency on coal, and providing a source of low-carbon energy when combined with carbon capture, use and storage (CCUS)" (BP, 2022).

The prospects for natural gas demand by economic sector also differ. In academic literature, natural gas is usually identified as a "transition" or as "interim" or as a "bridge" fuel into the carbon neutral era for a number of reasons.

First, natural gas can play a role in "reducing emissions and improving air quality by replacing coal and diesel, in sectors which are difficult to decarbonize with renewables, such as industry, the built environment and transportation" (Sever, 2022, p. 101). Gas demand in buildings is expected to decline after 2025–2030, but long-term gas demand is likely to be supported by industry (for high temperature heat and chemicals), particularly in Asia (McKinsey, 2022).

Second, "natural gas is considered a reliable baseload resource required for a stable transmission network. A commonly raised disadvantage of renewable resources is that they are intermittent and dependent upon the availability of resources, subject to natural circumstances. Natural gas can quickly compensate for decreases in solar or wind power supplies and it can quickly respond to sudden increases in demand" (Sever, 2022, p. 102). That is why the crucial role of natural gas in the energy transition period is to support the integration of renewables into the power system so long as the intermittency issue remains a challenge for the renewable energy sources. That is why even after 2035–2040, when gas demand in power is set to slow down, natural gas is still expected to play the role of a back-up to renewables. For instance, the rapid development of renewable energy sources in the last five years in Kazakhstan has exposed the problem of the lack of a sufficient number of generating units with a manoeuvrable generation mode (i.e. hydroelectric power plants and gas turbine power plants). Accordingly, in the foreseeable future only a combination of natural gas and renewables can offer any country, including developed ones, a predictable, reliable, flexible and cost-effective pathway to a lower emissions energy system.

Finally, by all accounts natural gas will play a new role even after 2030 in blue hydrogen and ammonia production, and gas infrastructure will be repurposed for low-carbon fuels such as hydrogen and biogas, or CO_2 transportation for CCUS (McKinsey, 2022). Hydrogen can be produced from fossil sources, like natural gas (so-called blue hydrogen), as well as from renewable sources (so-called green hydrogen). Natural gas so far accounts for virtually all the hydrogen produced today. The scientific literature notes that although natural gas is a fossil fuel, studies have shown that it remains the cleanest, least polluting and most hydrogen rich of all hydrocarbon energy sources. In the long run, therefore, the key potential for natural gas is in "contributing to the production of blue hydrogen and the powering of green hydrogen plants" (Olawuyi and Pereira, 2022, p. 6). According to BP (2022), in addition to being cost competitive in many parts of the world, the production of blue hydrogen helps enable the expansion of low-carbon hydrogen without relying solely on renewable power. Evidently, hydrogen is viewed by Europe as a "key energy carrier for achieving its ambitions" (Fleming, 2022, p. 126).

5 Just energy transition strategy

It has already become an axiom in the legal literature that "energy transition is determined by technology and economics, but influenced by government policies" (Mu and Jena, 2020, p. 15). Geopolitics influences government policies in the field of energy, so today one of the most burning questions is how the war in Ukraine will affect the global gas market and energy policies and laws around the world, in particular in terms of the impact on the process of energy transition. For instance, Russian officials claim that as of the end of summer 2022, the EU's gas market continues to shrink, while the consumption of coal and fuel oil in Europe is growing. If so, this calls into question the achievement of the EU's climate goals. In particular, Russian officials continue to insist that current energy crisis in Europe is caused by the unreasonable energy policy of "accelerated decarbonization" and liberalisation of energy markets pursued by the EU, which has led to a decrease in global gas demand (global gas demand in the first eight months of 2022 decreased by 40 billion m3) and to a sharp and uncontrolled increase in natural gas prices, which Gazprom estimates could reach $4,000/1,000 m3 in the coming winter (Neftegaz.RU, 2022).

The legal literature has traditionally advocated international cooperation to address the so-called "energy trilemma" of sustainability, security of supply and affordability, which affects both the developed and the developing world (Cameron et al., 2020, p. 2). Emergence of international law of energy as a new integral part of public international law that "formalizes the transition to a global energy system that provides sustainable and affordable energy for all" has been declared (Roeben and Mete, 2020, p. 99). Some legal scholars have even suggested introducing the notion of a "global energy transition" and have called for the urgent introduction of a "global energy law" by internationalizing existing national energy laws. Their justification is that "only binding international law provides states with the certainty that investment in transition will be matched by those of other states" (Cameron et al., 2020, p. 330).

However, the Russian invasion of Ukraine has dashed the hopes of many legal scholars for international cooperation in developing a global strategy for energy transition and a "global energy 2.0" as a novel general order for energy (Cameron et al., 2020, p. 329). On the contrary, we should expect an increase of energy nationalism in diverse forms as many gas-endowment states rightfully view their gas resources as a ticket to accelerated economic growth. For example, Russia is already developing a new energy strategy with a planning period until 2050, since the current version, although adopted in June 2020, is no longer relevant because it does not take into account global challenges and transformations in energy markets caused by its invasion of Ukraine. In particular, natural gas is likely to play a much larger role in Russia's new energy strategy than it used to do. Kazakhstan, another gas-endowment country within the EAEU, has also set new priorities in its energy policy. Its Comprehensive Development Plan of the Gas Industry with a planning period until 2026, adopted in July 2022, enunciates a key role for natural gas in Kazakhstan's future energy balance and national economy. Previously, the gas industry in Kazakhstan was largely neglected.

At the same time, it is worth considering that the regionalization of economies is actively taking place in the world, including in the form of integrations of national gas markets. In particular, within the framework of the EAEU, the EAEU law has emerged as a new regional legal system and a common gas market is being created, and the EAEU member states have pledged to pursue a coordinated energy policy (Chikanayev, 2021). Accordingly, since Russia uses its weight to determine the development of the EAEU, and the other EAEU member states welcome the prospect of gaining a competitive advantage due to cheap Russian gas, we should expect an increase in the role of natural gas in the energy balance of all EAEU countries. As EAEU law as a new regional law prevails over the domestic laws of individual EAEU member-countries, consent to obey common rules under the EAEU law by its member states is another example of states conceding powers over their national energy economies – i.e., a very rare exception from the predominant energy nationalism of the states. The only similar example internationally in the gas sector is, of course, the single gas market of the EU, based on the consent to common rules in an energy chapter of the European Union Treaty. Accordingly, although it is unlikely that an international community of states will emerge to make collective decisions on the energy transition in the coming decades, it is still worth paying attention to what state policies and legislative innovations at the regional level, for instance in the EU and the EAEU, will be carried out in the context of the role of natural gas in the energy transition.

Energy strategies of any country regarding the role of natural gas in the energy transition should take into account and be based on the prospects of natural gas in this particular country or region in the medium and long term, as mentioned in section 2 of this chapter. Depending on the prospects natural gas has in this particular country or region, each state needs to decide the speed and intensity of the natural gas phase-out and energy transition, set out clear objectives that mark the desired state of the energy system of the future within specific timeframes, and then determine the political, legal and economic actions needed to achieve them (Cameron et al., 2020).

At the same time, it is important that within the framework of the new energy strategies and gas policies currently being hastily developed, due to the unexpected war in Ukraine, both at the EU and EAEU regional levels and at the national level, there should be no excessive complacency regarding natural gas as a relatively clean energy source, and *vice versa*, excessive haste with the transition to renewable energy sources.

For gas-rich countries, the energy transition poses a special economic threat if the governments of these countries will not adequately plan for a future in which there is increased use of renewable energy and other low-carbon technologies. The risk is that, if the energy transition is slower than expected, a country may lose from divesting too early. On the other hand, if the global energy transition takes place much faster than expected, then a country that deliberately delays phasing out its natural gas will face a situation where all investments in the gas industry have depreciated, and natural gas itself as a commodity is not needed by anyone or is needed for much less money. For instance, there can be the conundrum of the so-called "stranded resources/assets", that are, for instance, fossil fuels yet to be explored and left in the ground or the gas pipeline infrastructure that has lost its economic value "as a direct result of an unforeseeable regulatory or legislative change specific to the industry in question" (Tscherning, 2022, p. 454). An ill-considered energy transition can also lead to the so-called "carbon lock-in" issue, that is "continued investment in carbon-intensive fossil fuel use due to the need to recoup the massive capital investment in the pipeline" (Aczel, 2022, p. 26). A lot has been written in the academic literature about other risks, in particular the risk that the investments allocated to natural gas can create a "crowd-out" effect, when the bridging technology taps financial resources of emerging renewable technologies and therefore delays lower carbon options. Moreover, "investments in natural gas, which are required for today's supply security, can hinder mid-term and long-term sustainability and climate targets by locking-in the energy systems into fossil fuels instead of low-carbon options" (Sever, 2022, p. 105).

In general, there is already a generally accepted understanding among experts that under decarbonization, the role assigned to the natural gas in the energy mix will ideally last for a couple of more decades until 2050, meaning that it may be the last window of opportunity for gas-rich states to exploit their reserves and revenues from gas (Sever, 2022, p. 111). The energy transition factor, therefore, has an important impact on future investment flows: it creates a perception that gas assets, unlike renewable energy facilities, will become riskier, since a long-term project of around twenty-five years encounters scenarios of peaking markets for the natural gas as a commodity (Cameron, 2021, p. 11). Modern legal scholarship has also demonstrated that for the natural gas, as a bridge fuel, "the speed of the transition comes down to the aggregate investment and resource allocation decisions of individual states, and most importantly in the developing world" (Cameron et al., 2020, p. 328).

Therefore, the main problem when working on a new energy strategy for states with rich natural gas deposits is to correctly determine the time and manner of their exit from gas assets, as well as the moment when it is necessary to reorient the flow of investments from hydrocarbons to renewable energy sources and related technologies. Indeed, as Olawuyi noted, "maximizing the full value of natural gas in resource-rich countries can contribute to a just global energy transition and green growth" (Olawuyi, 2022, p. 75). In the legal scholarship, four key strategies for energy transition by a government of a gas-rich state have so far been considered. The easiest one is known as "beating the climate clock", namely the acceleration of extraction and selling of gas reserves before the possible terminal decline in gas prices. At the same time, it is noted that this strategy, although the easiest to adopt and execute, in practice can lead to the so-called "green paradox", a situation in which gas-rich countries and gas companies in anticipation of a climate policy (such as carbon tax) or dramatic shifts towards more competitive renewable technology or rapid decline in gas prices on a global level, accelerate the production and sale of natural gas in a "race to the bottom" (Manley et al., 2020, p. 37). The paradox under this scenario is that the anticipation of a climate policy increases near-term carbon emissions. There is also a risk that accelerated production of gas is not transformed into lasting benefits for the country in terms of human and physical assets above ground (this process of transformation of the subsoil asset into above ground productive assets in the economic literature is called the Hartwick Rule) (Manley et al., 2020, p. 34).

Therefore, a gas-rich country should choose a strategy that will help with transformation of its gas assets into above ground productive assets and with divesting from gas and benefit from gas extraction in the most efficient and sustainable manner (Manley et al., 2020, p. 46). In most cases, it will be necessary to move first from coal to natural gas to reduce emissions from coal and provide the population and industry with the energy they need in the most cost-effective way, as many developing countries in the world have not completed even the transition from coal to natural gas, i.e., the so-called "third energy transition". That is why an important point underlined in the academic literature is that developing countries should be allowed to continue to exploit and develop their fossil fuel resources, which can then be used as a springboard towards transitioning to low-carbon economies. Some scholars describe this process as "energy progression" (as opposed to "energy transition") (Ladan et al., 2022, p. 586).

But even for most developed counties the "transition role assigns a two-step path for natural gas: a temporarily increased share in energy portfolios to replace dirtier fossil fuels and ensure baseload supplies, followed by a decreasing share so as to leave the floor to zero-carbon technologies" (Sever, 2022, p. 103). It is generally accepted that it is not fair for developed countries, especially those that have their own natural gas reserves, to insist that developing countries should switch from natural gas to renewable energy sources at an accelerated pace and bear the burden of energy transition on a par with developed countries, which in many cases developed partly because they previously colonized and exploited the subsoil of these developing countries. Therefore, it is important to avoid undue optimism when discussing national energy transition strategies, and the possible emergence of a more global energy transition strategy, as "it will be difficult to achieve a just and equitable global energy transition without reconciling the divergent narratives on the role of natural gas in promoting a just and equitable transition" (Olawuyi, 2022, p. 75). At the same time, the energy crisis of 2022, which has had a particularly strong impact on Europe, shows that the concept of a "just energy transition" should take into account not only the interests of developing countries, but also the interests of the poor in developed countries, because "a just energy transition is one that delivers a transition to lower carbon energy sources while also stimulating economic development, social inclusion, and respect for human rights, including the right to decent employment, health, and education, amongst others" (Olawuyi, 2022, p. 82). As mentioned above, Russian officials, including President Putin, explicitly blame the energy policy of the EU, including liberalisation of the energy markets, for the European energy crisis of 2021–2022, as in their opinion the EU too hastily neglected the importance of conventional energy sources and relied too heavily on renewable and alternative energy sources. There is obviously some truth in Putin's words in this case, since it has long been noted by researchers that "a focus on climate change objectives alone, without examining the overall implications of decarbonization policies on energy security, may result in increased energy poverty, stunted economic development, and human rights violations, especially economic, social, and cultural rights" (Olawuyi, 2022, p. 76).

As mentioned above, Russia's invasion of Ukraine has upset the global gas market, and Europe and Russia have been forced to frantically develop new energy strategies. The rupture of the "gas symbiosis" has been damaging both to Russia and to Europe, both from a economic point of view and from the point of view of disrupting their plans to achieve carbon neutrality in a rational manner. Moreover, the global energy crisis is spurring new investments in natural gas, including new LNG infrastructure, even in a world working towards net zero emissions by 2050. However, as the IEA stated, no one should imagine that Russia's invasion of Ukraine can justify a wave of new large-scale fossil fuel infrastructure in a world that wants to limit global warming to 1.5 C (IEA, 2022). The problem is that all measures the EC has taken so far involve the substitution of Russian gas with gas from other sources. This is evident from the EU's recent proposal to assign natural gas a 'green label' in the EU taxonomy (Regulation (EU) 2020/852), that will translate into streamlined investment into further gas infrastructure in Europe that creates a lock-in effect.

The world needs, therefore, international cooperation and a global energy transition strategy that will foster local laws and policies that promote a just and equitable energy transition for all through inclusive planning. As Olawuyi suggested, there is "the need for increased bilateral and multilateral cooperation by natural gas markets to coordinate a coherent agenda that maximizes the full value of natural gas in the energy transition. Several of the just transition challenges facing the natural gas industry and the energy sector as a whole, ranging from demand side management, efficiency in supply and consumption, energy pricing, mitigation of environmental impacts, climate change, business and human rights impacts, and addressing the resource curse concern, among others, are interconnected and cannot be addressed in isolation" (Olawuyi, 2022, p. 89). Given that multilateral cooperation and global energy transition strategy in a near future is unlikely, it is yet to be seen if at least cooperation for promotion of a just and equitable energy transition at regional level is possible. From this point of view, the EU's single gas market and the EAEU's common gas market are the best-case studies to analyze.

6 Legal pathways for natural gas markets reforms in advancing the energy transition

As mentioned above, international cooperation for the purposes of a coordinated energy transition has had some success at the regional level, within the framework of supranational organizations such as the EU and the EAEU. At the same time, it is not for nothing that these two organizations and their member countries have chosen different designs and approaches to regulating their supranational gas markets, as well as different approaches to reforming their national gas markets, which undoubtedly affects the role of natural gas in the energy transition in the respective regions of the world, that is, different so-called "legal pathways" (Bellantuono, 2019, p. 3). Moreover, the differences in their approaches to reforming their gas markets will now grow, since "in response to the war in Ukraine, diversification of supplies away from Russia is now a priority, increasing the importance of geopolitics in the EU gas market architecture" (Boute, 2022, p. 19).

There is a clear difference from both the legal and the economic perspectives between the concepts of a "common gas market" and a "single gas market", as they suggest different degrees of integration of domestic gas markets. In the EAEU's common gas market, unlike the EU's single gas market, domestic gas markets are preserved with a full-fledged national state regulation, as well as individual barriers to access to the national markets.

The EU's single gas market was created on the basis of the Anglo-Saxon liberalization and privatization "textbook", while the future design of the EAEU's common gas market is largely based on the architecture of the Russian domestic gas market. The Russian gas market in its turn continues to be organized on the basis of central command and control, and quasi-monopolistic principles, with Gazprom as a state-owned and vertically integrated gas company dominating gas production, supply and transportation through its direct and indirect subsidiaries.

For now, Russian domestic gas market consists of regulated and unregulated segments: Gazprom and so-called independent gas producers. Importantly, the current Russian Energy Strategy effective until 2035provides for a step-by-step transition from the regulation of wholesale gas prices of Gazprom to market pricing mechanisms. Gazprom sells gas on the Russian domestic market at regulated prices that remained below the economically viable level, thereby supporting the domestic economy (Katja Yafimava, 2015). QazaqGas plays the same strategic role for the national economy of Kazakhstan. In other words, cheap/cross-subsidised natural gas nowadays is used by governments of Russia and Kazakhstan as well as many other gas-exporting countries as an equivalent to the "bread and circuses" of ancient Rome: a palliative offered specifically to avert potential discontent. Unlike Kazakhstan, however, Russia is also able and willing to use natural gas as a geopolitical weapon.

EAEU's gas market target model also expects that all EAEU member countries would switch at some point in the future from the regulation of wholesale gas prices to the regulation of gas transport tariffs. Interestingly, the EAEU Treaty does not clearly provide a gas price setting model for the future common gas market, but only states the desire of the EAEU member states to achieve equal netback pricing on the territory of the EAEU. The concept of export netback-parity was, evidently, transplanted into the EAEU Treaty from Russian law and as in Russia the transition to export netback parity levels has been postponed repeatedly, it comes as no surprise that the EAEU Treaty does not formulate the principle of export netback parity in a binding way (Boute, 2022, p. 11).

Because of the war in Ukraine and the imminent gas embargo by the EC, Russia should not expect its exports of gas to make the same high profits as they did in previous years. This means that Gazprom will soon find it difficult to bear its social burden of cross-subsidization of local population and domestic industry. It is reasonable to expect, therefore, a revival of heated discussions among relevant stakeholders on the long-expected reforms of the Russian domestic gas market. Among the possible scenarios of gas market reforms is a radical proposal of full liberalization of the national gas market, including deregulation of wholesale gas prices. It is not surprising, therefore, that the most controversial issue for the proposed reforms of the domestic gas market in Russia remains deregulation of wholesale gas prices and the tariff for gas transportation services. The problem is, however, that there is a legitimate concern among different stakeholders in Russia that any drastic and poorly thought-through measures with liberalization of gas prices may jeopardize the nation's plans for the development of local industries and the expansion of its gas networks and gasification of remote areas of the country and may lead to uncontrolled growth of gas tariffs and even social riots.

According to international best practice, in some cases the main objective of the reform of a gas market (i.e. including as part of the creation of an interstate gas market) is to increase the efficiency of the industry and reduce gas prices due to increased competition (e.g. liberalization and creation of the EU's single gas market is a good example) (Mitrova et al., 2018, p. 5). In other cases, especially those of gas market reforms in gas-producing countries or economic unions that have gas-producing countries as member states, the main objective of gas market reform is a reduction of cross-subsidization and improvement of the efficiency of public administration management (i.e. due to the fact that in gas-producing countries gas prices normally are already extremely low, there is no point in gas exporting countries seeking to reduce gas prices for consumers). The objectives of the EAEU's proposed common gas market and the reforms of domestic gas markets required to realize this common market, however, are not yet clear. Moreover, because of the war in Ukraine and depleting gas export revenues, Russia is clearly not ready to countenance the equal treatment of all consumers in the EAEU's common gas market, irrespective of their country of origin, because this would require it first to abandon its current practice of cross-subsidizing its own local industry and population and to establish fair competition in the respective domestic gas markets of the countries of the EAEU. According to Boute, "the opening of gas markets to competition implies the deregulation of prices, and is thus opposed to the use of gas exports as geopolitical instrument" and "the 2021–2022 energy crisis, exacerbated by the war in Ukraine, undermines the political attractiveness of price deregulation, with increasing social and economic pressure on governments to intervene with prices" (Boute, 2022, p. 13).

As discussed in section 5 above, the government of a gas-rich state must choose its strategy for the energy transition carefully. In accordance with international best practice, one of the possible steps a government of a gas-rich country may take to increase social value from the natural gas extracted is to reduce subsidies on the consumption of gas by its own industries and population. Eliminating these subsidies not only releases more gas for export that secures more income for the state budget, but also helps with the energy transition, as a relatively cheap supply of natural gas makes the economies of gas-rich countries more carbon intensive and limits the competitiveness of renewable energy in these countries (Manley, D., Heller, P., & Cust, J., 2020, p. 39). It seems that the most profound effect of the war in Ukraine will be on the Russian gas market, as it will force Russia to curtail all its plans to liberalise its domestic gas market. This, in turn, means that the common gas market of the EAEU will also not be as liberal as originally envisaged. This, again, will slow down the process of the liberalization of gas markets, including the deregulation of wholesale gas prices, in all the EAEU countries for a long time and, most importantly, will slow down the process of their energy transition, since Russia will have to preserve its cross-subsidization mechanism in the coming decades for both political and economic reasons. Evidently, Russia will use its competitive advantage, viz. large reserves of relatively cheap natural gas, for as long as possible. At the same time, it is already clear that the political leadership of Russia has lost some of its former enthusiasm for renewable energy sources. Interestingly, while in Russia the role of the state in the economy, including the gas sector, will increase in the foreseeable future and reforms of its domestic gas market will be postponed indefinitely, in Kazakhstan, on the contrary, we should expect to see an acceleration of long-overdue reforms and a gradual liberalization of the local gas market. The newly adopted Comprehensive Development Plan of the Gas Industry of Kazakhstan for 2022–2026, in particular, sets as the long-term goal the creation of a competitive domestic gas market featuring the gradual deregulation of the gas market and the development of gas exchange trading.

Although the EAEU, including Kazakhstan, may push ahead with gas market reforms regardless of what happens in Russia, the role of the state is tending to increase globally, and with it state intervention in regulating gas markets in many countries of the world, particularly natural gas prices. For instance, due to the unprecedented and rapid increase in natural gas prices in 2022, even the countries of the EU are now considering the introduction of the EU-wide gas price cap, which flies in the face of the policy of the liberalisation of gas markets carried out in the EU so far, including the liberalisation of gas prices. The reason why the EU is considering the introduction of gas price regulation is because its priorities have changes. In response to the Russian invasion of Ukraine, it presently seeks not to increase private interest and private initiative in the gas sector, but to use public law to bolster social stability. As the noted Russian legal scholar Porkovsky observed more than a century ago, preference can sometimes reasonably be given to the "social value" of public law over the "social value" of private law (Pokrovsky, 1998, p. 47).

7 Conclusion

The energy transition has had a significant impact on the energy policies of nearly all countries, since in the light of this transition, investments in hydrocarbons, in particular in natural gas production, unlike investments in renewable energy, now seem to be risky investments. The challenges of the fourth energy transition have also had an impact on international investment law. In particular, work is underway to “modernize” the Energy Charter (this is discussed in greater detail in Chapter 6 of this Handbook), which in its current version prevents states from pursuing state policies aimed at transitioning to a low-carbon economy.

The main challenge for the further use of natural gas during the energy transition is the development of technologies that will make natural gas less “dirty”, since “the contribution of the natural gas industry to global energy transition will therefore depend to a great extent on the availability and accessibility of state of the art technologies and infrastructure that can reduce methane leakage, as well as other social and environmental impacts that erode the overall efficiency of natural gas as a transition fuel” (Olawuyi and Pereira, 2022, p. 6).

At the same time, we should remember that the “quest for global energy transition must be balanced with the search for energy security in some of the world’s energy poorest countries with abundant natural gas resources” (Olawuyi and Pereira, 2022, p. 14). Therefore, nearly everybody agrees that the goal is to achieve a low-carbon economy, the ways to achieve this goal, officially enshrined in the Paris Climate Agreement, adopted in 2015, as well as the 2015 UN Sustainable Development Goals, will inevitably be different for different countries and regions. Also, the strategies for such an energy transition currently require significant revision, taking into account the likely consequences of the war in Ukraine.

At the same time, due to the war in Ukraine and the much-touted “clash of civilizations” between West and East, it would be naïve to expect global international strategic cooperation and the development of a unified strategy for the energy transition, as well as the emergence of international energy law, which would give the force of law to the obligations assumed by states. On the contrary, we should expect even greater energy nationalism and regional differences in transition strategies, as well as an increasing role for public law in the regulation of the gas sector. At the same time, international cooperation on energy transition will be actively carried out at the regional level, within the framework of single or common energy markets of associations such as the EU and the EAEU. That is, instead of one global gas market, there will be several regional gas markets, possibly split between the West and the East. As time goes on, Russian pipeline gas will cease to be supplied to Europe. Instead, it will flow mainly to China and the EAEU countries. The “gas symbiosis” previously enjoyed by Europe and Russia will reappear in some form between China and Russia. This will give China a much-needed competitive advantage as it struggles to out-compete the US: cheap gas. In short, while the energy transition will still be determined in large part by technology, economics and government policies, it will also be increasingly influenced by geopolitics. The result is likely to be a transition that is less rational than it might have been, and for this the blame lies squarely with the gross violations of the rules-based international order mainly by Russia, but other great powers must take their share of the blame as well.

References

Aczel, M.R., 2022. Technological revolution in natural gas developments and LNG: policy advancements and their implications for national and international markets. In: D.S. Olawuyi and E.G. Pereira, eds., 2022. *The Palgrave handbook of natural gas and global energy transitions*. Cham: Palgrave Macmillan, pp. 21–72.

Bellantuono, G., 2019. Legal pathways of decarbonisation in the EU: the case of coal phase-out (June 29, 2019). *Oil, Gas and Energy Law Intelligence*, 17(3). Available at SSRN: https://ssrn.com/abstract=3411986. (Accessed: 1 September 2022).

Boute, A., 2022. Shaping the Eurasian gas market: the geopolitics of energy market regulation. *Geopolitics*, Online 5.7.2022.

Boute, A., 2020. The principle of solidarity and the geopolitics of energy: *Poland v. Commission* (OPAL Pipeline). *Common Market Law Review*, 57(3), pp. 889–914.

BP, 2022. *Energy Outlook*. Available at https://www.bp.com/content/dam/bp/business-sites/en/global/corporate/pdfs/energy-economics/energy-outlook/bp-energy-outlook-2022.pdf. (Accessed: 1 September 2022).

Cameron, P., 2021. *International energy investment law: the pursuit of stability*. 2nd ed. Oxford: Oxford University Press.

Cameron, P.D., Mu, X., and Roeben, V., 2020. The concept of global energy transition and its agenda. In: P.D. Cameron, X. Mu & V. Roeben, eds., 2020. *The global energy transition: law, policy and economics for energy in the 21st century*. Oxford: Hart Publishing, pp. 327–336.

Chikanayev, Sh., 2021. Gas market reform in Kazakhstan: problems, prospects and legal aspects. *Oil, Gas & Law Journal*. [e-journal] #1. pp. 44–54. Available through: https://gratanet.com/laravel-filemanager/files/3/ngp1-2021(with_cover)%20(2).pdf (Accessed: 1 September 2022).

CNBC, 2022. Europe admits it'll have to burn more coal as it tries to wean itself off Russian energy. Available at: https://www.cnbc.com/2022/05/20/eu-plans-renewables-expansion-says-coal-needed-a-little-while-longer.html (Accessed: 1 September 2022).

Daniel, P., Krupnick, A., Matheson, T. et al., 2020. How should shale gas extraction be taxed? In: P.D. Cameron, X. Mu & V. Roeben, eds., 2020. *The global energy transition: law, policy and economics for energy in the 21st century*. Oxford: Hart Publishing, pp. 273–310.

Fleming, R., 2022. The hydrogen revolution and natural gas: a new dawn in the European Union? In: D.S. Olawuyi and E.G. Pereira, eds., 2022. *The Palgrave handbook of natural gas and global energy transitions*. Cham: Palgrave Macmillan, pp. 123–140.

Henderson. J., 2019. *Lecture on global gas industry: new technologies and new market trends*. Presented at SKOLKOVO Summer Energy School. Available at: https://www.youtube.com/watch?v=xrxN0avNmJQ&list=PLt3UHIQuQ6NalFszLjLCSRt79zkXh3_vS&index=3&t=1856s (Accessed: 1 September 2022).

Huhta, K., 2022. The contribution of energy law to the energy transition and energy research, *Global Environmental Change*, 73, 102454.

IEA, 2019. *The role of gas in today's energy transitions*. Paris: IEA. Available at: https://www.iea.org/reports/the-role-of-gas-in-todays-energy-transitions (Accessed: 1 September 2022).

IEA, 2022. *A 10-point plan to reduce the European Union's reliance on Russian natural gas*. Paris: IEA. Available at: https://www.iea.org/reports/a-10-point-plan-to-reduce-the-european-unions-reliance-on-russian-natural-gas (Accessed: 1 September 2022).

IEA, 2022. *Coordinated actions across Europe are essential to prevent a major gas crunch: here are 5 immediate measures*. Available at: https://www.iea.org/commentaries/coordinated-actions-across-europe-are-essential-to-prevent-a-major-gas-crunch-here-are-5-immediate-measures (Accessed: 1 September 2022).

IEA, 2022. *Gas Market Report, Q3-2022*. Paris: IEA. https://www.iea.org/reports/gas-market-report-q3-2022 (Accessed: 1 September 2022).

Kremlin, 2022. *Vladimir Putin answered journalists' questions*. Available at: http://kremlin.ru/events/president/news/69036 (Accessed: 1 September 2022). (In Russian).

Ladan, M.T., Okukpon, I. and Maduekwe, N.C., 2022. Energy transitions and the future of natural gas law, policy, and research. In: D.S. Olawuyi and E.G. Pereira, eds., 2022. *The Palgrave handbook of natural gas and global energy transitions*. Cham: Palgrave Macmillan, pp. 567–594.

Manley, D., Heller, P. and Cust, J., 2020. Oil-rich countries' responses to energy transition: managing the decline. In: P.D. Cameron, X. Mu & V. Roeben, eds., 2020. *The global energy transition: law, policy and economics for energy in the 21st century*. Oxford: Hart Publishing, pp. 25–48.

McKinsey, 2022. *Energy Insights Global Energy Perspective*. Available at: https://www.mckinsey.com/~/media/McKinsey/Industries/Oil%20and%20Gas/Our%20Insights/Global%20Energy%20Perspective%202022/Global-Energy-Perspective-2022-Executive-Summary.pdf (Accessed: 1 September 2022).

Mitrova, T., Sergeeva, Z., Henderson, J. and Le Fevre, C., 2018. Foreign experience of deregulation and reforms of gas markets in the United Kingdom and EU: lessons learned for Russia. Moscow School of Management Skolkovo: The Oxford Institute of Energy Studies. Available at: https://energy.skolkovo.ru/downloads/documents/SEneC/Research/SKOLKOVO_EneC_Research_2018.12.01_Rus.pdf. (Accessed: 1 September 2022).

Mu, X. and Jena, D.K., 2020. Comparison of outlooks and implications for an energy transition. In: P.D. Cameron, X. Mu & V. Roeben, eds., 2020. *The global energy transition: law, policy and economics for energy in the 21st century*. Oxford: Hart Publishing, pp. 11–24.

Nalule, V.R. and Babajide, N.A., 2022. Protecting natural gas investments: trends in Investment Treaties and investors protections in Africa. In: D.S. Olawuyi and E.G. Pereira, eds., 2022. *The Palgrave handbook of natural gas and global energy transitions*. Cham: Palgrave Macmillan, pp. 461–481.

Neftegaz.RU, 2022. *A. Miller: The EU is reducing gas demand, but Gazprom's revenue for 2022 will be significantly higher than in 2021.* [online] Available at: https://neftegaz.ru/news/companies/749163-a-miller-es-sokrashchaet-spros-na-gaz-no-vyruchka-gazproma-za-2022-g-budet-sushchestvenno-vyshe-chem/ (Accessed: 1 September 2022). (In Russian).

Olawuyi, D.S., 2022. The role of natural gas in a just and equitable energy transition. In: D.S. Olawuyi and E.G. Pereira, eds., 2022. *The Palgrave handbook of natural gas and global energy transitions*. Cham: Palgrave Macmillan, pp. 73–95.

Olawuyi, D.S. and Pereira, E.G., 2022. Introduction: nature and scope of the international gas market. In: D.S. Olawuyi and E.G. Pereira, eds., 2022. *The Palgrave handbook of natural gas and global energy transitions*. Cham: Palgrave Macmillan, pp. 3–20.

Pereira, E.G. and Olawuyi, D.S., 2022. The future of natural gas: synthesis and summary for policy makers. In: D.S. Olawuyi and E.G. Pereira, eds., 2022. *The Palgrave handbook of natural gas and global energy transitions*. Cham: Palgrave Macmillan, pp. 595–610

Pokrovsky I.A., 1998. *Main problems of Civil Law*. Moscow. Statut. (In Russian).

Poudineh, R., 2022. Energy networks in the energy transition era. OIES Paper EL 48, May.

Robinson, T., 2022. Gazprom natural gas production drops sharply as Russia squeezes European supplies. Available at: https://www.naturalgasintel.com/gazprom-natural-gas-production-drops-sharply-as-russia-squeezes-european-supplies/ (Accessed: 1 September 2022).

Roeben, V. and Mete, G., 2020. What do we mean when we talk about international energy law? In: P.D. Cameron, X. Mu & V. Roeben, eds., 2020. *The global energy transition: law, policy and economics for energy in the 21st century*. Oxford: Hart Publishing, pp. 73–100.

Sever, S.D., 2022. Natural gas and energy security In: D.S. Olawuyi and E.G. Pereira, eds., 2022. *The Palgrave handbook of natural gas and global energy transitions*. Cham: Palgrave Macmillan, pp. 97–120.

Yafimava, K., 2015. Evolution of gas pipeline regulation in Russia: third party access, capacity allocation and transportation tariffs. Oxford Institute for Energy Studies, OIES paper NG 95, March.

Acknowledgement

The research underlying this chapter benefited from financial support from the Research Grants Council of Hong Kong (General Research Fund Grant No. CUHK14608118) and author greatly benefited from the discussions with Professor Anatole Boute, CUHK, Faculty of Law. The usual disclaimer applies.

Kangwa-Musole George Chisanga

Nuclear Energy and the Low-Carbon Transition: Exploring Potential Trade-Offs and Risks Involved with Enhancing Energy Access while Fighting Climate Change

Abstract: The transition to a low-carbon economy creates a dilemma for the energy sector; especially for developing countries. On one hand, enhancing access to energy is a developmental priority as this is a key driver of economic growth. On the other hand, combatting climate change is a cornerstone of the energy transition. Thus, pursuing these goals simultaneously presents the possibility of trade-offs. This is particularly evident in the context of enhancing energy access through nuclear power, a choice that has been made by Zambia and Kenya. These countries are presented as a case study to contextualise the issues associated with developing new nuclear energy programs.
While nuclear power provides the greatest output to energy production relative to other sources, it also carries enormous environmental and political risks if anything goes wrong. This chapter explores some of the potential risks and rewards of opting to include nuclear power to a country's energy mix. The chapter also describes some guiding principles drawn from treaties regulating nuclear energy access at international level and the guidelines provided by the International Atomic Energy Agency and explains the principles of energy justice and their role in the inclusion of nuclear energy in the low-carbon transition.

1 Introduction

The global energy sector is shifting away from reliance on fossil fuels towards low-carbon sources. In the current energy mix, the share taken up by low carbon sources (i.e. renewables and nuclear energy) is far lower than that of fossil fuels and this is set to change in the interest of fighting climate change. This transition to low-carbon energy creates a dilemma for countries still in the process of industrialising their economies. On one hand, they must enhance access to energy as a developmental priority to achieve economic growth. On the other, they must mitigate negative impacts on the environment and climate change. It is in this regard that conversations about the role of nuclear energy have resurfaced in recent years.

Kangwa-Musole George Chisanga is Lecturer, National Institute of Public Administration, Lusaka, Zambia.

https://doi.org/10.1515/9783110752403-017

Presently, peaceful use of nuclear material and technology has had significant benefits in a variety of fields from medicine and agriculture to electricity production and industry (IAEA, 2015; Stoiber, 2003, p. 3). Nuclear energy aids the health sector through cancer treatment while national food security is assured through enhanced shelf-life for agricultural products. Nuclear energy can also be applied in the mining sector where trace element analysis is used for determination of mineral contents in ores such as copper and material coloration of gemstones such as emeralds (Zambia Ministry of Higher Education, 2018, pp. 3, 7).

Enhancing access to energy without increasing the carbon footprint is a key driver of nuclear energy, especially for developing countries in the low-carbon transition. Another key driver is providing energy security while meeting energy demand, a historical driver for developed countries. In an effort to diversify their energy mix, various African countries established relationships with nuclear energy authorities from Russia (Postar, 2017, p. 407), South Korea and China (Van der Merwe, 2021, p. 7). The drivers behind the resurgence of nuclear power in both the developed and developing world, discussed in the third section of this Chapter, explain these developments.

There are, however, major trade-offs and risks inherent to the use of nuclear energy. From an economic perspective, nuclear energy can be a costly investment, especially at inception. This trades off with the need to provide affordable energy access. The technical knowledge needed to safely run nuclear plants necessitates training of personnel which can drive up costs. This is exacerbated by the security and environmental risks inherent in nuclear energy production. Each of these aspects need to be taken into careful consideration when adding this form of energy into a national energy mix. The fourth section of this Chapter discusses these trade-offs in light of the drivers of nuclear energy.

An exploration of prevailing international treaties and guidelines can reveal what principles guide the successful development of a nuclear energy program. For instance, within the guidelines published by the International Atomic Energy Agency (**'IAEA'**) and conventions such as the United Nations Framework Convention on Climate Change (**'UNFCCC'**), provision is made for sustainable development to play a guiding role in developing new nuclear energy facilities. Further, the concept of energy justice has implications for the future of nuclear power. Each of these is discussed in the penultimate section of the Chapter to present a balanced analysis of the important considerations involved with pursuing a course toward nuclear energy in the low-carbon transition.

2 Country-specific context

Kenya and Zambia have been selected as the case studies for this Chapter due to the similarity in their legal systems (i.e. they are both common law jurisdictions) and because they are both developing countries in the beginning stages of their nuclear energy programs. Both countries have set up Nuclear Energy Program Implementing Organisations ('**NEPIOs**') namely the Kenya's Nuclear Power and Energy Agency ('**NuPEA**') (formerly the Nuclear Electricity Board) and Zambia's formerly Zambia Atomic Agency ('**ZAMATOM**') (soon to be Zambia Nuclear Agency). These agencies are tasked with operating nuclear power plants once constructed (NuPEA, 2020, p. 1; Zambia Ministry of Foreign Affairs, 2019, p. 3).

The two countries have similar motivations for pursuing nuclear power programs as both are signatories to the Paris Agreement of 2015 and wish to fulfil their commitments to decarbonising their energy sectors while enhancing energy access to meet growing demand (Zambia Ministry of Higher Education, 2020, p. 3; NuPEA, 2020, p. 11). The countries have also set ambitious economic development strategies in Vision documents with a deadline of 2030 (Government of Kenya, 2008; Government of the Republic of Zambia, 2006). Zambia first officially announced it would pursue nuclear power in its National Development plan of 2017 (Zambia Ministry of National Development Planning, 2017, p. 130). This was seven years behind Kenya which started its plans in 2010 on the recommendation of its National Economic & Social Council (NuPEA, 2020, p. 1). For these reasons, the drivers for nuclear energy are equally applicable in both contexts.

Kenya has gone a step further than Zambia in its implementation program by undertaking and publishing a strategic environmental and social assessment report for its nuclear power programme (NuPEA, 2021). In this report, the Kenyan government highlights the anticipated environmental, social and economic impacts of its proposed nuclear program with mitigation measures and an environmental and social management and monitoring plan drafted for ease of NPP's environmental and social administration and follow-up. This is laudable as it addresses many of the risks discussed in this Chapter. Zambia has paused its plans to develop a nuclear program due to the high cost of the investment which would require debt financing as the country is working to restore itself to a more debt sustainable position (Government of the Republic of Zambia, 2020, p. 2,16; Chisanga and Zulu, 2021, p. 23). Against this background, reference will be made to these countries throughout the discussion in this Chapter starting with the drivers of nuclear energy.

3 Drivers of nuclear energy in the low-carbon economy

The revival of interest in nuclear energy has been justified on the basis of two policy priorities: security of energy supply and climate change mitigation (Cameron, 2007, p. 71). Kenya explicitly cites them among its justifications for pursuing a nuclear power program (Menya, 2014, p. 6). Decarbonizing the electricity sector in particular presents a central opportunity for nuclear energy over the next several decades (Buongiorno et al., 2019, p. xxiv). The nuclear energy industry has experienced a "nuclear renaissance": promoting nuclear technology as "clean energy" for its potential to mitigate greenhouse gas emissions. From 1995 onwards, nuclear power even received the support of the UNFCCC as a viable option to combat climate change. Some claim that nuclear energy is good for some sustainability indicators such as ozone depletion or photochemical smog (Aydın, 2020, p. 1051).

In this regard, it is worth exploring the two policy drivers for adopting nuclear energy. Securing energy supply is particularly important when justifying the use of nuclear energy over renewable sources. The argument that nuclear energy combats climate change serves as a major justification for its inclusion among the sources of energy in the low-carbon transition.

3.1 Security of energy supply

Security of energy supply has historically been a particularly important driver of nuclear energy and continues to play such a role. This can be observed from the oil crisis created in the wake of Russia's invasion of Ukraine which sent oil prices to record highs after sanctions were imposed on the importation of Russian oil (Reed, 2022). Historically, the oil crises of the 1970s led to huge price increases in imported oil and caused acute anxiety among Western governments about the security of oil supplies at prices they could afford. The response of some countries, especially ones with a high degree of import dependence, was to initiate programmes of nuclear power plant construction. By the mid-1980s, nuclear power had become one of the essential tools for governments that wished to see a diversification of their energy supplies away from oil. It accounted for over 16% of the world's electricity generation (Cameron, 2007, p. 73).

The benefit of adding nuclear energy is that it promotes energy security by substituting imported sources used for electricity production. This is true in Africa where Angola is the only oil producer in Southern Africa while Angola and Tanzania produce natural gas and South Africa produces gas and liquid fuel from coal, and has limited offshore gas reserves. Recent finds of natural gas in Mozambique will make the country a competitive player. Most of the region's countries are net importers of oil and gas, thereby compromising their energy security (UNECA, 2018, p. 36).

Further, although initial capital injection into nuclear power plants is relatively high, the operational costs are sufficiently low and some estimates hold that, in the long run, it has the lowest cost option for low-carbon sources (Nuclear Energy Agency & International Energy Agency, 2020, p. 14). On average, a nuclear plant takes five to eight years to be built, implying a longer cost recovery period and making it possible to produce cheap electricity. Further, nuclear power plants can produce electricity consistently even in cases of variation in weather patterns and drought.

3.2 Climate Change mitigation

The energy sector is the biggest contributor to greenhouse gas emissions in a number of countries (UNECA, 2018, p. 31). Fossil fuel-based power generation emits significant greenhouse gases that contribute to global warming and climate change. Climate change causes rises in ambient temperatures and rainfall variability, both of which have an impact on rainfall and water security. Preventing further climate change and enhancing water security is therefore a priority in the furtherance of the goal of enhanced energy access.

Rapidly rising demand for electricity, dire warnings about climate change, and a desire to keep electricity prices low have motivated growth in the nuclear industry. At present, there are at least three major concerns driving the need to add nuclear energy to the current energy mix, namely: (i) providing basic energy services to the world's poor; (ii) finding sources of energy that are less greenhouse gas intensive; and (iii) keeping costs low, both to ratepayers and to governments (Sovacool and Cooper, 2008, pp. 4, 15). These concerns are reflected in the African context.

Low access to clean and affordable energy sources is a blight on the economic development of Africa as a whole and the Southern African region in particular. There is overdependence on hydropower as Zambia relies on that for almost 100 per cent of its electricity while Kenya relies upon it for 52 per cent (UNECA, 2018, p. 9; Takase et al., 2021, p. 100015). The electricity mix in the region is still dominated by coal, at 62 per cent followed by hydropower at 2 per cent with renewable energy (excluding hydropower) representing less than 10 per cent. Over-dependence on coal and hydroelectric power each have their own shortfalls. Aside from contributing to increasing the carbon footprint, reliance on coal power has the drawback of having a finite resource which has been in shortage in recent years. The drawback of relying on hydro-electric power is that during droughts – as was experienced in Southern Africa in 2016 – power stations have to be shut down for lack of water. Reliance on hydropower has the setback of being highly susceptible to climate change (UNECA, 2018, pp. 11,36).

4 Trade-offs and risks inherent to nuclear energy

Africa is endowed with renewable energy resources such as hydro, biomass, solar and wind power that are yet to be fully developed. These developments face numerous barriers including lack of knowledge of the resource base; lack of capital (since they are still more capital-intensive than gas and diesel plants of equivalent nameplate capacity); limited skills base to plan, develop, operate and govern projects and grids with higher shares of renewables; poor institutional set-up to coordinate and promote renewables; and lack of public awareness (UNECA, 2018, p. 29). However, the growing demand for energy access necessitates a diverse set of sources of energy to be pursued simultaneously and this, as mentioned, is a driver for nuclear energy.

Nuclear power plants have been considered a poor choice for addressing energy challenges in a carbon-constrained world despite the positive aspects previously discussed (Sovacool and Cooper, 2008; Aydin, 2020). From an ecological perspective, nuclear energy poses the risk of impacting on biodiversity and ecosystems, air pollution, soil contamination, potential leakages from waste disposal or decommissioning, and emissions of harmful gases (e.g. sulphur dioxide). Well-known problems associated with the technology, such as radioactive waste, the risk of catastrophic accidents, and the link with atomic bombs, raise doubts over its sustainability. In addition, the cost of setting up nuclear power plants and the technical skills needed to run them safely can be inhibitive. Each of these aspects is discussed in detail below.

4.1 Environmental impacts of the uranium fuel cycle

Nuclear reactors typically use uranium as fuel. The processing cycle has been described as 'dirty, long, complex and dangerous' (Sovacool and Cooper, 2008, p. 6). This cycle comprises five major stages, namely: (i) the "front-end" of the cycle, where uranium fuel is mined, milled, converted, enriched, and fabricated; (ii) construction of the plant itself; (iii) operation and maintenance of the facility; (iv) the "back-end" of the cycle where spent fuel is conditioned, (re)processed, and stored; and (v) the final stage where plants are decommissioned and abandoned mines returned to their original state. Each of these stages has massive potential for environmental harm (Sovacool, 2008, p. 2950).

For instance, uranium mining at the front-end stage is dangerous and extremely damaging to the environment. This is due in part to the fact that up to 85% of the uranium is discarded as tailings resulting in toxic waste which must be stored under specific conditions to prevent leakage in the environment. Reliance on uranium also presents risks to water supply as uranium milling and mining, plant operation, and nuclear waste storage all consume, withdraw, and contaminate water supplies for cooling of reactors. This means most nuclear facilities cannot operate during droughts and can even cause water shortages (Sovacool and Cooper, 2008, p. 56).

Another complication is that the energy required to mine and process uranium and decommission a nuclear power plant can amount to over half of all the electricity that a typical reactor is expected to produce during its lifetime (Sovacool and Cooper, 2008, p. 10). Even in developed countries, nuclear waste disposal remains a major concern. The prevailing proposals are to dispose of radioactive waste in an underground repository, an option favoured by Belgium, France, Finland, Germany, Japan, Switzerland and the USA (Cameron, 2007, p. 80). However, none of them has yet operated such a facility. Further, the time-scales involved in disposal are unusually long as the process of implementation can take several decades and could last for as long as one or two generations. This raises concerns for countries planning to develop new nuclear power plants regarding how to deal with waste disposal when even the most experienced jurisdictions are so clearly struggling. As Kenya and Zambia are in the early stage of developing their nuclear energy programs, the issue of decommissioning should be properly planned for and, in this regard, the IAEA has published guidelines (IAEA, 2011).

A further, compounding problem is the decreasing availability of uranium as fuel for nuclear reactors. The ore grade of mined and milled uranium is diminishing as the quality of mined uranium reportedly peaked during the nuclear weapons programs of the 1940s and 1950s, when the highest grade deposits were depleted (Mudd and Diesendorf, 2008, p. 2624). In Africa, the main countries that can supply uranium for use in nuclear reactors are Congo, Niger, South Africa, Gabon, Madagascar, and Namibia (Hecht, 2012, p. 22.). Exploration for uranium continues in Botswana, Madagascar, Malawi, Mali, Namibia, Niger, South Africa, Tanzania, and Zambia (Postar. 2017, p. 405). However, uranium mining also poses risks to other important economic sectors.

Mining uranium in South Africa's Karoo, for instance, is done at a disadvantage to the agricultural and tourism sectors (Issah and Umejesi, 2018, pp. 286–288, 291). While most of the representatives of the South African government knew that some people would be adversely affected, they insisted that the majority of the people of South Africa would be positively impacted by the proposed mining operations. Implicitly, those that would be adversely affected are seen as making sacrifices for the majority of the people who would benefit in the region. In this way, the sacrifices to other sectors are justified on the basis that access fuel for nuclear energy is likely to bring about the greatest happiness to the greatest number of people. As will be seen, this is not in keeping with the tenets of energy justice and is not recommended as the approach to be taken by Zambia or Kenya.

4.2 Security and political risks

There also are significant political and security risks associated with developing and operating nuclear power plants. This is because nuclear power plants can be targeted by terrorists and fuel materials can be used for the development of nuclear weapons. The typical nuclear reactor produces enough plutonium every two months to create a nuclear weapon and commercial nuclear reactors already create, every four years, an amount of plutonium equal to the entire global military stockpile (Sovacool and Cooper, 2008, p. 77, 82). Terrorists could potentially attack at any stage in the nuclear fuel cycle. They could steal fuel material from mines, directly attack reactors, intercept nuclear material in transit or create nuclear weapons from radioactive tailings. These risks certainly dent the credibility of developing nuclear energy capability. However, this is undercut by the fact that before uranium becomes weapons-usable, it must be mined as ore, processed into yellowcake, converted into uranium hexafluoride, enriched, and pressed into bomb fuel (Hecht, 2012, p. 23); a fairly complicated set of processes for even sophisticated terrorist organizations to achieve. Despite the reality of this risk, the safeguards put in place by international non-proliferations treaties can be trusted to allay any fears that developing nuclear power plants can lead to enhanced terrorist capability.

Despite the existence of these safeguards, in practice, it has been observed that there is a trend to limit the spread of nuclear power generation to developing countries (Postar, 2017, p. 406). This anxiety is driven by the dual possibility of uranium and nuclear technology being used to make weapons or as an energy source. However, the existence of a connection between countries receiving assistance to develop peaceful nuclear power programs and whether they are more likely to acquire nuclear weapons is a highly debatable issue. Fuhrmann (2009), for instance, exploring the question of why the fear of spreading nuclear weapons capability has not stopped Western countries from assisting civilian nuclear programs in the Middle East, concludes that economic concerns override fears of weapon development. In a later work, Stulberg and Fuhrmann (2013) confess that the link between assitance in civilian nuclear programs and conflict remains debatable.

Africa is currently the world's largest nuclear-weapons-free-zone and it is in the world's interest to keep it this way (Bosman, 2021). While it may be assumed that the introduction of nuclear power in developing countries like Zambia with largely peaceful histories would not likely lead to the development of nuclear weapons, terrorist insurgency has risen in neighbouring Mozambique. This has been a cause for concern in recent years and the Southern African Development Community has been slow to respond in a decisive manner (Chingotuane et al., 2021, pp. 17–19). Kenya admits the presence of a threat posed by attacks by terrorist group Al-Shabab based in neighboring Somalia. However, the country commits to comply with international safeguards and cites its domestic legislation, the Nuclear Regulatory Act, 2019 as assurance that all material will be used for peaceful purposes and planning to create systems for accounting for and controlling nuclear material (NuPEA, 2021, pp. 22, 201). Aside from security concerns, the countries must also contend with the cost issues associated with nuclear energy.

4.3 High initial investment cost

There are significant cost implications for adding nuclear energy to the energy mix. Nuclear facilities rely almost entirely on government subsidies for construction, nuclear waste storage, and liability (Sovacool and Cooper, 2008, p. 25). This promotes the notion that renewable power sources such as wind, solar, hydroelectric, geothermal, and biomass have immense advantages over nuclear plants. However, some improvements in nuclear technology have addressed the cost of plant construction.

There are smaller and more environmentally friendly generators which cost less to construct, produce power in smaller increments, and need not rely on continuous government subsidies. These generate little to no waste, have less greenhouse gas emissions per unit of electricity produced, and do not substantially contribute to the risk of accidents and weapons proliferation (Cameron, 2007, p. 77).

Despite having lower greenhouse gas emissions, nuclear power plants may not be a suitable alternative due to the fact that reprocessing and enriching uranium requires a substantial amount of electricity. The electricity is often generated from fossil fuel-fired power plants. Further, uranium milling, mining, leeching, plant construction, and decommissioning all produce substantial amounts of greenhouse gas (Sovacool and Cooper, 2008, p. 64). The Oxford Research Group projects that because higher grades of uranium fuel will soon be depleted, assuming the current level of world nuclear output, by 2050 nuclear power will generate as much carbon dioxide per kWh as comparable gas-fired power stations (Van Leeuwen, 2007).

Nuclear generators face immense capital costs, rising uranium fuel prices, significant lifecycle greenhouse gas emissions, and problems with reactor safety, waste storage, weapons proliferation, and vulnerability to attack (Ayidin, 2020, p. 10). Nuclear units are too big for many small countries or rural users and nuclear power has higher costs than competitors per unit of net carbon dioxide displaced (Lovins, 2005, p. 13). Even in developed locations like the United States and Western Europe, new nuclear power plants are considered unprofitable investments due to their high capital costs (Buongiorno et al., 2019, p.xx). As previously mentioned, this high cost is the reason Zambia has had to pause its planned nuclear program. The high cost is exacerbated by the technical risk associated with running nuclear plants.

4.4 Technical risks

The technical risks of nuclear energy are exemplified by the three most significant nuclear power accidents: Three Mile Island in 1979; Chernobyl in 1986; and Fukushima in 2011.The first two were caused by human error while the third was due to a combination of human error and natural disaster.

The Three Mile Island incident was the result of poor training of operators who failed to monitor the loss of coolant which caused the reactor meltdown (Pogue, 2007, p. 463). No deaths or environmental damage resulted from this incident. The Chernobyl disaster was the result of engineers testing the cooling pump system of the nuclear reactor. This caused a meltdown that resulted in up to 4000 deaths and released more than two hundred times the radiation released by the atom bombs dropped on Nagasaki and Hiroshima. Traces of the radiation could be detected in every country in the Northern Hemisphere. This accident vividly illustrated the trans-boundary nature of nuclear accidents (Sovacool and Cooper, 2008, pp. 68, 70; Cameron, 2007, p. 73).

The Fukushima disaster occurred after an earthquake of magnitude 9.0 struck the Pacific coast of Japan caused a tsunami which, in turn, caused an accident at the Fukushima Daiichi Nuclear Power Station (Tsujikawa et al., 2016, p. 98). This resulted in a large quantity of radioactive substances released into the environment. Due to rapid evacuation of residents in the affected area, fewer than 5 deaths were recorded. However, the accident resulted in large amounts of radioisotopes being widely dispersed in the air, soil, fresh water, food and seawater over eastern Japan, covering an area of about 800 km^2 (Ohnishi, 2012).

The accident at Chernobyl and a string of incidents involving leaks at many of the nuclear plants around the world brought to an end the positive approach to nuclear power that had been seen for several decades. Since that time, there has been a significant growth in the number of international treaties, national laws and regulations, and specialist institutions designed to constrain the operation of nuclear power in the interests of safety, health and the environment (Cameron, 2007, p. 76). Anti-nuclear activists claim that disasters may and do happen despite strict safety measures, pointing to the Fukushima disaster for reference (Aydin, 2020, p. 100044). The trend in legal development has been driven by concerns to address the risks inherent in the use of nuclear energy and to make them acceptable for its use for civil purposes. The result is an industry that is highly regulated in all of the developed countries. This high level of regulation necessitates an exploration of the guiding criteria that can be drawn from different instruments regulating the sector.

5 Guiding principles for the development of nuclear energy

Nuclear energy is a highly regulated sector and this is justified due to the risks inherent to the application of this form of energy. Countries seeking to develop new nuclear energy programs can draw from various international treaties, conventions and guidelines to ensure their programs comply with global standards.

This section discusses some notable principles enshrined in treaties, namely nuclear safety and security and sustainable development. Further, the concept of energy justice has emerged parallel to these concepts to provide further guidance on the application of nuclear energy in the era of the transition to low-carbon energy sources.

5.1 Nuclear safety and security as global standards

The concept of nuclear safety means protection of people and the environment against radiation risks, and the safety of facilities and activities that give rise to these risks. Nuclear security means prevention and detection of, and response to, theft, sabotage, unauthorized access, illegal transfer or other malicious acts involving nuclear material, other radioactive substances or their associated facilities (IAEA, 2018, p. 2, 3).

In the wake of accidents such as Three Mile Island and Chernobyl, numerous international instruments were developed to promote nuclear safety. For example, the Convention on Early Notification of a Nuclear Accident, 1986; Convention on Assistance in the Case of a Nuclear Accident or Radiological Emergency, 1986; and the Convention on Nuclear Safety, 1994. The Nuclear Safety Convention particularly provides benchmark standards for the siting, design, construction and operation of nuclear installations, as well as the adequacy of human and financial resources, the assessment and verification of safety, quality assurance and emergency preparedness. The control mechanism in the Treaty is the peer-review mechanism of national reports on implementation.

To promote nuclear security, the United Nations passed numerous treaties starting with the Treaty on Non-Proliferation of Nuclear Weapons and, most recently, the Treaty on the Prohibition of Nuclear Weapons, 2017 which operates at global level. For African states, the most important treaty is the African Nuclear-Weapon-Free Zone Treaty (also known as 'the Pelindaba Treaty') of 1996. Signatories to this treaty are prevented from creating, acquiring, controlling, or possessing "nuclear explosive device[s]" (Article 3) or supplying "source" or "nuclear material" to non-nuclear weapon states without IAEA safeguards (Article 9(c)). The treaty also requires parties to prohibit nuclear explosive devices from being stationed in their territories (Article 4). Parties should not test, or encourage testing of, nuclear devices in their own territories or anywhere. (Article 5). Only non-nuclear weapon states meeting IAEA safeguards are allowed to receive exported "source" material in order to ensure civilian use. However, the ease with which states can withdraw from the Pelindaba Treaty has been noted as a weakness (Article 20; Postar, 2017, p. 406).

5.2 Sustainable development in international treaties

Sustainable development is a key guiding concept in the guideline governing nuclear power. For instance, Article 1 of the Joint Convention on the Safety of Spent Fuel and Radioactive Waste Management of 1997 recognises the inter-generational implications of nuclear waste, and requires more detailed national reporting requirements than the Nuclear Safety Convention. Parties must aim to avoid imposing 'undue burdens' on future generations, including burdens that are greater than those permitted for present generations.

The Sustainable Development Goals (SDGs) adopted by the UN General Assembly in 2015 include a goal to provide Affordable and Clean Energy (i.e. SDG number 7). This goal intersects with other goals such as the alleviation of poverty (SDG number 1), the resilience of infrastructure in sustainable industrialisation (SDG number 9) and sustainable production and consumption (SDG number 12). Taken together, the goals provide a guideline for future nuclear energy programs to be pursued in a sustainable way (Nerini et al., 2017, p. 16; Chisanga, 2020, p. 13).

Principle 5 in the Stockholm Declaration of 1972 provides that non-renewable resources of the Earth must be employed in such a way as to guard against the danger of their future exhaustion and to ensure that benefits from such employment are shared by all mankind. Article 3.4 of the UNFCCC requires Member States to promote sustainable development and Article 4.1 (d) requires them to reduce harmful atmospheric emissions and promote sustainable use of energy. The Paris Agreement of 2015 in Articles 4.4 and 4.6 requires countries to mitigate their environmental impact, develop its plans for a low-carbon future.

Applying sustainable development principles in the nuclear field entails an emphasis on long term safety for future generations without relying unduly on long term forecasts which are unlikely to be accurate due to the long timescales involved (Stoiber et al., 2003, p. 9). The issue of intergenerational justice is particularly important with respect to management of nuclear waste and the irreversibility of nuclear damage (Aydin, 2020, p. 53). Waste management and decommissioning processes, particularly for nuclear energy systems, can lead to the generation of inequalities (McCauley et al., 2019, p. 916).

5.3 Energy justice considerations

The meaning of the concept of energy justice is discussed by Bhullar in this volume and other recent literature (for example: McCauley et al., 2013; Guruswamy, 2015; Sovacool et al., 2016a; Heffron et al., 2018). For present purposes the tenets of energy justice most applicable are: distributional, procedural, recognition, cosmopolitan and restorative justice (Jenkins et al., 2017).

Distributional justice addresses the distribution of environmental benefits and ills of energy projects and their associated responsibilities. Kenya and Zambia both applied this concept by prioritising impact assessments when identifying potential physical locations for their planned nuclear reactors (NuPEA, 2021; Government of the Republic Of Zambia, 2019, p. 7).

Procedural justice highlights the importance of procedure in influencing whether outcomes for stakeholders are equitable or inequitable. This has implications where decisions may be taken without full disclosure of all relevant issues to affected parties, and bias and political pressure from powerful, vested interests unfairly influence proposed energy developments (Heffron et al., 2018). Kenya has applied this concept by publishing its findings on the social and environmental impacts of its planned program but Zambia has yet to do so.

Recognition justice seeks to ensure a level playing field for all stakeholders in energy development decision-making. An illustration of the disregard for recognition justice was observed in the dumping of nuclear waste in areas occupied by indigenous peoples in Australia (Marsh and Green, 2019). This will have implications for Kenya and Zambia when selecting the sites of storage of nuclear waste; an aspect that has not been addressed in detail by either country.

Cosmopolitan justice stems from the belief that we are all 'world citizens' and, as such, are all affected by energy projects in some way (Sovacool and Dworkin, 2014, p. 11). The universally felt effects of climate change have led to cosmopolitan philosophy being the basis of the approach to environmental protection and regulation (Mccauley et al., 2016, p. 146). This is clearly illustrated by the effects of the Chernobyl accident on the Northern Hemisphere. As discussed in heading 5.1 above, both Kenya and Zambia have committed to keeping nuclear material from polluting the environment or being used for warfare which is a positive indication that they respect cosmopolitan justice.

Restorative justice aims to repair the harm done to the person, society and nature and not just punishing the offender which is the usual focus of the legal system and can assist in pinpointing where prevention needs to occur (Heffron and McCauley, 2017, p. 658; Chisanga and Heffron, 2021, p. 250). Kenya has detailed its proposed mitigation measures for the harm its program may cause but Zambia has yet to do so.

For other countries, these concepts are relevant to both international issues and domestic issues relating to nuclear energy. International issues include the right of people in developing countries to escape the poverty trap by the provision of universal access to energy services and to avoid environmental damage resulting from the disposal of nuclear waste shipped from developed nations. Domestic issues include ensuring the affordability of energy supply for the poor or outlawing the forcible abandonment of homes and villages for instance in the development of new large-scale hydroelectric projects (Heffron et al., 2018: p. 42). In this way, the principles of energy justice serve as a measuring criteria for the implementation of nuclear programs in the low-carbon transition.

6 Conclusion

For a scholar of energy law, the prospect of Africa having nuclear energy as a result of the low-carbon transition is simultaneously exciting and thought-provoking. It is exciting because there would be an unprecedented level of new skills and expertise necessary to implement nuclear programs brought into the workforce. This coupled with having a proven, reliable source of low-carbon energy and its impact on the continent's industrialization fuels the impetus to study the development of this area of energy law.

The prospect of nuclear power is, however, thought-provoking due to the risks inherent to nuclear power. An accident at a nuclear plant can have irreversible consequences on the environment and this cannot be ignored. Further, even the running of nuclear power plants has environmental impacts, particularly on water use, which the public must accept as a necessary sacrifice for enhanced access to energy. These trade-offs are certain to affect the public acceptability of nuclear power in Africa. There is also cause to reflect on the approaches taken by the two countries in this Chapter as they have lessons for other countries that may plan to include nuclear energy into their energy mix.

The approaches taken by Kenya and Zambia differ in at least two respects: public availability of the details about the program and steps proving government commitment. To illustrate, while Zambia's Government (2019) reported to have an ambitious 200-year roadmap for its nuclear program, this roadmap remains unpublished and the national Nuclear Policy (2020) omits any reference to it. In contrast, Kenya shared its 15-year roadmap for public scrutiny. This is in keeping with the concepts of energy justice as the general public are being kept informed about the progress of the program.

Kenya has also passed legislation and published a report setting out the risks and mitigation measures associated with its nuclear program. Zambia has not yet implemented these steps despite enshrining them in its published Nuclear Policy. This may indicate that the government commitment may be weaker than previously announced; a sad development given the promise that nuclear energy has for the country. However, what can be drawn from other policy documents is that Zambia is likely taking a cautious approach as it makes itself more debt sustainable; a necessary step to finance its nuclear program (Government of the Republic of Zambia, 2020, p. 16; Chisanga and Zulu, 2021, p. 23). Whatever the case, there are positive lessons to be drawn from the current progress made by these two countries regarding the future of nuclear energy.

The patchwork of regulations and guidelines with which these countries must comply should be considered safe harbour against the risks of a nuclear project going wrong for safety reasons, security breach of environmental catastrophe. While accidents at nuclear plants, when they happen, have serious environmental impacts and high costs, they are far less frequent than those recorded from fossil-fuel generated plants or other renewables (Sovacool et al., 2016b, p. 3956). This is an important consideration to countering the doom-scenarios most members of the public associate with nuclear energy as consensus on the acceptability of the energy source is being formed.

Further, compliance with the principles of nuclear safety and security and promotion of sustainable development can lead to a successful introduction of nuclear energy in the transition to a low-carbon economy. Lessons drawn from experiences of countries where accidents have occurred should serve not as a deterrent to ever pursuing nuclear programs, but as guidance for how this can be done correctly. In addition, applying the principles of energy justice – particularly cosmopolitan, restorative and distributional justice – is key to the acceptability of nuclear energy in countries like Zambia and Kenya where no nuclear plants have ever existed. The continental and, arguably, global interest of keeping Africa as the world's largest nuclear-weapons free-zone should encourage these countries to double efforts at ensuring non-proliferation of nuclear weapons as they plan and implement their respective programs.

Even so, the decision to include nuclear energy into the energy mix is fraught with risks and trade-offs for the two countries discussed in this Chapter. In the interest of enhancing energy security and supply, a country must contend with the unavoidable cost implications of constructing nuclear reactors. Zambia's decision to halt its nuclear power ambition has shown how decisive such financial considerations are. This shouldn't slow efforts to set up a legal framework; a commitment Zambia indicated in its published Nuclear Policy. Further, an impact assessment must consider the environmental impact on water use caused by nuclear reactors fuelled by uranium. There is also the possibility of the uranium fuel being used for development of nuclear weapons. Arguably, even commitments to safeguard against this possibility may not be enough to deter terrorist groups in neighbouring countries from sabotaging nuclear plants once set up in Kenya or Zambia. It is hoped that serious cautionary measures will be taken in this regard. Further research will definitely be needed regarding how the benefits and risks of nuclear power play out in these countries and any others that adopt nuclear energy programs as they transition to a low-carbon economy.

References

African Nuclear-Weapon-Free Zone Treaty, 1996. Date of Adoption: April 11, 1996. Date entry into force: July 15, 2009.

Aydın, C., 2020. Nuclear energy debate in Turkey: stakeholders, policy alternatives, and governance issues. *Energy Policy*, 136, 111041.

Bosman, I., 2021. Nuclear disarmament: what the world can learn from Africa. *All Africa: South African Institute of International Affairs*.

Buongiorno, J. et al., 2019. *The future of nuclear energy in a carbon-constrained world*, Massachusetts Institute of Technology.

Cameron P.D. 2007. The revival of nuclear power: an analysis of the legal implications. *Journal of Environmental Law*, 19(1), pp. 71–87.

Chingotuane, E.V.P. et al., 2021. *Strategic options for managing violent extremism in Southern Africa: the case of Mozambique*. Friedrich-Ebert-Stiftung.

Chisanga, K.M.G. and Heffron, R.J., 2020. Nevsun Resources Limited v. Araya 2020 SCC 5. *Global Energy Law and Sustainability*, 1(2), pp. 248–251.

Chisanga, K.M.G. and Zulu, H., 2021. Growing the Zambian economy through energy. *JCTR Bulletin No. 124 – Second Quarter*, pp. 22–24.

Chisanga, K.M.G., 2020. Energy justice and nuclear power: considerations for Zambia Atomic Agency. *Centre Annual Review*, 19, pp. 1–20.

Fuhrmann, M., 2009. Spreading temptation: proliferation and peaceful nuclear cooperation agreements. *International security*, 34(1), pp. 7–41.

Government of Kenya, 2008. *The Kenya Vision 2030*. Government Printers.

Government of the Republic of Zambia, 2006. *Vision 2030*. Government of the Republic of Zambia.

Government of the Republic of Zambia, 2019. *Country Statement at the 63rd Regular Session of the International Atomic Energy Agency (IAEA) General Conference*. Vienna: IAEA.

Government of the Republic of Zambia, 2020. *Economic Recovery Programme 2020–2023*. Ministry of National Development and Planning.

Guruswamy, L., 2015. The contours of energy justice. In: A. Shawkat et al., eds., 2015. *International law and the Global South*. Cambridge: Cambridge University Press.

Hecht, G., 2012. An elemental force: uranium production in Africa, and what it means to be nuclear. *Bulletin of the Atomic Scientists*, 68, pp. 22–33.

Heffron, R.J. and McCauley, D., 2017. The concept of energy justice across the disciplines. *Energy Policy*, 105, pp. 658–667.

Heffron, R.J. et al., 2018. A treatise for energy law. *The Journal of World Energy Law & Business*, 11, pp. 34–42.

IAEA, 2011. *Safety of nuclear power plants: decommissioning and operation (No. SSR2/2)*.

IAEA, 2015. *Manual of good practice in food irradiation*.

IAEA, 2018. *IAEA safety glossary: terminology used in nuclear safety and radiation protection 2018 Edition*.

Issah, M. and Umejesi, I., 2018. Risks and vulnerability in uranium mining: a synthesis of local perspectives in the Great Karoo region of South Africa. *The Extractive Industries and Society*, 5, pp. 284–291.

Jenkins, K., McCauley, D. and Warren, C.R., 2017. Attributing responsibility for energy justice: a case study of the Hinkley Point nuclear complex. *Energy Policy*, 108, pp. 836–840.

Joint Convention on the Safety of Spent Fuel and Radioactive Waste Management. (1997). Date of Adoption: September 5, 1997. Date entry into force: June 18, 2001.

Lovins, A.B., 2005. *Nuclear power: economics and climate-protection potential*. Rocky Mountain Institute.

Marsh, J.K. and Green, J., 2019. First nations rights and colonising practices by the nuclear industry: an Australian battleground for environmental justice. *The Extractive Industries and Society*, 7(3), pp. 870–881.

Mccauley, D. et al., 2013. Advancing energy justice: the triumvirate of tenets. *International Energy Law Review*, 32, pp. 107–110.

Mccauley, D. et al., 2016. Energy justice in the Arctic: implications for energy infrastructural development in the Arctic. *Energy Research & Social Science*, 16, pp. 141–146.

Mccauley, D. et al., 2019. Energy justice in the transition to low carbon energy systems: Exploring key themes in interdisciplinary research. *Applied Energy*, 233-234, pp. 916–921.

Menya, L., 2014. *Experience in the development of Kenya's nuclear power programme*. IAEA.

Mudd, G.M. and Diesendorf, M., 2008. Sustainability of uranium mining and milling: toward quantifying resources and eco-efficiency. *Environmental Science & Technology*, 42(7), 2624-2630.

Nerini, F.F. et al., 2018. Mapping synergies and trade-offs between energy and the Sustainable Development Goals. *Nature Energy*, 3, 10-15.

Nuclear Energy Agency & International Energy Agency, 2020. *Projected costs of generating electricity 2020 Edition*. IEA.

NuPEA, 2020. *Strategic Plan 2020–2025*. Government of the Republic of Kenya.

NuPEA, 2021. *Strategic Environmental and Social Assessment Report (Sesa) for the Kenya's nuclear power programme*. Final Draft Report. NuPEA.

Ohnishi, T. 2012. The disaster at Japan's Fukushima-Daiichi nuclear power plant after the March 11, 2011 earthquake and tsunami, and the resulting spread of radioisotope contamination. *Radiation Research*, 177(1), pp. 1–14.

Paris Agreement, 2015. Date of Adoption: December 12, 2015. Date entry into force: November 4, 2016.

Pogue, E.R., 2007. The catastrophe model of risk regulation and the regulatory legacy of Three Mile Island and Love Canal. *Penn State Environmental Law Review*, 15, pp. 463–493.

Postar, S., 2017. The half-lives of African uranium: A historical review. *The Extractive Industries and Society*, 4, pp. 398–406.

Reed, S., 2022. Russian sanctions could create 'supply crisis' as oil output falls. *The New York Times* (16 March).

Sovacool, B.K. and Cooper, C., 2008. Nuclear nonsense: why nuclear power is no answer to climate change and the world's post-Kyoto energy challenges. *Wm. & Mary Envtl. L. & Pol'y Rev.*, 33, pp. 1–119.

Sovacool, B.K. and Dworkin, M.H., 2014. *Global energy justice*. Cambridge: Cambridge University Press.

Sovacool, B.K. et al., 2016a. Energy decisions reframed as justice and ethical concerns. *Nature Energy*, 1, pp. 1–6.

Sovacool, B.K. et al., 2016b. Balancing safety with sustainability: assessing the risk of accidents for modern low-carbon energy systems. *Journal of Cleaner Production*, 112, pp. 3952–3965.

Sovacool, B.K., 2008. Valuing the greenhouse gas emissions from nuclear power: A critical survey. *Energy Policy*, 36, pp. 2950–2963.

Stoiber, C. et al., 2003. *Handbook on nuclear law*. Vienna: International Atomic Energy Agency.

Stulberg, A.N. and Fuhrmann, M., eds., 2013. *The nuclear renaissance and international security*. Stanford, CA: Stanford University Press.

Takase, M., Kipkoech, R. and Essandoh, P.K., 2021. A comprehensive review of energy scenario and sustainable energy in Kenya. *Fuel Communications*, 7, 100015.

Tsujikawa, N., Tsuchida, S. and Shiotani, T., 2011. Changes in the factors influencing public acceptance of nuclear power generation in Japan since the 2011 Fukushima Daiichi nuclear disaster. *Risk Analysis*, 36(1), pp. 98–113.

United Nations Economic Commission for Africa (UNECA), 2018. *Energy crisis in Southern Africa: future prospects*, UNECA.

United Nations Framework Convention on Climate Change, 1992. Date of Adoption: May 9, 1992. Date entry into force: March 12, 1994.

United Nations, 1972. *Stockholm Declaration*. Report of the United Nations Conference on the Human Environment, 5–16 June. New York, NY: United Nations.

Van der Merwe, L., 2021. *International involvement in the African nuclear market*. South African Institute of International Affairs.

Van Leeuwen, J.W.S., 2007. Nuclear power and global warming: CO_2 emissions from nuclear power. In: F. Barnaby and J. Kemp, eds., 2007. *Secure energy? Civil nuclear power, security and global warming*. Oxford Research Group Briefing Paper.

Zambia Ministry of Foreign Affairs, 2019. *Zambia's follow up national report on the implementation of resolution 1540 (2004)*. Government of the Republic of Zambia.

Zambia Ministry of Higher Education, 2008. *Ministerial statement: nuclear science and technology programme in Zambia*. Parliament of the Republic of Zambia.

Zambia Ministry of Higher Education, 2020. *National nuclear policy 2020*. Government of the Republic of Zambia.

Zambia Ministry of National Development Planning, 2017. *Seventh National Development Plan 2017–2021*. Government of the Republic of Zambia.

John Wiseman

Accelerating the Phase Out of Coal in Australia: Key Trends and Drivers

Abstract: This chapter provides a concise overview of Australian experience and learning about policies and strategies for accelerating the rapid, well managed and equitable phase out of coal. Coal mining and coal fired power production have been important foundations for Australian economic and export growth for well over a hundred years. Coal based industries have also been key sources of economic prosperity and employment for many Australian regional communities. While Australian coal industry owners, investors and workers retain significant political influence, international pressure to reduce CO_2 fossil fuel emissions combined with sharp falls in the price of renewable energy are likely to continue to accelerate the phase out of coal. The most significant factors influencing coal phase out trends and impacts in Australia are the relative price of fossil fuels and renewable energy; international demand for Australian coal; and government climate and energy policy decisions. Climate activists and advocacy groups are also deploying an increasingly diverse, creative and effective array of legal, financial and corporate governance strategies highlighting the physical, financial and reputational risks of coal investment, mining and production. There is also increasing awareness of the importance of respectful, well-planned, well-resourced just transition strategies in broadening and deepening public support for a rapid, just and well managed transition away from coal.

1 Introduction

Coal mining and coal fired power production have been crucial foundations for Australian economic and export growth for well over a hundred years. Coal based industries have also been key sources of economic prosperity and employment for many Australian regional communities.

International pressure to reduce fossil fuel emissions combined with sharp falls in the price of renewable energy are now, however, intensifying debate about the need to accelerate the phase-out of coal production in Australia. Climate advocacy groups are successfully employing a wide array of legal, divestment and corporate governance strategies, highlighting the physical and transition risks of coal production and investment. There is also growing awareness of the importance of proactive and re-

John Wiseman is a Senior Research Fellow with Melbourne Climate Futures and an Adjunct Professor at the Melbourne School of Population and Global Health, University of Melbourne, Australia.

https://doi.org/10.1515/9783110752403-018

spectful just transition strategies in strengthening public support for a rapid and orderly shift away from coal.

Learning from the diverse ways in which Australian governments, communities, trade unions and business are responding to these challenges and opportunities provides a valuable source of learning about coal phase-out policies. Informed by relevant international experience and research, this chapter reviews and discusses recent Australian coal phase-out trends, debates and strategies. The key conclusion is that, while economic drivers remain crucial, climate related legal actions are playing an increasingly important role in shifting public opinion and in creating a more fertile policy and regulatory environment for accelerating the phase-out of coal.

2 Key factors and drivers influencing coal phase out strategies and outcomes

There is now widespread understanding that a rapid phase out of coal production is an essential basis for GHG emission reductions at the speed required to keep global warming as close as possible to 1.5 °C. Recent analysis of reductions in fossil fuel production required to achieve a 50% chance of keeping global warming below 1.5 °C finds that by 2050 nearly 90% of global coal reserves–and 95% of Australian coal reserves–must remain unextracted. (Welsby et al., 2021)

Systematic reviews of coal phase out strategies in diverse jurisdictions highlight a range of key concerns and obstacles preventing and delaying the phase out of coal (Diluiso, 2021; Jacobs and Steckel, 2022). These concerns and obstacles include negative impacts on national and regional economic growth and employment; loss of export income and taxation revenue; and the political and economic power and influence of coal producers, investors and workers.

Key factors and drivers with the potential to overcome these obstacles and to accelerate the phase out of coal include the following (Diluiso, 2021; Jacobs and Steckel, 2022):

- Production costs and price of domestic and export coal relative to other energy sources;
- Government policy and regulation including carbon tax and emission trading schemes;
- Subsidies for coal production and support for renewable energy (eg. feed in tariffs, renewable energy targets, infrastructure investment)
- Public concern about climate change and other environmental and health impacts of coal;
- Equitable, well managed transition strategies supporting regions, workers and communities impacted by the phase out of coal; and

- Legal, financial and corporate governance strategies focussing on the physical and transition risks of coal production and investment.

While all of these factors and drivers have played influential roles in Australian coal-phase out debates and strategies, progress in phasing out coal has remained extremely slow (Christoff, 2021). Coal industry owners and managers along with key allies in the media and finance sector have been highly successful in maintaining political support for the ongoing expansion of coal. Dramatic shifts in global energy demand and supply and in the Australian political landscape in the first half of 2022 may, however, now be strengthening the potential for a significant acceleration in Australian coal-phase out trends and outcomes.

3 Australian coal production and export trends

Australia's recoverable coal reserves are the third largest in the world, with 75,428 million tonnes (Mt) of black coal and 73,865 Mt of brown coal (Geoscience Australia, 2022; Geoscience, n.d.). Australia is the fifth largest producer of coal (behind the US, China, Russia and India). Coal mining employed about 36,000 workers (about 0.4% of Australia's workforce) in 2022 (Australian Bureau of Statistics, 2022).

Australia is responsible for approximately 5% of total global greenhouse gas (GHG) emissions, if emissions from both domestic and exported fossil fuel use are taken into account (Christoff, 2021). In 2021, Australian per capita GHG emissions from coal were higher than any other developed country (Redfearn, 2022). A 2021 report by the Australian Institute noted that new coal and gas projects currently under development in Australia would result in 1.7 billion tonnes of GHG emissions each year (equivalent to the annual emissions of over 200 coal-fired power stations – or twice as much as the annual emissions from global aviation) (Ogge et al., 2021).

Approximately 20% of Australian coal production is for domestic use. Over 90% of domestic coal is used to produce electricity with the remainder used for steel production. While the contribution to Australia's energy supply of gas and renewables continues to grow, coal still accounted for 59% of Australian electricity production in 2021. This is down from over 80% in 2000 (Clean Energy Council, 2022).

In 2010, Australia had 34 operational coal fired power stations. By 2021, 18 of these power stations had closed with a further 7 scheduled for closure by 2035 (Carbon Brief, 2022). The ongoing closure of coal fired power stations, combined with rapidly rising energy prices has led to a fierce debate between those (including Ministers in the 2018–2022 Liberal National Party (LNP) government led by Scott Morrison) who argued for subsidies to keep coal fired power stations open and those (including the newly elected Albanese Labor government) who support an orderly process for replacing coal fired power with renewable energy (Nelson and Gilmore, 2021). In June

2022, the Australian Energy Market Operator (AEMO) said it expected 60 percent of the eastern seaboard's coal fleet of coal fired power stations to exit the electricity grid by 2030 with the last remaining plant shut by 2042 (AEMO, 2022).

Ongoing falls in the price of renewable energy compared to coal have been a significant factor in driving the shift away from coal-based electricity production. Between 2010 and 2019, the cost of large, utility-scale solar photovoltaic projects fell by 82% with the cost of concentrating solar power falling by 47%. Over the same period, the cost of wind power fell by 39% (onshore) and 29% (offshore) (International Renewable Energy Agency, 2019). In 2021, the Commonwealth Scientific and Industrial Research Organisation (CSIRO) GenCost Report found that the levelised cost (LCOE) of wind energy in Australia had fallen to between \$45 and \$57 per megawatt hour (MWh) with the cost of solar PV electricity falling from between \$44 and \$65 per MWh (Graham et al., 2021). The LCOE of a new black coal generator was estimated to be between \$87 and \$118 per MWh.

The first half of 2022 saw remarkable increases in the overall price of energy in Australia with wholesale electricity prices averaging \$87 per MWh in the first three months of 2022, up 141% from a year earlier. By June 2022 soaring energy prices and concerns about potential blackouts led the Australian energy regulator to intervene in the electricity market, capping prices at \$300per MWh. Factors leading to this sudden rise in energy prices include increasing international demand for coal as a result of the Russia-Ukraine war; a shortage of gas available for domestic use (primarily as a result of the majority of Australian gas production being exported); and coal fired power generators going offline due to technical faults and breakdowns (Graham et al., 2021).

Australia is the world's biggest exporter of metallurgical coal, and the second biggest exporter of thermal coal. The value of Australian coal exports (mainly going to Japan, China, India, South Korea, and Taiwan) is predicted to rise to over \$110 billion in 2022–2023 (Beaven, 2022). This represents a sharp increase from \$69 billion in 2019, largely as a result of the impact of the Russia-Ukraine war on international coal prices. Longer term falls in demand, particularly from China, are, however, likely to lead to further reductions in the value of Australian coal exports over the next few years (Gosens et al. 2021).

Research published by the Reserve Bank of Australia (RBA) in September 2021 found that Australian coal exports would, in fact, fall by 80% if Australia's major trading partners implemented policies consistent with keeping global warming below 1.5 degrees (Kemp et al., 2021). Commitments to zero emissions by 2050 by South Korea, Japan and China, combined with the recent decision by China to end financing of all coal-fired power stations outside China, suggest that this is indeed the direction in which Australia's major trading partners are heading. The RBA paper also notes that 'the impact of a decline in fossil fuel exports would be significant for certain communities and regions, especially those in which mining accounts for a large share of employment' (Kemp et al., 2021, p. 36).

On the other hand, there is also mounting evidence that Australia's vast solar and wind resources, combined with well-planned, adequately funded investment in energy transmission, distribution and storage infrastructure, have the potential to rapidly expand Australia's access to secure and affordable renewable energy (Burdon et al., 2019).

The 2021 Beyond Zero Emissions (BZE) report, *Export Powerhouse, Australia's $333 billion export opportunity,* provides a compelling account of the huge potential for low-cost renewable energy to drive investment in high value, energy intensive export industries including green hydrogen, green steel and green aluminium (BZE, 2021). Importantly, as the BZE report also notes, 'to capture this growing momentum towards zero-emissions markets, Australia needs a cohesive industry strategy and an ambitious climate target to keep up with our key trading partners' (BZE, 2021, p. 5).

The rapid shift in views about Australia's energy future is also reflected in the following reflections made in 2021 by the Business Council of Australia: 'The momentum for moving towards net zero by 2050 is unstoppable. The pace and scale of change is accelerating globally. Australia is at a crossroads: we can either embrace decarbonisation and seize a competitive advantage in developing new technologies and export industries; or be left behind and pay the price' (Special Broadcasting Service (SBS), 2021).

4 Australian government climate and energy policies

The bitterly contested 'climate wars' engulfing Australian climate and energy debates over the last twenty-five years have created a long and sustained period of policy chaos and uncertainty (see also Godden chapter in this book).

Between 1996 and 2007, the LNP government, led by conservative climate-sceptic Prime Minister, John Howard, combined fierce opposition to climate action and emission reduction measures with strong and unwavering support for the coal industry (Pearse et al., 2013). The Rudd and Gillard Labor governments (2007–2014) did manage to implement a range of policies aimed at reducing GHG emissions and accelerating investment in renewable energy. While the Rudd government's attempt to introduce an emissions trading scheme (the Carbon Pollution Reduction Scheme) was defeated in 2009, the Gillard Labor government succeeded in implementing a national carbon price, a key component of its Clean Energy Futures Package (CEF) for three years between 2011 and 2014 (Hudson, 2019).

Many CEF initiatives, including the carbon price, were rapidly reversed following the 2013 election of the LNP government led by Prime Minister Tony Abbott, which replaced the CEF with a $2.55 billion Emissions Reduction Fund paying businesses, local government and community organisations for emission reduction projects (Hudson, 2019). LNP Prime Minister Malcolm Turnbull, who replaced Tony Abbott in September 2015, unsuccessfully attempted to implement a series of policy packages designed to create a more orderly transition to a low emissions energy system. These policy packages, which included a 'baseline and credit' scheme, a Clean Energy Target, and a National Energy Guarantee, were all rapidly undermined and defeated by LNP members firmly committed to ongoing support for coal (Hudson, 2019).

Scott Morrison, who in turn replaced Turnbull as LNP Prime Minister in August 2018, gained considerable notoriety by holding up a lump of coal in Parliament while confirming his view that coal industry jobs and profitability were a higher priority than reducing carbon emissions. The Morrison government also successfully mobilised concern about potential loss of jobs in coal dependent regions as part of the political strategy which helped him win the 2019 federal election (Hudson, 2019).

The Labor Government led by Prime Minister Anthony Albanese, elected in May 2022, has combined strong support for higher emission reduction targets and the acceleration of renewable energy investment with an ongoing commitment to protect employment in the coal industry. The management of rapidly escalating energy prices in fact became the Albanese Government's first major policy challenge. As noted above, the Australian energy crisis was driven by a range of factors including the Russia-Ukraine war, a shortage of gas available for domestic use and the increasingly fragile state of Australia's ageing coal fired power generators. As Prime Minister Albanese correctly noted, these problems were all accentuated by the chaotic and counter-productive climate and energy policies of previous LNP governments (Albanese, 2022).

> It's not acceptable that we have had a government previously, which was in office for three terms, announced 22 different energy policies and didn't land one.... You've had a decade of neglect ... you've had a decade where we have an energy grid that isn't fit for purpose for the 21st century. You've had too many arguments taking place rather than the investment certainty which comes from having an energy policy ... And what we find is the consequences of the former government's failure to put in place an energy policy is being felt right now, with problems in the market. (Albanese, 2022)

In June 2022, Climate Change Minister, Chris Bowen, announced that the new government would formalise Australia's Paris Agreement Nationally Determined Contributions (NDC) pledge to reduce greenhouse gas emissions by 43 per cent below 2005 levels by 2030 (Bowen, 2022). This commitment was formally enshrined in the *Climate Change Bill 2022* passed by the Australian Parliament in September 2022 (see Godden chapter in this book). While this was a significant improvement on the previous government's 2030 commitment of 26–28% reduction in GHG emissions, it still fell well short of the GHG reduction targets which the United Nations Environment Program (UNEP) noted would be required to keep global warming below 1.5 degrees.

Bowen also announced a wide range of other climate action commitments, including investments of over $23 billion designed to accelerate the transition to renewable energy and electric vehicles. The new Labor government has however been careful not to raise expectations about halting new coal and gas export projects. Prime Minister Albanese noted during the 2022 election campaign that, 'if coal mines stack up environmentally, and then commercially, which is the decision for the companies, then they get approved. ... Labor would welcome any jobs that would be created' (Foley and Toscano, 2022).

The determination of successive LNP governments to protect the interests of coal industry businesses and investors has certainly played an important role in undermining the possibility of a swift and well-managed transition away from coal in Australia. A range of other factors have, however, driven increased support for a just and well-managed energy transition. In addition to the supportive role which state governments have played in encouraging renewable energy, these factors include, a wide array of climate change advocacy initiatives, increasing recognition by households and business of the financial as well as environmental benefits of investing in renewable energy, heightened awareness of the importance of just transition strategies and the growing impact of climate risk litigation and divestment campaigns.

5 The importance of just and well managed regional energy transition strategies

Internationally and in Australia, there is growing awareness that broad public and political support for accelerating the phase-out of fossil fuels depends on workers and communities being fully convinced that governments and business are genuinely committed to inclusive, long term, well-resourced, just transition principles and policies (Jacobs and Steckel, 2022). The political sensitivity of coal phase-out strategies has been heightened in Australia by the fact that over 90% of Australian employment in coal production is concentrated in a small number of regions, including the Bowen Basin in Central Queensland, the Hunter Valley in New South Wales and the Latrobe Valley in Victoria (Centre for Policy Development, 2021).

Recent experience of regional transitions in the Latrobe Valley, Hunter Valley and Central Queensland, confirm and reinforce findings from international research highlighting the following key success factors for driving just and well-managed regional transition strategies (Wiseman and Wollersheim, 2021; Cahill, 2022).

- *Respectful and inclusive engagement with workers, communities and all relevant stakeholders.* Particular attention needs to be paid to ensuring inclusion of groups who are often sidelined from these discussions, including women, young people, Indigenous people and socio-economically disadvantaged groups.
- *Strong, proactive and well-coordinated leadership from all levels of government.* This leadership needs to include clear and compelling narratives about the necessity of phasing out fossil fuel industries to meet emissions reduction targets,

along with the significant employment opportunities which can be created through a proactive and well-managed transition to a clean energy economy.

- *Transition governance authorities combining national and state level policy coordination with local accountability, knowledge and expertise.* Dialogue and engagement needs to extend well beyond consultation, enabling all relevant stakeholders to contribute to fully informed and transparent discussions and deliberations (Smith, 2017).
- *Re-employment, retraining and early retirement support for workers affected by mining and plant closures.* Opportunities to access early retirement, redeployment and retraining need to be readily available to workers prior to workplace closures. Noting that new clean energy jobs will not necessarily be in the same locations as existing coal sector jobs, relocation and retraining packages will also be essential.
- *Economic renewal and diversification policies and strategies building on regional strengths and informed by local experience and insights.* Carefully facilitated and respectful conversations between government, workers, business and communities can play a crucial role in visualising, planning and building alternative economic pathways.
- *Maximising the creation of secure, high-quality jobs.* While reaffirming that 'managed well, transitions to environmentally and socially sustainable economies can become a strong driver of job creation, social justice and poverty eradication', the International Labor Organization (ILO) also cautions that, 'the job-creating potential of environmental sustainability is not a given: the right policies are needed to promote green industries while ensuring decent work within them' (ILO, 2015, p. 10).
- *Expanding employment opportunities and access to services for all community members.* The impact of energy transitions on households, communities and businesses affected by plant closures extends well beyond workers directly employed in plants and mines. Particular attention needs to be paid to addressing the employment and community support priorities of vulnerable individuals, including women, low-income households and Indigenous communities.
- *Adequately resourced, long-term rehabilitation plans for mine sites and power plants.* Sufficient funding needs to be available to rehabilitate mine sites in ecologically sound ways, and in line with community expectations.
- *Ensuring government and business commitments to just transition goals are underpinned by detailed implementation plans and adequate long-term resourcing.* The costs and responsibilities for addressing the impacts of coal transition strategies also need to be fully transparent and equitably shared.

6 Climate related litigation and divestment strategies

Australian and international climate change litigation interventions include an increasingly broad array of actions designed to; i) encourage and require climate risk disclosure by corporations and governments; ii) highlight the impact of fossil fuel emissions and climate change impacts on human rights; and iii) employ climate science evidence to challenge and halt fossil fuel projects (see Benjamin and McCallum in this book; see also Peel and Osofsky, 2021; UNEP and Sabin Center for Climate Change Law, 2020; Setzer and Higham, 2021).

6.1 Climate risk disclosure litigation

Litigation encouraging and requiring climate risk disclosure commonly builds on the recommendations of the Task Force on Climate-related Financial Disclosures (TCFD, 2017). The TCFD guidelines are now the widely accepted global standard for climate risk governance, strategy, risk management, metrics and targets for companies and investors. Climate risks as defined by the TCFD include *Transition Risks* (risks arising from the policy, legal, technological and financial actions required to meet climate change mitigation and adaptation goals) and *Physical Risks* (risks resulting from the acute and chronic impacts of climate change) (TCFD, 2017).

Australian financial regulators, including the Australian Securities and Investment Commission (ASIC), the Australian Prudential Regulation Authority (APRA), the Australian Securities Exchange (ASX) Corporate Governance Council and the Reserve Bank of Australia (RBA), have all issued increasingly strong advice requiring Australian companies to align their climate disclosure policies and practices with TCFD guidelines (Debelle, 2021).

The Reserve Bank of Australia noted in 2019, for example, that, 'climate change is exposing financial institutions and the financial system more broadly to risks that will rise over time, if not addressed' (RBA, 2019, p. 1). The 2021 APRA Prudential Practice Guide on Climate Change Financial Risks (2021, p. 19) also advises that 'APRA anticipates the demand for reliable and timely climate risk disclosure will increase over time, and for institutions with international activities there is a need to be prepared to comply with mandatory climate risk disclosures in other jurisdictions.'

In 2019, Noel Hutley SC published a highly influential legal opinion noting that the TCFD climate risk guidelines appeared to have become the Australian 'industry standard' and that company directors who failed to consider climate change risks could potentially be found liable for breaching their legal duty of care and diligence (Hutley and Hartford-Davis, 2019). The 2021 update of this legal opinion noted that 'it is clear the benchmark for directors on climate change and attendant risks and opportunities continues to rise' (Hutley and Hartford-Davis, 2021, p. 2). The 2021 opinion also highlighted the possibility that company directors could be found to have engaged in misleading or deceptive conduct by engaging in 'greenwashing' (ie. misrepresenting or exaggerating the extent to which company plans and strategies are aligned with publicly stated climate change and emissions reduction goals) (Hutley and Hartford-Davis, 2021). A number of legal actions have recently been instigated to test the extent to which Australian companies and company directors are liable for failing to adequately disclose and address climate risks and for engaging in greenwashing.

In 2017, Commonwealth Bank shareholders, Guy and Kim Abrahams, brought a claim against the Commonwealth Bank of Australia (CBA) alleging that the CBA's Annual Report failed to adequately disclose climate change related risks (Hutchens, 2017). The case was withdrawn shortly after being filed when the CBA agreed to; i) include acknowledgement in its Annual Report that climate change posed a significant risk to bank operations; ii) publicly commit to policies aligned with the goal of a net zero economy by 2050; and iii) not lend money to finance the development of the Adani coal mine (Hutchens, 2017). In 2021, Guy Abrahams successfully brought a second claim seeking access to documents providing information about seven CBA funded oil and gas projects in order to clarify the extent to which these projects were consistent with the Paris Agreement climate goals (Equity Generation Lawyers, 2021).

In 2018, Mark McVeigh, a 23 year old member of the Retail Employees Superannuation Trust (REST), commenced proceedings alleging that REST had breached the *Corporations Act 2001 (Cth)* and the *Superannuation Industry (Supervision) Act 1993 (Cth)* by failing to provide adequate information regarding climate change risks and the fund's management of such risks (*McVeigh v REST,* [2019]). The litigation was settled after REST acknowledged that 'climate change is a material, direct and current financial risk to the superannuation fund' and agreed to implement climate change risk management strategies.

In 2020, Kathleen O'Donnell, a 23 year old owner of government bonds, brought a class action against the Commonwealth of Australia arguing that the government should be held accountable for not disclosing the risks of climate change to sovereign bond investors (*O'Donnell v Commonwealth, [*2020]). The Court rejected the claim on the basis that the applicant did not have standing and suggested that the claim of misleading or deceptive conduct would, 'require improvement' to demonstrate that the relief sought had direct practical and financial importance for the applicant – rather than demonstrating an emotional or intellectual concern about climate change risks.

In 2021, the Australasian Centre for Corporate Responsibility (ACCR) brought an action against the mining company Santos arguing that the company was engaging in 'misleading and deceptive conduct' by claiming that natural gas and blue hydrogen are 'clean fuels' and that their use is consistent with the company's stated goal of reaching net zero emissions by 2040. As ACCR Executive Director, Brynn O'Brien notes, this case has the potential to create globally significant precedents, testing the extent to which companies can appear to set ambitious net zero emission targets without any real intention of meeting them, 'signalling corporations have the matter at hand when that is so far from the case' (Peacock, 2021).

The growing number of climate risk disclosure cases of this kind, combined with the increasing focus of regulatory agencies on climate risk transparency, is also creating a more fertile political environment for anti-greenwashing and disclosure actions being undertaken by shareholder action and divestment advocacy organisations such as Market Forces (2022), Greenpeace (2021) and the ACCR (2022).

6.2 Climate change and human rights litigation

There is growing recognition by the United Nations Human Rights Council and other international treaty bodies that climate change represents a significant threat to human rights (Godden in this book; Peel and Osofsky, 2021). In 2019, the UN Special Rapporteur on extreme poverty and human rights found that climate change threatens the right to life, water and sanitation, health, food, and housing, as well as a 'wide range of civil and political rights' (Bachelet, 2019).

Legal actions based on the human rights implications of climate change have now been initiated (with varying levels of success) in many international jurisdictions including the United States, Mexico, Germany, France, the UK, South Korea and Columbia (de Wit, 2022). In 2018, the Supreme Court of Justice of Colombia advised that the 'fundamental rights of life, health, the minimum subsistence, freedom and human dignity are substantially linked and determined by the environment and the ecosystem' (Future Generations v Ministry for the Environment and Others, [2018], p. 13). The Court therefore ordered that the Presidency of the Republic rapidly introduce short, medium and long term government climate action policies, including laws to offset the rate of deforestation in the Amazon (*Future Generations v Ministry for the Environment and Others,* [2018]).

In July 2022, the Supreme Court of Brazil handed down a landmark judgement recognising the Paris Climate Agreement as a Human Rights Treaty and concluding that, 'treaties on environmental law are a type of human rights treaty and, for that reason, enjoy supranational status' (Kaminski, 2022). In July 2022, Australia's newly elected Labor government announced at the Pacific Islands Forum that it would seek to add to this momentum by supporting an initiative by Vanuatu for the International Court of Justice to consider whether climate inaction is a breach of human rights (Bagshaw, 2022).

While the lack of a national human rights framework constrains the potential for legal challenges based on the human rights impacts of climate change in Australia, a number of recent cases have tested the implications of the principle of 'duty of care' for coal-phase out litigation.

The most influential case focussing on duty of care has been *Sharma v Minister for the Environment* (2021), in which eight Australian children sought an injunction to restrain the Commonwealth Minister for the Environment from approving the expansion of the Whitehaven Vickery coal mine (Bush, 2022). The applicants claimed that the expansion of this mine would increase carbon emissions by 100 million tons per year. In May 2021, Justice Bromberg of the Federal Court found that the Minister did owe children a duty of care to protect them from climate change. Justice Bromberg noted that 'trauma will be far more common and good health harder to hold and maintain… It will largely be inflicted by the inaction of this generation of adults, in what might fairly be described as the greatest inter-generational injustice ever inflicted by one generation of humans upon the next' (Sharma v Minister for the Environment, [2021], p. 72–73).

On March 15, 2022, the Federal Court of Australia upheld an appeal by the Minister, overturning the initial decision to impose a duty of care (Tigre, 2022; see also Godden in this book). Importantly, however, the court also continued to note and accept expert evidence that the burning of coal from the Whitehaven project was likely to increase the risk of global average surface temperatures increasing beyond 2°C above pre-industrial levels, causing catastrophic climatic hazards (Tigre, 2022).

A number of actions addressing human rights concerns have also been taken at state levels in Australia. In *Waratah Coal v Youth Verdict* (2020), the Queensland Land Court was asked to consider whether the application by Waratah Coal for a mining lease and environmental authority to develop a thermal coal mine was in breach of the *Human Rights Act 2019* (Qld). The objectors argued that the mine would contribute to climate change and approval would therefore be incompatible with human rights provisions, including the rights to recognition and equality before the law, right to life, property rights, the rights of children and the cultural rights of Aboriginal and Torres Strait Islander peoples.

In 2021, Bushfire Survivors for Climate Action (BSCA) sought an order compelling the NSW Environment Protection Authority (EPA) to develop guidelines and policies protecting the environment from climate change (Cox, 2021). While the Court held that the EPA had indeed failed in its duty to implement the necessary policies, the Court did not specify actions which the EPA should take, noting that the EPA has a discretion as to the specific content of the policies it develops and implements (Cox, 2021).

Australian climate advocacy organisations are also focusing greater attention on legislative as well as litigation strategies. In May 2021, the House of Representatives considered (and rejected) The *Liability for Climate Change Damage (Make the Polluters Pay) Bill 2021*. This Bill sought to make emitters of greenhouse gases greater than 1 million tonnes in any 12 month period liable for climate change damage (with retrospective effect), giving victims the right to bring an action against fossil fuel companies.

6.3 Litigation opposing specific coal projects

Australian climate activists have also employed a range of legal strategies aimed at halting specific coal mining projects and developments. In 2016, the Australian Conservation Foundation (ACF) challenged the Minister for Environment's decision to approve the Adani coal mine (Australian Conservation Foundation Inc (ACF) v Minister for the Environment, [2016]). Grounds for this challenge included the failure of the Minister to consider the impacts of the mine on Australian environments (such as the Great Barrier Reef) as well as the impact of GHG emissions arising from the transport and combustion of coal overseas. The Court rejected the ACF case, primarily on the grounds that there was insufficient evidence to show that the environmental impacts were a direct consequence of the proposed mining activities (*ACF v Minister for the Environment,* [2016]).

In 2017, the Chief Judge of the New South Wales Land and Environment Court, Brian Preston dismissed an appeal by Gloucester Resources Limited seeking approval to develop a new coal mine at Rocky Hill in the Gloucester Valley of NSW (Gloucester Resources Limited v Minister for Planning, [2019]). Reasons for this judgement included the climate change impacts of the emissions produced by the mine as well as its visual and social impacts.

In 2021, Environment Victoria commenced a proceeding in the Supreme Court of Victoria against the Victorian EPA seeking judicial review of its decision in relation to the three remaining coal power stations in Victoria (La Nauze, 2021). Environment Victoria argued that in failing to set limits on greenhouse gas emissions when making its decision regarding the licences, the EPA failed to require best practice management of toxic emissions and thus, failed to take proper account of the principles of environmental protection contained in the *Environment Protection Act* 1970 (Vic).

In November 2021, the Mullaley Gas and Pipeline community group challenged a decision of the Independent Planning Commission (IPC) to grant development consent to Santos for the Narrabri coal seam gas project (*Mullaley Gas and Pipeline Accord Inc v Santos* [2021]). The Federal Court upheld the IPC decision that the downstream GHG emissions were outside the control of Santos. In July 2022, Bushfire Survivors for Climate Action announced that it was bringing a further claim seeking to prevent the Narrabri expansion (Environmental Defenders Office, 2022a).

Australian climate advocacy organisations have continued to intensify and broaden their deployment of climate litigation strategies following the election of the Albanese Labor Government. In June 2022, the Environmental Defenders Office(2022b) sought a Federal Court injunction arguing that approval for the Scarborough gas project should be withheld unless the project was approved under the *Environment Protection and Biodiversity Conservation Act 1999* (Cth) (EPBC Act). The EDO argued that this decision should take account of the negative impact which GHG emissions from the Scarborough project would have on the Great Barrier Reef.

In July 2022, the Environment Council of Central Queensland (ECCQ) wrote to newly appointed federal Environment Minister, Tanya Plibersek, requesting that she reconsider the EPBC assessment of 19 coal and gas project approvals (Slezak and Sedghi, 2022). The request for reassessment of these projects (including the Narrabri, Warratah and Woodside projects) was made on the basis that the Minister has a legal obligation to consider the broader effects of GHG emissions and climate change when considering impacts on Australian and international environments (Schuijers, 2022).

This 'reconsideration request' rests on the argument that the most recent climate science provides substantial new evidence that GHG emissions from all new fossil fuel projects are accelerating global warming (Schuijers, 2022). These projects are therefore likely to have a significant negative impact on Australia's environmental heritage and biodiversity. The outcome of this request–and of subsequent legal appeals–will play an important role in clarifying the extent to which government policy makers and regulators now need to take account of climate change evidence and impacts in considering future coal mining projects.

7 Climate litigation: an increasingly powerful weapon in coal phase out plans and strategies

Recent Australian and international experience strengthens understanding of the importance of deploying multiple interlinked strategic interventions in order to accelerate a rapid, equitable and well-managed phase-out of coal.

Increases in the price of coal relative to renewable energy are clearly having a significant impact on investment decisions in relation to new and existing coal mining and coal industry projects. Strong, proactive and well-coordinated government policy and regulation will, however, also play a crucial role in ensuring that the phase- out of coal occurs at the speed required to keep global warming as close as possible to 1.5 °C. Political support for decisive government coal phase-out policies will in turn depend on strengthening public awareness of, the role which fossil fuel emissions play in intensifying climate risks; the economic opportunities created by a well-managed transition to renewable energy; and the possibility that accelerating the phase-out of coal can be achieved while protecting the jobs and livelihoods of coal-dependent workers and communities.

Recent Australian experience also demonstrates the increasingly powerful contribution which climate- related legal actions are making in directly challenging the social license of individual coal projects, as well as in strengthening the case for disclosing and addressing the climate risks of coal. Even in instances where legal actions are not fully successful, climate litigation can have a significant impact on the views and attitudes of corporations, investors, policy makers and the general public in relation to the desirability and inevitably of a rapid phase-out of coal. Recent evidence also suggests that while Australian courts are now often willing to accept scientific evidence about the climate risks of coal, substantial work is still required to strengthen the preparedness of courts to attribute specific climate-related harms to individual fossil fuel projects.

While the broader applicability of learning from Australian experience clearly depends on specific economic, legislative and judicial contexts, there is mounting evidence that climate-related litigation has growing potential to complement public advocacy, shareholder action and divestment as vital weapons in the armoury of activists and policy makers seeking to accelerate the phase-out of coal and other fossil fuels.

References

Albanese, A., 2022. *Doorstop interview – Brisbane: transcript.* Available at: <https://www.pm.gov.au/media/doorstop-interview-brisbane> [Accessed 8 July 2022].

Australasian Centre for Corporate Responsibility (ACCR), 2022. *Australasian Centre for Corporate Responsibility.* Available at: <https://www.accr.org.au/> [Accessed 15 July 2022].

Australian Bureau of Statistics (ABS), 2022. *ABS employment June 2022.* Available at: <https://www.abs.gov.au/statistics/labour/employment-and-unemployment/labour-force-australia/latest-release> [Accessed July 2022].

Australian Conservation Foundation Inc v Minister for the Environment [2016] FCA 1042.

Australian Energy Market Operator (AEMO), 2022. *Integrated system plan 2022.* AEMO. Available at: <https://aemo.com.au/en/energy-systems/major-publications/integrated-system-plan-isp/2022-integrated-system-plan-isp> [Accessed 10 July 2022].

Australian Prudential Regulation Authority (APRA), 2021. *Prudential practice guide: CPG 229 climate change financial risks.* APRA. Available at: <https://www.apra.gov.au/sites/default/files/2021-11/Final%20Prudential%20Practice%20Guide%20CPG%20229%20Climate%20Change%20Financial%20Risks.pdf> [Accessed 7 September 2022].

Bachalet, M., 2019. *Opening statement to the 42nd session of the Human Rights Council. Available at:* <https://www.ohchr.org/en/climate-change> [Accessed 10 July 2022].

Bagshaw, E., 2022. Australia prepares for likelihood of climate refugees, backs push for UN justice. *The Age, 11* July. Available at: <https://www.theage.com.au/politics/federal/australia-prepares-for-likelihood-of-climate-refugees-backs-push-for-un-justice-20220711-p5b0rg.html?cid=c234690058b64e8fdf4b6306ae30a7d4> [Accessed 13 July 2022].

Beaven, K., 2022. Coal exports forecast to smash record with value set to break $100 billion this financial year. *Australian Broadcasting Corporation (ABC) News,* 4 April. Available at: <https://www.abc.net.au/news/2022-04-04/australian-coal-exports-to-break-record/100964414> [Accessed July 8 2022].

Beyond Zero Emissions (BZE), 2021. *Export Powerhouse, Australia's $333 billion opportunity.* Beyond Zero Emissions. Available at: <https://bze.org.au/research_release/export-powerhouse/> [Accessed 1 July 2022].

Bowen, L., 2022. *Address to the IGCC 2022 climate change investment and finance summit.* Available at: <https://www.minister.industry.gov.au/ministers/bowen/speeches/address-igcc-2022-climate-change-investment-and-finance-summit> [Accessed 20 June 2022].

Burdon, R., Hughes, L., Lord, M., Madeddu, S., Ueckerdt, F. and Wang, C., 2019. *Innovation and export opportunities of the energy transition.* Energy Transition Hub. The Australian-German Energy Transition Hub. Available at: <https://www.energy-transition-hub.org/files/resource/attachment/innovation_and_export_opportunities_of_et_final_0.pdf> [Accessed 10 May 2022].

Bush, Z., 2022. Is climate change justiciable? Politics and policy in Minister for the Environment v Sharma. *Australian Public Law,* [blog] 29 June. Available at: <https://www.auspublaw.org/blog/2022/06/is-climate-change-justiciable-politics-and-policy-in-minister-for-the-environment-v-sharma> [Accessed 5 July 2022].

Cahill, A., 2022. *What regions need on the path to net zero.* Available at: <https://nexteconomy.com.au/work/what-regions-need-on-the-path-to-net-zero-2/> [Accessed 7 September 2022].

Carbon Brief, 2022. *Australia's biggest coal-fired power plant to shut years ahead of schedule.* Available at: <https://www.carbonbrief.org/daily-brief/australias-biggest-coal-fired-power-plant-to-shut-years-ahead-of-schedule/> [Accessed 10 July 2022].

Centre for Policy Development (CPD), 2021. *Who's buying? The impact of global decarbonisation on Australia's regions.* Centre for Policy Development. Available at: <https://cpd.org.au/2022/01/whos-buying-centre-for-policy-development/> [Accessed 20 May 2022].

Christoff, P., 2021. Mining a fractured landscape: the political economy of coal in Australia. In: M. Jacobs and J. Steckel, eds., 2022. *The political economy of coal: obstacles to clean energy transitions*, London: Routledge, pp. 233–257.

Clean Energy Council, 2022, *Clean energy Australia report.* Clean Energy Council. Available at: <https://assets.cleanenergycouncil.org.au/documents/resources/reports/clean-energy-australia/clean-energy-australia-report-2022.pdf> [Accessed 8 September 2022].

Corporations Act 2001 (Cth). Available at: <http://classic.austlii.edu.au/au/legis/cth/consol_act/ca2001172/> [Accessed 8 September 2022].

Cox, L., 2021. NSW bushfire survivors win legal battle ordering EPA to take action on climate crisis. The *Guardian,* 26 August. <https://www.theguardian.com/science/2021/aug/26/nsw-bushfire-survivors-win-legal-battle-ordering-epa-to-take-action-on-climate-crisis> [Accessed 7 September 2022].

Debelle, G., 2021. *Climate risks and the Australian financial system.* 14 October 2021, CFA Australia Investment Conference, Melbourne. Available at: <https://www.rba.gov.au/speeches/2021/pdf/sp-dg-2021-10-14.pdf> [Accessed 4 July 2022].

de Wit, E., 2022. *Climate change litigation update. Available at:*<https://www.nortonrosefulbright.com/en-au/knowledge/publications/901a1a41/climate-change-litigation-update> [Accessed 7 September 2022].

Diluiso, F., et al., 2021. Coal transitions – part 1: a systematic map and review of case study learnings from national, regional and local coal phase out experiences. *Environmental Research Letters*, 16(11), 113003.

Environmental Defenders Office (EDO), 2022a. *Bushfire survivors' legal challenge to massive Narrabri coal mine extension.* Available at: <https://www.edo.org.au/2022/07/05/bushfire-survivors-legal-challenge-to-massive-narrabri-coal-mine-extension/> [Accessed 12 July 2022].

Environmental Defenders Office (EDO), 2022b. *Injunction sought against Woodside's Scarborough Gas project.* Available at: <https://www.edo.org.au/2022/06/22/injunction-sought-against-woodsides-scarborough-gas-project-to-protect-great-barrier-reef/> [Accessed 7 September 2022].

Environment Protection and Biodiversity Conservation Act 1999 (Cth). Available at: <https://www.legislation.gov.au/Details/C2016C00777> [Accessed 8 September 2022].

Equity Generation Lawyers, 2021. *Abrahams-v-Commonwealth Bank of Australia.*
Available at: <https://equitygenerationlawyers.com/abrahams-v-commonwealth-bank-of-australia-2021/> [Accessed 10 July 2022].

Foley, M., and Toscano, N., 2022. Albanese aims for superpower status in global energy transition. *The Age,* 11 July. Available at: <https://www.theage.com.au/politics/federal/albanese-aims-for-superpower-status-in-global-energy-transition-20220711-p5b0sq.html> [Accessed 11 July 2022].

Future Generations v Ministry for the Environment and Others (2018), Radicación no. 11001-22-03-000-2018-00319-01.

Geoscience Australia, 2022. *Coal.* Available at: <https://www.ga.gov.au/digital-publication/aecr2021/coal> [Accessed 12 July 2022].

Geoscience Australia, n.d. *Solar energy.* Available at: <https://www.ga.gov.au/scientific-topics/energy/resources/other-renewable-energy-resources/solar-energy> [Accessed 12 July 2022.

Gloucester Resources Limited v Minister for Planning [2019] NSWLEC 7.

Gosens, J., Turnbull, A. and Jotzo, F., 2021. China's decarbonization and energy security plans will reduce seaborne coal imports: results from an installation-level model. *Joule*, 6(1), pp. 782–815.

Graham, P., Hayward, J., Foster, J., and Havas, L., 2021. *GenCost Report 2021–22. Commonwealth Scientific and Industrial Research Organisation (CSIRO). Available at: <https://publications.csiro.au/publications/publication/PIcsiro:EP2022-2576* > [Accessed 7 September 2022].

Greenpeace, 2021. *Dirty power.* Available at: <https://act.greenpeace.org.au/dirtypower> [Accessed 12 July 2022].

Hudson, M., 2019. 'A form of madness': Australian climate and energy. *Environmental Politics*, 28(3), pp. 583–589.

Human Rights Act 2019 (Qld). Available at: <https://www.legislation.qld.gov.au/view/html/asmade/act-2019-005> [Accessed 8 September 2022].

Hutchens, G., 2017. Commonwealth Bank shareholders drop suit over nondisclosure of climate risks. *The Guardian*, 21 September 2017. Available at: <https://www.theguardian.com/australia-news/2017/sep/21/commonwealth-bank-shareholders-drop-suit-over-non-disclosure-of-climate-risks> [Accessed 12 July 2022].

Hutley, N., and Hartford-Davis, S., 2019. *Climate change and directors' duties: memorandum of opinion.* The Centre for Policy Development. Available at: <https://cpd.org.au/wp-content/uploads/2019/03/Noel-Hutley-SC-and-Sebastian-Hartford-Davis-Opinion-2019-and-2016_pdf.pdf> [Accessed 12 July 2022].

Hutley, N. and Hartford-Davis, S., 2021. *Climate Change and Directors' Duties: Further Supplementary Memorandum Of Opinion.* The Centre for Policy Development. Available at: <https://cpd.org.au/wp-content/uploads/2021/04/Further-Supplementary-Opinion-2021-3.pdf> [Accessed 12 July 2022].

International Labor Organisation (ILO), 2015. *Guidelines for a just transition towards environmentally sustainable economies and societies for all.* Geneva: International Labour Office. Available at: <https://www.ilo.org/wcmsp5/groups/public/—ed_emp/—emp_ent/documents/publication/wcms_432859.pdf> [Accessed 7 September 2022].

International Renewable Energy Agency (IRENA), 2019. *Renewable Power Generation Costs In 2019.* IRENA. Available at: <https://www.irena.org/-/media/Files/IRENA/Agency/Publication/2020/Jun/IRENA_Power_Generation_Costs_2019.pdf> [Accessed 12 July 2022].

Jacobs, M., and Steckel, J. 2022. *The political economy of coal: obstacles to clean energy transitions.* London: Routledge.

Kaminski, I., 2022. Brazilian court world's first to recognise Paris Agreement as human rights treaty. *Climate Home News* (7 July). Available at: <https://www.climatechangenews.com/2022/07/07/brazilian-court-worlds-first-to-recognise-paris-agreement-as-human-rights-treaty/> [Accessed 4 July 2022].

Kemp, J., McCowage, M., and Wang, F., 2021. *Towards net zero implications for Australia of energy policies in East Asia.* Reserve Bank of Australia. Available at: <https://www.rba.gov.au/publications/bulletin/2021/sep/towards-net-zero-implications-for-australia-of-energy-policies-in-east-asia.html> [Accessed 25 June 2022].

La Nauze, J., 2021. Why we're taking the EPA to court. *Environment Victoria*, [blog] 23 September. Available at:<https://environmentvictoria.org.au/2021/09/23/why-were-taking-the-epa-to-court/> [Accessed 7 September 2022].

Market Forces, 2022. *Is your super fund's 'sustainable' option invested in companies expanding fossil fuel industry?.* Available at: <https://www.marketforces.org.au/sustainable-funds-analysis-2022/> [Accessed 8 September 2022].

McVeigh v Retail Employees Superannuation Pty Ltd [2019] FCA 14.

Minister for the Environment v Sharma [2021] FCA 560.

Morton, A., 2022. Labor faces decisions on approval of up to 27 coal developments including greenfield mines. *The Guardian*, 11 July.

Available at: <https://www.theguardian.com/environment/2022/jul/11/labor-faces-decisions-on-approval-of-up-to-27-coal-developments-including-greenfield-mines-analysis-shows> [Accessed 11 July 2022].

Mullaley Gas and Pipeline Accord Inc v Santos NSW (Eastern) Pty Ltd [2021] NSWLEC 11.

Nelson, T., Gilmore, J., 2021. The end of coal is coming 3 times faster than expected. Governments must accept it and urgently support a 'just transition'. *The Conversation*, 13 December. Available at: <https://theconversation.com/the-end-of-coal-is-coming-3-times-faster-than-expected-governments-must-accept-it-and-urgently-support-a-just-transition-173591> [Accessed 25 June 2022].

O'Donnell v Commonwealth of Australia [2021] FCA 1223.

Ogge, M., Quicke, A., and Campbell, R., 2021. *Undermining climate action the Australian way*. The Australia Institute. Available at: <https://australiainstitute.org.au/wp-content/uploads/2021/11/P1163-Undermining-climate-action-the-Australian-way-WEB.pdf> [Accessed 4 July 2022].

Peacock, B., 2021. Why the federal court case against Santos could have wide-reaching ramifications. *PV Magazine*, 21 September. Available at: <https://www.pv-magazine-australia.com/2021/09/21/why-the-federal-court-case-against-santos-could-have-wide-reaching-ramifications/> [Accessed 12 July 2022].

Pearse, G., McKnight, D. and Burton, B., 2013. *Big Coal: Australia's Dirtiest Habit.* Sydney: NewSouth.

Peel, J. and Markey-Towler, R., 2021. A duty to care, the case of Sharma v Minister for the Environment [2021] FCA 560. *Journal of Environmental Law*, 33(3), pp. 727–736.

Peel, J. and Osofsky, H., 2021. Climate change litigation. *Annual Review of Law and Social Science*, 16(1), pp. 21–38.

Redfearn, G., 2022. Australia's greenhouse pollution from coal higher per person than any other developed country, data shows. *The Guardian*, 20 May. Available at: <https://www.theguardian.com/environment/2022/may/20/australias-greenhouse-pollution-from-coal-higher-per-person-than-any-other-developed-country-data-shows?CMP=share_btn_tw> [Accessed 12 July 2022].

Reserve Bank of Australia (RBA), 2019. *Financial stability review – October 2019.* RBA. Available at: <https://www.rba.gov.au/publications/fsr/2019/oct/box-c-financial-stability-risks-from-climate-change.html> [Accessed 8 July 2022].

Schuijers, L., 2022. Times have changed: why the environment minister is being forced to reconsider climate-related impacts of pending fossil fuel approvals. *The Conversation*, 11 July. Available at: <https://theconversation.com/times-have-changed-why-the-environment-minister-is-being-forced-to-reconsider-climate-related-impacts-of-pending-fossil-fuel-approvals-186715?utm_source=twitter&utm_medium=bylinetwitterbutton> [Accessed 12 July 2022].

Setzer, J. and Higham, C., 2021. *Global trends in climate change litigation: 2021 snapshot.* Grantham Research Institute on Climate Change and the Environment and the Centre for Climate Change Economics and Policy. Available at: <https://www.lse.ac.uk/granthaminstitute/wp-content/uploads/2021/07/Global-trends-in-climate-change-litigation_2021-snapshot.pdf> [Accessed 12 July 2022].

Sharma v Minister for the Environment [2021] 391 ALR 1.

Slezak, M. and Sedghi, S., 2022. Labor asked to reassess decisions about coal and gas projects made by previous governments. *ABC News*, 11 July (Last updated 5:55 am on 11th July 2022). Available at: <https://www.abc.net.au/news/2022-07-11/legal-request-labor-coal-gas/101221006> [Accessed at 11 July 2022].

Smith, S., 2017. *Just transition: A report for the OECD.* Just Transition Centre. Available at: <https://www.oecd.org/environment/cc/g20-climate/collapsecontents/Just-Transition-Centre-report-just-transition.pdf> [Accessed 11 July 2022].

Special Broadcasting Service (SBS), 2021. Business Council of Australia backs 2030 climate target. *SBS News*, (Last updated 3:49 am on 9th October 2021). Available at: <https://www.sbs.com.au/news/article/business-council-of-australia-backs-2030-climate-target/evsbti0r4>

Superannuation Industry (Supervision) Act 1993 (Cth). Available at: <http://classic.austlii.edu.au/au/legis/cth/consol_act/sia1993473/> [Accessed 8 September 2022].

Task Force on Climate-related Financial Disclosures (TCFD), 2017. *Recommendations of the Task Force on Climate-related Financial Disclosures.* TCFD. Available at: <https://assets.bbhub.io/company/sites/60/2021/10/FINAL-2017-TCFD-Report.pdf> [Accessed 11 July 2022].

Tigre, M., 2022. Australian Federal Court dismisses the novel duty of care previously found in Sharma: what does it mean for future climate litigation in Australia?. *Sabin Center for Climate Change Law Climate Law Blog*, [blog] 21 March. Available at: <https://blogs.law.columbia.edu/climatechange/2022/03/21/australian-federal-court-dismisses-the-novel-duty-of-care-previously-found-in-sharma-what-does-it-mean-for-future-climate-litigation-in-australia/> [Accessed 20 June 2022].

United Nations Environment Programme (UNEP), and Sabin Center for Climate Change Law, 2020. *Global climate litigation report 2020 status review.* Nairobi: UNEP. Available at: <https://wedocs.unep.org/bitstream/handle/20.500.11822/34818/GCLR.pdf?sequence=1&isAllowed=y> [Accessed 28 May 2022].

Waratah Coal Pty Ltd v Youth Verdict Ltd [2020] QLC 33.

Welsby, D., Price, J., Pye, S. and Ekins, P., 2021. Unextractable fossil fuels in a 1.5 °C world. *Nature*, 597, pp. 230–234.

Wiseman, J., and Wollersheim, L., 2021. Building prosperous, just and resilient zero-carbon regions: learning from recent Australian and international experience. Melbourne: Melbourne Climate Futures, University of Melbourne. Available at: <https://law.unimelb.edu.au/__data/assets/pdf_file/0009/3934404/Wiseman-and-Wollersheim,-2021_MCF-Discussion-Paper_final.pdf> [Accessed 5 July 2022].

Anne Kallies

The Changing Role of Energy Networks in the Energy Transition

Abstract: Electricity networks are an essential part of a functioning electricity system. With the energy transition, generation is changing rapidly, becoming increasingly intermittent and decentralized. This change is creating new demands on networks. In most developed countries, liberalized electricity markets are the governance model to ensure efficient and reliable electricity supply. While differences exist, these markets are premised on a clear legal (and often ownership) separation between competitive generation and regulated network services. Transition is requiring a rethinking of the roles, responsibilities and objectives assigned to network providers, network operators and regulators, as well as the role of the state as guarantor of electricity supply as an essential service. Network regulatory reform required to facilitate a rapid transition includes network access, integrating network planning and investment with generation planning and investment, regulating the need for ancillary services as well adapting network regulation to new patterns of energy production and use that do not fit traditional energy flow such as microgrids, prosumerism and embedded networks. This chapter will provide an overview of how these challenges are addressed by different jurisdictions, drawing on selective case studies from the US, Australia and Europe, focusing on how energy governance models support or hinder these reforms.

1 Introduction

Electricity networks are an essential part of a functioning electricity system. With the energy transition, generation profiles are changing rapidly. They are becoming increasingly intermittent and decentralized. This change is creating new demands on networks.

In most developed countries, liberalized electricity markets are the governance model to ensure efficient and reliable electricity supply. While differences exist, these markets are premised on a clear legal (and often ownership) separation between competitive generation and regulated network services.

Much of the legal and policy literature engaging with energy transitions has been on supporting renewable energy generators in the wholesale electricity market. Legal

Anne Kallies is a Senior Lecturer at the RMIT Graduate School of Business & Law, Melbourne, Australia.

https://doi.org/10.1515/9783110752403-019

instruments such as feed-in-tariffs or renewable portfolio schemes and their respective advantages and disadvantages have long dominated the discourse.

However, the electricity sector (together with gas, water, and telecommunications) is an infrastructure industry. Often overlooked is the connection between the impact of a changing generation and user profile on the other parts of this interconnected system.

The uptake of renewable energy sources, but also the shift to demand side participation by consumer-producers of electricity (the so-called prosumers), interfaces with other parts of the industry – in particular the networks. Network regulatory reform is key to facilitating a rapid transition and takes centre stage in transition efforts of many countries. This includes reforms of network access, integrating network planning and investment with generation planning and investment, regulating the need for ancillary services as well adapting network regulation to new patterns of energy production and use. It also requires a rethinking of the roles, responsibilities and objectives assigned to network providers, network operators and regulators, as well as of the role of the state who is responsible for governing electricity supply as an essential service.

This chapter focusses on developed countries seeking to transition a mature electricity sector with existing grid infrastructure, governed by market frameworks. For many developing countries, which may not yet have a main grid and may still be in the process of electrification, the challenge is quite different. Here, innovative solutions, such as microgrids, may become the main mode of delivering electricity to a diverse range of customers in the future (see eg, Attanasio, 2021). At the same time, the urgency of providing access to energy to aid economic development, can lead to a lock-in of fossil fuel driven future energy pathways . Chapters in this volume (Zhang on Asia and the Pacific, Addaney and Kengni on Africa, and Shankar and Basu on India) provide valuable insights.

This chapter is structured as follows. In Part 2 it sets out the importance of electricity networks for the energy transition. Part 3 details basic structural elements of contemporary network regulatory frameworks, namely unbundling, third-party access and incentive regulation. Part 4 questions the ability of these frameworks to address transition challenges. Part 5 explains how network legal frameworks have to date sought to accommodate the energy transition. Part 6 concludes.

2 The Changing Roles and Functions of Electricity Networks

Electricity networks are the backbone of our traditional energy systems. They ensure that energy flows from where it is generated to where it is used. We distinguish transmission networks from distribution networks. The high voltage transmission networks transport electricity from the site of generation across large distances. Distribution and transmission networks are connected by substations which reduce voltage before disseminating the electricity further to the consumers through the distribution networks. Some very large users of electricity – such as aluminium smelters – may be connected directly to the transmission grid, but most users connect with the distribution network.

Networks are traditionally custom-built to connect generation sources, such as coal-fired or nuclear power stations, or hydro-electric resources, to big industrial users and load centres such as cities and other settlements. The installation cost of network infrastructure is enormous. For example, Australia's CSIRO estimates the capital cost of transmission line per km to be between 0.4 million AUD and 1.8 million AUD, depending on the size chosen. In addition, long planning horizons are required for installation. Generally speaking, electricity networks are planned and sized to ensure that at any given time the full electricity demand is covered.

The electricity grid is now subject to unprecedented challenges due to the decarbonisation of the energy sector. Support for renewable generation, in form of targets, tariffs and other schemes, has led to a rapid uptake of intermittent generation.

With the rise of renewables the existing network layouts are no longer fit for purpose. Renewable energy has to be generated at the location of the resource, as their energy sources, in particular wind or solar, are not easily transportable. Where these resources are remote to the existing grid, new infrastructure will be required. In addition, wind and solar in particular are intermittent sources of energy. This means that they are not always available and output is variable. They cannot be relied upon to provide for a continual output of electricity. One of the increasingly challenging tasks for network providers and operators is therefore to ensure they can reliably supply energy. This, in turn, leads to the need for additional so-called ancillary services to provide for system strength, frequency control and inertia.

Finally, the increase in (mostly renewable) generation that connects to distribution rather than transmission networks, as well as the rise in prosumerism, leads to changing patterns of network use.

The Australian Climate Change Authority succinctly summarised the renewable network challenge: 'wholesale market rules can affect the way renewable energy competes with other forms of generation, while network regulation can influence the cost and availability of access for renewable generation connecting to the grid' (Climate Change Authority, 2021). With the cost of renewable energy coming down rapidly, regulators and legislators are now turning to addressing the network, rather than the investment challenge for renewable energy.

3 An Introduction to the Regulatory Frameworks of Electricity Networks

Energy market liberalization has changed the way networks are regulated irreversibly. This section will introduce three central pillars of energy market liberalization, which determine the regulatory frameworks for network investment, planning and development. Market liberalization has seen principles of microeconomics embodied in competition law and energy regulation. Its key elements of third-party access, unbundling, and incentive regulation all seek to mimic competition and achieve efficiencies in network investment, management and use.

3.1 Unbundling

Traditionally the entire energy value chain would be delivered by a single entity, often in public ownership. The reasons for public ownership were twofold: Firstly, electricity is an essential service and therefore of national importance. Secondly, at this stage, the whole sector was considered to be a natural monopoly. A natural monopoly is one where 'the entire demand within a relevant market can be satisfied at the lowest cost by one firm, rather than two or more' (Posner, 1969, p. 548). While this holds no longer true for generation, networks continue to be considered a classic example of such a monopoly – it makes little economic sense to build competing networks in the same location. Market reform was implemented to separate potentially competitive upstream and downstream markets for generation and supply from networks in the electricity sector.

These reforms, introduced for efficiency gains, determine the regulatory frameworks of electricity markets in major developed countries to this day (Cameron, 2000). Unbundling is the term employed to describe the separation of the different functions of electricity provision, especially generation/production and retail/supply, from the network functions, i.e. transmission and distribution (Jamasb and Pollitt, 2005). Unbundling is necessary to ensure that network owners cannot abuse their monopoly position. A network business with simultaneous interests in electricity generation and retail would be in a position to exclude competitors from using their networks, or set higher tariffs (Talus, 2016). Unbundling, in particular of transmission network operation from generation, is therefore considered a central element of market reform. There are different degrees of unbundling employed in different jurisdictions around the world (for an overview see Kallies, 2021). In a nutshell, administrative unbundling requires the keeping of separate accounts for transmission and generation activities. Functional unbundling sets rules for a clear operational independence between network and generation activities within a firm or electricity utility. Legal unbundling entails the operation of these activities by separate legal entities –

with some jurisdictions, for example in the United States, favouring independent system operator models. Finally, ownership unbundling, increasingly favoured for transmission networks in the EU, requires strict separation of ownership and business interests of companies involved in the respective network and generation activities. In contrast, vertical integration of interests in supply and generation, continues to be fairly common, for example in Australia but also in Europe.

Unbundling is an ongoing process. Apart from the efforts to complete the separation of networks from competitive sector elements, further functions emerge as potentially subject to competition. These include in particular metering services and connections. Traditionally, metering was considered a core network activity (ENA, 2016). With the arrival of advanced metering infrastructure, new functions of metering and data management can be offered as competitive services. As an illustrative example, following reform, in some parts of Australia metering services are now no longer provided by the network (AEMC, 2015). Instead, separate roles of metering coordinator, metering provider and metering data provider will in future be provided through competitive markets (Godden and Kallies, 2018).

Similarly, Germany, in its roll-out of smart meters,[1] is creating new and market-exposed roles of metering operators (Godden and Kallies, 2018)

As will be discussed in the next section 4, unbundling, in particular of distribution and supply activities, can provide some barriers to the implementation of new and innovative models of electricity supply.

Unbundling is often accompanied by a move towards corporatization and ultimately privatization of the different segments of the electricity market segments, where they were previously state-owned (IEA, 2005).

3.2 Third-Party Access

Competition in electricity generation and retail markets is premised on the availability of networks for all competitors and aims to ensure consumer choice of retailers. Another central plank of electricity market reform is the so-called third-party access. General competition law does usually not require third-party access. Instead 'all firms, including dominant or monopoly firms, are free to determine their trading partners'. (Dunne, 2015, p. 129) The main exemption to this freedom of contract in Europe, but also applied in the United States and in Australia, is the 'Essential Facilities Doctrine'. This doctrine requires third-party access where 'a facility or infrastructure is essential for reaching customers and/or enabling competitors to carry on their business,

1 The Smart Metering Act 2016 (Messstellenbetriebsgesetz) implements the requirement of the Directive 2009/72/EC [2009] OJ L 211/55.

and which cannot be replicated by reasonable means'. Electricity network infrastructure provides a classic example of this.

General competition law rules often already require third-party access to natural monopolies. In many countries, general competition law is strengthened by energy sector-specific regulated ex ante third-party access regimes – so called "regulated" access. European Union member states, the United States and Australia all have introduced regulated third-party access regimes (in detail, Kallies, 2021).

Non-discriminatory access to networks for new generators has been crucial for new renewable generation to access the market. As will be seen, however, the historical co-development of networks and legacy fossil fuel-based generation means that third-party access rules alone are not sufficient to enable the emergence of a renewable-friendly, yet reliable future network.

3.3 Incentive Regulation

The final aspect of market reforms central to understanding the role and function of networks is the introduction of incentive regulation for transmission and distribution networks.

Incentive regulation is a further standard building block of modern network regulation. Traditionally, network regulation was often based on cost-of-service or rate-of-return regulation. Incentive regulation seeks to mimic competitive markets for networks (Jamasb and Pollitt, 2008, p. 6163). It relies on the regulator specifying a regulatory goal for the network operator, such as a certain degree of network reliability, and an estimated budget to achieve this goal. If the network can achieve these operational goals more efficiently, it can keep the savings. Incentive regulation is therefore thought to drive efficient investment in and management of networks.

Various variations of incentive regulation regulate network expenditure around the world. Yet, incentive regulation alone has not always been successful in incentivizing much needed new network infrastructure. As the experience with the British RPI-X regulatory model showed, incentive regulation may ensure 'efficiency in business as usual activities' (Shaw et al., 2010, p. 5932) but did not necessarily ensure long-term investment (McHarg, 2013).

Different approaches have been considered to incentivize new network investment, with different levels of success. In Australia major network investments proposals are required to pass a regulatory investment test. This cost-benefit test requires networks to apply to the economic regulator and show that the planned investment is economically viable and necessary to either reach reliability standards or maximize market benefits (Godden and Kallies, 2013). Several enquiries have found that the test has not prevented network overinvestment, also called 'gold-plating' (Productivity Commission, 2013, p. 66) while investment to expressly develop new renewable sources has not been sufficiently incentivized. The EU requires transmission network operators to 'develop' network infrastructure – a requirement that has been interpreted to include an 'obligation to invest in new transmission infrastructure' (Rumpf and Bjørnebye, 2019).

As will be discussed further, the energy transition, with its changing network usage patterns and new generation sources, often remote from the grid, requires new network infrastructure investment, more suited to the new generation profile.

4 Integrated Systems and Disintegrated Sector? Can Liberalized Markets Provide for Innovative New Solutions?

In summary, following market liberalization, the dominant model of electricity sector regulation is premised on vertical disintegration – the ownership and management of the different functions of the electricity is separated. However, the underlying physical electricity system remains integrated and highly interdependent. Damage and change to any part of the electricity system can impact other parts immediately (Beder, 2003). Constant and centralized management of supply and demand necessitates 'centralistic control' for dispatching energy (Künneke, 2008). Post-liberalization, system operators provide this central and important service. We therefore see a mismatch between a sector that relies on economic separation of functions, while still requiring integrated management (Scholten & Künneke, 2016). Consequently, there has been discussion on whether unbundling and the resultant clear separation of networks from retail and generation can provide barriers to future smart grid solutions and energy innovation (Rønne, 2016). Several studies (e.g., Sanyal and Ghosh, 2013; Jamasb and Pollitt, 2011) have argued that unbundling of networks from competitive functions of the markets has led to a decrease in energy innovation. Rønne, in the context of smart grids, states that innovation will require 'proper planning and coordination ... covering all elements of the supply chain and not only the particularly unbundled activity' (Rønne, 2016). She warns that the liberalization process and particularly the unbundling of networks from production and supply may become a barrier to the development of smart grids. Clearly, any changes to the electricity system impact all parts of the system. Arguably, they can be more easily delivered in a vertically integrated system. As unbundling is now a reality in modern electricity systems, the system-wide challenges that energy transitions pose will have to be addressed through regulatory intervention that enables coordination of the different segments of the electricity sector.

5 Network Regulation in the Age of the Energy Transition

Networks and their existing infrastructure layouts provide a physical and technological barrier to the uptake of renewable energy. Their legal frameworks, premised on the separation of network activity from retail and generation markets, can also provide serious regulatory barriers to integrated network and generation planning. In addition, the requirements on network providers are increasing to manage networks for the flexible needs of generators and, increasingly, prosumers whose generation may meet their own needs for only parts of the day. Finally, without appropriate regulatory reforms, a rapid uptake of intermittent renewable generators has the potential to destabilize the electricity system – endangering central system objectives of reliable and secure electricity supply. We are now seeing a number of legal reforms emerging which seek to enable innovative network solutions more suited to the highly distributed renewable focused generation profile of the future. The following section will explain where and how the focus of regulatory reform has been.

5.1 Getting Renewable Energy Connected to the Grid

Connecting renewable energy resources to the existing grid or extending the grid to reach the resource is central to the success of energy transitions. Third-party access regimes are crucial to get a range of new generation sources connected to the network, and thus ultimately to their downstream markets.

Challenges for renewables seeking to connect to the system are multifold. Where they are close to the existing grid, the access regime may be not suited to smaller intermittent generators. This issue has for example been identified in Australia, where grid connection regimes require costly upfront grid connection studies to be undertaken by generators, and, potentially, also finance any network augmentations necessitated by the connection request (Kallies, 2011) While these requirements do not seem unreasonable for say a large coal-fired power station, these costs can be forbidding for smaller generators.

A lack of suitable network infrastructure to connect renewable resources has been a recurring issue for energy transition efforts. Off-shore windfarms, for example, need to get dedicated network connections built. In Australia and some areas of the United States, some of the best on-shore wind and solar resources can be found remote to the existing network. Legal and regulatory frameworks for networks had to be adapted to incentivize the building of new network infrastructure.

In addition, even where the renewable energy resource is located close to the existing grid, connecting multiple new generation facilities to one particular area of the grid can lead to congestion. For example, in Germany the vast majority of new large-scale renewable generation has been wind farms. The best wind resources, however, are located in the north of the country. A central plank of the German transmission efforts is therefore to expand interconnections between the north and the south of the country.

Early efforts to ensure the timely connection of renewable energy generation were focused on connection regimes. One such example is the network arrangement accompanying the German feed-in tariff. German renewable energy legislation sets up a customized grid connection regime, which prioritizes renewable generators over other new generation seeking to connect to the shared network. The Renewable Energy Act 2021 (Germany) contains an express commitment to connect renewable generators "as a priority" (in section 8), and to "optimize, strengthen and expand" networks to ensure their availability for renewable generators (in section 12).

A range of other examples can be found for integrated network planning.

For example, the US state of Texas has nominated Competitive Renewable Energy Zones (CREZ). It legislated through Senate Bill 20 that the Public Utility Commission Texas, the regulator of the state's electric and telecommunications utilities, will oversee the CREZ process by designating CREZ and selecting transmission service providers, as well as reporting back regularly to legislature. The CREZ process was to ensure that the geographically best wind resources were being developed and recognised the overarching importance of transmission for successful large-scale renewable energy development. The process ensured that transmission lines were co-developed with future generation interest. The transmission investment was financed by the Transmission Network Service Providers, who could recoup the investment from the consumers through regulated rates of return (Zarnikau, 2011).

In another example, the UK has regulated offshore zones through substantive changes to regulatory and institutional framework through the Energy Act (2004). It adds a new competency for Ofgem, the regulator, to run competitive tender processes for new offshore transmission infrastructure needed to connect the vast offshore wind resources of the UK to the British mainland. Investment costs are socialized, with 20 years revenues guaranteed for the new Offshore Transmission Owners. These examples show that regulation around the planning of and investment into new networks will have to be reintegrated with changing patterns of demand and generation to allow the stationary electricity sector to fulfil its emissions reduction promise.

However, the focus has shifted increasingly to considering the impact of a geographically uneven investment in renewables on the whole grid system. Many countries have started to 'steer' renewable investment into specific locations or stagger investment, in order to ensure that the load on the existing grids does not destabilize electricity supply. In Germany, this has taken the form of legislated annual 'lid' on the build-out of specific categories of renewables, to ensure the system keeps up with network investment (Renewable Energy Act 2021 (Germany) part 3). A number of states in Australia have recently implemented renewable energy zones, as a way of coordinating network and generation investment. (ESB, 2021) Coordinated network investment is now increasingly done across state and national borders, to leverage economies of scale. In the US, FERC's Order 1000 requires transmission network providers participate in regional network planning processes to ensure cost-effective transmission investment to the benefit of all participants (FERC, 2011). On a subnational level, the European Union has revised the TEN-E regulation (Regulation (EU) 2022/869) in order to further the European energy transition. The revised regulation recognises energy infrastructure, such as electricity networks, as 'key enabler' of the energy transition and supports integrated and coordinated solutions to network planning, for example for offshore networks and smart grids (EC, 2020). Wiseman's chapter on Energy Governance Models (in this volume) provides further insights and examples on energy infrastructure planning, financing and siting.

While relatively slow to react to the changing generation profiles, legal frameworks have, overall, sought to find solutions to address the issues of network access and network extension for the energy transition. However, the next challenge for network providers is to manage the reliability and security of networks.

5.2 Changing Roles for Network Providers and Regulators: Reliability and Resilience of Networks

Networks are currently experiencing the double impact of a rapidly changing generation and demand profile as well as climate change. Both are challenging the ability of network providers and system operators to balance supply and demand at all times. New resources to manage power system flexibility are already required today, and regulators and network providers struggle to address these issues in a timely manner.

Power system reliability standards are set by law (Kuiken, 2021). As an example, the Australian National Electricity Market legal framework has set a reliability standard of 0.002% expected unserved energy. This means that 99.998% of electricity demand by customers should be met (AEMC, 2013). Where networks do not meet these standards they are penalized. Climate change related phenomena, such as fire, floods and storms are becoming more common and are already impacting on reliability and are forecast to do so even more in the future. At the same time the shift to prosumerism means that not only does supply become more intermittent, but so too does demand, as many consumers produce their own electricity through roof-top solar installations. Traditional incentive regulation has not been able to facilitate network investment that can address all of these challenges. Instead it usually incentivises the expansion of network capacity, rather than the smarter, more innovative use of network capacity.

New and innovative approaches are now discussed to address the network challenge of maintaining frequency and balancing an increasingly unpredictable grid. They often take place at the "edge of the grid" – at the interface of distribution networks and supply. The role of the distribution network provider is probably the most impacted by the energy transition. Traditionally, distribution network providers did not need to participate in balance supply and demand, but delivered electricity to a passive consumer. New approaches include *inter alia* demand side management, smart grids, microgrids and network storage. Some of these solutions, however, are currently limited by the regulatory frameworks.

One such example are microgrids. "Microgrids are electricity distribution systems containing loads and distributed energy resources … that can be operated in a controlled, coordinated way either while connected to the main power network, or while islanded" (CIGRE, 2015). An islandable microgrid can be more resilient to climate impacts, lower the high costs of the build and upkeep of the expensive transmission network, and allow prosumers to exchange the energy produced within their community. All functions of the power system – networks, generation and supply, are contained within a microgrid at a much smaller scale. Legal discussion centres on who should operate a microgrid and how access can be regulated. Currently there are no clear guidelines on how to support and finance microgrids in a fair and equitable way, although a range of smaller case studies are emerging around the world (Attanasio, 2021). Similarly, smart grids, seeking to leverage the use of information technology to better balance supply and demand, are requiring active engagement of the consumer and distribution networks to operate not only the energy network, but also manage data flow (Diestelmeier, 2021).

Energy transitions add complexities which the standard structure of a liberalised electricity sector is not well equipped to address. Essential services objectives of safe and reliable supply are challenged by the transition to a more sustainable system. Legal frameworks for networks will need to accommodate complex new products and services to ensure system reliability, and at the same time ensure consumer protections and safety considerations.

6 Conclusion

In a climate impacted world, networks have a central role to play in both climate mitigation and adaptation. In mitigation, they are crucial enablers for the transition to a high renewable electricity system. In adaptation, network innovation is one central element of a more climate change resilient electricity system. Regulators and lawmakers have now clearly recognized this challenge and legal and regulatory frameworks for networks are beginning to catch up on the big task to address network flexibility to these challenges for the future. This need for enhanced flexibility and resilience will need to be reflected in the legislated roles, responsibilities and incentives for network providers. One of the great challenges for a governance framework that seeks to regulate networks as separate from other parts of the electricity system, will be to recognize the integrated physical nature of the electricity system. An important role for legal researchers will be interdisciplinary engagement with power system engineers, economists and social scientists to translate this need for better planning and integration into a future-proof flexible regulatory framework for networks.

References

AEMC, National Electricity Amendment (Expanding competition in metering and related services) Rule 2015 (SA) No 12 (NER) New Rule 7.3.1.

AEMC, 2013. Fact Sheet: The NEM Reliability Standard.

Attanasio, D., 2021. The Regulation of microgrids. In: M.M. Roggenkamp et al., eds., 2021. *Energy law, climate change and the environment.* Cheltenham: Edward Elgar Publishing, pp. 656–667.

Beder, S., 2003. *Power play: the fight to control the world's electricity.* New York, NY: New Press.

Cameron, P. 2000. Reforming energy markets. *Journal of Energy and Natural Resources Law*, 18(4), pp. 353–377.

CIGRE Working Group C6.22, 2015. *Microgrids I, Engineering, Economics and Experience.*

Climate Change Authority, 2012. *Renewable energy target review: final report.*

Diestelmeier, L., 2021. A legal framework for smart grids. In: M.M. Roggenkamp et al., eds., 2021. *Energy law, climate change and the environment*. Cheltenham: Edward Elgar Publishing, pp. 645–655.

Dunne, N., 2015. *Competition law and economic regulation: making and managing markets*. Cambridge: Cambridge University Press.

Energy Association Networks (ENA) and Commonwealth Scientific and Industrial Research Organisation (CSIRO), 2016. *Future regulatory options for electricity network.*

Energy Security Board, National Electricity Amendment (Renewable Energy Zone Planning) Rule 2021.

European Commission, 2020. Proposal for a REGULATION OF THE EUROPEAN PARLIAMENT AND OF THE COUNCIL on guidelines for trans-European energy infrastructure and repealing Regulation (EU) No 347/2013. COM/2020/824 final

FERC (United States of America Federal Energy Regulatory Commission), 2011. *Transmission planning and cost allocation.* Order No. 1000. July 21.

Godden, L. and Kallies, A., 2013. Electricity network development: new challenges for Australia. In: M.M. Roggenkamp et al., eds., 2013. *Energy networks and the law.* Oxford: Oxford University Press.

Godden, L. and Kallies, A., 2018. Smart infrastructure: innovative energy technology, climate mitigation, and consumer protection in Australia and Germany. In: D. Zillman et al., eds., 2018. Innovation in energy law and technology: dynamic solutions for energy transitions. Oxford: Oxford University Press, pp. 391–411.

International Energy Agency, 2020. *Power systems in transition: challenges and opportunities*. Paris: OECD/IEA.

Jamasb, T. and Pollitt, M. 2005. Electricity market reform in the European Union: review of progress toward liberalization & integration. *The Energy Journal*, 26, pp. 11–41.

Jamasb, T. and Pollitt, M., 2008. Incentive regulation of electricity distribution networks: lessons of experience from Britain. *Energy Policy*, 35(12), pp. 6163–6187.

Jamasb, T. and Pollitt, M., 2011. Liberalisation and R&D in network industries: the case of the electricity industry. *Research Policy*, 37(6), pp. 995–1008.

Kallies, A., 2011. The impact of electricity market design on access to the grid and transmission planning for renewable energy in Australia: can overseas examples provide guidance. *Renewable Energy Law and Policy*, 2(2), pp. 147–159.

Kallies, A., 2021. Regulating the use of networks in liberalised markets. In: M.M. Roggenkamp et al., eds., 2021. *Energy law, climate change and the environment*. Cheltenham: Edward Elgar Publishing, pp. 599–610.

Kuiken, D., Regulating electricity network reliability markets. In: M.M. Roggenkamp et al. eds., 2021. *Energy law, climate change and the environment*. Cheltenham: Edward Elgar Publishing, pp. 611–620.

Künneke, R., 2008. Institutional reform and technological practice: the case of electricity. *Industrial and Corporate Change*, 17(2), pp. 233–265.

McHarg, A., 2013. Evolution and revolution in British energy network regulation: from RPI-X to RIIO. In: M.M. Roggenkamp et al. eds., 2013. *Energy networks and the law*. Oxford: Oxford University Press, pp. 321–332.

Posner, R., 1969. Natural monopoly and its regulation. *Stanford Law Review*, 21, pp. 548–643.

Regulation (EU) 2022/869 of the European Parliament and of the Council of 30 May 2022 on guidelines for trans-European energy infrastructure, amending Regulations (EC) No 715/2009, (EU) 2019/942 and (EU) 2019/943 and Directives 2009/73/EC and (EU) 2019/944, and repealing Regulation (EU) No 347/2013, OJ L152/45, 3.6.2022.

Rønne, A., 2013. Smart grids and intelligent energy systems: a European perspective. In: M.M. Roggenkamp et al. eds., 2013. Energy networks and the law. Oxford: Oxford University Press, pp. 141–160.

Rumpf, J., and Bjørnebye, H., 2019. Just how much is enough? EU regulation of capacity and reliability margins on electricity interconnectors. *Journal of Energy & Natural Resources Law*, 37(1), pp. 67–91.

Sanyal, P. and Ghosh, P., 2013. Product market competition and upstream innovation: evidence from the US electricity market deregulation. *The Review of Economics and Statistics*, 95(1), pp. 237–254.

Scholten, D. and Künneke, R., 2016. Towards the comprehensive design of energy infrastructures. *Sustainability*, 8(12), 1291

Shaw, R., Attree, M. and Jackson, T., 2010. Developing electricity distribution networks and their regulation to support sustainable energy. *Energy Policy*, 38(10), 5927–5937.

Talus, K., 2016. *Introduction to EU energy law*. Oxford: Oxford University Press.

Zarnikau, J., 2011. Successful renewable energy development in a competitive electricity market: a Texas case study. *Energy Policy*, 39(7), pp. 3906–3913.

Kennedy Chege

Legal/Policy Tools and Strategies for Hydrogen in the Low-Carbon Transition

Abstract: The decarbonisation of global energy systems drives markets today, hence the emphasis on the clean energy transition through the use of cleaner sources of energy such as hydrogen, as a viable resource to support the energy transition. Hydrogen is a preferred pathway towards decarbonisation since it is a clean and affordable fuel, it is versatile and is applicable in a diverse range of sectors, among other factors. Sub-Saharan Africa is well-placed for the development of a hydrogen economy, particularly as a result of its abundant natural resources such as solar and wind, as well as government, industry and civil society support. Governments across the region, together with private sector partners, are increasingly placing the hydrogen economy as a key priority area, as it constitutes an important pathway towards decarbonisation and is perceived to be the missing link towards achieving global net-zero targets by 2050. This chapter commences with a discussion of the significant role and utility of hydrogen as an appropriate decarbonisation pathway in the low-carbon transition. It proceeds to specifically evaluate whether the legal and policy tools that governments in Africa already have in place or are contemplating, either support or hinder the energy transition. This policy review, not only identifies policy gaps but also considers examples of national and international hydrogen strategies in selected countries, to highlight their legal underpinnings and assess the degrees of convergence and divergence between national, regional and international regulatory frameworks supporting the development of hydrogen economies. This review further presents policy options and recommends approaches to enhance hydrogen production and the energy transition from a fossil fuel-based economy to a hydrogen-based economy in Africa. Additionally, this chapter examines the regulation of hydrogen technologies (such as electrolysers and fuel cells), focusing on generation, transmission and distribution. It appraises the different enforcement mechanisms towards increasing the adoption of hydrogen in the selected African countries.

1 Introduction

Hydrogen is revolutionising the energy landscape, with global production set to more than double by 2030, following a series of public and private sector commitments

Kennedy Chege is a Researcher and PhD candidate at the DST/NRF SARChI: Mineral Law in Africa (MLiA) Research Chair at the University of Cape Town, South Africa.

https://doi.org/10.1515/9783110752403-020

and initiatives (Resource World, 2021). Hydrogen is presently experiencing unprecedented momentum across the world, as a viable decarbonisation pathway, amid the global energy transition imperatives to tackle the adverse effects of climate change and other environmental concerns. This transition drive relates to the move away from the use of fossil fuel sources of energy such as coal and oil, to cleaner sources of energy, including hydrogen. The COVID-19 pandemic has also accelerated the trend toward the decarbonisation of global economies by substantially reducing the demand for hydrocarbons (Muralidharan, 2020).

Hydrogen is a preferred pathway toward decarbonisation, not only the decarbonisation of the electricity component of the energy industry, but other sub-sectors (Whyte, 2021). The preeminent status that hydrogen enjoys is mainly because it is an affordable fuel, it is versatile, and it is applicable in a diverse range of sectors, among other factors (Office of Fossil Energy: United States Department of Energy, 2020, p. 11). Hydrogen, being the most abundant chemical element in existence, is also thought to be particularly appealing to countries such as South Africa that possess sizeable existing gas infrastructure that could be repurposed for hydrogen production, as will be discussed below.

Furthermore, the hydrogen industrial chain mainly constitutes upstream hydrogen production, midstream hydrogen storage and delivery, and downstream integrated applications in various economic sectors, as explained below (Pingkuo and Xue, 2022, p. 9486). To fully exploit the potential of hydrogen, a holistic approach is necessary, requiring that these aspects of the hydrogen industrial chain be viewed collectively and not separately. This chapter is concerned with these areas of the hydrogen economy.

It is evident that clean hydrogen is enjoying significant momentum, amid the rapid expansion of policies and projects around the world. Therefore, it is imperative to scale up technologies and bring down costs to allow hydrogen to become more widely used. It is in light of this that the focus today among both governments and corporations is on upscaling clean hydrogen production. This growing momentum in adopting hydrogen as a viable alternative source of clean energy is not only as a means of fulfilling international obligations toward a clean energy transition and tackling climate change under the Paris Agreement of 2015, but also the UN's Sustainable Development Goals (i.e. SDG 7 and SDG 13) as well as the commitments that were made at the 26th United Nations Climate Change Conference of the Parties (COP26) that was held in Glasgow (Scotland) in November 2021 (UNFCCC, 2015).

According to a 2020 report by the World Economic Forum (WEF), green hydrogen constitutes one of the most exciting technologies, with the potential to positively transform society and industry (Carbeck, 2020, p. 21). Similar sentiments were echoed at the COP26 conference to emphasise the significant role that hydrogen could play in the global clean energy transition (Koole and Blank, 2021).

The increased focus on hydrogen production, especially in developing countries, is also motivated by the desire to, among other objectives: enhance energy security, create new jobs, attract foreign direct investment (FDI), offer long-term energy storage, encourage the development of local industries in countries that do not have access to fossil fuel resources but possess renewable energy resources, and encourage a just transition by decarbonising value chains and the so-called hard-to-abate sectors such as heavy industries, aviation, steel production, shipping, *et cetera* (ESMAP, 2020, p. 10).

Today, green or renewable hydrogen, which is produced through the electrolysis of water, using electricity generated by renewable sources such as wind and solar, could be produced with zero greenhouse gas (GHG) emissions. The only by-product of this process is water, making green hydrogen to be perceived as the "holy grail" of decarbonisation (Scita, Raimondi and Noussan, 2020, p. 1). As the cleanest and most sustainable form of hydrogen, green hydrogen constitutes a key pathway to achieving global net-zero targets and towards the establishment of a global hydrogen economy. The International Energy Agency (IEA), published a report outlining the roadmap for the global energy sector towards achieving net-zero by 2050. This report advocates for a transformation of energy systems, and it identifies the adoption of green hydrogen as a key pillar toward the decarbonisation of this industry (IEA, 2021, p. 75).

Whereas the emphasis is on clean hydrogen (i.e. green and blue hydrogen) to decarbonise the energy sector, there is existing production across other categories of hydrogen. These are classified according to the ways that they are produced, and categorised according to "colours/ shades", including: grey, brown/ black, turquoise, pink, purple, red, white and yellow hydrogen – all comprising of hydrogen produced predominantly from fossil fuel feedstock, for example, either biomass, coal, oil, natural gas, methane and nuclear energy (Marchant, 2021). These categories could play fundamental roles in the energy transition by providing opportunities to switch to cleaner hydrogen as part of feasibility, or pilot studies, in the short-term (Norton Rose Fulbright, 2020). This temporary blending, especially of blue and green hydrogen, will enable detailed studies into production, transportation, storage and integration using existing hydrogen projects and transportation networks (Hydrogen Council, 2021, pp. 5–7).

According to a report by the Hydrogen Council, the flagship industry initiative of private stakeholders from the energy, transport and industry sectors, there is a need for a fact-based approach that leverages regional resources and includes a combination of different production pathways (Hydrogen Council, 2021, p. 5). This approach acknowledges that there is not a single hydrogen production pathway to achieve low GHG emissions. Therefore, incorporating other forms of hydrogen, at least in the short-term, will achieve both emission and cost reductions, thereby supporting decarbonisation efforts and alleviating global warming.

With respect to the African continent, which is the main focus of this chapter, it is expected that the coming years will prove to be significant for its growth and development. The clean energy transition specifically, not only offers development opportunities for regions with high renewable energy potential such as Africa, but it also would enable the continent to utilise its comparative advantage and leverage its natural endowments, and its full renewable energy potential, which hitherto remain largely untapped. Countries such as South Africa and Kenya already possess the requisite infrastructure that can be leveraged to take advantage of green hydrogen for both production and export (Roodbol, 2021).

As a result, the development of a hydrogen economy could accelerate the growth and diversification of Sub-Saharan African economies. Despite these opportunities, Africa faces numerous challenges – its endeavour to alleviate poverty and foster energy security remain some of the most significant historical challenges that have faced the continent. To address these and other challenges as well as to encourage the emergence and development of an African hydrogen economy, national governments across the continent need to make a number of interventions. They need to: ensure that a conducive policy framework is in place, invest heavily in research and development as a critical enabler to boost the development of a hydrogen economy and to drive local applications for hydrogen, promote the development of a clean hydrogen value chain, encourage the reduction of the costs in producing green hydrogen at scale, among other interventions that are canvassed in this chapter below.

It is against this backdrop that this chapter discusses the significant role and utility of hydrogen as the appropriate decarbonisation pathway in the low-carbon energy transition. It proceeds to the crux of the discussion, which is to specifically evaluate the legal/ policy tools and strategies in selected developed and developing countries. This policy review not only identifies policy gaps but also considers examples of national and international hydrogen strategies in selected countries, so as to highlight their legal underpinnings and assess the degrees of convergence and divergence between regional and national regulatory frameworks either supporting or hindering the development of hydrogen economies. Lastly, the review further presents policy options and recommendations for developing appropriate policy and legal frameworks to enhance hydrogen production and the energy transition from a fossil fuel-based economy to a hydrogen-based economy in Africa.

2 Roles and utility of hydrogen as an appropriate decarbonisation pathway in the low-carbon transition

Approximately 75% of global GHG emissions are generated by sectors outside of electricity (World Bank Group, 2021). These statistics make the case for deeper actions to decarbonise across sectors, thus the important role that low-carbon hydrogen will play in decarbonising the global energy industry is becoming increasingly widely recognised. However, presently, the majority of hydrogen production originates from fossil fuel sources. For example, grey hydrogen is generated through steam reformation of natural gas, methane or coal (Kaplan and Kopacz, 2020). Only a meagre 2% of hydrogen production consists of low-carbon hydrogen, being green and blue hydrogen (Day, 2022). To be truly "green", hydrogen needs to be produced exclusively through renewable sources. Therefore, there is significant potential for emissions reduction from clean hydrogen to meet global net-zero goals.

The utility of hydrogen stems from its versatility as an energy carrier and feedstock in multiple sectors, rather than merely as an energy source (Office of Fossil Energy: United States Department of Energy, 2020, p. 11). These sectors include the following: power generation (including energy storage), transportation (e.g. shipping and aviation sectors), industrial and chemical processes, and in heating for buildings as well as for private use in homes. Hydrogen is also renowned for its ability to decarbonise the hard-to-abate sectors such as iron and steel production, the chemicals sector, *et cetera.*

A major compelling future area for hydrogen usage is for both industrial heat and chemical feedstock and fuel (ESMAP, 2020, p. 76). The adoption of hydrogen for this purpose offers a plausible decarbonisation alternative for large-scale industrial heat users. With respect to industrial uses, hydrogen could be used as feedstock in the production of chemicals, iron and steel, by replacing methane gas as a reduction agent for producing iron that would then be used to produce steel (ESMAP, 2020, p. 76). Similarly, hydrogen could be instrumental in the decarbonisation of industries such as fertilisers, cement and petrochemicals (Office of Fossil Energy: United States Department of Energy, 2020, p. 8).

In the context of the global transportation sector, clean mobility solutions are key on the agenda, as a pathway towards the decarbonisation of this sector (Berger, 2021, p. 4). Hydrogen could be used to power fuel cell vehicles, a fast-growing alternative to battery-powered vehicles, and to produce fuels such as ammonia and methanol to decarbonise, for example, maritime transport. Fuel cell technology has been shown to be able to provide unparalleled performance for vehicles. In various forms of shipping, such as ferries, fuel cells are likely to become a “green” alternative to biofuels (Ludwig *et al.*, 2021). For other forms of shipping, ammonia and methanol derived from green hydrogen will likely become the most favoured alternative to the present use of battery-electric power in the foreseeable future (Ludwig *et al.*, 2021).

Hydrogen-powered fuel cell vehicles offer both high efficiency and low emissions (Office of Fossil Energy: United States Department of Energy, 2020, p. 8). Most importantly, these vehicles could play an increasingly important role in reducing emissions from long-haul trucks, buses, trains, ships and airplanes, thus revolutionising the transportation sector (Office of Fossil Energy: United States Department of Energy, 2020, p. 8). In the aviation and shipping industries, the ability of hydrogen to produce carbon-neutral fuels that can run through existing carbon-intensive technologies such as diesel engines and jet turbines, makes it unparalleled in terms of its potential to decarbonise the transportation sector.

In addition to the above uses, the deployment of green hydrogen could facilitate sector coupling among different economic sectors, thus minimising the cost of meeting each of their decarbonised energy needs, and increasing efficiencies by seamlessly utilising assets from one sector to another (Bhagwat and Olczak, 2020, p. 16). The speed at which hydrogen becomes cost-competitive in each of the above end-use applications is dependent on several factors and conditions, including the following: the speed at which the current insufficient supporting infrastructure and policy frameworks are addressed, industry investment to enhance the upscaling of hydrogen, increased focus and investment in research and development, among others. The development of hydrogen requires sufficient financial, infrastructural and policy support to facilitate wide deployment and get to commercial-scale projects. The financial aspect particularly requires leveraging both public and private investments.

In terms of energy storage, hydrogen could become the solution for long-term storage of energy for mini-grids, as a means to counter the intermittent supply challenges associated with renewable energy such as solar and wind (Office of Fossil Energy: United States Department of Energy, 2020, p. 8). Future large-scale hydrogen value chains will require a much broader variety of energy storage options to cushion the African continent from oil price volatility that has been prevalent, and energy supply disruptions. Since wind, solar and other sources of generation from renewables tend to be seasonal, countries currently lack the ability to effectively store surplus energy from these sources. Therefore, surplus energy needs to be captured and stored in an efficient way that allows for use, to meet the increasing demand when it rises (Office of Fossil Energy: United States Department of Energy, 2020, p. 8). The electrolysis process could be used to convert excess electricity into hydrogen during times of oversupply, which would then be used to generate power through either fuel cells or direct combustion in gas turbines when needed (Metcalfe, Burger and Mackay, 2020, p. 25). Green hydrogen thus appears to be the most appropriate solution to the challenge of facilitating easier storage and transportation of energy to international markets and enabling greater levels of deployment.

Furthermore, storage systems such as clean hydrogen are significantly cheaper and allow for energy to be stored for longer periods than conventional battery energy storage systems, which generally have higher production costs and geopolitical complications (Headley and Schoenung, 2020, p. 2). The advancements in hydrogen and storage technologies would thus enable Africa to fully utilise these resources and supply the world with large quantities of green hydrogen (Ayodele and Munda, 2019, p. 17, 670).

Green hydrogen could thus become the pre-eminent resource in these and other industries in the event that the costs of production and utilisation prove it to be competitive as compared to other alternatives. Electrolysers have historically been costly, thereby posing a significant barrier to upscaling the production of green hydrogen as a clean energy solution during its first major commercialisation wave in the 1990s and early 2000s (Kroposki *et al.*, 2006, p. 12). However, this situation is gradually changing, with the costs of electrolysers and fuel cells having reduced and projected to continue reducing across the world, having more than halved within the past decade (ACER, 2021, p. 3). This development as well as the decline in the costs of renewable sources of energy, coupled with advancements in fuel cell technologies, show green hydrogen's commercial viability and constitute factors that will facilitate its increased production (Ouziel and Avelar, 2021). Using low-cost wind and solar power to generate green hydrogen can result in its cost being comparable to the cost of hydrogen generated from fossil fuels – access to cheaper renewables will help to drive down operational costs.

Apart from its potential to considerably accelerate Sub-Saharan Africa's electrification rates, which are currently low *vis a vis* global standards, the hydrogen economy is expected to create much-needed jobs across Africa, thus playing a leading role in alleviating poverty (Bhagwat and Olczak, 2020, p. 6). A single green hydrogen plant has the potential to create hundreds of jobs throughout the project development process – from design and construction, to the commencement of operations. The following section of this chapter assesses the legal/ policy tools and strategies for the development of hydrogen economies in selected developed and developing countries.

3 Legal/policy tools and strategies for the development of hydrogen economies in selected countries

In previous years, global demand for hydrogen has substantially increased, supported by national hydrogen strategies and policies being adopted by countries such as the United States of America ("USA"), Germany, Japan, China, among others (Faris, 2020). The demand for hydrogen is expected to grow between six to ten times *vis a vis* 2020 volumes (Research Dive, 2022). It is also projected that by 2050, hydrogen could potentially meet up to 24% of the world's energy needs, with annual sales in the range of 630 billion Euros ($712 billion), according to analysts cited by the European Commission (European Commission, 2020, p. 2). Also, with the proliferation of hydrogen strategies and policies across jurisdictions, the private sector is increasingly investing in hydrogen-related projects and technologies in efforts to promote the achievement of global net-zero goals and achieve climate neutrality without compromising industrial growth and social development.

As in any other economic industry, regulatory uncertainty can inhibit investments and pose a barrier to competition between businesses seeking to establish themselves in the envisaged hydrogen economy. Moreover, the lack of clarity, transparency and harmonisation of legal and policy tools have been cited both by scholars and industry players as key barriers to market entry and the scaling up of a clean hydrogen economy in many countries (Norton Rose Fulbright, 2020). These are some of the challenges that countries across the world endeavour to address through the adoption of appropriate legal frameworks to support the emergence and development of hydrogen economies. There needs to be clear policy and regulatory environments across the African continent that encourages investment and emphasises capacity building, as without investment in renewable technologies, including green hydrogen, the ability of countries to achieve their net-zero targets by 2050 would be impossible.

Although the decarbonisation drive has been present for a number of years, countries have only fairly recently begun enacting laws and policies, and making significant investments into the manufacturing and deployment of emerging clean technologies, clean hydrogen being one of these technologies (Hiltbrand *et al.*, 2021). There are currently no clear frontrunners in the race to deploy green hydrogen, but countries such as China, EU member states (e.g. Germany), Japan, and South Korea, have thus far announced generous investment commitments and ambitious deployment goals (Hiltbrand *et al.*, 2021).

This section of the chapter provides an account of some of the most fundamental legal/ policy tools and strategies for the development of hydrogen economies. The discussion begins with a synopsis of the position internationally, particularly concerning the EU regional framework and Germany's national framework, as case studies from the perspective of developed countries. It then considers the position in the African continent and in selected jurisdictions within Africa, as case studies from the perspective of developing countries. The focus in this regard will mostly be on South Africa and Namibia, two of the countries in Africa that are projected to become green hydrogen powerhouses and that are continually intensifying efforts to create appropriate legal and policy frameworks to pave the way for the production and deployment of green hydrogen.

The analysis of these different perspectives is imperative to assess the degrees of convergence and divergence in regional and national regulatory frameworks for the adoption of hydrogen amid the global clean energy transition. This research evaluates the position in two developed jurisdictions and two developing jurisdictions, as they each represent the position in other countries with similar levels of development, whilst cognisant of contextual differences between countries, including those on similar levels of development. The various points of convergence and divergence between their hydrogen strategies are explored further in this chapter.

In terms of global governance, since Japan promulgated the world's first national hydrogen strategy in 2017, over 30 countries have since introduced hydrogen strategies and published hydrogen energy roadmaps in their respective jurisdictions (Hydrogen Council, 2021, p. 5). These include the major world economies, including the USA, China, Japan and Germany. Countries, especially from the developed world, have in recent times elevated the hydrogen sector to the pinnacle of their national energy strategies (Hydrogen Council, 2021, p. 5). Significantly, some of these countries are Member States of the EU.

3.1 European Union

Green hydrogen has quickly established itself as the cornerstone of Europe's energy transition plans. The impetus for the development of a green hydrogen sector is manifested by the European Green Deal, the overarching EU initiative toward a more sustainable economy and towards achieving net-zero goals by 2050 (European Commission, 2019). The "Hydrogen Strategy for a Climate Neutral Europe", which was adopted by the European Commission in 2020, is a fundamental component of the broader European Green Deal agenda (European Commission, 2020).

Among other goals, this Strategy charts the course towards establishing a European hydrogen eco-system across Europe (European Commission, 2020, p. 3). It outlines step-by-step courses of action that ought to be adopted, with the overall goal of exploring how producing and using green hydrogen can help to decarbonise the EU economy in a cost-effective way, in line with the aims of the European Green Deal, as well as help in post-COVID-19 economic recovery efforts by creating sustainable growth and jobs (European Commission, 2020, pp. 5–7).

Pursuant to the aforementioned EU hydrogen Strategy, both the EU collectively and its member states individually, are obligated to provide a regulatory framework that governs the upscaling of green hydrogen production (European Commission, 2020: p. 13). They also are required to provide financial support to establish a competitive hydrogen market and a well-developed transnational hydrogen network (European Commission, 2020, p. 20). It is in light of this that countries such as Germany, as is explained below, the Netherlands and other member states of the EU have accelerated efforts to introduce legal and regulatory frameworks to guide the adoption of green hydrogen into their economies. The Netherlands, for example, recently adopted its Climate Act, which aims at reducing carbon dioxide (CO2) emissions by 49%, by 2030, and 95% by 2050, compared with the levels of emissions in 1990 (Climate Act, 2019). The country was also mandated to reduce its overall GHG emissions by at least 25% by the end of 2020, in comparison to 1990 emission levels, following the landmark *Urgenda* judgment of 2019, handed down by the Dutch Supreme Court (*State of the Netherlands v. Urgenda Foundation*, 2019) (Benjamin and McCallum, in this volume).

Furthermore, in December 2021, the European Commission published its legislative "Package on Hydrogen and Decarbonized Markets", which proposes new rules, including providing legal clarity on the concepts and role of blue and green hydrogen, to encourage the development of a hydrogen market throughout the EU (European Commission, 2021). The Package, in line with the EU Hydrogen Strategy, aims to facilitate the uptake of renewable and low-carbon gases, including hydrogen, in the EU's energy infrastructure.

3.2 Germany

Germany actively seeks to become a leader and key exporter of green hydrogen. This endeavour is the reason why it is intensively building international partnerships to secure its future hydrogen supply, as it acknowledges that it unilaterally does not have the requisite capacity to produce the required quantities of hydrogen itself, and will therefore have to rely on importation (Fuhrmann, 2020, p. 8). Its hydrogen Strategy stipulates that "the energy partnerships will also be contributing to the decarbonization and economic development of the countries exporting the hydrogen", thus suggesting a symbiotic relationship and collaboration between countries (Huber, 2021).

For example, Germany has entered into a number of agreements with Namibia to support Namibia's development of green hydrogen to secure its long-term supply of the resource. Also, in December 2021, it was announced that Hive Hydrogen (a combination of English solar company, Hive Energy and South African investment organisation, Built Africa) and Linde plc (German chemical company) have teamed up to establish the "world's largest green ammonia export plant" in Nelson Mandela Bay, that will have a production capacity of more than 800,000 tonnes per year (HiveEnergy, 2021). Pre-feasibility studies for the project have already been completed and the first phase is planned to commence operations in 2025, with full operation expected by the end of 2026 (HiveEnergy, 2021).

In 2020, the German Federal Government announced its "National Hydrogen Strategy," also demonstrating its commitment to the European Green Deal (Strachan, 2020). The overarching principle of this Strategy prioritises the security of supply, affordability and environmental compatibility to be combined with innovative and smart climate action for the energy transition to be successful (Baltic Industry, 2021). In terms of climate change mitigation, the country's Climate Action Plan 2050 aims at reductions of between 80% to 95% of GHG emissions by 2050 in comparison with the levels in 1990 (Climate Action Plan 2050, p. 2).

Pursuant to its hydrogen Strategy, Germany favours the exclusive adoption of green hydrogen in the long-term as it considers only hydrogen produced from renewable energy to be sustainable (Huber, 2021). Northern Germany is renowned for possessing abundant renewable energy resources, therefore facilitating the production of green hydrogen (Michalski *et al.*, 2017). This focus on green hydrogen implies that the role of blue hydrogen as a possible bridging energy source remains unclear. However, the Strategy states that other low-carbon sources of hydrogen will "play a role" in a global and European hydrogen market (Huber, 2021). This issue culminated in Germany's Hydrogen Council, the government-appointed advisory body, calling for an urgent decision on the status of blue hydrogen (Huber, 2021).

Secondly, the German Parliament recently enacted an amendment to its Energy Act, which contains provisions relating to the regulation of hydrogen markets, thus further strengthening its national climate goals of achieving GHG neutrality by 2045 (Von Burchard – CMS). The purpose of these amendments is to gradually build up hydrogen infrastructure throughout Germany (Von Burchard – CMS).

3.3 South Africa

From an African continent-wide perspective, it is imperative that governments are well-equipped with effective policies and strategies to respond to the energy transition and its associated effects. South Africa and Namibia are two countries that are viewed as regional leaders in the future hydrogen economy.

South Africa is presently the leading emitter of GHG across the continent and one of the largest emitters globally, making the case for the adoption of greener sources of energy, including green hydrogen, even more compelling. The country's comparative advantage in producing green hydrogen is widely recognised, considering that it possesses abundant renewable energy resources, particularly wind and solar resources (Cliffe Dekker Hoffmeyr, 2021, p. 3). South Africa is also the global leader in producing platinum group metals (PGMs), which are crucial for the electrolysis process (Cliffe Dekker Hoffmeyr, 2021, p. 3). Thirdly, the country's expertise and capabilities around the *Fischer Tropsch* (FT) Process, through companies such as Sasol, is another major factor for its comparative advantage (Walwyn, and Crompton, 2020).

Hydrogen is a key priority area for South Africa towards achieving a just transition and its socio-economic objectives. In his 2021 State of the Nation Address (SONA), President Cyril Ramaphosa cited that hydrogen fuel cells are a national priority as an alternative energy source, to diversify the country's energy mix (Davis, 2021). While responding to a debate in Parliament regarding the aforementioned SONA address, the President highlighted the Hydrogen South Africa Strategy (HySA), confirming that after over a decade of research, the country is prepared to manufacture hydrogen fuel cells (FuelCellsWorks, 2021). To support this move, the Industrial Development Corporation (IDC) is placed with the responsibility to drive the commercialisation of the green hydrogen economy in South Africa by actively forging partnerships with the private sector to fund projects across the green hydrogen value chain (Coetzee, 2021, p. 2). Within the past year, several substantial developments with regard to South Africa's green hydrogen policy and public and private sector commitments have been announced.

Most importantly, South Africa's Hydrogen Society Roadmap was released in February 2022 (Mjwara, 2022). This Roadmap provides the appropriate supporting framework for developing and integrating hydrogen-related technologies across multiple sectors of the economy and for creating a green hydrogen economy by 2050, as envisaged. It indicates how hydrogen and fuel cell technologies could become a game-changer in the country's energy industry and enable it to fulfil its national and international climate change mitigation goals. A secondary objective of this Roadmap is to encourage economic recovery, in line with the country's Economic Reconstruction and Recovery Plan (ERRP). The Roadmap, therefore, enables the country's just transition away from coal as well as stimulates the post-COVID-19 economic recovery.

Another significant recent development was when the South African government, together with its domestic and international private sector partners released a feasibility study in October 2021 that identified three green hydrogen hubs in the country that had the potential to form a hydrogen valley (DSI, 2021). Nine pilot projects in the mobility, industrial and building sectors, were identified as part of the study (DSI, 2021, 8). The study found that these hydrogen hubs and their concomitant projects could be leveraged to kick-start the hydrogen economy in South Africa.

Also, during the COP26 Conference, the country managed to secure financial commitments of $8.5 billion cumulatively from the USA, the UK, France, Germany and the EU (Hanspal, 2021). These funds are intended to be used to speed up South Africa's transition to a green economy, with a particular focus on phasing out coal, which has thus far been the predominant energy source in South Africa's electricity sector. Additionally, this commitment will also support both domestic and foreign investments in green hydrogen production in South Africa.

3.4 Namibia

Namibia's vast solar and wind resources, as well as large tracts of unused land, provide it with a comparative advantage and a strong foundation for the development of a green hydrogen hub at cost-effective rates (von Oertzen, 2021: p. 16). Despite the country's considerable potential for producing green and blue hydrogen, it presently lacks a legal framework to regulate this industry (von Oertzen, 2021, p. 23). The Director-General of the National Planning Commission, Obeth Kandjoze previously asserted that the existing framework, consisting of the Petroleum Products and Energy Amendment Act, and the Minerals (Prospecting and Mining) Act, do not suffice to regulate green hydrogen (Newsbase, 2022). The government of Namibia perceives domestic renewable energy generation and green hydrogen production as key to decarbonisation (especially to decarbonise its electricity sector), to expand/ diversify its industrial sector and create both national and regional employment opportunities (Atlantic Council, 2021).

Namibia's recently launched Harambee prosperity plan II (covering the period 2021–2025) action plan toward economic recovery and inclusive growth, paves the way for the establishment of a national strategy for developing green hydrogen and ammonia (Harambee prosperity plan II, 2021). Its key pillars include propelling Namibia towards becoming a top exporter of green hydrogen, and achieving the country's socio-economic goals. However, the absence of specific policies and regulations relating to the regulation of green hydrogen in the country could pose a major barrier to attracting investments in sustainable energy in Namibia, as there is no legal protection, certainty, and quality standards/ assurances for investors, which are essential.

The utility of a conducive legal framework was highlighted by President, Hage Geingob, both in his 2022 New Year's speech and during the most recent State of the Nation (SONA) address, when he stated that a green hydrogen policy for Namibia would attract additional investment and position the country to become a regional and global leader in decarbonisation (State of the Nation Address (SONA), 2022, p. 17). The Namibian government sees this need for a legal framework as urgent, particularly to regulate its milestone green hydrogen project, which will be operating from Tsau Khaeb National Park (Afro News, 2022). This project is the most notable in the government's Southern Corridor Development Initiative (SCDI) in the Karas region in the southern part of the country. The region is especially suitable for green hydrogen production, owing to its large solar and wind resources, as well as its proximity to the sea and export routes (Afro News, 2022). This project aims to generate 5 GW of renewable energy, and it will eventually produce up to 300,000 tonnes of green hydrogen per year to serve both regional and international markets (Afro News, 2022). There are already approximately 3000 permanent employees working on this project, and it is projected that it will create about 15,000 direct jobs each year (Schutz, 2021). The first phase of this project is expected to enter production in 2026.

A major effort by the government of Namibia thus far has been focusing on stimulating private-public partnerships to support the development of domestic green hydrogen. A prime example is Germany, which as stated above, continues to invest large amounts of funds in Namibia's green hydrogen production and development. Also, during the COP26 Conference, Namibia signed a Memorandum of Understanding (MOU) with Belgium to collaborate in the efforts to enhance green hydrogen production and export (IEA, 2022). Most importantly, there are currently plans to develop a green hydrogen strategy that promotes investment opportunities for Namibia, and Germany has committed to play a central role in its implementation (von Oertzen, 2021, p. 23).

The legal underpinnings and recommendations for devising appropriate policy and legal frameworks to promote hydrogen economies, discussed under parts 4 and 5 below, would be instrumental in assisting nations such as Namibia to formulate appropriate laws and policies to support the development of a hydrogen economy. The following section of this chapter analyses the various degrees of convergence and divergence between regional and national frameworks for the adoption and development of green hydrogen.

4 Legal underpinnings and degrees of convergence and divergence between regional and national frameworks for the adoption/development of green hydrogen economies

The COP26 conference clearly showed that the global energy industry is eager to promote alignment and cooperation between countries and governments to accelerate the emergence of hydrogen economies (Hydrogen Forward, 2021). Multiple industry groups used this conference as a platform to call on global leaders to ensure that there are robust hydrogen policies that enable more efficient cross-border investments. Specifically, five international hydrogen associations urged the countries present at the conference to provide further clarity on hydrogen investment policies (Hydrogen Forward, 2021). This call to action by the various role players in the energy industry demonstrates a widespread desire for a more uniform approach to hydrogen standards and investment, key components to facilitate the acceleration of hydrogen production, deployment and use across the world. Similarly, a recent report by IRENA (2022, p. 71, 74) indicates that hydrogen will alter energy trade and regionalise relations between countries, therefore creating new centres of geopolitical influence. The report proceeds to assert that the desire by stakeholders in the global energy industry to shape the rules, standards and governance of hydrogen could usher in a new era of enhanced international cooperation.

It is evident from the discussions of the above regulatory frameworks for hydrogen that they each consider green hydrogen as essential to decarbonising their industrial processes and energy supply, to achieve both their international and domestic climate goals. However, it has been noted that there are significant variabilities in the decarbonisation ambitions of countries. According to Stephenson *et al.* (2021), domestic low-carbon ambitions are strongly cultural, depending on how individual countries view the role of energy, and the choices, policies, investments and actions that flow therefrom. They termed these factors as comprising the "energy culture" of countries. Therefore, this energy culture may influence the extent to which countries are willing to respond to the challenge of climate change.

The above scholars asserted that countries' low-carbon ambitions are the result of the following interacting factors, none of which is completely dominant in determining the degrees to which countries see their decarbonisation imperatives: a country's financial dependence on fossil fuels, its dependence on fossil fuels in the primary energy supply, its internal institutional paradigm – whether governments that are more permeable to the concerns of its citizens may be more willing to adopt a stronger low-carbon trajectory, and its externally facing paradigm – whether countries with a global outlook are more likely to have aspirational goals than those with an internal focus (Stephenson *et al.*, 2021, p. 1).

Also, although climate objectives are included in national hydrogen strategies, there is a general lack of comprehensive and prescriptive regulatory measures to achieve these objectives. For example, despite most countries having made net-zero pledges, several of them do not yet have plans to quit coal, including Australia, Japan, and the USA (de Hoog and Kirk, 2021). Therefore, there is a need for more stringent and prescriptive regulatory measures that would obligate countries to take measures to achieve their climate objectives.

Another area of convergence between national hydrogen strategies is that many countries envisage blue hydrogen as a transitory fuel and a stepping stone towards overall green hydrogen deployment in the long run (Patel, 2020: p. 8). However, the commitment to continue producing blue hydrogen in tandem with green hydrogen is lacking in some national strategies, such as in Germany, as shown above, and in Australia's National Hydrogen Strategy. Also, whereas countries clearly acknowledge hydrogen's potential for decarbonisation, it appears that there is a lack of uniformity with regard to the position of countries on hydrogen that is produced by fossil fuel sources. This uncertainty was manifested at the COP26 Conference through the Glasgow Climate Pact, a series of commitments from the world's biggest nations to make green solutions for businesses and governments operating in every economic sector. Specifically, these commitments are ambiguous about the proportions of renewable hydrogen and low-carbon hydrogen, as well as the emissions intensity thresholds for low-carbon hydrogen (COP26 Glasgow Climate Pact, 2021, p. 23). Moreover, about 40 countries committed to these Breakthroughs that emanated from the conference, therefore, albeit a significant number, not every country made these commitments.

Additionally, according to the national hydrogen strategies across several industrialised countries, it is clear that they perceive the development and application of advanced technologies as a key means of achieving large-scale deployment of hydrogen (Pingkuo and Xue, 2022, p. 9495). Therefore, these strategies emphasise technology innovation as a priority area. Germany’s hydrogen Strategy is similar to the strategy of Japan, another country that seeks to be a leader in the future green hydrogen revolution. Despite some context-specific differences and nuances relating to differing emphases and patterns, the two countries converge on three main drivers for hydrogen development: climate mitigation and other environmental goals, diversification of energy supply, and technological leadership (Narita, 2019, p. 3). In terms of climate change mitigation, whereas Germany aims at between 80% to 95% GHG emission reductions by 2050 in comparison with 1990, Japan aims for GHG emission reductions of 80% by 2050 in comparison to the levels of emissions in 2010 (Jensterle *et al.*, 2019). Also, as is the case with Japan, Germany has proposed the development of lightweight and safe liquid organic storage as a focus in the long-term (Michalski *et al.*, 2017). Also, both German and Japanese companies have a strong presence in the Hydrogen Council, depicting the role of the private sector in supporting the development of hydrogen in these countries.

As is the case with Germany's hydrogen strategy, South Africa's and Namibia's strategies also rely on the development of international partnerships and foreign investments to kick-start their hydrogen economies. At the beginning of 2022, the South African government announced a new collaboration with the German Ministry of Economic Cooperation and Development (BMZ), whereby the BMZ will provide €12.5 million in funding to support a project that will be launched through this collaboration to not only encourage green hydrogen production in South Africa, but also to coordinate the inclusion and involvement of a myriad of stakeholders, and ensure high environmental standards (Salma and Tsafos, 2022). Some examples of recent partnerships and collaborations by Namibia have been discussed above.

The above collaboration between South Africa and Germany follows the launch of a concessionary financing initiative by the KfW Development Bank, on behalf of the German government in July 2021 to support the development of the hydrogen economy in South Africa (Salma and Tsafos, 2022). As part of this initiative, a total of up to €200 million was availed by the bank, which would subsequently be allocated to several selected projects across South Africa (Salma and Tsafos, 2022). Such initiatives show the synergies between countries spurning both the developed and developing world, in terms of developing hydrogen economies.

In addition to the above, according to the International Renewable Energy Agency (IRENA), countries such as South Africa, Kenya, Egypt, Ethiopia, and Morocco are leading the energy transition efforts, as they are showing firm commitments toward accelerating the adoption of renewable sources of energy (IRENA, 2015, p. 3). Countries across the continent have in recent years been focusing on introducing or improving existing fiscal and financial incentives to support the adoption of renewable energy, including the deployment of hydrogen-related technologies.

The right mix of incentives and penalties is required for an effective hydrogen market. Incentives, particularly on the supply side would go a long way in assisting in the formation of pilot projects that feed into existing processes as well as set up independent production, which can be scaled as commercial viability is ascertained (TIPS, 2021). In South Africa for example, among several other incentives, section 11D of its Income Tax Act provides incentives for research and development activities (Income Tax Act, section 11D). Hydrogen manufacturers are resorting to this provision as a tax incentive to advance their research and development activities (Kaitwade, 2022). Similarly, Nigeria provides up to 120% of research and development expenses as tax-deductible, thus allowing investors to minimise costs (Oyewo, 2013, p. 35).

Lastly, in the context of Namibia, reflecting on the country's tendency to change policies and rules in the mining sector, the Institute for Public Policy Research (IPPR) advised that if the country is to achieve its mission to become a top green hydrogen exporter, its tax regime will need to be clear from the outset (New Era, 2022). As expressed above, the clarity and certainty of legislation are imperative to attracting investments, thereby ensuring the growth and development of the industry.

5 Recommendations for African countries for developing appropriate policy and legal frameworks to promote hydrogen economies

A key priority for African countries ought to be a focus on how to create appropriate legal and policy frameworks to attract investors and unlock their hydrogen economies. The Hydrogen Council in November 2021, identified six fundamental pillars for efficient policy design for clean/ green hydrogen (Hydrogen Council, 2021, p. 5). It is important for African countries to take these pillars into account in drafting and developing national hydrogen policies and the necessary regulatory frameworks to attract both domestic and foreign investments. These pillars are explained below.

First, the Hydrogen Council recommends that countries should leverage their local strengths as a starting point in policy design and complement this with cross-border cooperation and trade, to unlock efficiency gains (Hydrogen Council, 2021, p. 7). For example, in countries such as South Africa and Namibia that are considered to become future green hydrogen hubs, it is crucial that they develop uniform policy and regulatory frameworks to accelerate the development of hydrogen economies. Also, in light of the African Continental Free Trade Area Agreement (AfCFTA) that came into effect at the beginning of January 2021, harmonised regional policies that address *inter alia* the nature and types of incentives to be introduced, infrastructure and industry standards and certification, how the various barriers to hydrogen economies will be tackled on a regional level, among other pertinent issues, will need to be developed regionally, and eventually trickle down to inform domestic laws.

Additionally, in terms of countries leveraging their local strengths, they must address the interplay between existing gas infrastructure and hydrogen infrastructure. This could be achieved by, for example, repurposing existing gas infrastructure for transporting and storing hydrogen in gaseous form. There are several advantages to repurposing gas infrastructure. This process is more efficient and convenient because transportation networks for natural gas are already in place in many countries (ACER, 2021, p. 6). Also, natural gas networks can be converted to transport hydrogen with minimal modifications and at a cheaper cost *vis a vis* the costs of constructing new hydrogen networks (ACER, 2021, p. 6). In addition to the above, the requisite technologies for converting natural gas infrastructure to hydrogen are already available and proven, thus making it easier to repurpose existing networks (ACER, 2021, p. 6).

However, among other technical challenges, a significant problem that could arise for countries in this green revolution of adopting clean systems such as hydrogen, is the risk of having stranded assets where they cannot be repurposed, thus posing challenges relating to decommissioning, particularly for developed countries. In developing countries such as South Africa and Namibia, there is much less risk because oil and gas infrastructures may either not currently be in place or they may not be as extensive as in industrialised countries. This situation is a strong factor that would stand the continent in good stead in the process of adopting and developing green hydrogen into their energy systems.

The emphasis for African countries should be to use existing infrastructure better, rather than developing new solutions, therefore utilising storage and liquefied natural gas (LNG) infrastructure ought to be part of the long-term vision of nations to enhance efficiency. According to research by the National Business Initiative (NBI), Business Unity South Africa (BUSA) and the Boston Consulting Group (BCG), it was found that for South Africa to achieve its net-zero 2050 target, gas will need to be substituted with cleaner alternatives (Hako, 2022). This research advocates for the repurposing of existing gas infrastructure. A question arises relating to how the repurposing process should be regulated. This issue is at the core of energy debates today (Oil Field Africa, 2021). Gas Infrastructure Europe (GIE), which has approximately 70 members, representing 27 European nations that own and operate the existing infrastructure, provides several policy guidelines and recommendations that could be adopted globally to boost the establishment of hydrogen economies, as described below.

Some of these key policy recommendations include the following: countries need to develop and apply appropriate legislative frameworks that correspond with their existing legislation relating to gas (Oil Field Africa, 2021). This process could be conducted by building upon the existing basic principles for natural gas, whilst on the other hand, allowing countries the flexibility to consider their context-specific requirements and specifications. Also, these frameworks/regulations need to be capable of evolving with the respective market and the various developmental stages of infrastructure (Oil Field Africa, 2021). Additionally, they must acknowledge the role of gas infrastructure operators in integrating hydrogen into their energy systems (Oil Field Africa, 2021). Lastly, these frameworks ought to guarantee cost-recovery for investments into hydrogen infrastructure (Oil Field Africa, 2021).

A second policy recommendation by the Hydrogen Council is that governments can create certainty for investors by enacting legislation with clear terms that reduce risks and uncertainty in these industries (Hydrogen Council, 2021, p. 9). One of the most important factors that influence the decisions of investors in any economic industry is certainty relating to the relevant legislation to mitigate policy risk. Coupled with this, the Hydrogen Council recommends hydrogen-specific support be introduced through legislation and other policies in the different sectors where hydrogen is applied either as a source of energy or as feedstock for various chemical processes, as explained above (Hydrogen Council, 2021, p. 11). Such support could include the introduction of incentives such as loans, subsidies and grants for hydrogen infrastructure.

Fourthly, the Council recommends the building of carbon pricing mechanisms from existing schemes within African countries, to operate in tandem with hydrogen-specific support, to encourage uptake in the long-term, whilst simultaneously mitigating carbon leakage (Hydrogen Council, 2021, p. 14). These carbon pricing mechanisms, if properly implemented, could enable the deployment of hydrogen and allow low-carbon and clean hydrogen to compete alongside other technologies. The Council's fifth pillar for efficient policy design for clean hydrogen relates to the establishment of international standards and robust certification systems to aid in the development of the hydrogen economy and to enable cross-border trade in hydrogen (Hydrogen Council, 2021, p. 15). These international standards ensure uniformity across the industry, thus facilitating the commercialisation of hydrogen technologies. Also, the harmonisation of certification systems between countries or regions plays a major role in enhancing the global trade of hydrogen technologies and products.

The final pillar of the Hydrogen Council requires countries to factor in and incorporate societal values into their regulatory frameworks and policy decisions (Hydrogen Council, 2021, p. 17). For example, the relevant regulatory frameworks should take into account the fact that hydrogen is an explosive and flammable gas, therefore its production, storage and transport are subject to strict regulatory requirements to safeguard health and safety considerations. The Council notes that well-designed hydrogen policies can make positive contributions to several UN SDGs, therefore Environmental, Social and Governance ("ESG") standards are crucial for hydrogen policy design and development.

6 Conclusion

Hydrogen is rapidly emerging as a key enabler for the global clean energy transition, by supporting the decarbonisation of a wide range of industries, as countries take steps to mitigate the adverse effects of climate change. In order to solve the impending climate crisis quickly and cost-effectively, employing green hydrogen is inevitable, as it is gradually perceived as the missing link to achieving net-zero goals within the stipulated time frames. The growing number of countries that are adopting strategies and investing in hydrogen adds further weight to its utility for the future energy market.

This chapter has discussed the fundamental role and use cases for hydrogen in various economic sectors, laying the ground for the sentiment today that hydrogen is the appropriate decarbonisation pathway in the low-carbon transition. The premise of this chapter is that the development of low-carbon hydrogen (i.e. green or blue hydrogen), requires suitable financial, infrastructural and policy support to allow it to achieve wide deployment and to get to commercial-scale projects. The emphasis of this chapter has been on evaluating the legal/ policy tools and strategies that exist in selected countries, drawing from the experiences in both developed and developing economies. This policy review has considered examples of national and international hydrogen strategies, highlighting their legal underpinnings and assessed the degrees of convergence and divergence between these regional and national regulatory frameworks. Lastly, the review further presented policy options and recommendations for developing appropriate policy and legal frameworks to enhance hydrogen production and the energy transition from a fossil fuel-based economy to a hydrogen-based economy in Africa.

References

Afro News. 2022. *Namibia: Govt wants green hydrogen legal framework*. Available at: <https://afro.news/2022/01/13/namibia-govt-wants-green-hydrogen-legal-framework/> [Accessed 22 April 2022].

Atlantic Council. 2021. *Namibia: A green hydrogen hub for Africa*. Available at: <https://www.atlanticcouncil.org/event/a-green-hydrogen-hub-for-africa/> [Accessed 22 April 2022].

Ayodele, T.R. and Munda, J.L., 2019. Potential and economic viability of green hydrogen production by water electrolysis using wind energy resources in South Africa. *International Journal of Hydrogen Energy*, 44(33), pp. 17669–17687.

Baltic Industry, 2021. *Strategic plans reveal large-scale hydrogen expansion*. Available at: <https://bindustry.eu/strategic-plans-reveal-large-scale-hydrogen-expansion/> [Accessed 12 March 2022].

Berger, R. 2021. *Hydrogen transportation: The key to unlocking the clean hydrogen economy*. Available at: <roland_berger_hydrogen_transport.pdf> [Accessed 12 March 2022].

Bhagwat, S.R., and Olczak, M. (Africa- EU Energy Partnership), 2020. *Green Hydrogen: bridging the energy transition in Africa and Europe*. Available at: <https://africa-eu-energy-partnership.org/wp-content/uploads/2021/04/AEEP_Green-Hydrogen_Bridging-the-Energy-Transition-in-Africa-and-Europe_Final_For-Publication_2.pdf> [Accessed 14 February 2022].

Carbeck, J. 2020. *World Economic Forum: Top 10 Emerging Technologies of 2020*. Available at: <https://www3.weforum.org/docs/WEF_Top_10_Emerging_Technologies_2020.pdf> [Accessed 24 October 2021].

German Federal Ministry for the Environment, 2016. *Climate Action Plan 2050 – Germany's long-term low greenhouse gas emission development strategy*.

Climate Act of 2 June 2019 (The Netherlands). *Staatsblad* 2019 253.

Cliffe Dekker Hoffmeyr, 2021. *Energy Alert*. Available at: <https://www.cliffedekkerhofmeyr.com/export/sites/cdh/en/news/publications/2021/Energy/Downloads/Energy-Alert-7-April-2021.pdf> [Accessed 12 March 2022].

Coetzee, R. – IDC, 2021. *Commercialisation of the green hydrogen economy in South Africa*. Available at: <https://www.ee.co.za/wp-content/uploads/2021/06/Presentation-Rian-Coetzee.pdf> [Accessed 16 January 2022].

COP26 Glasgow Climate Pact, 2021. Available at: <https://ukcop26.org/wp-content/uploads/2021/11/COP26-Presidency-Outcomes-The-Climate-Pact.pdf> [Accessed 03 April 2022].

Davis, G., 2021. *SA ready to make hydrogen fuel cells as alternative energy source – Ramaphosa*. Available at: <https://ewn.co.za/2021/02/19/sa-ready-to-manufacture-hydrogen-fuel-cells-as-alternative-energy-source-ramaphosa> [Accessed 12 March 2022].

Day, P. 2022. *'Green' hydrogen offers a path to decarbonization, but it won't be easy*. Available at: <https://www.reutersevents.com/renewables/renewables/green-hydrogen-offers-path-decarbonization-it-wont-be-easy?utm_campaign=NEP%20HYGN%2026JAN22%20Newsletter&utm_medium=email&utm_source=Eloqua> [Accessed 03 April 2022].

de Hoog, N. and Kirk, A., 2021. *Current coal phaseout pledges 'absolutely not enough', warn experts*. Available at: <https://www.theguardian.com/environment/ng-interactive/2021/dec/23/why-cop26-coal-power-pledges-dont-go-far-enough-visualised> [Accessed 03 April 2022].

Department of Science and Innovation (DSI), 2021. *South Africa hydrogen valley Final Report*. Available at: <https://www.dst.gov.za/images/2021/Hydrogen_Valley_Feasibility_Study_Report_Final_Version.pdf> [Accessed 22 April 2022].

Energy Sector Management Assistance Program (ESMAP), 2020. *Green hydrogen in developing countries.* Available at: <https://documents1.worldbank.org/curated/en/953571597951239276/pdf/Green-Hydrogen-in-Developing-Countries.pdf> [Accessed 12 March 2022].

European Commission, 2020. *A hydrogen strategy for a climate-neutral Europe*. COM(2020)301. Available at: <https://ec.europa.eu/energy/sites/ener/files/hydrogen_strategy.pdf> [Accessed 14 February 2022].

European Commission – Press Release, 2021. *Commission proposes new EU framework to decarbonise gas markets, promote hydrogen and reduce methane emissions*. Available at: <Commission_proposes_new_EU_framework_to_decarbonise_gas_markets__promote_hydrogen_and_reduce_methane_emissions.pdf> [Accessed 14 February 2022].

European Union Agency for the Cooperation of Energy Regulators (ACER), 2021. *Transporting pure hydrogen by repurposing existing gas infrastructure: overview of existing studies and reflections on the conditions for repurposing*. Available at: <https://extranet.acer.europa.eu/Official_documents/Acts_of_the_Agency/Publication/Transporting%20Pure%20Hydrogen%20by%20Repurposing%20Existing%20Gas%20Infrastructure_Overview%20of%20studies.pdf> [Accessed 03 April 2022].

Faris, J., 2020. *Which countries are backing the hydrogen economy?* Available at: <https://www.h2bulletin.com/countries-hydrogen-economy-goals-policies/> [Accessed 8 December 2021].

Fuhrmann, M., 2020. *Germany's National Hydrogen Strategy – Serious efforts to realize a decarbonized society; development of green hydrogen supply infrastructure is the challenge*. Available at: <https://www.mitsui.com/mgssi/en/report/detail/__icsFiles/afieldfile/2021/02/19/2012_fuhrmann_e.pdf> [Accessed 14 February 2022].

FuelCellsWorks, 2021. *South Africa moves to manufacture, commercialize hydrogen fuel cell technology.* Available at: <https://fuelcellsworks.com/news/south-africa-moves-to-manufacture-commercialize-hydrogen-fuel-cell-technology/> [Accessed 8 December 2021].

Hako, N., 2022. *Research outlines key findings on the role of gas in South Africa's energy transition*. Available at: <https://www.esi-africa.com/southern-africa/research-outlines-key-findings-on-the-role-of-gas-in-south-africas-energy-transition/> [Accessed 14 March 2022].

Hanspal, J., 2021. *COP26: South Africa to receive $8.5bn to stop using coal*. Available at: <https://www.theafricareport.com/143773/cop26-south-africa-to-receive-8-5bn-to-stop-using-coal/> [Accessed 17 December 2021].

Harambee prosperity plan II, 2021. *Harambee prosperity plan II 2021-2025*. Available at: <http://hppii.gov.na/storage/2021/03/HPP2.pdf> [Accessed 22 April 2022].

Headley, J. and Schoenung, S., 2020. Hydrogen energy storage. In: US Department of Energy, ed., 2020. *Energy Storage Handbook*. Available at: https://www.sandia.gov/ess/publications/doe-oe-resources/eshb [Accessed 5 September 2022].

Hiltbrand, G., Herndon, W., O'Rear, E.G., and Larsen, J., 2021. *Clean hydrogen: a versatile tool for decarbonization*. Available at: <https://rhg.com/research/clean-hydrogen-decarbonization/> [Accessed 14 February 2022].

HiveEnergy, 2021. *World's largest green ammonia plant for Nelson Mandela Bay, South Africa*. Available at: <https://www.hiveenergy.co.uk/2021/12/15/worlds-largest-green-ammonia-plant-for-nelson-mandela-bay-south-africa/> [Accessed 14 February 2022].

Huber, I., 2021. *Germany's hydrogen industrial strategy*. Available at: <https://www.csis.org/analysis/germanys-hydrogen-industrial-strategy> [Accessed 14 February 2022].

Hydrogen Council, 2021. *Hydrogen decarbonisation pathways: a life-cycle assessment*. Available at: <https://hydrogencouncil.com/wp-content/uploads/2021/04/Hydrogen-Council-Report_Decarbonization-Pathways_Part-1-Lifecycle-Assessment.pdf> [Accessed 12 March 2022].

Hydrogen Council, 2021. *Policy toolbox for low carbon and renewable hydrogen: enabling low carbon and renewable hydrogen globally*. Available at: <https://hydrogencouncil.com/wp-content/uploads/2021/11/Hydrogen-Council_Policy-Toolbox.pdf> [Accessed 03 April 2022].

Hydrogen Forward, 2021. *Top 5 hydrogen takeaways from COP26*. Available at: <https://www.hydrogenfwd.org/top-5-hydrogen-takeaways-from-cop26/> [Accessed 03 April 2022].

International Energy Agency (IEA), 2022. *Belgium-Namibia MoU on green hydrogen*. Available at: <https://www.iea.org/policies/14754-belgium-namibia-mou-on-green-hydrogen> [Accessed 03 April 2022].

IEA, 2021. *Net Zero by 2050: a roadmap for the global energy sector*. Available at: <https://iea.blob.core.windows.net/assets/deebef5d-0c34-4539-9d0c-10b13d840027/NetZeroby2050-ARoadmapfortheGlobalEnergySector_CORR.pdf> [Accessed 03 April 2022].

International Renewable Energy Agency (IRENA), 2015. Africa 2030: *roadmap for a renewable energy future*. Available at: <A_Renewable_Energy_Roadmap.pdf> [Accessed 14 March 2022].

IRENA, 2022. *Geopolitics of the energy transformation: the hydrogen factor*. Available at: <IRENA_Geopolitics_Hydrogen_2022.pdf> [Accessed 23 April 2022].

Jensterle, M., Narita, J., Piria, R. *et al.*, 2019. *The role of clean hydrogen in the future energy systems of Japan and Germany*. Available at: <https://www.adelphi.de/de/system/files/mediathek/bilder/The%20role%20of%20clean%20hydrogen%20in%20the%20future%20energy%20systems%20of%20Japan%20and%20Germany%20-%20Study.pdf> [Accessed 12 March 2022].

Kaitwade, N., 2022. *Analysis: water electrolysis is a major key to a clean energy transition*. Available at: <https://www.esi-africa.com/industry-sectors/business-and-markets/analysis-water-electrolysis-is-a-major-key-to-a-clean-energy-transition/> [Accessed 23 April 2022].

Kaplan, R., and Kopacz, M., 2020. Economic conditions for developing hydrogen production based on coal gasification with carbon capture and storage in Poland. *Energies*, 13(19), 5074.

Koole, C., and Blank, T.K., 2021. *COP26 made clear that the world is ready for green hydrogen*. Available at: <https://rmi.org/cop26-made-clear-that-the-world-is-ready-for-green-hydrogen/> [Accessed 14 February 2022].

Kroposki, B., Levene, J., Harrison, K. *et al.*, 2006. *Electrolysis: Information and opportunities for electric power utilities*. Technical Report NREL/TP-581-40605. Available at: <https://doi.org/10.2172/892998> [Accessed 17 August 2021].

Ludwig, M., Luers, M., Lorenz, M. *et al.*, 2021. *The green tech opportunity in hydrogen*. Available at: <https://www.bcg.com/publications/2021/capturing-value-in-the-low-carbon-hydrogen-market> [Accessed 14 February 2022].

Marchant, N., 2021. *Grey, blue, green – why are there so many colours of hydrogen?* Available at: <https://www.weforum.org/agenda/2021/07/clean-energy-green-hydrogen/> [Accessed 14 February 2022].

Metcalfe, J., Burger, L.R., and Mackay, J., 2020. *Unlocking South Africa's hydrogen potential*. Available at: < https://www.pwc.co.za/en/assets/pdf/unlocking-south-africas-hydrogen-potential.pdf> [Accessed 09 September 2021].

Mjwara, P., 2022. *High level outcomes of the Hydrogen Society Roadmap*. Available at: <https://www.saasta.ac.za/saasta_wp/wp-content/uploads/2022/02/DG-Presentation-HSRM-Launch-17-February-2022-v2_17022022-002.pdf> [Accessed 22 April 2022].

Michalski, J., Bünger, U., Crotogino, F. *et al.*, 2017. Hydrogen generation by electrolysis and storage in salt caverns: potentials, economics and systems aspects with regard to the German energy transition. *International Journal of Hydrogen Energy*, 42(19), pp. 13427–13443.

Muralidharan, A., 2020. *COVID-19's impact on the energy sector*. Available at: <https://www.hydrocarbonengineering.com/clean-fuels/19112020/covid-19s-impact-on-the-energy-sector/> [Accessed 12 December 2021].

Narita, J., 2019. *The role of clean hydrogen in the future energy systems of Germany and Japan*. Available at: <https://www.nedo.go.jp/content/100899758.pdf> [Accessed 12 March 2022].

New Era, 2022. *Have clear tax regime to realise green hydrogen – IPPR*. Available at: <https://energycentral.com/news/have-clear-tax-regime-realise-green-hydrogen-ippr> [Accessed 12 March 2022].

Newsbase, 2022. *AfrElec: Namibia investigates legal framework to regulate fledgling green hydrogen industry.* Available at: <https://newsbase.com/story/namibia-investigates-legal-framework-to-regulate-fledgling-green-hydrogen-industry-231820> [Accessed 22 April 2022].

Norton Rose Fulbright, 2020. *Hydrogen paves the way to decarbonisation.* Available at: <https://www.nortonrosefulbright.com/en/knowledge/publications/44e51e98/hydrogen-paves-the-way-to-decarbonisation> [Accessed 22 August 2021].

Office of Fossil Energy: United States Department of Energy, 2020. *Hydrogen Strategy: Enabling A Low-Carbon Economy.* Available at: <https://www.energy.gov/sites/prod/files/2020/07/f76/USDOE_FE_Hydrogen_Strategy_July2020.pdf> [Accessed 8 December 2021].

Oil Field Africa, 2021. *GIE setting out future hydrogen infrastructure.* Available at: <https://oilfieldafricareview.com/gie-setting-out-future-hydrogen-infrastructure/> [Accessed 14 March 2022].

Ouziel, S., and Alevar, L., 2021. *4 technologies that are accelerating the green hydrogen revolution.* Available at: <https://www.weforum.org/agenda/2021/06/4-technologies-accelerating-green-hydrogen-revolution/> [Accessed 14 March 2022].

Oyewo, M.B., 2013. Taxation and tax policy as government strategy tools for economic development in Nigeria. *IOSR Journal of Business and Management (IOSR-JBM)*, 13(5), pp. 34–40.

Patel, M. (TIPS), 2020. *Green hydrogen: a potential export commodity in a new global marketplace.* Available at: <https://www.tips.org.za/images/TIPS_Green_hydrogen_A_potential_export_commodity_in_a_new_global_marketplace.pdf> [Accessed 8 December 2021].

Pingkuo, L. and Xue, H., 2022. Comparative analysis on similarities and differences of hydrogen energy development in the World's top 4 largest economies: A novel framework. *International Journal of Hydrogen Energy*, 47, pp. 9485–9503.

Research Dive, 2022. Demand: hydrogen generation market expected to grow at a CAGR of 6.9% and amass a revenue of $212,877.4 million in the 2021 to 2028 timeframe. Available at: <https://www.globenewswire.com/news-release/2022/03/30/2412948/0/en/Demand-Hydrogen-Generation-Market-Expected-to-Grow-at-a-CAGR-of-6-9-and-Amass-a-Revenue-of-212-877-4-Million-in-the-2021-to-2028-Timeframe-200-Pages-Confirmed-by-Research-Dive.html> [Accessed 05 April 2022].

Resource World, 2021. *Hydrogen production to double by 2030.* Available at: <https://resourceworld.com/hydrogen-production-to-double-by-2030/> [Accessed 8 December 2021].

Roodbol, A., 2021. *Hydrogen, financing the energy transition and climate change.* Available at: <https://www.miningreview.com/energy/hydrogen-financing-the-energy-transition-and-climate-change-enlit-africa/> [Accessed 22 August 2021].

Salma, T., and Tsafos, N., 2022. *South Africa's Hydrogen Strategy.* Available at: <https://www.csis.org/analysis/south-africas-hydrogen-strategy> [Accessed 22 April 2022].

Schutz, E., 2021. *The African nation aiming to be a hydrogen superpower.* Available at: <https://www.bbc.com/news/business-59722297> [Accessed 28 December 2021].

Scita, R., Raimondi, P.P, and Noussan, M., 2020. Green hydrogen: the Holy Grail of decarbonisation? An analysis of the technical and geopolitical implications of the future hydrogen economy. *Future Energy Program – Working Paper.*

State of the Nation Address (SONA), 2022. *8th State of the Nation Address.* Available at: <https://hppii.gov.na/storage/2022/04/2022-SONA-6-April-Digital.pdf> [Accessed 22 April 2022].

State of the Netherlands v Urgenda, ECLI:NL:HR:2019:2007.

Stephenson, J.R., Sovacool, B.K., and Inderberg, T.H.J., 2021. Energy cultures and national decarbonisation pathways. *Renewable and Sustainable Energy Reviews*, 137, pp. 1–15.

Strachan, E., 2020. *The emerging hydrogen economy: regulation, policy and industry update.* Available at: <https://www.akingump.com/en/experience/industries/energy/speaking-energy/the-emerging-hydrogen-economy-regulation-policy-and-industry-update.html>[Accessed 12 March 2022].

Trade & Industrial Policy Strategies (TIPS), 2021. *Green hydrogen-potential new export for South Africa.* Available at: <https://tips.org.za/images/TIPS_Press_release_Green_hydrogen_Potential_new_export_for_South_Africa_23_February_2021.pdf> [Accessed 22 August 2021].

United Nations Framework Convention on Climate Change (UNFCCC). 2015. *Paris Agreement*. Available at: <https://unfccc.int/files/meetings/paris_nov_2015/application/pdf/paris_agreement_english_.pdf> [Accessed 22 August 2021].

Urgenda.nl. *Landmark decision by Dutch Supreme Court*. Available at: <https://www.urgenda.nl/en/themas/climate-case/> [Accessed 14 February 2022].

Von Burchard – CMS. *Hydrogen law and regulation in Germany*. Available at: <https://cms.law/en/int/expert-guides/cms-expert-guide-to-hydrogen/germany> [Accessed 12 March 2022].

von Oertzen, D., 2021. *Issues, challenges and opportunities to develop green hydrogen in Namibia*. Available at: <https://www.kas.de/documents/279052/279101/Issues%2C+Challenges+and+Opportunities+to+Develop+Green+Hydrogen+in+Namibia.pdf/a4729b11-5f95-11fc-3203-737fad34543a?version=1.0&t=1638951171809> [Accessed 22 April 2022].

Walwyn, D.R., and Crompton, R., 2020. *South Africa has huge 'green fuels' potential. But it needs to act now*. Available at: <https://theconversation.com/south-africa-has-huge-green-fuels-potential-but-it-needs-to-act-now-129009> [Accessed 22 August 2021].

Whyte, K., 2021. *South Africa's green hydrogen potential*. Available at: <https://www.bizcommunity.com/Article/196/834/215148.html> [Accessed 28 December 2021].

World Bank Group, 2021. *Apoyo del Banco Mundial a la Implementación del HidrógenoVerde*. Available at: <https://www.unepfi.org/wordpress/wp-content/uploads/2021/09/5_Fernando-de-Sisternes_BM_H2V_Financiamiento_Octubre_2021_compartir.pdf> [Accessed 12 March 2022].

Liebrich M. Hiemstra

The Financial Side of Energy Markets

Abstract: This chapter focuses on the regulatory frameworks for financial energy markets in the EU and the USA. Specific attention is paid to the consequences of climate policies. The first part is devoted to financial energy contracts and markets structures. The second part is devoted to incentives for financial trading and the distinction among hedging, speculation and arbitrage. The third part discusses regulatory and supervisory regimes.

1 Introduction

This chapter will explain the characteristics of the financial side of energy markets. It aims to clarify why financial contracts are needed in the energy sector and how such transactions are conducted by energy companies. A specific focus in this chapter is the low-carbon transition. This focus is also reflected in the description of the different types of financial contracts discussed herein, including derivatives relating to cap-and-trade schemes for CO2 emissions and environmental, social and governance (ESG) financial products. In addition, this chapter addresses how these financial contracts in the energy sector are regulated and will pay attention to anti-manipulation rules in the European Union and the United States. In line with the other chapters in the book, this chapter will take the low-carbon transition and climate finance as a guidance in discussing the topics above and pursues to shed light on the question how financial contracts in the energy sector may contribute to a low-carbon transition.

2 Energy markets and trading in financial contracts

The energy market can be seen and defined from different angles. Examples include the perspective of consumers and their off-take agreements with energy providers, the perspective of transport- and grid connections and the cross-border operators of these grids, the different sources of commodities which are used to generate electricity and the wholesale market for trading energy products. As a consequence, there is no fixed notion of *the energy market.* The variety of different facets is further in-

Liebrich M. Hiemstra is Researcher at the University of Tilburg, School of Law, The Netherlands and Senior Legal Counsel at Vattenfall, Amsterdam, The Netherlands.

https://doi.org/10.1515/9783110752403-021

creased by the cross-border element of trading in energy products such as coal, electricity and liquified natural gas and global interdependencies of energy prices of these products. Energy prices are highly volatile and dependent on external elements such as weather, climate policy, political developments and technology. Companies producing electricity, or trading in energy products, have an interest in pro-actively responding to these forces as they may impact the price of energy products. One of the tools to try to mitigate the impact of external factors on the price of a physical energy product, is to conduct trading in financial instruments – which value is derived from the physical energy products they trade in – simultaneously to trading in physical products. In addition, there may be other reasons why energy companies trade in financial contracts too. The paragraphs below will explain how these financial products are traded by energy companies and what the reasons and incentives are for energy companies to conduct these transactions.

2.1 How does trading in financial contracts work?

In order to investigate how trading in financial contracts work, let's first see how trading in physical energy products works. Energy companies generate electricity through gas- or coal fired power plants or through renewable sources such as wind turbines, hydrogen facilities or solar panels. In addition to such production task, many energy companies trade in energy commodities to meet an underlying demand to run a power plant – such as the trade in coal to fuel the coal fired power plant – or to meet a contractual obligation to deliver an agreed volume to a purchaser. Energy companies do not know the future price level of these commodities or the daily spot price of the electricity they generate, whilst they have a commercial interest to limit their exposure to these price fluctuations or uncertainties. As indicated above, one way to control such exposure is conducting a transaction whereby the energy company is entering into a financial contract simultaneously to the physical transaction. This is called hedging. Please see the example below on how hedging in the energy sector may work in practice.

A fictive energy company called Alpha is generating electricity through its power plant. Alpha does not want to be exposed to the daily spot price of electricity generated by its plant when selling the electricity and decides to see how it can mitigate this price risk. Alpha expects that the price of electricity on 1 January 2025 will be EUR 40 per megawatt hour. At the same time, another energy company Bravo – which is in need for electricity and therefore at the demand side of the market – expects that the spot price of electricity on 1 January 2025 will be EUR 60 per megawatt hour. Both parties agree to sell and purchase a set amount of megawatt hour for a price of EUR 50 per megawatt hour on 1 January 2025 and they both think they concluded a profitable transaction. This contract is called a forward contract with a physical delivery. What if Bravo changes its mind on the future spot price and expects this price to be lower than EUR 50 per megawatt hour? It does not want to be committed to paying Alpha the high spot price on 1 January 2025 and decides to sell the forward contract to another energy company called Charlie. The forward contract is tradable and has a value which is derived from the price of electricity: an energy derivative. Alpha, Bravo and Charlie entered into the world of energy derivative trading in order to hedge their price risks.

In case financial products have a value which is derived from the price of an energy product, the trading therein can be described as Energy Trading (Hiemstra, 2020a). Derivatives can exist in all types of shapes, but they do not identify a fixed set of financial instruments (Biggins, 2012). Energy Trading is not limited to trading in derivatives with an underlying based on the price of electricity. Energy derivatives may also be based on renewable energy products as well, such as guarantees of origin which serve as a proof for the renewable generation source of electricity or CO_2 certificates (Dagoumas and Koltsaklis, 2017). Trading in energy derivatives can be conducted through multiple financial products, in multiple forms and on multiple venues. One distinction can be made between bilateral trades (so-called over-the-counter trades) or trades conducted through exchange platforms. Examples of exchanges where energy derivatives are traded are the European Energy Exchange (EEX) for the European Power market, Eurex as the largest derivative exchange in Europe, the Chicago Mercantile Exchange (CME), ICE Futures US (ICE) or the New York Mercantile Exchange (NYMEX). Recent developments on these exchanges show a shift in trading in sustainable derivatives. CME has launched E-mini S&P 500 ESG Index futures, a new derivative portfolio to align market participants financial goal with ESG values. Also Eurex introduced equity index futures contracts tied to ESG benchmarks. Next to the derivatives which have clear link to decarbonization, such as emission allowances, there are different classes of derivatives which measure sustainability targets or ratings: ESG derivatives. These ESG-index based derivatives are one of the fastest growing segments for exchanges and an increasingly popular hedging and trading tool (Lannoo and Thomadakis, 2020).

3 Incentives for trading

3.1 Hedging, arbitrage and speculation

There are three main reasons why energy companies trade in energy derivatives: hedging, speculation and arbitrage. This division plays a role in the regulatory exemptions at EU level for those trades conducted to mitigate the (price) risks related to the physical commodities necessary for the conduct of an energy company's business as opposed to proprietary trading for direct gain (the so-called hedging exemption). With respect to energy companies, there are generally two risks involved in physical trading. One is the risk associated with the market price for energy (the price risk) and the other is the risk associated with the amount of energy that will be bought (the volume risk) (Hull, 2012, p. 761). It is not always clear how to distinguish hedging from other reasons for trading, such as speculation or arbitration (Hull, 2012; Partnoy, 2002). Cheng and Xiong (2014) reflect that the classification of market participants into the categories of "speculators" and "hedgers" very poorly aligns with the economically relevant distinction: reducing versus increasing risk. They state that many "hedgers" appear to take bets on prices that are insensitive to their current exposure. Disregarding the identity of the trader as a factor of classifying trades, and instead emphasizing the motive of a trade, may increase the difficulties in applying the distinction. It is already difficult for regulators to distinguish trading motives in a bilateral trade environment, and would be much harder in an anonymous market in which orders may be split by algorithms and allocated to a wide range of counterparties (Duffie, 2014). A market participant trading in (heavily) subsidized renewable products, where margins and risks are lower than for the old and grey commodities, is less likely to enter into risky derivative trades and less likely to qualify as a speculator (Hiemstra, 2020a).

3.1.1 Hedging

Hedging plays an important role in trading in energy derivatives as prices are volatile with large price fluctuations and therefore high price risks. Hedging can be risk mitigation in order to offset an exposure. Market participants engage in hedging activities in order to manage risks for future instability in the price or rate on which a derivative is based. Hedging can therefore be considered as a form of insurance against changes in the market. Derivatives also play an essential role in helping firms to manage climate-related and transition risks. By facilitating the transfer of risks from counterparties that do not wish to have risk exposures to those that are willing to do so, derivatives offer an effective tool to hedge physical and transition risks by reducing uncertainty over future prices (ISDA, 2021). Academic literature suggests several questions: What risks do firms hedge? How much do they hedge? How far ahead do they hedge? What determines corporate hedging policy? Should firms hedge at all? Can corporate risk management create value? It is indicated that "as straightforward as it might appear, these questions are still largely unresolved" (Mackay and Moeller, 2010, p. 2) and that academic guidance is still lacking (Poitras, 2013, p. 48). However, it is only a tool to, potentially, minimize or control a price risk, since there is no guarantee that the outcome with hedging will be better than the outcome without hedging. In addition, the risk that a counterparty defaults or may not be able to fulfill its contractual obligations is not mitigated. Hedging entails entering into multiple transactions at the same time for different prices and concluding hedging transactions is in certain aspects parallel to trading in multiple derivatives at the same time. This is because the hedge transaction is linked to a physical trade, so market participants spread the market risk. Without having a possibility to hedge, market participants would face large risks relating to price fluctuations. There is a difference, however, between hedging using future- and forward contracts or using options for hedging purposes. Since the difference between futures, forwards and options is the optionality of the possessor of the option to exercise its right to sell or purchase, the option for hedging purposes is more likely to be seen as an insurance tool.

3.1.2 Arbitrage

Arbitrage is a process whereby market participants profit from price discrepancies. This is done by simultaneously entering into transactions relating to a similar product in two or more markets. Since one trade stands in for the other, arbitrage can be risk free. The possibility to arbitrage only exists if a product is priced differently on different markets or if this difference is the result of the difference in currency rates. Interesting in the process of arbitrage is that there is a short window of opportunity for market participants, since the forces of supply and demand will eventually create a balance between the different markets (Hull, 2012, p. 16).

3.1.3 Speculation

Speculation is the activity where a market player takes a position in order to make profit, whilst hedgers want to avoid exposure to adverse market movements in the price of an asset. It is therefore the opposite of hedging: taking upon a risk in order to make profit instead of mitigating a risk with the objective to avoid a loss. Speculation can be a business in itself and the return for speculators is not sure. The in-house professional execution of speculative trading is proprietary trading. The objective of these (in-house) departments is to make money and in planning to do so, they use working capital. Usually, speculators trade for their own account without a client portfolio and the activities are not related to the core business of their undertaking. As for hedgers, there is a difference in speculating with futures or options (Hull, 2012, p. 15). When a speculator uses futures, the potential loss as well as the potential gain is very large. When options are used, and the speculator has the possibility to choose whether it writes the option, the loss is limited to the purchase price of the options, no matter how low the market price becomes.

3.2 Sustainable finance derivatives as a tool to reach decarbonization targets

Derivatives may play a role in pricing several energy products which may have an impact on climate change, such as a barrel of oil or guarantees of origin relating to megawatts generated by a green production facility. In that way, derivatives may help to make the true costs of climate change tangible (Futures Industry Association, 2021). This leads to the assumption that there are other reasons for energy companies or large industries to trade in sustainable finance derivatives next to the more financial driven reasons to trade – as those reflected above – and which can very bluntly be summarized as a *buy low, sell high* business strategy. Especially large industrial parties involved in chemical or heavy industries show a focus on the ambition to decarbonize their output and engage in purchasing renewable certificates as a tool to mitigate their carbon emissions. This comes with a risk of 'greenwashing', which implies that sustainable efforts do not reflect actual climate performance (Coen et al., 2022). This would be the case if a company active in a highly polluting industry trades in emission certificates and uses this activity for marketing purposes whereby the polluting activities are reflected as ancillary to its emissions trading business. Sustainability efforts across the derivatives ecosystem differ in their details, but share a common trait: they are born out of industry-led innovation and adaptability. Climate change-related innovation is evident in big efforts, like the creation of carbon marketplaces that did not exist until relatively recently (FIA, 2022).

One important tool in combating climate change is a market-based concept called cap-and-trade. In short, the idea behind the cap-and-trade approach is to help control emissions by putting a price on carbon, and providing economic incentives through an allocation of a limited number of permits that must be purchased by those who pollute more and can be sold by those who pollute less. This concept is further elaborated by Richards in this volume. There is a distinction between primary- and secondary markets for trade in emission certificates (ESMA, 2022a). Primary markets consist of auctions to which most market participants whose main business relates to generating CO_2 are able to participate. Here is where the emission certificates are created. Secondary markets consist of exchanges where all other parties may participate and where those emission certificates are traded (Hedges, 2009). Hence, a separate market for the trade in these financial instruments is created which attracts investors, industrials and parties searching for trading opportunities with either hedging, speculative or arbitrage motives. In Europe, these secondary markets are EEX in Germany, ICE Endex in the Netherlands and Nasdaq Oslo in Norway. Derivatives based on US emission certificates such as California carbon allowances and RGGI (as further described in paragraph 3.2.2) are traded on ICE.

Another specific type of sustainable financial instruments are ESG derivatives, which are trades measuring certain ESG components. Although a fixed definition for ESG derivatives is lacking, ESG derivatives may have a value derived from an underlying interest rate with an additional premium in case the pre-set ESG targets are not met. The premium would turn into a discount if the targets are met. Therefore, market participants have an interest in meeting the ESG targets which are linked to the derivatives they trade in. Sustainability-linked products can attract much needed investment for research and the low-carbon transition. Derivatives play a role in these objectives as they: i) enable governments and investors to raise capital towards sustainable investments; ii) help firms hedge risks; iii) facilitate transparency, price discovery and market efficiency; and iv) contribute to long-termism (Lannoo and Thomadikis, 2020). As the route to decarbonization requires a long-term view instead of a short-term incentive to make profit, derivatives are vital for investors to manage these long-term risks and being able to realize the long-term goal of climate change.

3.2.1 European Union

In July 2021, the European Commission launched its Renewed Sustainable Finance Strategy to support meeting the commitments from the European Green Deal, which include becoming the first climate-neutral continent by 2050 and to reduce greenhouse gas emissions by at least 55% by 2030 (European Commission, 2021a). In this strategy, the European Commission emphasizes that a framework for sustainable finance can make it easier for public authorities to raise sustainable capital which is relevant as the scale of investments required to achieve the commitments as described above is well beyond the capacity of the public sector on its own. Such framework should include labels for financial instruments and sustainability derivatives could help bring clarity, transparency and coherence to sustainable finance markets. Such label could include a reference to the energy transition or more sustainability-linked labels such as ESG. Based on this strategy, it appears that there is an increasing space for financial instruments to be used as a tool to reach the climate change and decarbonization targets.

3.2.2 United States

Next to specific emission trading programs such as the Regional Greenhouse Gas Initiative (RGGI, 2021) and the Western Climate Initiative (WCI, 2020) which are covered elsewhere in this Handbook, the interest in ESG issues is on the rise. Apart from the implementation of ESG factors in investment strategies of large industrial players, several new financial instruments relating to sustainability appear on the horizon. One of these is the so-called conservation finance instruments which are characterized by a mechanism through which a financial investment into an ecosystem is made that aims to conserve the values of that system for the long term (United Nations Environment Programme, 2016). The US Commodity Futures Trading Commission (CFTC) underlines that commodity derivatives exchanges could address climate and sustainability issues by incorporating sustainability elements into existing contracts and by developing new derivative contracts to hedge climate-related risks, which may include weather, ESG and renewable generation and electricity derivatives (CFTC, 2020).

The Federal Reserve Board – the governing body with a mandate to oversee the federal reserve banks in the US – recognized climate change and climate-related risks as increasingly able to influence financial risks and US financial stability (Board of Governors of the Federal Reserve System, 2020). In addition, US regulators such as the Securities and Exchange Commission (SEC) and the CFTC have increased their focus on ESG financial products since the beginning of the Biden administration in January 2021 (SEC, 2021 and CFTC, 2021). A specific example can be found in the SEC proposed rule which would require registrants under the Securities Act and the Securities Exchange Act to include certain climate-related disclosures in their registration statements and periodic reports, including information about climate-related risks that may have impact on their business, results of operations, or financial condition (SEC, 2022). Even though this proposal is still open for comments, it is a sign that focus on climate is enlarged. However, such increased focus has not yet led to increased regulatory initiatives in this field in relation to climate change.

4 Regulation and supervision

The market for trading in energy derivatives has been subject to increased regulation since the financial crisis in 2007, with a general aim to make the market more transparent and safer for both investors and – ultimately – end consumers of electricity and gas (Lannoo and Thomadakis, 2020; Hiemstra, 2020a). This tighter regulation includes the implementation of specific anti-manipulation rules in the energy sector. Supervision and enforcement of these regulatory frameworks are limited to the territorial jurisdiction of specific regulatory authorities, whilst the trade in energy derivatives is characterized by cross-border relationships between market players. This section continues with an overview of the specific regulatory frameworks in the EU and the US and further investigates how these frameworks interlink with each other.

4.1 EU

4.1.1 Relevant regulatory framework

At a European level there are several regulatory frameworks to supervise energy derivative trading: Markets in Financial Instruments Directive (MiFID II), the European Market Infrastructure Regulation (EMIR), the Regulation on Wholesale Energy Market Integrity and Transparency (REMIT) and the Market Abuse Directive and Regulation (MAD/MAR). The objective of REMIT is to increase integrity and transparency in the wholesale energy market and to foster competition for the benefit of final consumers of energy, whilst EMIR aims to reduce systemic risk by increasing market transparency and to mitigate counterparty risk by introducing a clearing obligation for OTC derivatives. MiFID II aims to make financial markets more transparent and to increase the level of protection for investors. Under MiFID II, emission allowances are listed as a specific category of financial instruments no matter where and how they are traded, which in practice means that primary markets as well as secondary markets are under surveillance of ESMA. There is discussion on activities of speculators or pure financial actors – whom may not even be based in the European Union – and whether they should be restricted from trading as certain buy-and-hold strategies may lead to a reduction of allowances available to compliance entities (Energy Post, 2022). Such buy-and-hold strategy may be the basis for anti-manipulative market behavior. Anti-manipulation rules are mostly derived from MAD/MAR and the trading in financial derivatives – including emission certificates – is subjected to statutory prohibitions of market manipulation and insider trading. More specifically, according to article 12 MAR these prohibitions entail: i) entering into transactions which are likely to secure its price at an abnormal or artificial level; ii) entering into transactions which affects the price of a financial instruments and which employs a fictitious device or any other form of deception; iii) disseminating information through media which gives misleading signals as to the supply, demand, price of the financial instrument, where the person who made the dissemination knew that the information was misleading.

4.1.2 Supervisory regime

Market supervision of Energy Trading is not a purely national matter in the European Union. As directives form the European framework for financial regulation, the implementation and scope of regulation on a national level, as well as supervision and enforcement, may vary along the Member States. The regulatory frameworks mentioned in the previous sub-section have their own supervisory agencies; the Agency for the Cooperation of Energy Regulators ('ACER') and the European Securities and Markets Authority ('ESMA'). As the trade in energy derivatives is characterized by cross-border activities, national- and European Supervisory agencies benefit from cooperation at a horizontal (between EU supervisors or between national supervisors) and a vertical level (between EU supervisors and national supervisors) (Hiemstra, 2020b).

The supervision of anti-manipulation rules under MAD/MAR takes place at different levels. The first line of defence against market abuse is at firm level, whilst the second line of defence, complementing the one at firm level, lies with market operators and investment firms operating a trading venue (ESMA, 2022a). Finally, a third line of defence is regulatory market surveillance, where national regulatory authorities with jurisdiction over carbon markets put in place their (digital) market surveillance systems.

Newly developed sustainable derivatives, which qualify as financial instruments under MiFID II, would be subjected to the same anti-manipulation rules under MAD/MAR as described above. In addition, market participants trading in these financial instruments are subjected to mandatory reporting obligations which could provide regulatory agencies at different levels with information triggers to detect suspicious market behaviour.

4.2 US

4.2.1 Relevant regulatory framework

In the US, the relevant regulatory framework at a federal level for trading in sustainable derivatives is based on the Commodity Exchange Act, which was amended in 2010 by the Dodd Frank Wall Street Reform and Consumer Protection Act. The latter increased the scope of the regulatory framework by including the types of financial products regulated by the CFTC. In addition, the regulations of the CFTC and the rules of specific exchanges where these financial instruments are traded are part of the regulatory framework. CFTC points out that the current regulatory framework – and especially the lack of common definitions and standards for climate-related data and financial products is – is not yet fit to provide regulatory authorities and market participants with the tools to monitor and manage climate risk (CFTC, 2020).

When it comes to anti-manipulation rules, the scope of the prohibitions within the US system is similar to the one in Europe under MAR. According to the Commodity Exchange Act, the following – non-limitative – list of behaviour is prohibited: i) fraud and manipulation of by using manipulating devices or providing untrue statements; ii) pre-arranged trading; iii) fictitious trades such as wash trades which lack the intention to actually execute them; iv) disruptive trading practices such as violating bids or offers or spoofing (trading with the intent to cancel the transaction before execution); and v) position limit violations.

4.2.2 Supervisory regime

The CFTC has been charged with regulatory supervision in the US derivative market since 1974 and has broad authority to both supervise and enforce market manipulation and insider trading activities. The CFTC could contribute to the transition to a net-zero economy by facilitating the development of new financial products that help the private sector mitigate its climate-related risks and should ensure that these products actually provide the climate benefits they claim (Phillips, 2022). Enforcement at a federal level is shared with the Federal Energy Regulatory Commission (FERC) which has a mission to assist consumers in obtaining reliable, safe, secure and economically efficient energy services. FERC has targeted the prohibition of market manipulation in the energy sector as one of its four priorities (FERC, 2020). Under article 18 of the Code of Federal Regulations, it is unlawful for any entity in connection with the purchase or sale of gas or electricity to conduct fraudulent acts or to make untrue statements. Next to the federal CFTC and the FERC, a market participant is subjecting itself to market regulation and supervision from exchanges when it starts trading on these venues by agreeing to be bound by the exchange rules.

5 Overlap and cooperation between regulatory authorities

Trade in sustainable derivatives is not limited to national- or even continental borders. European based enterprises may enter the US Future Exchange and a New York based commodity trader may enter the EEX. From that perspective, the two regulatory systems are compatible. However, supervision and enforcement of violations of anti-manipulative actions are supervised by ESMA in the European Union and CFTC in the US. In practice this means that a cross border trading activity which conflicts with anti-manipulation rules under both MAR and the Commodity Exchange Act, might be subjected to enforcement actions of both ESMA and the CFTC. Such dual submission to supervision is not desirable from the point of view of market participants and also very inefficient from the point of view of the regulator. Such problem is partially avoided through the recognition of central counterparties established in third-countries under EMIR, which implies the delegation of monitoring of some financial instruments traded via those central counterparties (ESMA, 2022b). Supervisory activities conducted outside a regulatory agency's jurisdiction might conflict with the principle of legality. This is a key principle in the protection of citizens against acts of a government (Tridimas, 2006; Lavrijssen, 2006). Therefore, it is vital that supervisory authorities in different jurisdictions cooperate. In 2019, a joint statement of the European Commission and the CFTC was published on cross-border derivatives regulatory issues (European Commission, 2019). This statement reflected discussions between CFTC and ESMA on regulatory developments such as the European Commission's plans to implement a new version of EMIR and the CFTC's invitation to comment on proposed rules pertaining to non-US market participants and emphasized the importance of effective supervisory oversight on both sides of the Atlantic. A more tangible initiative is the memorandum of understanding between ESMA and the CFTC signed in 2021 regarding cooperation and the exchange of information with respect to certain registered derivatives clearing organization which are recognized in both jurisdictions (ESMA and CFTC, 2021).

As a consequence of the above, it seems that coordination and supervision at a global level is lacking. Only a truly global initiative on regulation and supervision of sustainable derivatives will close the legality loophole the regulatory authorities find themselves in (Heffron, 2021, p. 10). However, this is only a fictious solution which does not take into account sovereignty arguments of countries, local characteristics of supervision, enforcement and insurmountable differences between political views and legal systems. Meanwhile, cooperation initiatives between regulatory authorities are contributing to the overall goal of fighting climate change and decarbonization by making use of legal possibilities.

6 Conclusions

The Intergovernment Panel on Climate Change (IPCC, 2021) repeatedly warned that greenhouse gas emissions must decline sharply to limit global warming to 1.5°C. It is clear that industries and governments have a responsibility to cooperate to meet these targets. As seen in this chapter, sustainable derivatives may contribute to achieving these goals by enabling industries to mitigate their future price risks and being able to decide on large scale sustainable investments. Sustainable derivatives and secondary markets for emissions trading are not limited to national or even continental borders. This international component conflicts with the legal mandate of regulatory authorities. This legality loophole in the law will not be solved unless national parliaments agree on far reaching global regulations to facilitate the trade in sustainable derivatives and emission trading whilst adhering to principles of legality. But such legal framework remains a pipedream. Meanwhile, cooperation between governments and regulatory agencies and the willingness of investors to choose for climate change-related innovation is our best option for now.

References

Biggins, J., 2012. 'Targeted touchdown' and 'partial liftoff': Post crisis dispute resolution in the OTC derivatives markets and the challenge of ISDA. *German Law Journal*, 2012, 13(12), pp. 1297–1328.

Board of Governors of the Federal Reserve System, 2020. *Financial Stability Report*. <https://www.federalreserve.gov/mwg-internal/2535425/progress?id=N2jb8R6Pf-Uk1Qwk0djd-UHCVL0F3bJigducsvm3PwE>, (Accessed 9 April 2022).

Cheng, I.H., Xiong, W., 2014. Why do hedgers trade so much? *The Journal of Legal Studies*, 43(S2), pp. 183–207.

Coen, D., Herman, K., Pegram, T., 2022. Are corporate climate efforts genuine? An empirical analysis of the climate 'talk-walk' hypothesis. *Journal of Business Strategy and the Environment*, Early View 29 March.

Commodity Futures and Trading Commission (CFTC), 2020. *Managing Climate Risk in the U.S. Financial System*. Report of the Climate-Related Market Risk Subcommittee, Market Risk Advisory Committee of the U.S. Commodity Futures Trading Commission.

Commodity Futures and Trading Commission (CFTC), 2021. *Interdivisional Group Will Focus on Derivatives Markets' Role in Addressing Climate-Related Risk and Transitioning to Low-Carbon Economy*, Press release 9368-21, <https://www.cftc.gov/PressRoom/PressReleases/8368-21> (Accessed 9 April 2022).

Dagoumas, A. and Koltsaklis, N., 2017. Price Signal of Tradable Guarantees of Origin for Hedging Risk of Renewable Energy Sources Investments. *International Journal for Energy Economics and Policy*, 7(4), pp. 59–67.

Duffie, D., 2014. Challenges to a policy treatment of speculative trading motivated by differences in beliefs. *Journal of Legal Studies*, 43(2), pp. 173–182.

Energy Post, 2022. Online Roundtable 31 March 2022: "Options to Reform the EU ETS", <https://energypost.eu/options-to-reform-the-eu-ets-coping-with-price-volatility-and-speculation-event-summary/> and <https://youtu.be/7bRNZwN_FIE> (Accessed 15 April 2022).

European Commission, 2019. *Joint Statement of the European Commission and CFTC Following Meeting on Cross-Border Derivatives Regulatory Issues*. < https://ec.europa.eu/info/sites/default/files/business_economy_euro/banking_and_finance/documents/190913-joint-statement-ec-cftc_en.pdf> (Accessed 9 April 2022).

European Commission, 2021a. *Communication from the Commission to the European Parliament, the Council, the European Economic and Social Committee and the Committee of the Regions: Strategy for Financing the Transition to a Sustainable Economy* (COM(2021)390 final, <https://eur-lex.europa.eu/resource.html?uri=cellar:9f5e7e95-df06-11eb-895a-01aa75ed71a1.0001.02/DOC_1&format=PDF> (Accessed 9 April 2022).

European Commission, 2021b. *International Carbon Market* < https://ec.europa.eu/clima/eu-action/eu-emissions-trading-system-eu-ets/international-carbon-market_en> (Accessed 9 April 2022).

European Securities and Markets Authority (ESMA) and Commodity Futures and Trading Commission (CFTC), 2021. *Enhanced Memorandum of Understanding Related to ESMA's Assessment of Compliance and Monitoring of the Ongoing Compliance with Recognition Conditions by Certain Derivatives Clearing Organizations Established in the United States*. < https://www.esma.europa.eu/press-news/esma-news/cftc-and-esma-sign-enhanced-mou-related-certain-recognized-central> (Accessed 9 April 2022).

European Securities and Markets Authority (ESMA), 2022a. *Final Report. Emission allowances and associated derivatives*, ESMA70-445-38, <esma70-445-38_final_report_on_emission_allowances_and_associated_derivatives.pdf> (europa.eu)> (Accessed 9 April 2022).

European Securities and Markets Authority (ESMA), 2022b. *Public Statement: ESMA updates on third-country CCP recognition decisions*, ESMA91-398-4844, < https://www.esma.europa.eu/press-news/esma-news/esma-updates-third-country-ccp-recognition-decisions> (Accessed 15 April 2022).

Federal Energy Regulatory Commission, 2020. *2020 Report on Enforcement*, <https://www.ferc.gov/sites/default/files/2020-11/2020%20Annual%20Report%20on%20Enforcement.pdf> (Accessed 15 April 2022).

Futures Industry Association (FIA), 2021. *How derivatives markets are helping the world fight climate change*. [pdf] Available at <https://www.fia.org/resources/markets-need-be-part-climate-change-solution-says-fia> (Accessed 9 April 2022).

Hedges, A., 2009. The Secondary Market for Emissions Trading: Balancing Market Design and Market Based Transaction Norms. In: D. Freestone and C. Streck, eds., 2009, *Legal aspects of carbon trading: Kyoto, Copenhagen, and beyond*. Oxford: Oxford University Press.

Heffron, R. J., 2021. *Achieving a just transition to a low-carbon economy*. Cham, Switzerland: Palgrave Macmillan.

Hiemstra, L., 2020a. Energy trading and the exchange of information between supervisors: effectiveness of fragmented supervision and information sharing. *Journal of Energy and Natural Resources Law*, 39(2), pp. 159–182.

Hiemstra, L., 2020b. REMIT: ten years and counting. An exploration of the regulatory paradigm for commodity derivative trading in the energy market. *Law and Financial Markets Review*, 14(4), pp. 237–248

Hull, J., 2012. *Options, futures & other derivatives*. Harlow: Pearson.

Intergovernmental Panel on Climate Change, 2021. Summary for Policymakers. In: *Climate Change 2021: The Physical Science Basis. Contribution of the Working Group I to the Sixth Assessment Report of the Intergovernmental Panel on Climate Change.* < https://www.ipcc.ch/report/ar6/wg1/#FullReport> (Accessed 15 April 2022).

International Swaps and Derivatives Organisation, 2021. *The Role of derivatives in carbon markets*, < https://www.isda.org/a/soigE/Role-of-Derivatives-in-Carbon-Markets.pdf> (Accessed 9 April 2022).

LaMotte, R., Williamson D.M., Hopkins L.A., 2009. Emissions Trading in the US: Legal Issues. In: D. Freestone and C. Streck, eds., 2009, *Legal aspects of carbon trading: Kyoto, Copenhagen, and beyond.* Oxford: Oxford University Press.

Lannoo,K. and Thomadakis, A., 2020. *Derivatives in sustainable finance*, CEPS – ECMI Study, Centre for European Policy Studies.

Lavrijssen,S.A.C.M., 2006. *Onafhankelijke mededingingstoezichthouders, regulerende bevoegdheden en de waarborgen voor good governance*, Den Haag: Boom Juridische Uitgevers.

Mackay, P. and Moeller, S., 2010. Corporate risk management: the hedging footprint. *SSRN Electronic Journal*.

Partnoy, F., 2002. Enron and derivatives. Available at SSRN: https://ssrn.com/abstract=302332

Phillips, T., 2002. *A Climate and Competition Agenda for the Commodity Futures Trading Commission*, Center for American Progress, < https://www.americanprogress.org/article/a-climate-and-competition-agenda-for-the-commodity-futures-trading-commission/> (Accessed 9 April 2022).

Poitras, G., 2013. *Commodity risk management. Theory and application*, New York: Routledge.

Regional Greenhouse Gas Initiative (2021). *101 Factsheet*, < https://www.rggi.org/sites/default/files/Uploads/Fact%20Sheets/RGGI_101_Factsheet.pdf> (Accessed 9 April 2022).

Securities and Exchange Commission, 2021. SEC Division of Examinations Announces 2021 Examination Priorities. Enhanced Focus on Climate-Related Risks. Press release 2021-39, <SEC Division of Examinations Announces 2021 Examination Priorities> (Accessed 9 April 2022).

Securities and Exchange Commission, 2022. *Proposed Rule on the Enhancement and Standardization of Climate-Related Disclosures for Investors*, Release Nos. 33-11042; 34-94478; File No. S7-10-22], < https://www.sec.gov/rules/proposed/2022/33-11042.pdf> (Accessed 15 April 2022).

Tridimas, T., 2006. *The general principles of EU law*. 2nd [rev.] ed. Oxford: Oxford University Press.

United Nations Environment Programme, 2016. *The State of Sustainable Finance in the United States.* < https://wedocs.unep.org/bitstream/handle/20.500.11822/9828/-The_state_of_sustainable_finance_in_the_United_States-2016The_State_of_Sustainable_Finance_in_the_US.pdf.pdf?sequence=3&amp%3BisAllowed=> (Accessed 9 April 2022).

Western Climate Initiative, Inc., 2020. *Annual Report – Activities and Accomplishments*, <https://wcitestbucket.s3.us-east-2.amazonaws.com/amazon-s3-bucket/documents/annualreport-2020-20210512-en-1635541015.pdf> (Accessed 9 April 2022).

Katerina Mitkidis

Greening Global Value Chains

Abstract: Most regulatory tools for low-carbon transition are jurisdiction-specific, respecting the principle of national sovereignty. Although possibly locally successful, they typically capture only scope 1 and scope 2 emissions. Value chains-related (scope 3) emissions remain largely unregulated. This is problematic, as global value chains are commonly organized across multiple jurisdictions with different climate policy ambitions. Products are often produced at different location than where they are consumed, and production-related emissions are transferred with the products. These emissions embedded in imported products amount to large volumes (e.g. in the EU estimated to about 30% of member state's national emissions). This chapter gathers the scientific evidence on upstream scope 3 emissions and discusses the available regulatory toolbox for reducing those. Both private and public regulatory tools are represented as well as soft and hard regulatory tools, and modifications between those categories. The interactions between the various types of regulation are discussed with the aim to identify possible synergies and conflicts. The chapter takes the EU as its starting point and draws in examples from other jurisdictions where relevant.

1 Introduction

Global value chains (GVCs) are not frequently mentioned in the low-carbon transition discourse. This is natural: while the problem of climate change is inherently universal, regulatory tools for low-carbon transition are jurisdiction-specific, targeting scope 1 and 2 emissions and reflecting the individual country's climate policy. Countries' climate policy ambitions differ based on political preferences, available resources, geographical location, and the level of development. Such differences allow for outsourcing of energy-heavy production from jurisdictions with stricter (usually developed countries) to jurisdictions with weaker regulation (usually developing countries). This entails transfer of production-related emissions to developing countries, emissions that then return to the developed countries embedded in the imported final products.

But the picture is more complicated. While sustaining the living standard in developed countries is dependent both on the import of fossil fuels and products with embedded emissions, the extraction and use of fossil fuels in production represents

Katerina Mitdikis is Associate Professor at the Department of Law, School of Business and Social Sciences, Aarhus University, Denmark.

https://doi.org/10.1515/9783110752403-022

not only a legal right of developing countries, but also their possibility for economic and social progress (Mitkidis and Šefčíková, forthcoming 2023). This interdependence leads to up to four times higher per capita fossil fuels footprints in developed countries than in developing countries (HLPF, 2018, p. 2).

When a product reaches the lead firm of a GVC, it carries with it a load of embedded emissions generated in relation to activities upstream in the value chain, such as extraction, processing, and transportation of the product ('upstream scope 3 emissions'). These emissions are indirect to the activities of the lead firm. In developed countries, upstream scope 3 emissions amount to significant volumes. However, as national carbon accounting only covers emissions generated in connection to activities taking place within the territory of the specific state, upstream scope 3 emissions are counted under the national emissions of the country of production, even though the product is aimed for use elsewhere.

Thus, to achieve a successful low-carbon transition globally, upstream scope 3 emissions must be curbed. While staying outside of the international and national legislative focus so far, we cannot speak of a regulatory vacuum in respect to upstream scope 3 emissions. A plethora of international and industrial guidelines, creative use of existing legal tools, and developing of new meta-regulatory tools provide incentives and assistance to the lead firms of GVCs to manage their upstream scope 3 emissions.

This chapter proceeds as follows. After a brief introduction to GVCs, it gathers the scientific evidence on upstream scope 3 emissions and discusses the available regulatory toolbox for reducing them. The interactions between the various types of regulatory tools and their public and private variants are discussed.

2 GVCs

Increased interconnectedness of the world brought about by the cable connection, and a simplified and increased mobility of people, goods and capital has led to a geospatial separation of production and consumption. Today, production is predominantly organized in GVCs, passing through several jurisdictions: chains of legally separate entities 'that are constituted through equity ownership (e.g., corporate groups) or contractual relationships (e.g., supply chains) but centrally governed by lead firms' (Salminen and Rajavuori, 2021). The ability of companies to optimize their production through selecting the appropriate structure of their value chains (Gereffi et al., 2005) allows them to efficiently manage costs and risks. This has both positive and negative impacts on society: consumers have access to more, cheaper, and readily available products, but production can lead to extensive negative social and environmental externalities. In the climate change context, this may lead to so-called 'carbon leakage', a situation where businesses, facing costs related to climate policies adopted in a country, transfer their production to another country with more lenient climate policies. The produced goods then partly return to the country of the lead firm through import with embedded emissions that do not count against the lead firm's or its home country's climate performance.

The negative externalities of GVCs often stay invisible to consumers and regulators in the countries of import. Thus, they may skew the perception of environmental footprints of firms and products, leading to ill-informed purchase choices and, ultimately, undermining the low-carbon transition. As Sobel-Read (2014) argues, it is not appropriate anymore to focus in legal research on lead firms, but GVCs should be treated as the basic value of analysis. This remains, however, difficult for legal scholarship that is organized along the three traditional axes of public/private law, hard/soft law, and national/international law. Governance of GVCs transcends all these categories and, therefore, challenges both legal theory and practice, despite the increasing understanding of GVCs' climate impacts.

3 Distribution of emissions along GVCs

In the world characterized by a geospatial fragmentation of consumption and production, goods move across the globe. A typical product's lifecycle starts with extraction of raw materials for its production at one place and disposal of the (rest of the) product at another. Each step in a product's life cycle inevitably leads to emissions. Emissions from the upstream value chain embedded in the product follow it, as it crosses borders within international trade. Researchers find that emissions mostly flow from developing to developed countries (e.g., Wiedmann and Lenzen, 2018, p. 314; Zhong et al., 2018).

Emissions embodied in international trade inevitably distort the picture of national carbon accounting. For example, Herrmann and Hauschild (2009) calculated the impact of embedded emissions in products imported from China to the UK between the years 1992 and 2004 due to intensified outsourcing of production. The authors found that while the amounts of UK's emissions avoided due to outsourced production increased from ca 3 to 16 million tons of CO_2, this saving did not cover the increase from ca 25 to 130 million tons of CO_2 emissions embedded in the goods imported from China to the UK. These numbers provided a different shading to the otherwise bright result of UK's only 1% increase in national CO_2 emissions from the consumption of energy in the same period. Furthermore, the authors highlighted two important climate-related consequences of the outsourced production. First, production in China in comparison to the UK led to a higher CO_2 emission per produced unit of output, pointing towards lower energy-efficiency of the production processes in developing countries. Second, consumption in developed countries increased because of lower prices of imported goods. In combination, these impacts have been increasing the global emissions and emasculating the low-carbon transition efforts.

China as the 'world's factory' and a net carbon exporter has been a frequent object of study of emissions embodied in international trade (Zhang et al., 2017). Mi et al. (2018) concluded that Chinese export of embedded CO_2 emissions peaked in 2008. This is good news for global climate change mitigation, but the authors stress that countries that may partly replace China should do so with the deployment of low carbon technologies, a point emphasized also by others (Arce et al., 2016). The problem of international trade embodied emissions is not pertinent only to China though; most developing countries and some developed countries (such as Canada, the Netherlands, and Czechia) are all net-exporters of CO_2 emissions (OECD, 2021).

Focusing on emissions from production when looking on emissions embodied in international trade is a natural consequence of the territorial 'production-based' monitoring and accounting requirements found in international law instruments (Paris Agreement, Article 13(7)a). What follows is that we lack policy measures to account for and regulate emissions embedded in traded products. That is why an alternative 'consumption-based' approach to carbon accounting has been discussed (Davis and Caldeira, 2010). However, the 'consumption-based' approach is not as methodologically developed (Heinonen, 2020). Moreover, in the current production systems organized in GVCs, it seems ill-fitted to follow territorial borders in carbon accounting, whether using the 'production-' or 'consumption-based' approach.

Proposals for GVCs theory-informed methods of accounting for CO_2 emissions embodied in international trade have been emerging (Zhang et al., 2020; Zhu et al., 2022). Yet, it is difficult to imagine how these methodologies can be included in the international climate law regime that is agreed among sovereign states because such methodologies entail a complex apportioning of responsibility for emissions. Nevertheless, GVCs-based carbon accounting methodologies reflect the reality of international trade and are being adopted at various degrees by GVCs' lead firms.

Businesses and researchers agree that scope 3 emissions represent the largest share of emissions within GVCs. The CDP (2022) found that '... GHG emissions in a company's supply chain are, on average, 11.4 times higher than its operational emissions.' Some companies report even larger shares of scope 3 emissions. For example, the LEGO Group reports that in 2020, scope 3 missions represented 98% of the group's total emissions, while only 2% were connected to the group's direct operations (The LEGO Group, 2021, p. 4–5). BASF SE reports more moderate results for 2020, where 19% of emissions were connected to the direct operation of the company, while 81% represented scope 3 emissions (50% upstream and 31% downstream) (BASF, 2021, p. 5). The results of BASF closely correspond to the findings of Meinrenken et al. (2020) that on average total value chains emissions break down into 45% upstream value chain emissions, 23% emissions connected to companies' direct operations, and 32% downstream value chain emissions (Meinrenken et al, 2020, p. 1). However, the authors emphasize that the actual distribution of emissions along GVCs largely depends on the specific industry, company, and most importantly product (Meinrenken et al., 2020, p. 4).

The intricacy of upstream scope 3 emissions' accounting, characterized by large amounts of data and the use of complex mathematical models, has slowed down the deployment of relevant methodologies (Mitkidis, 2017, p. 1–2, 8). While difficult, it has been greatly improving (Mehling et al., 2019, p. 436), as proven by the emergence of various standards on upstream scope 3 emissions as well as product carbon footprint. GHG Protocol's Corporate Value Chain (Scope 3) Accounting and Reporting Standard adopted in 2011 is the best known in the former category. The ISO 14067:2018 – Carbon footprint of products standard, Publicly Available Specification (PAS) 2050 of the GHG Protocol, and the Product Environmental Footprint (PEF) of the European Commission can be named in the latter. These methods provide invaluable information on the emissions' distribution along GVCs, information that can be further used to curb and regulate those emissions.

4 Legal tools for greening GVCs

This section discusses legal tools for greening GVCs. The author acknowledges that the choice, design, and effects of the legal tools depend on the broader concept of legal pathway of decarbonization (Bellantuono, 2019, p. 3; Bellantuono et al., Introduction, in this volume). The narrower focus on legal tools is chosen to contain the complexity of GVCs' governance defined by their transnational character and a web of political, economic, social, and technological aspects (Humphrey and Schmitz, 2001; Gereffi et al., 2005; Ponte and Sturgeon, 2014).

Tools that are in some form employed by most of the developed countries hosting the chains' lead firms and/or by the firms themselves are included here. Both private and public regulatory tools are represented as well as soft and hard regulatory tools, and modifications between those categories. GVCs are transnational in nature yet consist of private entities. Thus, they are neither fully covered by one national nor by the international legal system. Therefore, each GVC is governed by a plurality of legal orders and legal tools. The individual tools are most often mutually complementary rather than competing, and thus can be seen as facilitating the low-carbon transition. Yet, some potential conflicts exist.

Tools for decarbonization can be classified in many ways (Dernbach, 2018, p. 321; also see Richards, in this volume). This chapter builds on the classification introduced by Light and Vandenbergh (2015) as further discussed by Light and Orts (2015, p. 23–53) within the context of parallels between private and public regulatory tools of environmental governance. This classification and identified parallels are loosely employed here to provide an account of legal tools for greening GVCs within the low-carbon transition context. Below, the individual tools are briefly introduced with the public and private varieties and their interactions. An outline of interfaces between the tools follows.

4.1 Procurement

Procurement processes are regularly used to drive environmental standards throughout GVCs both by private and public buyers (Light and Orts, 2015, p. 46). The phenomenon of environmental contractual governance has been extensively studied by legal scholars (for private procurement perspectives, see, e.g.: Vandenbergh, 2007; Cafaggi, 2013; Mitkidis, 2015; Poncibò, 2016; Affolder, 2018; for public procurement perspectives, see e.g.: Bolton, 2008; Sjåfjell and Wiesbrock, 2015; Andhov et al., 2020). Environmental requirements appear in all stages of the procurement process: the planning/pre-contractual/pre-tender phase, the acquiring/negotiation phase, the contract execution, and the contract implementation phase (Andrecka and Mitkidis, 2017, p. 69). However, while public procurement largely focuses on the first two phases, private procurement focuses on the latter two (Andrecka and Mitkidis, 2017, p. 88). The overall idea is that contracts are awarded to suppliers that fulfil environmental requirements prescribed by the buyers. However, a GVC consists of more tiers than a buyer and a supplier. Thus, supply chain contracts are used to cascade environmental provisions throughout all the value chain's tiers. There is a growing scholarship on the best way such flow-down contractual provisions can be optimally designed and used (e.g. Raj et al., 2018; Groschopf et al., 2021).

Environmental requirements in procurement processes relate to various issues, such as environmental regulation compliance, waste handling, and water use. They can and often do refer also to climate impacts. However, this is frequently done in a vague manner. For example, the BASF's Supplier Code of Conduct (September 2021) that is incorporated in the company's procurement processes refers to emissions as follows: 'You [the respective supplier] minimize your negative impact on biodiversity, climate change and water scarcity.' The vagueness can have both positive and negative impacts for the lead firms of GVCs as well as for the environment (Peterkova, 2014). However, it hampers the legal enforceability of such requirements (Mitkidis, 2015, p. 181–187). Possibly even a bigger issue for the requirements' enforceability is their disconnection from the subject-matter of the contract. In private contracts, such a disconnection hinders awarding of contract law remedies in case of breach (Mitkidis, 2015, p. 172–175). In public procurement, the authorities may be discouraged to include such 'disconnected' criteria into a tender process (Andhov et al., 2020 p. 38). For example, although the EU's public procurement directive of 2014 allows for inclusion of environmental criteria in the procurement process, these must be linked to the subject matter of the contract (Directive 2004/24/EC). While this condition has been developed by the Court of Justice of the EU to protect tender participants against the use of sustainability criteria for the purpose of hidden unequal treatment and discrimination, nowadays, it mainly presents a hinder to the use of public procurement for sustainability goals (Semple, 2015). The case law of Court of Justice has been developing the requirements towards including the whole lifecycle of a product rather than limiting it to the product's physical qualities (*Max Havelaar* case, C-368/10). Therefore, climate-related aspects can be included in the procurement criteria as far as those are connected to the purchased product, e.g. by stipulating its energy efficiency (Martinez Romera and Caranta, 2017).

4.1.1 Interactions among public and private procurement

The use of climate requirements in private and public procurement interact on several levels. Public procurement serves as a natural inspiration to private procurement (Mitkidis, forthcoming 2023), since private companies are those competing for public contracts. However, inspiration can also flow from the private to the public sector. Private companies have been developing experience, expertise, and knowledge of the market conditions regarding environmental sustainability in general and emissions reduction in particular over several decades. Yet, mutual learning and reinforcement between the public and private sphere has been limited so far. The know-how of climate contractual governance is an asset that companies can use to compete for public contracts. Public regulation could therefore search to create a level playing field, encouraging sharing of know-how and experience beyond one's corporate or industrial borders.

4.1.2 Legal hinders to the use of procurement

Contract law is based on the principle of freedom of contract and, thus, contractual parties are free to include climate aspects in their agreements.

However, the *effective* use of requirements in contracts and other stages of procurement processes to drive sustainability provisions through GVCs is based on the presumption of their legal enforceability. As outlined above, they may not be though enforceable due to their vagueness and disconnection from the contract's subject matter. Moreover, considering private procurement, the question of legitimacy can be raised (Mitkidis, 2015).

4.2 Transparency regulation

Transparency in the form of provision of relevant information has been identified as the third wave of pollution control regulation, after the first wave of command-and-control measures and the second wave of market-based approaches (Tietenberg,

1998, p. 587–588). Information disclosure has certain advantages over other types of regulation. It is perceived as less intrusive to business operation, it is cheaper for the regulator (substituting the regulator's costs of standards' setting and enforcement with the companies' costs of information gathering, monitoring and reporting), it is flexible and less prone to changes (rather than stipulating concrete measures or limits, it 'only' requires information), and it takes advantage of technological development, which makes information handling easier and cheaper (Cohen, 2001; Light and Orts, 2015, p. 40–42). Most importantly for this chapter, it can reach with its impacts across borders without interfering with states' sovereignty. The last characteristic makes transparency regulation particularly suitable for regulating GVCs.

Information disclosure can relate to companies' and their value chains' performance or to products' characteristics. When directed towards consumers, information disclosure requirements are rooted in the consumers' right to know/right to information (Tietenberg, 1998, p. 589). It is presumed that if consumers are in possession of relevant information, they will make rational choices, not only in the context of money, but also the planetary, and thus also their individual health. When related to corporate performance rather than a specific product, information disclosure requirements capitalize on the so-called business case of corporate social responsibility. Information disclosure allows companies to show to their stakeholders that they 'care', thus, to utilize 'green advertising' and build reputation, to monitor their own progress and to compare themselves to their peers, and importantly to provide information to investors.

Information disclosure comes in different forms and requirements to disclose come from both public and private regulators. Below, three main types of information disclosure regulatory tools are discussed.

4.2.1 Reporting

The requirements to regularly report on corporate emissions is the first transparency regulatory tool discussed here. It comes in several forms.

First, climate impacts are often covered within broader sustainability reporting. While usually not naming emissions specifically, national and supranational laws and regulation on sustainability reporting encourage transparency about corporate climate impacts under the request to disclose information on environmental impacts. For example, the EU's Non-Financial Reporting Directive (NFRD, 2014/95/EC) obliges large undertakings to report on their environmental policies, performance, results, non-financial KPIs and related principal risks. Yet, some EU member states chose to mention climate impacts expressly in their national implementation of the directive (e.g., Danish Financial Statements Act, §99a). Moreover, in 2022, a proposal for a replacement of NFRD has been adopted (COM/2021/189 final). The new Corporate Sustainability Reporting Directive, coming into effect in 2023, extends reporting obligations so that they expressly include, among others, corporate scope 3 emissions (EFRAG, 2021). Sustainability reporting laws are typical examples of the meta-regulatory approach (Parker, 2007); they do not prescribe concrete actions and/or targets, but rather steer corporate behaviour by creating stimuli for firms to develop their self-regulatory capacity (Scott, 2008). The same approach is taken by numerous voluntary compliance-based regulation, most notably the United Nations Global Compact (2000) and the OECD Guidelines for Multinational Enterprises (2011 update).

Secondly, some voluntary compliance-based regulation focuses specifically on climate impacts' reporting. The most prominent is the not-for-profit charity CDP that has been running a global environmental disclosure for companies, cities, regions, and nations for 20 years. Started with reporting of scope 1 and 2 emissions, CDP has increasingly embraced scope 3 emissions (CDP, 2022). Most companies reporting their value chain emissions to CDP use the GHG Protocol's Corporate Value Chain (Scope 3) Accounting and Reporting Standard to do so. In November 2021, a new International Sustainability Standards Board (ISSB) was founded by the International Financial Reporting Standard Foundation. In March 2022, the ISSB published a draft of Climate-related Disclosures Standard for public consultation. The standard aims to facilitate the understanding of the financial impacts of climate-related risks and opportunities, thus making clear links between financial and climate-related corporate reporting. This will also include reporting on the effects of climate-related risks and opportunities on companies' value chains.

Finally, when the issue of emissions is subject to a targeted mandatory public regulation, it generally focuses only on scope 1 and 2 emissions. For reasons related to states' sovereignty as well as to feasibility, these regulations omit scope 3 emissions, therefore not reaching beyond the GVC's lead firm. Instead, such regulation is often connected to the issuance of an operating license or the access to climate-focused market-based mechanisms, e.g. the EU's emissions trading scheme (2003/87/EC).

4.2.2 Product labelling

Product labelling is used as a tool to drive consumers' purchase choices to the safe and ecologically friendly ones. It has been used successfully regarding products' environmental impacts that may also negatively impact human health, e.g., dangerous household chemicals labelling, and/or individuals' finances, e.g., energy input labelling. These labels are often mandatory, as is the case for example in the EU (Regulation (EU) 1272/2008; Regulation (EU) 2017/1369).

Product labelling that was initially introduced as a regulatory tool for consumers' protection has gradually developed to target a broader scope of negative environmental externalities. Eco-labels are a prominent example here (Iraldo et al., 2020). Even narrower use of product labels to communicate products' climate impacts to consumers has been discussed both by academia and regulators (e.g., Vandenbergh,

2011) for over a decade now. Cohen and Viscusi (2012, p. 1250020-9) pointed out that the effectiveness of carbon labelling may be compromised by the time and spatial distance between consumers and the climate change impacts of their purchase decisions. The authors also identified criteria for effective product labels: '… the consumer must receive the information, process the information, believe the information and use it to update beliefs that potentially can influence decisions regarding the product' (Cohen and Viscusi, 2012, p. 1250020-10). Fulfilling these criteria is difficult for carbon labels. Acquiring reliable and standardized data of corporate value chain carbon footprint is challenging (section 3 above) and it is even more so in respect to individual products. If data are available a question arises, how should they be communicated to consumers so that they believe and understand them.

Multiple private voluntary carbon labelling schemes have been established employing in general four different styles of communicating products' carbon footprint to consumers: (i) low-carbon labels indicating products with low amount of embedded emissions among products from the same category, (ii) carbon rating labels tagging products from the same category into various levels of climate performance (such as 'platinum', 'golden', etc.), (iii) carbon score labels indicating the actual quantity of embedded emissions in a product, and (iv) carbon neutral labels presenting the achievement of zero carbon emissions of a product via off-setting. Carbon Trust developed the first product carbon label in 2007 in the UK (https://www.carbontrust.com/what-we-do/assurance-and-certification/product-carbon-footprint-label). Other private carbon labelling schemes followed in, among others, Canada, Switzerland, and Japan. Up to now, there is no mandatory public regulation of product carbon labelling. The EU's proposal for Ecodesign for Sustainable Products Regulation (COM(2022) 142 final) from March 2022 opens up the possibility for the European Commission to stipulate requirements regarding life-cycle environmental impacts for selected product categories, including their carbon footprint and the use of an adequate labelling scheme. However, the proposed regulation needs first to be adopted and come into force, and the Commission needs to agree and decide on the requirements tailored to specific product groups. This process will foreseeably take years to be completed. Until then, voluntary product labelling schemes can be employed.

When used by a GVC lead firm, product labelling in respect to energy input and product carbon footprint affects the whole chain. Suppliers' production processes and the used materials must abide by the rules of the specific labelling scheme, otherwise sanctions apply (e.g., label retraction).

4.2.3 Supply chain due diligence and certification

The efforts to monitor and assess suppliers' climate performance are not new. Companies do that voluntarily through their value chain policies, suppliers' codes of conduct and corporate standards. Since 2015, companies can seek a certification of their value chains' emissions' measuring, managing, and reducing with Carbon Trust. Similarly, when European companies seek the certification under the EU Eco-Management and Audit Scheme (Regulation (EC) No 1221/2009), they are required to consider emissions created along their value chain in their continuous improvement process.

The voluntariness of value chain's performance monitoring has been 'hardening'. Following the introduction of the requirement to conduct a human rights risk-based due diligence in companies' value chains (UN Guiding Principles on Business and Human Rights), the tool has spread also to the environmental area. It has been implemented into the OECD Guidelines for Multinational Enterprises in 2011 (General Policies, para. 10). While it is not mandatory for companies to comply with the OECD Guidelines, they enjoy big authority and are widely used by business in managing their non-financial impacts.

A surge of national legislation on risk-based due diligence in GVCs followed the international soft law instruments (e.g. in Germany, the Netherlands, and France). The most recent addition to risk-based due diligence laws is the EU's proposal for the Corporate Sustainability Due Diligence directive (CSDDD) (COM(2022) 71 final). The proposal is instrumental to the fulfilment of EU's climate policies, as enshrined, among others, in the EU's Green Deal and the union's international obligations. The proposal has been adopted as the European Commission fears that the lack of legal clarity and proper enforcement of the international soft law instruments do not prevent serious environmental and social harmful impacts in GVCs and endanger the value chains' resilience. The proposal introduces a legal obligation for large companies to conduct human rights and environmental due diligence of their own operations and their value chain. Within the due diligence process (CSDDD, Art. 4(1)), companies shall (i) identify, prevent, and mitigate actual or potential adverse impacts of their and their value chains' activities, (ii) establish and maintain a complaints procedure for trade unions, civil society organisation, and persons negatively affected by companies' and their value chains' activities, (iii) monitor and publicly communicate on the effectiveness of their due diligence policy and measures. The CSDDD would be enforced through a combination of remedies; a remedial action to be taken by the non-compliant company within an appropriate time and substantial financial penalties. The proposal includes a special provision regarding climate impacts (CSDDD, Art. 15) according to which companies would need to adopt a plan ensuring that the business model and strategy of the company are aligned with the Paris Agreement and include emission reduction targets. Most interestingly, the fulfilment of the plan would be linked to the variable remuneration of companies' directors.

4.2.4 Interactions among transparency tools

The various forms of disclosure tools relate closely to each other. For instance, the use of carbon labels and due diligence processes are regularly disclosed in companies' sustainability reports, and due diligence processes generate data for acquiring carbon labels and preparing sustainability reports. These tools are complementary and together build a transparent picture of the companies' and their value chains' climate performance.

The interaction between private and public regulation of transparency in GVCs is particularly interesting. Some authors argued that private regulation aims to avoid the adoption of a more stringent public regulation (Reich, 2008) and, thus, built an argument for the need to harden the disclosure requirements. However, private disclosure may be seen as a necessary predecessor of public regulation, paving the way to understanding of what is feasible and desirable, and delivering background data for further public disclosure regulation. Finally, public hard disclosure regulation has 'given teeth' to private and soft regulation. For example, the EU's NFRD recognizes global standards, so companies reporting based on those standards do not need to prepare a separate report based on NFRD.

4.2.5 Legal hinders to the use of transparency tools

The legal hinders to the use of transparency tools are connected to their meta-regulatory character. In respect to reporting and due diligence obligations, the relevant regulations do not prescribe the substantive behaviour, but are focused on the procedural aspect. That may incentivize companies to employ creative compliance strategies (Nurse, 2015). The effective use of carbon label might then be reduced by the limited possibilities of their enforcement through consumer law and their potential clash with the international trade law regime when required through public regulation or procurement.

4.3 Market-based tools

As national climate ambitions differ, regulators turn their focus to leverage the markets to prevent carbon leakage and to reduce upstream scope 3 emissions. There are two possible ways: regulators can either take advantage of the existing markets or create new ones (Light and Orts, 2015, p. 33).

Emissions trading systems are an example of the latter. While having a jurisdictionally limited scope, they may try to exert influence over markets to create an international level playing field. The free allocation of allowances under the EU Emissions Trading System (Directive 87/2003/EC) is a typical example here (Mehling et al., 2019, p. 435). To prevent negative impacts of the system on the competitiveness of selected carbon leakage-sensitive industries, those are allocated allowances for free. Therefore, the climate law-related incentives for displacing of the production are taken away.

The other market-based approach is to leverage existing markets by imposing taxes, fees, and charges on undesired behaviour, such as carbon emissions, and providing benefits to desired behaviour, such as contracting with suppliers actively reducing their carbon footprint (Light and Orts, 2015, p. 33–34). These approaches can be used both by public and private regulators through financial regulation and procurement processes. From the angle of public regulators, especially, carbon tax imposed as a border adjustment measure has been discussed in the context of greening GVCs. Carbon border adjustments, their form and legal and climate implications, are frequent topics of academic literature (e.g. Gros and Egenhofer, 2011; Mehling et al., 2019; Böhringer et al., 2022). Recently, academics and practitioners have focused their interest on the EU's proposed carbon border adjustment mechanism (CBAM) (European Commission, 2021). The EU announced that CBAM would be gradually introduced (fully operating as of 2026) and applied to the most carbon leakage-sensitive industries. The leading idea is that EU importers will be obliged to buy carbon certificates for the imported products that will equal the carbon price that would have been paid if the goods were produced under the EU's carbon pricing rules. This policy, thus, aims to reduce the asymmetry between foreign and domestic products (Mehling et al., 2019, p. 435). Similar policy tools already exist in some jurisdictions, for example California (European Commission, 2021), and are considered in others, including the USA (Bacchus, 2021a), Japan (European Commission, 2021), and Canada (Carbon Pulse, 2021).

4.3.1 Interactions among market-based tools

Market-based mechanisms are primarily tools of public regulation. Private regulation can contribute through individual companies' internal fees on carbon (Light and Orts, 2015, p. 34–37) and procurements processes. The public and private approaches exist next to each other and together can create a stronger incentive than each of them individually could.

There are interactions also between the different tools. For example, the EU's proposed CBAM will rely on setting the price to imported products based on the price of EU ETS allowances applicable at the time of import. This can create tensions under the international trade law regime that is discussed immediately below.

4.3.2 Legal hinders to the use of market-based tools

The use of public market-based tools raises concerns under the international trade law regime. The announced main features of EU's planned CBAM's are a prototype for analysis. Possible violation of the most favoured-nation treatment and national treatment WTO rules have been analysed (e.g. Bacchus, 2021b; Marcu et al., 2020).

The possible violations would depend on whether high carbon products coming from outside the EU would be considered 'like' products with domestic low-carbon products (Marcu et al., 2020, p. 19) and whether the amount charged on imported products would be exactly the same as the carbon price for the domestic product under the EU ETS (Bacchus, 2021b). Here, especially the phasing out of the free allocation of allowances under the EU ETS would be relevant. Other issues would be whether the CBAM would be considered an internal regulation or whether it would be activated at the moment of import, and, thus, considered a quantitative restriction on import (Bacchus, 2021b), and whether CBAM could be subsumed under the GATT environmental exceptions (Mehling et al., 2019, pp. 464–470). While all these issues have already been partially discussed in legal scholarship, we must bear in mind that the analysis is only preliminary, as CBAM has so far only the form of policy announcement and its exact design is not settled yet.

5 Synergies and conflicts

The legal tools for greening GVCs interact not only among the private/public axis (e.g., Berger-Walliser and Shrivastava, 2015), but also, and intensively, among the individual types (e.g., Cafaggi and Iamiceli, 2013; Ulfbeck and Rott, 2015; Ulfbeck et al. 2019). Together, they create a web of rules that compensate for the lack of prescriptive regulation for greening GVCs, which is missing due to the principle of national sovereignty. There are many more or less conspicuous, recognized and utilized synergies.

Contracts (and procurement processes more broadly) seem instrumental in deploying several of the other tools. They can facilitate the use of carbon labels as they pass the requirements of the labelling schemes upstream GVCs. They can require suppliers to deliver data necessary for reporting of scope 3 emissions as well as for providing evidence on embedded emissions in imported products for the purpose of the planned CBAM. They can similarly bind suppliers to cooperate in risk-based due diligence and improvement of the lead company's and its value chain's carbon footprint. However, there is a major issue with using private contracts for driving GVCs' decarbonization and that is their unenforceability through contract law. Here, transparency regimes, and especially reporting is of help. The use of procurement has become a standard measure included in corporate sustainability reports. This transparency also creates accountability, increasing the contracts' binding power. Corporate sustainability reports also regularly cover the use of labels and should address corporate due diligence processes. The increasingly legalized risk-based due diligence then requires companies to take action to mitigate any major risks connected to the business operation, products, and partners. This legalization became clearly visible in the 2021 decision of the District Court in Hague (HA ZA 19-379), ordering Royal Dutch Shell to mitigate the group's CO_2 emissions globally, thus also including its scope 3 emissions. Carbon labels, contractual clauses requiring emissions monitoring and reduction and participation in carbon disclosure regimes can all aid such mitigation among GVCs.

6 Conclusion

Since most emissions are generated in the upstream part of value chains, greening GVCs is necessary in order to move towards global and local decarbonization. GVCs cross national boundaries and, therefore, are difficult to regulate. Yet, as the legal tools discussed above show, we certainly cannot speak of a regulatory vacuum in this context. Quite the opposite, a range of private and public regulatory tools utilizing procurement, transparency, and markets all aim to decarbonize GVCs. They are all non-prescriptive; they do not mandate concrete actions to be taken by the regulated subjects. This can be seen both as an advantage and disadvantage. On the one hand, they take advantage of expertise of the regulated subjects, motivate technological, business, and regulatory innovation and voluntary action. On the other hand, they cannot be easily controlled and enforced. To improve that, existing and potential synergies among the various tools and their public and private variants should be fully recognized and utilized.

At the end, it should be noted that this chapter addresses the main direct regulatory tools for GVCs' decarbonization. Many indirect tools, such as the CO_2 emission performance standards for heavy-duty vehicles (e.g., Regulation (EU) 2019/1242) or focus on local sourcing in the wake of recent global crises, will create further indirect pressure on climate performance in GVCs.

References

Affolder, N., 2018. Looking for law in unusual places: cross-border diffusion of environmental norms. *Transnational environmental law*, 7(3), pp. 425–449.

Andhov, M. et al., eds., 2020. *Sustainability through public procurement: the way forward – Reform proposals.* SMART Project Report.

Andrecka, M., and Mitkidis, K. P., 2017. Sustainability requirements in EU public and private procurement – a right or an obligation? *Nordic Journal of Commercial Law*, 1, pp. 55–89.

Arce, G. et al., 2016. Carbon emissions embodied in international trade: The post-China era. *Applied Energy*, 184, pp. 1063–1072.

Bacchus, J., 2021a. Striking a balance on climate change and global trade. *The Hill*, 19 July 2021. Available at: https://thehill.com/opinion/energy-environment/563680-striking-a-balance-on-climate-change-and-global-trade/ (Accessed: 8 April 2022).

Bacchus, J., 2021b. Legal issues with the European Carbon Border Adjustment Mechanism. CATO Institute, Briefing Paper no. 125, 9 August 2021. Available at: https://www.cato.org/briefing-paper/legal-issues-european-carbon-border-adjustment-mechanism (Accessed: 8 April 2022).

BASF, *Scope 3 GHG Inventory Report.* February 2021. Available at: https://www.basf.com/global/en/who-we-are/sustainability/we-produce-safely-and-efficiently/energy-and-climate-protection/corporate-carbon-footprint.html (Accessed: 28 March 2022).

Bellantuono, G., 2019. Legal pathways of decarbonization in the EU: the case of coal phase-out. *Oil, Gas & Energy Law Intelligence*, 17(3).

Berger-Walliser, G. and Shrivastava, P., 2015. Beyond compliance: sustainable development, business, and proactive law. *Georgetown Journal of International Law*, 46(2), pp. 417–474.

Bolton, P., 2008. Protecting the environment through public procurement: the case of South Africa. *Natural Resources Forum*, 32(1), pp. 1–10.

Böhringer, C. et al., 2022. Potential impacts and challenges of border carbon adjustments. *Nature climate change*, 12, pp. 22–29.

Cafaggi, F., 2013. The regulatory functions of transnational commercial contracts: new architectures. *Fordham International Law Journal*, 36(6), pp. 1557–1618.

Cafaggi, F. and Iamiceli, P., 2014. Supply chains, contractual governance and certification regimes. *European Journal of Law and Economics*, 37(1), pp. 131–173.

Carbon Pulse, 2021. *Canada eyes CBAM consultation as budget sets out more stringent climate target* (19 April). Available at: https://carbon-pulse.com/126741/ (Accessed: 8 April 2022).

CDP, 2022. *Engaging the chain: driving speed and scale.* CDP Global Supply Chain Report 2021, February.

Cohen, M. A., 2001. Information as a policy instrument in protecting the environment: what have we learned? *Environmental law reporter*, 31(4), pp. 10425–10431.

Cohen, M. A. and Viscusi, W. K., 2012. The role of information disclosure in climate mitigation policy. *Climate Change Economics*, 3(4), 1250020.

Curtin, D. and Senden, L., 2011. Public accountability of transnational private regulation: Chimera or reality? *Journal of Law and Society*, 38(1), pp. 163–188.

Davis, S. J. and Caldeira, K., 2010. Consumption-based accounting of CO_2 emissions. *Proceedings of the National Academy of Sciences – PNAS*, 107(12), pp. 5687–5692.

Dernbach, J. C., 2018. The dozen types of legal tools in the deep decarbonization toolbox. *Energy Law Journal*, 39(2), pp. 313–352.

European Commission, *Carbon Border Adjustment Mechanism: Questions and Answers*. Available at: https://ec.europa.eu/commission/presscorner/detail/en/qanda_21_3661 (Accessed: 8 April 2022).

European Financial Reporting Advisory Group (EFRAG), 2021. Climate standard prototype. Working Paper, 8 September.

Gasper, D. et al., 2019. The framing of sustainable consumption and production in SDG 12. *Global policy*, 10(S1), pp. 83–95.

Gereffi, G. et al., 2005. The governance of GVCs. *Review of International Political Economy*, 12(1), pp. 78–104.

Greenhouse Gas Protocol, 2011. *Corporate Value Chain (Scope 3) Accounting and Reporting Standard.* World Resources Institute and World Business Council for Sustainable Development, September.

Gros, D. and Egenhofer, C., 2011. The case for taxing carbon at the border. *Climate policy*, 11(5), pp. 1262–1268.

Groschopf, W. et al., 2021. Smart contracts for sustainable supply chain management: conceptual frameworks for supply chain maturity evaluation and smart contract sustainability assessment. *Frontiers in Blockchain*, 4, 506436.

Heinonen, J. et al., 2020. Spatial consumption-based carbon footprint assessments – A review of recent developments in the field. *Journal of Cleaner Production*, 256, 120335.

Herrmann, I. T. and Hauschild, M. Z., 2009. Effects of globalization on carbon footprints of products. *CIRP Annals – Manufacturing Technology*, 58(1), pp. 13–16.

High-Level Political Forum on Sustainable Development, 2018. *HLPF Review of SDGs implementation: SDG 12 – Ensure sustainable consumption and production patterns*. Available at: <https://sustainabledevelopment.un.org/content/documents/196532018backgroundnotesSDG12.pdf> accessed 25 October 2021 [HLPF Review 2018].

Humphrey, J. and Schmitz, H., 2001. Governance in Global Value Chainss. *IDS bulletin*, 32(3), pp. 19–29.

Iraldo, F. et al., 2020. The future of ecolabels. *The international journal of life cycle assessment*, 25(5), pp. 833–839.

Light, S.E. and Orts, E.W., 2015. Parallels in public and private environmental governance. *Michigan Journal of Environmental and Administrative Law*, 5(1), pp. 1–72.

Light, S. E. and Vandenbergh, M. P., 2016. Private environmental governance. In: L. Paddock, R.L. Glicksman and N.S. Bryner, eds., 2016. *Decision making in environmental law*. Cheltenham: Edward Elgar Publishing, pp. 253–267.

Marcu, A. et al., 2020. *Border Carbon Adjustments in the EU: issues and options*. ERCST report. Available at: https://ercst.org/border-carbon-adjustments-in-the-eu-issues-and-options/ (Accessed: 8 April 2022).

Martinez Romera, B. and Caranta, R., 2017. EU public procurement law: purchasing beyond price in the age of climate change. *European Procurement & Public Private Partnership Law Review*, 12(3), pp. 281–292.

Mehling, M. A. et al., 2019. Designing Border Carbon Adjustments for enhanced climate action. *The American Journal of International Law*, 113(3), pp. 433–481.

Meinrenken, C. J. et al., 2020. Carbon emissions embodied in product value chains and the role of Life Cycle Assessment in curbing them. *Scientific Reports*, 10(1), 6184.

Mi, Z. et al., 2018. China's 'exported carbon' peak: patterns, drivers, and implications. *Geophysical Research Letters*, 45(9), pp. 4309–4318.

Mitkidis, K. P., 2014. Using private contracts for climate change mitigation. *Groningen Journal of International Law*, 2(1), pp. 54–80.

Mitkidis, K. P., 2015. *Sustainability clauses in international business contracts*. The Hague: Eleven International Publishing.

Mitkidis, K., 2017. Life-Cycle based climate regulation through supply chain contracts. Working paper presented at the SMART conference *Life-cycle based management and reporting for sustainable business*, 29–30 November 2016, University of Oslo Faculty of Law Legal Studies Research Paper Series No. 2017-21, https://doi.org/10.2139/ssrn.2975292.

Mitkidis, K., forthcoming 2023. Sustainable procurement of pharmaceuticals – a tool to combat global antimicrobial resistance. In: O. Rubin, E. Baekkeskov and L. Munkholm, eds., 2023. *Steering against superbugs – The global governance of antimicrobial resistance*. Oxford: Oxford University Press.

Mitkidis, K. and Sefcikova, A., forthcoming 2023. SDG12: Sustainable Consumption and Production. In: I. Bantekas, F. Seatzu and K. Akestoridi, eds., 2022. *Oxford Commentary on the Sustainable Development Goals*. Oxford: Oxford University Press.

Nurse, A., 2015. Creative compliance, constructive compliance: corporate environmental crime and the criminal entrepreneur. In: G. Mcelwee and R. Smith, eds., 2015. *Exploring criminal and illegal enterprise: new perspectives on research, policy & practice*. Bradford: Emerald Group Publishing Limited, pp. 97–119.

OECD, 2021. *Trade in embodied CO2 (TeCO2) Database*. Available at: https://www.oecd.org/greengrowth/carbondioxideemissionsembodiedininternationaltrade.htm (Accessed: 28 March 2022).

Palmujoki. A. et al., 2010. Green public procurement: analysis on the use of environmental criteria in contracts. *Review of European, Comparative & International Environmental Law*, 19(2), pp. 250–262.

Parker, C., 2007. Meta-Regulation: legal accountability for corporate social responsibility. In: D. McBarnet, A. Voiculescu and T. Campbell, eds., 2007. *The new corporate accountability: corporate social responsibility and the law*. Cambridge: Cambridge University Press, pp. 207–240.

Peterkova, K., 2014. General or specific? Wording matters in a supplier's code of conduct. *Contracting Excellence*, November/December.

Poncibò, C., 2016. The contractualisation of environmental sustainability. *European Review of Contract Law*, 12(4), pp. 335–355.

Ponte, S. and Sturgeon, T., 2014. Explaining governance in GVCs: a modular theory-building effort. *Review of International Political Economy*, 21(1), pp. 195–223.

Raj, A. et al., 2018. Designing supply contracts for the sustainable supply chain using game theory. *Journal of Cleaner Production*, 185, pp. 275–284.

Reich, R. B., 2008. The case against corporate social responsibility. Goldman School of Public Policy Working Paper No. GSPP08-003.

Salminen, J. and Rajavuori, M., 2021. Private international law, GVCs and the externalities of transnational production: towards alignment? *Transnational Legal Theory*, 12(2), pp. 230–248.

Scott, C., 2008. Reflexive governance, meta-regulation and corporate social responsibility: the "Heineken Effect". In: N. Boeger, R. Murray and C. Villiers, eds., 2008. *Perspectives on corporate social responsibility*. Cheltenham: Edward Elgar Publishing, pp. 170–185.

Semple, A., 2015. The link to the subject matter: a glass ceiling for sustainable public contracts? In: B. Sjåfjell and A. Wiesbrock, eds., 2015. *Sustainable public procurement under EU law: new perspectives on the state as stakeholder*. Cambridge: Cambridge University Press, pp. 50–74.

Sjåfjell, B. and Wiesbrock, A., 2015. *Sustainable public procurement under EU law: new perspectives on the state as stakeholder*. Cambridge: Cambridge University Press.

Sobel-Read, K. B., 2014. GVCs: a framework for analysis. *Transnational Legal Theory*, 5(3), pp. 364–407.

The LEGO Group, 2021, *Our 2020 carbon footprint*, available at: https://www.lego.com/cdn/cs/aboutus/assets/bltf22cba10c9d59016/LEGO_Group_2020_Carbon_Report.pdf (Accessed: 28 March 2022).

Tietenberg, T., 1998. Disclosure strategies for pollution control. *Environmental & Resource Economics*, 11(3), pp. 587–602.

Ulfbeck, V. G. and Rott, P., 2015. Supply chain liability of multinational corporations? *European Review of Private Law*, 23(3), pp. 415–436.

Ulfbeck, V. G. et al., eds., 2019. *Law and responsible supply chain management: contract and tort interplay and overlap*. London and New York, NY: Routledge.

Vandenberg, M. P., 2007. The new Wal-Mart effect: the role of private contracting in global governance. *UCLA Law Review*, 54(4), pp. 913–970.

Vandenbergh, M P. and Cohen, M. A., 2010. Climate change governance: boundaries and leakage. *New York University Environmental Law Journal*, 18(2), pp. 221–292.

Vandenbergh, M. P. et al., 2011. Time to try carbon labelling. *Nature Climate Change*, 1(1), pp. 4–6.

Wiedmann, T. and Lenzen, M., 2018. Environmental and social footprints of international trade. *Nature Geoscience*, 11(5), pp. 314–321.

Zhang et al., 2017. Embodied carbon in China's foreign trade: an online SCI-E and SSCI based literature review. *Renewable & sustainable energy reviews*, 68, pp. 492–510.

Zhang et al., 2020. Embodied carbon emissions in the supply chains of multinational enterprises. *Nature Climate Change*, 10(12), pp. 1096–1101.

Zhong, Z. et al., 2018. Transnational transfer of carbon emissions embodied in trade: characteristics and determinants from a spatial perspective. *Energy*, 147, pp. 858–875.

Zhu, K. et al., 2022. Reevaluation of the carbon emissions embodied in GVCs based on an inter-country input-output model with multinational enterprises. *Applied Energy*, 307, 118220.

Part III: **Regional Experiences**

Editorial introduction

The regional chapters offer critical insights into the regulatory efforts, developments and barriers at the regional level that either initiate and facilitate or inhibit energy decarbonisation. The ongoing and potential regional collaborations will benefit from looking into the progress and pitfalls of the paths toward energy decarbonisation. Three common issues are identified across the regional chapters that deserve particular attention by policymakers at the national and regional levels. The first issue is that many nations, such as those in Africa, Latin America, and Asia-Pacific, have abundant renewable resources. However, they lack the financial capacity to exploit those resources. Notably, the high level of sovereign debt currently shouldered by many countries in the said regions has limited the effects of public funding to play a positive role in developing renewable energy. Given the significant upfront investment required for renewable energy generation projects and the infrastructure, the need for private investment is clear. However, the lack of public funding to mitigate the risks attached to low carbon projects and programmes has seen few private investments flowing into the said areas. The lack of public funding and private investment has been particularly the case in developing and least developed nations where energy infrastructure is significantly lacking and substantial investments are required. The national legal framework can also inhibit the much-needed low carbon energy transition because the current policies in many nations of the said regions (especially Africa) prohibit private investments in energy generation and infrastructure. To what extent the private investment can be mobilised through leveraging public funding, such as those in the form of fiscal incentives and capital injections, remains a critical factor that will determine the pace and scale of renewable energy deployment.

The second issue from the experiences discussed in the regional chapters is that the domestic legal framework underpinning the investments in renewable energy and energy-related infrastructure (such as gas pipelines and electric grids) often lacks flexibility and foresight to accommodate the market changes. Like in the other regions, one of the essential decarbonisation policy tools in the Asia-Pacific has been feed-in tariffs, which have led to an unprecedented deployment of renewable energy. Nevertheless, the energy market and its regulatory framework have yet to catch up with such developments to manage the allocation of benefits among generators, often leading to the curtailment of renewable energy. The North American experience provides another example of how some provisions in the domestic laws can be abused to prevent energy infrastructure investment to facilitate the integration of natural gas (as transitional energy) and renewable energy into the overall energy portfolio. These experiences remind us to factor in the need when improving the energy legal framework to remain flexible in future policies while providing essential regulatory stability to investors.

https://doi.org/10.1515/9783110752403-023

Finally, regional collaboration and uniformity regarding energy transition need to be given more attention in the future. Several chapters on regional experiences elaborate on the regional initiatives and uniform approaches that have been adopted to accelerate the low carbon energy transition. They provide helpful insights on how supranational and multilateral organisations are uniquely placed to advance regional decarbonisation efforts and progress through standard making that transcend the national boundaries. For instance, the European Union is well known for its proactive and top-down approach to promulgating laws and regulations supporting energy decarbonisation and carbon neutrality. The established legal framework contains detailed regulatory arrangements and techniques to pursue the energy transition, which can be a source of lessons for other regions. Nonetheless, despite the leading role that the European Union has played in promulgating regulations through the top-down, such an approach is challenged by the limited enforcement at the national level, which needs to be addressed through more robust monitoring and enforcement mechanisms. Others also highlight the potential roles of multilateral organisations, such as multilateral development banks and sub-regional organisations. They can leverage their positions to foster increased uniformity in policies and standards making in the energy transition process. The collaborative approach at the regional level presents opportunities to enhance further the economic benefits attached to low carbon development through increased renewable electricity investment, economic growth and trade openness.

Michael Addaney, Bernard Kengni

Energy Transitions and the Emerging Energy Law in Africa

Abstract: Access to modern energy is crucial to addressing challenges such as poverty, famine and gender inequality in Africa, where over 600 million people do not have access to electricity and clean cooking facilities. Additionally, the anticipated population growth, urbanisation and industrialization will naturally require the utilization of all the available energy resources due to the increase in energy demand and consumption. With existing energy sources such as fossil fuels being the main contributor to climate change, African governments are faced with the dilemma of addressing the energy and economic challenges on the continent and at the same time transition to a low-carbon development pathway. This chapter explores the emerging regional regulatory policies, initiatives and programmes governing the main energy resources in Africa. Specifically, the regulation of renewable energy sources and technologies will be examined, focusing on their generation, transmission and distribution. Considering traditional challenges in the energy sector in Africa, such as climate change, low technologies, inadequate energy infrastructure and capital, the chapter argues for legal and policy reforms relating to the energy market to ensure sustainable and just energy transitions.

1 Introduction

Access to modern energy is crucial to addressing challenges such as poverty, famine and gender inequality in Africa, where over 600 million people do not have access to electricity and clean cooking facilities (Nalule, 2018). Additionally, the anticipated population growth, urbanisation and industrialization in Africa will naturally require utilising all the available energy resources due to an increase in energy demand and consumption (IEA, 2019). With existing energy sources such as fossil fuels being the main contributor to climate change (IPCC, 2018), African governments are faced with the dilemma of addressing the energy and economic challenges on the continent and, at the same time, transitioning to a low-carbon development pathway. Fossil fuels

Michael Addaney is a Lecturer in environmental policy and sustainability planning at the University of Energy and Natural Resources, Ghana, an Earth System Governance Fellow and Research Associate of the Centre for Public Management and Governance of the University of Johannesburg, South Africa.
Bernard Kengni is Postdoctoral Research Fellow, NRF/DST SARChI Research Chair: Mineral Law in Africa, Department of Private Law, University of Cape Town, South Africa.

https://doi.org/10.1515/9783110752403-024

are critical in enhancing access to energy in Africa by offering short- and medium-term solutions to access challenges as countries on the continent make efforts to meet the United Nations sustainable developmental goal 7 (SDG 7) – expanding access to affordable and clean energy for all (UN, 2015). Enhancing access to clean and renewable energy is key in effectively responding to other developmental challenges such as poverty and famine as an estimated 3 billion people (40% of the world population) rely on high polluting and unhealthy household fuels for cooking and lighting (UNDP, 2022). The African continent boasts of substantial renewable energy sources such as wind, solar and hydropower which could be harnessed to meet the energy needs of the projected urbanisation dynamics and population growth.

Moreover, the projected explosion in population growth, rapid urbanisation and industrialisation in Africa will require a corresponding increase in energy demand and consumption (Cobbinah and Addaney, 2021, pp. 2–3). However, the traditional energy sources, particularly fossil fuels, account for 60 percent of greenhouse gases (GHGs) that contribute to climate change. Thus, energy transitions in Africa focus on the need to address climate change by shifting from fossil fuels to renewable energy sources. Despite its inherent challenges, the global efforts to transition to a low-carbon economy are associated with positive impacts. African governments have to be well-equipped with effective policies and strategies to respond to the energy transition and its associated effects. For instance, the transition is likely to escalate energy access challenges and poverty on the African continent, mostly due to reduced levels of finance for fossil fuel energy projects (Nalule, 2020, p. 261). This chapter explores the emerging regional regulatory policies, initiatives and programmes governing the main energy resources in Africa. Specifically, the regulation of renewable energy sources and technologies will be examined, focusing on their generation, transmission and distribution. The chapter further explores low-carbon initiatives involving multiple states at regional and sub-regional levels. In particular, it identifies and examines how challenges related to cross-border energy infrastructures, market coupling and inter-state trade of renewable energy are dealt with. Considering traditional challenges in the energy sector in Africa, such as climate change, low technologies, inadequate energy infrastructure and capital, the chapter argues for legal and policy reforms relating to the energy market to ensure sustainable and just energy transitions.

2 Energy Resources and the Transition to Renewable Energy in Africa

This section discusses the energy resources and potential for transitioning to low-carbon development in Africa. The African continent has the world's lowest energy access rate at only 32 percent (Africa Renewable Energy Initiative, 2015, p. 8). In 2019, only 43% of the population had access to modern energy in Africa in comparison to Asia (86%), South America (95%), and the Middle East (92%) (Tracking Energy SDG7, 2019). There is therefore a high priority to enhance access to energy to drive socio-economic development in Africa including realising the UN sustainable development goal 7 (SDG 7). Sub-Saharan African in particularly is endowed with renewable energy resources. For instance, the region boasts of solar energy potential estimated at 10,000 GW; wind potential of 109 GW largely in the coastal countries; geothermal capacity appraised at 15 GW (e.g. in the Rift Valley in East Africa); and available hydropower projected at 300–350 GW (Nalule, 2021, pp. 23; Morrissey, 2017). These energy resources can be harnessed to meet the rapidly increasing demand for energy on the continent. However, for African countries to take advantage of the vast energy resources to increase the percentage of renewables in the energy mix, there is the need to adopt policies that incentivize renewable energy utilisation, enabling legal frameworks, pioneering financing mechanisms, and energy supply strategies prioritising the diverse resources (Avila et al., 2017).

More broadly, the drivers of the global energy transition include climate action, energy demand, enhancing energy access, and utilisation of oil and gas resources (Olawuyi, 2021). The significant driver is the need to address climate change under the UNFCCC and the 2015 Paris Agreement. The energy transition thus focuses on addressing climate change through the reduction in energy-related CO_2 emissions in order to increase renewable energy and energy efficiency measures while concurrently decreasing the use of fossil fuels (Bridge et al., 2013, pp. 331–333). Despite emitting least carbon dioxide, African countries are already subjected to extreme climate events and conditions such as droughts, floods and famine (UNDP, 2022; USAID, 2017). In this respect, African countries must set targets and strategies to respond to climate change impacts and the global quest to transition to clean energy sources through their nationally determined contributions (NDCs) under the UNFCCC. The transition to renewable energy is also increasingly becoming attractive due to the decline of fossil fuel investments and the lowering costs of installation and maintenance of renewables (IRENA, 2019). Despite the global move to transition to renewable energy, the majority of African countries still depend on fossil fuels in meeting their energy demand. In South Africa, for instance, large part of the electricity grid is powered by an ageing coal-fired fleet. There are ongoing efforts to introduce natural gas, concentrating solar power (CSP) and renewables to diversify the energy mix. The global energy transition consequently raises challenges for African countries due to declines in fossil fuel investments and the need to decommission ageing energy systems.

The various geographic sub-regions in Africa boast of diverse energy resources that can potentially be harnessed to facilitate the transition to renewable energy. For instance, the Rift Valley in East Africa has a projected 15 GW of geothermal capacity particularly in Ethiopia and Kenya (Castellano et al., 2015). Additionally, Eastern and the Horn of Africa region has a vast hydropower energy resource which is estimated at 350 GW due to the presence of the Congo and the Nile Rivers largely sited in Angola, Cameroon, the Democratic Republic of Congo, Ethiopia and Gabon (Castellano et al., 2015). The Sub-Saharan African region generally contains rich fossil energy resources comprising of petroleum, coal and gas, with discovered natural gas alone estimated at 400GW. There are also estimated coal resources of 300 GW concentrated mainly in Botswana, Mozambique and South Africa (Kebede et al., 2010, pp. 532–537).

In recent times, Mozambique has become a primary energy producer in Southern Africa through exportation of electricity due to the rapid expansion of the hydropower sector and the vast discoveries of natural gas and coal within its territory. For instance, the Cahora Bassa Dam in Mozambique is one of the biggest hydroelectric power schemes in Africa with an installed capacity of 2075 MW (SADC, 2015). Mozambique currently exports electricity to Botswana, South Africa, Zimbabwe and the SAPP which is largely enabled by the favourable investment framework (UENP/AfDB, 2017). Also, in 2010, the US energy company Anadarko discovered significant gas reserves at the coast of Cabo Delgado province in Mozambique. In 2011, ENI, an Italian energy company also found a substantial gas field in the same area (Planting, 2019). The country has since experienced an influx of foreign energy companies exploring for profitable energy contracts. Consequently, the Cabo Delgado province in Mozambique currently hosts the three largest liquid natural gas (LNG) projects in Africa. For instance, the Mozambican LNG led by US-based Anadarko committed $20 billion to the development of integrated offshore and onshore gas fields in 2019. Similarly, in the same year, Rovuma LNG managed by Exxon-Mobil and ENI planned to commit $30 billion to develop integrated offshore and onshore gas fields in the same region (Planting, 2019).

Despite the cost-effectiveness of large power plants in generating electricity to a wider population, the energy markets in most countries across the African continent are evolving with costly small-scale power systems (Cartwright, 2015). These small-scale power systems makes it possible to connect remote rural communities to the national grid. The high transmission and distribution costs associated with the small-scale power systems further undermine the potential energy trade on the African continent and the sub-regions including the South African Power Pool (SAPP) and West African Power Pool (WAPP). The WAPP and SAPP rely on ineffective and low performing power systems with poor financial backing. The inadequate finance undermines the ability of participating countries to invest in new technologies to enhance their generating and distribution capacities despite the substantial renewable energy potential in the regions. For instance, the solar energy resources in the West and Southern African regions are estimated at 10,000GW with a total technical solar resource for photovoltaic valued at 6500 Terawatt Hours (TWh) annually (International Renewable Energy Agency, 2015). In terms of wind energy sources, most of the coastal countries in both regions have suitable wind conditions that can contribute to redefining the energy transformation agenda in Africa with a total wind power resource of about 109 Giga Watts (IEA-International Energy Agency, 2016). Energy resources are fairly distributed across the African continent, making it a fertile ground to engage in regional trade for the anticipated energy transformation in the region.

The energy transition in Africa is therefore influenced by various factors including geography, social and economic situation, political environment, availability of energy resources and a country's energy framework. The majority of the energy systems in African countries rely on geothermal sources and are obsolete with large transmission and distribution losses leading to high costs of electricity and more challenges in the energy market. There is however a promising trend in the increased deployment of renewable energy projects on the African continent. For example, in 2019, Kenya launched the Lake Turkana Wind Power (LTWP) farm which is the largest in Africa to provide 310 MW of power to the national grid.[1] Similarly, Senegal launched the Taiba Ndiaye Wind Project in 2018 to generate 158 MW of reliable and low cost energy.[2] The intended Nzema Solar Power Station in Ghana also promises to be the largest installation in Africa involving 630,000 solar photovoltaic modules. It is expected to increase Ghana's power generating capacity by 6% (Eshun and Amoako-Tuffour, 2016). However, this location advantage enjoyed by countries in Africa, especially in the West, Eastern and Southern regions, is not yet fully harnessed. The key hindrances include lack of strong political will and commitment by the individual governments and regional groups as well as ineffective planning for land use in a dual manner for different energy source (Irowarisima, 2021). From this discussion, Africa's energy transition is severely hindered by the lack of proper strategic energy planning systems which undermines energy access on the continent, not by the lack of generation and distribution capacity. Transitioning the African energy sector therefore demands scaling up of energy laws, policies and strategies that are compatible with the global energy transition developments. It would take time, more finances, advanced technology and preparation to jump from fossil fuels to renewables on the African continent.

3 Emerging Legal and Policy Framework Governing Africa's Energy Transition

Energy transition is presented as a crucial enabler of sustainable development and climate resilience (Cantarero, 2020; Chen et al., 2019, p. 1565). It equally offers a global opportunity to pursue alternative and environmentally-friendly energy sources (Cantarero, 2020, p. 3). This is intended to enable increased access to energy in regions

1 See, 'Lake Turkana Wind Power', https://ltwp.co.ke/.

2 See, 'Taiba Ndiaye Wind Project', http://www.taibaeolien.com/news/parc-eolien-taiba-ndiaye-celebrates-groundbreaking-on-west-africas-first-utility-scale-wind-farm/.

such as Africa, where some countries still depend highly on fossil fuels for energy generation and electrification rates remain quite low (Arimah and Ebohon, 2000, p. 202). Africa's energy transition can be enhanced by scaling-up regional utility-scale renewable energy generation capacity (Abbas et al., 2020, p. 36283). This is key to accelerate the transition from fossils to low-carbon initiatives, which is necessary to advance access to energy on the continent. To achieve such a scale-up, the African continent requires clear measures or structures at regional and sub-regional levels to guide a successful energy transition. While there is no existing unified regional or sub-regional law or policy between states on energy transition, there are initiatives and plans that could serve as the base for regional and sub-regional policy and regulatory frameworks. Therefore, the following discussion highlights existing low-carbon initiatives at regional and sub-regional levels involving multiple states and examines challenges relating to the cross-border generation and transmission of renewable energy.

3.1 Emerging low-carbon plans

Considering the advantages of power pools and the different capacities to generate energy from renewable sources, inter-state trade of renewable energy is vital to ensure sustainable regional and sub-regional energy transition (Pavičević and Quoilin, 2020). As a result, African countries are taking measures at different levels to accelerate the energy transition on the continent.

3.1.1 Continental level

At a continental level, initiatives have been adopted to promote energy transition through coordinated efforts to achieve states' shared goal of realising sustainable development and climate resilience through low-carbon initiatives (Abbas et al., 2020). The Africa Energy Commission (AFREC), a specialised energy agency of the African Union (AU), is a vital initiative addressing the security of supply and other critical energy issues, including renewable energy.[3] This is pursued through the African energy transition programme. The programme provides an understanding of short-, medium- and long-term energy system transformations necessary to achieve energy transition in Africa.[4] For that effect, it identifies "frameworks to support the development of sectoral and technologically detailed, policy-relevant" strategies consistent,

3 See, AFREC "Programme", available at https://au-afrec.org/en/programs (accessed on 16 April 2022).

4 AFREC "Energy Transition Programme", available at https://au-afrec.org/en/programs/energy-transition-programme (accessed on 16 April 2022).

amongst others, with the Paris Agreement's goal.[5] The programme is further intended to transform energy development in Africa in terms of AU's Agenda 2063. This Agenda supports the idea that energy is a critical resource that drives the economy and development and should, therefore, strengthen and develop the African economy, including reliance on renewable energy.[6] Further, the AU's Programme for Infrastructure Development in Africa (PIDA) energy vision promotes the development of "efficient, reliable, affordable and environmentally friendly energy networks to increase access to modern energy services for all Africans".[7] PIDA is a crucial continental initiative comprising 51 cross-border infrastructure projects, including energy generation. All African countries support PIDA as it aims to raise the necessary resources to transform Africa with modern infrastructure, including in the renewable energy sector (Germany's KfW Development Bank, GIZ and IRENA, 2020, p. 84). The sub-regional initiatives discussed below show more vital inter-state collaboration compared to efforts at a continental level.

3.1.2 Sub-regional level

There is inter-state coordinated plans and initiatives at the African sub-regional levels to promote and achieve energy transition. Significant work is being carried out at the sub-regional level to improve energy security across Africa, notably through regional power pools. The existing five power pools, including the Southern African Power Pool (SAPP), Eastern Africa Power Pool (EAPP), Central African Power Pool (CAPP), West African Power Pool (WAPP) and North African Power Pool (NAPP), all seek to achieve energy efficiency, including from renewable energy sources. Member states of the SAPP plan to increase investment projects, interconnected grids, electricity access, and a competitive electricity market.[8] Investment projects, in particular, include revenue creation for hydropower and other forms of clean energy (SAPP, 2021, pp. 15, 34). Another initiative is to improve the integration of renewable energy technologies on the SAPP grid to shift to clean energy sources in the sub-region (NELSAP, 2019, p. 4).

An inter-state renewable energy initiative in the EAPP involves the plan to generate 80 MW from a run-of-river hydropower station near the tri-point between Tanzania, Rwanda, and Burundi, who will share the power generated (NELSAP, 2019, p. 4).

5 Ibid.

6 AFREC "Agenda 2063: The Africa we Want", available at https://au-afrec.org/en/agenda-2063 (accessed on 16 April 2022).

7 PIDA "PIDA Vision" available at https://www.au-pida.org/pida-vision/ (accessed on 17 April 2022).

8 SAPP "Agreed Objective of the PAU", available at https://www.sapp.co.zw/agreed-objective-pau (accessed on 17 April 2022).

On the other hand, through the New and Renewable Energies Commission, the NAPP member states aim to develop essential renewable energy resources and are currently coordinating renewable energy programs, particularly solar energy (MEDELEC, 2015). The commission also seeks to master different technologies that will enable integration into the electrical systems under the best technical and economic conditions (Ibid., 2015). The WAPP, on its part, through the ECOWAS Master Plan for the Development of Regional Power Generation and Transmission Infrastructure, seeks to integrate diverse renewable energy resources into the energy mix (TRACTEBEL, 2018, pp. 3, 10). It also seeks to better integrate initiatives such as the West Africa Clean Energy Corridor (WACEC), intended to address energy challenges in the sub-region (Ibid.). The WACEC forms part of the Africa Clean Energy Corridor (ACEC). The ACEC, launched in 2014, is a regional initiative intended to "accelerate the development of renewable energy potential and cross-border trade of renewable power" in the Eastern African Power Pool and Southern African Power Pool, covering the proposed region for the PIDA north-south corridor.[9] The energy ministries of relevant regions adopted the ACEC, and the West African regional heads of state, for example, endorsed the WACEC in 2017 and incorporated it into the ECOWAS Treaty (Germany's KfW Development Bank et al., 2020, p. 69).

Clean Energy Corridors are regional initiatives whose objectives are to transform the fuel mix by promoting clean and cost-effective renewable power initiatives and supporting regional efforts to create and develop sustainable electricity markets (Omitaomu et al., 2012, p. 293). The design of those corridors takes into consideration the specific needs and priorities of different regions and is aligned under five main pillars, including resource assessment, national and regional planning, frameworks to enable investment, capacity building and public awareness (Germany's KfW Development Bank et al., 2020, p. 69). The practical implementation of the corridors depends on high-level political commitment in the respective regions since country-level commitment is crucial for realising inter-state projects (Wu et al., 2015, pp. 17, 62). Despite the various initiatives at continental and sub-regional levels promoting low-carbon energy generation, existing challenges are slowing down effective energy transition at those levels, as explained below.

3.1.3 Challenges to low-carbon initiatives

The potential of renewable energy sources in Africa is limited by various challenges. First, the lack of a unified regulatory framework for the energy transition in Africa and at the sub-regional level is a severe barrier to the transition from fossils to low-

9 IRENA "Africa Clean Energy Corridor", available at https://irena.org/cleanenergycorridors/Africa-Clean-Energy-Corridor (accessed on 17 April 2022).

carbon initiatives. For effective energy transition to happen, there is a strong need for regulatory frameworks that provide innovative ancillary services and approaches to financing, which are crucial energy transition enablers (Akinyemi et al., 2019, p. 519). For this reason, African governments and their development partners must design regional and sub-regional predictable enabling frameworks to facilitate cross border energy generation necessary to bridge the energy gap by improving the power pools and inter-state energy trade (Ibid.). One main challenge arises because African countries often have different power sector structures, including vertically integrated with no private sector participation, vertically integrated with private sector participation, and vertically unbundled (Mostert, van den Berg, and Kengni, 2021, pp. 245–246). Even more severe, many countries on the continent do not allow private investments in their power sectors. Such private investments are essential to facilitate the energy transition where states lack the financial capacity, as is often the case in developing countries (Choukri, Naddami, and Hayani, 2017, p. 3).

Those structures highlight the main regulatory obstacles that hamper the direct investments necessary to provide the much-needed capital to fund and acquire the expertise required to improve energy security in Africa. This implies that future continental and sub-regional regulatory frameworks and policies must support the systemic innovation necessary to harness renewable energy potential on the African continent. This is because Africa desperately needs a system's approach in which innovative technologies, business models, hybridisation, improved regulatory frameworks, policy support and financing frameworks will be taken into consideration (Germany's KfW Development Bank et al., 2020, pp. 73–74).

Second, cross-border energy infrastructures, market coupling, and inter-state renewable energy trade are very poor in many instances (Eberhard et al., 2016, p. 4). The Central African Power Pool ranks the lowest in terms of cross-border energy generation and distribution. In Central Africa, where hydropower is the primary source of energy, the electrical energy sector is experiencing a severe infrastructure deficit, both in terms of the development of production capacities and access to electrical energy (Matija and Quoilin, 2020). To achieve effective cross-border low-carbon initiatives and inter-state energy trade, there is a strong need to strengthen and modernise the grids of different power pools. To enhance the grid and productivity, cheaper renewable energy sources like solar and wind, planning, operation and maintenance of grids must be carried out and upscaled (Mahmud, 2014, pp.Vii–viii). In addition, as part of the energy transition initiative in Africa, it is necessary to expand the interconnectors required for cross-border electricity trade (Adeoye and Spataru, 2020, p. 12). Such interconnectors are essential to improve and support energy security and ensure the flexibility needed to generate more energy from renewable sources (Ibid., p. 1).

Third, due to the difficult financial situations in which most African countries often find themselves, financing renewable energy projects is usually a nightmare (Ibid., p. 5). This is further exacerbated by the fact that in some countries, private investors are excluded from the energy sector though they dispose of the required capital to finance innovative technologies (Uhunamure and Shale, 2021, p. 10). As a result, the inter-state generation of low-carbon energy generation initiatives is lagging because of limited investment in new business models such as system operating procedures (eg. dynamic line rating and virtual power plants: see Pueyo (2018)). Another financial constraint results from countries' continuous investment in non-renewable sources of energy, such as fossils, despite much discussion about the importance of energy transition (Pueyo, 2018, p. 87). While many countries' failure to invest in low-carbon development is due to a lack of capital and new and innovative infrastructure for that purpose. It is also evident that the lack of political will is a crucial reason for some countries' failure to invest in low-carbon initiatives (Shahbaz et al., 2019, p. 611). This is explained by the fact that many countries are either not doing the needful to attract much-needed capital or simply lack the appetite to invest in renewable energy even when there is the capacity to do so (Chirambo, 2018, pp. 606–607).

The lack of regional and sub-regional frameworks for energy transition highlighted above are in stark contrast with significant advances witnessed in various countries, including Egypt, Ethiopia, Kenya, Morocco and South Africa which are currently leading transition efforts on the continent (Obonyo, 2021). In South Africa, for example, the key policy in the sector is the Renewable Energy Independent Power Producers Procurement Programme (REIPPP) which in 2011 became the first real step towards adopting the green economy in the country. It is in line with the REIPPP that South Africa's electricity public utility, Eskom, set up its Just Energy Transition (JET) programme in 2020 to champion "transition towards a cleaner and greener energy future" (Eskom, 2022). JET's main goal is to achieve a "Net Zero" carbon emissions by 2050 (Ibid.).

4 Conclusion

There are many initiatives driving the transition to sustainable energy in Africa despite the critical role of fossil fuels to their economies. Renewable energy is no doubt the path to a sustainable future for all. African countries are taking initiatives and developing plans to transition from fossils to low-carbon energy at continental and sub-regional levels. This includes initiatives such as the Africa Clean Energy Corridor, of which objectives are currently being implemented in the West African Power Pool and the Southern African Power Pool. Despite these critical initiatives, this chapter finds that regional and sub-regional energy transition measures in Africa are still limited. This is due to the lack of essential regional and sub-regional regulatory frameworks designed to enable and enhance energy transition. There is currently no African regional or sub-regional legal framework or policy providing guidelines for cross-border renewable energy production or development of infrastructure for that purpose. Such are key for renewable energy generation as demonstrated by countries and regions where strides are being made towards transition to cleaner energy. For instance, the EU through the Energy Union (EC, 2015) seeks to speed up clean energy transition to support EU's economy. As a result, energy transition forms part of the EU regional policy main goals. The aim is to promote increased dependence on energy from renewable sources to ensure sustainable and affordable energy (EC, 2019). In Morocco, the energy sector transformation started in 2009 with the National Energy Strategy. The strategy served, amongst others, as the basis for policies to promote energy transition. Subsequently, Morocco enacted legislation to enable investment in large-scale solar and wind projects through the Moroccan Agency for Sustainable Development which pilots' renewable energy programs in the country.

Therefore, closing the energy gap in Africa and transitioning to renewable sources involves sound reforms targeting energy utilities and regulatory frameworks to improve regional and sub-regional cooperation that leads to operational efficiency. To improve on existing initiatives by addressing the challenges slowing down energy transition on the continent, it is necessary that continental organisations such as the AU and the African Development Bank (AfDB) drive continent-wide progress by ensuring coordination and facilitating best practices. The AU can champion a continental policy on energy transition, while the AfDB can create finances specifically to support renewable energy investment initiatives.[10]

References

Abbas, W., Khan, A.R., Bashir, A. et al., 2020. Scaling up renewable energy in Africa: measuring wind energy through econometric approach. *Environmental Science and Pollution Research*, 27(29), pp. 36282–36294.

Addaney, M., and Cobbinah, P.B. (2019). Climate Change, Urban Planning and Sustainable Development in Africa: The Difference Worth Appreciating. In: Cobbinah, P.B., Addaney, M. (eds) *The Geography of Climate Change Adaptation in Urban Africa*. Cham: Palgrave Macmillan. https://doi.org/10.1007/978-3-030-04873-0_1

Adeoye, O. and Spataru, C., 2020. Quantifying the integration of renewable energy sources in West Africa's interconnected electricity network. *Renewable and Sustainable Energy Reviews*, 120, 109647.

Africa Clean Energy Corridor, 2015. *Analysis of infrastructure for renewable power in Eastern and Southern Africa*. International Renewable Energy Agency Report. www.irena.org/DocumentDownloads/Publications/IRENA_Africa_CEC_infrastru cture_2015.pdf

Africa Renewable Energy Initiative, 2015. *A framework for transforming Africa towards a renewable energy powered future with access for all*. International Finance Corporation, 'Getting Electricity', Doing Business Report IFC (Washington, DC, 2018).

10 The AU and AfDB have continental mandates that can enable them to promote low-carbon energy generation initiatives. See their renewable energy initiatives at http://www.arei.org and https://www.afdb.org/en/topics-and-sectors/initiatives-partnerships/sustainable-energy-fund-for-africa.

Akinyemi, O., Efobi, U., Osabuohien, E. and Alege, P., 2019. Regional integration and energy sustainability in Africa: exploring the challenges and prospects for Ecowas. *African Development Review*, 31(4), pp. 517–528.

Arimah, B.C. and Ebohon, O.J., 2000. Energy transition and its implications for environmentally sustainable development in Africa. *International Journal of Sustainable Development & World Ecology*, 7(3), pp. 201–216.

Avila, N., Carvallo, J.P., Shaw, B. and Kammen, D.M., 2017. The energy challenge in Sub-Saharan Africa: a guide for advocates and policymakers. https://www.oxfamamerica.org/sta tic/media/files/oxfam-RAEL-energySSA-pt1.pdf.

Bridge, G., Bouzarovski, S., Bradshaw, M. and Eyre, N., 2013. Geographies of energy transition: space, place and the low-carbon economy. *Energy Policy*, 53, pp. 331–340.

Cantarero, M.M.V., 2020. Of renewable energy, energy democracy, and sustainable development: a roadmap to accelerate the energy transition in developing countries. *Energy Research & Social Science*, 70, 101716.

Cartwright, A., 2015. Better growth, better cities: rethinking and redirecting urbanization in Africa. New Climate Economy – Working Paper (London and Washington, DC).

Castellano, A., Kendall, A., Nikomarov, M., and Swemmer, T., 2015. *Brighter Africa: the growth potential of the Sub-Saharan electricity sector*. McKinsey Report. http://www.mckinsey.com/industries/electricpower-and-natural-gas/our-insights/powering-africa (accessed 13 February 2020).

Chen, B., Xiong, R., Li, H. et al., 2019. Pathways for sustainable energy transition. *Journal of Cleaner Production*, 228, pp. 1564–1571.

Chirambo, D., 2018. Towards the achievement of SDG 7 in Sub-Saharan Africa: creating synergies between power Africa, Sustainable Energy for All and climate finance in order to achieve universal energy access before 2030. *Renewable and Sustainable Energy Reviews*, 94, pp. 600–608.

Choukri, K., Naddami, A., and Hayani, S., 2017. Renewable energy in emergent countries: lessons from energy transition in Morocco. *Energy, Sustainability and Society*, 7(1), 25.

Eberhard, A., Gratwick, K., Morella, E., and Antmann, P., 2016. *Independent power projects in Sub-Saharan Africa: lessons from five key countries*. World Bank Publications.

European Commission, 2015. *A framework strategy for a resilient energy union with a forward-looking climate change policy*. COM(2015)80, February 25.

European Commission, 2019. *The European Green Deal*. COM(2019)640, December 11.

Eshun, A.E., and Joe Amoako-Tuffour Eshun, J., 2016. A review of the trends in Ghana's power sector. *Energy Sustainability Society*, 6(9).

Germany's KfW Development Bank, GIZ and IRENA, 2020. *The Renewable energy transition in Africa: powering access, resilience and prosperity*. Available at https://www.irena.org/-/media/Files/IRENA/Agency/Publication/2021/March/Renewable_Energy_Transition_Africa_2021.pdf (accessed on 17 April 2022).

Hossain, J. and Mahmud, A., 2014. *Large scale renewable power generation advances in technologies for generation, transmission and storage*. Singapore: Springer.

IEA, 2019. *Africa Energy Outlook 2019*, Paris: IEA.

IEA, 2016. *World Energy Outlook 2016*. Paris: IEA.

Intergovernmental Panel on Climate Change (IPCC), 2018. *Global warming of 1.5 °C – A special report.*

IRENA, 2019. *Renewable power generation costs in 2019*. Available at, https://www.irena.org/-/media/Files/IRENA/Agency/Publication/2020/Jun/IRENA_Power_Generation_Costs_2019.pdf.

Irowarisima, M., 2021. African energy challenges in the transition era: the role of regional cooperation. In: Nalule, V.R., ed., 2021. *Energy transitions and the future of the African energy sector law, policy and governance*. Cham: Palgrave Macmillan.

Kebede, E., Kagochi, J., and Jolly, C.M., 2010. Energy consumption and economic development in Sub-Sahara Africa. *Energy Economics*, 32, pp. 532–537.

Morrissey, J., 2017. *The energy challenge in Sub-Saharan Africa: a guide for advocates and policymakers. Part 1: generating energy for sustainable and equitable development*. Oxfam Research Backgrounder Series, https://www.oxfamamerica.org/static/media/files/oxfam- RAEL-energySSA-pt1.pdf

Mostert, H., van den Berg, H.M., and Kengni, B., 2021. Frameworks for energy governance and regulation in Africa. In: M.M. Roggenkamp, K.J. de Graaf and R.C. Fleming, eds., 2021. *Energy Law, climate change and the environment*. Cheltenham: Elgar Publishing, pp. 245–246.

Mungai, E.M., Ndiritu, S.W., and Da Silva, I., 2022. Unlocking climate finance potential and policy barriers – A case of renewable energy and energy efficiency in Sub-Saharan Africa. *Resources, Environment and Sustainability*, 7, 100043.

Nalule, V.R., 2018. *Energy poverty and access challenges in Sub-Saharan Africa: the role of regionalism*. Cham: Palgrave Macmillan.

Nalule, V.R., 2020. Transitioning to a low-carbon economy: is Africa ready to bid farewell to fossil fuels?. In: G. Wood and K. Baker, eds., 2020. *The Palgrave handbook of managing fossil fuels and energy transitions*. Cham: Palgrave Macmillan, pp. 261–286.

Nalule, V.R., 2021. How to respond to energy transitions in Africa: introducing the energy progression dialogue. In: V.R. Nalule, ed., 2021. *Energy transitions and the future of the African energy sector law, policy and governance*. Cham: Palgrave Macmillan, pp. 3–35.

Olawuyi, D.S., 2021. Can MENA extractive industries support the global energy transition? Current opportunities and future directions. *The Extractive Industries and Society*, 8(2), 100685.

Omitaomu, O.A., Blevinsa, B.R., Jochema, W.C. et al., 2012. Adapting a Gis-based multicriteria decision analysis approach for evaluating new power generating sites. *Applied Energy*, 96, pp. 292–301.

Pavičević, M., and Quoilin, S., 2020. Modeling the impact of power generation on the water sector in the North, Eastern and Central African Power Pools. Working Paper presented at the 2020 IEEE PES/IAS PowerAfrica.

Planting, S., 2019. Gas in Mozambique – A $128bn opportunity. Business Maverick, September, https://www.dailymaverick.co.za/article.

Pueyo, A., 2018. What constrains renewable energy investment in Sub-Saharan Africa? A comparison of Kenya and Ghana. *World Development*, 109, pp. 85–100.

SADC, 2015. *Regional Indicative Strategic Development Plan 2015–2020*. Southern African Development Community Report (Gaborone), https://www.sadc.int/about-sadc/overview/strate gic-pl/regional-indicative-strategic-development-plan/

Shahbaz, M., Balsalobre-Lorente, D., and Sinha, A., 2019. Foreign direct investment – CO_2 emissions nexus in Middle East and North African countries: importance of biomass energy consumption. *Journal of Cleaner Production*, 217, pp. 603–614.

The Energy Progress Report, 2019. *Tracking Energy SDG7*. https://trackingsdg7.esmap.org/data/files/download-documents/2019-Tracking%20SDG7-Full%20Report.pdf accessed 15 March 2022.

TRACTEBEL, 2018. *Ecowas Master Plan for the development of regional power generation and transmission infrastructure 2019–2033*. Available at https://www.ecowapp.org/sites/default/files/volume_0.pdf (accessed on 17 April 2022).

Uhunamure, S.E. and Shale, K., 2021. A swot analysis approach for a sustainable transition to renewable energy in South Africa. *Sustainability*, 13(7), 10.

UNEP and AfDB, 2017. *Atlas of Africa energy resources.* Nairobi: United Nations Environment Programme Report.

United States Agency for International Development, 2017. *Southern Africa drought.* Fact Sheet. USAID. https://scms.usaid.gov/sites/default/files/documents/1866/southern_africa_dr_fs04_01-30-2017.pdf.

Wu, G.C., Deshmukh, R., Ndhlukula, K. et al., 2015. *Renewable energy zones for the Africa Clean Energy Corridor: multi-criteria analysis for planning renewable energy*. The International Renewable Energy Agency and Lawrence Berkeley National Laboratory. https://www.irena.org/publications/2015/Oct/Renewable-Energy-Zones-for-the-Africa-Clean-Energy-Corridor

Hao Zhang

Energy Transition Pathways for Asia and the Pacific: Regulatory Policies and Challenges for Renewable Energy Development

Abstract: The Asia-Pacific region has an important role to play in the global energy transition. As a fast-growing region in terms of population, economy and energy demand, countries in Asia and the Pacific face a common challenge of meeting the increased energy demand with clean energy. Although the region holds nearly half of the global renewable energy investment, its energy portfolio is still heavily fossil-fuel dependent because the deployment of renewable energy significantly lags behind that of coal-fired power plants in supplying the energy needs of the region. By examining the various regulatory policies for renewable energy development in this region, including feed-in tariffs (FiTs) and renewable energy auctions or tenders, this chapter analyses the convergent and divergent regulatory challenges of promoting renewable energy investment in countries of this region. Regulatory policies for renewable energy are present in most countries in Asia and the Pacific. Still, their effectiveness is challenged by the domestic energy infrastructure and the regulatory systems for the power sector that are incompatible with large scale renewable energy uptake. This chapter provides insights into the diverse effort and the dynamic regulatory landscapes developed at various jurisdictional levels in the Asia Pacific region for renewable energy development that may guide other countries in the region towards energy transition.

1 Introduction

The Asia-Pacific region has an important role to play in the global energy transition. As a fast-growing region in terms of population, economy and energy demand, countries in Asia and the Pacific face a common challenge of meeting the increased energy demand with clean energy. Countries in the Asia-Pacific represent more than 50% of the global GDP, and the region's demand for electricity accounts for approximately 60% of the world total (Zafar et al., 2019). Given its largest population size, fast-growing economy, and energy demand, the region's economic transformation, supported by a decarbonized energy system, is indispensable to the global success of realizing sustainable development and climate mitigation goals (ESCAP, 2018; REN21, 2019).

Hao Zhang is Associate Professor at the Faculty of Law, The Chinese University of Hong Kong.

https://doi.org/10.1515/9783110752403-025

Although the region holds nearly half of the global renewable energy investment, its energy portfolio is still heavily fossil-fuel dependent because the deployment of renewable energy significantly lags behind that of coal-fired power plants in supplying the energy needs of the region (ESCAP, 2018). The study by Nathaniel and Khan (2020) provides a specific example that urbanization in ASEAN (the Association of Southeast Asian Nations) countries has triggered more non-renewable energy consumption, which in turn, contributes to the inadequate investment in renewable energy. Overall, the region's renewable energy supply is still primarily sourced from hydropower, especially large-scale hydropower and bioenergy. These renewable energy sources contribute to the higher penetration of renewables in certain countries such as Myanmar, Sri Lanka, the Philippines and Indonesia (REN21, 2019), while modern renewable energy (such as photovoltaics and wind) is still very much underdeveloped. The region's fast economic development and soaring energy demand have not seen a significant increase in modern renewable energy in the final energy consumption (Xu et al., 2019). For instance, some of the largest economies in the region still have relatively low shares of renewable energy in the overall energy consumption portfolio. China's modern renewable energy accounts for around 10.06% of its final energy consumption in 2019 (IEA, 2019a). India had around 16% modern renewable energy share in its final energy consumption of the same year (IEA, 2019b).

The major hindrance to modern renewable energy deployment in the Asia-Pacific region is the high investment cost compared to the cost of fossil fuels and hydropower (ESCAP, 2018; Nguyen et al., 2019; Kardooni et al., 2018). The low cost of hydropower remains a barrier to deploying non-hydro renewables in countries where hydro resources are abundant (Nguyen et al., 2019). The high cost of modern renewable energy requires policy and regulatory support in various ways, such as feed-in tariffs (FiTs) and favourable grid access for renewable energy generators. The broader energy market structure and regulation also affect the integration of renewable energy in countries (such as China) where coal-fired generation still plays a dominant role (Zhang, 2019). Therefore, it is critical to understand the various support policies for renewable energy development in the context of the electricity market and regulation in the Asia-Pacific region.

Existing studies also highlight the positive roles of increased renewable energy consumption and trade in economic development in the Asia-Pacific region (Murshed et al., 2021; Ghazouani et al., 2020; Liu et al., 2018; Tran et al., 2016). These results provide policymakers in the Asia-Pacific region with some critical insights when designing the overarching national economic and energy policies to support continued economic growth and also to achieve the energy transition. There is a direct link between increased renewable electricity consumption, economic growth and trade openness. This means that ensuring renewable energy integration is a decisive factor for the latter two. This argument makes it clear that deploying renewable energy requires ambitious political will with explicit milestones at the national level and concrete policy/regulatory support in support of industries and technologies in the field of renewable energy.

By examining the various regulatory policies for renewable energy development in this region, including FiTs and renewable energy auctions or tenders, this chapter analyses the convergent and divergent regulatory challenges of promoting renewable energy investment in countries of this region. This chapter largely focuses on national experiences given the diverse and dynamic regulatory policies for renewable energy at the domestic level. That being said, there are discussions and proposals that promote regional collaboration and connectivity of the electricity infrastructure at the sub-regional level, such as the proposed roadmap for power connectivity in the Asia-Pacific by regional and sub-regional organizations (ESCAP, 2019; ASEAN, 2017). Power connectivity in the region has numerous benefits in the context of energy decarbonization. However, realizing this ambitious policy agenda faces a wide array of challenges, ranging from building trust and political consensus to harmonizing the policy and regulatory frameworks across jurisdictions in the region and developing intergovernmental agreements (ASEAN, 2017). All of these issues require dedicated attention and research in the future.

Regulatory policies for renewable energy are present in most countries in Asia and the Pacific. Still, their effectiveness is challenged by the domestic energy infrastructure and the regulatory systems for the power sector that are incompatible with large scale renewable energy uptake. This chapter provides insights into the diverse effort, and the dynamic regulatory landscapes developed at various jurisdictional levels in the Asia Pacific region for renewable energy development that may guide other countries in this region towards energy transition. This chapter is structured as follows. Section two discusses the various regulatory policies for renewable energy in the Asia-Pacific region, and it looks at successful and unsuccessful cases related to policy support for renewable energy development. Section three examines the factors that affect renewable energy integration. Section four concludes this chapter and sheds some light on the areas for future research.

2 Regulatory policies for renewable energy in Asia and the Pacific

The Asia-Pacific region has more than 60 countries with diverse geographical and population sizes, differing energy circumstances and varying potential and progress related to renewable energy development. This region hosts some of the most prominent countries in both areas and populations, notably China and India, which exercise substantial influence over the regional trend towards energy transition. Meanwhile, Asia and the Pacific are also home to some of the smallest, least developed and most remote countries in the world, where energy infrastructure is under development and access to electricity is still not realized for some populations and local communities. These characteristics of the region indicate that countries are at varying degrees of development in the energy industry, market and policy. At the one end of the population and energy demand spectrum, an increasing number of countries in Asia have placed great emphasis on tackling energy security challenges, due to the large population size and continuing expansion of cities and industries (Hanif et al., 2019). The energy data in 2020 suggest that four countries, China (57.3%), India (12.6%), Japan (6.7%) and South Korea (4.6%), account for 81.2% of the primary energy consumption in the Asia-Pacific (BP, 2021). These key energy parameters and the overall demography of the region have made Asia-Pacific a dominant player in energy markets, and its energy demand is still on the rise at an unprecedented rate. Accelerating energy transition is fundamentally challenged by the political imperative to secure energy supply at a reasonable cost (i.e. fossil fuels) and the need to mitigate pollution and greenhouse gas emissions from the booming industrial activities, such as supplying electricity from renewables. Energy law and the support policy framework in these countries are often tasked with the objective to balance the two challenges of energy security and energy transition. These two challenges were often perceived as competing and contradictory, especially in the context of developing countries where energy efficiency is relatively low and energy supply is dependent on imports (Zhang, 2019). However, there has been an increasing recognition that renewable energy development contributes to resolving the energy security challenge, reflecting the synergies between renewable energy and energy security (Cox et al., 2019; Hache, 2018).

At the other end of the spectrum related to energy demand, the least developed (notably Pacific countries) and some developing countries face a very different array of energy and development challenges (Sinha et al., 2020; Raza et al., 2018; Guerreiro and Botetzagias, 2018). Due to the challenging geographical circumstances and limited availability of conventional energy resources, the most pressing issue for these countries is to improve access to clean and affordable energy, particularly for those remote and small communities (Raza et al., 2018; ESCAP, 2018). Renewable energy provides the solution to source indigenous energy. It promotes local energy communities without the need to secure a large amount of investment to expand the energy network and improve the energy infrastructure. It also helps these countries reduce or even remove their reliance on expensive fossil fuel imports (ESCAP, 2018). Although the economies and energy circumstances of the countries in the Asia-Pacific are extremely varied in size and complexity, renewable energy provides the common solution to address the two primary sets of challenges related to energy security and transition and improved access to energy services.

2.1 The changing landscape of regulatory policies

Given the diverse economic and energy parameters of countries in Asia and the Pacific, the national regulatory and policy framework to support renewable energy in this region varies significantly in terms of scope and comprehensiveness across countries. Renewable energy targets and support mechanisms are present at various degrees and at different levels of government. Overall, high-income countries in this region have promulgated laws or national policies that specify the various support measures to deploy renewable energy. These countries have also adopted targets to increase the share of renewable energy in the power generation mix (Zhu et al., 2020; Kim et al., 2021; Zhang, 2019). Developing countries with fast-growing industries, such as China, India, Vietnam, and the Philippines, have adopted policies aiming to reduce the carbon intensity of economic growth and increase energy efficiency (Sinha et al., 2020; Roxas and Santiago, 2016). Through various forms of incentives, these measures have promoted the uptake of renewable energy in Asia-Pacific. Nonetheless, countries in this region with abundant fossil fuel resources or dependencies or countries with limited financial capacity have seen little progress in renewable energy development, mainly because of the weak or absent support for renewables from the political will or national policies (Cole and Banks, 2017; REN21, 2019).

The power generation sector provides the most promising arena to kick start the energy transition in Asia and the Pacific because the sector consumes much higher, if not the most, fossil fuels to produce electricity. The power sector is often considered the bloodline of national economic development (Oyewunmi et al., 2020). It is also the sector where policy and regulatory support to promote renewables are available, and deployment of renewable energy generation can happen more quickly throughout the supply chain, with large scale renewable energy at the upstream and small distributed renewables at the consumer end (ESCAP, 2018). As discussed above, increasing the share of renewable energy in the overall power generation mix facilitates the most fundamental energy transition required to achieve the Sustainable Development Goals and climate mitigation targets. It has also become a core regulatory demand facing national policymakers to improve the domestic policy and regulatory framework that governs the internal energy market (Heffron and Talus, 2016; Oyewunmi et al., 2020; Zhang, 2022).

Across the countries in Asia-Pacific, setting renewable energy targets constitutes the first step to developing a pathway towards a clean energy future. The targets are essential because they signal to markets that the governments are committed to supporting the sector's development, thus attracting public and private capital to invest. To date, a vast majority of countries in the region have adopted renewable energy targets of various sorts, with varying degrees of bindingness on domestic performance. Besides targets, the cost and price of renewables are at the centre of the policy and regulatory framework for renewable energy because it drives the speed and scale of renewable energy deployment in a country's specific context. The existing studies so far suggest that the support policies and regulatory mechanisms introduced to increase renewable energy uptake are broadening (ESCAP, 2018; Chang et al., 2016). However, there is yet to be a one-size-fits-all solution, given the complexity of assessing the impact of various support policies and regulatory mechanisms in different social and legal contexts (Wall et al., 2019; IRENA, 2021).

The range of instruments and incentives introduced in the power sector is diverse, and national policymakers are acutely aware of the need to tailor these measures based on local circumstances. The successful and unsuccessful cases, elaborated in the below section, demonstrate the importance of finding the appropriate policy and regulatory framework for concrete goals in a given context. Generally speaking, FiTs, commonly used by countries across the Asia-Pacific region and beyond, have driven up the initial uptake of renewable energy generation. However, the scheme has been revised, discontinued, or abruptly terminated, mainly because it is fiscally unsustainable. Countries in the region have resorted to auctions to harness the market trend of the declining cost of renewables and make the tariffs more cost-reflective or grid parity in some counties when the conditions are mature. Several countries in the Asia-Pacific have also experimented with other policy instruments, such as renewable energy portfolio standards, green certificate schemes and feed-in premiums, but they are much less common across countries in the region. Finding the right policy or mix of instruments requires dedicated efforts and, in most cases, learning through trial and error. Furthermore, the energy market structure and operation, underscored by the energy market regulation, are essential. The cases of higher auction prices for solar PV projects in Japan and the renewable energy curtailment in China exemplify that the energy market regulation may facilitate or hamper the integration of renewable energy. The additional cost incurred from curtailment is likely to jeopardize the economies of scale for renewable energy. Understanding the lessons learned provides helpful insights to national policymakers about the policy options and the critical issues that need to be addressed by the domestic policy and regulatory framework.

2.2 Effectiveness of regulatory policies

The most common mechanism to incentivize renewable energy development in the region is FiTs, and it has been proven to be somewhat effective to promote the uptake of renewable energy, at least in terms of generation capacity (Zhu et al., 2020; Kim et al., 2021; Zhang, 2019, Wall et al., 2019). FiTs are typically supported and underscored by three essential regulatory components, including guaranteed grid access, long-term power purchase contracts and cost-based purchase price (Lu et al., 2020). Countries in the Asia-Pacific region where FiTs policy exist follow this typical design approach, although the implementation leads to contrasting results of renewable energy penetration (Zhang, 2019). The FiTs work effectively during the early stage of the renewable energy market because they are price driven, where the government offers a guaranteed and above market purchasing price for electricity produced from renewable sources. As the leading developer of wind and solar energy, China has enacted detailed provisions through its Renewable Energy law framework to subsidize centralized and distributed solar PV generators, as well as onshore and offshore projects (Zhang, 2019). India relied on FiTs to realize its capacity addition in wind power till 2011 before using auctions to permit utility-scale renewable energy projects (ESCAP, 2018). To increase the share of clean energy in its generation mix after the Fukushima nuclear accident in 2011, Japan introduced FiTs for wind and solar to boost investment in the sector. Vietnam has improved its FiTs system by differentiating the rates for solar based on the solar irradiance, installation type and operation date (REN21, 2019).

However, the popularity of FiTs to boost renewable energy in the region has had a sharp turn in countries where investments were driven up more quickly than expected due to the high subsidies. Given the burden of FiTs on the public budget and the rapid decline of the cost of renewable energies, several countries have decided to discontinue or gradually phase out FiTs to prevent over-subsidization. For instance, China has significantly reduced FiTs as the country prepares for grid parity prices in light of the significant decline in the cost to generate wind and solar power. China's National Development and Reform Commission has decided that from 2021, newly permitted solar PV projects (including centralized generation and distributed projects for industrial and commercial use) and newly approved onshore wind power projects are not entitled to subsidies from the Chinese central government (NDRC, 2021). Starting from 2022, FiTs for newly built distributed solar PV projects in China are also removed. These changes are considered necessary to relieve the financial burden on China's Renewable Energy Development Fund, which had already accumulated a deficit of over RMB 100 billion (US$14.5 billion) by the end of 2018 (Hang, 2019). In response to the market trend and the mounting pressure of FiTs on government expenditure, Japan cut the FiTs for large scale solar generation approved between 2012 and 2014, which failed to reach completion by September 2019 (Sheldrick and Tsukimori, 2018).

In other cases, the FiTs scheme has been replaced by, or used in tandem with renewable energy auctions to reflect the declining cost of renewables. Auctions with ceiling prices and reverse auctions for renewable energy deployment have gained momentum in Asia-Pacific. These new mechanisms have produced some positive results. Auctions with ceiling prices have been piloted in Kazakhstan and Uzbekistan to boost renewable energy capacity with tariff levels that are more cost reflective. Kazakhstan approved the new set of FiTs, which are also the ceiling prices in renewable energy auctions (PWC, 2021). The ceiling prices help stabilize the national budget aimed at promoting renewable energy development. An increasing number of countries in the region (such as India, Thailand, China, the Philippines, Indonesia etc.) have conducted several successful reverse auctions where governments invite investors to bid for a specific capacity of renewable energy generation based on predetermined requirements and the bidder with the lowest price per unit of electricity wins the tender. Reverse auctions are arguably ideal for large scale projects because the experiences so far in Asia and the Pacific indicate that they achieved significantly lower prices per unit of electricity from wind and solar (ESCAP, 2018). In addition, auctions are also easily adaptable to a country's specific context. For instance, the reverse auctions held in India have seen the price of solar plummeting by around 85% from 2010 (US$ 250 per MWh) to 2019 (US$ 37 per MWh), and recently the lowest-ever wind bid (US$ 38 per MWh) was also achieved in an auction of a 500 MW wind project (REN21, 2019; ESCAP, 2018). Similarly, the auctions conducted in Thailand have also achieved prices well below the ceiling bidding price.

Nonetheless, in some cases, auctions alone have not generated promising results or even led to higher average prices to purchase renewable electricity, increasing the burden on public expenditure (IRENA, 2021). Japan's experiences provide a relevant example. Japan discontinued the FiTs and introduced renewable energy auctions in 2017. After five solar PV and two biomass auctions, only one-third of the initially announced volumes were awarded, yet no biomass project has been successfully contracted through tendering. Furthermore, the average price awarded (e.g. US$115 MWh in one of the auctions) is also much higher than those in other countries (IRENA, 2021). The case of Japan demonstrates that the cost of renewable energy can be significantly increased when considering factors including grid connection and access, and land availability, in addition to relatively higher expenses arising from equipment, installation and building costs. Due to the risk of high curtailment rates without compensation and uncertainties related to grid connection, investors in the Japanese market will have to adjust their risk perception and factor in the cost of curtailment.[1]

The failure of economies of scale in the Japanese context reveals a common problem facing many countries in Asia-Pacific and beyond. For instance, the issue of renewable energy curtailment in China is well documented in the relevant legal and policy scholarship (Zhang, 2019; Qi et al., 2018; Schuman and Lin, 2012; Kahrl et al., 2011). The amount of renewable energy curtailment in China is astonishing, with data revealing that in 2016 alone, the curtailment of wind power in China reached 49,700 GWh, which is higher than the total electricity consumption of Bangladesh, with a total population of 163 million in 2016 (49,000 GWh) (Zhang, 2019). Despite the promising role of FiTs and other price-driven policies in boosting renewable energy development, in practice, however, implementing the FiTs provision depends on the interconnection of renewable energy generators to the grid network. An essential component of power systems is that energy generators (both renewable and other fuel sources) are not only physically connected to the grid but also produce electricity expected to be dispatched by grid operators. When this does not occur, renewable energy supplies from some generators are curtailed, and investors must bear financial

1 Please refer to the chapter on Japan in this volume that provides some detailed discussion on this issue.

losses (Luo et al., 2016). There are various reasons for this curtailment, including transmission and congestion constraints, system balancing challenges, as well as legal and regulatory aspects underpinning technology, safety and grid operations (Kane and Ault, 2014). In light of the fast development of renewable energy and public policy goals to accelerate a transition of the power system to be clean and low carbon, countries across Asia and the Pacific have faced challenges in integrating renewable energy into their grid network (Duncan and Sovacool, 2011; Bird et al., 2016). Clearly, promoting renewable energy development requires an integrated view of renewable energy and energy market regulation. Updating the law and regulations that govern grid interconnection and operations is essential to ensure the reliability of power systems and establish an enabling environment for renewable energy development.

3 Factors affecting the effectiveness of supporting policies in Asia and the Pacific

The fast development of renewable energy in Asia-Pacific benefits from the supportive policies developed by governments to provide cost-effective solutions. The use of FiTs and other price discovery mechanisms to boost uptake of renewables reduces the investment cost and thus enhances the affordability of renewable energy at various scales. The national experiences in the region suggest that governments benefit from paying particular attention to developing a national policy and regulatory framework to support its renewable energy market, which is a crucial step to aligning domestic energy strategy with the national commitments to Sustainable Development Goals and the Paris Agreement. In this regard, an important lesson learned from the Asia-Pacific region is that the national policy framework needs to be carefully designed, considering the lack of a one-size-fits-all solution to increasing the market share of renewables. The national policy framework also needs to be reviewed and revised when the market conditions change because a mismatch between policy and market can hamper the progress and development of the renewable energy sector. Clearly, a significant challenge facing national policymakers is how to balance the effectiveness of policymaking and the predictability and stability of investment decision making by firms and investors (Heffron and Talus, 2016; Oyewunmi et al., 2020).

Some first-mover countries in the Asia-Pacific region have witnessed that certain types of modern renewable energy technologies are already cost-efficient to achieve grid parity so that they can compete with power generators that are fossil fuel-intensive. Nevertheless, most countries in the region still face the challenge that renewable energy technologies are costly and require governments' support in the first place to enable access. The Asia-Pacific experiences demonstrate that policy and technology for renewables are both context-dependent. They require policymakers to be mindful of the local circumstances and collect evidence and generate data to convince private investors that the investments are financially viable. Although government support is indispensable when the renewable energy market is at its infant stage, national policymakers in a number of countries have become acutely aware of the challenge to ensure the financial sustainability of the support programmes and regulatory policies. The success and failure of the price-driven mechanisms, as examined in the above section two, reveal that national policymaking needs to take into account the factors discussed below that are likely to affect the effectiveness of the support mechanisms. These factors include (a) identification of the appropriate policy instrument or a mix of instruments; (b) responsiveness of support mechanisms to market trends; (c) a holistic approach to integrating renewable energy into the national energy market regulation.

3.1 Identifying the appropriate policy instruments

The choice of modern renewable energy technology is determined by a range of local factors, among which the right policy instrument provides the much-needed push for market formation and technology dissemination. The policy instruments ideally aim to signalling the market and providing incentives to investors at the inception. Over time a transition from fiscal support to a price discovery policy instrument is required to reflect the declining cost of deployment. The instruments adopted should be adapted to the country's policy environment and technology availability. Policymakers also need to adapt these instruments to balance the projects with various lead times (small/distributed vs large/centralized projects) because they benefit stakeholders at different scales and speeds. Considering the long lead time for large-scale power generation projects, supportive policy instruments are immediately required to incentivize the market and investors.

The price-driven mechanisms, including FiTs and auctions, are preferred policy options in Asia-Pacific countries. Each has advantages and disadvantages, depending on the local context factors. The national practices in the region reveal that FiTs are the most crucial policy instrument that mobilizes and channels capital to the renewable energy sector. The subsidies provided by the government to renewable energy projects are often part of the overall national policy framework, which also shows the government's commitment to energy decarbonization. All of these are helpful to secure financing from private sector banks and financiers. To ease the pressure on the national budget, policymakers may consider setting clear guidance on the total expenditure budgeted to subsidize projects based on predetermined conditions, such as duration of payment, installed capacity and annual indexation of rates based on market conditions and inflation. Pilot programmes are an excellent option to demonstrate the project's feasibility and financial viability. Depending on the country's specific context, FiTs can also be restricted to distributed projects only to enable more access to energy services by local communities.

Auctions provide a policy option for countries where the renewable energy sector evolves and cost management becomes plausible. It is also a practical approach to understanding the cost level and testing the market reaction. Renewable energy auctions are particularly effective to achieve cost-effectiveness for utility-scale projects. The region has witnessed a few successful auctions, resulting in the lowest-ever prices for wind and solar projects (e.g. India and Thailand) and competitive costs of renewables at grid parity levels (e.g. China). Auctions are not alien to governments, and they can be tailored for renewable energy to suit the institutional and policy settings of a country and to acquire more mature technologies. Auctions can also be used in tandem with FiTs to achieve the duo results of incentivizing the market and achieving lower prices.

3.2 Ensuring responsiveness of support mechanisms to market trends

A significant challenge in the Asia-Pacific region when implementing the support mechanisms for renewable energy deployment is to ensure their responsiveness to market trends. The FiTs are being phased out due to the lack of financial sustainability, which is mainly caused by the fact that the rates of FiTs are not being adjusted regularly enough to reflect the market prices of renewable energy. Consequently, the public budget is overly burdened, causing investment disputes due to delayed and suspended payment of FiTs to renewable energy developers and shattering the market confidence. The experiences from countries in the Asia-Pacific region that have implemented the FiTs regime indicate that the FiTs are better supported and complemented by the holistic planning of the energy sector development in a country's specific context and tailored incentives for different types of renewables-based on criteria that go beyond the traditional parameters such as resources zones and the general category of renewables (such as onshore and offshore wind). Other essential factors, including capacity scale and technological class, shall also be considered when determining the levels of FiTs. The evidence from the region suggests that the absence of specificity in the FiTs regime will attract renewable energy with the lowest cost, which will crowd the market and prevent the proliferation of other renewable technologies that are more desperately dependent on government support. Adjustment of FiTs to reflect the market trend is also a difficult task for policymakers who are often not familiar with the technological development or market conditions of renewable energy. Abrupt reduction or termination of FiTs, as happened in several jurisdictions in the Asia-Pacific region, also has a negative impact on regulatory stability.

Renewable energy auctions provide an excellent option to boost renewable energy deployment by focusing on developmental aspects (such as capacity addition and location) while leaving the cost issues and technology selection to the market. The experiences from India, Kazakhstan and Japan are sources of regional lessons to be learned, both of which demonstrate that the auction design needs to consider local circumstances that are impactful on the success of auctions, notably land use and renewable energy access to the grid. Auctions, when used in tandem with the FiTs as the ceiling prices, also provide a clear signal and incentive to the market. It signals the investors that cost-effectiveness is the main objective if the market conditions allow lower prices to be achieved. Nonetheless, even if the lower prices are not feasible at the moment, the fixed rates of FiTs will guide investors to make their investment decisions and drive the development of research and development. Ensuring the responsiveness of support mechanisms to market trends is critical to countries that plan to expand large-scale renewable energy generation while facing public expenditure constraints.

3.3 Adopting a holistic approach to market integration

The lack of a holistic or integrated view of renewable energy and energy market regulation has become a significant challenge in some Asia-Pacific countries. One of the consequences arising from the absence of this holistic approach is the curtailment of renewable energy (such as in Japan and China). Countries with regulated energy markets are more likely to encounter curtailment due to the persistency of forecasting, planning and grid operations that are suited for conventional types of generation (such as coal power). Although countries implementing FiTs often require guaranteed access of renewables to the grid network, transmission companies struggle or resist coping with the integration of renewable energy because the upgrade of forecasting, planning and grid operation and their reinforcement plans are costly and time-consuming. There is also a lack of incentives or legal obligations for grid companies to do so due to the legal system's slow response.

In the case of China, for instance, the dispatch regulation is yet to be fundamentally changed to prioritize renewables. China's Renewable Energy Law requires the grid companies to bear the cost of connection and access, and such costs can be partially recovered from the Renewable Energy Development Fund. The Renewable Energy Law allows grid companies to curtail renewable energy under circumstances that their access to the grid will endanger grid stability and reliability. This provision is also incorporated in the power purchase agreement to exempt grid companies from their liability. However, the Law does not specify circumstances endangering grid stability and reliability, leaving a loophole in the legal system that allows grid companies to exercise discretion (Zhang, 2019). Since 2016, the Chinese central government has taken numerous administrative measures to reduce the curtailment rate. One effective policy requires that grid companies are still obliged to pay the FiT rates to renewable energy producers when curtailment happens (Hover, 2020). Despite the easing of curtailment in recent years, China's National Energy Administration has acknowledged that the adjustment of benefits caused by these regulatory measures amongst generators has not been effectively managed (NEA, 2018). Since the announcement of China's carbon neutrality target, the Chinese central leadership has stressed that the laws and regulations that are maladaptive to the carbon neutrality development shall be amended, signalling an important step to address the mismatch between renewable energy uptake and the outdated grid dispatch rules that do not support renewable energy integration to the grid.

In Japan, the grid companies are also obliged to accept the grid access needs of renewable energy producers. However, grid companies determine the costs, which are entirely borne by the producers. Renewable energy developers also assume risks of high curtailment probability because grid companies are allowed to curtail renewable energy for up to 30 years annually without needing to pay any compensation (IRENA, 2021). As a result, curtailment drives up prices of renewable energy in Japan, leading to higher prices in auctions. Kimura estimates that a 10% curtailment rate can increase generation costs of solar power up to JPY 6.3 kWh (US$ 50 MWh) (Kimura, 2019). Looking forward, tackling this challenge requires a holistic view of market integration rules and energy market regulations that go beyond just price reduction. Some key elements include improved grid interconnection rules and a compensation system for curtailment.

4 Conclusion

The economic development in the Asia-Pacific region has been accompanied by soaring energy consumption, especially fossil fuels. This development model has generated challenges and problems at multiple levels, notably environmental pollution, energy supply shortage and climate change. Countries in the region have increasingly realized that moving towards a clean and decarbonized energy system is fundamental to achieving the Sustainable Development Goals and the target endorsed by the Paris Agreement and long-term economic prosperity. Renewable energy provides a somewhat universal solution to energy sector decarbonization in the region due to its versatility to be adopted in the energy supply chain and its positive impact on economic activities, indicating a solid business case for renewable energy. The support mechanisms and regulatory policies to promote renewable energy deployment that many countries in the region have adopted add to this imperative.

Asia and the Pacific have demonstrated a robust and steady increase in renewable energy in the past decade, with significant country differences. However, the challenge faced by Asia and the Pacific is still profound. Fossil fuel consumption in many countries has had a sharp rise, leaving the share of renewable in the overall energy mix relatively low. The national experiences suggest that government support for renewable energy development is indispensable. The price-driven instruments implemented by different countries provide valuable insights and lessons to policymakers about their effectiveness. Given that policy and technologies are both context-sensitive, finding the right policy or mix of instruments requires dedicated efforts and, in most cases, learning through trial and error. While price and costs are critical factors determining the progress and scale of renewable energy deployment, other vital factors such as the responsiveness of the policy instrument to market trends and a holistic approach to market integration are also highly influential. With new policies and instruments to boost renewable energy unfolding across countries in the region (such as green certificate trading and re-introduction of FiTs in certain countries), future research is much needed to understand their progress, implementation and effectiveness. The energy transition is a long-term effort, but it needs to be accelerated in the Asia-Pacific to achieve the sustainable development goals and decarbonization objectives.

References

Abdullah, W.S.W., Osman, M., Ab Kadir, M.Z.A. and Verayiah, R., 2019. The potential and status of renewable energy development in Malaysia. *Energies*, 12(12), 2437.

ASEAN, 2017. *Master plan on ASEAN connectivity 2025*. December 2017. https://asean.org/wp-content/uploads/2018/01/47.-December-2017-MPAC2025-2nd-Reprint-.pdf

Bird, L. et al., 2016. Wind and solar energy curtailment: A review of international experience. *Renewable and Sustainable Energy Review*, 65, pp. 577–586.

BP, 2021. *Statistical Review of World Energy 2021*. July 2021. https://www.bp.com/content/dam/bp/business-sites/en/global/corporate/pdfs/energy-economics/statistical-review/bp-stats-review-2021-full-report.pdf

Chang, Y. et al., 2016. Renewable energy policies in promoting financing and investment among the East Asia Summit countries: Quantitative assessment and policy implications. *Energy Policy*, 95, pp. 427–436.

Cole, P. and Banks, G., 2017. Renewable energy programmes in the South Pacific – Are these a solution to dependency? *Energy Policy*, 110, pp. 500–508.

Cox, S. et al., 2019. *Renewable energy to support energy security*. National Renewable Energy Laboratory, October 2019. https://www.nrel.gov/docs/fy20osti/74617.pdf

Duncan, D. and Sovacool, B.K., 2011. The barriers to the successful development of commercial grid connected renewable electricity projects in Australia, Southeast Asia, the United Kingdom and the United States of America. *Renewable Energy Law and Policy Review*. 2(4), pp. 283–301.

Economic and Social Commission for Asia and the Pacific (ESCAP), United Nations Economic and Social Council, 2018. *Energy transition in Asia and the Pacific: pathways to ensure access to affordable, reliable, sustainable and modern energy for all*. https://www.unescap.org/sites/default/files/APEF2018_2.PDF

ESCAP, 2019. *Electricity connectivity roadmap for Asia and the Pacific.* https://www.unescap.org/sites/default/d8files/knowledge-products/Electricity%20Connectivity%20Roadmap%20in%20Asia%20and%20the%20Pacific.pdf

Ghazouani, T. et al., 2020. Causal interactions between trade openness, renewable electricity consumption, and economic growth in Asia-Pacific countries: Fresh evidence from a bootstrap ARDL approach. *Renewable and Sustainable Energy Reviews.* 133, 110094.

Guerreiro, S. and Botetzagias, I., 2018. Empowering communities – the role of intermediary organizations in community renewable energy projects in Indonesia. *Local Environment: The International Journal of Justice and Sustainability*, 23(2), pp. 158–177.

Hache, E., 2018. Do renewable energies improve energy security in the long run? *International Economics*, 156, pp. 127–135.

Hang, A. 2019. Is China ready for subsidy-free renewables', Greentech Media, 31 May 2019. https://www.greentechmedia.com/articles/read/is-china-ready-for-subsidy-free-renewables

Hanif, I. et al., 2019. Carbon emissions across the spectrum of renewable and non-renewable energy use in developing economies of Asia. *Renewable Energies*, 143, pp. 586–595.

Heffron, R. and Talus, K., 2016. The development of energy law in the 21st century: a paradigm shift? *Journal of World Energy Law and Business*, 9, pp. 189–202.

Hover, A., 2020. *Trends and contradictions in China's renewable energy policy.* Center on Global Energy Policy, Columbia University, August 2020. https://www.energypolicy.columbia.edu/research/commentary/trends-and-contradictions-china-s-renewable-energy-policy#_edn22

International Energy Agency (IEA), 2019a. *Key energy statistics, 2019: China.* https://www.iea.org/countries/china

IEA, 2019b. *Key energy statistics, 2019: India.* https://www.iea.org/countries/india

International Renewable Energy Agency (IRENA), 2021. *Renewable energy auctions in Japan: Context, design and results.* January 2021. https://www.irena.org/-/media/Files/IRENA/Agency/Publication/2021/Jan/IRENA_Auctions_Japan_2021.pdf

Kahrl, F., Williams, J., Jianhua, D. and Junfeng, H., 2011. Challenges to China's transition to a low carbon electricity system. *Energy Policy*, 39, pp. 4032–4041.

Kane, L. and Ault, G., 2014. A review and analysis of renewable energy curtailment schemes and principles of access: Transitioning towards business as usual. *Energy Policy*, 72, pp. 67–77.

Kardooni, R., et al., 2018. Public opinion on renewable energy technologies and climate change in Peninsular Malaysia. *Renewable Energy*, 116, pp. 659–668.

Kim, H. et al., 2021. Is renewable energy acceptable with power grid expansion? A quantitative study of South Korea's renewable energy acceptance. *Renewable and Sustainable Energy Reviews*, 139, 110584.

Kimura, K., 2019. *Solar power generation costs in Japan: Current status and future outlook.* Renewable Energy Institute, October 2019. https://www.renewable-ei.org/pdfdownload/activities/Report_SolarPVCostJapan_EN.pdf

Liu, X. et al., 2018. Renewable energy, trade, and economic growth in the Asia-Pacific region. *Energy Sources, Part B: Economics, Planning, and Policy*, 13(2), pp. 96–102.

Lu, Y. et al., 2022. A Critical Review of Sustainable Energy Policies for the Promotion of Renewable Energy Sources. *Sustainability*, 12, 5078.

Luo, G. et al., 2016. Wind curtailment of China's wind power operation: Evolution, causes and solutions. *Renewable and Sustainable Energy Review*, 53, pp. 1190–1201.

Murshed, M. et al., 2021. The effects of regional trade integration and renewable energy transition on environmental quality: Evidence from South Asian neighbors. *Business Strategy and the Environment*, 30(8), pp. 4154–4170.

Nathaniel, S. and Khan, S.A. R., 2020. The nexus between urbanization, renewable energy, trade, and ecological footprint in ASEAN countries. *Journal of Cleaner Production*, 272, 122709.

National Development and Reform Commission (NDRC), 2021. *Notices on matters related to on-grid tariffs for renewable energy in 2021.* (关于2021年新能源上网电价有关事项的通知), NDRC Order No. (2021) 833, 7 June 2021.

National Energy Administration (NEA), *Press Conference of NEA on Performance of China's Electricity Sector in 2017.* (国家能源局新闻发布会介绍2017年度相关能源情况等), January 2018. www.nea.gov.cn/2018-01/24/c_136921015.htm

Nguyen, P.A., et al., 2019. *The development and cost of renewable energy resources in Vietnam*. Utilities Policy, 57, pp. 59–66.

Oyewunmi, T. et al., 2020. Decarbonization and the Energy Industry: An Introduction to the Legal and Policy Issues. Tulane Public Law Research Paper No. 20-9, March 2020.

PricewaterhouseCoopers (PWC), 2021. *Renewable Energy Market in Kazakhstan: Potential, Challenges, and Prospects.* May 2021. https://www.pwc.com/kz/en/assets/pdf/esg-dashboard-eng.pdf

Qi, Y. et al., 2018. *Deepening reform of electric power system and resolving the issue of wind power curtailment.* (深化电力体制改革 解决弃风限电问题), Brookings-Tsinghua

Center for Public Policy, April 2018. https://www.brookings.edu/wp-content/uploads/2018/04/fixing-wind-curtailment-with-electric-power-system-reform-in-china.pdf

Raza, M.Y. et al., 2018. Development of renewable energy technologies in rural areas of Pakistan. *Energy Sources, Part A: Recovery, Utilization, and Environmental Effects*, 42(6), pp. 740–760.

REN21, 2019. *2019 Asia and the Pacific Renewable Energy Status Report*. https://www.ren21.net/wp-content/uploads/2019/05/REN21_Asia_Report_2019_Web.pdf

Roxas, F. and Santiago, A., 2016. Alternative framework for renewable energy planning in the Philippines. *Renewable and Sustainable Energy Reviews*, 59, pp. 1396–1404.

Schuman, S., and Lin, A., 2012. China's Renewable Energy Law and its impact on renewable power in China: Progress, challenges and recommendations for improving implementation. *Energy Policy*, 51, pp. 89–109.

Sheldrick, A. and Tsukimori, O., 2018. Japan threatens to cut solar power subsidies, angering investors. Reuters, 21 November 2018. https://www.reuters.com/article/us-japan-renewables-litigation-idUSKCN1NQ0UE

Sinha, A. et al., 2020. Technology policy and environmental quality at crossroads: Designing SDG policies for select Asia Pacific countries. *Technological Forecasting and Social Change*, 161, 120317.

Tran, T.T. et al., 2016. Realizing the Intended Nationally Determined Contribution: The role of renewable energies in Vietnam. *Energies*, 9(8), pp. 587–604.

Wall, R. et al., 2019. Which policy instruments attract foreign direct investments in renewable energy? *Climate Policy*, 19(1), pp. 59–72.

Weir, T., 2018. Renewable energy in the Pacific Islands: Its role and status. *Renewable and Sustainable Energy Reviews*, 94, pp. 762–771.

Xu, X. et al., 2019. Global renewable energy development: Influencing factors, trend predictions and countermeasures. *Resources Policy*, 63, 101470.

Zafar, M. W. et al., 2019. From non-renewable to renewable energy and its impact on economic growth: The role of research & development expenditures in Asia-Pacific Economic Cooperation countries. *Journal of Cleaner Production*, 212, pp. 1166–1178.

Zhang, H., 2019. Prioritizing Access of Renewable Energy to the Grid in China: Regulatory Mechanisms and Challenges for Implementation. *Chinese Journal of Environmental Law*, 3(2), pp. 167–202.

Zhang, H., 2022. Exploring energy resilience in China's energy law in the carbon neutrality era. *Asia Pacific Law Review*, 30(1), pp. 167–187.

Zhu, D. et al., 2020. Analysis of the robustness of energy supply in Japan: role of renewable energy. *Energy Reports*, 6, pp. 378–391.

Acknowledgement

The work described in this chapter was fully supported by a grant from the Research Grants Council of the Hong Kong Special Administrative Region, China (Project No. CUHK 24602421).

Sirja-Leena Penttinen

Governing for Net-Zero in the European Union

Abstract: The European Union is often portrayed as the forerunner in the clean energy transition, with its ambitious policies adopted at EU level concerning the increase of renewable energy in the energy mix, reduction of energy consumption and increase of energy efficiency as well as the reduction of greenhouse gas emissions. The tools to reach these policy targets have been provided by legislative instruments, such as directives on renewable energy and energy efficiency. The creation of policy, regulatory and legislative framework concerning such a politically charged sector has, however, been challenging. The development has been hindered in particular by the diverse views of EU Member States concerning the future directions of the energy and climate policies and adoption of tools to that end, as well as the limited competence granted to the EU by the Treaties. In order to overcome these barriers, the EU has often relied on softer governance mechanisms to adopt and implement measures concerning energy. This chapter focuses on the Governance Regulation, which was adopted in 2018 as a part of the latest legislative package concerning the energy sector, the Clean Energy Package. With the inevitable need for a cleaner energy future, energy and climate policies cannot be held in separate silos as the EU approach has been for a long time. To this end, the chapter first discusses the importance and the concreate measures of the Governance Regulation in strengthening the coherence of energy and climate policies. Second, the chapter analyses the governance mechanisms embedded in the Governance Regulation, and identifies elements of 'hardening' governance to ensure that the EU is on track to meet its increasingly ambitious policy targets that are binding at EU level. Before concluding remarks, some recent developments outlining the most recent legislative proposals by the Commission are presented.

1 Introduction

For decades the European Union (EU) has been considered one of the forerunners in deploying a toolbox of various successful policies to stimulate the transition towards a low-carbon energy future and achieve reductions in greenhouse gas emissions. The robust policy and legislative frameworks put in place include, inter alia, government support for the uptake of renewable energy technologies (Penttinen, 2022a), voluntary and mandatory policies concerning the energy performance of a wide array of

---

Dr. Sirja-Leena M. Penttinen is Assistant Director of the Tulane Center for Energy Law, Tulane University, United States.

https://doi.org/10.1515/9783110752403-026

subjects (Penttinen 2021a, b, c) as well as the world's first emissions trading scheme (under Directive 2003/87/EC, the 'ETS Directive 2003').

The origins of the EU's robust regulatory interventions in these areas can be traced back in particular to the '20-20-20' targets that the EU was committed to achieving by 2020 (2020 framework) (EU Commission, 2008). These targets comprised a 20% reduction of EU greenhouse gas emissions compared to 1990 levels, increasing the share of EU gross final energy consumption supplied from renewable energy sources to 20%, and a 20% improvement in energy efficiency within the EU through a 20% reduction in primary energy consumption (EU Commission, 2008). The post-2020 framework extending to 2030 was adopted in 2014. According to the 2030 framework, the key targets are at least 40% cuts in greenhouse gas emissions (compared to 1990 levels), at least a 32% share for renewable energy as well as at least a 32.5% improvement in energy efficiency (European Council, 2014). Whereas under the 2020 framework the renewable energy target translated into Member State specific national binding targets, under the 2030 framework only the target concerning greenhouse gas emissions is binding at national level. The 40% target for greenhouse gas emissions was nevertheless considered too low, and was accordingly revised upwards to 55% (Article 4(1) of the Regulation (EU) 2021/1119 (the 'Climate Law')).

Growing concerns over climate change together with the adoption of the Paris Agreement led to the adoption of more ambitious goals, which have recently culminated in the agreement on the European Green Deal (EU Commission, 2019a), as well as in the adoption of the Climate Law, which lays down the goal of climate neutrality in binding EU legislation. Article 2(1) of the Climate Law provides that 'Union-wide greenhouse gas emissions and removals regulated in Union law shall be balanced within the Union at the latest by 2050, thus reducing emissions to net zero by that date, and the Union shall aim to achieve negative emissions thereafter'.

The achievement of the increasingly ambitious targets adopted during the past few decades has been and still is hampered by limited competences at EU level. Article 194 of the Treaty on the Functioning of the European Union (TFEU) sets out the EU's competences on energy matters. The common EU energy policy objectives defined at Treaty level include the establishment of an EU wide energy market, security of supply, promotion of energy efficiency and renewable energy as well as interconnection of energy networks in the EU. However, Member States remain competence over their 'energy rights', i.e. decisions on energy sources in their national energy portfolio.

Energy is a very politically charged sector. There are as many views on the future directions of the sector as there are EU Member States. The weighing of different energy policy objectives depends on the Member States, the traditional view being that the eastern Member States' priorities lie in securing energy supply and reducing reliance on Russian gas deliveries. This policy discourse has recently gained new ground in respect of the emergence of the 'energy solidarity' principle (Buschle and Talus, 2019; Boute, 2020). Some Member States, in particular the Nordic countries and

Germany as well as France after the election of President Macron, have pushed for an ambitious sustainable energy agenda (Knodt et al., 2020). The varying views on the future directions that might be taken recently came to the fore in the context of the adoption of the 2030 targets, as it became clear relatively early on that common ground that would enable adoption of binding national targets – similar to the renewable energy target in the 2020 framework – could not be found. In particular, the negotiations were marked by a clear impasse along East/West lines (Bocquillon and Maltby, 2020).

Furthermore, the targets contained in the 2020 framework may initially have contributed to the 'silo' thinking that has dominated the implementation of the various legislative tools each of which is designed to further the realization of its sector-specific target: just consider the directives on renewable energy, energy efficiency and greenhouse gas emission allowance trading within the EU, all of which provide tools to promote their respective policy domain. The horizontal coherence of EU energy as well as EU energy *and* environment (widely understood also to encompass climate change mitigation and adaptation, the latter being nevertheless relatively overlooked in the EU legislative framework to date) policies has been questioned. Each policy domain has developed in its own silo without much interaction with others.

The EU's supranational governance structure naturally also complicates policy-making as power is redistributed from the national level to supranational and subnational actors, as well as to quasi-state and non-state actors (Rosenow et al., 2018; Langlois-Bertrand et al., 2015). This multilevel governance structure within the EU requires careful design of policy mixes and policy coordination, as realization of stated policy objectives may be hindered if policy decisions, adopted measures and their effects are not taken into account at other governance levels (Rosenow et al., 2018; Penttinen et al., 2021). Likewise at national level conflicting interests between different government departments may hamper efficient realization of stated policies due to differing interpretations of objectives and preferences regarding their regulation. The impact of underlying politics is often overlooked in relation to the combination of policy instruments (Rogge and Schleich, 2018).

The EU has developed a holistic approach over the years. While climate related policies and implementing measures were previously separate from those relating to energy (also in a global context: see Eriksson and Reschl, 2019), the EU's governance has evolved towards more comprehensive climate policy integration (von Homeyer et al., 2021). Research also notes the energy sector's traditional resistance to addressing environmental concerns – climate change concerns in particular (Eriksson and Reschl, 2019). Furthermore, traditionally energy security is prioritized over combating climate change, thus underlining the central importance of a secure, continuous energy supply to societies in general (Nisbet, 2009). Climate change, instead, is portrayed more as a global environmental challenge (Nyman, 2018). This view is, however, rather ironic from the perspective that the (EU) energy sector is known for its cross-cutting character, perfectly illustrated, for example, by the flexible use of power to adopt various legislative acts under different competence articles prior to the adoption of the energy-specific legal base to be found in Article 194 TFEU (for an overview, see e.g. Hancher and Salerno, 2012; Talus and Aalto, 2017; Penttinen, 2020). Despite these traditional views, the EU's policy discourse today revolves around climate *and* energy, the development of which can be seen in the sphere of new measures adopted and/or proposed, as discussed in greater detail below.

Given the difficulties in adopting measures that fall within the scope of 'hard governance' (i.e. rules that arise from binding law: treaties, directives and regulations), the EU has traditionally relied on 'soft' governance frameworks and policy coordination (i.e. non-binding rules) (for a more detailed account, see e.g. Maggetti, 2015), such as Open Method Coordination (OMC), to overcome the challenges, as outlined above, that have complicated dependence on authority-based governance regimes to achieve the targets set. OMC, as an EU policy-making process, does not result in 'hard' EU legislation, but is instead a method of soft governance which aims to spread best practice and achieve convergence towards EU goals in those policy areas which fall under the partial or full competence of Member States (Szyszczak, 2006). OMC has been characterized as implying softer steering mechanisms to enhance communication and policy coordination, thus replacing the missing competences (Blomqvist, 2016). However, the common weakness of this particular governance model is that it is dependent on the willingness of national governments to initiate policy change. To address such weaknesses, a process of hardening of soft law governance can be seen in several EU policy areas (Bocquillon et al., 2020).

In order to overcome the challenges outlined above in respect of the realization of the increasingly ambitious targets within the energy sector, the EU Commission launched a new type of governance strategy in 2016. This strategy found expression in the form of Regulation (EU) 2018/1999 (the 'Governance Regulation'), which aims to enhance policies' horizontal coherence (Knodt et al., 2020). The Governance Regulation seeks to enhance cooperation between Commission Directorates-General and the inclusion of other policy considerations within previously separate 'silos'.

This chapter focuses on the development of EU energy governance. In particular, it examines the recently adopted Governance Regulation and the EU's Energy Union framework against the decarbonization framework. First, it illustrates how the EU has sought to overcome the issues considered as barriers to deepening integration in energy – lack of competence and varying policy priorities in particular – to adopt increasingly ambitious decarbonization targets and measures by which to achieve them. Second, it examines the current governance framework to show how the soft governance framework has started to incorporate harder elements in step with the increasingly ambitious decarbonization targets being set. It appears this trend is not only taking place in the EU, but also in other organizations to push countries in the desired direction with regard to decarbonization (Knodt and Schoenefeld, 2020).

The structure of the chapter is as follows. After the introductory part, the following section presents the concept of the Energy Union. In addition, the most important provisions of the Governance Regulation are discussed. This section illustrates how the Governance Regulation seeks to enhance the coordination of policies between the EU and its Member States as well as between the areas of energy and climate change. The third section discusses the legal nature of the main provisions as well as their enforcement. This section analyses the harder elements of the Governance Regulation. Finally, some concluding thoughts are provided.

2 In search of coherence: strengthening diffuse sub-sectoral governance via the Governance Regulation

The Energy Union was launched in 2015. It is built on five dimensions that are closely related and mutually reinforcing: (1) security, solidarity and trust; (2) a fully integrated internal energy market; (3) energy efficiency; (4) climate action, decarbonizing the economy; and (5) research, innovation and competitiveness. Through these dimensions, the Energy Union framework seeks to tie the previously separate silos together in an integrated and coordinated manner. The Energy Union is considered as the most significant policy idea that has been developed, and is aimed at reforming European energy governance, policy and reginal cooperation, with a view to streamlining these with long-term climate protection goals (Szulecki et al., 2016).

Turning the five dimensions into one strategy requires a robust governance framework in order to improve coordination between various policy instruments, measures and levels of government (Vandendriessche et al., 2017). The Governance Regulation seeks to integrate, streamline or repeal more than 50 existing individual planning, reporting and monitoring obligations of the EU energy and climate *acquis* (Proposal 2017). In this respect, the Commission emphasizes that the Energy Union needs strong governance 'ensuring that policies and measures at various levels are coherent, complementary and sufficiently ambitious' (Proposal 2017).

The Governance Regulation was adopted in 2018 as a part of the Clean Energy for All Europeans legislative package (EU Commission 2016). It is a key instrument, a 'novelty element' (as described by Vandendriessche et al., 2017) and an 'innovative piece of legislation' (Bocquillon et al., 2020) in ensuring that the policy measures adopted in order to achieve the Energy Union's objectives and the targets of the 2030 policy framework are implemented and coordinated in a coherent manner. As the Regulation's full name (Regulation on the Governance of the Energy Union *and* Climate Action) highlights, it was adopted under the legal bases of both environment and energy, namely Articles 192(1) and 194(2) TFEU.

The Governance Regulation seeks to build upon and streamline the existing governance mechanisms. In this respect, it draws to a great extent on existing planning and reporting obligations in the context of the 2020 targets, in particular national energy efficiency action plans (NEEAPs) and national renewable energy action plans (NREAPs). The key areas that the Regulation seeks to cover are planning, reporting and monitoring. It also aligns with the 'ratchet mechanism' contained in the Paris Agreement (Vandendriessche et al., 2017; Kulovesi and Oberthür, 2020); a concept that refers to the continuous reporting requirements coupled with an increasing level of ambition. The international linkages in this respect are visible in the Governance Regulation, as many provisions on reporting and monitoring reflect the mechanisms of the Paris Agreement.

The NEEAPS were first considered to be mainly a reporting tool and were adopted in Directive 2006/32/EC (the 'Energy Services Directive') in 2006. This is considered as being the first measure to have employed 'Open Method Coordination' within the field of sustainable energy law (Ringel and Knodt, 2018), which required Member States both to achieve energy savings by introducing new or upgrading existing energy saving measures and to report the adopted measures to the Commission every three years.

The successor to the Energy Services Directive, Directive 2012/27/EU (the 'Energy Efficiency Directive' or 'EED'), which was first adopted in 2012 and amended in 2021, obliges Member States to specify indicative national energy efficiency contributions towards the EU's 2030 target. Under the EED, the Commission's role is strengthened as compared with the NEEAPs initially adopted in the Energy Services Directive in terms of reviewing and providing feedback to the Member States on their plans and progress. Furthermore, the template established for the NEEAPs in the EED allows for more structured dialogue between the Commission and the Member States, which was critically needed (Ringel and Knodt, 2018; Proposal 2017).

A similar tool to that employed in the field of energy efficiency was also employed within the field of renewable energy. Directive 2009/28/EC (the 'Renewable Energy Directive of 2009') initially laid down an obligation for Member States to draft, publish and notify the Commission of their NREAPs (Article 4). As with the obligations arising from the EED, the Commission evaluated the action plans and had the power to issue recommendations to Member States in response to inadequate action. No further enforcement mechanism or any kind of follow-up was established.

The Governance Regulation sought to streamline and reduce overall planning obligations in the light of the 2030 targets. The new forms of planning, reporting, and monitoring revolve around the integrated National Energy and Climate Plans (NECPs) which are required to take into consideration the five dimensions of the Energy Union (Chapter 2 of the Governance Regulation). The NECPs follow the template set out in Annex I of the Regulation and are to be drafted once every ten years. Member States are required to state their objectives and the policies they will adopt to achieve them in respect of the next ten-year period. Impacts on neighbouring Member States must also be taken into consideration, in addition to which the Governance Regulation includes a specific provision on regional cooperation (Article 12). The draft

NECPs are reviewed by the Commission, which may issue Member State specific recommendations. These may focus, in particular, on the level of ambition of objectives, targets and contributions, especially from the perspective of *collectively* achieving the Energy Union objectives, as well as on policies and measures relating to those objectives and in particular measures of potential cross-border relevance (Article 9). Furthermore, Member States are required to publish the draft NECPs in order to be able to receive feedback from the public, thus increasing transparency and accountability.

Following the Commission's assessment, Member States have one year to consider the Commission's recommendations, after which they are to publish the final versions of the NECPs. Member States are required to take the Commission's recommendations into 'due account' in the final versions of their NECPS: if they choose not to address them, Member States must make public their reasons in this regard. The Governance Regulation provides the possibility for the Member States to update their NECPs if they wish to reflect increased ambition within them.

The NECPs thus implement the governance framework's planning obligation. In order to ensure reporting and monitoring respectively, Member States are obliged to submit national energy and climate progress reports biannually, following strict guidelines laid down in the Regulation. The Commission evaluates the progress reports to analyse the progress made at EU level towards achieving the 2030 goals, as well as to analyse the progress made at Member State level towards achieving the goals set out in the NECPs. If the Commission concludes that a Member State is not making enough progress, it can issue recommendations to that Member State. On the other hand, if it considers that not enough is being done to achieve targets collectively at EU level, it may issue recommendation to all Member States or adopt additional measures.

It should be noted that the first review of the NECP revealed significant gaps in the Member States' ambition level, concerning both renewable energy and energy efficiency. Several Member States were required to increase their level of ambition when submitting their final NECPs (European Commission, 2019).

In addition to the NECPs, the Governance Regulation includes an obligation on long-term Low Emissions Strategies (Article 15). The Low Emissions Strategies should cover a longer period, a 30-year horizon with a view to integrating the EU's commitments and those of its Member States towards achieving net zero greenhouse gas emissions within the EU by 2050 and negative emissions thereafter, in line with the recently adopted Climate Law. The Low Emissions Strategies are also aligned with the Paris Agreement, because under Article 4(19) of the Paris Agreement, all Parties were invited to communicate their long-term low greenhouse gas emission development strategies by 2020. Under the Governance Regulation, Member States must submit their Low Emissions Strategies to the Commission every ten years. The elements required to be present in Member States' long-term strategies are set out in Annex IV of the Regulation. As distinct from the NECPs, a similar review procedure is not envisaged for the low emissions strategies. Instead the Commission evaluates whether the national long-term strategies are adequate for the collective achievement of the objectives and targets of the Energy Union and advises as to any remaining gaps in collective action. Furthermore, the European Environmental Agency is specifically granted a role under the Governance Regulation in assisting the Commission with its tasks (Article 42).

In addition to the integrated planning and reporting obligations outlined above, the Governance Regulation contains provisions on greenhouse gas reporting and monitoring (Article 18) and on national adaptation actions, financial and technology support provided to developing countries and auction revenues (Article 19).

Despite strengthening the EU governance framework for energy and climate policies, the Governance Regulation was criticized for leaving some important gaps unaddressed. These include the absence of long and mid-term emission reduction targets and an independent scientific advisory body (Kulovesi and Oberthür, 2020). The recently adopted Climate Law fills these gaps and therefore complements the Governance Regulation. First, it lays down the binding EU level climate-neutrality target for 2050. In order to ensure that the EU and the Member States remain on track to achieve this objective and make progress on climate change adaptation – the rules in respect of which have been laid down in the Climate Law for the first time in EU law – the Commission has the competence to regularly assess progress. The Climate Law also sets the intermediate target of reducing net greenhouse gas emissions by at least 55% by 2030, as compared to 1990 levels. In addition, another target is to be set for 2040 to enable monitoring of the progress and to ensure the realization of the target (s) set. Furthermore, the Climate Law is aligned with the Paris Agreement as it specifically requires for the publication of the conclusions of such an assessment every five years 'in order to allow for a timely preparation for the global stocktake referred to in Article 14 of the Paris Agreement' (preamble para. 36).

The Climate Law also specifically empowers the Commission to 'take necessary measures' in the event that the collective progress made by Member States towards the achievement of the climate-neutrality objective or on adaptation is insufficient or if the measures adopted by the EU are inconsistent with the climate-neutrality objective or inadequate to enhance adaptive capacity, strengthen resilience or reduce vulnerability (preamble para. 36). The Commission should also regularly assess relevant national measures and issue recommendations where it finds that a Member State's measures are inconsistent with the climate-neutrality objective or inadequate to enhance adaptive capacity, strengthen resilience and reduce vulnerability to climate change. In this regard, the Climate Law is directly linked to the Governance Regulation and provides that the system for the measurement of progress towards the climate-neutrality targets as well as the consistency of the measures taken to that effect should be built upon and be consistent with the Governance Regulation. Considering especially that one of the objectives of the Governance Regulation was to lighten Member States' administrative burden by streamlining planning and reporting obligations, it is important that the regular reporting and Commission's evaluations are consistent with the existing requirements of the Governance Regulation. In this respect, the Climate Law amends the Governance Regulation (Article 13) to reflect the obligations adopted in the Climate Law.

Furthermore, the Climate Law established the European Climate Change Council (ECCC) (Article 3). The ECCC is an independent expert advisory body at EU level, which serves 'as a point of reference for the Union on scientific knowledge relating to climate change by virtue of its independence and scientific and technical expertise.' Furthermore, considering the need to enhance 'the role of science in the field of climate policy', those Member States that do not yet have a national climate advisory body are encouraged to establish one.

Considering that the EU has adopted ambitious targets for renewable energy and energy efficiency for the 2030, the Commission has special measures provided by the Governance Regulation in its toolbox to ensure that the EU stays on track to achieve the collective targets in particular within the fields of renewable energy and energy efficiency. The following section analyses the legal nature of these measures and their enforcement.

3 Embedding harder elements of governance to support the realization of EU level targets

It should be noted that the governance of renewable energy is considered especially important in the absence of national binding targets for renewable energy. While the 2020 framework on renewable energy relied on mandatory national targets for every EU Member State (i.e. a particular Member State-specific target for renewables within total energy consumption), the 2030 target is binding at EU level only. The 2020 framework targets remain as indicative targets for Member States, thus signalling *you cannot do worse than that*. This is laid down also in Directive (EU) 2018/2001 (the 'Renewable Energy Directive of 2018') (Article 3(4)). Given the relative success of the 2020 framework (at both EU and Member State level), an advanced system of governance was required to ensure ambition and progress.

The EU's relatively new governance structure is built upon long-term energy and climate planning, short-term reporting and frequent monitoring. The chosen legal instrument in this regard was a regulation, which under EU law is directly applicable in all EU Member States and does not require the adoption of national transposition measures to this effect.

It should be recalled that one of the main objectives of the Energy Union framework is to ensure coherent implementation of a combination of policies with a view to achieving the *overarching* EU energy and climate policy goals. This approach was implemented by the adoption of the five interrelated dimensions of the Energy Union Framework Strategy, which are in turn reflected in the Governance Regulation. The latter requires Member States, inter alia, to cover and integrate all five dimensions in their NECPs. This is emphasized both in the substantive articles of the Regulation and in its annexes, which contain templates for NECPs and their reporting. In this respect, the EU has clearly sought to break with the traditional silo thinking that has played a dominant role in EU energy policy.

The OMC method the EU has traditionally relied on has long been criticized for its 'softness': the national plans established under this governance model tend to follow national paths with very little learning taking place, especially considering that no harder elements are included in the event that 'advice' received from EU institutions is disregarded. This inward-looking approach was also identified as a weakness in the EU's Impact Assessment 2016, which notes that Member States often fail to take into account the wider implications of their national policies. A question therefore arises as to the exact legal nature of the measures introduced in the Governance Regulation and how they are enforced.

The Governance Regulation sets out several obligations for EU Member States. The most important of these are the NECPs and reporting towards the progress of the objectives set out therein. These mark the 'planning' and 'reporting' elements included in the Governance Regulation. The third element, 'monitoring', falls within the scope of the competences of the EU Commission. This particular task is twofold: the Commission assesses the progress that Member States have made in terms of achieving the energy and climate objectives and related policies as well as providing feedback in the event of insufficient ambition or progress. More importantly, the Commission's enforcement toolkit includes measures to address the 'ambition and delivery gaps' in Member States' NECPs.

While in the past the tendency has been to evade the monitoring element by setting targets whose implementation can be assumed, or by relying upon soft modes of governance such as reporting and peer reviewing (Jordan et al., 2010), a significantly stronger enforcement toolbox is built into the Governance Regulation by the introduction of the following elements: first, the Governance Regulation empowers the Commission to 'to take corrective action' in the event of inconsistencies, the achievement of insufficient progress towards the overarching EU objectives and insufficient action in the NECPs (ambition gap); and second, the Commission assesses the implementation of the national policies and related measures adopted against the policy objectives set out in the NECPs (delivery gap). In the event of any ambition and/or delivery gap the Commission issues a recommendation to the Member State concerned.

Recommendations, under EU law, are soft law tools that allow an EU institution that issues one to make its views known and to suggest a course of action. However, under Article 288 TFEU, recommendations do not have legally binding force.

With regard to legally binding rules, the Commission has the possibility to resort to judicial proceedings in the form of infringement proceedings under Article 258 TFEU. Such proceedings may ultimately lead to the imposition of fines on any Member State held to have breached its obligations under EU law. However, since there are no Member State-specific binding targets, Member States cannot be sanctioned for failure to achieve any such targets. Instead, Member States are only obliged to draw up national plans, submit them for review and take into account the Commission's recommendations. However, as these are laid down in a legally binding instrument, a Regulation, the Commission may take action if a Member State fails to fulfil its obligations under the Governance Regulation, such as by failing to submit an NECP.

The emergence of harder elements in the Governance Regulation is hidden in the details. If the Commission has issued recommendations, 'the Member State concerned shall take due account of the recommendation in a spirit of solidarity between Member States and the Union and between Member States' (Article 34(2(a))). The Member State concerned must include in its NECP progress report information on the policies and measures adopted that are aligned with the recommendation, in addition to a detailed timetable for implementation if applicable. If a Member State does not follow the Commission's recommendations, it is required to provide reasoning to that end, with the burden of proof remaining with the respective Member State. This is a novel process that marks the direct influence of EU law and policy on Member States' national policymaking and is indicative of the EU's growing influence on national energy and climate policies (Ringel and Knodt, 2018). At the same time, this process is necessary in order to ensure coherence and coordination, as emphasized in the Regulation, so to say to 'keep everyone in line'.

Within the areas of renewable energy and energy efficiency – both of which rely purely on EU level collective action in the absence of national mandatory targets – the Commission is empowered to take corrective action. Within the area of energy efficiency, the Commission is empowered to take additional measures at EU level; whereas within the area of renewable energy, the Commission can cover the delivery gap by adjusting the share of renewable energy in specific sectors or by making a financial contribution to an EU-level renewable energy financing platform (Article 33), or it may 'propose measures and exercise its power at Union level' (Article 32(2)). In addition, if the Commission concludes that a Member State has fallen below the baseline share over a one-year period, that Member State will be required to introduce additional measures within one year and close the gap within one further year. The additional measures include (i) implementing national measures to increase deployment of renewable energy; (ii) adjusting the share of renewable energy in the heating and cooling sector; (iii) adjusting the share of renewable energy in the transport sector; (iv) making a voluntary financial payment to the EU's renewable energy financing mechanism, as set out in Article 33 of the Governance Regulation; and (v) using the cooperation mechanisms set out in in the Renewable Energy Directive of 2018 (Article 32(3)).

Annex II of the Governance Regulation provides a formula for the calculation of an individual renewable energy target for each Member State that allows the Commission to assess their progress. Although the target is not binding, the formula allows the calculation of a numerical target for each Member State that is taken into consideration as a reference value when assessing Member States' ambition levels. It provides a clear benchmark by which to assess individual national failures, and therefore apportion blame and shame (Bocquillon et al., 2020).

Perhaps the most interesting of the 'additional measures' is the contribution to the EU's renewable financing mechanism. The Member State concerned is asked to make a voluntary financial contribution to the EU's renewable energy financing mechanism, which is managed by the Commission. The mechanism is used to contribute to the most cost-efficient renewable energy projects across the EU, with a view to providing Member States with the option to contribute to achievement of the EU's target at the lowest possible cost. However, the Governance Regulation does not provide any details on this particular tool and its implementation.

Furthermore, the Commission may also propose new measures and exercise its power at EU level to ensure achievement of the target in question. The Commission's powers to 'propose measures and exercise its power at Union level' has been considered controversial. Although there are no specific legal remedies that exist for the enforcement of EU level collective targets, the formulation of the provision in the Governance Regulation is seen as a justification for EU intervention in national energy policies that can conflict with the sovereign energy rights provided for in Article 194 (2) TFEU (Ringel and Knodt, 2018; Monti and Martinez Romera 2020). This discussion, however, is nothing new, as various views have been expressed over the years on this energy rights caveat and its linkages to the mandatory national targets as enshrined in the Renewable Energy Directive of 2009 (see Johnston and van der Marel, 2013; Hancher and Salerno, 2012, who note that the legal basis for the adoption of the Renewable Energy Directive of 2009 was the environmental legal basis, i.e. Article 192 TFEU that enabled the EU to adopt a measure laying down mandatory national targets for renewable energy). Furthermore, it appears that the Commission is not interested in using the reporting and monitoring system to design a system that is 'binding by the back door' (Bocquillon and Maltby, 2020). On the other hand, the design of the provisions on the NECPs has been praised, especially as they enable national sovereignty concerns to be taken into account (Bocquillon et al., 2020).

The monitoring role does not only include the Commission. It can be interpreted to extend even further as a result of the transparency added by the Governance Regulation. The Commission is required to report on its assessment based on the NECPs as well on indicators, European statistics and data, where available, on progress towards achieving the EU level targets through collective action. This information forms part of the State of the Energy Union Report, which is to be submitted every year by the Commission to the European Parliament and to the Council (Article 35). In the context of the State of the Energy Union, the European Parliament and the Council are to address on an annual basis the progress achieved by the Energy Union on all dimensions of energy and climate policies (Article 36).

In this respect, the increased transparency integrated into the Governance Regulation is considered a key tool by which to ensure ambition and compliance (Bocquillon and Maltby, 2020). In particular, greater transparency allows for 'public review', thus revealing those Member States whose level of ambition and delivery are to be praised as well as those whose actions still leave room for improvement. It appears that the European Parliament, in particular, was in favour of this tool, which relies on naming and shaming to strengthen the softer governance framework (Bocquillon and Maltby, 2020). The same applies in relation to conforming with the Commission's recommendations: sheer peer pressure is considered crucial to delivering the required changes.

These core elements included in the Governance Regulation – namely increased transparency to allow for 'naming, shaming and blaming' (in the form of the yearly State of the Energy Union Report delivered to the Parliament and the Council together with the biannual assessment summary of Member States' progress), the requirement to publicly respond to (in)action as to reporting in respect of the NECPs, thus imposing a burden of proof on Member States, linking voluntary financial contributions to insufficient actions, and empowering the Commission to adopt new measures or sharpen existing ones at EU level are all established mechanisms that integrate harder elements into the soft governance framework (Knodt and Schoenefeld, 2020; Knodt et al., 2020; Bocquillon et al., 2020).

The drivers for the hardening elements that have been integrated into the soft governance framework relate in particular to the issues described as a starting point in this chapter. The soft governance approach is particularly appealing in situations where there are limited possibilities to agree on hard legislation (Bocquillon et al., 2020). The failure to adopt mandatory targets for the Member States in respect of renewable energy in the 2030 framework is one example of this situation. Harder elements are introduced in order to increase the effectiveness of the chosen approach (Knodt and Schoenefeld, 2020). Effectiveness, in turn, relates to the urgency with which action needs to be taken, thus generating political pressure to act. In the context of the Governance Regulation, this concerns, in particular, the ambitious targets adopted in the aftermath of the Paris Agreement, which were further spurred by increasing scientific evidence on the state of affairs at the time (IPCC, 2021). Finally, this particular governance model is considered to fit particularly well within the context of the low-carbon energy transition the dynamics of which are still uncertain in various fields, which makes the future even more uncertain. In this respect, the flexibility provided by soft governance frameworks that include harder elements in the form of 'pledge and review' (Oberthür, 2019) is noteworthy as it allows for the revision of targets and adaptation to the revised targets (Bocquillon et al., 2020).

4 Recent developments: EU Commission Fit for 55 proposal on energy efficiency

As discussed above, the NECPs submitted to the Commission for review by the end of 2019 revealed a serious ambition gap. While the EU's target ambition level for 2030 is a 32.5% reduction for final energy consumption, the NECPs only paved the way to achieve a collective reduction of 29.4% for final energy consumption and 29.7% for primary energy consumption as compared with the projections from the 2007 reference scenario for 2030 (Proposal 2021).

Against this background, the Commission took the view that the agreed 32.5% energy efficiency target is insufficiently ambitious to achieve the target of a 55% reduction by 2030. A higher ambition level requires more robust promotion of energy efficiency in all areas of the energy system and in all relevant sectors where the activity carried on affects energy demand. With that in mind, the Commission proposed a set of measures for energy efficiency that range from cross-sectoral to sector-specific measures and which present the energy efficiency target as a binding legal obligation.

Articles 1 and 4 of the Proposal offer perhaps the most interesting developments in this area. First, they propose that the energy efficiency principle be embedded into binding legislation and thus subject to judicial review and enforcement. This underlines the importance of the principle, in addition to which the Commission has been very innovative in proposing the obligation to public entities to ensure the verification of the application of the principle. Much of the success of the provision clearly depends on how Member States transpose the obligation into their national legislation as no further direction to that end is provided in the Proposal. Such direction might include, for example, guidance as to the strictness of the requirements relating to verification of the application of the principle (e.g. as to what documentation is needed to prove that an assessment upon which the verification can be based has been made). This approach, aimed at concretizing the principle of energy efficiency, seeks to ensure that it goes beyond fine words and requires that action be taken.

In addition to the energy efficiency first principle, the Commission proposes a more ambitious target for the collective achievement of EU level energy efficiency. Instead of the previously agreed 32.5% target by 2030, the Commission suggests increasing the target level to 39% and 36% of energy efficiency savings in primary and final energy consumption respectively (representing a 9% reduction by 2030 compared to the 2020 baseline scenario). The revised targets reflect the relative success of the governance framework as established by the Governance Regulation: the NECPs revealed the existing ambition gap in Member States' national plans and, under the powers granted to the Commission by the Governance Regulation, more ambitious targets, new measures and improvements to existing measures are proposed to realize the target set and ensure that the 2050 climate neutrality objective is met.

In this respect, energy efficiency is subjected to a similar process as renewable energy currently is under the Governance Regulation. The Proposal sets out indicative national energy efficiency contributions towards the collective targets and provides Member States with a formula by which to calculate their contributions. The new targets reflect the additional efforts required as compared with those currently in place as enshrined in the NECPs. However, the Commission emphasizes that the national targets are of indicative nature only, due to strong opposition on the part of a majority of the Member States to the idea of mandatory, binding national targets. Moving towards harder governance mechanisms similar to those in place in the field of renewable energy, as well as benchmarks and delivery gap mechanisms, is also proposed to complement those measures that already form part of the Governance Regulation.

The Proposal provides, in this regard, that if the Commission concludes, on the basis of its assessment of the biannual progress reports, that insufficient progress has been made towards meeting the energy efficiency contribution targets, Member States that are above their indicative trajectories referred to above are required to undertake 'additional measures' that must be implemented within one year following the date of reception of the Commission's assessment. Such additional measures include, for example, (i) national measures delivering additional energy savings, including stronger project development assistance for the implementation of energy efficiency investment measures; (ii) increasing the energy savings obligation; (iii) adjusting the obligation for public sector; and (iv) making a voluntary financial contribution to the National Energy Efficiency Fund or another financing instrument dedicated to energy efficiency. The annual financial contributions are to be equal to the investments required to reach the indicative trajectory. Furthermore, in order to ensure contingent monitoring, the Member State involved is required to include in its NECP progress report an explanation as to how it will bridge the gap to ensure that it meets its national energy efficiency contributions target. In similar vein as currently provided for under the Governance Regulation, if the Commission deems the measures insufficient to meet the collective energy efficiency target, 'the Commission shall, as appropriate, propose measures and exercise its power at Union level' to ensure the realization of the 2030 targets.

In addition to these requirements, as well as other reporting related obligations enshrined in the Proposal, increasing transparency also clearly underlines the Commission's use of hardening governance elements in the sphere of energy efficiency in order to ensure the achievement of the ambitious targets. In this respect, the Proposal is a coherent instrument, extending its reach – as required by the principle of energy efficiency – outside the energy efficiency silo (Penttinen, 2022b).

Naturally, it should be emphasized that what has been published is at this stage only a proposal. It is subject to negotiation, potential change and needs to be adopted by the European Parliament and the Council, the EU co-legislators, to become law.

5 Concluding thoughts

The governance of the 2020 framework relied on planning and reporting, as the sectoral legislative tools required Member States to establish separate plans for renewable energy, energy efficiency as well as non-ETS sector emissions, detailing the sectoral objectives and measures (to be) adopted to that effect. The previously separate reporting obligations defining the Member States' contributions towards the EU's renewable energy and energy efficiency targets are now codified in the Governance Regulation under NECPs, following the model set up by the Paris Agreement.

However, while the measures required by the Paris Agreement have been characterized as bottom-up, the EU's approach diverges from this to some extent. The Governance Regulation provides for a clear structure in the form of the templates for Member State reporting. NECPs are produced in an iterative process, which is based on a dialogue between the Member States and the Commission. Further, the Governance Regulation provides considerable authority to the Commission to monitor Member States' policy planning and implementation and provides a clear route to ever-deeper influence on EU Member States' national energy and climate policies. Furthermore, the EU's strengthened procedural obligations contrast with those of the Paris Agreement's in relation to Nationally Determined Contributions, reporting and review (Oberthür, 2019).

In the context of the energy and climate framework, the scientific evidence increases the pressure to act. Traditional soft governance mechanisms are perceived as being too weak to meet the increasing ambition level. As a response, it appears that it is necessary to embed harder elements in the governance framework to ensure efficient action to achieve the desired goals.

As highlighted above, the framework for energy and climate is not the only policy area of the EU to rely on soft governance methods. Within the energy sector, and in the context of the Governance Regulation in particular, it appears that the EU 'has turned a weakness into strength, and developed a set of tools that sharpen the way soft power is exercised' (Goldthau and Sitter, 2015). In this respect, the EU can provide examples of both good practices to deploy, as well as potential pitfalls and what to avoid, for those regions that are still struggling with the absence of regional cooperation, trust and political consensus as discussed in chapters of this volume on Asia-Pacific (Zhang), Africa (Addaney and Kengni) and Latin America (Bellera Landa, Trahan and Nemeth). This is so, in particular, as regards to how to create effective policies and strategies towards decarbonization and implement these in the regulatory framework – despite the lack of consensus and in presence of diverse views. Similarly to the North American experience (Coleman, in this volume), and the US in particular, one of the main barriers to further increase the share of renewable energy in the EU are the national permitting procedures. While the current legislative framework seeks to encourage Member States to streamline existing procedures, national diversity is yet flourishing and delaying many renewable energy projects. Likewise, with the lowest hanging fruit picked up in terms of the location for the renewable energy production plants, the EU is also experiencing limitations with regard to infrastructure, network in particular, development. While the EU Commission has already started to address these issues in a more determined manner (EU Commission, 2022), these will be among the next governance challenges for the European Union, considering in particular the Member States national competencies in their renewable energy permitting and authorization procedures.

References

Blomqvist, P., 2016. Soft and hard governing tools. In: C. Ansell and J. Torfing, eds., 2016. *Handbook on theories of governance*. Cheltenham: Edward Elgar Publishing, pp. 267–278.

Bocquillon, P. and Maltby, T., 2020. EU energy policy integration as embedded intergovernmentalism: the case of Energy Union governance. *Journal of European Integration,* 42(1), pp. 39–57.

Bocquillon, P., Brooks, E. and Maltby, T., 2020. Speak softly and carry a big stick: hardening soft governance in EU energy and health policies. *Journal of Environmental Policy and Planning*, 22(6), pp. 843–856.

Boute, A., 2020. The principle of solidarity and the geopolitics of energy: Poland v Commission (OPAL pipeline). *Common Market Law Review*, 57(3), pp. 889–914.

Buscle, D. and Talus, K., 2019. One for all and all for one? The General Court ruling in the OPAL Case. *Oil, Gas and Energy Law* 5.

Directive (EU) 2018/2001 of the European Parliament and of the Council of 11 December 2018 on the promotion of the use of energy from renewable sources, OJ L 328, 21.12.2018, p. 82–209.

Directive (EU) 2018/2002 of the European Parliament and of the Council of 11 December 2018 amending Directive 2012/27/EU on energy efficiency, OJ L 328, 21.12.2018, p. 210–230.

Directive 2003/87/EC of the European Parliament and of the Council of 13 October 2003 establishing a scheme for greenhouse gas emission allowance trading within the Community and amending Council Directive 96/61/EC, OJ L 275, 25.10.2003, p. 32–46.

Directive 2006/32/EC of the European Parliament and of the Council of 5 April 2006 on energy end-use efficiency and energy services and repealing Council Directive 93/76/EEC [2006] OJ L114/64.

Directive 2009/28/EC of the European Parliament and of the Council of 23 April 2009 on the promotion of the use of energy from renewable sources and amending and subsequently repealing Directives 2001/77/EC and 2003/30/EC, OJ L 140, 5.6.2009, p. 16–62.

Directive 2012/27/EU of the European Parliament and of the Council of 25 October 2012 on energy efficiency, amending Directives 2009/125/EC and 2010/30/EU and repealing Directives 2004/8/EC and 2006/32/EC, OJ L 315, 14.11.2012, p. 1–56.

Eriksson, J. and Reschl, G., 2019. Worlds apart, worlds together: converging and diverging frames in climate and energy governance. *Globalizations*, 16(1), pp. 67–82.

European Commission Staff Working Document, Impact assessment accompanying the document proposal for a regulation of the European Parliament and the Council on the Governance of theEnergy Union, amending Directive 94/22/EC, Directive 98/70/EC, Directive 2009/31/EC, Regulation 663/2009/EC, Regulation 715/2009/EC, Directive 2009/73/EC, Council Directive 2009/119/EC, Directive 2010/31/EU, Directive 2012/27/EU, Directive 2013/30/EU and Council Directive (EU) 2015/652 and repealing Regulation (EU) No 525/2013, SWD(2016) 394.

European Commission, 2008. Communication from the Commission to the European Parliament, the Council, the European Economic and Social Committee and the Committee of the Regions, '20 20 by 2020, Europe's climate change opportunity', 23.1.2008, COM(2008) 30 final.

European Commission, 2016. Communication from the Commission to the European Parliament, the Council, the European Economic and Social Committee, the Committee of the Regions and the European Investment Bank, 'Clean Energy for All Europeans' COM(2016) 860 final.

European Commission, 2019a. Communication from the Commission to the European Parliament, the European Council, the Council, the European Economic and Social Committee and the Committee of the Regions, 'The European Green Deal'. COM(2019) 640 final.

European Commission, 2019b. Communication from the Commission to the European Parliament, the Council, the European Economic and Social Committee and the Committee of the Regions, 'United in delivering the Energy Union and Climate Action – Setting the foundations for a successful clean energy transition', COM(2019) 285 final.

European Commission, 2022. Speeding up permit-granting and PPAs. SWD(2022) 149.

European Council, 2014. Conclusions on 2030 Climate and Energy Policy Framework, SN 79/14 (23 October 2014).

Goldthau, A. and Sitter, N., 2015. Soft power with a hard edge: EU policy tools and energy security. *Review of international Political Economy*, 22(5), pp. 941–965.

Hancher, L. and Salerno, F. M., 2012. Energy policy after Lisbon. In: A. Biondi et al., eds., 2012. *EU law after Lisbon* (Oxford University Press), pp. 365–400.

IPCC, 2021. Climate Change 2021. The Physical Science Basis. Summary for Policymakers. Intergovernmental Panel on Climate Change.

Johnston, A. and van der Marel, E., 2013. Ad Lucem? Interpreting the new EU energy provision, and in particular the meaning of Article 194(2) TFEU. *European Energy and Environmental Law Review*, 22(5) pp. 181–199.

Jordan, A., Huitema, D., van Asselt, H. et al., 2010. Governing climate change in the European Union: understanding the past and preparing for the future. In: A. Jordan, D. Huitema, H. van Asselt et al., eds., 2010. *Climate change policy in the European Union: confronting the dilemmas of mitigation and adaptation*. Cambridge: Cambridge University Press, pp. 253–275.

Knodt, M. and Schoenefeld, J. J., 2020. Harder soft governance in European climate and energy policy: exploring a new trend in public policy. *Journal of Environmental Policy and Planning*, 22(6), pp. 761–773.

Knodt, M., Ringel, M., and Müller, R., 2020. Harder soft governance in the European Energy Union. *Journal of Environmental Policy and Planning*, 20(6), pp. 787–800.

Kulovesi, K. and Oberthür, S., 2020. Assessing the EU's 2030 Climate and Energy Policy Framework: Incremental change toward radical transformation? *Review of European, Comparative & International Environmental Law* 29(2), pp. 151–166.

Langlois-Bertrand, S., Benhaddadi, M., Jegen, M., Pineau, P.-O., 2015. Political-institutional barriers to energy efficiency. *Energy Strategy Reviews*, 8, pp. 30–38.

Maggetti, M., 2015. Hard and soft governance. In: K. Lynggaard, I. Manners and K. Löfgren, K., eds., 2015. *Research methods in European Union studies*. Cham: Palgrave Macmillan, pp. 252–265.

Monti, A. and Martinez Romera, B., 2020. Fifty shades of binding: appraising the enforcement toolkit for the EU's 2030 renewable energy targets. *Review of European, Comparative & International Environmental Law*, 29(2), pp. 221–231.

Nisbet, M. C., 2019. Communicating climate change: why frames matter for public engagement. *Environment: Science and Policy for Sustainable Development*, 51(2), pp. 12–23.

Nyman, J., 2018. *The Energy security paradox: rethinking energy security in the United States & China*. Oxford: Oxford University Press.

Penttinen, S.-L., 2020. *Free movement and the energy sector in the European Union: the role of the European Court of Justice*. London and New York, NY: Routledge.

Penttinen, S.-L., 2021a. Energy efficiency. In: O. Woolley, eds., 2021. *Encyclopedia of European Union Law, Energy Law Volume*. Oxford: Oxford University Press, 2022.

Penttinen, S.-L., 2021b. Energy performance of buildings. In: O. Woolley, eds., 2021. *Encyclopedia of European Union Law, Energy Law Volume*. Oxford: Oxford University Press, 2022.

Penttinen, S.-L., 2021c. Ecodesign and energy labelling. In: O. Woolley, eds., 2021. *Encyclopedia of European Union Law, Energy Law Volume*. Oxford: Oxford University Press, 2022.

Penttinen, S.-L., 2022a. Regulatory and policy instruments to promote decarbonization in the energy sector. In: L. Reins and J.M. Verschuuren, eds., 2022. *Research handbook on climate change mitigation law*. Cheltenham: Edward Elgar Publishing. pp. 337-362.

Penttinen, S.-L., Kallioharju, K., Sorri, J., Heljo, J. and Harsia, P., 2021. Building electrification: policy implications and interactions. In: P. Aalto, eds., 2021. *Electrification: accelerated transition to climate neutrality*. Amsterdam: Elsevier, pp. 175–196.

Penttinen, S.-L., Nippala, E., and Kallioharju, K., 2022b. Energy efficiency in the Fit for 55 framework: increasingly ambitious targets coupled with hardening governance. *Oil, gas and energy law, Special issue on the EU 'Fit for 55' Legislative Package*, 19(5).

Proposal for a Directive of the European Parliament and of the Council on energy efficiency, Brussels, 14.7.2021. COM(2021) 558 final.

Proposal for a Regulation of the European Parliament and of the Council on the Governance of the Energy Union, Brussels, 23.2.2017, COM(2016), 759 final/2.

Regulation (EU) 2018/1999 of the European Parliament and of the Council of 11 December 2018 on the Governance of the Energy Union and Climate Action, OJ L 328, 21.12.2018, p. 1–77.

Regulation (EU) 2021/1119 of the European Parliament and of the Council of 30 June 2021 establishing the framework for achieving climate neutrality and amending Regulations (EC) No 401/2009 and (EU) 2018/1999 ('Climate Law'), OJ L 243, 9.7.2021, p. 1–17.

Ringel, M. and Knodt, M., 2018. The governance of the European Energy Union: efficiency, effectiveness and acceptance of the Winter Package 2016. *Energy Policy*, 112, pp. 209–220.

Rogge, K. S., and Schleich, J., 2018. Do policy mix characteristics matter for low-carbon innovation? A survey-based exploration of renewable power generation technologies in Germany. *Research Policy*, 47, pp. 1639–1654.

Rosenow, J., Fawcett, T., Eyre, N., Oikonomou, V., 2018. Energy efficiency and the policy mix. In: R. Lorch et al., eds., 2018. *Building governance and climate change: regulation and related policies*. London and New York, NY: Routledge, pp. 89–101.

Szulecki, K., Fischer, S., Gullberg, A. T. and Sartor, O., 2016. Shaping the 'Energy Union': between national positions and governance innovation in EU energy and climate policy. *Climate Policy*, 16(5), pp. 548–567.

Szyszczak, E., 2006. Experimental Governance: The Open Method of Coordination. *European Law Journal*, 12(4), pp. 486–502.

Talus, K. and Aalto, P., 2017. Competences in EU energy policy. In: J. Wouters and R. Leal-Arcas, eds., 2017. *Research handbook on EU energy law and* policy. Cheltenham: Edward Elgar Publishing, pp. 15–29.

Vandendriessche, M., Saz-Carranza, A. and Glachant, J.-M., 2017. The governance of the EU's Energy Union: bridging the gap? *EUI Working Paper* RSCAS 2017/51.

von Homeyer, I., Oberthür, S. & Jordan, A. J., 2021. EU climate and energy governance in times of crisis: towards a new agenda. *Journal of European Public Policy*, 28(7), pp. 959–979.

James W. Coleman

The Low-Carbon Transition in North America

Abstract: North America will be at the heart of the global low-carbon transition and the governance challenges it will bring to the fore. The United States is the world's biggest economy and the biggest producer and consumer of both oil and gas. Canada is also a top five producer of both oil and gas. And these two countries have the fastest growing populations in the G-8 so they are a key testing ground for the crucial global question of how to provide energy for a growing population while achieving a transition to cleaner energy sources such as renewable power. Mexico also is a petroleum powerhouse with a growing population but inconsistent policies have thus far frustrated efforts to better coordinate markets and policies across North America. This chapter will unravel the tangled multi-jurisdictional energy policy struggle unfolding across these three federal republics and explore how these countries can manage their resource wealth to help clean up the energy system in North America and in the increasing number of countries reliant on North American natural gas exports.

1 Introduction

North America will be at the heart of the global low-carbon transition and the governance challenges it will bring to the fore. The United States is the world's biggest economy and the biggest producer and consumer of both oil and gas. Canada is also a top five producer of both oil and gas. And these two countries have the fastest growing populations in the G-8 so they are a key testing ground for the crucial global question of how to provide energy for a growing population while achieving a transition to cleaner energy sources such as renewable power. Mexico also is a petroleum powerhouse with a growing population but inconsistent policies that have thus far frustrated efforts to better coordinate markets and policies across North America (Anglés-Hernández and Valenzuela, in this volume). This chapter will unravel the tangled multi-jurisdictional energy policy struggle unfolding across these three federal republics and explore how these countries can manage their resource wealth to help clean up the energy system in North America and in the increasing number of countries reliant on North American natural gas exports.

James W. Coleman is Professor of Law, Southern Methodist University, Dedman School of Law.

https://doi.org/10.1515/9783110752403-027

2 Oil & Renewable Energy Booms & The Rebirth of North America Energy Exports

North American energy was the historic drive of the modern global economy and in recent years, increased production of oil and gas has made the continent again the center of global energy flows. At the same time, North America's growing production of renewable energy has made it a model for the global transition to clean energy sources. And its growing population and economy has made it a crucial model for developing countries around the world looking to expand prosperity and energy access at the same time that they address the environmental and climate costs of energy.

The modern oil industry began with the discovery of oil in Texas and rise of the internal combustion engine at the beginning of the previous Century (Coleman 2020). This oil boom made globalization possible because oil's energy density made it the fuel you could carry with you, enabling growing international shipping and soon powering growing international aviation.

The early decades of the oil industry were dominated by North America. The United States dominated oil production for the first half of the Twentieth Century, at times producing over two thirds of world oil. Mexico was the world's second largest producer for years after World War I, although it fell back after the 1938 expropriation of its oil fields, which strained relationships between the United States and Mexico. Canada also became a significant oil producer after the 1914 discovery of oil in the Turner Valley in Western Canada.

All three countries remained important oil producers through the second half of the Twentieth Century and the United States and Canada became leading producers of natural gas as well. Natural gas is much more expensive to transport and store than oil because it is more voluminous and can easily escape to the atmosphere. But it burns much more cleanly and efficiently than oil, making it a natural choice for power plants in urban areas and use in home heating and appliances. So the industry in both countries spent billions building millions of miles of airtight pipelines crisscrossing the continent and delivering natural gas from oil and gas fields to homes, businesses, and power plants around the country.

United States oil production, however, fell after 1970, as the world's oil center of gravity shifted to growing production in the Soviet Union and Middle East. Oil production kept rising in Canada and growing oil exports from Canada and Mexico fueled the United States booming economy and its huge refining centers in the Midwest and on the Gulf Coast. But the United States inevitably was forced to import increasing volumes from overseas, especially from Venezuela and the booming oil producers in the Middle East. As the Twentieth Century came to a close, the United States also began importing more and more natural gas from Canadian pipelines.

Thus, North America, and the United States in particular, entered the Twenty-first Century as a major energy importer, driving global oil production. But the last two decades have seen a dramatic reversal as successive booms of unconventional oil and gas resources in the United States and Canada have made North America a crucial source of energy exports to support economic growth across the globe. In 2003, Canada proved that it could economically extract oil from its vast reserves of oil sands in Western Canada, beginning a steady expansion of heavy oil production (Coleman, 2014). In 2006, the United States production of natural gas began a continuing rise as new hydraulic fracturing techniques unlocked production from shale gas resources. The same techniques were extended regions with shale oil, inaugurating a decade-long oil boom in 2009. Oil production grew in spurts, rising as much as 2 million barrels per day in one twelve-month period – the biggest oil boom in world history (Coleman, 2020).

Two decades of booming oil and gas production have made North America a center of oil production for the global economy. In 2015, Congress and the President removed severe restrictions on US oil exports that had been in place since 1975 (Congressional Research Service, 2019). For the decade preceding 2020, the United States accounted for two of every three barrels of oil added to global supply (Johnston, 2022). Although Mexico's production has been steadily declining over the past decade (Garcia Sanchez, 2018), Canada's more significant oil production has steadily increased, roughly tripling from 1991 to 2019 (Canada Energy Regulator, 2022).

As US natural gas production increased, it began exporting more and more around the world. First, it built pipelines to carry natural gas to Mexico, then in 2016, it began operating liquefied natural gas (LNG) facilities to refrigerate natural gas most of the way down to absolute zero to turn it into a liquid and reduce its volume so it can be shipped overseas to countries in need of natural gas. In just five years, the United States became the world's number one source of liquefied natural gas to world markets.

At the same time, renewable energy production has boomed in both Canada and the United States. For decades, hydropower has provided the majority of Canadian electricity. Although many of the first electrification projects in the United States were hydroelectric, hydropower has now been overtaken by solar and wind power, which are rapidly becoming cheaper.

Even without subsidies, solar and wind power are now the cheapest source of electricity over large swaths of North America (Coleman, 2019). In 2021, renewable sources – hydropower, solar, and wind – surpassed both coal power and nuclear power to become 21% of the US electricity mix and its second largest source of electricity after natural gas, which represents 40% of the US mix (US Energy Info. Admin., 2022). The US Energy Information Administration projects that the majority of new electric generation capacity additions will also come from renewable energy and that renewable energy will surpass natural gas by 2050 and make up 42% of US electric generation.

Canada also has been adding further renewable energy to its grid and projects significantly more wind power production in the future (Canada Energy Regulator

2022). Mexico, by contrast, is not increasing its renewable production, although there are many opportunities for further production, particularly if it is able to forge more links with US electricity markets seeking more renewable energy (Garcia Sanchez & Coleman, 2022). Finally, both Canada and the United States are significantly increasing their sales of electric vehicles (Kohn et al., 2022).

3 Growing Legal Challenges to Cleaner Energy Infrastructure and Energy Integration

Although North American energy production and trade has continued to increase, in the most recent decades increasing legal challenges have faced plans to build infrastructure to help these new energy sources reach consumers in North America and abroad. In particular, linear infrastructure such as oil and gas pipelines, and power-lines for electricity have faced increasing challenges in gaining permits, surviving environmental review, and using eminent domain for construction. This has created bottlenecks to bringing cleaner energy sources to market, which are key obstacles to further deployment of clean energy in North America.

One challenge has been securing construction permits from national and subnational regulators. In the United States, construction of both power-lines and oil pipelines is primarily regulated by the states. By contrast, interstate natural gas pipelines are approved by the federal government under the Natural Gas Act (Coleman, 2019). But, in recent years, states have found new ways to block federally-approved gas pipelines using state Water Quality Certifications required by Section 401 of the Clean Water Act. States have begun denying these certifications for broader reasons and, although the Environmental Protection Agency adopted regulations to focus and speed these reviews in 2020, it changed its mind and proposed rolling back those changes in June 2022.

Similarly, the federal government has found new ways to block state-approved oil pipelines and power-lines. For example, the Dakota Access Pipeline was approved by the four states whose approval it required but, in 2016, the federal government asserted that it would need to conduct a full National Environmental Policy Act environmental impact statement for the project even though the government had concluded it had no significant environmental impacts (Coleman, 2017). This step was very significant because the federal governments sole role in reviewing interstate pipelines is approving their crossing of federal waters. In that limited role, the federal government has typically concluded that a full environmental review is not required; those reviews take over five years on average. Federal courts have also required full environmental impact statements for power-lines approved by state siting authorities (Salzman & Ruhl 2020; Coleman, 2019).

Furthermore, international energy transport projects generally need approval from both national governments, even projects such as power-lines and oil pipelines that are generally regulated by the states. (Coleman, 2018). The fate of the Keystone XL pipeline proposal – permit denied twice under President Obama, approved under President Trump, then revoked under President Biden – illustrates the challenge of securing a steady course of approval from even one jurisdiction. This challenge is equally applicable to new renewable energy projects such as the Plains & Eastern Clean Line, designed to carry wind energy from Oklahoma to Tennessee, which was supported by the federal government during the Obama administration but then shelved at the beginning of the Trump administration (Gold, 2019). Renewable energy projects in Mexico, promoted by the Mexican Energy Reform of 2015, are now opposed by the current President, Andres Manuel Lopez Obrador, who took office in 2018 (Farmer, 2020).

Canada and Mexico both have somewhat more federalized procedures for approving energy transport projects but are nonetheless facing growing permitting challenges for pipeline and power-line projects. For example, Canada has not been able to build sufficient interprovincial power-lines to support growing use of renewable power, with famous roadblocks such as one province refusing to transport hydropower from another and repeated US rejection of power-lines designed to export hydropower to the US northeast (Van de Biezenbos, 2022). In Mexico, federal policies in favor of further renewable electricity have run into opposition from Indigenous communities concerned that such projects could transform their traditional territories (Martinez, 2020). These challenges are particularly important given the substantial transmission upgrades that will be necessary to support expanded renewable energy in Mexico.

At times, ongoing energy trade has been threatened by subnational actors. During the 2021 winter storm in Texas, Governor Abbott purported to forbid contracted exports of natural gas that had not been first offered to Texas companies. This was particularly dangerous given Mexico's dependence on the United States for 94% of the natural gas imports that ensure reliable electricity from its power grid (Garcia Sanchez & Coleman, 2022). A similar subnational challenge by the state of Michigan is currently threatening the Line 5 project that carries oil from western Canada, through the United States, to eastern Canada (Van de Biezenbos & Coleman, 2021).

As a result, energy transport project investors increasingly need support from both federal and state policymakers and the number of veto gates for these projects is increasing, raising the risk of investment in new energy transport (Coleman, 2021). As challenging as these hurdles are for traditional energy sources, they present disproportionate challenges to clean energy for two reasons.

First, a sustainable transition requires first building out new sources of energy and then replacing traditional energy sources such as oil and coal. New roadblocks to energy transport primarily constrain those new sources of energy, making it harder to displace long-established transport routes for traditional energy. For example, well over half of United States crude oil pipelines were built before 1970, before the National Environmental Policy Act was enacted, and thus before the advent of modern environmental review (Sider, 2016). In fact, the modern network of national oil pipelines was motivated in part by the need to protect oil transport from German submarines in World War II; remarkably, the pipelines such as the Big Inch and Little Inch oil pipelines that were built as an emergency matter during the war are still in service to this day (Klass & Meinhardt, 2015).

Second, cleaner sources of energy are far more dependent on long-distance linear infrastructure than traditional sources of energy. Coal and oil can be transported by tanker, barge, truck, or rail, and oil can also be sent by pipeline. Natural gas, by contrast, generally must be shipped by airtight steel pipelines and is only sent overseas if it can be cooled most of the way to absolute zero at a multi-billion-dollar liquefaction facility and then loaded on to a quarter billion dollar refrigerated vessel so it can be brought to markets in Europe and Asia. Electricity is even more infrastructure dependent because it can only be shipped by powerline (Coleman, 2019). As a result, renewable energy projects often end up waiting months or even years for approval to connect with transmission to bring their product to market (Salzman & Ruhl, 2020).

4 Policy Initiatives Toward an Integrated North America Clean Energy Powerhouse

North America's simultaneous energy booms, energy exports, and growing economies mean it will play a crucial role in the world's energy future and in determining the pace and feasibility of the clean energy transition. To make North America a clean energy powerhouse, it must build infrastructure to enable clean energy sources, gradually support a transition to those sources, and leverage its energy trade to assist other countries in achieving their clean energy transition.

The most urgent challenge is reforming permitting to make it easier to build the linear infrastructure that is required for the energy transition. The United States government has begun to take some steps ease roadblocks for energy transport. The bipartisan 2021 Infrastructure Investment and Jobs Act gives the Federal Energy Regulatory Commission (FERC) backstop authority to approve electric transmission over the objection of the states in National Interest Electric Transmission Corridors chosen by the Department of Energy. The Department of Energy has issued a notice of intent to begin this process (US Department of Energy, 2022). FERC is also currently taking steps to speed up interconnections of new renewable projects with the electric grid (FERC, 2022). The crucial state of California has created a new review pathway just for projects supporting clean energy that promises to have them finish both permitting and judicial review in a matter of months (Mudge *et al.*, 2022). Further suggested reforms could involve reducing national permitting requirements and limiting state and local roadblocks to energy projects (Salzman & Ruhl, 2020; Coleman, 2019; Van de Biezenbos, 2022).

A continuing challenge is finding the correct instrument to promote cleaner energy sources or restrain carbon emitting sources of energy. Canada has implemented a nationwide carbon price that is implemented in each province by its own choice of cap-&-trade or carbon tax systems (Snoddon, 2022). The federal government in the United States has largely confined itself to subsidies for wind and solar power, rather than penalizing carbon emissions, whereas the states have taken a wide range of approaches from cap-and-trade, to bans on new coal power, to renewable portfolio standards that set a required percentage of renewable electricity (Coleman, 2014). It is unclear what direction Mexico will take with President Obrador deeply skeptical of market mechanisms such as cap-and-trade and carbon taxes and also wary of raising fuel prices (Lucatello, 2022).

The final question is how the continent, and especially key energy exporters such as the United States and Canada can leverage their trade relationships to aid cleaner energy supplies. Coal is still the world's largest source of electricity, so growing United States exports of natural gas may help other countries substantially reduce their greenhouse gas emissions and clean their air by replacing coal with natural gas power – the same trade that has allowed the United States to significantly cut pollution from its electricity sector (Kasumu et al., 2018). The full environmental footprint of these natural gas exports, however, can be substantially improved by reducing greenhouse gas emissions throughout the gas supply chain, especially wasteful emissions from flaring, leaking, and venting methane (Coleman, 2021). Even within the continent, there are substantial opportunities for cooperation in enabling the energy transition. Because renewable energy is weather-dependent, it often is most valuable if it can be shipped from resource-rich areas to urban centers that can be in another country. For example, Montana ships wind energy north to populations in Canada and Mexico might be well-served by sending wind power in Tamaulipas north to Texas (Klass, 2013; Garcia Sanchez & Coleman, 2022).

References

Adebola S., Kasumu, V.L., Coleman, J.W. et al., 2018. Country-level life cycle assessment of greenhouse gas emissions from liquefied natural gas trade for electricity generation. *Environ. Sci. Technol.*, 52(4), pp. 1735–1746.

Canada Energy Regulator, *Canadian crude oil exports: a 30 year review.* https://www.cer-rec.gc.ca/en/data-analysis/energy-commodities/crude-oil-petroleum-products/report/canadian-crude-oil-exports-30-year-review/index.html

Coleman, J.W., 2014. Importing energy, exporting regulation. *Fordham L. Rev.*, 83, pp. 1357–1399.

Coleman, J.W., 2017. Policymaking by proposal: how agencies are transforming industry investment long before rules can be tested in Court. *Geo. Mason L. Rev.*, 24, pp. 497–532.

Coleman, J.W., 2018. Beyond the pipeline wars: reforming environmental assessment of energy transport. *Utah L. Rev.*, pp. 119–167.

Coleman, J.W., 2019. Pipelines & power-lines: building the energy transport future. *Ohio St. L.J.*, 80, pp. 263–307.

Coleman, J.W., 2021. State energy cartels. *Cardozo L. Rev.*, 42, pp. 2233–2280.

Coleman, J.W., 2021. The jurisdictional anticommons. In: *Getting to yes on linear infrastructure projects*. Macdonald-Laurier Institute. https://perma.cc/Q4UT-F68Y

Congressional Research Service, 2019. The world oil market and U.S. policy: background and select issues for Congress. Apr. 23.

Farmer, M., Mexico's fight against renewable energy: the story so far. *Power Technology*, Sep. 9, 2020. https://www.power-technology.com/analysis/mexico-renewable-energy-fight-state-power-company-andres-manuel-lopez-obrador-pemex-cfe-cenace-legal-block-investment-greenpeace/

Gold, R., 2019. *Superpower: one man's quest to transform American energy*. New York, NY et al.: Simon & Schuster.

Johnston, R., 2022. Shale struggles, May 10. https://www.commoditycontext.com/p/shale-struggles

Klass, A.B. and Meinhardt, D., 2015. Transporting oil and gas: U.S. infrastructure challenges. *Iowa L. Rev.*, 100, pp. 947–1053.

Klass, A.B., Takings and transmission. *N.C. L. Rev.*, 91, pp. 1079–1160.

Kohn, E., Huang, C., Kong, N. and Hardman, S., 2022. Electric vehicle incentives in 15 leading electric vehicle markets. Institute of Transportation Studies University of California, Davis (January 2022) https://escholarship.org/content/qt0tn2p4x6/qt0tn2p4x6.pdf

Lucatello, S., 2022. *Towards an emissions trading system in Mexico: rationale, design and connections with the global climate agenda*. Cham: Springer.

Martinez, N., 2020. Resisting renewables: the energy epistemics of social opposition in Mexico. *Energy Res. & Soc. Sci.*, 70, 101632.

Mudge, A.E., Weiner, P.H. and Hull, R.C., 2022. California opens new permitting pathway for renewable energy projects, https://www.coxcastle.com/news-and-publications/2022/california-opens-new-permitting-pathway-for-renewable-energy-projects (July 2022).

Ruhl, J. B. and Salzman, J., 2020. What happens when the Green New Deal meets the Old Green Laws?. *VT. L. Rev.*, 44, pp. 693–721.

Sanchez, G.J.G. and Coleman, J.W., 2021. North American energy in the crossfire. (November 18, 2021) https://ssrn.com/abstract=3966733

Sanchez, G.J.G., 2018. The fine print of the Mexican energy reform. In: D. Wood, ed., 2018. *Mexico's new energy reform*. Washington, DC: Wilson Center Mexican Institute, pp. 36–52.

Sider, A., 2016. More than half of U.S. pipelines are at least 46 years old. Wall Street Journal, Nov. 2. https://www.wsj.com/articles/aging-pipelines-raise-concerns-1478128942

Snoddon, T., 2022. Policy Forum: carbon taxes and fiscal federalism in Canada – A new wrinkle to an old problem. *Canadian Tax Journal*, 70, 73–95.

U.S. Department of Energy, 2022. *Building a better Grid Initiative to upgrade and expand the Nation's electric transmission grid to support resilience, reliability, and decarbonization*. 87 *Fed. Reg.* 2769 (Jan. 19).

U.S. Energy Info. Admin, 2022. *Annual Energy Outlook 2021*. https://www.eia.gov/outlooks/aeo/pdf/AEO_Narrative_2021.pdf

U.S. Environmental Protection Agency, 2022. *Clean Water Act Section 401 Water Quality Certification Improvement Rule*. 87 *Fed. Reg.* 35318 (June 9).

U.S. Federal Energy Regulatory Commission, 2022. Improvements to Generator Interconnection Procedures and Agreements. 179 FERC ¶ 61,194.

van de Biezenbos, K. and Coleman, J.W. A 40-year-old Treaty could save Line 5, C.D. Howe, https://www.cdhowe.org/intelligence-memos/van-de-biezenbos-coleman---40-year-old-treaty-could-save-line-5 .

van de Biezenbos, K., 2022. Lost in transmission: a constitutional approach to achieving a nationwide net zero electricity system. *Osgoode Hall Law Journal*, 59(3), pp. 629–666.
Viscidi, L., Mexico's renewable energy future in Mexico's new energy reform. In: D. Wood, ed., 2018. *Mexico's new energy reform*. Washington, DC: Wilson Center Mexican Institute, pp. 146–163.

Isabella Bellera Landa, Blair Trahan, Ashley Otilia Nemeth

Legal Pathways to Decarbonization in Latin America

Abstract: Countries and relevant stakeholders around the world are looking to implement new legislative schemes to address the climate crisis and comply with the Paris Climate Agreement. Latin America has formed part of this trend, with States, multilateral organizations, and think tanks implementing or proposing legal paths to promote decarbonization. This chapter discusses the current state of such legal schemes and proposals through specific examples at the national and multilateral level. The chapter also discusses what the authors perceive as challenges to such efforts in the region, including: the significant impact that the COVID-19 pandemic has had in the region; how that will affect plans for sustainable recovery; and legal hurdles that may affect investors' incentives to develop clean energy projects in Latin America. Another important consideration will be the role that international investment treaties may have. This issue is of critical importance for Latin America as countries in the region have faced the majority of international claims since the enactment of the ICSID Convention; a statistic that some detractors to the investment law system have argued could lead to a "regulatory chilling effect." Nevertheless, investment treaties can be an incentive for states to plan policies and legislation thoughtfully that can meet climate goals while simultaneously respecting the rights of existing investments impacted by the transition.

1 Introduction: Decarbonization and Energy in Latin America

Latin America is a region of vast energy sources, including the world's second-largest oil reserves outside of the Middle East (Tissot, 2020: p. 5). Currently, Latin America is

---

Note: Any views expressed in this publication are strictly those of the authors and should not be attributed in any way to White & Case LLP. White & Case means the international legal practice comprising White & Case LLP, a New York State registered limited liability partnership, White & Case LLP, a limited liability partnership incorporated under English law, and all other affiliated partnerships, companies, and entities. This paper is prepared for the general information of interested persons. It is not, and does not attempt to be, comprehensive in nature. Due to the general nature of its content, it should not be regarded as legal advice.

Isabella Bellera Landa is an Associate at White & Case LLP, Washington, D.C., United States.
Blair Trahan is an Associate at White & Case LLP, Washington, D.C., United States.
Ashley O. Nemeth is an Associate at White & Case LLP, Washington, D.C., United States.

https://doi.org/10.1515/9783110752403-028

– collectively – energy self-sufficient, and predominately relies on fossil fuel resources, with coal, natural gas, and oil comprising approximately two-thirds of the total energy supply in the region (International Energy Agency, 2019; Tissot, 2020: p. 31).[1] While Latin America's energy consumption per capita remains below the global average, the region's population is projected to grow by more than 70 million people by 2050. Living standards in the region are also expected to increase in tandem with population growth, therefore increasing projected energy needs and energy-related CO_2 emissions (International Renewable Energy Agency, 2020, p. 42–43; Investopedia, et al., 2022); Mactrotrends, 2022). Nevertheless, commentators agree that Latin America has "all the right conditions to become a global renewable energy hub" and has important resources and advantages that make it an attractive place for energy generation activities (Economic Commission for Latin America and the Caribbean, 2021). Latin America has significant untapped resources for wind, solar, biomass, and hydro generation (FS-UNEP Collaborating Centre for Climate & Sustainability Energy Finance, 2020, p. 49–50; International Energy Agency, 2021, p. 10). Indeed, as indicated by the Inter-American Development Bank ("IDB"), a combination of solar, wind, marine, geothermal, and biomass nominal peak energy capacity from Latin America would be enough to power global electricity demand "several times over." Vergara, et al., 2013, p. 9).

Moreover, certain jurisdictions have implemented policies aimed at promoting investment and fostering local expertise, which have attracted the participation of international developers and lenders (FS-UNEP Collaborating Centre for Climate & Sustainability Energy Finance, 2020, p. 49–50; Leal and Miranda, 2022, p. 4). Indeed, leading up to the COVID-19 pandemic, the region had been experiencing significant growth in renewable energy capacity investment. Between 2010 and 2015, renewable power generation investments in Latin America rose to nearly US $120 million, with hydropower and biomass representing the largest sources (International Renewable Energy Agency, 2019). By 2021, several countries in the region were among the top 40 most attractive markets in the world for renewable energy investment and deployment opportunities (Ernst & Young, 2021).

As will be discussed in the following sections, the COVID-19 pandemic has negatively impacted the development of renewable energy infrastructure in Latin America. Despite the recent setback, however, Latin America's renewable capacity remains vast and commentators agree that scalability in the region is both technically and economically feasible. Tapping into just 4% of the available technical potential of re-

1 The region, however, is not a monolith. For example, sources of electricity generation vary significantly by country and country-groupings. While Central America and the Caribbean rely significantly on oil for power generation, countries in the Andean Zone of South America instead depend on hydroelectricity. Nevertheless, the region is discussed as a whole for the purposes of this chapter (Tissot, 2020, p. 31).

newable energy could satisfy the projected 2050 electricity demand for the region (Vergara, et al., 2013, p. 9).

Emerging technologies also may expand the region's renewable capacity. Technologies like floating photovoltaic solar systems not only could produce electricity at greater performance rates than traditional solar panels, but also could reduce water evaporation and eutrophication of water bodies (Colomina, et al., 2021). In this regard, the World Bank estimates that using only 5% of the water reservoir surface in Latin America for this technology would produce gigawatts of energy, equivalent to the total installed capacity of hydroelectricity in the region (Colomina, et al., 2021).

Further, numerous Latin American governments have entered into commitments concerning decarbonization and renewable energy growth, seemingly indicating that these are important policy goals. Indeed, all Latin American countries have ratified the Paris Climate Agreement (Páez-Salgado and Westphalen, 2021, p. 448), and have submitted their first Nationally Determined Contributions ("NDCs") in accordance thereof.

The meeting in Glasgow of the Conference of the Parties ("COP26") in November 2021 resulted in significant pledges and commitments, including:

- Chile and Ecuador signed the Global Coal to Clean Power Transition Statement, thereby committing to cease all new coal investments, scale up clean power, and phase out coal entirely by 2040 (UN Climate Change Conference UK 2021, April 2021).
- Sixteen states in the region signed the One Sun Declaration, committing to creating a global framework for investing in and developing solar and wind energy (UN Climate Change Conference UK 2021, February 2021).
- Six states are now part of the PPCA, a coalition working to advance the transition from unabated coal power generation to clean energy (Powering Past Coal Alliance, 2022) and
- Five states launched the LAC Green Hydrogen Action alliance to collaborate on regulatory, financing, certification, and other strategic issues in the hopes of positioning Latin America as a global hub for hydrogen energy (Heynes, 2021).

Latin America's challenge over the next two decades will not be one of natural resources or apparent political will, but rather, one of establishing institutions and stable regulatory frameworks to implement these goals. The following subsections thus will focus on challenges and opportunities for decarbonization, with a particular focus on legal solutions that have been proposed by certain jurisdictions and multilateral institutions.

2 Challenges to Decarbonization

While most Latin American jurisdictions have taken steps towards decarbonization, challenges abound, including the ongoing impact of the COVID-19 pandemic, and the need to attract significant investments due to high levels of sovereign debt across the region.

COVID-19 Pandemic: The pandemic has taken a significant macroeconomic toll on Latin America. The region experienced its sharpest GDP contraction since 1900 (6.8%), resulting in the most severe contraction among developing regions and backtracking the progress achieved in the past decade (Economic Commission for Latin America and the Caribbean, 2021; Fastmarkets, 2021). While some economic recovery was achieved in 2021, GDP forecasts for 2022 and 2023 anticipate that Latin American GDP will expand by only 2.5% and 1.9% respectively, maintaining the region on course for what has been defined by commentators as "a lost decade" (Jelmayer, 2022; Powell and Valencia, 2022).

COVID-19 similarly impacted foreign direct investment ("FDI") inflows in the region. In 2020, FDI inflows in Latin America decreased by 35% and the total value of investment project announcements fell by 50% (Economic Commission for Latin America and the Caribbean, 2021, p. 19–20). FDI project announcements in renewable energy, in particular, decreased by US$ 5.5 billion as compared to 2019 (Economic Commission for Latin America and the Caribbean, 2021, p. 33). Public tenders and auctions, which had driven more than 80% of the current renewable capacity in the region, were also set back (Atxalandabaso, 2021). These decreased investments from both the private and public sector pose a formidable challenge to decarbonization.

While the negative effects of the pandemic could arguably be translated into an opportunity to re-allocate resources in line with international commitments on decarbonization, Latin America's recovery spending thus far casts doubt on said opportunity. In 2020, while the region allocated US$ 318 billion to stimulus and fiscal measures, it earmarked only 0.5% for projects consistent with environmental and climate goals (Economic Commission for Latin American and the Caribbean, 2021, p. 28). Spending on environmental protections has decreased steadily since 2016 and the COVID-19 pandemic has only diminished the amount of those expenditures. Indeed, in some jurisdictions such as Argentina, Brazil, Chile, Colombia, Costa Rica, the Dominican Republic, Honduras, Mexico, Peru, and Uruguay, environmental spending fell by 35% in 2020 (Economic Commission for Latin American and the Caribbean, 2021, p. 28). Experts reason that a lack of fiscal space and existing high borrowing rates are the cause of low environmental investment rates (Moloney, 2021).

Sovereign Debt Burden: In addition to the challenges created by the effects of the COVID-19 pandemic, high levels of sovereign debt further underscore the need to attract private investment to meet decarbonization goals, which is a significant challenge to some jurisdictions in the region. Indeed, Latin America has the greatest external debt burden on GDP (56.3%) and the highest external debt service in terms of exportations of goods and services (59%) than any other region (Economic Commission for Latin American and the Caribbean, 8 Jul. 2021). Such constraints do not bode well for the outstanding investments needed for achieving climate goals. A renewable energy matrix will necessitate cumulative investments of US$ 800 billion by 2050 (United Nations Environment Programme, 2019). Importantly, the workforce needed to install, operate, and maintain renewable energy capacities will not materialize on its own. States will thus have to invest in education and across economic sectors to ensure that the workforce required to successfully transition and achieve decarbonization exists across the entire value chain (IRENA, 2020, p. 101–102).

In light of these challenges, it may be necessary for Latin American states to undertake legal and regulatory actions to improve the conditions that will allow them to increase investments in renewable energy. In this regard, experts recommend the implementation of incentives and market-based mechanisms, including mapping renewable energy resources in order to develop a portfolio of financeable projects, developing financing mechanisms (such as loans, grants, guarantees, and bonds) to incentivize investment, and supporting regulatory and pricing policies that are stable, predictable, and create enough confidence to stimulate long-term investments (Vergara, et al., 2013, p. 24–25; International Renewable Energy Agency, 2020, p. 134; Salman, F., et al., 2020, p. 51).

3 Incentives and Opportunities for Decarbonization

While the challenges facing the region are significant, there also are existing incentives and opportunities to assist in overcoming them. Potential benefits of adopting decarbonization policies include: increased GDP, reduced capital investment requirements (as compared to fossil fuels) to meet projected increased demand, lower electricity costs, increased energy security, employment generation, and health benefits resulting from cleaner air, among others (United Nations Environment Programme, 2019, p. 34–47).

Electricity demand in Latin America is expected to almost triple by 2050, and will require additional capital investments to meet projected demand, irrespective of the source chosen (United Nations Environment Programme, 2019, p. 35). In Brazil alone, the energy sector is predicted to emit 25.35 percent more CO2 in 2031 than 2021 (Leal and Miranda, 2022, pg.3). A renewable energy power matrix, however, would reduce needed capital investments by US$ 283 billion by 2050, as compared to fossil fuel sources (United Nations Environment Programme, 2019, p. 35). In fact, in many parts of Latin America, the cost of generating renewable energy is already the lowest-cost source of new power generation (Vogt-Schilb, A., et al., Inter-American Development Bank, 2019, p. 10; International Labor Organization and Inter-American Development Bank, 2020, p. 32). These energy sources, along with geothermal and hydropower, which have lower capital and operational costs, have the potential to lower electricity generation costs for the entire region (United Nations Environment Programme, 2019, p. 37). Moreover, for states reliant on imported non-renewable sources, such as Chile, Costa Rica, and Uruguay, energy security could lower the risk of disruption to national economies (United Nations Environment Programme, 2019, p. 40).

In addition to a reduction in expenditures, decarbonization efforts also may result in attractive economic returns. A recent IRENA report confirms that investments in the renewable energy sector can catalyze significant growth over the next three decades (IRENA, 2020, p. 15, 16, 40, 41, 48). For instance, IRENA reports that for every dollar that is invested in Latin American renewables there is a potential return on investment between US$ 3 and US$ 8 (IRENA, 2020, p. 35). Commentators also estimate that decarbonization could generate 15 million net jobs by 2030, and over 35 million new jobs by 2050 – an increase that is critical to Latin America, a region with a rapidly expanding work-age-population (Bataille et al., 2020; United Nations Environment Programme, 2019, p. 46); Latin America Center, 2014). This population growth presents a vital opportunity to drive cross-generational economic development by investing across sectors to build-up a workforce capable of achieving a transition to renewable energy sources.

A transition to renewables also is expected to have significant impacts on the well-being of people in the region, beyond employment. Welfare improvements driven by social and environmental gains (measured by the "welfare indicator") would increase by 14.8% in Latin America (IRENA, 2020, p. 155). This increase includes sizeable improvements in education, and reductions in illness and disease caused by air pollution (IRENA, 2020, p. 156). As one study indicates, a shift to renewables in the region will help reduce urban air pollution, improve health conditions and quality of life, and avoid US$ 30 billion in the costs of illness by 2050 (IRENA, 2020, p. 124; United Nations Environment Programme, 2019, p. 45).

While the COVID-19 pandemic has been a significant challenge to decarbonization, the renewable industry has proven to be resilient. Since 2010, Latin America has accounted for approximately 17% of global renewable energy investment projects, and this share remained unchanged in 2020 despite renewable energy investment project announcements declining in the world overall (Economic Commission for Latin American and the Caribbean, 2021, p. 33). As of May 2021, the share of renewable energy projects increased to 33%, nearly matching Europe's increase of 35% (Economic Commission for Latin American and the Caribbean, 2021, p. 33). Auctions and tenders in the region have also returned in 2021 in numerous countries, including Colombia, Brazil, Chile, Peru, and Ecuador (Atxalandabaso, 2021).

In this regard, experts project that new renewable capacity installations will exceed 10GW for the first time in the region by the end of 2021 (BloombergNEF, 2021). Driven in part from pent-up demand during the pandemic, Latin America is expected to increase cumulative utility-scale wind and solar capacity by two-thirds through

2023 (BloombergNEF, 2021). What remains to be seen is whether private and public investment figures, in absolute terms, will exceed pre-pandemic figures as is needed.

Although fiscal measures during the pandemic have not fully accounted for decarbonization efforts, states are not the only relevant market player. Energy companies outside of the region continue to invest in Latin America. For example, one of 2021's most significant announcements was made by an Australian company that plans to build the world's largest green hydrogen plant in Brazil at a cost of US$ 5.4 billion (Economic Commission for Latin American and the Caribbean, 2021, p. 33). National oil companies (NOCs) have also begun to play an important role. For instance, Colombia's Ecopetrol has sought to diversify its business model with non-fossil fuel sources of revenue and has pledged to be net zero by 2050 (Palacios et al., 2021; Viscidi et al., Inter-American Development Bank, 2020, p. 15–16).

Financial institutions and sovereign financiers also are making impactful decisions for decarbonization. Major international lenders, like HSBC and Fidelity International, committed to ending funding for unabated coal at COP26.[2] When coupled with state-commitments, these promises toll the death knell for "all significant public international financing for coal powers." Such a collapse in international coal financing represents an opportunity for shifting funding into renewable energy – estimated at US$ 17.8 billion a year – which may benefit the region.

While challenges abound, the incentives and opportunities for decarbonization in Latin America are also abundant. The region has the available natural resources to transition to renewables while remaining collectively self-sufficient. What remains to be solved is the means to the decarbonization-end – a proper pathway that is mindful of the challenges awaiting the region.

4 Decarbonization in Practice

The transition to renewable energy will require significant changes in society that are not likely to result from voluntary actions alone. Regulations and policies are important tools that can wield significant influence over industry and individual behavior when formulated and implemented correctly. Latin America has achieved important progress in this respect. According to a World Bank-partnered study, "on indicators such as the legal framework for renewable energy and planning for renewable energy expansion" Latin America has scores that surpass the global average (Global Energy and Extractives Practice, 2020, p. 41). Between 2017 and 2019, Latin America was among the "fastest improving regions in the adoption of energy efficiency poli-

2 See, *End of Coal in Sight at COP26*, [press release] 4 Nov. 2021. Available at: https://unfccc.int/news/end-of-coal-in-sight-at-cop26 [Accessed 15 June 2022].

cies" and scored higher in electricity access as compared to other access-deficit regions (Global Energy and Extractives Practice, 2020, p. 31). Regulations and policies are not, however, an all-encompassing solution. Despite these average scores, Latin America's energy efficiency is below the global average and it remains dependent on fossil fuel sources (Global Energy and Extractives Practice, 2020, p. 41).[3]

There remains room for progress within legal frameworks that foster the region's transition to renewables. While Latin America's progress is often analyzed at the regional level, it is important to understand that the region is not a monolith. Decarbonization policies and progress vary markedly by country. The following subsections consider examples of the types of legal frameworks in place to support decarbonization efforts in two Latin American states: Chile and Colombia.

4.1 Chile

Chile is a high-income country with a population of 19.12 million people (World Bank, *Population Statistics*), which produces 0.01% of global emissions (Grantham Research Institute on Climate Change and the Environment). Decarbonization efforts in Chile largely began in 2004, with lawmakers exempting renewable plants from transmission fees, opening the renewable energy spot market, and guaranteeing small plants the right to be connected to the country's power grid, which in turn benefitted renewable generators (*Law No. 19.940 modifying the General Electrical Services Law (LGSE) of 1982*). Since then, numerous laws and policies have been enacted to position Chile as a regional leader in renewable energy. In 2008, certain electricity companies were mandated to sell a percentage – that gradually increases from 5% to 10% by 2024 – of their electricity from renewable sources (*Law No. 20.257 on Non-Conventional Renewable Energies*). In 2010, tax deductions were granted for solar thermal systems installed in new housing developments (*Law No. 20.365 on Tax Exemption for Solar Thermal Systems*). By 2012, further subsidies were granted to renewable energy installations to enable their access to powers lines and the grid (*Resolution 370 regulating the subsidies for power transmission lines to facilitate access to the grid for renewable energy installations*).

In 2013, a concession system was created to foster the exploration and development of geothermal energy (*Law No. 19.657 on Geothermal Energy and its Regulation by Decree 114*). One year later, in 2014, a comprehensive tax reform was enacted that brought about carbon taxes (*Law No. 20571 on environmental taxation (carbon tax)* and *Law 20.780 (tax reform implementing a green tax)*). In 2017 and 2018, reducing

3 Also see, International Energy Agency, 2022. *IEA World Energy Balances*. [online] Available at: https://www.iea.org/data-and-statistics/data-product/world-energy-statistics-and-balances [Accessed 1 July 2022] (65% of the region's total energy supply is sourced from fossil fuels).

greenhouse gas emissions became a focus of various laws–specific, energy-sector reduction targets were introduced and a long-term vision for the country's energy policies was established, which included actions plans for low emissions energy generation (*Climate Change Mitigation Plan for the Energy Sector* and *Energy Route 2018–2022*). Already a leader with the largest electric bus fleet outside of China, in 2019 Chile committed to electrify all public transport by 2040 (Bartlett, 2019). Additionally, in 2020, the National Green Hydrogen Strategy was passed, which seeks to position Chile as a global producer and exporter of hydrogen power by 2040 (*National Green Hydrogen Strategy 2020*; REN21, 2021, p. 72).

In 2020, unlike many countries in the region, Chile earmarked part of its COVID-19 Recovery resources for sustainable and green projects. (Jaramillo, 2020). Moreover, in 2021, Chile announced that it would be exceeding prior announcements and closing half of all coal fired power plants by 2025.[4] The remaining plants are expected to close by 2040 (Reyes, 2019). Chile also inaugurated the region's first concentrated solar power plant in 2021, which will power approximately 380,000 homes with renewable energy (OLADE 2021).

Chile's efforts have resulted in substantial progress in its efforts to decarbonize. The proportion of renewable sources in Chile's overall total energy supply has steadily increased in the last ten years, from 22% in 2010 to 30% in 2020, and is closely approaching the region's average proportion of 35%. Chile substantially lags behind the regional average, however, in renewable electricity generation supply sources (47% as compared to the region's 68%), demonstrating the need for further policy enactment (International Energy Agency, *Chile* and *Central & South America*).

While Chile's current policies have been deemed "insufficient" by the Climate Action Tracker,[5] its planned policies, if implemented, "would peak emissions before 2025, overachieve the 2030 NDC targets and put Chile's emissions on a declining trend slightly above the 1.5-degree compatible pathway range." Chile was also the first Latin American state to submit its Long Term Low Emissions Strategy during COP26, in accordance with the Paris Agreement. This Strategy includes over 400 actions to reduce carbon emissions, including a goal to have 80% of its power generation supplied from renewable sources by 2030. These targets are expected to become legally binding in a forthcoming law that is being drafted.

4 Moore and Azzopardi, 2021. Chile speeds up plans to close coals plants, to retire half its fleet by 2025. *S&P Global Commodity Insights*, [online] 28 April. Available at: https://www.spglobal.com/platts/en/market-insights/latest-news/electric-power/042821-chile-speeds-up-plans-to-close-coal-plants-to-retire-half-its-fleet-by-2025 [Accessed 1 July 2022].

5 The Climate Action Tracker is an "independent scientific analysis that tracks government climate action and measures it against the globally agreed Paris Agreement," produced by Climate Analytics and the New Climate Institute. Climate Action Tracker. *About.* [online] Available at: https://climateactiontracker.org/about/ [Accessed 1 July 2022].

While Chile's emissions will need to peak and decline sooner than current estimates in order to meet the Paris Climate Agreement's 1.5°C temperature limit, the country's current political dynamics suggest decarbonization will remain relevant in Chilean political discourse and policies. Both Gabriel Boric, the recently elected President, and Maria Elisa Quintero, the recently elected President of the constitutional assembly, ran on platforms committed to environmental protection and climate change action (Bonnefoy and Londoño, 2021; El Desconcierto, 2021; Galaz, 2021; Malinowski and Fuentes, 2022; Sengupta, 2022).

Unlike other countries in the region, the bulk of the work facing Chile is the execution of current planned policies, rather than the pre-requisite step of formulating and passing the underlying legal frameworks. Chile's net-zero emissions targets have been lauded by climate scientists as "a detailed methodological framework" that not only "covers all sectors and gases" but also substantiates sector-specific targets with "detailed emissions pathway analysis." (Climate Action Tracker, *Net Zero Targets: Chile*). Chile's climate change and renewable energy record of accomplishment suggests decarbonization is achievable in the country.

4.2 Colombia

Colombia is an upper middle-income country with a population of 50.89 million people (World Bank, *Population Statistics*) and produces 0.49% of global emissions (Grantham Research Institute on Climate Change and the Environment, *Overview and Context: Colombia*). Using legal instruments to promote renewable energy in Colombia largely began in 2002, through the creation of a dedicated renewable energy program, the introduction of tax exemptions for the sale of electricity from wind and biomass sources, and the declaration of non-conventional energy sources as a national priority (*Law 697 promoting the Rational and Efficient use of Energy and the Use of other Non-Conventional Energy Sources* and *Law 788/2002, establishing the Tax Reform*). By 2014, a legal and tax incentive framework was established to encourage investment in clean energy generation (*Law 1715/2014, regulating the integration and promotion of non-conventional renewable energy (FNCER)*). 2015 and 2016 brought about a renewed focus on tax mechanisms, with the introduction of additional tax benefits to promote the development of non-conventional energy sources (Adam, 2021, p. 163) and an upstream carbon tax that charges importers and producers of liquid fossil fuels (USAID, 2020, p. 60). The benefits of doing so accrued swiftly – between 2017 and 2018, the carbon tax catalyzed a reduction of fossil fuel emissions of approximately 38% (USAID, 2020, p. 60). In 2018, public institution guidelines were established to foster both low carbon development and a comprehensive management plan for climate change in the mining sector (*Law no 1931 establishing guidelines for the management of climate change* and *Comprehensive management plan for climate change in the energy mining sector*).

A slew of executive decrees and actions followed in 2019 and 2020, placing climate change, the environment, and decarbonization front and center. In 2019, a comprehensive strategy for deforestation control and forest management set out Colombia's vision for reducing deforestation to zero by 2030 – representing an important development, as deforestation-based emissions accounted for almost half of the total emissions for the country in 2014 (Climate Transparency Report 2020, *Colombia*, p. 4). That same year, taxation of electric vehicles was limited to 1% and new measures were set for the promotion of electric and zero-emissions vehicles (*Law 1964/2019 promoting the use of electric vehicles*). As a result, all major cities must have five or more public fast charging stations by 2023 irrespective of consumer demand (Climate Transparency Report 2020, *Colombia*, p. 11). By 2025, at least 30% of cars rented or purchased for official fleet and 10% of buses must be electric, with a related goal of 100% electric buses by 2035 (Climate Transparency Report 2020, *Colombia*, p. 11). Various resolutions followed, establishing frameworks to facilitate long-term contracts for photovoltaic and wind power generation projects (*Resolutions 4 0590, 4 0141 and 4 0179 on long-term contracting for electric power generation projects*). Finally, in 2019 and 2020, concurrent executive actions were passed, setting long-term objectives for low-carbon development in Colombia (*Colombian Low-Carbon Development Strategy* and *Long Term Strategy E2050*).

Despite these renewable energy efforts, Colombia remains heavily dependent on fossil fuel energy sources. While Colombia's electricity generation is cleaner than the entire region – 71% is sourced from renewables as compared to the region's 68% – the country derives 77% of its total energy supply from fossil fuels (International Energy Agency, *Colombia*). According to the Climate Action Tracker, Colombia's current policies are "insufficient" and not compatible with the Paris Climate Agreement's 1.5° C temperature limit (Climate Action Tracker, *Colombia*). Even if current planned policies are implemented, emissions are still projected to reach near 40% above the 1.5°C limit (Climate Action Tracker, *Colombia*).

Recent commitments paint a mixed picture for the future of decarbonization in Colombia. In some respects, the country is a "regional climate ambition leader," but in others, the country appears unprepared to fully part ways with fossil fuels (Herrera, et al., 2021). In 2021, for example, Colombia announced that its second NDC would aim to reduce greenhouse gas emissions by 51 percent by 2030 – representing a significant increase from its prior target of 20 percent (Maxwell, et al., 2020). Colombia has also committed to becoming carbon neutral by 2050, and it is expected to achieve 14% clean electricity by August 2022 (Herrera, et al., 2021).

At the same time, however, a new 2020 regulatory framework provided for pilot projects to explore and exploit fracking-based, non-conventional oil and gas (Climate Transparency Report 2020, p. 1). Further, the carbon intensity of Colombia's total energy source has increased by 2% since 2015 figures (International Energy Agency, *Colombia*). While renewable energy received support within Colombia's COVID-19 recovery plan, so too did coal (Climate Action Tracker, *Colombia*). Moreover, Colombia has yet to announce a clear phase-out date for coal power generation or fossil fuel vehicles (Climate Action Tracker, *Colombia, Policies & Action*).

Even so, there are indications that political appetite remains strong for decarbonization and other climate change-related initiatives. In its most recent NDC, Colombia indicated it would announce new, and presumably more ambitious, mitigation targets (Climate Action Tracker, *Colombia, Policies & Action*). Further, throughout 2021 and within various multilateral forums, former Colombian President Iván Duque called for debt-for-climate actions swaps that would allow countries like Colombia to spend on climate without affecting their overall cost of capital in international debt markets (UN News, 2020; Herrera, et al., 2021).

This suggests that Colombia is prepared to commit to climate action if provided the necessary fiscal support. Public polling also demonstrates that the Colombian people view climate action favorably. A BBC World Service poll found that an impressive 74% of Colombians, the highest of all countries surveyed, are "enthusiastic about having their governments take on a leadership role in setting ambitious targets to address climate change as quickly as possible" (Global Scan, 2021). Such support, alongside the commitments already made, may manifest the measures needed to achieve decarbonization.

Nevertheless, the future in both Colombia and Chile remains difficult to predict. At the time of writing this chapter, both countries are undergoing political changes that have created significant uncertainty regarding the legal stability of investment regimes and related energy regulatory frameworks. Colombia, for its part, has elected the first left-leaning President in Colombian history – Gustavo Petro – who has vowed to retool the Colombian economy away from fossil fuels and put a halt to exploration efforts. This promised energy transition has been met with varying skepticism as commentators warn of the difficulties the Colombian people and economy may face if said transition is not executed thoughtfully given the country's high level of dependence on oil and gas for its energy production (Fajardo, 2022). Other commentators however, predict that Petro will respect existing contracts concerning fossil fuels (The Dialogue, Latin America Advisor, 2022, p. 1, 3).

Chile, for its part, voted in a September 2022 referendum to reject a new draft Constitution that would have replaced the Constitution that has been in effect since 1980. The 388-articles-long draft Constitution was wide-ranging in substance and placed the environment, among other issues, at its core (Elliott, 2022; Propuesta Constitución Política de la República de Chile, 2022, Arts. 39, 97, 104, 106, 119.8, 184, 197, 333, Capitulo III.). The recent plebiscite rejection, caused by voters' disillusionment with the reform process and initiatives to gather support for the preparation of another draft Constitution, extends the uncertainty and unpredictability experienced by investors (Barry, 2022; Elliott, 2022). Only time will tell whether the two new administrations will deliver on energy-related campaign promises in a way that meets the Paris Climate goals while preserving the relative regulatory stability that has fostered foreign investment in their respective energy sectors.

5 Multi-lateral Efforts

As has been detailed in prior sections, decarbonization in Latin America will not only require political momentum and technical expertise, but also significant financial resources. The countries considered above paint a common picture for the region: constrained fiscal space presents a formidable challenge in achieving the systemic changes needed for carbon neutrality (Crete, 2021). External investment – be it private, bilateral, or multilateral – will be pivotal in achieving net zero emissions in Latin America. The quandary, however, is that decarbonization efforts are occurring in a Latin American context of multilateralism mistrust (Fleiss, 2021; Stuenkel, 2021). Multilateral efforts and organizations in the region will have to strategically face the challenges of nationalism and political polarization in their attempt to foster cooperation (Stuenkel, 2021). Even so, the COVID-19 pandemic may provide unexpected opportunities. The extensive need for public and external funding brought about by the pandemic not only may increase Latin American appetite for multilateralism, but also put multilateral institutions in a position to demonstrate their capacity to deliver "regional public goods" (Stuenkel, 2021). As countries begin building back their economies with sustainable development in mind, multilateral organization may prove instrumental in addressing the collective action problem that is climate change and decarbonization.

Looking at past, current, and planned decarbonization efforts of a multilateral organization in Latin America, and in particular a multilateral development bank (MDB), provides valuable insight into the role that multilateralism can play in the path to decarbonization. Regardless of the issue – be it infrastructure, climate change, social needs, etc. – MDBs "have historically played a significant role in addressing [Latin America's] main regional development challenges" (Fleiss, 2021). MDBs have supported the region throughout all of the crises it has faced since the 1980s (Fleiss, 2021). While there are 14 MDBs serving the region, the four largest MDBs account for over 95% of the development lending received in Latin America: the World Bank Group, the Inter-American Development Bank (IDB Group), the Central American Bank for Economic Integration, and the Development Bank of Latin America (Fleiss, 2021). The IDB Group, in particular, is the main multilateral creditor in Latin America and has the largest outstanding portfolio in the region as compared to other MDBs (Fleiss, 2021). In 2021 the IDB Group set a record US$ 23.4 billion in new financing approvals, commitments, and private-sector mobilizations for the region (IDB, *IDB Sets Record $23.4 Billion in 2021 Financing & Mobilization, Surpassing Prior Estimate*). The IDB Group, therefore, provides an instructive case study as to the decarbonization efforts made thus far by an active multilateral organization in the region.

The IDB Group is a relatively complex organization, comprised of the Inter-American Development bank (IDB), IDB Invest, and IDB Lab. The IDB serves governments, and both IDB Invest and IDB Lab serve the private sector (Fleiss, 2021; IDB, *Lending and Grants*). Across these three separate institutions, the IDB Group provides concessional and traditional loans, grants, guarantees, and equity investments to public and private entities, as well as regional technical cooperation programs in Latin America (IDB, *Lending and Grants*).

The IDB Group's first climate change initiative, the Sustainable Energy and Climate Change Initiative (SECCI), was launched in 2007 with the aim of "expanding investment in renewable energy and energy efficiency technologies, increasing access to international carbon finance, and the mainstreaming of adaptation to climate change into []policies and programs" (IDB, *SECCI Funds*). Since then, sustainable energy and climate change has remained a "priority area" for the IDB Group's sector work (IDB, 2009, *Annual Report 2008*; IDB, 2011, *Annual Report 2010*; IDB, 2014, *Annual Report 2013*; IDB, 2015, *Annual Report 2014*; IDB, 2021, *Annual Report 2020*). In 2008, US$ 610 million in loans and US$ 21.3 million in grants was approved for renewable energy and other SECCI projects (IDB, 2009, *Annual Report 2008*). By 2010, loans in projects related to "environmental sustainability, climate change, and sustainable energy" increased to US$ 3.6 billion, representing 27.6 percent of lending – up significantly from the proportion seen just four years prior (6.2%) (IDB, 2011, *Annual Report 2010*). In 2011, the IDB Group launched the Emerging and Sustainable Cities Initiative (ESCI) with the aim of "supporting sustainable growth in those intermediate cities in Latin America that have the potential to develop in an environmentally responsible way" (IDB, 2014, *Annual Report 2013*). By 2014, the ESCI reached 40 cities in the region, benefitting approximately 41 million people (IDB, 2015, *Annual Report 2014*) Since then, the IDB Group has continued to make significant investments in renewable energy, decarbonization, and sustainability in Latin America.

In 2015, the Climate and Clean Energy Facility doubled to US$ 100 million and has since financed two of the largest rooftop solar projects in Latin America (IDB, 2015, *IDB Expands Climate and Clean Energy Facility to Finance Energy Efficiency, Self-supply Renewables and Adaptation*). That same year, the IDB Group partnered with the Caribbean Development Bank to create a US$ 71.5 million Sustainable Energy Facility to fund renewable energy and institutional capacity projects in the Eastern Caribbean and later expanded the project with an additional US$ 85.5 million in 2018 (IDB, 2018, *IDB and CDB to expand the Sustainable Energy Facility (SEF) for the Eastern Caribbean*). The following year, the IDB supported Suriname in creating the first Electricity Act, laying the legal foundation for public energy auctions for large-scale renewable projects and a net metering system to allow customers to generate their own solar energy (Colomina, 2021). In the last five years, the IDB Group has doubled down on its commitment to renewable energy and other climate change initiatives. For example, 2018 brought about significant investments: US$ 230 million for low-carbon infrastructure in Mexico, Brazil, Peru, and Colombia (Navacerrada and Fernandez-Baca, 2022), US$ 125 million in financing for the modernization of a hydroelectric power plant in Paraguay (IDB, 2018, *IDB supports program in Paraguay to modernize the Acaray hydroelectric power plant*), US$ 130 million in financing for the modernization of the Argentine-Uruguayan binational hydroelectric power plant (IDB, 2018,

Modernization hydroelectric plant, productive and tourism competitiveness of Salto Grande), US$ 400 million in loans to boost energy efficiency in the Dominican Republic (IDB, 2018, *Dominican Republic to boost energy efficiency with IDB loan*), and a US$ 1 billion loan for the construction of the largest hydropower facility in Colombia (IDB, 2018, *IDB Invest signs largest renewable energy project in Colombia*) among others. The IDB Group provided similar commitments and financing from 2019 to 2021 (IDB, 2019, 2020, 2021 (*Guatemala*), 2021 (*Uruguay*)).

In 2021, the IDB Group's funding for climate-related projects hit a record high of US$ 4.5 billion. The IDB Group also deployed a financing structure that is expected to serve as a replicable model for the region with the aim of accelerating decarbonization. The pilot financial instrument, related to a US$125 million financing package for the construction and operation of a wind farm in Chile, involves "monetizing the displacement of greenhouse gas emissions when closing thermoelectric coal plants early and replacing them with clean technology projects" (IDB, 2021 (*Chile*)). Offsets from the wind turbines reduce loan interest payments, therefore incentivizing the early closure of two coal-fired plants. Further, the IDB Group's "current focus areas" for energy investments and its active portfolio in the sector indicate it will continue to make significant strides in helping the region achieve decarbonization.

In light of the aforementioned, it becomes evident that the IDB Group has been a powerful catalyst in the region in more than just times of crises. The IDB Groups' commitment to clean energy has produced sizeable investments and brought about some of the largest renewable power plants in the region. Even so, the Achilles heel of the case for decarbonization in Latin America remains the issue of resources. Fiscal constraints for states in the region were already at the fore prior to the costly COVID-19 pandemic that remains ongoing to date. Achieving carbon neutrality will require significant investments of all relevant market players. MDBs, and the IDB Group in particular, will continue to have an instrumental role in achieving decarbonization in Latin America.

6 Investor-State Dispute Settlement Implications

While legal policies and actions are an important tool to achieving decarbonization, they also create costs and challenges. As states change regulatory schemes and subsidies that support carbon intensive industries in order to pivot resources to renewable energy, existing investments, especially those in carbon-intensive sectors, face uncertainty. Governments thus may face a challenging balancing act between implementing legislation to meet their climate goals while simultaneously respecting the rights of investors and companies that own assets impacted by the transition (and indeed protecting themselves from risk). Finding such a balance will be top of mind for Latin American governments, as numerous countries in the region are among the list of most frequent respondent states for investment-treaty disputes. This trend has continued, with Peru facing the highest number of filed cases in 2020 (UNCTAD, 2020. *Investor–State Dispute Settlement Cases: Facts And Figures 2020*).

The two states considered above in Section II are no strangers to investment-treaty claims – Chile has received five claims and Colombia has received 17 (UNCTAD, 2020. *Investor–State Dispute Settlement Cases: Facts And Figures 2020*). Latin American states would be remiss not to consider the investment-treaty implications of the actions they take in furtherance of decarbonization. Respondent states incur, on average US$ 4.7 million in investment-treaty disputes and the average amount awarded to successful claimants is US$ 438 million (Hodgson, et al., 2021).

Nevertheless, there are ways to ensure that policies in favor of decarbonization do not result in significant litigation/arbitration risks for States, while not severely affecting investors' rights. States can learn from the experience of existing investor-state disputes to properly design policies and contracts that allow for flexibility when underlying conditions make the case for regulatory change. Proactive planning and careful contract drafting should take into account the requisite policy space a State may need in order to change fiscal and regulatory frameworks in ways that do not conflict with international investment treaties. Importantly, decarbonization efforts may be achieved where: (1) long-term policies are announced transparently and implemented with advance notice; and (2) States compensate companies for measures that negatively impact their investment (Wiwen-Nilsson, 2006). This shows that states can engage in fundamental regulatory change, without running afoul of investment treaties.

Investors' "legitimate expectations," regarding their investments and the regulatory frameworks they invest under, is an important factor for states to consider when contemplating regulatory changes that foster decarbonization. The violation of an investor's legitimate expectations has gained particular prominence in investor-state disputes as one of the key tenets of the Fair and Equitable Treatment ("FET") standard enshrined in multiple investment treaties (Potestà, 2013).

The basic argument made by investors regarding legitimate expectations and regulatory frameworks is as follows: a given regulatory framework reasonably induced the investment in question and the investor had the legitimate expectation that said regime would remain stable. Should such framework (or key provisions of it) later arbitrarily change, causing an investor to suffer damages as a result, an investor can assert claims based on the violation of its legitimate expectations protected by the FET standard. Of note, some tribunals have held that a regulatory framework specifically created to attract and retain foreign investment can give rise to legitimate expectations.

Nevertheless, notice and engagement can be a powerful tool to combat the risk of international arbitration. The emerging "global climate politics" favors decarbonization – countless nations, including the world's largest economies have announced plans for net-zero carbon emissions. Further, these announcements are often made years in advance of any actual domestic changes, at highly publicized global events like COP26. Absent specific commitments, it may be argued that with such transparent and advance notice, older fossil fuel investments no longer have legitimate expectations that the general legal frameworks that originally induced their investments will not change.

As States begin or continue to make legal changes for the inevitable carbon-neutral future, transparent and advance notice and potential engagement with investors may prove to be a helpful defense in treaty arbitration.

7 Lessons from Other Global Regions

Other chapters in this book have similarly analyzed regional experiences, including in Africa, the European Union, and the Asia-Pacific region. Latin American states would be wise to look to these regions to learn from both their progress and pitfalls on the path to decarbonization.

Similar to Latin America, many African nations have substantial renewable resources but lack the requisite finances to develop that capacity due, in large part, to significant levels of sovereign debt (Addaney & Kengi, this volume). The need for private investment in both regions is clear, but their respective postures towards said investments differ. Unlike Latin America, many African nations' current policies limit private investment in energy generation and infrastructure (Addaney & Kengi, this volume). Regional stability presents yet another point of distinction between these two regions (PSC Report, 2021) and a further reason for why Latin American states should be hesitant to adopt nationalized approaches to decarbonization. Large-scale, Western, energy purchasers inform their choices with pricing and geopolitics alike (Brown, 2022). With a reliable source of energy and solid, democratic institutions, "Latin America is singularly well-placed" to attract foreign demand for sustainable energy (Brown, 2022). Private investment will remain an important factor in achieving decarbonization locally while creating a robust sustainable export market.

The experience in the Asia-Pacific region further reminds Latin American states to factor in the need to remain nimble and flexible in future policies. As is the case in Latin America, the Asia-Pacific has a diverse group of nations with economies of vastly varying size and debt levels. One of the Asia-Pacific region's more popular decarbonization policies has been feed-in tariffs. (Zhang, this volume). These programs have led to a rapid introduction of renewable energy, but such expansions have then led to the curtailment of such policies during peak renewable generation as it occurred in Spain to the detriment of existing generators. Like the Asia-Pacific, Latin American countries looking to adopt feed-in tariffs must be proactive in embedding flexibility and foresight in their policy making to both lessen costs and ensure infrastructure can support excess energy generation.

Finally, the experience in the European Union demonstrates how multilateral organizations, like the IDB, may be uniquely placed to advance regional standards and progress. The European Union takes a regional approach in its decarbonization efforts, promulgating regulations top down, but is limited in its enforcement – largely relying on naming and shaming noncompliance (Penttinen, this volume). Multilateral organizations, through the use of investment and lending stipulations, may be able to leverage contractual obligations to foster greater regional uniformity regarding decarbonization. Importantly, investors are already discussing the importance and economic attractiveness of "regional, physical energy integration" in the form of cross-border infrastructure (Brown, 2022). Only time will tell whether multilateral organizations and investors in the Latin American region will seize this unique opportunity to coalesce the region's efforts towards decarbonization.

8 Conclusion

Latin America – like most regions today – is looking to implement new legislative policies to address the climate crisis and comply with the Paris Climate Agreement. Chief among those goals is the decarbonization of the energy industry. The current state of regulatory frameworks demonstrates that there is significant room for progress in Latin America. Challenges abound – the region has been severely impacted by the COVID-19 pandemic, the costs to decarbonize are significant, and a fresh memory reminds Latin American states that regulatory changes may produce investment-treaty claims. Importantly, however, the incentives and natural resources available for decarbonization in the region are also abundant. Further, experience demonstrates that properly designed policies, careful contract drafting, advance and transparent notice, and – where relevant – adequate compensation, can create the requisite regulatory space for states to change policies without running afoul of investment treaties. Ultimately, a proper pathway to decarbonization, that is mindful of the challenges awaiting the region and the need for multilateralism, remains possible.

References

Adam, J., 2021. Renewable Energy Arbitration in Latin America. In: Alvarez, G.M. et al., eds. 2021. *International arbitration in Latin America: Energy and natural resources disputes.* Kluwer Law International. Ch.7.

Atxalandabaso, I., 2021. How are auctions changing the solar market in Latin America? *RatedPower*, [online] 21 Oct. Available at: <https://ratedpower.com/blog/auctions-solar-market-latin-america/> [Accessed 15 June 2022].

Bartlett, J., 2019. As UN climate talks near, host Chile charges up electric transport. *Reuters*, [online] 9 October, https://www.reuters.com/article/us-climate-change-chile-transport-featur/as-un-climate-talks-near-host-chile-charges-up-electric-transport-idUSKBN1WO1LA [Accessed 23 February 2022].

Barry, E., Chile Is Trying To Shed the Last Remnants of Its Pinochet-Era Dictatorship, *Time*, [online] 5 July, https://time.com/6193719/chile-constitution-reform-boric/ [Accessed 12 July 2022]

BloombergNEF, 2021. Latin America Set for Record Wind, Solar Expansion in 2021, *BloombergNEF Blog* [online] 11 May. Available at: <https://about.bnef.com/blog/latin-america-set-for-record-wind-solar-expansion-in-2021/> [Accessed 15 June 2022]

Bonnefoy, P. and Londoño, E., 2021. Gabriel Boric, a Former Student Activist, Is Elected Chile's Youngest President. *New York Times*, [online] 20 December. Available at: https://www.nytimes.com/2021/12/19/world/americas/chile-president-election.html [Accessed 1 July 2022].

Brown, A, 2022. How Latin America can reap the benefits of the energy transition. *BNAmericas*, [online] 8 July. Available at: https://app.bnamericas.com/article/section/all/content/xkyvf7keq-how-latin-america-can-get-shiny-eggs-from-energy-transition-golden-goose [Accessed 12 July 2022].

Climate Action Tracker. *Chile.* [online] Available at: https://climateactiontracker.org/countries/chile/ [Accessed 1 July 2022].

Climate Action Tracker. *About.* [online] Available at: https://climateactiontracker.org/about/ [Accessed 1 July 2022].

Climate Action Tracker. *Net Zero Targets: Chile.* [online] Available at: https://climateactiontracker.org/countries/chile/net-zero-targets/ [Accessed: 1 July 2022].

Climate Action Tracker. *Colombia.* [online] Available at: https://climateactiontracker.org/countries/colombia/ [Accessed: 1 July 2022].

Climate Action Tracker. *Colombia, Policies & Action*. [online] Available at: https://climateactiontracker.org/countries/colombia/policies-action/ [Accessed: 1 July 2022].

Climate Transparency Report 2020. *Colombia.* [pdf] Available at: https://www.climate-transparency.org/wp-content/uploads/2021/01/Colombia-CT-2020.pdf [Accessed 1 July 2022].

Colomina, J.A., 2021. *Consolidating a Sustainable Energy Sector in Suriname*. IDB, [blog] Available at: <https://blogs.iadb.org/energia/en/consolidating-a-sustainable-energy-sector-in-suriname/> [Accessed 5 July 2022].

Colomina, J.A., et al., 2021. *It's time for solar to get its feet wet,* [online] Available at: <https://blogs.iadb.org/energia/en/its-time-for-solar-to-get-its-feet-wet/> [Accessed 15 June 2022].

COP25 Chile, 2021. *Chile Delivers Long-Term Climate Strategy to the UN Executive Secretary of Climate Change.* [online] Available at: https://cop25.mma.gob.cl/en/chile-delivers-long-term-climate-strategy-to-the-executive-secretary-of-un-climate-change/ [Accessed 1 July 2022].

Crete, E., 2021. *South American Finance Ministers Discuss Incentives and Mechanisms to Finance the Decarbonization of their Economies, Sustainable Development Solutions Network.* [online] UNSDSN. Available at: <https://www.unsdsn.org/south-american-finance-ministers-meet-to-discuss-the-decarbonization-of-their-economies> [Accessed on 2 July 2022].

Economic Commission for Latin America and the Caribbean, 2021. *Latin America and the Caribbean Has All the Right Conditions to Become a Renewable Energy Hub with Great Potential in Green Hydrogen.* [online] Available at: https://www.cepal.org/en/news/latin-america-and-caribbean-has-all-right-conditions-become-renewable-energy-hub-great [Accessed 15 June 2022].

Elliott, L., 2022, Draft Chile constitution puts environment and indigenous rights at its core, *Financial Times*, [online] 4 July. Available at: https://www.ft.com/content/25a20fc7-ae6e-4fe7-82a4-26635b3e96b8 [Accessed 12 July 2022].

Ernst & Young, 2021. *Renewable Energy Country Attractiveness Index.* [pdf] Available at: https://assets.ey.com/content/dam/ey-sites/ey-com/en_gl/topics/power-and-utilities/ey-recai-58th-edition-top-40-ranking-october-2021.pdf [Accessed on 2 July 2022].

Economic Commission for Latin America and the Caribbean, 2021. *The recovery paradox in Latin America and the Caribbean*. [pdf] Available at: <https://repositorio.cepal.org/bitstream/handle/11362/47059/4/S2100378_en.pdf> [Accessed 15 June 2022].

Economic Commission for Latin America and the Caribbean, 2021. *Foreign Direct Investment in Latin America and the Caribbean*. [pdf] Available at: <https://repositorio.cepal.org/bitstream/handle/11362/47148/4/S2100318_en.pdf> [Accessed 15 June 2022].

Economic Commission for Latin America and the Caribbean, *Growth in Latin America and the Caribbean in 2021 Will Not Manage to Reverse the Adverse Effects of the Pandemic*. [press release] 8 Jul 2021. Available at: <https://www.cepal.org/en/pressreleases/growth-latin-america-and-caribbean-2021-will-not-manage-reverse-adverse-effects> [Accessed 15 June 2022].

El Desconcierto, 2021. *Boric firma compromiso de descarbonización y el fin de las termoeléctricas en Ventanas.* [online] Available at: https://www.eldesconcierto.cl/nacional/2021/08/20/boric-firma-compromiso-de-descarbonizacion-y-el-fin-de-las-termoelectricas-en-ventanas.html [Accessed 1 July 2022].

Fajardo, L., 2022. Petro presidente: 3 ambiciosas propuestas económicas para transformar Colombia (y las dificultades que plantean). *BBC News Mundo*, 20 June. [online] Available at: https://www.bbc.com/mundo/noticias-america-latina-61861055 [Accessed: 1 July 2022].

Fastmarkets, 2021. *How Latin America lost a decade of economic progress.* [online] Available at: <https://www.fastmarkets.com/insights/how-latin-america-lost-a-decade-of-economic-progress> [Accessed: 1 July 2022].

Fleiss, P., 2021. *Multilateral development banks in Latin America*. [pdf] p. 8, 9, 14, Economic Commission for Latin America and the Caribbean (ECLAC). Available at: <https://repositorio.cepal.org/bitstream/handle/11362/46916/1/S2100262_en.pdf> [Accessed on 2 July 2022].

FS-UNEP Collaborating Centre for Climate & Sustainability Energy Finance, 2020. *Global Trends in Renewable Energy Investment.* [pdf] Available at: <https://www.fs-unep-centre.org/wp-content/uploads/2020/06/GTR_2020.pdf> [Accessed 15 June 2022] (showing that Latin America and the Caribbean as a region has raised renewable energy capacity investment by 43%).

Galaz, F.P., 2021. Chile's presidential candidates and their environmental plans. *Diálogo Chino,* [online] 3 September. Available at: https://dialogochino.net/en/climate-energy/45926-chile-presidential-candidates-environment/ [Accessed 1 July 2022].

Global Energy and Extractives Practice, World Bank Group, 2020. *RISE 2020, Regulatory Indicators for Sustainable Energy: Sustaining the Momentum.* [pdf] Available at: https://rise.esmap.org/data/files/reports/2020-full-report/RiseReport-010421.pdf [Accessed 23 February 2022].

Grantham Research Institute on Climate Change and the Environment. *Overview and Context: Chile.* [online] Available at: https://climate-laws.org/geographies/chile [Accessed 1 July 2022].

Grantham Research Institute on Climate Change and the Environment. *Overview and Context: Colombia.* [online] Available at: https://climate-laws.org/geographies/colombia [Accessed: 1 July 2022].

Global Scan, 2021. New Global Poll ahead of COP26 in Glasgow Shows Growing Support for Governments to Take Strong Action on Climate Change. *Globe Scan*, 21 October. [online] Available at: https://globescan.com/2021/10/27/global-poll-cop26-growing-support-governments-take-strong-action-climate-change/ [Accessed: 23 February 2022].

Heynes, G., 2021. *LAC Green hydrogen alliance to be established to accelerate green hydrogen adoption in Latin America*. [online] Available at: https://www.h2-view.com/story/lac-green-hydrogen-alliance-to-be-established-to-accelerate-green-hydrogen-adoption-in-latin-america/ [Accessed 15 June 2020].

Herrera, C, et al., 2021. Latin America at the Leaders Summit on Climate. *NRDC*, [blog] 23 April. Available at: https://www.nrdc.org/experts/carolina-herrera/latin-america-leaders-summit-climate [Accessed: 1 July 2022].

Hodgson, M., Kryvoi, Y., Hrcka, D., 2021. 2021 Empirical Study: Costs, Damages and Duration in Investor-State Arbitration. *British Institute of International and Comparative Law*, [e-journal] pp. 4–5. Available at: <https://www.biicl.org/documents/136_isds-costs-damages-duration_june_2021.pdf> [Accessed 5 July 2022].

IDB, *Lending and Grants*. [online] Available through: IDB website <https://www.iadb.org/en/fin> [Accessed on 5 July 2022].

International Energy Agency, 2022. *IEA World Energy Balances*. [online] Available at: https://www.iea.org/data-and-statistics/data-product/world-energy-statistics-and-balances [Accessed 1 July 2022].

International Energy Agency (IEA), 2019. *Central & South America*. [online] Available at: <https://www.iea.org/regions/central-south-america> [Accessed 15 June 2022].

International Energy Agency (IEA), 2021. *Hydrogen in Latin America*. [pdf] Available at: https://www.iea.org/reports/hydrogen-in-latin-america [Accessed 23 June 2022].

International Renewable Energy Agency (IRENA), 2019. *Regional Action Plan: Accelerating Renewable Energy Deployment in Latin America*. [pdf] Available at: https://www.irena.org/-/media/Files/IRENA/Agency/Regional-Group/Latin-America-and-the Caribbean/IRENA_LatAm_action_plan_2019_EN.PDF?la=en&hash=12D7D12BF816911D9ED12AFEA0F34E73258B18F2 [Accessed 15 June 2022].

International Renewable Energy Agency (IRENA), 2020. *Global Renewables Outlook 2020*. [pdf] Available at: <https://www.irena.org/-/media/Files/IRENA/Agency/Publication/2020/Apr/IRENA_Global_Renewables_Outlook_2020.pdf> [Accessed 15 June 2022].

International Energy Agency. *Chile*. [online] Available at: https://www.iea.org/countries/chile/ [Accessed 1 July 2022] (spreadsheet on file with authors demonstrating proportion calculated using IEA source data).

International Energy Agency. *Central & South America*. [online] Available at: https://www.iea.org/regions/central-south-america [Accessed 1 July 2022] (spreadsheet on file with authors demonstrating proportion calculated using IEA source data).

Inter-American Development Bank (IDB), 2022. *IDB Sets Record $23.4 Billion in 2021 Financing & Mobilization, Surpassing Prior Estimate*. [Online] 1 February. Available at: <http://iadb.org/en/news/idb-sets-record-234-billion-2021-financing-mobilization-surpassing-prior-estimate> [Accessed on 5 July 2022].

IDB. *Lending and Grants*. [online] Available through: IDB website <https://www.iadb.org/en/fin> [Accessed on 5 July 2022].

IDB. *SECCI Funds*. [online] Available at: <https://www.iadb.org/en/climate-change/secci-funds> [Accessed on 5 July 2022].

IDB, *Inter-American Development Bank Annual Report*, various years. [online] Available at: www.iadb.org .

IDB, 2015. *IDB Expands Climate and Clean Energy Facility to Finance Energy Efficiency, Self-supply Renewables and Adaptation*. [online] Available at: <https://www.iadb.org/en/news/idb-expands-climate-and-clean-energy-facility-finance-energy-efficiency-self-supply-renewables> [Accessed 5 July 2022].

IDB, 2018. *IDB and CDB to expand the Sustainable Energy Facility (SEF) for the Eastern Caribbean*. [online] Available at: <https://www.iadb.org/en/news/idb-and-cdb-expand-sustainable-energy-facility-sef-eastern-caribbean> [Accessed 5 July 2022].

IDB, 2018. *IDB supports program in Paraguay to modernize the Acaray hydroelectric power plant*. [online] Available at: <https://www.iadb.org/en/news/idb-supports-program-paraguay-modernize-acaray-hydroelectric-power-plant>[Accessed 5 July 2022].

IDB, 2018. *Modernization hydroelectric plant, productive and tourism competitiveness of Salto Grande*. [online] Available at: <https://www.iadb.org/en/news/modernization-hydroelectric-plant-productive-and-tourism-competitiveness-salto-grande> [Accessed 5 July 2022].

IDB, 2018, *Dominican Republic to boost energy efficiency with IDB loan*. [online] Available at: <https://www.iadb.org/en/news/dominican-republic-boost-energy-efficiency-idb-loan> [Accessed 5 July 2022].

IDB, 2018. *IDB Invest signs largest renewable energy project in Colombia*. [online] Available at: <https://www.iadb.org/en/news/Largest_renewable_energy_project_in_Colombia> [Accessed 5 July 2022].

IDB, 2019. *Suriname to increase the electricity coverage in rural areas with IDB support*. [online] Available at: <https://www.iadb.org/en/news/suriname-increase-electricity-coverage-rural-areas-idb-support> [Accessed 5 July 2022].

IDB, 2020. *Ecuador moves ahead in transformation of energy grid with IDB support.* [online] Available at: <https://www.iadb.org/en/news/ecuador-moves-ahead-transformation-energy-grid-idb-support> [Accessed 5 July 2022].

IDB, 2021. *Guatemala will contribute to mitigate climate change with efficient use of firewood.* [online] Available at: <https://www.iadb.org/en/news/guatemala-will-contribute-mitigate-climate-change-efficient-use-firewood> [Accessed 5 July 2022].

IDB, 2021. *IDB Invest Closes Financing for Uruguay's First Green Transmission Line, Boosts the Energy Sector.* [online] Available at: <https://www.idbinvest.org/en/news-media/idb-invest-closes-financing-uruguays-first-green-transmission-line-boosts-energy-sector> [Accessed 5 July 2022].

IDB, 2021. *IDB Invest and ENGIE Chile debut the world's first pilot project to monetize the cost of decarbonization.* [online] Available at: <https://www.idbinvest.org/en/news-media/idb-invest-and-engie-chile-debut-worlds-first-pilot-project-monetize-cost-decarbonization> [Accessed 5 July 2022].

IDB. *Energy: Sustainable, Reliable, and Diversified Energy For Latin America And The Caribbean.* [online] Available at: <https://www.iadb.org/en/sector/energy/overview> [Accessed 5 July 2022].

International Renewable Energy Agency (IRENA), 2020. *Global Renewables Outlook 2020.* [pdf] at 101-102 Available at: <https://www.irena.org/-/media/Files/IRENA/Agency/Publication/2020/Apr/IRENA_Global_Renewables_Outlook_2020.pdf> [Accessed 15 June 2022].

International Energy Agency. *Colombia.* [online] Available at: https://www.iea.org/countries/colombia/ [Accessed: 1 July 2022] (spreadsheet on file with authors demonstrating proportion calculated using IEA source data).

Jelmayer, R., 2022, World Bank reduces Latin America and Caribbean growth forecasts, *BNAmericas*, [online] 8 June. Available at: <https://app.bnamericas.com/article/section/all/content/xbj5lmbde-spotlight-world-bank-economic-forecasts-for-latin-america-and-caribbean> [Accessed 15 June 2022].

Jaramillo, C.J., 2020. A green recovery of Latin America and the Caribbean is possible and necessary. *World Bank Blogs*, [blog] 11 September. Available at: https://blogs.worldbank.org/latinamerica/green-recovery-latin-america-and-caribbean-possible-and-necessary [Accessed 1 July 2022].

Malinowski, M. and Fuentes, V., 2022. Chile Assembly That's Rewriting Constitution Taps New Leadership. *Bloomberg*, [online] 5 January. Available at: https://www.bloomberg.com/news/articles/2022-01-05/chile-assembly-that-s-rewriting-constitution-taps-new-leadership [Accessed 1 July 2022].

Maxwell, A., et al., 2020. Latin America's 2020 Climate Leaders and Laggards. *NRDC*, [blog] 21 December. Available at: https://www.nrdc.org/experts/amanda-maxwell/latin-americas-2020-climate-leaders-and-laggards [Accessed: 1 July 2022].

Macrotrends, 2022. *Latin America and The Caribbean Life Expectancy.* [online] Available at: <https://www.macrotrends.net/countries/LCR/latin-america-and-the-caribbean/life-expectancy> [Accessed 15 June 2022].

Moloney, A., 2021. Hard-hit by COVID-19, Latin America seen skimping on climate cash. *Reuters* [online] 10 June. Available at: https://www.reuters.com/article/us-latam-climate-change-coronavirus-fina/hard-hit-by-covid-19-latin-america-seen-skimping-on-climate-cash-idUSKCN2DM29E [Accessed 15 June 2022].

Nationally Determined Contributions (NDCs), United Nations Framework Convention on Climate Change, https://unfccc.int/process-and-meetings/the-paris-agreement/nationally-determined-contributions-ndcs/nationally-determined-contributions-ndcs.

Navacerrada, P., Fernandez-Baca, J., 2022. *The IDB and UK join forces to invest in sustainable infrastructure in Peru.* IDB, [blog] Available at: <https://blogs.iadb.org/energia/en/the-idb-and-uk-join-forces-to-invest-on-sustainable-infrastructure-in-peru/> [Accessed 5 July 2022].

OLADE. *Chile becomes the first country in Latin America to inaugurate a Concentrated Solar Power Plant*. [pdf] Available at: https://www.olade.org/en/noticias/chile-becomes-the-first-country-in-latin-america-to-inaugurate-a-concentrated-solar-power-plant/#:~:text=Olade%20App-,Chile%20becomes%20the%20first%20country%20in%20Latin%20America,a%20Concentrated%20Solar%20Power%20Plant&text=Cerro%20Dominador%20is%20the%20name,CSP)%20plant%20in%20Latin%20America . [Accessed 1 July 2022].

Páez-Salgado, D. and Westphalen, E., 2021. Climate Change and International Arbitration in Latin America. In: G.M. Alvarez, M. Riofrio Piché, F.V. Sperandio, eds. *International Arbitration in Latin America: Energy and Natural Resources Disputes*. Den Haag: Wolters Kluwer, pp. 447–492.

Powering Past Coal Alliance, 2022. *PPCA Members*, [online] Available at: <https://www.poweringpastcoal.org/members> [Accessed 1 July 2022].

Worldometer, *Mexico Coal*, [online] Available at: https://www.worldometers.info/coal/mexico-coal/ [Accessed 1 July 2022].

Powell, A., and Valencia, O., 2020. Avoiding a New Lost Decade for Latin America and the Caribbean, *IDB* [online] 15 Oct. Available at: <https://blogs.iadb.org/ideas-matter/en/another-lost-decade-for-latin-america-and-the-caribbean/> [Accessed 15 June 2022].

Potestà, M., 2013. Legitimate Expectations in Investment Treaty Law: Understanding the Roots and the Limits of a Controversial Concept. *ICSID Review*, 28(1) Spring (2013), pp. 88–122.

Propuesta Constitución Política de la República de Chile, 2022.

PSC Report, *African Conflicts to Watch in 2022* (Dec. 17, 2021), https://issafrica.org/pscreport/psc-insights/african-conflicts-to-watch-in-2022.

Reyes, V., 2019. Piñera confirma que las 28 termoeléctricas a carbón que hay en Chile serán cerradas antes de 2040. *Biobiochile.cl*, [online] 4 June. Available at: https://www.biobiochile.cl/noticias/economia/negocios-y-empresas/2019/06/04/pinera-confirma-que-todas-las-termoelectricas-a-carbon-que-hay-en-chile-seran-cerradas-gradualmente.shtml [Accessed 1 July 2022].

Sengupta, S., 2022. Chile Writes a New Constitution, Confronting Climate Change Head On. *New York Times*, [online] 6 January. Available at: https://www.nytimes.com/2021/12/28/climate/chile-constitution-climate-change.html [Accessed 1 July 2022].

Stuenkel O, 2021. *The Complex Task of Reviving Multilaterals in Latin America*. Americas Quarterly, [online] 1 February. Available at: <https://www.americasquarterly.org/article/the-complex-task-of-reviving-multilaterals-in-latin-america/> [Accessed on 5 July 2022].

Salman, F., et al., USAID, 2020, *Environment and Energy Landscape in Latin America and the Caribbean: An Analysis of Trends 2020–2030*. [pdf] Available at: <https://www.climatelinks.org/sites/default/files/asset/document/2021-06/PA00XCV9.pdf>.

Tissot, R., 2020, *Infrastructure and Environment Department, Latin America's Energy Future*, Inter-American Development Bank. [pdf] Available at: <https://publications.iadb.org/publications/english/document/Latin-America-Energy-Future.pdf> [Accessed 15 June 2022].

The Investopedia Team, Boyle, M.J. and Eichler, R., 2022. *Standard of Living*. [online] Available at: <https://www.investopedia.com/terms/s/standard-of-living.asp> [Accessed 15 June 2022].

The Dialogue, Latin America Advisor, 2022. What Does Petro's Plan to Decarbonize Colombia Involve? [pdf] Available at: < https://www.thedialogue.org/latin-america-advisor/> [Accessed 12 July 2022].

REN21, 2021. *Renewables 2021 Global Status Report*. [pdf] Available at: https://www.ren21.net/wp-content/uploads/2019/05/GSR2021_Full_Report.pdf [Accessed 1 July 2022].

United Nations Conference on Trade and Development, 2020. *Investor–State Dispute Settlement Cases: Facts And Figures 2020*. [pdf] p. 2, Available at: <https://unctad.org/system/files/official-document/diaepcbinf2021d7_en.pdf> [Accessed 5 July 2022].

United Nations Climate Change, Nationally Determined Contributions Registry. [online] Available at: <https://www4.unfccc.int/sites/NDCStaging/Pages/All.aspx> [Accessed 15 June 2022].

UN Climate Change Conference UK 2021, April 2021. *Global Coal to Clean Power Transition Statement*. [online] Available at: https://ukcop26.org/global-coal-to-clean-power-transition-statement/ [Accessed: 1 July 2022].

UN Climate Change Conference UK 2021, February 2021. *Green Grids Initiative – One Sun One World One Grid: One Sun Declaration*. [online] Available at: <https://ukcop26.org/one-sun-declaration-green-grids-initiative-one-sun-one-world-one-grid/> [Accessed: 1 July 2022].

UN News, 2020. Colombia calls for global financial consensus to avert COVID debt crisis. *UN News*, 21 September. [online] Available at: https://news.un.org/en/story/2021/09/1100512 [Accessed: 1 July 2022].

USAID, 2020. *Environment and Energy Landscape in Latin America and the Caribbean: An Analysis of Trends 2020–2030*. [pdf] Available at: https://www.climatelinks.org/sites/default/files/asset/document/2021-06/PA00XCV9.pdf/ [Accessed 1 July 2022].

United Nations Environment Programme, *Latin America and the Caribbean could save US$ 621 billion by 2050 through the decarbonization of energy, transport sectors*. [press release] 12 Dec. 2019. Available at: <https://www.unep.org/news-and-stories/press-release/latin-america-and-caribbean-could-save-us-621-billion-2050-through> [Accessed 15 June 2022].

Wiwen-Nilsson, T., 2006. Phasing-Out of Nuclear Power in Sweden. *Journal of Energy & Natural Resources Law*, 24, pp. 355–361.

Vergara, W., Alatorre, C. and Alves, L., Inter-American Development Bank, 2013. *Rethinking Our Energy Future*. [pdf] Available at: <https://idbdocs.iadb.org/wsdocs/getdocument.aspx?docnum=37836720> [Accessed 15 June 2022].

Part IV: **National Experiences: Introduction**

Editorial introduction

The *United Nations Framework Convention on Climate Change* envisages a global community of nations that act in consensus to reduce emissions to avoid dangerous climate change. That vision has proved hard to realise since 1992. Successive measures under the Convention have moved from common but differentiated responsibility principles in early years, economic flexibility measures under the Kyoto Protocol, and now to the Nationally Determined Contributions under the Paris Agreement 2015. These trends reflect national geopolitical imperatives, nation-state energy agendas, and enforcement difficulties around national sovereignty. Significantly, the trends also acknowledge the variability of national circumstances and the different legal pathways for decarbonisation. This is a central premise informing the research in this book. It confirms the complex legal and policy choices around energy, climate change and transition that operate in national settings. Collectively, the section charts the progress of legal and regulatory change as these nations move along the decarbonisation pathway; influenced by interactions between global drivers and national settings.

The chapters come from India, Poland, Japan, Brazil, China, Mexico and Australia, so the analyses are drawn principally from the Asia Pacific, South Asia, and Latin America, with Poland, the European Union (EU) representative. They explore national approaches that are typical national decarbonisation pathways (and the barriers) in the Global South, and in strongly emergent economies in Asia and South America. Many of these nations will play vital roles in achieving emissions reduction targets globally, and include nations with entrenched economic dependency on carbon. Setting these seven nations together to learn of their comparative experiences provides insights for designing more effective law and policy and avoiding dangerous climate change. Also, it illustrates the extent of the task to re-orient national legal and socio-economic systems to accelerate decarbonisation.

The group comprises nations such as China and India whose economic and trading power has intensified in recent decades – and which have adopted ambitious sustainability and climate change laws and policies. Shankar and Basu comment on Indian transition initiatives, wedged between global drivers of climate risk and the need for orderly transition of national laws suggesting, 'the flexibility, cost effectiveness and resilience of renewable energy are supposed to be the winners but the challenges are humongous'. The authors illustrate these challenges for legal pathways to decarbonisation indicating that with 'its National Electricity Plan in place, India exuberantly sets the ambition to achieve 275 GW of renewables by 2027. This necessitates frantic commitment to minimize the reliance on the non-clean sources of energy.' The gap between legislative and policy ambition on renewable uptake and energy transition, and its actual achievement in sectors such as electricity is a common thread across several national chapters. This chapter reveals the complexity and potential for internal inconsistencies in the national legal pathways to decarbonisation.

https://doi.org/10.1515/9783110752403-029

China too has adopted an ambitious carbon neutrality goal in its updated NDC as identified by Claire Nan Guo. Nationally, China has worked to implement a low-carbon transition with the chapter outlining key long-term strategies and development objectives, including adjustments in the regulatory systems, legal decision-making processes, legal orders, and regulation. Importantly, in its legal pathway to decarbonisation, China has introduced an Emissions Trading Scheme (ETS), piloted in 7 provinces that now has a high transactional volume- although long-term effectiveness is not fully clear. Attention to the ETS design provides valuable comparative experience for how market measures perform in a major economy. The problematic status of offset mechanisms in driving deeper decarbonisation is noted – again with parallels in other national chapters.

Japan offers an interesting contrast to the other Asian nations, given its specific energy settings emphasising energy security, with a low carbon emissions profile predicated on a high ratio of nuclear power. Yet, as Kurokawa identifies, the ramifications of the Fukushima Daiichi nuclear power plant disaster in 2011 continue to reverberate in Japan's decarbonisation pathway. As energy transition occurs in Japan, the continuity of supply in liberalised electricity markets is foregrounded. Ensuring system reliability in electricity markets with thermal plant phase-out is a theme taken up in several chapters. Achieving a balance between reliability and transition is a pressing issue in the liberalised market models that distinguish the decarbonisation experience of many national systems.

As a point of contrast, Anglés-Hernandez and Valenzuela outline how Mexico's legal framework for energy transition faces multiple challenges in seeking to promote good governance and private investment in the sector, as well as environmental protection and human rights – all while maintaining state control of the economy. In this way the Mexican chapter highlights the significant influence of government institutions on energy transition. It finds parallels with other national experiences including the state system in Poland. In federal nations such as India and Australia multilayered law and policy across jurisdictions add complexity to the implementation of energy transition laws.

Brazil too has a complex energy law and normative framework that regulates the fragmented and multiple elements of its energy sector, as described by Leal and Miranda. Brazil like many nations has a long-standing dependency on carbon-intensive sources. While such dependencies hinder decarbonisation, Brazil has unique potential to diversify its renewable sources, and it has long been seen as a model for sustainable energy. Yet the balance between energy security (gradual transformations) and climate crisis management (urgent action) in decarbonisation is delicate and requires proper planning and regulation. Brazil's regulation promotes flexibility, but energy and climate policies lack sufficient synergy, and the energy sector grows without clear priorities and mitigation goals. The lack of an overarching clear framework law to drive decarbonisation besets several nations covered here. It illustrates the difficulties of translating International goals into existing legal systems where many laws have competing policy objectives around energy sustainability, and ensuring security of supply.

Although Australia's total emissions are lower than larger economies such as China and India, its per-capita carbon footprint is inequitably high. Australia is a major of exporter of coal and LNG, largely into Asia. It has climate adaptation challenges given effects of increased extreme events are already evident. Yet until recently it had only weak NDC targets. Climate litigation sought to spur stronger government and industry action. As Godden explores, however, subnational governments have promoted regulatory models for renewable energy transition, and this is well underway in the national electricity sector. Even so, the legacy of a centralised national energy system provides barriers, such as high transmission costs. With new national climate change laws poised to take effect, internal transition will be boosted – but the geo-political ramifications of current energy shortages mean that Australia may remain a major carbon-based exporter for the foreseeable future.

The need to transcend an energy system and economy originally built on coal to institute a more sustainable energy profile is explored in the Polish chapter by Swora. Poland is at an important point of structural and legal reform. The dilemma of energy transition is captured – 'Poland as the EU Member State is obliged to implement EU laws and policies related to energy transition [...], energy transition in Poland has to take into account individual factors, related to the country's economy and historical dependence on fossil fuels.' Transition for Poland though reveals a potential for decoupling of GDP and emissions growth. Moreover, Poland is in a *just transition* where socio-economic factors are significant. The imperative of a just transition resonates across other national experience. The chapter concludes that the country has the legal framework necessary to assist policy efforts towards just transition. Major amendments to Energy law in 2021 are designed to capture technological improvements for flexibility in energy markets. The drawing together of new technologies and supporting regulation also characterises the experience of many nations.

In summary, the chapters all provide important insights into the diversity of approaches to decarbonisation pathways as each nations seeks to implement UNFCCC targets. While national diversity of decarbonisation is accepted, the chapters also reveal some commonalities in the barriers faced and the legal and regulatory models that are adopted to facilitate transition.

Lee Godden

Energy Law and Regulation in Australia

Abstract: This chapter analyses the structural transformation of the energy sector in Australia over the past decade, while noting the resistance to renewable energy transition at a national policy level under a previous conservative government. That government dismantled one of the most comprehensive but short-lived carbon pricing legislative regimes in 2014, to replace it with weak NDCs under the Paris Agreement and land sector focused (voluntary) greenhouse gas emissions reduction schemes. A new national government has introduced the Climate Change Act 2022 to statutorily embed Paris Agreement NDC targets. Even so, Australia continues to be distinguished by a dichotomy in its energy law and policy. On the one hand it is a major energy exporter – largely coal and LNG, while subnational governments have been active in legislative and policy incentives for renewable energy. South-eastern Australia has one of the highest penetrations of residential solar generation in the world. The promotion of renewable energy and more recently battery storage has been countered by a national policy insistence on energy security that favours fossil fuel generation and gas as a transition power source while holding out for the technological revolution of hydrogen. The former national policy vacuum was challenged by a proactive climate ligation strategy. This complexity is increased by a highly regulated, but largely privatised national electricity and gas markets that are governed by detailed energy market rules developed around market liberalisation, unbundling and competition agendas. These legislative objectives are being tested in an era of increasing government intervention, and the rise of decentralised energy supply. The chapter provides a prognosis of the legal measures that may enhance the prospects for rapid decarbonisation in Australia.

1 Introduction: Energy Transition – Internal and External Settings

Australia's current energy system developed from a publicly-owned, fossil fuel-dependent foundation in the nineteenth and early twentieth centuries where access to 'cheap' energy resources was a boon to economic development (Butlin, 1994). The pattern of primary extraction and global export of natural resources, set in place under British Imperial rule (Merrett, 2014) continued with the later federation of colonies

Lee Godden formerly was Professor at the Centre for Resources, Energy and Environmental Law, Melbourne Law School, The University of Melbourne, Australia.

https://doi.org/10.1515/9783110752403-030

that formed the Australian nation (Johnson and Storr, 2021). In this formative period, the legal system was largely oriented to facilitating energy exploration and production with few environmental constraints. Transformation in the orientation of the energy regulatory system began in the late 20th century, with legal requirements for greater environmental sustainability being adopted almost concurrently with the privatisation of energy assets, and the introduction of liberalized energy markets in fossil fuels – electricity and gas from the 1990s onwards (Kallies, 2021b). Fossil fuels continue to be major power sources in Australia – and to be exported, although there are increasing amounts of renewable energy now in the domestic electricity generation profile, especially in south-eastern Australia.

Significantly, there is increasing external and internal pressure from a climate change perspective for Australia to reduce its fossil fuel exports as a contribution to global emission reduction targets. The pathways for internally and externally focused energy transition are complicated by a diverse range of legal and non-legal factors. The interplay of such factors, especially economic dependencies, indicate a growing divergence between the rates of energy transition and decarbonisation within Australia's energy system and in its export profile. In this manner, the Australian national experience confirms the premise of this handbook that, '[l]egal pathways of decarbonisation represent the set of (formal and informal, public and private) institutions, (formal and informal, public and private) legal tools and interpretative practices available in a specific legal system to pursue decarbonisation goals. Legal pathways interact with political, economic, technological and social drivers of decarbonization and influence the design and effects of climate policies'.

Within Australia as a federal nation, 'cooperative' federal governance institutions play a major role in energy law and policy (Kallies, 2021b). The origins of such cooperative (and at times not so cooperative arrangements) lie in the national constitutional settings whereby it is subnational governments that legally 'hold' the energy resources, such as coal and petroleum. The federal government however can exercise intergovernmental policy 'controls' in the energy space through, what is now known as, National Cabinet, as well as legislative controls in related fields, such as through the *Environment Protection and Biodiversity Conservation Act 1999* (Cth) (*EPBC Act*) (Godden et al., 2018). The main domestic regulatory focus is the national electricity market (NEM) and the national gas market (NGM), which are integrated into complex multilevel and multi-authority statutory regulatory systems (e.g. National Electricity Law and Rules), together with the respective legislative frameworks in the Northern Territory and Western Australia which do not participate in the 'national' markets.

Historically, domestic energy law and policy were regarded as largely separated from environmental law, and there have been policy efforts to separate energy projects from climate change laws (e.g. the lack of a climate assessment trigger in the EPBC Act). More recently, in the Australian legal system there has been stronger convergence of energy legislation and policy, environmental law requirements (particularly environmental impact assessment and project development controls), and climate change mitigation and adaptation law and policy. A recent driver for convergence has been the upsurge in climate litigation against fossil fuel extraction and use (Schuijers, 2021a; 2021b; 2021c), in association with third-party regulator or 'surrogate regulator' models such as financial disclosure requirements (Peel et al, 2019; Schuijers and Young, 2021). Nonetheless, the degree of interaction between these three fields of law and policy has varied significantly over the last two decades depending upon the policy orientation of the national government (Godden et al, 2018) and energy pricing concerns (Godden, 2020).

After a long period of relative inaction on climate initiatives at a national level, an incoming national Labor government in 2022 committed to a more proactive stance on climate change, including setting more ambitious Nationally Determined Contributions (NDCs) under the United Nations Framework Convention on Climate Change (UNFCCC) *Paris Agreement* 2015 (for discussion of the Paris Agreement see Bodansky, Brunnée and Rajamani, 2017, p. 3).

Thus, multilevel laws, from international law to energy sector specific laws, and diverse structural economic patterns distinguish Australia's energy legislation and policy package, which influence the scale, extent and rapidity at which energy transition is occurring. Moreover, Australia represents a paradox; there is clear momentum building internally to effectively integrate renewable energy sources into domestic power generation and to transition sectors such as transport. Decarbonisation is clearly underway in specific contexts, but the energy transition pattern is lumpy and not being driven uniformly by a consistent and coherent legal and policy framework that applies internally and externally.

This chapter investigates these multilevel patterns. It outlines federal (national and subnational jurisdictions) energy law and regulation, including export regulation, it discusses the laws governing the liberalised electricity and gas markets, and analyses the recent trends and prospects for transition (Australian Energy Regulator, 2021). It outlines the role played by public and private law including statutory reform, third party financial institutions and civil society litigation. It concludes that while Australia has great potential to transform its internal reliance on fossil fuels in electricity generation, transformation in other sectors such as in planning and transportation remains relatively slow. There are few policies to enhance vehicle efficiency or to seriously adapt planning systems to climate change impacts. Australia has a highly carbon-intensive vehicle sector (Liebman and Dargaville, 2022).

Moreover, Australia's long term economic reliance on primary resource exports such as coal and gas remains a more daunting barrier to substantial energy transition in a global context. The pattern of Australia's external emissions profile transition reflects both colonial and contemporary transnational economic dependencies (Merrett, 2014) and trading interactions, as well as multinational resource and capital structures.

2 Energy Resources and Policy in Australia

Australia has an abundance of energy resources – renewable energy from wind and solar, potential for tidal power, and plentiful carbon-based sources, such as coal and petroleum – including 'unconventional' and shale gas (Geosciences Australia, 2020). The domestic energy law and policy for many years has reflected this abundance of carbon-based resources in terms of Australia's continuing economic dependency on fossil fuel exploitation and exports, with liquified natural gas LNG predicted in coming years to rapidly overtake coal-based exports (Wiseman, in this book). Coal resources are widespread across the continent but the extraction of carbon-based exports (and other natural resources) varies across the continent (Geosciences Australia, 2020). The geographically large northern and western jurisdictions of Queensland, Western Australia and the Northern Territory are more exposed to dependency on resource exports than the metropolitan regions of those jurisdictions, and the southern Australian states. Coal mining and petroleum production remain major regional industries, although a slow phase out of coal-fired power generation is occurring (Wiseman, this book). Southern states such as New South Wales, South Australia and Victoria, are more proactive on climate change, yet still have not fully transitioned from fossil fuel power generation despite vigorous subnational law and policy supporting renewable energy (see e.g. *Climate Change and Greenhouse Emissions Reduction Act 2007* (SA) and *Climate Change Act 2017* (Vic)). South-eastern Australia has one of the highest rates of solar rooftop penetration in the world, strong investment in renewable generation and battery storage, and experimentation with community power generation and microgrids (Duck, 2020). In August 2022, there was a landmark event where there was more solar power generation running the national electricity grid than energy sourced from coal (Lowrey, 2022).

On the other hand, Australia has approved large new coal projects such as the Carmichael Mine (Adani project) in central Queensland, amid much controversy (*Australian Conservation Foundation Inc v Minister for the Environment* (2016) FCA 1042; Schuijers and Young, 2021) as well as the expansion of existing coal mines, including under water catchments (Sydney Knitting Nannas, 2022). There have been some high profile exceptions, (*Gloucester Resources Limited v Minister for Planning* (2019) NSWLEC 7; 234 LEGRA 257; Wiseman, in this book). Even given current trends to phase out coal, existing projects will support large coal export volumes over the life of the projects. Thus the extent to which already approved coal mine projects, and the accompanying investments may become stranded assets (Carney, 2015) might be queried. China is predicted to still prioritise energy security in its energy law and planning despite a national policy on reducing carbon intensity (Zhang, 2022). Thus, despite international trading tensions between these nations, China is likely to remain a strong market for Australian coal exports. By contrast, there is a trend toward divestment of coal assets by some multinational companies such as BHP (a resources company with origins in Australia) and litigious and regulatory pressure for disclosure of assets at risk due to climate change (see below).

Set against the variable trend to reduce dependency on coal resources by Australia, is the expansion of offshore and unconventional gas exploitation. Developments in technologies, such as hydraulic fracturing have made extraction of unconventional petroleum resources commercially feasible in areas which were previously unviable. Political lobbying by the gas sector to position itself as a 'bridge' in the energy transition has proved highly successful, with several large unconventional gas projects approved as part of the post COVID-19 economic incentives (Peel et al, 2022).

Ironically, this expansion in unconventional gas production destined for export is occurring at a time of domestic gas shortages, high consumer prices due to an absence of a domestic gas reserve, and growing energy poverty (Godden, 2020). Much of the country's export of Liquid Petroleum Gas (LPG) goes to Asian markets such as Singapore, Japan, China and Korea. Internally, conflicts and trade-offs around gas exploitation, economic development and environmental and social impacts are long-standing (Kennedy et al, 2017). Those states where there is substantial coal seam and shale gas extraction have progressively implemented tighter controls, although environmental damage, especially to groundwater, has already occurred in many regions (Holley, et al., 2019). Following a moratorium, and then a scientific report (The Independent Scientific Inquiry, 2018) that sanctioned unconventional gas exploitation (albeit with environmental controls), the Northern Territory Government has allowed shale gas extraction to occur over half of the land area of the Territory. Unconventional gas exploitation is well established in NSW, Queensland and the Northern Territory despite deep-seated land use and water management conflicts.

Significant offshore oil and gas reserves occur on the northwest Australian continental shelf with over 80 per cent of oil and gas production produced offshore, regulated under the complex *Offshore Constitutional Settlement Act 1979* (Cth) and legislation administered by the National Offshore Petroleum Safety and Environmental Management Authority (NOPSEMA) (Marsden, 2013). The regulatory failings of that regime were highlighted by the Montara Oil spill, caused in November 2009 by a well blowout from an oil rig located in Commonwealth waters off the north coast of Western Australia. The well was owned by Seadrill (Norwegian) but operated by PTTEP Australasia, a subsidiary of PTT (a Thai State-owned oil and gas company). The grossly inadequate safety capping of the wellhead and the risk assessment for the drilling program were approved by the Northern Territory as a delegate of the Commonwealth government agency (NOPSEMA). Following a Royal Commission, there was a tightening of the NOPSEMA offshore petroleum regime. In 2021, a class action by Indonesian seaweed farmers whose crops were affected was successful in the Federal Court of Australia in obtaining (relatively meagre) compensation (*Sanda v PTTEP Australasia (Ashmore Cartier) Pty Ltd (No 7)* (2021) FCA 237). Major oil spill disasters in other jurisdictions, such as the Deep Horizon oil spill in the Gulf of Mexico, have been a catalyst for energy transition in the light of the substantial environmental, economic and social costs of such disasters. To date, there has been relatively limited attention in Australia to any potential phase-out of offshore petroleum production. This may be changing given the filing of an action by the Australian Conservation Foundation seeking an injunction to prevent the extensive Woodside Scarborough-Pluto gas project in the offshore of Western Australia (Peel et al, 2022).

Australia, due to a long term policy constraint, does not use nuclear energy for electricity generation, despite sporadic efforts to argue for its utilisation. Australia is actively investigating, through its research and development processes, the potential for green hydrogen to operate in conjunction with renewable energy generation. As yet, there is no commercial production of green hydrogen.

The abundance of fossil fuel resources, and a politically and socially entrenched path dependency upon their utilisation, to date has posed a significant challenge for comprehensive energy transition in Australia. The political fallout from efforts to put into effect a cap and trade carbon price mechanism nationally has been immense – contributing to the political 'defeat' of five Australian Prime Ministers. The progressive carbon pricing mechanism and associated regulatory structure introduced in 2011 was short lived and quickly dismantled with a change of national government in 2014 (Godden et al, 2018). Effectively, for more substantial energy transition to occur in Australia beyond the admittedly strong gains made in renewable energy in the power generation profile, will require known economic carbon resources to be 'left in the ground' and for investment in at least some of the existing energy production to be 'stranded' – with issues of either economic or 'political' compensation looming. Moreover, in many regional areas of Australia it will require significant economic and workforce structural adjustment (University of Technology Sydney, 2021; Wiseman, in this book). Such structural factors do not have the same impact in urban areas. Thus, the disparity of circumstances and impacts of energy transition typically has precipitated a political divide between many rural communities and the major metropolitan centres, where energy transition is more actively championed. The 2022 federal election saw a large electoral swing to independent political candidates, many of whom campaigned on a platform for stronger action on climate change. The Labor Opposition also campaigned on the basis of stronger climate change action (albeit with a less comprehensive package of reforms). There is now stronger momentum for more effective energy transition and a new national legislative platform for more ambitious climate change mitigation targets.

3 Climate Change Act 2022

The Climate Change Act 2022 derived from two climate change instruments introduced into the post-election national Parliament – the Climate Change Bill 2022 (Cth) and the Climate Change (Consequential Amendments) Bill 2022 (Cth). The Act gives practical effect to the incumbent government's election commitment to cut greenhouse gas emissions to 43% below 2005 levels by 2030, and to reach net zero by 2050. The Act has four main functions with the primary one related to setting Australia's greenhouse gas emissions reduction targets and to articulating future ambition around reduction targets. In this way it is a legislative codification of Australia's Nationally Determined Contribution (NDC) pursuant to Article 4 of the UNFCCC 2015 Paris Agreement. Secondly, it provides for an annual climate statement to be tabled in Parliament, which must chart progress towards the targets, and examine the effectiveness of policies in reducing emissions. The Act confers advisory functions on the Climate Change Authority to advise the Minister for Climate Change regarding the annual climate statements, and to provide advice on revised emissions reductions targets for any new or adjusted NDC.

The Climate Change (Consequential Amendments) Bill, incorporated emissions reductions targets into 14 existing pieces of legislation, including: existing climate change emissions reporting, renewable energy and carbon farming legislation, certain infrastructure and financing statutes as well as legislation governing relevant government agencies such as the Commonwealth Scientific and Industrial Research Organisation (CSIRO) (research organisation), Clean Energy Finance Corporation (CEFC), Clean Energy Regulator (CER), and Australian Renewable Energy Agency (AREA).

While the Climate Change Act offers a more certain basis for climate policy to facilitate decarbonisation, including in power generation, the legislation does not mandate specific pathways for energy transition beyond setting relevant targets and objectives and in embedding emissions reduction objectives into government functions. In this way, the Act constitutes a 'Framework for Action' rather than a prescriptive regulatory scheme. This model replicates UK climate change legislation and that already established in Australian subnational jurisdictions such as Victoria and South Australia.

The Climate Change Act also does not mandate substantive changes to the underpinning regulatory regime that facilitates liberalised energy markets in electricity and gas, nor prescribe exactly how the federal government will pursue emissions reductions in energy exports. The Climate Change Act will continue to operate in a heterogenous energy system overlain by a complex policy, regulatory, and institutional structure. Energy transition in Australia must still be negotiated within multi-layered constitutional and institutional requirements, and across a diversity of interests. In the vital electricity sector, Niall and Kallies (2017, p. 501) identify that substantial reform to electricity generation, distribution and consumption has been made complex by the number of State (provincial government) and private interests, the different, sometimes competing incentives of private and State actors and by the types, size and nature of generation that range from large State-owned coal and gas generators to home solar. In light of the need to negotiate so many different interests, the following section describes energy law and regulation and evaluates the potential to drive transition.

4 Energy Law and Regulation: Governing the Energy System in Australia

Energy resources are extracted, produced (e.g. power generated), distributed, and regulated in various systems across Australia. The most important for transition purposes is the governance of the hybrid regulatory, institutional and 'physical infrastructure' systems collectively known as the national energy markets (National Electricity Market (NEM) and National Gas Market (NGM)). The NEM and NGM comprise both the physical systems (generation, transmission, distribution, and energy retailing) and related legal and institutional governance frameworks (National Electricity Law and Rules). This liberalised 'market' energy system, despite its high degree or privatisation of assets, is distinguished by comprehensive levels of government regulation. The guiding objectives of the legislation are strongly informed by competition and consumer protection principles.

Neither the NEM nor NGM actually cover the entire country. Instead, these markets are concentrated in the densely populated parts of eastern and southern Australia. The actual laws governing the electricity market are comprised of the *National Electricity (South Australia) Act 1996*, along with mirror legislation adopted in all Australian jurisdictions participating in the NEM. Electricity and gas production, transport, and supply across state borders thus rely on a cooperative scheme between the provincial governments and the Australian government in its regulatory capacity. A similar national mirror legislative model to the NEM is in place for gas supply, and it includes the National Gas Rules, with the gas market covering conventional (natural) gas and LNG for domestic and export markets. Each market system comprises high-level policy direction, economic regulation, rule-making and rule enforcement (Godden and Kallies, 2021). The Australian national gas and electricity markets are governed under the same institutional structure – the Australian Energy Market Operator (AEMO), the Australia Energy Regulator (AER) and the Australia Energy Market Commission (AEMC). Sector regulation is guided by similar legislated objectives focusing on efficiency, reliable, safe, and secure supply, and the long-term interests of consumers with respect to price, quality, and safety.

The NEM operates within an unbundled energy market paradigm (Godden and Kallies, 2021) with divided responsibilities between government law and policies, third party regulators, and private operators. This interplay can limit systemic transition as, in the past, it has deferred energy system adaptability to cost imperatives (Niall and Kallies, 2017). The NEM has a wholesale spot market for selling electricity with the spot price indicating physical supply and demand across the NEM. The spot price acts as a price signal for investors (Australian Government Department of Climate Change, Energy, the Environment and Water, n.d.). Associated financial markets interact with the wholesale market, allowing electricity retailers and generators to contract to buy and sell electricity at an agreed price, with the electricity then ultimately supplied to customers.

NEM's physical component comprises 40,000 kilometres of transmission and distribution lines – a major cost factor influencing energy transition as grid access costs for renewable energy can be a barrier (Kallies, 2021a). Australia's metropolitan areas still largely obtain electricity primarily from centralised large generators. Although, more devolved electricity distribution is occurring as residential solar penetration in south-eastern Australia increases. The Australian Energy Regulator's (2021, p. 6) State of the Market Report reported that,

> The National Electricity Market (NEM) is undergoing a profound transformation from a centralised system of large fossil fuel (coal and gas) generation towards an array of smaller scale, widely dispersed wind and solar generators, grid scale batteries and demand response. This transition has required adaptation by all participants, ... and is driving a significant package of reforms to ensure the market framework remains fit for purpose.

Nonetheless, without further strategic planning and changes to the NEM rules to facilitate more cost effective distributed electricity supply, this transformation may stall. The AER also noted that, '[a]side from reliability and security challenges, Australia's energy market transition poses risks to efficient investment in, and use of, energy infrastructure. The market lacks a coordinated framework to locate generators efficiently and provide transmission capacity where it is needed' (AER, 2021, p. 57).

There has been a surge of renewable energy (solar PV and wind) in the market in the last decade. Community concerns about fossil fuel generation and carbon emissions are a major catalyst, which have coincided with policy and legislative initiatives, especially by subnational governments, and behavioural change by energy consumers. Government incentives for lower emissions generation has resulted in investment in wind, solar farms and small scale solar PV systems, while rising energy prices assisted transition by encouraging customers to adopt more efficient energy use and to generate their own power (AER, 2021, p. 23). Even so, the legislative objectives that guide the regulatory system tend to prioritize reliability (energy security) over flexibility of market supply. To that extent, they may pose a barrier to more rapid decarbonisation, and a more adaptive electricity network system – one which is responsive to climate change adaptation imperatives (Godden, 2021).

Moreover, as Liebman and Dargaville (2022) suggest, a comprehensive review of the National Electricity Market legal frameworks and institutional directions is needed. They stress that the review of the governing market rules needs to be more fundamental than the reform proposals from the Energy Security Board (ESB) which, inter alia, seek to modify the overarching statutory objectives for electricity market design. Current objectives are not focused on resilience and system transformation (Godden, 2022). A concern for systemic stability precipitated the introduction of the Energy Security Board in 2017. Greater levels of renewable generation were regarded as challenging stability, so retention of fossil fuel generation was advocated. Thus, the direction of electricity regulatory reform has been driven, in part, by the need for a fossil fuel and technology-based response to perceived extreme event threats to the system – ironically enough, due to climate change impacts (Kallies and Johnston, 2021).

An overhaul of the existing electricity market design – the wholesale energy trading and network regulation – is pivotal to continued effective transition as coal still remains the main source of electricity generation (AER, 2021). Liebman and Dargaville (2022; cf. AER, 2021) argue that central aspects of the market design are no longer fit for purpose, as they were designed for an era of centralised fossil fuel generation, and not for distributed energy resources. To achieve a more effective transition, market regulation in the NEM should better incorporate the functionality of renewable energy technologies and storage capacity (Liebman and Dargaville, 2022). By contrast, the most recent State of the Energy Market report (see AER, 2021, pp. 11–16) identifies 'conventional' market concerns with supply and demand, supply risks (including gas), and pricing.

The regulatory model is yet to shift substantially toward transition as a guiding priority, given the systemic emphasis in the Australian national energy regulatory system on market efficiency, competition, energy security, and meeting increased demand. The question then is whether the current regulatory design will allow the rapidity of decarbonisation required to meet the more ambitious emission reduction targets now being set for internal energy transition. Other drivers beyond market regulation, such as divestment of coal and gas investment interests in generation and distribution of fossil fuels, may provide added impetus for energy transition within national markets (see below and for more detail, see Wiseman, in this book).

Liebman and Dargaville (2022) place their hopes on a reinvigorated cap-and-trade scheme similar to the European Union model, with a key objective of driving an accelerated and orderly retirement of coal-fired generation plants. However, without an effective global carbon market working in synchronisation with a carbon pricing scheme within Australia, the prospects for cap and trade legislation appear slight – at least in the short term. Politically, there is unlikely to be an appetite for a national government to chance its hand again, given the successive political backlash against a 'carbon tax' within the Australian community. A perverse outcome of a cap and trade scheme or a carbon tax may also be a price pass-through to consumers in an era of rising costs of living. The Independents in the national Parliament may negotiate some future concessions around carbon pricing but the framework nature of the Climate Change Act does not signal a strong move in the direction of an economy-wide carbon price. Further, the type of economic incentives for decarbonisation that the earlier Carbon Pricing legislation sought to achieve (Caripis, et al., 2011) are no longer as relevant for internal energy transition. Subnational governments adopting specific legislative and policy measures, such as rooftop solar rebates and 'buy-outs' of ageing coal-fired plants as occurred with Hazelwood in Victoria, offer more targeted 'incentives'.

Also, as the AER's (2021, p. 23) State of the Energy Market report makes clear, '... the declining costs of renewable plant (both commercial and small scale) have made them the most economic options for new build generation. This cost advantage over thermal plant is forecast to widen over the next 2 decades as economies of scale and technology improvement further reduce costs, particularly for solar plant and batteries.' Accordingly, the barriers to transition become not so much the 'source of generation' but other systemic factors such as how to deal with large volumes of renewable energy in the national grid (AER, 2021) – the major investments made by subnational governments in battery storage may alleviate some such problems around generation and transmission but regulatory barriers may continue to hinder timely transition.

5 Other Emission Reduction Measures

Australia does have an Emissions Reduction Fund (ERF) that operates as a voluntary scheme where proponents put forward projects for emissions reductions – many of which are tied to initiatives in the land sector. The main objective of the ERF is to assist Australia in meeting its international obligations under the UNFCCC and the Kyoto Protocol, to reduce emissions of greenhouse gases and meet an emissions reduction target of 5% below 2000 levels by 2020 (de Wit and Quinton, 2018). That target has now been superseded by the emissions reduction target set in 2022 by the Albanese Labor government. Emission reduction activities that are eligible under the ERF can create carbon credits (carbon offsets) that can be sold to businesses and organisations that require offsets to meet compliance requisites, or to entities which voluntarily offset their emissions. Australian governments may also purchase credits.

The ERF has a 'safeguarding mechanism' that is 'designed to stop the benefits achieved through carbon offsetting being negated by emissions increases elsewhere in the economy' (de Wit and Quinton, 2018, p. 766). The viability of the safeguard mechanism in driving transition has been questioned. Calls have been made to strengthen it to a baseline and credit model (Liebman and Dargaville, 2022). The ERF has been important for maintaining a skeleton of emission reduction activities that support the Carbon Credits (Carbon Farming Initiative) Act 2011 and an associated Rule introduced in 2015. The carbon credits under the Act and Rule are geared to meeting international reduction obligations. Essentially, though, the ERF is a weak offsetting mechanism that has done little to drive substantial emission cuts in the industrial, commercial and transport (e.g. airline) sectors. More recently, the integrity of the system has been questioned with regard to whether approved projects meet the requisite additionality standards (i.e. that it really is a new basis for reductions and not simply continuing existing land-based activities). In the past, Australia has made 'special pleading' under the UNFCCC Kyoto Protocol around its reduction targets which were largely achieved by reducing land clearing, alongside a rapid increase in timber plantations on agricultural land. But, 'the capacity to further reduce land clearing is limited' (Pouton, Keenan and Godden, 2022, p. 4). Moreover, as de Wit and Quinton (2018, p. 766) pertinently observe, 'carbon offsetting alone will not be sufficient to achieve the deep emissions cuts required to meet the Paris targets and avoid dangerous climate change'.

Therefore, a distinct divergence is emerging in Australia in terms of the extent, viability and rapidity of energy transition between internal economic sectors such as power generation, transport and (possibly) the land sector, and Australia's export sector. Australia's contribution to climate change via 'scope 3 emissions' from coal exports are still highly controversial (Wiseman, in this book). Moreover, given current project approvals and investment patterns in Australia, petroleum, especially LNG exports, now pose a bigger challenge for Australia to achieve its new emission reduction targets (Hepburn, 2022). Relevantly, the 2021 State of the Market report notes:

> The gas market is also undergoing a fundamental shift. In 2020 we saw a move to more flexible use of our gas resources to meet the competing demands of Australian industry and households, and liquefied natural gas (LNG) export businesses. Focus has turned to identifying and encouraging development of new sources of gas as the traditional sources decline. (AER, 2021, p. 7).

This trend highlights the importance of effective drivers for decarbonisation that operate in the financial and investment sector, and of third party activities, such as climate change advocacy and climate change litigation (Peel et al., 2022).

6 Drivers for transition beyond energy law and regulation

With the new legislation in place, Australia is set to resume a more comprehensive statutory footing for national climate change initiatives and measures to reduce emissions and enhance energy transition. The policy and legislative vacuum that distinguished the previous liberal government's approach to climate change laws, however, saw the development of a vigorous civil society response that sought to prod national government law and policy in the direction of stronger action on climate change. Other avenues for decarbonisation were explored, such as 'encouraging' influential institutions within the legal and financial regulatory systems, as well as business and industry groups to advance energy transition (Peel et al., 2019). Community groups, frustrated by a lack of action from the previous national government, sought avenues such as climate change litigation to challenge government decisions and institutional positions that entrenched the fossil fuel dependency in Australia (Schuijers and Young, 2021).

Broadly speaking, the climate change litigation and associated civil society actions in Australia can be characterised as falling into identifiable groups (Schuijers and Young, 2021; Wiseman, in this book). These groupings comprise:

1. applications for judicial review and merits review of government decisions which approve projects for carbon energy resource extraction or the extension of existing projects, such as coal mines that increase Australia's GHG emissions, together with applications for injunctive relief;
2. legal actions in relation to corporate compliance with financial regulation, including for greater disclosure of information related to climate risk, and in respect of corporate duties to disclose substantial risks;
3. legal actions taken in regard to claims for compensation for climate change impacts or for costs incurred given the need for climate change adaptation; and
4. human rights claims, especially by Indigenous peoples, in respect of rights to life, home and culture, where those are threatened by inaction on climate change.

Included in the first group are a series of legal actions taken by litigants such as the Australian Conservation Foundation (and supported by community public interest legal organisations such as the Environmental Defender's Office and Environmental Justice Australia) to challenge government approvals of fossil fuel energy resource projects under various legislative regimes. The national environmental legislation, the *EPBC Act,* which provides for judicial review of Ministerial approvals of controlled actions such as coal mines and petroleum projects, and applications for injunctions, has figured prominently in climate litigation (Schuijers, 2021b). Controlled actions under the *EPBC Act* are those actions which have or are likely to have a significant impact on 'Matter[s] of National Environmental Significance' which are designated under the Act. These include matters such as, World Heritage places including the Great Barrier Reef, wetlands of international significance, and listed threatened species and ecological communities. The extent to which the Environment Minister under the *EPBC Act* (and other decision-makers) might owe a duty of care to future generations to have regard to climate change impacts such as increased bushfire risk, was tested by an application for an injunction in respect of the decision to approve an extension to the Whitehaven coal mine project – a controlled action for *EPBC Act* purposes. While the concept that a Minister must have regard to such a duty of care to prevent physical harm to at risk children was accepted in the first instance decision in the Federal Court, the injunctive relief was reversed on appeal to the Full Federal Court (see Wiseman, in this book, and later relevant cases). While innovative jurisprudence is developing in climate litigation which is stretching existing judicial authority in order to deal with climate change exigencies, a more coherent pathway for decarbonisation may be to seek law reform of substantive legislation, such as the *EPBC Act*, and to ensure its better alignment with specific climate change and energy regulation statutes at national and federal level. Environmental impact assessment and development control legislation has, in most Australian jurisdictions, not expressly required consideration of climate change or energy transition priorities.

Such considerations could also dovetail with corporate and financial sector disclosure requirements in respect of energy, transport and infrastructure projects that are emissions intensive.

7 Climate Risk and Financial Regulation as Drivers of Transition

In Australia, the necessity for financial regulation of climate risk now is well established. To date the measures rely largely on information transparency measures, process-based regulation and normative codes of practice. In a corporate setting, the scope of directors' duties now includes consideration of climate risk to a corporation and specific corporate disclosure obligations (Schuijers and Young, 2021). Specific risks might include; physical risks impacting insurance liabilities and the value of financial assets; liability risks relating to compensating loss or damage; and transition risks resulting from the shift toward a low-carbon economy (Foerster et al., 2017). Given normative requirements for disclosure – (Australian regulators have not mandated disclosure) legal action can be taken by those with financial interests in a company, such as shareholders, or as investors in a bank or fund, because, for example, directors or superannuation fund managers did not adequately consider and manage the foreseeable risks posed by climate change (Wiseman, in this book).

The efforts to engage the financial and the corporate business community have proved to be quite effective; energy transition is clearly on the corporate radar. Moreover, litigation has seen some change in investment strategies by major institutions such as superannuation funds which are (sometimes) investing in renewables and slowly divesting from carbon-based industries. The funding of multinational coal and petroleum projects in Australia, though, has shown little change (Wiseman, in this book). The approval of 10 new exploration sites for carbon based projects (Hepburn, 2022), by the new national government suggest that the divergence between energy transition in the domestic electricity sectors and the continuation of large, export oriented carbon projects will escalate.

8 Climate Adaptation and Human Rights Claims

Litigation around climate adaptation to date in Australia has included challenges to regulatory efforts to adapt through planning systems (see e.g. NSW coastal sea-level rise cases) as well as claims for compensation and assistance as communities face costs in respect of growing rates of extreme events such as floods and bushfires (Wiseman, in this book). Australia's formal human rights framework is likely to be tested by reference to international obligations and protocols, by a series of claims, including a recent action by Torres Strait Islanders that seeks stronger mitigation of climate change but also compensation for cultural loss due to a failure by the previous national government to provide adequate adaptation (Wiseman, in this book).

In summary, there have been some significant gains made toward emission reductions and energy transition in the climate litigation sphere. As Schuijers and Young (2021, p. 78) note, 'Australian climate change litigation is expanding in the contemporary context of rising community awareness, escalating harm and ongoing legal and political change'. Yet much climate litigation does not achieve substantive change by itself – often it raises awareness and is a catalyst for longer-term statutory change.

9 Conclusion

Decarbonisation across multiple sectors and jurisdictions is needed to ensure that Australia is well positioned to meet more ambitious climate mitigation targets under the UNFCCC to avoid dangerous climate change, and progressively to 'ratchet up' its NDCs under the Paris Agreement. Over almost two decades, the well-established package of climate change and policy legislation, especially at a subnational level, has driven some substantial gains in renewable energy utilisation with consequent emission reductions. The pattern nationally has been chequered – to say the least, ranging from a comprehensive package of climate change legislation introduced in 2011 to weak UNFCCC targets and skeleton emission reduction legislation from 2014 to 2022. Climate litigation and stronger attention to the contribution to be made by the Australian financial sector and businesses in reducing emissions, drove some momentum for change but there were barriers to substantive transition in the absence of strong supporting legislation. The economic dependency of Australia on carbon resource exports and the multinational entities that facilitate them is a continuation of a legacy from colonial economic history (Merrett, 2014). In the twenty-first century, it remains one of the most serious challenges that the national government will have to address if it is to achieve deep decarbonisation.

References

Australian Conservation Foundation Inc v Minister for the Environment (2016) FCA 1042.

Australian Energy Regulator (AER), 2021. State of the Energy Market 2021 Report. [pdf] Available at: <https://www.aer.gov.au/system/files/State%20of%20the%20energy%20market%202021%20-%20Full%20report_1.pdf> [Accessed 30 August 2022].

Australian Government Department of Climate Change, Energy, the Environment and Water, n.d. The National Energy Market. [online] Available at: <https://www.energy.gov.au/government-priorities/energy-markets/national-electricity-market-nem> [Accessed 30 August 2022].

Bodansky, D., Brunnée, J. and Rajamani, L., 2017. *International climate change law*. Oxford: Oxford University Press.

Butlin, N.G., 1994. *Forming a colonial economy: Australia, 1810–1850*. Cambridge: Cambridge University Press.

Carbon Credits (Carbon Farming Initiative) Act 2011 (Cth).

Caripis, L., Peel, J., Godden, L. and Keenan, R., 2011. Australia's carbon pricing mechanism. *Climate Law*, 2(4), pp. 583–603.

Carney, M., 2015. Breaking the tragedy of the horizon – climate change and financial stability. 29 September, Bank of England, London.

Climate Change Act 2017 (Vic).

Climate Change Act 2022 (Cth).

Climate Change and Greenhouse Emissions Reduction Act 2007 (SA).

Climate Change Bill 2022 (Cth).

Climate Change (Consequential Amendments) Bill 2022 (Cth).

de Wit, E., and Quinton, A., 2018. Creating, buying and safeguarding emissions reductions under the emissions reduction fund. *Australian Law Journal*, 92(1), pp. 766–773.

Duck, T., 2020. Improving resilience: electricity law, microgrids and solar in the context of climate change. *Environmental and Planning Law Journal*, 37, pp. 443–458.

Environment Protection and Biodiversity Conservation Act 1999 (Cth).

Foerster, A., Peel, J., Osofsky, H. and McDonnell, B., 2017. Keeping good company in the transition to a low carbon economy? An evaluation of climate risk disclosure practices in Australia. *Corporate and Securities Law Journal*, 1(1), pp. 154–183.

Geosciences Australia, 2020. Australian Energy and Minerals Resources Investor Guide 2020 Australian Government. [pdf] Available at: <https://d28rz98at9flks.cloudfront.net/133857/133857_00_0.pdf> [Accessed 30 August 2022].

Gloucester Resources Limited v Minister for Planning (2019) NSWLEC 7; 234 LEGRA 257.

Godden, L., 2020. Energy justice in Australia: from remote access to consumer protection. In: I. del Guayo, L. Godden, J. Gonzales, M. Montoya and D. Zillman, eds. 2020. *Energy justice and energy law*. Oxford: Oxford University Press, pp. 178–199.

Godden, L., 2022. Law, resilience, and natural disaster management in Australia: the 'Bushfire Summer' and critical energy networks. In: C. Banet, H. Mostert, L. Paddock, M, Montoya and I. del Guayo, eds. 2022. *Resilience in energy, infrastructure, and natural resources law: examining legal pathways for sustainability in times of disruption*. Oxford: Oxford University Press, pp. 116–134.

Godden, L. and Kallies, A., 2021. Governance of the energy market in Australia. In: M. Roggenkamp, K. de Graad and R. Fleming, eds. 2021. *Energy law, climate change and the environment*. Cheltenham, United Kingdom: Edward Elgar Publishing, pp. 204–215.

Godden, L., Peel, J. & McDonald, J., 2018. *Environmental law*. Oxford, United Kingdom: Oxford University Press.

Hepburn S., 2022. Opening 10 new oil and gas sites is a win for fossil fuel companies – but a staggering loss for the rest of Australia. The Conversation [online] 1 June. Available at: <https://theconversation.com/opening-10-new-oil-and-gas-sites-is-a-win-for-fossil-fuel-companies-but-a-staggering-loss-for-the-rest-of-australia-189374> [Accessed 30 August 2022].

Holley, C., Kennedy, A., Mutongwizo, T. and Shearing, C., 2019. Governing energy transitions: Unconventional gas, renewables and their environmental nexus. *Environmental and Planning Law Journal*, 36(5), pp. 427–436.

Johnson, M. and Storr, C., 2021. Australia as empire. In: P. Cane, L. Ford & M. McMillan, eds. 2021. *The Cambridge legal history of Australia*. Cambridge: Cambridge University Press, pp. 258–280.

Kallies, A., 2018. The national energy guarantee: solving the energy crisis? *Australian Environment Review*, 33(1), pp. 20–23.

Kallies, A., 2021a. Regulating the use of energy networks in liberalised markets. In: M. Roggenkamp, K. de Graad and R. Fleming, eds. 2021. *Energy law, climate change and the environment*. Cheltenham, United Kingdom: Edward Elgar Publishing, pp. 599–610.

Kallies, A., 2021b. The Australian energy transition as a federalism challenge: (Un)cooperative energy federalism? *Transnational Environmental Law*, 10(2), pp. 211–235.

Kallies, A. and Johnston, V., 2021. How the law contributes to protecting energy infrastructure from extreme weather events: an Australian case study. In: R. Grears, ed. 2021. *The Palgrave handbook of climate resilient societies*. Cham, Switzerland: Springer, pp. 1–23.

Kennedy, A., Schafft, K. and Howard, T., 2017. Taking away David's sling: environmental justice and land-use conflict in extractive resource development. *Local Environment*, 22(5) pp. 1–17.

Liebman, A. and Dargaville, R., 2022. Here's what you need to know about the Australian government's climate change bills. [online] Available at: <https://lens.monash.edu/@technology/2022/05/27/1384734/four-urgent-next-steps-on-energy-policy-for-australias-31st-prime-minister> [Accessed 30 August 2022].

Lowrey, T., 2022. Solar briefly overtakes coal in Australia as number one source of power nationally. ABC News, [online] 20 August. Available at: <https://www.abc.net.au/news/2022-08-20/solar-briefly-overtakes-coal-australia-number-one-source-power/101354054> [Accessed 30 August 2022].

Marsden, S., 2013. Regulatory reform of Australia's offshore oil and gas sector after the Montara Commission of Inquiry: What about transboundary Environmental Impact Assessment? *Flinders Law Journal*, 15(1), pp. 41–53.

Merrett, D., 2014. Big business and foreign firms. In: S. Ville & G. Withers, eds. 2014. *The Cambridge economic history of Australia*. Cambridge: Cambridge University Press, pp. 309–329.

National Electricity (South Australia) Act 1996.

Niall, S. and Kallies, A., 2017. Electricity systems between climate mitigation and climate adaptation pressures: can legal frameworks for "resilience" provide answers? *Environmental and Planning Law Journal*, 34(6), pp. 488–502.

Offshore Constitutional Settlement Act 1979 (Cth).

Peel, J. and Osofsky, H., 2020. Climate change litigation. *Annual Review of Law and Social Science*, 16(1), pp. 21–38.

Peel, J., Neville, B. and Markey-Towler, R., 2022. Why this new climate case against the high-polluting Scarborough gas project is so significant. *The Conversation*, [online] 23 June. Available at: <https://theconversation.com/why-this-new-climate-case-against-the-high-polluting-scarborough-gas-project-is-so-significant-185578#.> [Accessed 30 August 2022].

Peel, J., Osofsky, H., and Foerster, A., 2019. A 'Next Generation' of climate change litigation? An Australian perspective. *Oñati Socio-legal Series*, 9(3), pp. 275–307.

Pouton, E.P., Keenan, R. and Godden, L., 2022. An Australian Climate Accord: A New Way Forward for Climate Crisis Governance? [pdf] Available at: <https://apo.org.au/sites/default/files/resource-files/2022-04/apo-nid317943.pdf> [Accessed 30 August 2022].

Sanda v PTTEP Australasia (Ashmore Cartier) Pty Ltd (No 7) (2021) FCA 237.

Schuijers, L., 2021a. Climate science is now more certain than ever – here's how it can make a difference in Australian court cases. *The Conversation*, [online] 13 August. Available at: <https://theconversation.com/climate-science-is-now-more-certain-than-ever-heres-how-it-can-make-a-difference-in-australian-court-cases-165874> [Accessed 30 August 2022].

Schuijers, L., 2021b. Environmental law: climate of change in the courtrooms. *Law Society Journal*, 84, pp. 76–78.

Schuijers, L., 2021c. In a landmark judgment, the Federal Court found the Environment Minister has a duty of care to young people. *The Conversation*, [online] 27 May. Available at: <https://theconversation.com/in-a-landmark-judgment-the-federal-court-found-the-environment-minister-has-a-duty-of-care-to-young-people-161650> [Accessed 30 August 2022].

Schuijers, L., 2022. Compelled by the Court to act on climate change: Bushfire Survivors for Climate Action Incorporated v Environment Protection Authority [2021] NSWLEC 92. *Journal of Environmental Law*, 34(1), pp. 223–232.

Schuijers, L. and Young, M., 2021. Climate change litigation in Australia: law and practice in the sunburnt country. In: I. Alogna, C. Bakker and J. Gauci, eds. 2021. *Climate change litigation: global perspectives*. Leiden, Netherlands: Brill Publishers, pp. 47–78.

Simes, L., 2022. Here's what you need to know about the Australian government's climate change bills. [online] Available at: <https://lens.monash.edu/@politics-society/2022/08/16/1384980/heres-what-you-need-to-know-about-the-australian-governments-climate-change-bills> [Accessed 30 August 2022].

Sydney Knitting Nannas, 2022. No coal mining in Sydney's water catchment. [online] Available at: <https://knittingnannas.org/2022/08/13/no-coal-mining-in-sydneys-water-catchment/> [Accessed 30 August 2022].

The Independent Scientific Inquiry into Hydraulic Fracturing in the Northern Territory, 2018. The Independent Scientific Inquiry into Hydraulic Fracturing of Onshore Unconventional Reservoirs in the Northern Territory 2018 final report. [online] Available at: <https://frackinginquiry.nt.gov.au/> [Accessed 30 August 2022].

University of Technology Sydney, 2021. UTS Conference: Decarbonisation & Energy Transition Session 5 Visions for transition – energy justice, energy commons, energy democracy. Online conference, 7–9 December 2021.

Zhang, H., 2022. China's energy law and energy sector in the context of carbon neutrality objective. 21 July, The Center for Resources, Energy and Environmental Law Seminar, Melbourne Law School.

Guilherme J. S. Leal, Mariana Miranda

Brazil's Energy Transition and Climate Litigation

Abstract: Brazil's energy law emerges from a vast body of normative acts that regulate in a rather fragmented manner multiple aspects of the energy sector. This decentralized regulation, albeit favours flexibility and dynamism in the government of the energy sector, may lead to incoherencies in the formulation, interpretation, and application of the law. Inconsistencies may occur horizontally (i.e., between acts with the same legal hierarchy, but with different cores, such as climate change and energy transit) and vertically (i.e., between top strategic policies and operational rules). Although the discussion about just transition to a low-carbon economy permeates the whole legal landscape applicable to the energy sector, Brazil lacks a clear framework law that fosters better decision-making on this subject. Against this backdrop, our contribution aims to provide an overview of the energy law in Brazil and discuss how decisionmakers (lawmakers, regulators and courts) should deal with the transition to a low-carbon economy.

1 Introduction

Brazil has vast oil and natural gas fields, mainly in offshore areas (such as the Pre-Salt region); extensive lands where biofuel production may thrive; and favourable natural conditions for renewable energy generation. Although more than half of its energy supply is accounted for by fossil fuels, Brazil has an enormous potential, yet to be explored, to expand, beyond hydropower, the share of wind, solar and biomass in its energy mix (EPE, 2022) and champion the transition towards a low-carbon economy. Whilst Brazil's long-standing dependency on carbon-intensive sources to secure domestic energy supply has been hindering the energy sector's decarbonisation, the country has a unique opportunity to boost the diversification of renewable sources.

But the balance between energy security (which involves gradual transformations) and climate crisis management (which requires urgent actions) is a delicate one. It cannot be achieved without proper planning and regulation. Both are critical to ensure foreseeability (key to the sustainable development) and ambitious progress

Guilherme Junqueira de Sousa Leal is Partner at Graça Couto Advogados. LL.M in Energy Law from the University College London, UK, and in Environmental Law from the George Washington University, USA.
Mariana Fernandes Miranda is a Lawyer at Graça Couto Advogados. Master in Energy from the Energy and Environment Institute of the São Paulo University, Brazil.

https://doi.org/10.1515/9783110752403-031

towards a low-carbon energy matrix. Notwithstanding, Brazil's current climate commitment, established on 7 April 2022 under the Paris Agreement, does not stipulate sectorial goals, but rather economy-wide absolute targets that "will be translated into policies and measures to be detailed and implemented" (UNFCCC, 2022). Meanwhile, energy and climate policies lack sufficient synergy, and the energy sector grows without clear priorities and mitigation goals. In this context, following the global trend of resorting to adjudication to improve climate governance (IPCC, 2022), ad hoc political decisions encouraging the use of fossil fuels (such as coal) are being challenged before the Brazilian Supreme Court. This chapter will address all these aspects, highlighting the rising risk of climate change litigation against energy policies laid down without broad public debate and in the absence of clear planning and regulation setting forth a low-carbon economy pathway.

2 Brazil's energy supply mix and GHG emissions

The monitoring and analysis of Brazil's energy supply is conducted by the Energy Research Office ('Empresa de Pesquisa Energética – EPE'), a state-owned entity created in 2004 to provide the Ministry of Mines and Energy with relevant information for the making of energy planning and policies (Law no. 10,847/2004, Article 4, sole paragraph). In this regard, the Energy Research Office publishes several reports, including the annual *Ten-Year Energy Expansion Plan*, which provides for assessments on the main aspects of Brazil's energy sector, as well as prospects of this sector's development within a ten-year horizon. The Energy Research Office is not empowered to make political decisions. Thus, it does not set national priorities or goals for the energy sector. It rather produces technical material to support the government's decision-making on energy-related matters, such as the low-carbon transition.

On 6 April 2022, the Ministry of Mines and Energy approved the Energy Research Office's 2031 Ten-Year Energy Expansion Plan (GM/MME Norm no. 40/2022). Its key findings include the following: In 2021, renewable sources (i.e., hydropower, biomass, wind, and solar) accounted for 83 percent of Brazil's *electricity supply*, being 63 percent hydropower (EPE, 2022). However, (i) renewables accounted for 47 percent of Brazil's total *energy supply* (i.e., 18 percent biomass; 12 percent hydropower; 9 percent firewood and charcoal; and 8 percent others, v.g., wind, solar, and biogas), and (ii) non-renewable sources represented 53 percent of the country's energy supply mix (i. e., 34 percent oil; 12 percent natural gas; 5 percent coal; 1 percent uranium; and less than 1 percent others) (EPE, 2022). Thus, in spite of the significant share of renewable sources in its electricity matrix (with a noteworthy participation of hydropower), Brazil's total energy supply still depends on fossil fuels.

Such reliance on carbon-intensive sources for attending domestic energy demand is perceived not only in Brazil, but in most countries. As pointed out in Chart 1 below, the main fossil fuels used by the energy sector (i.e., oil, natural gas, and coal) accounted for 80.9 percent of the world's energy supply in 2019, and 77.8 percent of the OECD countries' energy mix in 2020 (IEA, 2021).

Table 3: Share of total energy supply by source (fossil fuels). Source: *Brazil*: EPE, 2020; EPE, 2021; and EPE, 2022. *World and OECD*: IEA, 2021.

	Brazil				World	OECD
Source (fossil fuels)	**2019**	**2020**	**2021**	**2031**	**2019**	**2020**
Oil	34.4%	33.1%	34%	30%	30.9%	34%
Natural gas	12.2%	11.8%	12%	14%	23.2%	30.6%
Coal	5.3%	4.9%	5%	5%	26.8%	13.2%
Total	51.9%	49,8%	51%	49%	80.9%	77.8%

But despite its dependency on fossil fuels, the energy sector is not Brazil's main greenhouse gases (GHG) emitter. In 2020, it accounted for 18.2 percent (393.7 $MtCO_2eq$) of national emissions, whilst 46 percent (998 $MtCO_2eq$) derived from land use changes (deforestation and forest fires); 27 percent (577 $MtCO_2eq$) were caused by livestock and agriculture; 4.6 percent (100 $MtCO_2eq$) were originated from industrial activities; and 4.3 percent (92 $MtCO_2eq$) derived from wastes (SEEG, 2021). In 2021, the energy sector released 422 $MtCO_2eq$ in the atmosphere (EPE, 2022), jumping 7 percent compared with the 2020 levels of GHG emissions.

Against this backdrop, much attention has been paid – not only domestically, but also in the international sphere – to Brazil's failure in halting deforestation. For example, in 2020, when deforestation rates soared (Silva Junior et al., 2021), political leaders in Europe suspended the negotiations on a free-trade treaty between the European Union and Mercosur, claiming that Brazil's environmental policy was "against the commitments made in the Paris Agreement, in particular as regards combating global warming and protecting biodiversity" (EU, 2020). Indeed, as seen, in 2020, land use changes accounted for 46 percent of Brazil's GHG emissions (998 $MtCO_2eq$), raising international concerns. But when it comes to energy transition, historical emissions and responsibilities are the developed countries' Achilles heel, and the Brazilian government often brags about the important share of renewables in its energy mix, stating that "this already qualifies Brazil as a low carbon economy" (UNFCCC, 2016), and that "Brazil has one of the cleanest energy mixes in the world" (UNFCCC, 2022).

However important this accomplishment might be, such narrative, one may argue, disregards socioenvironmental constraints for the expansion of Brazil's main renewable source (hydropower) and ends up favouring business-as-usual planning. Consequently, as the projected post-Covid 19 economic recovery accelerates without a clear transition pathway, the energy sector's GHG emissions will eventually rise.

Brazil's total energy supply is projected to grow at a rate of 2.7 percent per year until 2031 (EPE, 2021), when the energy sector is expected to emit 529 $MtCO_2eq$ in the atmosphere (25.35 percent above the 2021 levels) (EPE, 2022). Furthermore, as projected by the Energy Research Office, the ratio of renewables and non-renewables expected by 2031 (48 against 52 percent) will be roughly the same as that found in 2021 (47 against 53 percent, as seen) (EPE, 2022). Moreover, as shown in Chart 1 above, the oil supply is expected to have just a slight decrease (from 34 to 30 percent) and the offer of natural gas is likely to have a small growth (from 11 to 14 percent), whilst the amount of coal tends to stay around 5 percent. Therefore, fossil fuels will still be critical sources for securing Brazil's energy supply in 2031 – and beyond.

On 16 December 2020, the Ministry of Mines and Energy approved the Energy Research Office's *2050 National Energy Plan* (MME Norm no. 451/2020), which pointed out key long-term energy-related challenges and set forth broad recommendations for the government's decision making (EPE, 2020). In addressing challenges concerning climate change, decarbonisation, and energy transition, the report recognised, inter alia, the need of connection between energy and environmental policies, and suggested further analysis on possible institutional, regulatory and market arrangements aiming at promoting energy transition without risking energy security. Moreover, the report stated that the economic gains expected from the exploration of the oil and natural gas fields at the Pre-Salt region (located in Brazil's exclusive economic zone, where large, ultradeep oil and gas reservoirs have been discovered in 2006, under Lula Administration) would probably facilitate the country's energy transition. Under this assumption, and projecting the 2050 scenario, the report recommended the maintenance of oil production at the rate expected to be reached in 2030 (5.5 million barrels per day) (EPE, 2020). Therefore, even though renewables are likely to grow in the long-term, Brazil does not have a clear, comprehensive plan or target to reduce the production and the use of fossil fuels by mid-century.

The 2009 National Policy on Climate Change (Law no. 12,187, of 29 December 2009) was almost passed by the National Congress with a provision determining a gradual replacement of fossil fuels, by encouraging the development of renewable energies and the progressive increase of their participation in the energy mix. But President Lula – big advocate of the exploration of the Pre-Salt region, discovered under his Administration – exercised his veto power against such provision, maintaining that it disregarded Brazil's energy demands and could weaken the national energy system's security and reliability. The veto was also grounded on the argument that the gradual replacement of fossil fuels neglected the potential use of hydropower, which makes the Brazilian energy matrix one of the cleanest in the world (Brazil, 2009).

Considering this reasoning, it is worth noting that, although hydropower has been accounting for a big share of the renewable sources of Brazil's energy mix, the prospect of its expansion is rather contentious, due to the socioenvironmental impacts associated with the installation of large hydroelectric projects (Goldemberg, 2015). Furthermore, the connection between isolated hydropower plants and consumer centres often requires long electricity grids, crossing extensive areas and causing socioenvironmental conflicts (IEA, 2021).

In addition to the impacts caused by hydropower, it should be stressed that, according to the IPCC (2021), many South American regions "are projected to experience an increase in frequency and/or severity of agricultural and ecological droughts". Therefore, as Caceres et al. (2021) point out, climate change can affect hydropower generation through changes in the timing and magnitude of precipitation, not only in Brazil, but in other South American countries, like Peru and Colombia.

And this is not just a hypothetical risk. In 2021, for example, Brazil faced a severe water crisis. From March to May, its South-Central region experienced a grave drought, which led to a 267 km^3 shortage of water resources compared with the seasonal average for the past 20 years (Getirana et al., 2021). As a result, big hydropower plants' reservoirs were reduced to less than 20 percent of their capacity. In the Paraná River Basin – which accounts for two-fifths of Brazil's installed hydropower capacity – the rivers' water flows have dramatically fallen to the lowest levels in 91 years (Getirana et al., 2021; National Water Agency Norm no. 77/2021). Against this backdrop, to tackle the water crises and avoid energy and water rationing, the government resorted to fossil fuel-based thermoelectric power plants. They generated 13.2 percent of the country's power in July 2021, the highest rate in its history (Getirana et al., 2021). In this context, the Energy Research Office's 2031 Ten-Year Energy Expansion Plan predicts that non-renewable thermal power is likely to increase 50 percent by the 2031 (EPE, 2022).

Given the limitations and vulnerability of the hydropower, energy planning should seek diversification of renewable sources, e.g., wind, biomass, and solar. Accordingly, the Energy Research Office states that hydropower, which in the beginning of this century represented 83 percent of Brazil's installed capacity, should reduce its relative share to 46 percent by 2031 (EPE, 2022). In this regard, as Espinosa (2021) put it, "a swift and broad transition to renewable energy will be essential to achieve the emission reduction goals laid down by the Paris Agreement".

Wind and biomass are particularly important and have been given special attention by the Brazilian government more recently. On 25 January 2022, the Decree no. 10,946 filled a key regulatory gap regarding the development of wind projects, providing for rules on the concession of offshore areas. And as to biomass-based energy, on 22 March 2022, the Decree no. 11,003 established the 'Federal Strategy to Incentivise the Biogas and Biomethane Sustainable Use', following the Global Methane Pledge undertaken at the 26th Conference of the Parties (COP26), held in Glasgow (EC, 2021). This act sets forth incentives for biomethane and biogas production and stipulates that methane credits may be issued and traded in the carbon market, which is likely to be regulated in 2022.

Biomass also has the potential to contribute for the reduction of GHG emissions caused by the transport sector, by complementing the use of oil derivatives (e.g., gasoline and diesel) with biofuels (EPE, 2022). In this regard, Law no. 13,576, of 26 December 2017, created the National Biofuels Policy (RenovaBio). In a nutshell, under this Law, the National Council of Energy Policy sets forth annual GHG emissions reduction targets for the downstream distribution sector, and, on an annual basis, such targets are allocated amongst individual fuel distributors according to their market shares. Individual targets are met through the acquisition of Credit Decarbonisation by Biofuels (CBIO). Thus, this regulation sets forth a sectorial cap-and-trade scheme, which aim at reducing emissions from the national fuel matrix and stimulating biofuels production. Although one may find this is a modest market mechanism to tackle climate change (Confraria and Khouri, 2021), it is a pivotal step for the decarbonisation of Brazil's transport sector.

The abovementioned initiatives to enhance the participation of wind and biomass in Brazil's energy supply mix must be praised. Notwithstanding, however important they might be, Brazil's energy supply mix, as projected by the Energy Research Office, will be dependent on fossil fuels in a long-term scenario, and those initiatives have not been taken in a broader context of clear, comprehensive energy transition policy. Even though renewables are expected to grow, Brazil does not have a clear plan or target to reduce the production and the use of fossil fuels by mid-century.

3 Brazil's GHG mitigation targets

The Paris Agreement became a key instrument to leverage the decarbonisation of the energy sector worldwide (Wörsdörfer and Howes, 2020). By abandoning the Kyoto Protocol's binary architecture – in which Annex I Parties (mainly developed countries) have committed to mitigate GHG emissions, and Non-Annex I Parties (mostly developing countries) have been exempted from setting their own emission reduction targets (Voigt and Ferreira, 2016) – the Paris Agreement urged all Parties to achieve net zero emissions in the second half of this century, in light of their national circumstances (Bodansky and Rajamani, 2018). Since then, the pursuit of this long-term goal has been driven by flexible mechanisms that have spurred the adoption of progressive, self-determined commitments (i.e., Nationally Determined Contributions – NDCs), which ought to reflect the countries' highest possible ambition. Against this backdrop, almost all Parties have incorporated into their NDCs sectorial targets, including the energy sector (UNFCCC, 2021), which is a key contributor to climate change (IEA, 2021).

But the speed of this low-carbon transition is not following the rapid aggravation of the climate crisis (IPCC, 2021), as the commitments expressed in the countries' NDCs are falling short of the Paris Agreement's goals (UNFCCC, 2021). In this context, Brazil's NDC has become particularly contentious. Its original version, submitted in 2016, was replaced by a less ambitious contribution, presented in 2020 (UNEP, 2021). In 2022, another updated – and still contentious – NDC was submitted. Unlike the first

NDC, both updated versions did not indicate specific targets for the energy sector, raising doubts on the government's political willingness to accelerate the energy transition, which remains significantly subject to business-as-usual decision making.

To better understand the evolution of Brazil's race to achieve a low-carbon energy mix, it is worth noting the trajectory of its international commitments on GHG emissions reductions – which include economy-wide mitigation targets to be achieved in 2025 and 2030, and net-zero emissions by 2050 – examining whether they comprise energy-related goals. Besides, it is important to verify whether the domestic regulatory landscape enables a consistent and foreseeable pathway towards the energy transition.

Brazil's first pledge of emissions reduction was announced at the 15th Conference of the Parties (COP15), which took place in Copenhagen, from 7 to 19 December 2009. President Lula personally attended the meeting, where he committed to reduce Brazil's emissions by 36.1 to 38.9 percent in 2020, considering the business-as-usual emissions projected for such year. This reduction would result from the carrying out of Nationally Appropriate Mitigation Actions (NAMAs), which provided for, inter alia, the following energy-related measures: energy efficiency increment; increase of the use of biofuels; expansion of the energy supply by hydroelectric power plants; and increase of alternative sources of energy (UNFCCC, 2010). As Franchini and Viola (2019) put it, with this initiative, Brazil emerged "not only as a major power leading the developing countries, but as a global role model for mitigation governance".

To give an extra layer of strength to its international pledge, Brazil's 2020 target was explicitly incorporated into the domestic law as a "voluntary national commitment", pursuant to the 2009 National Policy on Climate Change, passed by the Law no. 12,187, of 29 December 2009. This Law was regulated by the Decree no. 7,390, of 9 December 2010, which reproduced the abovementioned NAMAs as means to achieve the 2020 goal, and, more broadly, pointed out the Ten-Year Energy Expansion Plan – which, as seen, is annually updated by the Energy Research Office – as a key technical ground to inform decision making and enforcement of climate policies.

In spite of some controversies regarding the methodology used by the government in the setting of the 2020 target, it is generally acknowledged that at least its 36.1 percent floor was achieved (SEEG, 2021). As to the indicated energy-related measures, according to SEEG, they lacked a clear benchmark, which undermined their assessment. Yet, given that, from 2010 to 2020, there has been a growth in the share of renewables in Brazil's energy mix and an emergence of biofuels policies, it has been assumed that such measures were fulfilled (SEEG, 2021).

Brazil's 2025 and 2030 mitigation targets and 2050 net-zero pledge are part of its NDC, which, as anticipated, is rather controversial.

On 28 September 2015 – thus, nearly two months before the 21st Conference of the Parties (COP21), which took place in Paris from 30 November to 11 December 2015 – Brazil, under Rousseff Administration, communicated to the UNFCCC secretariat its intended Nationally Determined Contribution (iNDC). On 21 September 2016, under Temer Administration, Brazil submitted to the secretariat its instrument of ratification of the Paris Agreement, thereby converting its iNDC into NDC, pursuant to paragraph 22 of Decision 1/CP.21.

In this first NDC, Brazil took into account the estimated levels of GHG emissions in 2005 (2.1 $GtCO_2e$) to commit to pursue an economy-wide reduction of 37 percent by 2025 (thereby reaching the amount of 1.3 $GtCO_2e$) and, as an indicative contribution, of 43 percent by 2030 (1.2 $GtCO_2e$). This commitment was accompanied by explanatory remarks concerning, inter alia, Brazil's target of zero illegal deforestation in the Amazon by 2030; its plan to restore 12 million hectares of forests by 2030; the development of a low carbon agriculture programme; and the energy sector's goals. Within this later topic, Brazil set forth the following targets: (i) to increase the share of sustainable biofuels in the energy mix to nearly 18 percent by 2030, and (ii) to achieve 45 percent of renewable sources in the energy mix by 2030, highlighting, amongst other aspects, that the share of non-hydro renewable sources in the energy mix should reach 28 to 33 percent by 2030 (UNFCCC, 2016). This first NDC did not have any 2050 net-zero pledge, which would only be added in 2021.

On 9 December 2020, under Bolsonaro Administration, Brazil submitted to the UNFCCC secretariat an "updated" version of its NDC, replacing the previous one. According to this new document, the 2025 target (37 percent reduction) was maintained and the 2030 target (43 percent reduction), rather than indicative contribution, became a commitment. Moreover, the new NDC stated that these goals would be "compatible with an indicative long-term objective of reaching climate neutrality in 2060" (UNFCCC, 2020). This 2060 net-zero pledge was anticipated to 2050, as explained in a letter submitted on 31 October 2021 to the UNFCCC secretariat. Unlike the original NDC, the 2020 version did not have any energy-related goal (Romeiro et al., 2021). Besides, this NDC was widely criticised because, although it presented the same reduction targets, revisions of the 2005 baseline led to increases in the absolute emissions (Caio et al., 2021). In view of this, on 13 April 2021, six youngsters filed a lawsuit against the government with the aim to annul the updated NDC (Popular Action no. 5008035-37.2021.4.03.6100, still pending).

On 7 April 2022, the Bolsonaro Administration submitted a "second update" of the NDC to the UNFCCC secretariat. It confirmed the 2025 mitigation pledge (37 percent reduction), raised the 2030 target (to 50 percent reduction), and highlighted its "long-term objective to achieve climate neutrality by 2050". Furthermore, it should be noted that this new version did not stipulate sectorial goals, but rather economy-wide absolute targets, which "will be translated into policies and measures to be detailed and implemented" (UNFCCC, 2022).

Therefore, more than five years after the submission of its first NDC, the Brazilian government does not have GHG emissions reduction goals for the energy sector and will still translate its economy-wide absolute targets into national policies. Although the first NDC, one may argue, could have lacked ambition in the setting of energy-related targets, the fact that it fixed certain goals for the energy sector conveyed a sense of need to shift the business-as-usual approach. When the updated versions of the NDC suppressed such sectorial targets, the government failed to enhance ambition in the pursuit of the energy transition.

At the national level, Brazil does not have clear energy transition regulation. As seen, the 2009 National Policy on Climate Change (Law no. 12.187, of 29 December 2009) almost established a gradual replacement of fossil fuels, but such provision was vetoed by the President. The 1997 National Energy Policy, as amended in 2011, indicates the mitigation of GHG emissions as a general objective, amongst others. However, this is far from establishing a uniform, coherent energy transition plan. As also mentioned, the Energy Research Office is responsible for delivering a Ten-Year Expansion Plan. This study, however, makes projections for the coming decade without determining new policy routes. The setting of a transition pathway is a political decision that has not yet been made in Brazil. Indeed, it has recently eliminated energy-related targets from its international commitments.

It should be acknowledged that Brazil has a relevant share of renewables in its energy supply mix (more than the global average). Relevant initiatives regarding wind and biomass have taken place. Though, it should not be ignored that Brazil lacks a clear, comprehensive transition plan. Against this backdrop, ad hoc political decisions encouraging the use of fossil fuels (mainly coal) are being challenged before the Brazilian courts, bringing the discussion on energy and climate policies to a new arena.

4 Climate litigation and energy transition

In its 'Climate Change 2022: Mitigation of Climate Change' report, the IPCC's Working Group III acknowledged that there is robust evidence and high agreement on the fact that, "outside the formal climate policy processes, climate litigation is another important arena for various actors to confront and interact over how climate change should be governed" (IPCC, 2022). Accordingly, the number of climate-related lawsuits in the world has been on a rise since 2015, year when the Paris Agreement was adopted and a historical ruling in a climate dispute was delivered by a Dutch court (Setzer and Higham, 2021; Benjamin and McCallum, in this volume). The *Urgenda* case illustrates the role climate litigation "can play, is playing, and is likely to play in shaping decision making and regulatory landscape relating to climate change across various levels of governance" (Peel and Osofsky, 2015). Indeed, the 2015 decision triggered the so-called '*Urgenda effect*', stimulating the filing of many climate lawsuits against public and private actors across the world, including in the Global South (Setzer and Vanhala, 2019). Some of these cases, like Urgenda, are deemed as 'strategic' (Bouwer, 2018), as they seek ground-breaking shifts in public policies and governmental behaviour (Setzer and Higham, 2021). In the Global South, strategic climate litigation, rather than pursuing more ambitious regulatory action, has focused on the enforcement of existing legislation. As Setzer and Benjamin observe, “asking national governments to implement stringent mitigation measures at the expense of poverty reduction, energy security needs or other developments agendas will be taxing for the judiciary in the Global South” (Setzer and Benjamin, 2019).

In Brazil, climate litigation is still incipient, and there is a continued evolution of strategies and legal arguments underpinning the disputes. Such cases have been brought by many types of plaintiffs, which, besides individuals, non-governmental organisations, and public prosecutors, also include political parties. The Brazilian political parties have the right to pursue judicial relief on alleged violations of constitutional rights and human rights directly before the Supreme Court. After the country’s democratisation process in the 1980s, political parties have made extensive use of their power to request judicial review of legal and administrative measures established by the legislative and executive branches. On the back of this long history of constitutional litigation, political parties are now turning their focus to the adjudication of climate change before the Supreme Court (Setzer et al., 2019).

Two climate change lawsuits brought by political parties due to the Government’s failure to combat deforestation (ADPF no. 760 and ADO no. 59) are part of a package of seven environment-related cases that the Supreme Court started to hear on 30 March 2022 (Bicalho et al., 2022). Much attention has been paid to these cases (Toni et al., 2022), given that deforestation, as seen, is Brazil’s major GHG emitter and a reason for international discredit. But there is another case (ADI 7095), which has not been included in that ‘green package’, but deserves further discussion, for it submitted to the Supreme Court the analysis of whether certain energy law stimulating the use of coal as energy source would be aligned with Brazil’s climate law.

Before describing this case, it should be highlighted that the elimination of coal as an energy source has been a major topic of discussion at the international level. OECD countries are assessing the possibility of phasing out unabated coal (IEA/OECD, 2021) and, according to the UN Secretary-General António Guterres, “coal needs to be phased out in OECD countries by 2030 and by 2040 everywhere else” (UN, 2022). And regardless of the setting of long-term elimination target, the existing use of coal is already at the core of climate change disputes (for the Australian case law, see J. Wiseman, in this volume).

In Brazil, the use of coal as an energy source has led to judicial disputes. In 2021, for example, the Federal Court of the State of Rio Grande do Sul, based on the National and State Policies on Climate Change, ordered the operator of the “largest Thermoelectric Power Plant in the State of Rio Grande do Sul” to incorporate climate-related analysis in the environmental impact assessment of such project. The ruling acknowledged that energy generation projects shall consider climate risks in the assessment of their potential negative externalities.

In a broader perspective, a discussion on a specific energy programme approved by the National Congress was submitted to the Supreme Court, expanding the debate on energy and climate policies to the judiciary. In March 2022, three political parties filed a lawsuit (ADI 7095) directly before the Supreme Court questioning the constitutionality of a Law that stimulates the use of coal as a energy source. The case refers to the Law no. 14,299, of 5 January 2022, which created a 'Just Energy Transition Programme' for the coal production region of the State of Santa Catarina, located in the southern part of Brazil. In a nutshell, this act aims to prepare such region for the likely elimination of unabated coal-fired thermoelectric generation by 2040. Furthermore, it admits the possibility of continuing coal-fired thermoelectric generation beyond 2050, upon the achievement of net zero GHG emissions.

One may understand that this programme is consistent with the discussions held by OECD countries regarding the phasing out of unabated coal. On the other hand, in the context of the existing legislation in Brazil (which is not an OECD party), it is important to note that one of the main objectives of the National Energy Policy (Law no. 9,478, of 6 August 1997) is the mitigation of GHG emissions by energy and transport sectors. Thus, there is a discussion on which legal grounds the 'Just Energy Transition Programme' on coal could be justified, given the framework mitigation goal established by the National Energy Policy.

In the case submitted to the Supreme Court, the plaintiffs highlight that the coal-fired powerplants in operation in the State of Santa Catarina emit significant amount of GHG (4,3 million tons CO_2e in 2020), and argue that the Law no. 14,299, of 5 January 2022, is inconsistent with Brazil's climate policies and international commitments taken under the Paris Agreement. Moreover, the plaintiffs sustain that the subsidies to coal use passed by Law at issue violate the constitutional right to a healthy environment (Article 225 of the Federal Constitution).

Thus, following the global trend of resorting to adjudication to improve climate governance (IPCC, 2022), ad hoc political decisions encouraging the use of fossil fuels (mainly coal) are being challenged before the Brazilian Supreme Court, which, in 2022, has given climate-related cases special attention, demonstrating that the government's failure to enforce environment and climate policies may lead to judicial review.

5 Conclusion

As seen, despite the relevant participation of renewable energies in its electricity mix (mostly due to the large operation of hydropower plants), Brazil's total energy supply still depends on fossil fuels. And although non-hydro renewables are likely to expand in a long-term horizon, Brazil does not have a clear, comprehensive plan or target to reduce the production and the use of fossil fuels by the mid-century. Pursuant to Brazil's current climate pledge, established on 7 April 2022 under the Paris Agreement, the country's economy-wide absolute targets "will be translated into policies and measures to be detailed and implemented" (UNFCCC, 2022). Therefore, more than five years after the submission of its first NDC, the Brazilian government still does not have GHG emissions reduction goals for the energy sector and will still translate its economy-wide absolute targets into national policies. In this context, ad hoc political decisions encouraging the use of fossil fuels (mainly coal) are being challenged before the Supreme Court, following the global trend of climate litigation. Therefore, without proper planning and regulation setting forth a clear, uniform energy transition plan, it is more difficult to ensure foreseeability and ambitious progress towards a low-carbon energy matrix.

After this chapter was concluded, the new Lula administration took office in January 2023. Its strong commitment to fight climate change might influence all government's departments, including the energy sector.

References

Alberto, M. and Mendes, C.H., 2019. Litigância climática e separação de poderes. In: J. Setzer, K. Cunha, A. Fabbri, eds., 2019. *Litigância climática: novas fronteiras para o direito ambiental no Brasil*. São Paulo: Thomson Reuters Brasil, pp. 117–138.

Bodansky, D. and Rajamani, L., 2018. *General issues in elaborating the Paris Rulebook*. Center for Climate and Energy Solutions.

Borges, C., Prolo, C.D. and La Rovere, E.L. 2021. Análise científica e jurídica da nova contribuição nacionalmente determinada (NDC) Brasileira ao Acordo de Paris. https://www.climaesociedade.org/_files/ugd/d19c5c_9bc29d5e06a14fd0af3d38c042ac0cb7.pdf

Bouwer, K., 2018. The unsexy future of climate change litigation. *Journal of Environmental Law*, 30(3), pp. 483–506.

Brazil, 2009. *Presidential Veto Message* no. 1,123/2009.

Caceres, A.L., Jaramillo, P., Matthews, H.S. et al., 2021. Hydropower under climate uncertainty: Characterizing the usable capacity of Brazilian, Colombian and Peruvian power plants under climate scenarios. *Energy for Sustainable Development*, 61, 2021, pp. 217–229.

Gloucester Resources Limited v Minister for Planning [2019] NSWLEC 7. Available at: https://www.caselaw.nsw.gov.au/decision/5c59012ce4b02a5a800be47f#_Toc431199

Confraria, J. and Khouri, A., 2021. Economia, regulação e direito: a contribuição de sua intersecção para a descarbonização do setor elétrico brasileiro. In: C. Pimentel and M.J.C. Pereira Rolim, eds., 2021. *Caminhos jurídicos e regulatórios para a descarbonização no Brasil*. Belo Horizonte: Fórum, 2021, pp. 251–269.

Dernbach, J.C., 2021. Introduction. In: C. Pimentel and M.J.C. Pereira Rolim, eds., 2021. *Caminhos jurídicos e regulatórios para a descarbonização no Brasil*. Belo Horizonte: Fórum, 2021, pp. 19–22.

Energy Research Office – EPE and Ministry of Mines and Energy, *2050 National Energy Plan*. Brazil, 2020.

Energy Research Office – EPE and Ministry of Mines and Energy, *Ten-Year Energy Expansion Plan 2031*. Brazil, 2022.

Energy Research Office – EPE and Ministry of Mines and Energy, *Ten-Year Energy Expansion Plan 2030*. Brazil, 2021.

Energy Research Office – EPE and Ministry of Mines and Energy, *Ten-Year Energy Expansion Plan 2029*. Brazil, 2020.

Espinosa, P., 2021. *The world needs a swift transition to sustainable energy*. Available at: https://unfccc.int/news/the-world-needs-a-swift-transition-to-sustainable-energy

European Union (EU), 2020. Motion for a resolution – Paragraph 36 – Amendment 36. A9-0160/36 and A9-0160/2020.

Franchini, M. and Viola, E., 2019. Myths and images in global climate governance, conceptualization and the case of Brazil (1989–2019). *Rev. Bras. Polít. Int.*, 62(2), e005.

Getirana, A., Libonati, R. and Cataldi, M., 2021. *Brazil is in water crisis – it needs a drought plan. Nature*, 600, pp. 218–220. Available at: https://www.nature.com/articles/d41586-021-03625-w

Goldemberg, J., 2015. *O estado atual do sistema elétrico*. Revista USP., 104, pp. 37–44.

Intergovernmental Panel on Climate Change – IPCC, 2021. *Climate Change 2021: The Physical Science Basis*. Working Group I.

Intergovernmental Panel on Climate Change – IPCC, 2022. *Climate Change 2022: Impacts, Adaptation and Vulnerability*. Working Group II.

Intergovernmental Panel on Climate Change – IPCC, 2022. *Climate Change 2022: Mitigation of Climate Change*. Working Group III.

International Energy Agency – IEA, 2021. *Phasing out unabated coal: current status and three case studies*. Paris: OECD Publishing.

International Energy Agency – IEA, 2021. *World energy balances: overview*, Paris: IEA.

Monzoni, M. and Vendramini, A., 2016. *Renewable energy overview: industrial sector and Latin America*. Fundação Getútilo Vargas – FGV and Konrad Adenauer Stiftung – KAS (November). Available at: http://hdl.handle.net/10438/18476

Moreira, A., 2022. *OCDE aprova convite para Brasil negociar entrada na entidade. Valor Econômico*. Available at: https://valor.globo.com/brasil/noticia/2022/01/25/exclusivo-ocde-aprova-convite-para-brasil-negociar-entrada-na-entidade.ghtml

Peel, J., and Osofsky, H.M., 2015. *Climate change litigation: regulatory pathways to cleaner energy*. Cambridge: Cambridge University Press.

Romeiro, V., Genin, C. and Felin, B., 2021. *Nova NDC do Brasil: entenda por que a meta climática foi considerada pouco ambiciosa*. World Resources Institute Brazil. Available at: https://wribrasil.org.br/pt/blog/clima/nova-ndc-do-brasil-entenda-por-que-meta-climatica-foi-considerada-pouco-ambiciosa

Setzer, J. and Higham, C., 2021. *Global trends in climate change litigation: 2021 snapshot*. London: Grantham Research Institute on Climate Change and the Environment and Centre for Climate Change Economics and Policy, London School of Economics and Political Science.

Setzer, J., Vanhala, L.C., 2019. Climate change litigation: A review of research on courts and litigants in climate governance. *WIREs Clim Change*, 10:e580.

Setzer, J., and Benjamin, L., 2020. Climate litigation in the Global South: constraints and innovations. *Transnational Environmental Law*, 9(1), pp. 77–101.

Setzer, J., Leal, G.J. and Borges, C., 2021. Climate change litigation in Brazil: will green courts become greener? In: I. Alogna, C. Bakker and J.-P. Gauci, eds., 2021. *Climate change litigation: global perspectives*. Leiden: Brill/Nijhoff, pp. 143–172.

Setzer, J. and de Carvalho, D. W., 2021. Climate litigation to protect the Brazilian Amazon: establishing a constitutional right to a stable climate. *Reciel*, 30(2), pp. 197–206.

Silva Junior, C.H.L., Pessôa, A.C.M., Carvalho, N.S. *et al*. 2021. The Brazilian Amazon deforestation rate in 2020 is the greatest of the decade. *Nat. Ecol. Evol.*, 5, pp. 144–145.

Sistema de Estimativas de Emissões e Remoções de Gases de Efeito Estufa – SEEG. *Emissões por setor*, 2021. Available at: https://plataforma.seeg.eco.br/sectors/energia

Supreme Court. *Partido Socialista Brasileiro et al. v. Brazil*. Case no. ADI 6932, 2021.

Supreme Court. *Partido Socialista Brasileiro et al. v. Brazil*. Case no. ADO 60, 2020.

Supreme Court. *Rede Sustentabilidade et al. v. Brazil*. Case no. ADI 7095, 2022.

UNFCCC, Brazil – NDC, 2016. Available at: https://www4.unfccc.int/sites/ndcstaging/PublishedDocuments/Brazil%20First/BRAZIL%20iNDC%20english%20FINAL.pdf

UNFCCC, Brazil – NDC, 2020. Available at: https://www4.unfccc.int/sites/ndcstaging/PublishedDocuments/Brazil%20First/Brazil%20First%20NDC%20(Updated%20submission).pdf

UNFCCC, Brazil – NDC, 2022. Available at: https://www4.unfccc.int/sites/ndcstaging/PublishedDocuments/Brazil%20First/Updated%20-%20First%20NDC%20-%20%20FINAL%20-%20PDF.pdf

United Nation, 2022. *UNEP combats pollution, restores ozone and protects seas, UN chief tells 50th anniversary session*. Available at: https://news.un.org/en/story/2022/03/1113202

Voigt, C. and Ferreira, F., 2016. Differentiation in the Paris Agreement. *Climate Law*, 6, pp. 58–74.

Wörsdörfer, M. and Howes, T., 2020. *As we mark the Paris Agreement's 5th anniversary, we continue to expand our work on energy and climate*. Paris: IEA. Available at: https://www.iea.org/commentaries/as-we-mark-the-paris-agreement-s-5th-anniversary-we-continue-to-expand-our-work-on-energy-and-climate

(Claire) Nan Guo

Legal Pathways of Decarbonization in China: The Emissions Trading Perspective

Abstract: This Chapter starts with introducing the broad carbon neutrality goal in China's energy sector, and significant steps have been taken to start moving toward this new growth pathway. To identify the interpretative criteria shaping legal reactions in the low-carbon transition, key long-term strategies and development objectives will be listed out in specific institutional dimensions, including regulatory systems, legal decision-making processes, legal orders, and tools of regulation. Furthermore, this chapter discusses the challenging issues to implement the overall scope into near-term actions, especially focusing on how the legal system would affect institutional complementarities, enforcement mechanisms, sustainable finance, and low-carbon technology. In the end, this chapter explores pathways to confirm the crucial factors in low-carbon transition by legal instruments in a comparative perspective.

1 Introduction: China's policy mixes of decarbonization

Under the Paris Agreement, China is committed to addressing climate change as specified in its updated Nationally Determined Contributions (NDC), with carbon dioxide (CO_2) emissions peaking before 2030 and achieving carbon neutrality before 2060 (SCIO, 2020). China has made positive progress in implementing its NDC through comprehensive measures, including administrative regulations, economic instruments, and technological innovation for low-emission development.

First, China integrates climate mitigation targets into mid-term and long-term planning for socio-economic development. For example, the 14th Five-Year (2021–2025) Plan (FYP) proposes to reduce CO_2 emissions per unit of gross domestic product (GDP) by 18% compared to 2020 levels, and introduces an official appraisal to assess the performance of controlling greenhouse gas (GHG) emissions at provincial level (provinces, autonomous regions, and municipalities)(SCIO, 2021). In addition, the Action Plan for Carbon Dioxide Peaking Before 2030 sets out ten key actions throughout the circular economy, low carbon science and technology, public involvement, industrial sectors, urban and rural construction, and transportation (State Council, 2021).

(Claire) Nan Guo is Associate Professor, Faculty of Law, Jiangnan University, China.

https://doi.org/10.1515/9783110752403-032

Second, China improves laws and regulations that are incompatible with decarbonization. For example, the revision of the Atmospheric Pollution Prevention and Control Law provided a legal basis for controlling GHGs in coordination with air pollutants (SCIO, 2021). Furthermore, the process of amending existing laws, such as the Energy Conservation Law, the Electric Power Law, the Coal Industry Law, the Renewable Energy Law, and the Law on Promoting the Circular Economy, will expedite reconciliation with the new reduction targets (The Communist Party and State Council, 2021). Some crucial legislations, however, such as climate change law and energy law, are still pending.

Third, China is starting to build a clean energy system, with the commitment to increase the proportion of non-fossil fuels to about 25% in primary energy consumption and install 1.2 billion kilowatts of wind and solar power capacity by 2030 (SCIO, 2020). Under the principle of low carbon development, the coal and coal-fired power industry will be shrinking throughout the 14th – 15th FYPs period, along with other energy-intensive industries sticking to a tightened control. With the reduction of coal-fired electricity generation, renewables, on the other hand, emerge as an important substitute in power capacity. For instance, clean winter heating in northern households will proportionally replace coal consumption. Furthermore, policy support and economic incentives have been given to energy saving and low carbon technologies, including the demonstration and industrial application of carbon capture and storage technologies (CCUS), photovoltaic poverty alleviation programs, and power battery recycling pilots (SCIO, 2020).

Moreover, China has introduced carbon pricing to achieve decarbonization. In the form of carbon taxation, Article 3 of the Environmental Protection Tax Law (2018 Revision) stipulates that air pollutants, water pollutants, solid wastes, and noises are 'taxable pollutants'. The Resource Tax Law imposes a levy on mineral products and water usage. In the form of emission trading, China has selected seven provinces and municipalities – Beijing, Chongqing, Guangdong, Hubei, Shanghai, Shenzhen, and Tianjin – as ETS pilot projects since 2011 and started operating a national emission trading system (ETS) on July 16, 2021, after accumulating the pilot experiences (SCIO, 2021). By the end of December 2021, China's national ETS reached a cumulative transaction volume of 179 million allowances, representing a turnover of CNY 7.66 billion (USD 1.2 billion); the closing price was 54.22 CNY (USD 8.40)/ton, making an increase of 12.96 % from the starting price of CNY 48.00 (USD 7.44)/ton in July (ICAP, 2022). In addition, other economic instruments, such as carbon sink trading, energy utilization rights trading, and ecological compensation programs, will be integrated into the national ETS progressively (SCIO, 2021).

Among the policy mixes of decarbonization, the objective of the ETS is to use a market-based mechanism to control emissions and achieve GHG reduction gradually, as confirmed as part of the 1+N policy framework in October 2021 (ICAP, 2022). While reaching net-zero emissions by or around mid-century has become a mutual goal covering the majority of the global economy, ETSs are well suited to achieve climate change mitigation since the EU launched its ETS in 2005, followed by other mature systems, including New Zealand, South Korea, Switzerland, California, Quebec, and the US Regional Greenhouse Gas Initiative. Meantime, there is a growing number of ETSs in developing economies, such as Ukraine, Brazil, Chile, Indonesia, Pakistan, Thailand, Turkey, and Vietnam, which either have started establishing domestic ETS or set out a plan. At the end of 2021, there were 25 ETSs in force, covering 37% of global GHG emissions. In this context, emissions trading, which provides emissions cap and market signals needed to stimulate the low-carbon transition, will be critical for the global economy to achieve decarbonization (ICAP, 2022).

This chapter focuses on the institutional feasibility of China's national ETS. After illustrating how China adopted increasingly ambitious decarbonization targets and measures to achieve them, it focuses on the regulatory framework of the national ETS to analyze its contributions and challenges as a pathway to net-zero. The rest of the chapter is structured as follows. Section 2 elaborates on the internal elements of China's national ETS, to analyze the legal impediments preventing the ETS from supporting a just low carbon transition and the possible solutions by learning from other countries' experiences. Section 3 addresses how to improve the Chinese ETS from an external perspective.

2 Design features of ETS in China: friendly to decarbonization?

2.1 Regulatory bodies

China's national ETS involves multi-level governance. As the competent national authority, the Ministry of Ecology and Environment (MEE) is in charge of rule-setting, allowance pre-allocation, and verification of GHG emissions. It also oversees trading activities together with the National Development and Reform Commission, Ministry of Industry and Information Technology, and National Energy Administration (Interim Regulation, 2021, Article 4). The provincial ecology and environment departments, known as the MEE's subsidiaries, are in charge of rules implementation and management duties extending to their respective jurisdiction (Measures, 2020, Article 13). Additionally, agencies which manage emissions trading registration and exchange, such as Hubei Carbon Emission Trading Center and Shanghai Environmental Energy Exchange, are subject to the supervision of the MEE, State Administration for Market Regulation, the People's Bank of China, and China Securities Regulation Commission (Interim Regulation, 2021, Article 6).

2.2 Emissions cap

The emissions cap in China is set bottom-up, i.e., the total allowances issued in every province constitute the national cap. Covered emitters within the cap receive free emission allowances from the MEE's subsidiaries or buy extra allowances in the carbon market. China pledges to decline its CO_2 emissions per unit of GDP by over 65% from 2005 levels (SCIO, 2020), meaning that China introduced an intensity-based cap of over 4,500 MtCO2/year for 2019 and 2020. In comparison, the EU ETS has introduced an absolute cap fixed at 1,571,583,007 allowances in phase 4 (2021–2030) with an annual linear reduction factor of 2.2% (European Commission, 2017a), while China's intensity-based cap has the flexibility of ex-post adjustment according to the actual output and emission levels (Notice, 2020). Additionally, Article 8 of the Interim Regulations (2021), published by the MEE as a revised draft for public consultation, stipulates that MEE, together with other competent departments of the State Council, formulates the national emissions cap, hence its subsidiaries break down the overall cap region by region, implying the possibility of a top-down cap setting procedure in future (ICAP, 2022).

An intensity-based cap, which is friendly to rapid economic growth and accelerated structural adjustment (Pang and Duan, 2016), seems rational under China's current situation. While minimizing the risk of dragging down the economy, it helps to reduce emissions and enhance carbon efficiency (Afriat et al., 2015). In China's case, however, not every provincial government breaks down the national cap into quantitative targets, nor do most of the covered emitters have explicit emission reduction targets (Li et al., 2021). Meantime, the current carbon price – ranging from CNY54.22-62.29 (USD 9.79) – may not be high enough to make covered emitters stingy with CO_2 emissions (EDF, 2022), raising the risk that ongoing economic expansion makes the reduction targets hard to achieve (Shen, 2016).

Therefore, the emissions cap, whether set bottom-up or top-down, will have limited feasibility unless local governments and covered emitters have explicit reduction objectives. While setting out regional quantitative targets according to local circumstances, in return, brings empirical results to improve and adjust the national cap-setting (Liu and Zheng, 2016; Cheng and Mu, 2017).

2.3 Sectors and thresholds

The participants in national ETS – also known as GHG key emitters – are specified organizations and individuals formulated by the MEE, albeit the provisions for individuals have yet to be clarified (Measures, 2020, Article 21). To be clear, greenhouse gas, not included in air pollutants in China's legal terms (Atmospheric Pollution Prevention and Control Law, 2018, Article 2), covers CO_2, methane (CH_4), nitrous oxide (N_2O), hydrofluorocarbons (HFCs), perfluorocarbons (PFCs), sulfur hexafluoride (SF_6), and nitrogen trifluoride (NF_3) according to the definition of the Measures (2020). China's national ETS, however, is the exclusive measure for trading CO_2 credits at the initial stage.

In 2021, ETS participants covered more than 2160 key emitters from the power generation sector, including combined heat and power and captive power plants of other sectors, emitting over 26,000 tCO_2 annually in any year from 2013 to 2019 (World Bank, 2021). In comparison, the seven ETS pilots in China include 3,000 key emissions companies throughout 20 industries, such as power, steel, and cement (SCIO, 2021), while the Tokyo and Saitama ETSs target the commercial and industrial buildings (Li et al., 2021). Concerning the limited participants in the ETS, China has planned to gradually expand to the high emission industries across other sectors, such as petrochemical and steel (ICAP, 2021), albeit a specific timetable to incorporate other industries is pending.

2.4 Allowances Allocation

In 2020, the MEE issued the 2019–2020 National Carbon Emission Trading Cap Setting and Allowance Allocation Implementation Plan (Power Generation Industry) (short form: Allocation Plan), which adopted historical output and benchmarking as the primary approach. Specifically, each covered emitter in a given year receives a free allocation equal to 70% of its historical output in 2018 multiplied by the corresponding benchmark and correction factors, followed by ex-post adjustments according to the actual power generation during 2019–2020 (Karplus and Valerie, 2021; ICAP, 2022). At the end of 2021, the MEE announced that 99.5 % of emissions from covered entities had been surrendered successfully during the first compliance cycle of 2019–2020 (ICAP, 2022).

The Allocation Plan (2020) provides a larger share of free allowances for emitters with higher historical output, implying that emitters with lower generation outputs receive a smaller share of free allowances (Boute and Zhang, 2019). In other words, the current allocation method has a loophole to induce emitters to increase historical emissions to obtain more free allocations deliberately (Sun and Wang, 2017). Similarly, Li et al. (2021) found that entities are incentivized to consider abatement costs in production and develop emission reduction mechanisms if the free allowance allocation is tightened. Despite the ETS pilots adopting benchmarking and a historical intensity-based method mainly resulting in emitters with emissions gaps slightly outnumbering the emitters with emissions surplus (Li et al., 2021), it is worth noting that the average turnover rate[1] of China's national ETS (2%) is lower than in China's pilot

1 The turnover rate is the annual transaction volume divided by the total amount of allowances issued in the year. In China's national ETS, the cumulative trading volume of allowances is 179 million tons, while the total emission allowances issued for the first compliance cycle is 9 billion tons.

ETSs (5%) and the EU ETS spot market (more than 80% in 2020) (ICAP, 2022). Therefore, China's national Allocation Plan needs to be vigilant about major market surplus and price dropping (Verde et al., 2021) and to improve its incentive mechanisms to reward emitters contributing to emission reduction, such as the beneficial provisions for power plants equipped with the CCUS technology.

Furthermore, it has not been clear whether MEE will adopt the same Allocation Plan (2020) for the second compliance period, making covered emitters and potential market participants eager to know the new allocation criterion to adjust their generation capacity accordingly (Verde et al., 2021). Given the lesson learned in the EU ETS phase 1 (2005–2007) that an estimated cap and over-allocation made carbon prices fall to zero in 2007 (European Commission, 2017b), China's national ETS should move toward an explicit emission cap aligned with a long-term allowance allocation plan which contributes to internalizing the negative externality of GHG into the cost of production.

2.5 Compliance mechanism

There is a threshold equal to 20% of the verified emissions in the compliance mechanism. Power plants whose emission gap surpasses the threshold are obligated to surrender free allowances plus 20% of verified emissions, while others whose gap exceeds less than the threshold should surrender verified emissions with no discount (Notice, 2020). Additionally, compared with art. 40 of the Measures (2020) in force, art.24 of the draft Interim Regulation (2021) increases a fixed administrative fine from 20,000–30,000 (USD 1,449-4,347) to CNY 100,000 – 500,000 (USD 15,506 – 77,532), if power plants fail to rectify the omission within a limited time. Moreover, an overdue payment of the emission gap results in an allowance deduction in the following year's allocation (Measures, 2020, Article 40).

2.6 Monitoring, reporting, verification (MRV)

MEE issued 24 Guidelines for GHG Monitoring and Reporting for various sectors from 2013 to 2015 (SCIO, 2021) and two guidelines on enterprise GHG emissions accounting and reporting in 2021 (MEE, 2021b; MEE, 2021c). In 2022, MEE urged power plants emitting over 26,000 tCO_2 in 2020 or 2021 to submit reports of GHG emissions before March 31, 2022 (Notice, 2022).

Nonetheless, China's MRV regulations are relatively weak compared to the EU ETS (Shen, 2016). First, a monitoring plan without elaborating on mandatory rules and monitoring methodologies may affect the implementation rate (Tang et al., 2018). Based on the experiences of the ETS pilots, higher implementation rates of monitoring plans mostly result from incurring liability costs (Li et al., 2021). Second, Article 26 of the Measures (2020) authorizes that the provincial ecology and environment departments, or their commissioned technical service agencies, are responsible for verifying the GHG reports. However, the Measures (2020) lack provisions to specify the qualifications and responsibilities of the technical service agencies, covering the risk of reports being falsified or collusion with interested parties. For instance, some typical cases of MRV falsification had appeared in the preceding quarter of 2022 (Disclosure, 2022), during which entities were required to submit emission reports. Hence, it is progress that Article 26 of the draft Interim Regulations (2021) adds liabilities in this regard for the technical service agencies to use, such as cancelling commissions, impairing entities' credit record, and even terminating entities' operation for three years under severe circumstances. Although Article 37 of the Measures (2022) and Article 27 of the draft Interim Regulations (2021) both stipulate the punishment of official misconduct, the integrity of technical service agencies may be preserved in a better way if they are unhooked from the affiliation of the MEE's subsidiaries, leaving no space for rent-seeking in the commission process. Therefore, the MEE and its subsidiaries should focus on rule-setting, allowance allocation, and inspection (Notice, 2021, No.491), reserving the responsibility of emission verification to independent third parties. Additionally, MRV rules should enhance data quality control, clarify verification management requirements, and raise the liability costs to make the potential violators in awe of consequences (United Nations, 2017; ICAP, 2022).

3 Further improvements needed to achieve decarbonization

3.1 Clarify the legal status of carbon emission rights

Albeit the Measures (2020) clarify the definition of carbon emission rights, which are the carbon allowances distributed to the key emitters, it is still an ongoing debate about the legal status of carbon emission rights among domestic scholars. On the one hand, Ni (2022) suggests that the carbon emission right is a property right because it is tradable within the carbon market. For example, the Ministry of Finance published an interim policy that considers only purchased allowances (not those received for free) as financial instruments (MF, 2019). The free allowances issued by MEE's subsidiaries, on the other hand, derive from chartered credits. Hence, Yang & Fang (2021) argue that a carbon emission right is a new compound right in environment protection.

In a practical sense, the legal status of the carbon emission right relates to the judicial procedure to settle disputes. Specifically, disagreements between MEE's subsidiaries and key emitters in the process of allowance allocation and verification bring out the administrative status of the emission right and are subject to an administrative procedure in court (Administrative Litigation Law, 2017); while disagreements among private participant in the carbon market require a civil procedure to settle disputes. Since China's national ETS starts with a clean slate in regard to judicial review, it is necessary to clarify the legal status of the carbon emission right and the corresponding judicial procedures (Notice of the Supreme People's Court, 2021).

3.2 Refine the CCER offset mechanism

While removals from carbon sink projects have already been included in some ETSs as offset credits, China Certified Emission Reduction (CCER) system, a domestic offset mechanism, was initially launched in 2013 alongside the development of the seven ETS pilots (ICAP, 2022). The Beijing Green Exchange, the former Beijing Environmental Exchange, has been operating the CCER registry since 2015. However, because of limited trading volume and standardization issues, the CCER projects have stopped being registered since 2017 (Notice, 2017). Although CCERs could offset up to 5% of verified emissions in the first compliance cycle (Measures, 2020, art. 39; MEE, 2021a; Notice, 2021, No.492), it is unclear how the CCER credits generated during the suspension should integrate into the national ETS in the second compliance cycle, such as the specific timeline for CCER reinstatement, the quantitative limits and qualitative criteria for offset use, and the legal liability if CCERs fail to meet the offset provisions (ICAP, 2022). Furthermore, since China has been working on climate change cooperation initiatives with 28 countries (SCIO, 2021), it may be necessary to enact regulations on CCER transference through state parties to facilitate ecological conservation projects. In order to ensure broader trading opportunities, it is likely that such requirements will be made compatible with the accounting methodologies agreed at COP26 for the implementation of Article 6 of the Paris Agreement.

4 Concluding remarks

Based on the main characteristics of China's ETS discussed in Section 2, it is clear that a group of policy documents released by the MEE constitute the regulatory framework of the national ETS, giving it the appearance of a policy instrument. Hence, a mature legal system for ETS requires formal regulations enacted by the State Council or the national legislature, specific provisions, and exercisable mechanisms to direct cap-setting, allowance allocation, and MRV. Fortunately, the publication of the drafted Interim Regulations (2021) sends out a positive signal that the legal hierarchy of the ETS will move from the MEE upward to the State Council. Compared to the Measures (2020) remaining in force, the drafted Interim Regulations (2021) proposed new changes in various aspects, including the regulatory bodies other than the MEE (art.4; art.6), a top-down procedure of cap setting (art.8), the liability of verification institutes (art.26), and credit discipline on the trading participants and the technical service agencies (art.30). Although there is not enough publicly available data to evaluate the integral effectiveness of China's ETS, the experiences from China's ETS pilots and foreign ETSs play an important role in analyzing the possible outcome in the current situation and the improvements needed in the near future. While the newly launched national ETS covers over 40% of the overall CO_2 emissions in China, it remains to be seen how the climate change policy will interact with the legal system of ETS, and to what degree the ETS could contribute to China's commitment to decarbonization.

References

Administrative License Law of the People's Republic of China (2019 Amendment)[中华人民共和国行政许可法], Standing Committee of the National People's Congress Order No. (2019) 29, 23 April 2019.

Administrative Litigation Law of the People's Republic of China (2017 Revision)[中华人民共和国行政诉讼法], Standing Committee of the National People's Congress Order No. (2017) 71, 7 January 2017. [online] Available at: <http://lawinfochina.com/display.aspx?id=23600&lib=law&SearchKeyword=&SearchCKeyword=%d0%d0%d5%fe%cb%df%cb%cf%b7%a8 > [Accessed 9 December 2022].

Atmospheric Pollution Prevention and Control Law of the PRC (2018 Revision) [中华人民共和国大气污染防治法], Standing Committee of the National People's Congress Order No. (2018) 16, 26 October 2018.

Allocation Plan, 2020. Notice of Ministry of Ecology and Environment on Issuing 2019–2020 National Carbon Emission Trading Cap Setting and Allowance Allocation Implementation Plan (Power Generation Industry) [关于印发《2019–2020年全国碳排放权交易配额总量设定与分配实施方案(发电行业)》并做好发电行业配额预分配工作的通知], Ministry of Ecology and Environment, 30 December 2020. [Online] Available at: <https://chinaenergyportal.org/en/implementation-plan-for-the-2019-2020-national-carbon-emission-trading-quota-setting-and-allocation-power-generation-industry/> [Accessed 9 December 2022].

Afriat, M., Alberola, E., Swartz, J. and Kouchakji, K., 2015. *China: an emissions trading case study.* Available at: < https://www.ieta.org/resources/2016%20Case%20Studies/China%20case%20study.pdf > [Accessed 9 December 2022].

Boute, A, Zhang, H., 2019. Fixing the emissions trading scheme: carbon price stability in the EU and China. *Eur Law J.*, 25, pp. 333–347.

Cheng, Y.W., Mu, D., 2017. Study on the operation efficiency evaluation of pilot carbon trading markets in China [我国试点碳市场运行效率评价研究], *Science and Technology Management Research [科技管理研究]*, 4, p. 96–100.

Disclosure, 2022. Disclosure of typical cases on falsified carbon emission reporting of Zhong Tan Neng Tou etc. (the First Batch of Outstanding Environmental Issues in 2022) [生态环境部公开中碳能投等机构碳排放报告数据弄虚作假等典型问题案例 (2022年第一批突出环境问题]. Ministry of Ecology and Environment (MEE), 14 March 2022. Available at:<https://www.mee.gov.cn/ywgz/ydqhbh/wsqtkz/202203/t20220314_971398.shtml> [Accessed 9 December 2022].

Environmental Defense Fund (EDF), 2022. *China carbon pricing newsletter (Issue No. 13, 2022)*. Available at: < https://www.edf.org/sites/default/files/2022-10/ETS_Newsletter_Issue_No.13_2022.pdf > [Accessed 9 December 2022]

European Commission, 2017a. *Emissions cap and allowances*. Available at: <https://ec.europa.eu/clima/eu-action/eu-emissions-trading-system-eu-ets/emissions-cap-and-allowances_en> [Accessed 1 March 2022]

European Commission, 2017b. *Development of EU ETS (2005–2020)*. Available at: <https://ec.europa.eu/clima/eu-action/eu-emissions-trading-system-eu-ets/development-eu-ets-2005-2020_en> [Accessed 1 March 2022]

Heggelund, G., Stensdal, I., Duan, M. S., 2022. China's carbon market: potential for success? *Politics and Governance*, 10, pp. 265–274.

International Carbon Action Partnership (ICAP), 2021. *China national ETS*. Available at: < https://icapcarbonaction.com/en/ets/china-national-ets > [Accessed 9 December 2022].

International Carbon Action Partnership (ICAP), 2022. *Emissions trading worldwide: status report 2022*. Available at: <https://icapcarbonaction.com/system/files/document/220408_icap_report_rz_web.pdf > [Accessed 9 December 2022]

International Energy Agency (IEA), 2020. *China's emissions trading scheme: designing efficient allowance allocation*. Available at:< https://www.oecd.org/china/china-s-emissions-trading-scheme-e0f664f3-en.htm> [Accessed 9 December 2022]

International Energy Agency (IEA), 2021. *The role of China's ETS in power sector decarbonization*. Available at: <https://iea.blob.core.windows.net/assets/61d5f58d-4702-42bd-a6b6-59be3008ecc9/The_Role_of_China_ETS_in_Power_Sector_Decarbonisation.pdf> [Accessed 9 December 2022]

Interim Regulations, 2021. Interim Regulations for the Management of Carbon Emissions Trading (Revised Draft) [碳排放权交易管理暂行条例 (草案修改稿)], Ministry of Ecology and Environment, 30 March 2021. Available at: <https://www.mee.gov.cn/xxgk2018/xxgk/xxgk06/202103/t20210330_826642.html> [Accessed 9 December 2022].

Karplus, V.J., 2021. *China's CO_2 emissions trading system: history, status, and outlook*. Available at: < https://heep.hks.harvard.edu/files/heep/files/karplus_china_national_ets_june_2021_english.pdf > [Accessed 9 December 2022].

Li, D.Y., Duan, M.S., Deng, Z. and Zhang, H.J., 2021. Assessment of the performance of pilot carbon emissions trading systems in China. *Environmental Economics and Policy Studies*, 23, pp. 593–612.

Liu, H.Y. and Zheng, S., 2016. Analysis on Beijing's emissions trading pilot program[北京市碳排放权交易试点分析]. *Energy of China [中国能源]*, 12, pp. 32–36.

Liu, L.W., Chen, C.X., Zhao, Y.F. and Zhao, E.D., 2015. China's carbon-emissions trading: overview, challenges and future. *Renewable and Sustainable Energy Reviews*, 49, pp. 254–266.

Measures, 2020. Measures for the administration of carbon emissions trading (Trial) [碳排放权交易管理办法 (试行)], The Ministry of Ecology and Environment Order No. (2020) 19, 25 December 2020,

Ministry of Ecology and Environment (MEE), 2021a. *The procedure of using CCER offsets in the first compliance circle [全国碳市场第一个履约周期使用 CCER 抵销配额清缴程序]*. Available at:<https://www.mee.gov.cn/xxgk2018/xxgk/xxgk06/202110/W020211026635445691967.pdf> [Accessed 9 December 2022].

Ministry of Ecology and Environment (MEE), 2021b. *The Guidelines on Enterprise Greenhouse Gas Emissions Accounting and Reporting (Power Generation Facilities) [企业温室气体排放核算方法与报告指南 发电设施]*. Available at:<http://gdee.gd.gov.cn/attachment/0/419/419153/3265655.pdf> [Accessed 9 December 2022].

Ministry of Ecology and Environment (MEE), 2021c. *The Guidelines on Enterprise Greenhouse Gas Emissions Accounting and Reporting (Power Generation Facilities) (2022 Revision) [企业温室气体排放核算方法与报告指南 发电设施 (2022年修订版)]*. Available at:< https://www.mee.gov.cn/xxgk2018/xxgk/xxgk06/202203/W020220315357528424119.pdf > [Accessed 9 December 2022].

Ministry of Ecology and Environment (MEE), 2021d. *Guidelines on Enterprise Greenhouse Gas Emissions Reporting and Verification (Trial) [企业温室气体排放报告核查指南 (试行)]*. Available at:<http://www.tjjh.gov.cn/zyjkq/zwgk/yqgg/202107/P020210709617516696212.pdf> [Accessed 9 December 2022].

Ministry of Finance (MF), 2019. *Interim Regulations on the Accounting Methods of Emissions Trading[碳排放权交易有关会计处理暂行规定]*. Available at: http://www.gov.cn/xinwen/2019-12/25/5463857/files/5c11c14a22ce419a8e92cdde3ed8509c.pdf [Accessed 9 December 2022].

Ni, S., 2022. On the right attribute of carbon emission right – Also on the improvement of carbon market trading rules of China [碳排放权权利属性论——兼谈中国碳市场交易规则的完善]. *Political Science and Law[政治与法律]*, 2, pp. 2–14.

Notice, 2012. Notice of the National Development and Reform Commission (NDRC) on issuing the interim measures for the management of voluntary GHG emission reduction transactions [温室气体自愿减排交易管理暂行办法], National Development and Reform Commission (NDRC), No. (2012)1668, 13 June 2012.

Notice of National Development and Reform Commission on initiating the National Carbon Emissions Trading Market[国家发展改革委办公厅关于切实做好全国碳排放权交易市场启动重点工作的通知], National Development and Reform Commission (NDRC), 22 January, 2016. Available at:<http://www.gov.cn/xinwen/2016-01/22/content_5035432.htm> [Accessed 9 December 2022].

Notice of the National Development and Reform Commission No. 2 in 2017[国家发展和改革委员会公告], National Development and Reform Commission, 13 March 2017. Available at: <https://www.ndrc.gov.cn/xxgk/zcfb/gg/201703/t20170317_961176.html?code=&state=123>[Accessed 9 December 2022].

Notice of the Ministry of Ecology and Environment on issuing the management rules for the registration, trading, and settlement of the National Carbon Emission Rights (Trial) [关于发布《碳排放权登记管理规则 (试行)》《碳排放权交易管理规则 (试行)》和《碳排放权结算管理规则 (试行)》的公告], Ministry of Ecology and Environment (MEE), No. (2021)21, 17 May 2021. Available at: <https://www.mee.gov.cn/xxgk2018/xxgk/xxgk01/202105/t20210519_833574.html> [Accessed 9 December 2022].

Notice on implementing data supervision on National Carbon Trading Market [关于做好全国碳排放权交易市场数据质量监督管理相关工作的通知], Ministry of Ecology and Environment, No. (2021) 491, 25 October, 2021.

Notice on the first compliance cycle of emission allowance surrendering for the National ETS [关于做好全国碳排放权交易市场第一个履约周期碳排放配额清缴工作的通知]. Ministry of Ecology and Environment (MEE), No. (2021) 492, 26 October 2021. Available at: <https://www.mee.gov.cn/xxgk2018/xxgk/xxgk06/202110/t20211026_957871.html> [Accessed: 9 December 2022].

Notice of GHG emissions reporting management[关于做好2022年企业温室气体排放报告管理相关重点工作的通知], Ministry of Ecology and Environment No. (2022) 111, 15 March 2022. Available at: <https://www.mee.gov.cn/xxgk2018/xxgk/xxgk06/202203/t20220315_971468.html> [Accessed 9 December 2022].

Notice of the Supreme People's Court on Strengthening and Innovating Trial for Environment and Resources to Provide Judicial Service and Guarantee for the Modernization of Harmonious Co-existence Between Human and Nature[最高人民法院关于新时代加强和创新环境资源审判工作为建设人与自然和谐共生的现代化提供司法服务和保障的意见]. The Supreme People's Court of the People's Republic of China, 8 October 2021.

Pang, T. and Duan, M.S., 2016. Cap setting and allowance allocation in China's emissions trading pilot programmes. *Climate Policy*, 16(7), pp. 815–835.

State Council Information Office of the People's Republic of China (SCIO), 2020. *China's achievements, new goals and new measures for nationally determined contributions[中国落实国家自主贡献成效和新目标新举措]*. Available at: <https://unfccc.int/sites/default/files/NDC/2022-06/China%E2%80%99s%20Achievements%2C%20New%20Goals%20and%20New%20Measures%20for%20Nationally%20Determined%20Contributions.pdf> [Accessed 9 December 2022].

State Council Information Office of the People's Republic of China (SCIO), 2021. *Responding to climate change: China's policies and actions [中国应对气候变化的政策与行动2021]*. Available at:<http://english.scio.gov.cn/whitepapers/2021-10/27/content_77836502.htm> [Accessed 9 December 2022].

State Council, 2021. *Action plan for carbon dioxide peaking before 2030 [2030年前碳达峰行动方案]*. Available at:<https://english.www.gov.cn/policies/latestreleases/202110/27/content_WS6178a47ec6d0df57f98e3dfb.html> [Accessed 9 December 2022].

Shen, Y., 2016. Crossing the river by groping for stones: China's pilot emissions trading schemes and the challenges for national scheme. *Asia Pacific Journal of Environmental Law*, 18, pp. 1–42.

Sun, Y.P. and Wang, K.Y., 2017.*Annual Report of China Carbon Emissions Trading Scheme (2017) [中国碳排放权交易报告(2017)]*. Beijing: China Social Sciences Academic Press, pp. 22–30.

Tang, R., Guo, W., Oudenes, M. et al., 2018. Key challenges for the establishment of the monitoring, reporting and verification (MRV) system in China's National Carbon Emissions Trading Market. *Climate Policy*,18 (sup1), pp. 106–12.

The Communist Party of China Central Committee, State Council, 2021.*Working guidance for carbon dioxide peaking and carbon neutrality in full and faithful implementation of the new development philosophy[中共中央 国务院关于完整准确全面贯彻新发展理念做好碳达峰碳中和工作的意见]*. Available at: <https://english.www.gov.cn/policies/latestreleases/202110/25/content_WS61760047c6d0df57f98e3c21.html> [Accessed 9 December 2022].

United Nations, 2017. *International recommendations for energy statistics*. Available at: < https://unstats.un.org/unsd/energy/ires/IRES-web.pdf> [Accessed 9 December 2022].

Verde, S., Galdi, G., Alloisio, I. and Borghesi, S., 2021. The EU ETS and its companion policies: any insight for China's ETS? *Environment and Development Economics*, 23(3), pp. 203–230.

World Bank, 2021. *State and trends of carbon pricing 2021.* [online] Available at: < https://openknowledge.worldbank.org/handle/10986/35620> [Accessed 9 December 2022].

Yang, B. Y. and Fang, K., 2021. The Study on legal attributes of carbon emission rights [碳排放权的法律属性研究]. *Environmental Protection[环境保护]* 49(16), pp. 55–59.

Zhang, Y.F., Harris, J. and Li, J., 2018. China's carbon market: accelerating a green economy in China and reducing global emissions. Available at: <https://www.bu.edu/eci/files/2019/08/18-01_ZhangHarris_ChinasCarbonMarket.pdf>] [Accessed 9 December 2022].

Uday Shankar, Arindam Basu

Chronicling Energy Law in India in the Era of Low-Carbon Transition

Abstract: Within India's federal set up which typically fosters individual and shared responsibility between the centre and the states, 'electricity' falls under the Concurrent List, allowing both levels of governments to legislate and formulate policy on different facets of power market. Consequently, the Electricity Act, a central legislation, after coming into effect on 2003, exclusively revamped the power sector in India by de-licensing the generation segment, introducing multi-buyer model, establishing specialized court and conferring autonomy to regulatory bodies. But the Act largely deals with the sector-specific conventional sources of energy and notwithstanding early promise and the transformational reform it holds limited references on renewables which is persistently hurting India's ambitious socio-political and legal expression in the context. As of now, in the midst of Covid-induced environment, India's aspiration to achieve 175 GW of grid-connected renewable electricity by March 2022 appears to be epic. Additionally, with its National Electricity Plan in place, India exuberantly sets the ambition to achieve 275 GW of renewables by 2027. This necessitates frantic commitment to minimize the reliance on the non-clean sources of energy. The flexibility, cost effectiveness and resilience of renewable energy are supposed to be the winners but the challenges are humongous. As the global economy is gingerly getting prepared to embrace the low-carbon future, it is imperative that law eases such transition in orderly and just fashion while addressing global climate risk. For India, a profound plea for greater disclosure on emissions baselines, GHG reduction targets and transition plans are likely to be translated into larger investment risks. Hitherto, international investment law, covering an extensive global grid of investment treaties and trade agreements, oddly remains shy on the climate change issues. This makes the pitch for India slippery as its legal and policy response must entail sustainability as a guiding principle for domestic finance and investment scenario. The chapter will capture the unfolding drama scripted largely by the Electricity Act in the context of renewable energy and the low carbon transition in India. The narrative will also examine the policy perspective and the judicial interventions made in the renewable sector, thus far.

Uday Shankar is Registrar & Professor of Law at Hidayatullah National Law University, India.
Arindam Basu is Assistant Professor at the Indian Institute of Technology Kharagpur, Department of Rajiv Gandhi School of Intellectual Property Law, India.

https://doi.org/10.1515/9783110752403-033

1 Introduction

The frontier of global energy market is shifting. The transformation, coalesced with geopolitics, offers us a glimpse of future that is seduced by the irresistible siren song – 'go for renewables'. Attractive as it sounds, however, the makeover towards this major shift is not going to be tip-toe through tulips.

In the global energy market, India has always been an important player simply because of its untapped demand potential and to that end, the Indian energy policy approach is quite spartan. Currently, its generation capacity under various renewable energy projects stands at 152.90 Gigawatt.[1] This is surely encouraging, especially if we read it with India's climate commitment that effectively is about defining its own Nationally Determined Contribution (NDC). The target that India has set is threefold – making the economy sustainable by altering the pattern of consumption, to increase the forest cover of the country and generation of electricity by using non-fossil based resources. One of the stated goals is also to enhance nuclear power generation capacity in next decade.

This apparently simple-looking proposition stands on too many assumptions. Though we accept that this shift is necessary and acknowledge the importance of putting in place a long-term plan, in the current state, India's flamboyant visions inadvertently advances a circular argument. To boost generation capacity, India requires major investments in the renewable energy sector. The potential dominant markets are obviously electric vehicles, green hydrogen and manufacturing solar equipment. Clearly, a large part of the investment is expected to come from overseas markets. As a matter of fact, since 2014, investment in India's renewable energy sector is on the constant rise.[2] This, quite unsurprisingly, has catapulted India's global rank to fourth in terms of holding renewable energy capacity. But this silver lining has an almost invisible yet perilous grey tinge around it that holds the potential to upset India's dream.

From three different dimensions we need to look at this threat. Firstly, India must ensure that its increased economic activity remains carbon neutral. This is not simply in terms of what it is aimed to produce. Rather, the crucial issue is what has to be given away as a consequence of generating green energy en masse. Second, laying down the bump-free investment avenues inevitably requires loosening up the uncomfortable knots of environmental rules and regulations. It does not make any sense to support sustainable development that is disproportionately tilted towards unruly technology-driven environment. At the one end of the spectrum there is a

1 This total generation capacity is a combination of 50.78 GW from solar, 40.13 GW from wind, 10.63 GW from bio-power, 4.84 GW from small hydropower and 46.52 GW from large hydropower.

2 Information released by the Department for Promotion of Industry and Internal Trade (DPIIT), reveals that incoming FDI in the Indian energy sector is quite substantial. Only in between April 2000 and June 2021, India has received approximately US$ 10.28 billion in non-conventional energy sector.

need to uplift the domestic capacity and on the other, the confidence of the foreign investors has to be maintained. Thirdly, India's energy narrative is integrally connected to its international climate pledge which is thus far, blemished with dichotomy. If India is right about pointing out the lack of meaningful binders from the world's major carbon emitters, it fails to remain consistent in its own approach. India's aim to achieve energy transition should be backed up by strong legal accountability at the domestic level. However, the Indian government has preferred to dilute important environmental laws, relegating those laws to mere ornamental status at present. India's commitment at the COP 26 to achieve Net Zero emissions by 2070 and reduction of carbon emissions by one billion tonnes within 2030 for that reason is at variance. Subsequently, the COP27, held in Sharm El Sheikh, Egypt was concluded with an important agreement, providing 'loss and damage' funding to those countries that are already vulnerable because of climate change related events. But, except for amending the pledge on mitigation efforts, in general no further advancement was made in terms of enhancing the emission reduction commitments. India always has claimed for more space to choose its own energy mix. It has no serious reason reason to be unhappy with what happened at COP27. In Particular, the Sharm el-Sheikh Implementation Plan, the final resolution passed at COP27 which is to establish a work programme on just transition into renewable energy is in sync with India's long-term climate change planning. But parallely the burden is on India to prove that its climate pledges must not turn into the high-sounding dialect, devoid of any significant triumphs. Internally it just cannot afford to miss the mark when it comes to strike a right balance between conservation, the process of transformation and expansion of economic plinth.

For decades, electricity law has remained controversial for several issues. However, with its current energy policy outlook, India holds the promise to offer much more to the international mission for energy transition. Especially focusing on privatization and subsidy, last year, the Ministry of Power of India has circulated a draft Electricity (Amendment) Bill that proposes crucial amendments to the Electricity Act, 2003. The objective is to give a boost to the power sector. However, we need to proceed with caution to accept that the changes can really make the energy sector more workable and investor-friendly while achieving clean energy targets.

In this chapter we aim to capture the Indian time, brewing with an unique vivacity and full of prospects. Our aim is to tell a story that will offer a balanced chronicle, touching some of the most controversial legal issues related to energy, especially within the electricity sector along with climate change and green investment. Overall, what we desire to propose is that 'going green' cannot be an insulated agenda that can be perused by one-dimensional doggedness. Rather, there is a constant disclaimer that urges us to understand the limits of finite resources offered by our planet and make a sensible move to improve prosperity at all levels.

The chapter is divided into seven parts. Part I introduces the theme and prepares the ground for a narrative that gets unfolded into discussion on Indian energy policy with special emphasis on electricity law. Part II asks us to examine our wisdom about how we appreciate the 'green' in a flourishing energy market. The argument somewhat alarmingly suggests that not all Indian actions can be crowned as 'green'. Part III offers us a glimpse of the Indian energy market where green investmest is now the fashionable idea. Part IV informs us about the past and present of Indian electricity law and its importance to attain the green growth. Part V reconnoiters India's past, present and future climate pledges. We learn that it is an opportune time for India to align with the global climate pledge which with India's current legal and policy approaches does appear uncertain. Part VI offers a few alternatives that India can think of to make its presence more visible in global energy market and future climate talks. Part VII concludes the chapter.

2 Understanding 'Green' in Green Energy Market

The rising demand for renewable energy in various forms reflects a somewhat morbid situation that bluntly reminds us how unsustainable had been our consumption patterns. In point of fact, we have learned to accept, in a hard way, that there is imbalance in our social order, leading to intense distribution conflicts. Yet, the geopolitics involved in connection with renewable energy is complex and thus far, have received sporadic attention. One key reason for this lassitude is the failure of international or domestic laws to create enough incentives for stakeholders who are expected to be rewarded for their participation in the energy transition process.

At the heart of this discourse lies the tension between those who promote the idea of 'freer' free market and conservation of natural resources that are finite by their very nature of existence. So, there has been a long-standing dilemma regarding how to strike a right balance in between politics and regulations. Because our understanding towards environment-friendly technologies gets developed within this open-ended set up, there are obvious tendencies to either overestimate the credibility or outrightly downplay the benefits that certain technologies bring with them. However, the focus should not be actually on how we are going to benefit by renewable energies. That part is given and it hardly can be denied that the requirement of more utilization of renewable energies is obvious. Rather, a more pressing concern is about how viable are those technologies that are deployed to utilize renewable energies. This is certainly impregnated by the mainstream views of economics, *i.e.*, 'environmental goods and services are like normal ones except that they suffer from market failures'. Hence, the goal is to correct that market failure and make a move routinely. According to this insight, we can see how an incumbent technology should be priced or how the activities based on that technology should be taxed (Nordhaus, 2021: p. 74).

But this internalization mechanism accepts, tacitly though, that some forms of externalities are unavoidable and for the love of development, must be acceptable to all of us. There are disagreements on this version of development because it fails to provide us the guidance on how we should interpret the idea of sustainability within the prevalent economic dogma. Robert Solow opines that "a sustainable path for the national economy is one that allows every future generation the option of being as well-off as its predecessors. The duty imposed by sustainability is to bequeath to posterity not any particular thing....but rather to endow them with whatever it takes to achieve a standard of living at least as good as our own and to look after their next generation similarly. We are not consume humanity's capital, in the broadest sense" (Solow, 1993: p. 168).

This formulation is a stylized representation of how our society should function. Our energy consumption and energy harvesting for future generations are connected by a single thread and therefore, our understanding of 'green' technologies is essentially conditioned by the requirement to keep that thread unbroken. In other words, it refers to correct estimation of the effects of externalities on profits which is a delicate task. A fundamental requirement of the effective operation of a green economy is that profits must not provide the wrong signals. If that happens the economic development can go in the wrong direction. For instance, in the context of air pollution, Nicholas Muller had shown that 'in some cases the cost of pollution was so high the actual profits or net social value of a product were estimated to be negative'. Muller and his team (2011) conducted their study in seven industries and concluded that the net social value of production in those industries was negative because of permissive and tolerant emission regulations. This also meant that the price of emissions was set at a point that effectively failed to reflect the actual cost of pollution.[3]

It is not very difficult to see why this cannot be a matter of concern in other examples such as generation of electricity and carbon emissions. Similarly, if the articulated policies on harvesting renewable energy is not done correctly, then the value of expected or already in existence products can be negative and our understanding of 'green' shifts from conservation to unbalanced utilization, essentially driven by profit-maximizing motives.

Interestingly, this entire evolution is shaped up under acute controversy on the right to use fossil and renewable sources. The postulation that the classification of energy is nearly universal is not without controversy and often the disagreements rage on whether a particular type of energy should be deemed renewable or not. Consequently, uncertainty follows regarding exclusion of such energy entirely from the regulatory net or even setting a seemingly lower parameter of regulation (Crossley, 2019: p. 19). The latter path, if chosen, as we have already mentioned, always runs the

3 These industries include plants using coal, stone quarrying, sewage treatment, oil-fired power plants, solid waste incineration, marinas and petroleum and coal product manufacturing units.

risk of not reflecting social cost correctly. The first option is, however, the extreme form of ignoring the need to reflect social cost through regulatory process which ideally should happen when we can repose absolute faith in technology and resulting process of resource extraction. Needless to mention, such scenario is still not in sight.

Alarms have already been raised about the environmental benefits (or problems) that come with few forms of renewable technologies such as large-scale hydropower, woody biomass and peat. On the other hand, there are claims that technologies, dependent on energy sources that are not renewable, such as geothermal and nuclear energy, should be included in the definition of renewable energy, especially if the goal is to encourage the quicker deployment of low carbon electricity generation (Crossley, 2019).

How 'green' is India's state of affairs? In the power sector, India advances a vision that includes 'improving electricity distribution business and operations, enabling renewables and distributed energy resources, and promoting energy resilience and local manufacturing of renewable energy and energy storage technologies' (NITI Aayog and Rocky Mountain Institute, 2020: p. 5).

Therefore, there is a need to focus on four-pronged strategies – investing in least-cost energy solutions, supporting resilient and secure energy systems, prioritizing efficiency and competitiveness and promoting social and environmental equity. The first three mechanisms are essentially market driven that are visibly intended to be balanced by the fourth one. On paper, the social and environmental equity requires balancing investment in renewables that predominantly comes with the rider of technological solution. Even if the assessment of 'green' quietly alighted with the growth in job market, the sustainability of the process must be understood from how much impact it has on the environment. As we have already noted, this simply means that the regulatory aspects must be set up at the optimal level to reflect the social cost correctly. It is entirely one-dimensional, for example, to say that because air pollution is severe in most of the major cities in India, the green investment should be justifiable (this is exactly the example used in NITI Ayog's (2020: 12) assessment). Rather, the approach should be inclusive. India fails in that aspect badly. If the idea is to assess the impact of a technology driven green market, then the environmental impact assessment must be done with the clear conviction. It is unclear how India plans to do that when it has been found guilty of constantly diluting its environmental impact assessment regulations to accommodate market players whose claims are fairly unproven.

Let us simply look at it from India's euphoria about green hydrogen as an alternative to fossil fuels. On February, 2022, India's Ministry of Power released the first part of National Hydrogen Mission policy on green hydrogen and green ammonia (the second part is yet to be released). The idea is to find an alternative clean energy source, reduce dependency on fossil fuel and decrease crude oil imports in future. Green hydrogen is not the new kid in the block, though. The genesis can be traced back to the Nazis who ingeniously used hydrogen to produce synthetic fuels from coal. The prospecting reverie resurfaced today in a new avatar, holding the potential to offer significant climate change solution. But underneath the euphoria, lies the uncertainties. To use hydrogen as an alternative, it must be produced in enough quantity. As of now, the by-products generated while producing hydrogen by using certain technologies (*e.g.* steam reforming of natural gas), are causing enough apprehensions because one of them is CO_2. Even from this perspective one can bring cost-benefit analysis by citing other cleaner methods of producing hydrogen to justify its use. But the actual catch is something else. Professor Ad van Wijk of Delft University of Technology in the Netherlands says that efficiency is no longer the benchmark and in a sustainable energy system, calculation should be in terms of system costs, *i.e.* how much it would take to convert an existing system into a new one. It surely, must not be prohibitive (Van Renssen, 2020).

But there is a paradox in a clean hydrogen market. European experience reveals that the industries can be the main beneficiaries because they are the biggest hydrogen consumers today. But looking from the potential profit margin angle, the transport sector is the hot bed. As Europe is aiming for climate neutrality by 2050, interests are certainly picking up in clean hydrogen, especially from sectors like steel and chemicals. But these industries are extremely price-sensitive and therefore, they are very much reluctant and are just not ready to pay 'grey' price for a climate-friendly alternative. So, what are they doing to avoid such cost? They push to get green hydrogen into road transport as much as possible so that private car owners bear some of the initial costs (Van Renssen, 2020: 800).

For India this is a difficult pitch. If it accedes to such demands, especially to those overseas companies holding important technologies and patents, then its domestic investment scenario will be prone to misgivings. Indeed, we have observed that recently India is pushing aggressively its transport market by introducing electric vehicles run by hydrogen fuel cells and it has plans to manufacture five million tonnes of green hydrogen per annum by 2030. On the other hand, to make that important move India needs to be assured that long run benefits outpace the initial hick ups, if any. At present, with National Hydrogen Mission in place, India is desperately linking its climate obligations with the clean energy generation process, including hydrogen. Hence, its understanding of 'green' is further required to be seen from its climate change obligations point of view.

3 Linking Climate Change, Energy Transition and Green Investment

When in 1992 India became a party to the United Nation Framework Convention on Climate Change (UNFCCC), its economy was just about to be liberalized. India's demand, however, remained consistent over the period of time even if it gradually became one of the lucrative markets for the global conglomerates. Therefore, its persistent opposition to any legally binding quantitative GHG mitigation targets for itself, is to be seen in the light of its changing economy.

Today, India is following the policy of decarbonization, that includes achieving better energy efficiency, a gradual shift towards renewable energies and altering production and consumption patterns (Rajamani, 2017: 6). As per the Paris Agreement, India proposed its NDCs under which it had agreed to reduce the emissions intensity of its GDP by 33–35% from 2005 levels by 2030. This means that India needs to increase the share of non-fossil fuel-based electricity to 40% cumulative electric power installed capacity and significantly increase its forest and tree cover (Rajamani, 2017).

Last year in Glasgow, at COP 26, India once again repeated its tried and tested lines of thought *i.e.* acknowledgment for historical emission responsibilities, more carbon space and inequity. But, the most controversial announcements made by India at COP 26 were its Net Zero target by 2070 and decision to go ahead with the exploitation of its coal-reserves. Yet, the succeeding developments have put India at slight discomfort. For instance, in Egypt, COP27 delivered a decision on a mitigation work programme which parties agreed to commence following the conclusion of COP27, continuing up to 2026 with a possibility of further revision. States that are already committed on 2030 targets are to review their achievements in one year's time and if possible will speed up their coal phasedown efforts along with phasing out of inefficient fossil fuel subsidies. Here, India's concern was about identifying only coal usage as a source of potent greenhouse gas emission. What India wanted was to include other greenhouse gases within the future mitigation plan as well which did not happen under COP27 mitigation work programme.

Though, this minor setback is not entirely an outlier, to justify its climate pledge, India is heavily relying on three strategies – enhancing solar power capacity, promoting electric transport and using hydrogen reserves as an alternative to other fossil fuels. Central to the claim affirms a simple postulation that becoming energy efficient is the only solution and net zero seems to be an attractive appeal. But India is looking at net zero emission on a limited basis and not from the perspective of achieving carbon balance in all respects. There can be no net zero without appropriate infrastructures and these are never going to be built if it is purely left to the private sector alone. The private sector will distribute what is profitable to them and may fall short of the desirable length and breadth of social welfare (Helm, 2020: p. 3).

Yet, India's insistence on a market economy has been tenacious since the middle part of the last decade. An important dimension to India's energy chronicle is its budget allocation. Its 2022-23 budget provides for green bonds to finance environment friendly projects. Green bonds, typically debt instruments issued by the governments, are considered to be beneficial for addressing climate change. Green bonds are also part of Environmental Social Governance (ESG) investment process and currently regulated by the Securities and Exchange Board of India (SEBI) which in 2017, had issued necessary guidelines. Under the guidelines mainly the identified companies are required to disclose their business sustainability report to stock exchanges and based on that ESG related elements can be identified which includes isolating environmental risk factors that can impact a company's business, hence its ability to do credible business. Because India is already committed to net zero race, it relies a great deal on market mechanisms like green bonds (Ghosh *et al.*, 2021: 67-8). In reality, it is a part of green financing mechanism which also includes carbon tax and establishment of green banks or green funds. All these by and large are read with a country's efforts to achieve sustainable development. The main focus is on environment friendly projects in any form. Interestingly, a decoupling takes place when the need to contribute exclusively towards climate change mitigation gets interpreted in a generic sense.

Hitherto, among all these, we can still single out green bonds as it has its presence felt in the renewable energy sector. At present that influence is slowly on the rise and green bonds till 2020 covered only 0.7 per cent of all the bonds issued in India. Simultaneously, bank's lending to the non-conventional energy sector stood only 7.9 per cent of outstanding bank credit to the power sector by March 2020 (Ghosh *et al.* 2021). In a communication made on November 9, 2022, Union Finance Minister Smt. Nirmala Sitharaman confirmed that India has approved its first Sovereign Green Bonds Framework, developed in accordance with the provisions of the framework, Green Finance Working Committee (GFWC). This is expected to provide necessary support to India's climate pledge taken at COP26.

But this is just one side of the entire market. What if the investment made to a project is not environmentally benign? Can it be then called 'greenwashing'?[4] What will be the responsibility of the fund managers? A nagging unease settles in almost immediately given the fact that some fund managers can be dishonest enough to invite otherwise sensible investors by wrongly projecting the United Nations Principles for Responsible Investment (PRI). Ideally, these managers should not deviate from their own promise of integrating ESG into their investment decisions. This concern adequately gets reflected in a report published by KPMG (2020). According to this report, hedge fund managers may greenwash due to inadequate expertise, shortage of data, or uncertainties associated with the value of ESG (also see Hao Liang et al., 2020).

There is hardly any doubt that such tendency can only be tackled by reviewing the impact of the project itself. The Indian market provides an unique experience to those who wish to offer investment for greening the environment. The market for electricity, particularly is on the rise. However, any investment opportunity there is supposedly to be seen from how the regulatory aspects are taking shape. In the next segment we focus on that scenario.

---

4 Greenwashing is a deceitful tendency of some companies to gain market advantage by promoting their activities under the environmentally conscious tag, whereas in reality they are not.

4 Looking through the Lens of Electricity Law

The Constitution of India distinctly establishes a federal set up by distributing responsibilities between central and state governments, individually or jointly. Seventh Schedule of the Constitution embraces three lists *viz.*, Union List, State List and Concurrent List, identifying the subject matters of legislation for the centre and the states. Among all the three Lists, the Concurrent List holds the key for regulating 'Electricity' as the subject falls within it, primarily indicating the role of state governments on the subject. This of course is buttressed by the possibility of timely intervention by the centre to maintain uniformity at the national level. For that matter the centre enjoys a constitutionally enunciated supremacy over the states, though theoretically speaking, to regulate 'Electricity' within the Concurrent List, both do have shared responsibilities (Seventh Schedule of the Constitution of India).

During the colonial period, the electricity sector was being regulated to channel the production and distribution in major cities and towns through private players (Garg *et al.*, 2008: 2). In 1887, a law (Act XIII) was enacted to protect person and property from the risks connected with the supply and use of electricity for lighting and other purposes. In time, the Electricity Act No. 9 of 1910, a comprehensive law, came into existence, replacing the earlier Electricity Act of 1903. This Act laid down a basic regulatory framework for the electricity supply industry by introducing the provisions of 'grant of license for bulk supply' (Section 3, Part II of the Act dealt with Grant of licenses) and for purchase of electrical undertakings by the state (Section 6 of the Act dealt with purchase of Undertakings). However, the Act did not dwell upon the non-conventional source of energy and dealt only with electrical energy (Section 2(g) of the 1910 Act). Besides, the focus, thus far, was mainly on cities, leaving rural areas largely out of the purview. Therefore, it was the matter of time for India to witness another spell of legislative process.

Just after a year of independence, a new law materialized with the mandate to promote 'access to energy' in rural areas along with the cities through newly created statutory bodies known as 'State Electricity Boards'. These Boards were specifically entrusted with the three major responsibilities – 'production' 'transmission' and 'distribution' of electricity (Act no. 54 of 1948, The Electricity (Supply) Act, 1948). The Act also described the statutory powers and functions of the 'Central Electricity Authority' and provided for the rationalization of the production and supply of electricity in order to boost up the energy sector through 'Grid System'. The Act further dealt with 'water-power' whereby it allowed the Board to consider the installation of hydro-electric plants without adversely affecting the irrigation, navigation and flood control (Section 30 of the 1948 Act). This framework was revisited by the Parliament when it introduced the Electricity Regulatory Commission Act, 1998 to bring transparency, accountability and professionalism in the fixation of tariff for meeting energy crisis (Act No. 14 of 1998). Yet, with the onslaught of time, all these legislations became old-fashioned and needless to mention, 'clean energy' did not find any place in any of them.

The electricity regulatory framework received the timely update when in 2003 the Electricity Act came into being, replacing all three earlier legislations, namely Indian Electricity Act, 1910, the Electricity (Supply) Act, 1948 and the Electricity Regulatory Commissions Act, 1998. By this time the complexities in the sector increased manifold and environmental concerns started to permeate the related legislative process significantly. Hence, the enactment of Electricity Act, 2003 was an important move by the Parliament and to date it remains a crucial legislation. Most notably, it attempts to introduce renewable source of energy in the league of conventional sources through its provisions.

The Act essentially mandates that Regulatory Commissions, autonomous corporate bodies, shall deal with tariff and issue of licenses along with recommending the restructuring of State Electricity Boards into separate generation, transmission and distribution entities. It also mandates licensee-free thermal generation, non-discriminatory open access of the transmission system and gradual implementation of open access in the distribution system which is expected to pave the way for creation of a robust power market in India (Bhattacharya, 2003).

Then how does the Electicity Act, 2003 deal with the renewable energy? Clearly, the Act does not define renewable energy. Instead, several regulations are issued under the Act that hold the significance in terms of addressing issues related to the renewable energy.[5] With that the Act (Section 3(1)) requires the central government to issue, in consultation with the state governments, a national energy policy and tariff policy, from time to time. In April 2021, the Ministry of Power has issued the draft National Energy Policy 2021 to replace the existing National Electricity Policy 2005. There is a mandate to develop the power system based on optimal utilisation of resources such as coal, natural gas, nuclear, hydro, and renewable sources of energy. For renewable energy, the Central Government is responsible to prepare, publish and revise, in consultation with state governments, national policy for stand-alone systems for rural areas based on renewable and non-conventional energy sources (Section 4 of the Act). The State Electricity Regulatory Commission is required to consider the promotion of co-generation and generation of electricity from renewable energy sources while specifying the terms and conditions of the tariff (Section 61 of the Act). Further, the Commission is entrusted with the functions, *inter alia*, to promote cogeneration and generation of electricity from renewable sources of energy by

5 CERC (Terms and Conditions for Tariff determination from Renewable Energy Sources) Regulations, 2020, regulation 2(1)(w) – electricity generated from renewable energy sources; the Ministry of Power (MoP) in 2019 categorised large hydopower projects having a capacity of more than 25MW under the ambit of RE sources – https://powermin.gov.in/sites/default/files/webform/ accessed on February 09, 2022.

providing suitable measures for connectivity with the grid and sale of electricity to any person. For purchase of electricity from such sources it can also specify a percentage of the total electricity consumption in the area (Section 81 of the Act).

Undoubtedly, the above-mentioned provisions of the Electricity Act, 2003 offer a silver lining amidst the structurual uncertainties in the energy market. A crucial component of the entire framework under the Act is the Renewable Purchase Obligation (RPO) which mandates State Electricity Regulatory Commissions to specify a RPO target on obligated entities such as distribution licensees, open access consumers and captive consumers (Section 86(1)(e) of the Act). The targets vary widely across states. The legal enforcement of RPO is yet to be realised in fullest sense. The non-committal approach of power distribution companies in different states to procurement of a certain amount of renewable power is mulling the need for legally enforceable obligation to purchase of the energy from non-conventional sources.[6]

Giving a great impetus to the cause of clean energy, the Supreme Court validated the regulation made by the Rajasthan Electricity Regulatory Commission on the mandatory purchase of a minimum energy from renewable sources by captive power plants and open access consumers. Notably, the Court legitimised the regulation on the premise of pollution free environment, a facet of the right to life under Article 21 of the Constitution.[7] The judicial intervention has not only approved the regulatory power of the Commission to impose obligation on the utilities on RPO but also integrated the drive of 'renewable' with the constitutional goals.

Nonetheless, there is hardly any doubt that the current electricity regulatory framework contains necessary provisions to make India's renewable energy dream possible. At least it cannot be assumed that law does not tender any motivations to operationalize the renewable energy market. Additionally, the renewable energy policies framed thus far are expected to strengthen the integration of renewables in country's energy mix. For example, the National Electricity Policy, 2005 broadly prescribes that the development of power system should be based on optimal utilization of resources. Should it be realized through accurate planning or not largely depends on the cautious use of fossil fuel and to tap the cleaner sources of energy to meet the energy requirement of the country. As we will note in the next section, India fails to acquit itself completely from the guilty-pleasure of using fossil fuels yet. The nit-picking of plausible reason for this visible dichotomy is not possible though.

For the moment, as per the current Tariff Policy, distribution companies are under obligation to purchase a fixed percentage of renewable power as determined by the State Electricity Commisions (SERCs). The Policy requires fixation of a minimum percentage of RPO from such sources taking into account availability of such re-

6 Available on http://www.downtoearth.org.in/content/amendment-proposed-electricity-act-enforce-renewable-energy-purchase-obligation accessed on March 21, 2022.

7 Hindustan Zinc Limited v. Rajasthan Electricity Regulatory Commission, 2015 (6) SCALE 706.

sources in the region and its impact on retail tariffs. Para 6.4 of the Tariff Policy also states that procurement of renewable power for future requirements shall be done through a competitive bidding process and in the long-term, renewable energy technologies would need to compete with other sources in terms of full costs.

The Ministry of New Renewable Energy that emerged from erstwhile Ministry of Non-Conventional Energy Sources in 2006, keeps on issuing necessary guidelines for competitive procurement of electricity in order to make the renewables sustainable in the electricity market.[8] While the allocation for solar has already been done through competitive bidding under the National Solar Mission and state solar policies, these guidelines also seek to cover all other renewable energy sources, such as wind, small hydro, geothermal, biomass, tidal, etc. More importantly, the guidelines seek to create competition in the grid-connected renewable energy sector, bring transparency and fairness in allocation, reduce information asymmetries among bidders, bring standardization, and hence reduce ambiguity in the whole process of project allocation (Krithika and Mahajan, 2014).

These benefits are not distributed to cities only. Villages are also made beneficiaries. Section 5 of the Act mandates for the formulation of a National Rural Electrification Policy to develop and manage rural distribution networks utilizing local institutions. Accordingly, the Rural Electricity Policy, 2006 came into light that promises access to electricity in rural areas and strategically to promote renewables in the form of a stand-alone power system (Section 6 of the Electricity Act, 2003). On top of it, power generation and distribution system have been freed from the licensing in the rural areas (including those based on renewable sources of energy and non-conventional sources of energy) (Section 4 of the Electricity Act, 2003). To foster technological innovation, the Policy encourages using isolated lighting technologies like solar photovoltaic in any rural areas where off-grid or standalone system of electrification is not feasible. Overall, the goal is to promote decentralized distribution facilities in tandem with reinforcing the local distribution network based on renewable energy resources.

A draft Renwable Energy Act 2015, was published by the MNRE, with salient features of the establishment of National Renwable Energy Committee and National Renwable Energy Advisory Group to ensure effective coordination for promotion of non-conventional sources of energy. The proposed institutional design was aimed towards the growth of the renewable energy sector. The legislative initiatives foreclose the argument that the renewables are to be looked at as supplanting factor in the energy market (Shankar and Kumar 2020). The draft Act was released for the comments from various stakeholders. Surprisingly, the proposal was shelved by the Government. In 2021, the Government has proposed amendment in the Electricity Act, 2003

8 http://mnre.gov.in/file-manager/UserFiles/guidelines_sbd_tariff_gridconnected_res/guidelines_tariff_-grid_re.pdf. Accessed on January 21, 2022.

to provide the desired ecosystem for the upscaling of renewables in energy mix of the country. On the lines of National Energy Policy, it has been suggested that the Central Government shall notify National Renwable Energy Policy in consultation with the State Governments for growth of renewables and to prescribe a minimum percentage of purchase of electricity from renewable and hydro sources of energy (Insertion of Section 3A in the Electricity Act, 2003). The Policy needs to be considered while determining tariff by the Commission. In order to attach more statutory authority to RPO, the power to determine the obligation of utilities towards RPO has been transferred to the Central Government from the State Commission along with higher penalities for non-compliance (Amendment to Sections 142 and 146 of the Electricity Act, 2003). Hopefully, the proposals to embrace renewable energy sectors in legislative cover gets parliamentary approval at the earliest.

5 Path that India has Chosen

It is just not prudent to discount India's overall efforts when it comes to address the problems of climate change. Being the third-largest energy consuming country in the world, India's energy feasting has almost doubled since 2000. Nearly 80% of this demand, however, is still being met by coal, oil and solid biomass. The one good thing for India is that its per capita energy consumption and emissions are still less than half the world average. But it hardly can afford to be self-complacent. With gigantic population and rising economy, it is expected that India's energy consumption will increase exponentially in the next decade.

Needless to mention that its electricity demand will also be at an all-time high. We have already understood that the pitch for India is quite uncomplicated – meet the bulk of that demand from renewables and create a market where it can attract enough investment, preferably green investment. Yet, there exists an uncomfortable impression about India regarding its almost arrogant stance against any time-bound personal greenhouse gas reduction commitment under international climate change law. Thus far, India has successfully put the ball in the court of the developed nations and to certain extent it cannot be called unjustified from an equity point of view. All India is required to do is maintain a steady climate friendly domestic policy that clearly includes showing restraint in not diluting domestic environmental laws further to accommodate business interests. Here, India is found seriously deficient.

As we have already pointed out, along with sustainable green financing India is looking forward to create enough job opportunities and any green finance initiative must be tested at the altar of exiting environmental rules and regulations. Because green investment is almost always technology dependent, the industries that intend to deploy those technologies must show at the upfront the environmental harms are minimal or at least do not cross the permissible threshold. India has in place a very elaborate system of testing the impact of industrial activities for giving necessary permission to operate.

Environmental impact assessment (EIA) in India started to gain significance during 1980s. After India enacted the important Environment (Protection) Act in 1986, an EIA notification (required by Section 3(1) of the Environment (Protection) Act, 1986) was published in 1994. The structure, originally envisaged was based on notification of listed activities that failed to meet a prescribed threshold. In general, to start any project or for the expansion of any existing project, the project proponents are required to take prior permission from the Ministry of Environment, and Forest and Climate Change (MoEF & CC). This is to assesses the environment and social impacts of the projects. Public consultation and public hearings are the two very important components that project proponents must ensure at this stage.

Quite inexplicably, between 2006 and 2020, the Indian government brought 50 amendments to the EIA notification. It feels obvious that India's ambitious environmental commitments, including its policies to address the problems of climate change, is getting uneasily qualified by these flurry of amendments. Among all these amendments, the last one brought in March 2020 is the most provocative. Two controversial aspects of this new draft have been post-clearance compliance and post-facto clearance. Under the post-clearance compliance project proponents must ensure environmental safeguards and therefore, are required to follow certain rules once a project gets approved. The post-facto clearance envisages a bizarre notion of granting post approval to those projects that had failed to take clearance previously.

An obvious difficulty that may be felt in the entire process is the vanishing importance of public participation, an important and indispensable component of EIA. One can visualize the situation when a project is already away and EIA is yet to be done. The proposal is out rightly offensive to the object of EPA, 1986 under which it is originally notified. Because environmental laws are socially beneficent legislations, a purposive interpretation is desirable. No socially beneficial purpose possibly can be achieved by shoving practice like post-facto clearance (Ishita, 2021).

Adding to this, on January 17, 2022, the MoEF & CC, came up with another ingenious directive when by an office memorandum it introduced a rating system of State Environment Impact Assessment Authorities (SEIAA). The faster the appraisal with clearance, the higher the rating for the state agencies. Because the government is stubbornly pursuing its policy of promoting ease of doing business, this rating idea is seen to be a part of it. But this is entirely an irrational move as now the onus is on the authority to clear the projects in a hurry because their incentive lies in doing so (Aggarwal, 2022). The Terms of Reference (TOR) for conducting environmental impact assessment have traditionally been the responsibility of the project proponents. Contrary to the usual obligation, they have less incentive now to submit TOR reflecting their due diligence. It is entirely unclear in a booming investment environment how this relaxed regulatory criteria can address adequately the environmental concerns. The trap India allowed itself into is classic. The lure of development at the cost of sacrificing its conservation spirit for an indefinite period of time or at least till that time when it becomes self-sufficient enough to manage environmental issues by sheer economic and technological competency. The analogy of India's version of sustainable development breaks down when we understand that such future is dependent on rapidly shrinking conservation space-time. Besides, India's old claim for more carbon space due to caring disproportionately about the environment should be viewed from its growth trajectory. In 1990s its economy was closed and its demand could have been a rational one. In 2020s its economy is booming and therefore, the same ideology is inappropriate.

Nonetheless, it is not easy to comprehend how this entire process and also other environmental laws, interact with electricity laws. Even if we accept that reasonable amount of compatibility is desirable between the two legal regimes, the means of achieving that is going to be complex affairs. Apparently, one can miss the connection if one does not delve carefully. We know that the Electricity Act, 2003 lays down a framework that at the core is conducive to expand the frontier of the renewable energy sector. This preception fairly reflects in the Preamble of the Act that highlights the 'promotion of efficient and environmentally benign policies' for the development of the power market in India.

Needless to say, the diction preferred in the Premble is carefully chosen as the birth of the Act itself principally was to cover unexplored yet contemporary areas, such as renewables. Therefore, the language ostensibly to be interpreted to include environment friendly policy prescription, symbolising the integration of 'clean energy' in the energy mix that would certainly ensure energy security by minimising the damage to our natural environment. However, this is just a telling mandate. To make it work the regulatory bodies must respect the boundary laid down by the Act in the broadest sense that already has embraced the salient environmental tenets. Neither the existing environmental legislations nor the Electricity Act stands in opposition to each other. Instead, it is necessary to find an agreeable premise where the basic understandings envisaged by these two apparently different regimes can be further promoted together. It is also imperative to understand that the process of greening uncompromisingly depends on strengthening the regulations with pragmatic incentivisation for all the stakeholders and not by designing escape pods on which perpetrators get away without any sanctions. In the next section, we will discuss some of such promises.

6 A Reflection

India's energy policy and environmental laws in current condition are the sources of bewilderment. It is quite clear that India wants to create a business environment where investors feel encouraged to particate and strictly speaking, such beliefs should fairly be acceptable. Where India falters, however, is not apparent from its policy choices. Instead, the blemishes are subtle yet perilous in nature. On the one hand, India is providing (or nudging) business communities for more opt-in choices wherein it is reducing their motivation to care more for the environment. To that end, we believe that weak enforcement of laws and ambitious economic policies will only end up promoting inequitable forms of development (Hedlin and Sunstein, 2016).

We also understand that the call for renewables is overwhelmingly saturated by India's climate obligations. But the problems of climate change touch multiple fronts, requiring liberal and forward-looking solutions. India's standing in international climate change negotiations will largely depend on how it fares domestically. There is always a possibility that too much 'paternalistic' approach can lead to one-dimensional and often unsuccessful conservation measures. It is well acknowledged that a shift to renewables can play an important role in computing a country's NDCs. Additionally, NDCs under Paris Agreement are increasingly seen as integral mechanisms within SDGs and complementary national plans and targets. It is submitted that India's current renewable energy planning is somewhat hollow at the core in the absence of strong environmental spirit, especially from the climate change point of view. Though technically it may be possible to show certain improvements in the country's economic front with financed projects, such improvements are likely to be short-lived as climate change will keep on pushing the mitigation and adaptation requirements further in the near future. At this point India's non-binding climate stance, coupling with its continuation of coal usage and tremendous push for renewables under almost non-existent environmental regulations is just too uneven and full of incongruities.

If the target is to alter the demand and consumption patterns, then the policies must have the effect of proper nudging. Richard Thaler and Cass Sunstein (2009: pp. 185–98) give the wonderful idea of libertarian paternalism, under which energy users will spontaneously restrict themselves from consuming more. The duo recommend that such practice largely depend on making energy use visible by conceiving constructive programmes. If India promotes such policies rather than adopting a top-down approach, such as outrightly diluting environmental laws to accommodate industries, that might just work for it perfectly. Else, India's climate pledge relying profoundly on net zero emissions by 2070 merely seems a proud aspiration.

It is already mentioned that the electricity laws do contain important provisions on renewables. Together with the policies that have already come up under the Electricity Act, 2003, the opportunities are humongous. The integration of such laws and policies with the environmental laws is almost given. However, we have long passed the time when any tacit reference could have been hailed as a winner. We have already noticed that India's electricity laws and environmental laws already have provisions that can at the best be termed as implicit testimonials, uneasily depending upon progressive reading of both laws. Instead, we need laws and policies where the connection is more prominently established. In other words, we must mitigate the tendency of seeing environmental laws as 'cost of doing business'. Hence, we need to fashion a regime where the harmonization will take place seamlessly with clear mandates being offered to all stakeholders.

Much is being said about the Draft Electricity Bill. But the Bill does not exactly deal with renewable energies. Therefore, the optimism that the proposed Bill is going to revolutionize our energy market by focusing more on customer orientation, compliance, competition and climate protection is somewhat premature. Moreover, it is largely unclear whether states will agree entirely with the proposed contents. This potential hurdle further gets enlarged when we notice unsettling gaps in the draft, such as ignoring the issues related to energy storage and grid stability. One encouraging point obviously is giving more focus on competition and compliance. But again the complete realization of the dream depends on alleviating conflicts among conflicting interests.

7 Conclusion

The chronological narratives brought forth the initiatives undertaken to promote green energy along with extant legislation. The legislative prescription and policy enunciation promises a desirable ecosystem to the stakeholders committed to clean energy. It is pertinent to mention that India is persistently engaging with neigbours to enlarge the energy market and ensure energy security. The agenda of clean energy requires strengthening at the national, regional, and global levels because a healthy environment can become reality with an interdependent and integrative approach to the matter of renewables source of energy.

The position of India in South Asia warrants a forethought. The state of affairs that are slowly getting unfolded reveal somewhat different prioritization processes across the nations in this region. For example, if achieving mere electrification is the target, then countries like Bangladesh, Sri Lanka, Bhutan have already achieved more than India (Khasru, 2022). But we should not miss the fact that the territorial limit of India is much wider compared to these countries and as of now India has adopted a combined strategy of completing electrification alongside adding more renewable energy mix in it. Comparing to this, in Pakistan the situation is far from encouraging as it is badly struggling to meet its energy demands.

But this is also a fact that the priorities in these countries are set based on diverse conditions and availability of resources from which energy demands can be made. Besides, some of these countries' population size and density surely should make it even more challenging to improve upon all parameters at the same time, such as generation, transmission and distribution. But more so, it is important for these countries to curve a way out to achieve some of the primary objectives mentioned in Sustainable Development Goals, such as ensuring access to affordable, reliable, sustainable and modern energy for all (SDG 7) and building resilient infrastructure, promote inclusive and sustainable industrialization and foster innovation (SDG 9).

For India, establishing a healthy relationship with its other regional member states is important not only for re-defining the scope of green growth but also for geopolitical stability. As a key member of the South Asian Association for Regional Cooperation (SAARC), a certain amount of decisiveness is expected from India for regional integration. Just to fulfil this objective, in 2014 all SAARC members signed the SAARC Framework Agreement for Energy Cooperation for two core purposes. Firstly, the members thought that the Agreement would make it easy for integrated regional grid operation. Secondly, it was largely expected that the Agreement would enlarge the cross-border trade of electricity on voluntary basis, subject of course to the laws, rules and regulations of the trading countries. These were fairly modest aspirations to start with. However, after eight years of quivering presence, the Agreement is just barely surviving, not offering much to talk about. Instead, there exists important bilateral understandings between member states. For example, India and Nepal already have opened an oil product pipeline. With Bhutan, Bangladesh and Myanmar too, India has established cooperation which is vital for these countries for strategic reasons. Therefore, it will not be mere supposition if we claim that India has performed reasonably well in carrying out its regional responsibility.

Away from Asia, another saga is gradually shaping up now. The ongoing crisis in Ukraine has forced Europe to look for alternatives. European Union President Ursula Von der Leyen's recent visit to India may pave the way for establishing a joint Trade and Technology Council, aiming to reduce EU's dependence on Russian energy supply.[9] But the continuation of such Council, if established, will depend on how EU shapes up its renewable energy policies in days ahead. Till now, a major challenge before the EU was to keep the wholesale electricity price low so that markets remain balanced. Ironically, India is nurturing the same aspiration but with a different geopolitical set up. Hence, we can conceive that the viability of any potential co-operation between India and the EU must stand on a stable long-term vision and should not be planned merely based on any regional crisis the outcome of which is difficult to predict.

But even after all promises, a significant blemish on the part of India, as mentioned already, is its decision to continue with coal-based operations without any satisfactory projection to phase out the coal usages. Even though India is not the largest coal producer in the Asian region (that credit goes to Indonesia, India being the third in ranking after Vietnam), it is certainly one of the biggest consumers of coal, along with China. Now, if India moves towards alternative sources, too soon and too quickly, then it would alter the demand side of the market in the Asian region. There-

9 See the Press release EU-India: Joint press release on launching the Trade and Technology, available at https://ec.europa.eu/commission/presscorner/detail/en/ip_22_2643 (Last visited 30/06/2022).

fore, a weak, nonetheless plausible argument can be made in support of India's delaying tactic in phasing out coal consumption. However, it also becomes obvious for India that it should put in place long-term sustainable objectives and assess its short-term energy security and affordability goals periodically to address geopolitical consequences (IEA, 2022: p. 83).

The discussion in this paper should sufficiently alert about the conflicts that have saturated the energy and environmental laws and policies. A rider becomes obvious as we search for a tussle-free cohesive framework – our laws are required to be designed to accelerate the transition to green energy at affordable cost by ensuring flexibility of the entire regulatory framework. It is important that the increasing reliance on renewables must not come at the cost of operational excellence. Policies that leave it to the market entirely may fail to create enough incentives in the absence of an integrated legal regime. We accept that competition can oust the weak players from the market eventually and infrastructure will be improved in the process over the period of time. But we also posit that such less-interventionist and market-oriented vision cannot ensure accountability unless we create an environment where every move in the energy market will start with sufficient trust over the regulatory regime. In India we are sincerely waiting to have such future of trust.

References

Aggarwal, A., 2022. *Ease of Doing Business Takes Precedence over Environmental and Social Concerns in Project Review Process*, available at https://www.downtoearth.org.in/blog/environment/ease-of-doing-business-takes-precedence-over-environmental-and-social-concerns-in-project-review-process-81225 (Last accessed 2/4/2022).

Bhattacharya, S.C. *Review of the Electricity Act 2003 of India*, CEPMLP, Dundee University, Nov. 2003.

Crossley, P., 2019. *Renewable energy law: an international assessment*. Cambridge Cambridge University Press.

Garg, A. *et al.*, 2008. *Regulation in practice, impact of tariff orders on the Indian electric sector*. TERI.

Ghosh, S. et al., 2021. Green finance in India: progress and challenges. *Reserve Bank of India Bull.*, pp. 61–72 (January).

Hedlin, S. and Sunstein, C.R., 2016. Does active choosing promote green energy use? Experimental evidence. *Ecology L. Q.*, 43(1), pp. 107–41.

Helm, D., 2020. *Net zero: how we stop causing climate change*. Glasgow: William Collins.

IEA, 2022. *Southeast Asia energy outlook*. Paris: OECD/IEA.

Ishita, G., 2021. *Environment Impact Assessment: India needs to revamp its public consultation framework*, available at: https://www.downtoearth.org.in/blog/governance/environment-impact-assessment-india-needs-to-revamp-its-public-consultation-framework-75630 (Last accessed 2/4/2022).

Khasru, S.M., 2022. The Goal of an Energy-Secure South Asia; Available at https://www.thehindu.com/opinion/op-ed/the-goal-of-an-energy-secure-south-asia/article65354570.ece (30/06/22).

KPMG, 2020. *Sustainable Investing: Fast-forwarding its Evolution*.

Krithika, P.R. and Mahajan, S. Governance of renewable energy in India: issues and challenges, Background paper, March 2014, TERI-NFA Working Paper Series No.14, available on http://www.teriin.org/projects/nfa/pdf/working-paper-14-Governance-of-renewable-energy-in-India-Issues-challenges.pdf, accessed on February 21, 2022.

Liang, H. et al. Greenwashing, available at https://corpgov.law.harvard.edu/2020/11/17/greenwashing/ (last accessed April 2, 2022).

Muller, N.Z. et al., 2011. Environmental accounting for pollution in the United States economy. *Am. Econ. Rev.*, 101(5), pp. 1949–75.

NITI Aayog and Rocky Mountain Institute, 2020. *Towards a clean energy economy: post-COVID-19 opportunities for India's energy and mobility sectors*.

Nordhaus,W.D., 2021. *The spirit of green: the economics of collisions and contagions in a crowded world*. Princeton: Princeton University Press.

Rajamani, L., 2017. India's approach to international law in the climate change regime. *Indian J. Int. L.*, 57(1-2), pp. 1–23.

Shankar, U. and Kumar, S.P.P., 2020. A critical analysis of renewable energy act, 2015. CULR 69.

Solow, R., 1993. An almost practical step toward sustainability. *Resources Pol'y*, 19(3), pp. 162–172.

Thaler, R.H. and Sunstein, C.R., 2009. *Nudge: improving decisions about health, wealth, and happiness*. London: Penguin.

Van Renssen, S., 2020. The hydrogen solution? *Nature Climate Change*, 10, pp. 799–801.

Satoshi Kurokawa

Energy Law in the Low-Carbon Transition in Japan: The Tough Road to a Low-Carbon Society after the Fukushima Nuclear Crash

Abstract: Japan's carbon reduction policy was frustrated by the major accident at the Fukushima Daiichi nuclear power plant in 2011 as it was too dependent on nuclear energy. The FIT, which replaced the RPS, has facilitated renewable energy successfully, but it has also led to the shortage of electricity supply due to the closure of old-fashioned thermal power plants in the liberalized electricity market. Japan is working to reduce greenhouse gas emissions, while ensuring a stable supply of electricity, which is Japan's top energy policy priority. The FIP, non-fossil energy certificates, and the capacity mechanisms are expected to work, as well as the revival of nuclear energy.

1 Introduction

This chapter explores the energy law in Japan from the perspective of low-carbon transition. Japan has committed itself to achieving carbon neutrality by 2050 and promised to cut greenhouse gas (GHG) emissions by 46%–50% in 2030 compared to the 2013 levels. This 2030 target seems less ambitious than that of the European Union, which promises to cut GHG emissions by at least 55% in 2030 from the 1990 levels (European Climate Law 2021, §4(1)). However, this seems difficult to achieve as Japan's energy policy still suffers from the impact of the Fukushima Daiichi nuclear disaster in 2011. The 2021 Strategic Energy Plan (ANRE, 2021b) set an aggressive roadmap toward 2030, which forecasts that fossil fuels would contribute to 68% of the total primary energy supply (TPES) and 41% of the overall power generation.

Japan used to be an important player in global climate politics before 2011 with 54 installed nuclear reactors. However, the disaster at the Fukushima Daiichi Nuclear Power Plant caused a setback to the climate policy that depended on nuclear energy. Nuclear reactors stopped operation across the country after the accident. The shortfall in electricity supply has been covered by thermal power plants emitting tremendous amounts of CO_2.

Japan is the third-largest economy in the world. Therefore, its energy consumption and CO_2 emissions are also enormous. According to the International Energy

Satoshi Kurokawa is Professor at the Faculty of Social Sciences, School of Social Sciences, Waseda University, Japan.

https://doi.org/10.1515/9783110752403-034

Agency (IEA, 2021b), Japan's total energy supply (TES) was 17.4EJ in 2019. It was fifth in the world after China, the United States, India, and Russia. Furthermore, Japan was the fifth-largest electricity generator in the world, generating 1.04PWh. In addition, 88% of Japan's primary energy source were fossil fuels in 2019 (IEA, 2021a). Therefore, Japan was globally ranked fifth in terms of energy-related CO_2 emissions. It emitted 1.03Gt of CO_2, which constituted 3.1% of the global CO_2 emissions (33Gt) in 2019(IEA, 2020a).

More than 90% of Japan's CO_2 emissions are attributable to energy consumption. Therefore, reducing energy consumption and fossil fuel combustion are keys to CO_2 emission reduction. The Energy Saving Act (Act on the Rational Use of Energy and the Promotion of the Shift to Non-fossil Energy) plays a key role in reducing energy consumption. The Nuclear Policy Act encouraged nuclear energy and the Feed-in Tariff (FIT) Act encouraged renewable energy production to reduce fossil fuel combustion. However, securing a stable energy supply is the priority goal of the energy law scheme in Japan. Therefore, the climate change mitigation policy cannot jeopardize it. In addition, the liberalization of energy markets induced the construction of thermal power plants. In these ways, the energy and climate laws are being integrated into the low-carbon transition.

In this chapter, Japan's energy-related data are based on the Comprehensive Energy Statistics delivered every year by the Agency for Natural Resources and Energy (ANRE) unless otherwise noted.

2 Energy and climate laws

2.1 Development of climate law

Japan played a significant role in global climate change politics in the 1990s. It hosted the COP3 of the UN Framework Convention on Climate Change (UNFCCC) in Kyoto in 1997. Furthermore, Japan promised to reduce GHG emissions by 6% compared with its 1990 emission levels during the first commitment period (2008–2012) of the UNFCCC Kyoto Protocol. Due to the 2008 global financial crisis and recession, it seemed easy for Japan to meet the target. However, the nuclear disaster of 2011 changed the situation. Japan managed to fulfill its commitment using the Kyoto mechanisms. However, it rejected the second commitment period target, because the Japanese government knew that CO_2 emissions would increase unless the nuclear reactors resumed operation. Subsequently, Japan's GHG emissions peaked in 2013.

The Act on the Promotion of Global Warming Countermeasures was enacted in 1998. Later, the Cabinet submitted the Bill for the Global Warming Countermeasures Policy Act to the Diet in March 2010. The bill tried to set a legally binding emission reduction target and to introduce an emission trading scheme (ETS) in 2013. However, the bill did not pass the Diet before the Fukushima Daiichi nuclear disaster and was dropped in 2012. The Prime Minister "was unable to push the legislation forward under pressure from the growing antinuclear movement" (Kameyama, 2017, p. 132). Instead of this bill, the FIT Act was legislated in 2011, and the law that levied a carbon tax on the import of coal and oil was enacted in 2012.

The government started Japan's Voluntary Emissions Trading Scheme (JVETS) in 2005 as a drill for a legal ETS. In JVETS, participating business operators committed to reducing CO_2 emissions in exchange for government subsidies for emission-reduction facilities. If a participant could not meet the reduction target, it was required to buy allowances from other participants who exceeded their targets or to return the subsidy. Then, the Trial Implementation of Integrated Domestic Market for Emission Trading started in 2008, which incorporated JVETS. Despite these drills, Japan gave up on introducing ETS at the national level. In contrast, local governments have introduced the ETS. For example, Tokyo introduced a cap & trade system in 2010 by the Tokyo Metropolitan Environment Security Ordinance, which targeted office buildings' energy use. Saitama prefecture followed Tokyo in 2011.

2.2 Energy law as a tool of climate change mitigation

Companies that emit more than 3000t of CO_2 annually are required to report their periodic GHG emissions to the government according to the Act on Promotion of Global Warming Countermeasures (§26) and the Energy Saving Act (§16). These CO_2 emissions include the indirect emission from electricity consumption. The CO_2 emissions from energy sources account for >90% of the total CO_2 emissions in Japan. Therefore, energy law schemes are connected to climate law schemes. The Energy Policy Act of 2002 stated that the mitigation of global warming should be a consideration of the energy supply-demand policy in Japan. Energy laws that regulate energy markets, energy consumption, renewable energy, and nuclear energy have become a part of the low-carbon transition law. Furthermore, the Sophisticated Structure of Energy Supply Act of 2009, the Electricity Business Act, and the Energy Saving Act have formed a framework to reduce CO_2 emissions in terms of energy supply and consumption, as well as nuclear energy and renewable energy laws.

2.3 Priority on a stable energy supply

The priority goal of energy law and policy has been put on securing a stable energy supply. It should be noted that securing a stable energy supply is more important than reducing CO_2 emissions as a policy goal under the Energy Policy Act. This has been one of the reasons why Japan was not aggressive in abandoning coal power plants.

Japan's energy demand increased rapidly, and imports of crude oil also increased in the 1960s. In FY1973, when the oil crisis began, more than 75% of the domestic primary energy supply came from oil. At that time, most of the crude oil was imported from the Middle East. Japan faced soaring prices and an unstable supply of crude oil. Thus, energy security became a priority goal of Japan's energy policy. The government intended to reduce its dependence on oil by diversifying energy sources into coal, natural gases, nuclear energy, and so on. In 1980, the Act on Promotion of Development & Introduction of Alternative Energy (Petroleum Alternative Energy Act) was legislated. It encouraged alternative energy sources to petroleum, such as nuclear power, coal, natural gas, hydropower, and geothermal energy. The Energy Policy Act of 2002 stated that securing a stable supply of energy by diversifying energy supply sources and increasing energy self-sufficiency was its priority (§2).

Due to these legislations, the share of oil in the domestic primary energy supply market decreased significantly. Oil accounted for 40%, coal for 23%, and natural gas for 18% of the energy supply, respectively, in FY2010. However, from the perspective of climate change mitigation, replacing petroleum with other fossil fuels, such as coal and natural gas, was not preferable. Therefore, in 2009, the Petroleum Alternative Energy Act was amended and renamed the Act on Promotion of Development & Introduction of Non-fossil Energy (Non-fossil Energy Act). The Act aimed to secure both a stable energy supply and the protection of the environment.

3 Energy policy and energy market liberalization

3.1 Energy Policy Act and Strategic Energy Plan

The Energy Policy Act of 2002 has represented Japan's fundamental energy policy. "Securing stable supply," "environmental suitability," and "utilization of market mechanisms" were described as energy policy goals. As for climate change mitigation, Article 3 states, "with regard to energy supply and demand, measures must be promoted to realize energy supply and demand allowing for the prevention of global warming . . . by improving energy consumption efficiency, by such measures as promoting the conversion to non-fossil-fuel energy use such as solar and wind power and the efficient use of fossil fuels." As shown, climate change mitigation is only one of the considerations in the energy supply and demand policy. Therefore, the government cannot implement an energy policy that prioritizes climate change mitigation over a stable energy supply.

The government's energy policy is expressed in detail in the Strategic Energy Plan. The Energy Policy Act required it to include a "basic policy on measures on energy supply and demand," "measures that should be taken in relation to energy supply and demand on a long-term, comprehensive and systematic basis," and so on.

Therefore, it is important to analyze the Strategic Energy Plan to realize the energy policy in Japan. The 2021 Strategic Energy Plan (6th), promulgated by the Cabinet in October 2021, shows the current energy policy in Japan. In this Plan, "the key theme is to show the path of the energy policy to realize carbon neutrality by 2050 (announced in October 2020) and reduce greenhouse gas emissions by 46% in FY 2030 from its FY 2013 levels" (ANRE, 2021b).

The regulation on energy supply and its business is conducted by respective energy business legislations such as the Electricity Business Act, the Gas Business Act, the Heat Supply Business Act, and so on. Regarding non-fossil energy regulation, the Sophisticated Structure of Energy Supply Act and the FIT Act played a significant role in addition to the law regulating nuclear energy. The Ministry of Economy, Trade, & Industry (METI) and its external agency, ANRE are in charge of energy management.

As energy supply often impacts the environment, it is regulated by environmental laws such as the Environmental Impact Assessment (EIA) Act. Some construction plans for coal-fired thermal power plants were abandoned due to the negative comments submitted in the EIA process by the Ministry of Environment, which referred to their adverse impact on climate change (Kiko-network, 2015).

3.2 Energy market liberalization and its impact on low-carbon transition

The government of Japan has engaged in electricity market reform. It has improved the functioning of the electricity market for securing a stable and affordable electricity supply. Ironically, power companies rushed to make plans for building new thermal power plants to survive in the liberalized competitive market, because the cost of electricity from thermal power plants was lower than that from PVs or windfarms in the 2010s in Japan.

Ten utility-level electric power companies (hereafter, referred to as "utilities") regionally dominated electricity markets in Japan before the electricity market reform started in 1995. The Electricity Business Act supported the regional monopoly by the utilities which vertically consolidated the generation, transmission-distribution, and retail of electricity. The 1995 amendment of the act allowed independent power producers to sell electricity at a wholesale rate to utilities. Then, the electricity retail market was also deregulated, and it was completely liberalized in 2016. Moreover, utilities were forced to be unbundled into electricity generation companies, transmission-distribution network companies, and retail companies. The act prevents the transmission-distribution network companies from engaging in electricity generation and retail businesses (§22-2). The act requires the utilities to be unbundled legally. It does not require capital unbundling. Therefore, the network companies still have capital connection with generation and distribution companies. For example, Kansai Electric Power Company, Inc., which generates and retails power, owns Kansai Transmission and Distribution, Inc. as a subsidiary. Instead, the act requires the network companies to be fair to all generators and retail companies.

Furthermore, the liberalization of the electricity market has prompted competition among power generators and among retailers. The wholesale power market was established and named Japan Electric Power Exchange (JEPX) in 2003. The Organization for Cross-Regional Coordination of Transmission Operators (OCCTO) was established in 2015 to maintain a stable supply of electricity nationwide. It balances the supply and demand of electricity across regional service areas, which are connected by cross-regional interconnection lines. The Electricity Business Act requires every electricity company to participate in OCCTO. It is a similar organization to ENTSO-E (the European Network of Transmission System Operators for Electricity), but it also has regulatory functions. The act delegates OCCTO to issue instructions to electricity companies for the sake of the security of an interconnected power system. For example, it instructs grid companies to supply electricity beyond their service areas to fill the electricity shortage in the accepting service area (OCCTO, 2022, p. 18). Furthermore, the act orders OCCTO to make cross-regional network development plans.

Power network companies still have regional monopoly licenses, but they have the legal obligation to secure fair access to the network for all market participants. The government expected that securing fair access to the network and liberalizing the retail market would lead to renewable energy expansion. Ironically, the electricity market reform endorsed the construction of thermal power plants. The construction plans for 50 units of new coal-fired power plants were made after 2012, but one-fourth of them were canceled (Japan Beyond Coal 2020, Table 1).

In terms of the levelized cost of electricity generation in Japan, gas and coal were cheaper than wind and hydro (IEA, 2020b). As for the cost of electricity generation by category, coal cost JPY 12.5/kWh, LNG cost JPY 10.7/kWh, mega-solar cost JPY 12.9/kWh, and onshore wind cost JPY 19.8/kWh in 2020. It also projected that mega-solar would cost JPY 8.2–11.8/kWh and onshore wind would cost 9.9–17.2/kWh in 2030 (ANRE 2021a, pp. 4–5). However, the cost of electricity generation using renewable energy is expected to decrease rapidly. The FIT price for PV (50kw–250kw-peak) in FY2022 was JPY 10/kWh and that for onshore wind power (less than 250kw-peak) was JPY 16/kWh (ANRE FIT Rate). At the auction held in December 2021 for an offshore wind farm project in Akita Prefecture, which will start electricity generation in 2030, the strike price for the project was as cheap as JPY 11,990/MWh (JPY 11.99/kWh) (METI, 2021). Therefore, electricity companies were afraid that coal power plants would become stranded assets. Subsequently, many coal power plant installation projects were canceled under international pressure against coal power plants. Furthermore, electricity generators have begun to close old-fashioned inefficient thermal power plants for the same reason. This led to the electricity shortage in these years in Japan. In addition, the rising prices of coal and natural gas due to the Russia–Ukraine war has made thermal power plants even more economically unattractive.

Given the current energy supply and demand situation, the reduction in thermal power plant investment would cause an energy supply shortage in Japan. In addition, the electricity supply from renewable energy sources might be unstable. Therefore, the government set up a capacity market as a capacity system in 2020 to secure the electricity supply. The 2021 Strategic Energy Plan, which estimated the power generation mix of FY2030, states that 19% of the total energy supply will come from coal and that 20% will come from LNG.

The liberalization of the electricity market led to the endorsement of the aggregation business. The 2021 amendment to the Electricity Business Act gave the aggregator a legal position (§2(7)) and expected it to integrate an increasing number of small-scale distributed renewable energy generation facilities into the network.

4 Renewable energy penetration

4.1 Renewable energy policy in Japan

Japan used to be a world leader in the development of renewable energy. It was the largest global producer of solar cells from 1999 to 2007. In addition, it was the largest solar power generator in the world in 2004 and 2005. The Sunshine Project (1974–1992) and the New Sunshine Project (1993–2000) have contributed to renewable energy development in Japan. They were large national projects that promoted the development of alternative energies to petroleum, such as solar energy, geothermal energy, and hydrogen energy. However, the government was more enthusiastic about promoting nuclear power than about expanding renewable energy. This led to the unambitious target for renewable energy under the Renewable Portfolio Standard (RPS) Act of 2002. Only 0.6% of the total domestic electricity supply was generated by solar PV and wind turbines, even in FY2010. Consequently, Japan had fallen behind other leading countries in terms of renewable energy penetration.

The government seriously considered renewable energy once again after the Fukushima Daiichi nuclear disaster. The FIT Act was enacted in 2011, and it replaced the unsuccessful RPS scheme and absorbed the net-metering scheme for small-scale PVs, which started in 2009. Since the beginning of FIT, the electricity supply generated by renewable energy sources has increased steadily. The 2018 Strategic Energy Plan (METI, 2018, pp. 20–21) projected that renewable energy would be a major power source by 2030.

In 2019, Japan generated 69TWh of solar power electricity, which was 10.1% of the total global solar PV electricity generation and ranked third in the world after China and the United States (IEA, 2021b, p. 25). This accounted for 6.6% of the total domestic electricity generation in 2019. As for hydropower, Japan ranked ninth in the world with 87TWh electricity generation in 2019. However, the hydropower at a large dam site is not supported by the FIT scheme in Japan. Only 7.5TWh was generated by wind power in 2019 in Japan. However, the installed wind capacity has doubled from 2.0GW-peak in 2009 to 4.0GW-peak in 2020.

4.2 RPS, net-metering, and FIT

The RPS was introduced by the RPS Act (the Act on Special Measures Concerning New Energy Use by Operators of Electric Utilities) of 2002. At that time, Japan was among the leading countries in terms of renewable energy development. Japan's RPS scheme seemed sophisticated because it admitted the transaction of RPS credits (Tradable Green Certificates), which could be separated from the electricity generated by renewable energy sources. It also admitted the banking and borrowing of RPS credits. However, the RPS failed to encourage renewable energy penetration. The renewable energy obligations were only less than 5.0TWh for the first 4 years, which was no more than 0.5% of the total electricity supply. Even in 2010, the RPS required only 12.2TWh of renewable-energy electricity to be sold, which was 1.35% of the total electricity supply in Japan. As the Japanese RPS scheme covered biomass waste combustion, the requirement for solar and wind electricity was too small to create the demand for renewable-energy electricity and RPS credits in the market. Therefore, it failed to call for investment in renewable energy development. The unsuccessful RPS was replaced by FIT after the Fukushima Daiichi nuclear disaster in 2011.

In fact, Japan's first version of FIT was a net-metering scheme for small-scale PV facilities, which was based on the Sophisticated Structure of Energy Supply Act of 2009. The net-metering scheme was applied only to PV electricity, and it excluded PV facilities with a generation capacity greater than 500kW. This scheme targeted household-scale PV facilities. The surplus electricity that was not consumed at the house was purchased at a fixed generous price for 10 years. As most electric utilities had already started a voluntary program to buy excess PV electricity from households, it was easy for them to adapt to the net-metering scheme. The PV net-metering was successful in increasing PV installation. Therefore, it continued substantially as a part of the FIT scheme.

The FIT scheme in Japan made utilities purchase all eligible renewable-energy electricity (except small-scale PV) at a fixed price for a fixed duration. It includes solar, wind, small hydro, geothermal, and biomass power. However, tidal and ocean thermal powers are yet to be covered. The FIT has been extremely successful in solar PV penetration. For example, PV electricity generation increased from 3.5TWh in FY2010 to 69.4TWh in FY2019. It has increased 20 times in 10 years. The EIA Act did not require an environmental impact assessment before installing a mega solar facility until 2020. Therefore, the FIT led to a dramatic expansion of solar PV. However, the EIA scheme has become an obstacle in constructing wind farms (Schumacher,

2017). Therefore, the expansion of wind power took time. The amount of wind power electricity generation nearly doubled from 4.0TWh in 2010 to 7.6TWh in 2019.

Initially, the Japanese government set generous tariff rates to promote renewable energy installations; for example, JPY 40(JPYUSD=0.013, Sep.1, 2012)/kWh for PV facilities (≧10kW-peak) and JPY 22/kWh for wind power (≧20 kW-peak). The additional cost for the tariff is collected as a renewables surcharge from electricity end-users. In FY2021, it was JPY 3.36(JPYUSD=0.009, May 1, 2021)/kWh, which was one-tenth of the electricity bill (TEPCO 2021).

As renewable-energy electricity generation increased rapidly, the government improved the network connection rule to solve the frequency constraint problem, which was related to the supply-demand imbalance. The 2017 amendment of FIT Act authorized the network companies to require the renewable energy companies to curtail outputs when excessive renewable-energy electricity was present in the grid. This imbalance happens due to the lack of population and industries that consume renewable energy in the areas where such energy is abundant. For example, in Hokkaido and Kyushu, which are full of renewable energy sources and open spaces, many wind farms and solar farms were installed; however, the population and industrial size are not large enough to consume the generated electricity. Therefore, sending surplus electricity to metropolitan areas, such as Tokyo, Osaka, and Nagoya, is necessary to balance the supply and demand of electricity in Kyushu and Hokkaido. The OCCTO balances electricity supply and demand on a nationwide level across regional grids. A well-integrated national grid will facilitate the integration of variable renewable electricity (IEA, 2021a, p. 141).

The OCCTO is working to interconnect the divided network areas and to increase the capacity to accept renewable-energy electricity. The 2020 amendment to the Electricity Business Act reinforced the OCCTO's role to balance electricity supply and demand on a nationwide level and to improve power exchanges across Japan's regional grids.

The renewable penetration raised the electricity bills. So, the government introduced market mechanisms into FIT to curb rising electricity bills. The renewable-energy electricity generation capacity that was eligible for the FIT began to be allocated through auctions. The auction for the capacity of large-scale PV and onshore wind began in 2017 and 2021, respectively. The price competition in the auctions has contributed to lower prices of renewable-energy electricity.

4.3 FIP and integration into the market

The FIP scheme was initiated in 2022, and it intends to integrate renewable-energy electricity transactions into the wholesale market. The FIT Act was amended in 2021 and renamed the FIP Act (the Act on Special Measures Concerning Promotion of Utilization of Electricity from Renewable Energy Sources). The FIP scheme uses a "supply promotion subsidy," generally called "a premium," to promote the renewable-energy electricity transaction. The FIT scheme has required network companies (previously utilities) to purchase the eligible renewable-energy electricity at a fixed rate. However, the FIP encourages the generators of renewable-energy electricity to sell electricity at the wholesale market (or over-the-counter transactions) by providing them with premiums. The FIP encourages the autonomous transaction of renewable-energy electricity in the competitive market and expects a decline of renewable-energy electricity cost. In addition, it provides an incentive for renewable-energy electricity suppliers to supply electricity during peak-demand hours when price surges and to store electricity in batteries during off-peak hours. This mechanism is expected to balance the supply and demand of electricity and to mitigate the electricity shortfall during peak-demand hours. As a result, the electricity supply from renewable energy sources will be optimized.

The premium is calculated monthly for each renewable energy category. The FIP price, which is equivalent to the FIT price in Japan, is determined for each category by considering both the cost of renewable-energy electricity generation and the cost of dealing with imbalance. The reference price is, then, set based on the average spot-market price. The difference between the FIP price and the reference price becomes the premium. As the premium changes monthly according to the changing market price of electricity, the FIP in Japan is a kind of sliding FIP scheme. The Japanese government studied the FIP schemes in Europe, especially that in Germany. So, Japan arranged the German FIP to suit the situation in Japan. In terms of large-scale PV systems, the FIP price is determined via auctions. The FIP does not apply retrospectively to the already certified FIT facilities unless the FIT facility operators apply for the status change. The premium is paid by the end-user of electricity as the renewable energy surcharge collected through the electricity bills.

The tariff in FIT scheme is independent of the market price. However, the FIP links renewable-energy electricity price to the market price. Thus, the FIP scheme is a step toward the integration of renewable-energy electricity into the electricity market. As the electricity generation costs of solar PV and offshore wind turbines are becoming close to that of coal burning, it is supposed that the premium for solar and wind will be reduced to zero shortly and that in the market they will beat down the thermal power plant electricity. This will result in the closure of thermal power plants. However, the electricity demand cannot be fulfilled without the electricity supply from thermal power plants now in Japan. Therefore, the OCCTO opened its capacity market in 2020 to secure a stable supply of electricity in the future. It has secured the power supply capacity for the next 4 years. The capacity market works to secure investments in thermal power plants.

4.4 Aggregator

The 2020 amendment to the Electricity Business Act provided the aggregator with a legal status for the first time. The aggregators aggregate distributed energy sources such as solar PV facilities and wind farms and smooth out variations of electricity supply to networks. They work as an adjustment capacity, and as virtual power plants (VPPs). The Japanese government has recognized that the aggregators are indispensable for renewables penetration, which might make networks unstable. In addition, aggregators are expected to control the electricity consumption in households and offices by using demand response programs. Matching the supply and demand of electricity is of benefit. METI intends to make the saved amount of electricity to be tradable as "negawatt power" in the market (METI, 2020b).

4.5 Renewables penetration and NIMBY syndrome

The Japanese government and many local governments have been encouraging renewable energy penetration. The Act on Promoting Generation of Electricity from Renewable Energy Sources Harmonized with Sound Development of Agriculture, Forestry & Fisheries, legislated in 2013, has been encouraging the installation of PV facilities on farmlands and fishing villages. With the income from farming and electricity sales together, farmers obtain sufficient income to continue farming. The Act on Promoting the Utilization of Sea Areas for the Development of Marine Renewable Energy Power Generation Facilities of 2018 has been promoting offshore wind farms. The 2021 Amendment to the Act on Promotion of Global Warming Countermeasures established the scheme for regional decarbonization promotion project plans, which deregulated and streamlined the process of renewable energy installations. Moreover, a lot of municipal governments have invested in the community powers that engage in renewable energy generation. However, solar farms and wind farms are often exposed to the not-in-my-back-yard (NIMBY) syndrome. The number of local governments that have enacted local ordinances to deal with the troubles between renewable energy installations and their neighbors is increasing. As of December 2021, more than 170 local governments had this kind of ordinances.

5 Depending on nuclear energy

5.1 Indispensable non-fossil energy source

Despite the Fukushima Daiichi nuclear disaster, it seems difficult for Japan to quit its nuclear power. The nuclear power plants generated one-fourth of the domestic electricity supply in 2010. Japan produces little fossil fuel; thus, nuclear energy has been an attractive alternative with high energy density to secure a stable energy supply, even though the uranium supply depends on imports.

The government is prompting a nuclear fuel cycle policy that seeks to efficiently utilize the uranium ore. The policy is based on the Nuclear Policy Act (§7). The nuclear fuel cycle policy seeks the recycling of used nuclear fuel by extracting valuable radioactive materials such as uranium and plutonium. However, a fast-breeder reactor has not been successfully developed yet, and the prototype fast-breeder reactor, which was named "Monju," shut down due to a fire accident and is being decommissioned. Without fast-breeder reactors, the nuclear fuel cycle policy has stagnated. The government is promoting the plutonium-thermal use (Pluthermal) strategy, in which uranium and plutonium mixed-oxide (MOX) fuel, made of recovered plutonium and uranium, is burnt in light water reactors.

The 2010 Strategic Energy Plan highlighted nuclear energy as a path to carbon reduction. It projected that at least 14 new reactors would be installed by 2030, and the ratio of zero-emission electricity sources in all electricity sources would be approximately 70% in 2030. It was expected that more than 50% of the electricity would come from nuclear power and renewables by 2020. However, the Fukushima Daiichi nuclear disaster ruined the expectation for nuclear energy.

The government considers nuclear energy an important baseload energy source. The 2014 Strategic Energy Plan (METI, 2014, p. 24) stated, "nuclear power is an important base-load power source as a low-carbon and quasi-domestic energy source, contributing to stability of energy supply-demand structure." This nuclear-energy policy was maintained in the 2021 Strategic Energy Plan. It stipulated that the public trust in nuclear power would be gained on the major premise that the stable use of nuclear power must be promoted, and that safety should be secured. However, it also stipulated that the government would prioritize the safety of nuclear power and reduce dependency on it as much as possible, while expanding renewable energy. Even though only 6.2% of the total electricity supply came from nuclear power plants in FY2019, the 2021 Strategic Energy Plan expected 20%–22% of it would come from nuclear power plants in FY2030. To meet this target, it is inevitable to install several new nuclear reactors.

The Japanese government has especially encouraged the development of high-temperature gas reactors that produce hydrogen from water using a hot temperature. It can be a fundamental social infrastructure that supports a hydrogen society. In addition, the government is thinking of the introduction of small modular reactors, which seem safer than traditional reactors.

The disposal of used nuclear fuel is a critical problem in Japan. The Act on Final Disposal of Specified Radioactive Waste of 2000 stipulated that the high-level radioactive waste (HLW), which was separated from used nuclear fuel at fuel reprocessing facilities, should be geologically disposed of at depths >300 m. However, the location for such a facility is yet to be determined. This issue has been discussed from the perspectives of intergenerational and inter-regional equity. Without the HLW disposal site, nuclear power plants will be unable to continue operations and the low carbon transition of Japan will be frustrated.

5.2 Nuclear safety regulation

The Atomic Energy Policy Act of 1955 established a fundamental policy concerning nuclear energy in Japan. It has promoted the research, development, and utilization of nuclear energy (§ 1). The military use of nuclear energy is banned; it can only be used for peaceful purposes in Japan. Many people are apprehensive of nuclear power because hundreds of thousands of people were killed in Hiroshima and Nagasaki with atomic bombs during WW2. This factor has put the use of nuclear energy in a complicated political situation, which produced an irrational belief that serious accidents never occur in nuclear power plants in Japan. It was called "the safety myth of the nuclear." As the proponents of nuclear energy repeatedly said that nuclear power plants were safe, they were unable to talk about the possibility of a serious nuclear accident. Therefore, the nuclear safety regulatory scheme was developed on the unrealistic assumption that serious nuclear accidents, such as core meltdown, would not occur. The Fukushima Daiichi nuclear disaster destroyed the safety myths. The 2011 amendment to the Reactor Regulation Act assumed that serious accidents, such as core meltdowns, could occur. It employed defense-in-depth regulation to prepare for such a serious scenario.

The 2011 amendment required all nuclear reactors to meet the latest safety regulations. This means that new safety regulations retroactively apply to the nuclear reactors that were licensed based on obsolete safety regulations. This back-fit requirement has prevented the existing nuclear reactors from resuming operations because it is not easy for them to meet the new safety regulations and to obtain the operation license again. In principle, the operation period of nuclear reactors is limited to 40 years. However, the Nuclear Regulation Authority can approve 20 years of extended operation period after the safety scrutiny. Due to these regulations, as of February 2022, only 10 out of 54 reactor units resumed operation. Moreover, 24 units were waiting to be decommissioned.

6 Reducing energy consumption

In addition to increasing the use of non-fossil energy sources, reducing energy consumption is important for a low-carbon society. As Japan has few energy resources, it has rigorously engaged in policies that prompt long-term efficient energy usage. Reduction efforts have become even more important after the Fukushima Daiichi nuclear disaster. The final energy consumption has decreased from 14.7EJ in FY 2010 to 12.1EJ in FY2020.

The Energy Saving Act of 1979 requires factories, transportation, buildings, and machinery & equipment to improve their energy efficiency. For example, the legislation sets energy-efficiency standards for cars and other machines. This energy efficiency standard is called the "top-runner standard" because the next term standard is determined based on the best energy performance machine at the moment. The Corporate Average Fuel Economy (CAFE) regulation for automobile fuel efficiency is among the top-runner standard regulations. The CAFE regulation in Japan has come to reflect the well-to-wheel energy efficiency instead of the tank-to-wheel fuel efficiency because the share of battery electric vehicles (BEVs) and plug-in hybrid electric vehicles (PHEVs) is supposed to increase. However, the ratio of electricity generated by burning fossil fuels is high in Japan; thus, the increase in BEVs will not reduce CO_2 emissions dramatically. The capacity for renewable-energy electricity generation in Japan remains limited. The additional consumption of electricity leads to a demand for electricity generated by thermal power plants. Therefore, the Japanese government and automobile manufacturers do not believe that an increase in BEV contributes to a higher reduction of CO_2 emissions in the short term.

7 Non-fossil fuel value certificate

The Sophisticated Structure of Energy Supply Act requires that a certain percentage of the electricity each retailer sells should be non-fossil fuel electricity. The retailer can achieve the target ratio of non-fossil fuel electricity by purchasing renewable-energy electricity, hydropower electricity, or nuclear electricity. Otherwise, they can achieve their target by acquiring the environmental value of non-fossil fuel energy certificates in the market. The non-fossil fuel value can be separated from the electricity generated without the use of fossil fuels. This scheme encourages not only renewables but also nuclear energy. The RPS was replaced by FIT in Japan, but this non-fossil fuel electricity portfolio scheme seems to be a revival of the RPS.

8 Conclusion

Japan's renewable energy supply has increased significantly due to the success of FIT. ANRE (2021c) reported, "renewable energy continued to increase for the eighth consecutive year." In addition, the total energy consumption is decreasing. As the priority of its energy policy is to secure a stable energy supply, Japan cannot rush to increase the ratio of renewable energy with endangering stable supply. From now on, FIP is expected to accelerate renewable energy penetration. However, Japan cannot abandon nuclear energy to meet its energy demand. METI (2020a, pp. 2–3) predicted that "the power demand in 2050 will increase by 30%–50% compared with the current demand level due to electrification in the industrial, transportation and household sectors," and "it is practical to think it impossible to cover all electricity demands by renewable energy alone." To realize a zero-carbon-emission society in 2050, nuclear energy is indispensable and requires some breakthroughs.

References

ANRE (Agency for Natural Resources and Energy, Japan), 2021a. *Power generation cost verification* (in Japanese: 発電コスト検証について). Available at https://www.enecho.meti.go.jp/committee/council/basic_policy_subcommittee/2021/048/048_004.pdf (Accessed: 6 July 2022).

ANRE, 2021b. *Outline of Strategic Energy Plan*. Available at https://www.enecho.meti.go.jp/en/category/others/basic_plan/pdf/6th_outline.pdf (Accessed: 6 July 2022).

ANRE, 2021c. *FY2020 energy supply and demand report (Preliminary Report)*. Available at https://www.meti.go.jp/english/press/2021/1126_002.html(Accessed: 6 July 2022).

ANRE, *Comprehensive energy statistics* (in Japanese; 総合エネルギー統計). Available at https://www.enecho.meti.go.jp/statistics/total_energy/(Accessed: 6 July 2022).

ANRE, *FIT rate* (in Japanese:買取価格). [Online] Available at https://www.enecho.meti.go.jp/category/saving_and_new/saiene/kaitori/fit_kakaku.html (Accessed: 6 July 2022).

IEA, 2020a. *Global CO_2 emissions in 2019*. Available at https://www.iea.org/articles/global-co2-emissions-in-2019(Accessed: 6 July 2022).

IEA, 2020b. *Levelized cost of electricity calculator: interactive table of LCOE estimates from projected costs of generating electricity 2020*. Available at https://www.iea.org/articles/levelised-cost-of-electricity-calculator (Accessed: 6 July 2022).

IEA, 2021a. *Japan 2021 Energy Policy Review*. Available at https://iea.blob.core.windows.net/assets/3470b395-cfdd-44a9-9184-0537cf069c3d/Japan2021_EnergyPolicyReview.pdf(Accessed: 6 July 2022).

IEA, 2021b. *Key World Energy Statics 2021*. Available at https://iea.blob.core.windows.net/assets/52f66a88-0b63-4ad2-94a5-29d36e864b82/KeyWorldEnergyStatistics2021.pdf(Accessed: 6 July 2022).

Japan Beyond Coal, 2020. We're Really Going to Operate 15 Coal Plants Under Construction? Available at https://beyond-coal.jp/en/archives/15_coal-fired-power-plants-under-construction-2/ (Accessed: 6 July 2022).

Kameyama, Y., 2017. *Climate change policy*. New York, NY: Routledge.

Kiko-network, 2015. Japan's Env. Minister Disapproves Plan for Coal-Fired Plant in Aichi: Zero-Based Review Inevitable. Available at http://www.kikonet.org/wp/wp-content/uploads/2015/08/15de3b7219679afdd238064e7410049c.pdf (Accessed: 6 July 2022).

Ministry of Economy, Trade and Industry, Japan (METI), 2014. *Strategic Energy Plan* (Cabinet Decision, April, 2014) (Provisional Translation). Available at https://www.enecho.meti.go.jp/en/category/others/basic_plan/pdf/4th_strategic_energy_plan.pdf(Accessed: 6 July 2022).

METI, 2018. *Strategic Energy Plan* (Cabinet Decision, July 2018). Available at https://warp.da.ndl.go.jp/info:ndljp/pid/11663694/www.meti.go.jp/english/press/2018/pdf/0703_002c.pdf(Accessed: 6 July 2022).

METI, 2020a. *Green Growth Strategy through achieving carbon neutrality in 2050* (Provisional Translation). Available at https://www.meti.go.jp/english/press/2020/pdf/1225_001b.pdf(Accessed: 6 July 2022).

METI, 2020b. *Guidelines for energy resource aggregation business revised*. Available at https://www.meti.go.jp/english/press/2020/0602_002.html(Accessed: 6 July 2022).

METI, 2021. News Release December 24, 2021(in Japanese). Available at https://www.meti.go.jp/press/2021/12/20211224006/20211224006.html (Accessed: 6 July 2022).

OCCTO, 2022. *Annual Report-Fiscal Year 2021*. Available at https://www.occto.or.jp/en/information_disclosure/annual_report/files/220324_OCCTO_annualreport_2021.pdf (Accessed: 6 July 2022).

Regulation (EU) 2021/1119 of the European Parliament and of the Council of 30 June 2021 establishing the framework for achieving climate neutrality and amending Regulations (EC) No 401/2009 and (EU) 2018/1999(European Climate Law 2021), OJ L243/1, 9.7.2021.

Schumacher, K., 2017. Large-scale renewable energy project barriers: environmental impact assessment streamlining efforts in Japan and the EU. *Environmental Impact Assessment Review*, 65, pp. 100–110.

TEPCO, 2021. *FIT surcharge rates* (in Japanese: 再生可能エネルギー発電促進賦課金単価). Available at https://www.tepco.co.jp/corporateinfo/illustrated/charge/1253678_6290.html (Accessed: 6 July 2022).

Marisol Anglés-Hernández, José María Valenzuela

Mexico: Energy Transition in an Uncertain Legal and Institutional Setting

Abstract: Mexico's legal framework for the energy transition faces major challenges to promote investment while protecting the environment and human rights, in the middle of contestation over the formal roles of state control and private markets. The conflict between multiple public objectives, within an uncertain institutional setting, has hindered the development of an appropriate legal system to decarbonize the economy, manage physical risks of climate change, and direct the country toward the goals of the Sustainable Development Agenda 2030. Within this context, the chapter reviews the implication of the oil and gas industry deeply entrenched in the neoliberal economies of North America. It describes the specific Mexican legislation on climate change and energy transition and its institutions, and how it is still failing to provide adequate policy tools or governance systems to guide public spending and industrial regulation for decarbonization. We critically consider the constraints and opportunities imposed by a model of state-owned companies' dominance, on the one hand, and by the model of liberalization and state de-risking of private investment on the other. Finally, we discuss how principles on human rights and sustainable development could serve as leverage to guide the energy transition.

1 Introduction

Mexico is one of the countries most vulnerable to climate change due to its geographical location, topography, and socioeconomic characteristics (Lachinet et al., 2012; Murray-Tortarolo, 2021). Climate variability has been increasing drought and water scarcity, storms, intense rainfall, and flooding across the country (Mora et al., 2018). If this situation prevails, it could affect the realization of the human rights to access to water, food security, and a healthy environment, among others.

Even though Mexico has enormous potential for renewable energy generation, the legal and institutional framework associated with energy transition does not focus on it. On the contrary, it presents a series of inconsistencies and contradictions

Marisol Anglés Hernández is Researcher at the Institute for Legal Research, National Autonomous University of Mexico (UNAM), Mexico.
Jose Maria Valenzuela Robles Linares is Research Fellow at the Institute for Science, Innovation and Society, University of Oxford, United Kingdom.

https://doi.org/10.1515/9783110752403-035

that distance the country from fulfilling its obligations in terms of reducing greenhouse gases and guaranteeing human rights.

Energy transition requires experimentation and deployment of novel legal, regulatory and policy solutions, which can only be constructively pursued within an appropriate legal framework (Sabel and Victor, 2017). Therefore, it is necessary to have a clear energy policy that is aligned with climate goals and focused on the just and equitable energy transition. Mexico's legal pathway does not yet reflect the needs and requirements of energy transition and deep decarbonization, and has merely focused on reducing emission intensity of the energy system, despite having a robust climate change law (Valenzuela and Buira, 2021). This has created an uncertain environment which hinders the development of policy and regulatory experimentation required to find the appropriate conditions to decarbonize the energy system.

The country is still immersed in a long-standing political division over the form of economic governance of the energy sector: whether the state's role is to enable private investment or to directly manage the industry through state-owned enterprises (SOEs). Climate ambition has been secondary to both projects' focus on economic development. But the lack of progress towards more climate ambition in the energy sector can be seen from a regional perspective: Mexico has progressively veered towards integration with North America, a region that lacks climate ambition and with conflicting political paradigms on energy security (see Rodríguez Padilla, 2018; Coleman, in this volume). On the one hand, the liberalization paradigm focused on integration into international markets to secure timely and cost-effective supply notwithstanding the level of energy imports. On the other hand, the energy sovereignty paradigm emphasizes a high reliance on domestic production of fuels – including those required for electricity generation – with significant skepticism of the reliability of international markets in difficult times.

Mexican institutions are still in need of a minimal legal consensus about the priority of energy transition, beyond the private vs state debate. If this does not happen autonomously it might be driven through changes in North American markets, which might not result in addressing the particularities of Mexican legal traditions and domestic institutional capacities. We stress a key challenge: securing a just energy transition given the local development conditions and legal framework for the use of natural resources.

2 International and domestic climate legal mandates

Mexico has a broad and innovative climate legislation, which derives from the constitutional mandate –in Article 25, stating that national development must be comprehensive and sustainable. Based on this precept, the General Climate Change Law (Ley

General de Cambio Climático – LGCC) embodies the regulation of climate change in the Mexican legal system. It establishes the concurrent competencies relating to mitigation and adaptation in the three levels of government; provides for the creation of the Inter-ministerial Commission comprised of fourteen Ministries at the federal level: Interior, Foreign Affairs, Navy, Treasury and Public Credit, Welfare, Economy, Agriculture, and Rural Development, Communications and Transportation, Education, Health, Tourism, Agrarian, Territorial and Urban Development, Energy, and Environment and Natural Resources (Secretaría de Medio Ambiente y Recursos Naturales – SEMARNAT), the latter holds the presidency. This Inter-ministerial Commission for Climate Change oversees the coordination of actions between the ministries and entities of the Federal Public Administration in matters of climate change.

However, to date, true coordination of inter-institutional action has not been achieved. What really happens is that each Ministry develops some effort related to climate actions, but these are not discussed and agreed upon among them, so the results may even be contradictory (Pacheco-Vega, 2021; Von Lüpke and Well, 2020). As an example, the Ministry of Welfare promotes the "Sowing Life Program," which implies the planting of introduced species and, therefore, affects ecosystems and their functions; while the Ministry of the Environment implements the Payment for environmental services, aimed at maintaining forest areas.

Similarly, despite the bases for a low-carbon economy being legally and institutionally established, each Ministry has its own objectives. For example, the one for Agriculture promotes the expansion of the agricultural frontier, and the one for Energy (Secretaría de Energía – SENER) the production and utilization of fossil energy, which makes it difficult to integrate a true energy policy aimed at energy transition (Anglés-Hernández and Otero-Rovalo, 2019). In addition to the institutional complexity, the LGCC mandates the adoption of several planning instruments, including the National Climate Change Strategy (Estrategia Nacional de Cambio Climático), developed by the National Institute of Ecology and Climate Change (Instituto Nacional de Ecología y Cambio Climático – INECC), with a long-term vision. It identifies critical cross-cutting issues for long-term climate policy; including market-based approaches to pricing carbon, increased innovation, research and development of new technologies, and the need to move from fossil energies to renewable (not clean: see below) energies.

It is also important that there are other laws that regulate the energy sector with a clear impact on climatic aspects. So, in accordance with the Energy Transition Law (Ley de Transición Energética – LTE), Mexico recognizes the need to take actions to diversify the energy matrix and improve energy efficiency that contributes to the achievement of national climate goals, namely the achievement of 35% participation of clean energies in the electricity generation matrix by 2024. This law defines renewable energies as those whose source resides in natural phenomena, processes, or materials that can be transformed into usable energy by human beings, that regenerate naturally and are continuously or periodically available, and that when generated do not release polluting emissions. And as clean energies those energy sources and electricity generation processes whose emissions or residues, if any, do not exceed the efficiency criteria issued by the the Energy Regulatory Commission (CRE) and emissions criteria established by the SEMARNAT. Therefore, they are not necessarily clean energies, since their categorization depends on a range allowed by law.

Additionally, the LTE ordered the publication of a Transition Strategy to Promote the Use of Cleaner Technologies and Fuels. Following the first published version in December 2014 and revised in 2016, clean energy generation goals of 37.7% by 2030 and 50% by 2050 were proposed (SENER 2016). As a tool to reduce GHGs, the Electrical Industry Law of 2014 (Ley de la Industria Eléctrica – LIE) created Clean Energy Certificates (CELs). Each CEL accredits the production of one megawatt-hour (MWh) from clean energy and serves to comply with the obligations established by the SENER associated with consumption in charging stations.

In the international context, Mexico affirmed its commitment to fighting climate change, consequently, it signed and ratified the United Nations Framework Convention on Climate Change (UNFCCC) and its derived instruments, at the time the Kyoto Protocol and, subsequently, the Paris Agreement. In this context, Mexico formulated its NDC, which states an intention to reduce unconditionally its emissions of GHG by 22% by 2030, or up to 36% conditional to the implementation of international technology transfers and carbon pricing, among other factors.

Despite the legal advances in Mexico, key challenges to climate action still need to be addressed in order to limit the country's emissions. Nowadays, the NDC conditional and non-conditional goals are not consistent with the 1.5°C temperature limit, and do not necessarily put the country on a path to achieving the country's mid-century target, which is only aligned to the 2°C temperature limit as argued by the official Long Term-Low Emission Development Strategy (LT-LEDS) presented to the UNFCCC. Moreover, the country has not developed the policy instruments required to set the emission reductions needed by 2050 and the subsequent sectoral decarbonization plans.

Instead, Mexico is invested in a development path reliant on natural gas considered as a cleaner fuel. This path leads the country away from the long-term GHG reduction goals and discourages private investments in renewable energy – which have already fallen sharply in 2019–2020 (Demôro et al., 2021). This situation has become more complex since the election of the incumbent government (2018–2024), with a vision of nationalist development that leverages fossil fuels as instruments of energy sovereignty. Therefore, the energy sector, which has been formally and legally liberalized, is materially monopolized and locked into the fossil fuel economy, not unlike its North American partners.

3 The institutions of a fossil fuel economy in North America

Mexico is known as a major oil producer and exporter in the international economy. But for almost a decade already, the country has been a net energy importer due to a decreasing oil and gas production platform and a secular growth in fossil fuel demand across the economy. For instance, in the middle of the oil price crash at the beginning of the COVID-19 pandemic, the Mexican government made headlines as it held up an agreement between OPEC and other major oil producers to cut global production (Reuters, 2020).

In the 2010s, several large economies in Europe initiated a severe turn towards deep decarbonization in the energy sector. At the same time, Mexico engaged in major legal reforms to reinvigorate the fossil fuel industry in line with North American energy economics and politics (IEA, 2017; Wood, 2018; Hernández Ochoa, 2018). The constitutional reform in 2013 and ensuing implementation legislation served to harmonize the domestic legal framework with the dominant North American business model of private investment to develop conventional and unconventional hydrocarbons (shale/gas oil) that require fracking and emit significant amounts of methane into the atmosphere. Methane has an atmospheric life of approximately 12 years, and a global warming potential 25 times greater than that of carbon dioxide (Howarth et al., 2011), and remains an unsolved problem in the region.

These reforms were the culmination of a two-decades long attempt to liberalize the energy sector (Valenzuela and Studer, 2017), and represented a drastic change to the existing oil & gas sector, since they allowed the participation of private actors in the exploration and production of oil and natural gas, as well as in the refining of oil and the basic petrochemical sector –previously reserved for SOEs. The electric sector was liberalized by enabling market entry and a wholesale pool market. This encouraged the modernization of supply infrastructure, mainly from fossil fuels, and to a lesser degree in new renewable energy facilitated by state-backed long-term contracts. With the constitutional reform of 2013, Mexican Petroleum (Petróleos Mexicanos – Pemex) and the Federal Electricity Company (CFE), both SOEs, became productive state companies, to be managed according to market principles.

Pemex has been identified as one of the top corporations by historical aggregate emissions globally (Ekwurzel et al., 2017), which speaks to the relative size of the footprint of the national hydrocarbon sector in global climate change. However, in light of the still-rising global demand and the historical rise of unconventional hydrocarbon production in the US, Mexico's 2013 reforms did not seek to contain the climate footprint of the oil industry but instead to reverse the production decline through new private investment. Government reports on the achievements between 2012–2019 refer to commitments of 8,600 million USD on clean energy, more than 12,000 million only on new gas pipelines, and more than 160,000 million USD in hydrocarbons production. In addition to domestic production, natural gas import capacity from the US increased by 220% (Gobierno de México, 2018).

In the electricity sector, liberalization meant going beyond the inclusion of Independent Power Producers to sell to a single buyer and limited private bilateral contracts markets. The reforms made wholesale market competition the backbone of the industry – at the expense of the market share of the state-owned company CFE (Hernández Ochoa, 2018; Ibarra-Yunez, 2015). However, equally influential to the transformation of the electricity industry was the government's decision to lock the electricity system into natural gas-based power generation, making CFE a fossil fuel trading company, planning for natural gas to account for two-thirds of generation, and in the long-term, capping the share of clean energy at 50 percent by 2050. But this electricity target is hardly close to what the scientific literature considers appropriate for Mexico to achieve long-term climate ambition – the electricity sector already has technological alternatives, and it is fundamental to decarbonize other sectors (Buira and Tovilla, 2015; Buira et al., 2021; Veysey et al., 2016; Elizondo et al., 2017).

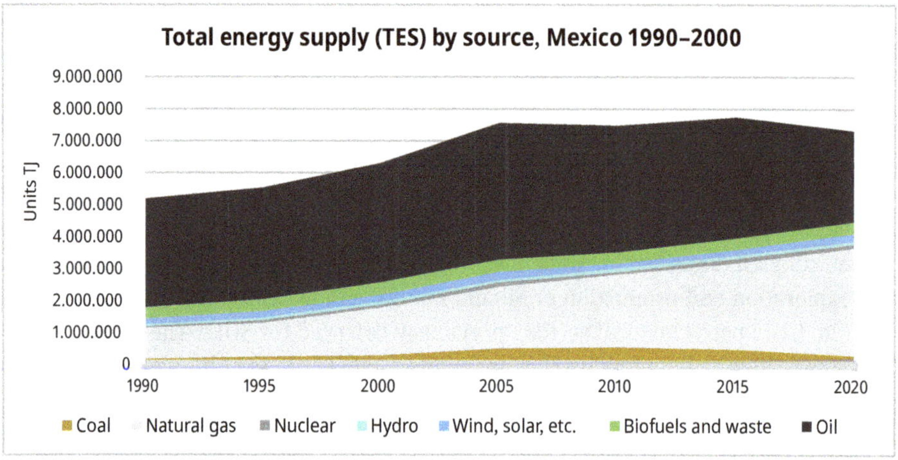

Figure 3: Energy supply in Mexico. Source: IEA, 2021.

Mexico's turn to natural gas is based on two historical conditions. The first condition is the technological progress on natural gas combined cycle power plants (NGCC) with high efficiency and consumption. They are intended to substitute heavy fuel oil and meet growing demand in the country, just as natural gas substituting for coal is considered a climate policy success in the United States. But more generally, the energy sector policy in the North American region has simply not reflected the requirements of decarbonization in the three countries.

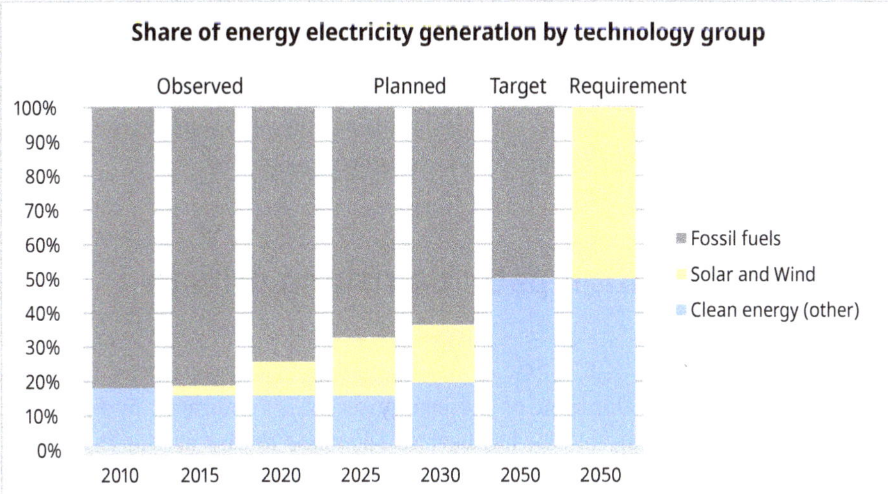

Figure 4: Indicative planning and the requirements of decarbonization. Source: Buira and Tovilla, 2015; SENER, 2018.

Climate policy shows a certain parallelism of integration. Mexico is unique in the region for having a national climate change law that does not yet exist in the United States or Canada. But there has been synchrony in other aspects, primarily on the policy reforms to enable the growth in the use of natural gas through electricity market reforms (Carreón-Rodríguez et al., 2006; Victor and Heller, 2006). The second condition was the shale gas boom in the United States, which led to an abundance of supply and a rapid and consistent drop in the price of natural gas to the lowest level among major economic regions. Government and economic stakeholders are expected to grasp benefits from abundant low-price natural gas and develop a domestic natural gas industry that could resemble that of the US. As events later showed, these expectations were incompatible, as the favorable economics of importing gas created inappropriate conditions to produce domestically. Ultimately, the state-owned electricity company, CFE, deployed the largest-ever expansion of natural gas import capacity infrastructure, which resulted in the electricity industry relying up to 90 percent on imported natural gas – essentially through pipelines from the United States.

Mexico's energy industry has converged towards a North American fossil fuel economy, both materially based on integrating infrastructure and markets, and institutionally in modes of governance and policy priorities. The governing coalition from 2018 has stopped the process of liberalization and turned towards protecting the current market share and role of state-owned companies. Similarly, there are intentions to make only minor changes to the structural integration of the fossil fuel economy in North America. In the 2020s, this integration is best described by Pemex's decision to purchase Shells' participation in the jointly owned Deer Park refinery in the state of Texas (Martinez, 2022).

Ultimately, domestic policy has not yet challenged the incumbent businesses in the fossil fuel industry. Instead, it has remained focused on developing the hydrocarbon industry, which, up until 2019, was based on the progressive expansion of private investment. The following sections will further discuss the nature of the two conflicting legal pathways and their implications for energy transition.

4 The liberalization path: de-risking private investment

A key pillar for the development of the energy sector, as embraced by reformists since the late 1990s and up to 2019, has been to allow and de-risk private investment in the energy sector. In contrast to common notions of liberalized markets as a setting for private risk-taking, developing countries' energy sector liberalization is much more characterized by the evolution of means to de-risk investment. This can happen by allowing for a high concentration of markets (as in Chile since the 1980s); through the development of Independent Power Producers contracts guaranteed by government agencies (IPPs with a single buyer); or through price regulation that allows investors to have certainty at power plant level (as in the Chinese fair price regulation).

De-risking mechanisms can target both fossil fuels and renewable energy industries. Promoters of de-risking argue these legal, regulatory, or contractual measures are central to achieving the best market conditions in developing countries. De-risking policies are based on the notion that there is an optimal distribution of risk allocation between private investors and governments (Gabor, 2021; Dafermos et al., 2021). As the government pushes forward the frontier to allow for increased private sector participation in infrastructure businesses, they can choose multiple mechanisms to distribute the risk from investors participating in the industry. The Mexican governing coalition deployed two mechanisms to de-risk private investment that are consequential to the energy transition.

The first and most straightforward is the issuance of long-term contracts for supply. This became particularly relevant in the electricity industry, where natural gas supply contracts and electricity supply contracts have a length of over 25 years for gas or 20 years for renewable energy contracts. CFE has anchored the expansion of natural gas transport infrastructure through long-term supply contracts and most of the wind and solar energy investment through the auction system. Government choices have led the company to simultaneously bet on both the expansion of natural gas power generation and renewable energy power generation.

In addition to this, between 2015 and 2018, the SENER and the National Energy Control Center (CENACE) held three long-term auctions in which CFE and other suppliers purchased CELs, energy and power – at the most competitive prices worldwide – to fulfill their obligations. As a result, over the next three years, 70 new power plants would be built in 19 states, adding 7,600 MW to Mexico's current generation capacity (García, 2016). The CELs were oriented to new projects, those installed from 2014 onwards, and to the generation of clean electricity.

However, in 2019, in direct opposition to the de-risking mode of governance, the government changed the rules of the game to benefit the CFE, by determining that power plants installed before 2014 could also acquire CELs. This fact makes evident the lack of legal certainty for investors, national and foreign, and puts at risk the development of renewable and clean energies in the country. The federal executive then proceeded with the project for a major overhaul of the legal regime. In 2021 the federal executive power sent to the Chamber of Deputies a preferential initiative with various reforms to the LIE, to eliminate the Wholesale Electricity Market as it currently stands, an act that could jeopardize the achievement of the commitments assumed by Mexico (on environment, climate or investment), the constitutional reform of 2013 and various human rights, the exercise of which depends on the quality of the environment.

Given these actions by the Mexican State, investors have resorted to the judiciary in defense of their rights. Until now, the court rulings have been in favor of maintaining current regulations, so legal reforms have not materialized. However, the climate of uncertainty and insecurity remains, which does not favor investment in the energy sector and causes harm to climate and human rights objectives. Although the revised North America trade agreement (USMCA in the US or TMEC in Mexico), which entered into force in 2020, allows constitutional modifications, this does not exclude the national treatment obligations that Mexico must give to the companies of its commercial partners and the rules of indirect expropriation, typical of investment treaties.

The second mechanism for de-risking is containing and dismantling dominant market players in ways that constrain their capabilities to outcompete new entrants into the industry. In private markets, this happens through anti-trust and unbundling policies, but in the case of state-owned companies that remain under the direct control of the government, this can take the form of policy. In the case of Mexico, the constitutional reform of 2013 focused on the figure of Coordinating Regulatory Bodies in Energy Matters to regulate energy markets, through the intervention of the CRE and the National Hydrocarbons Commission (CNH), with a view to developing a competitive market based on eminently technical and non-discriminatory criteria. So, the energy SOEs have been partially unbundled, and legal mandates have been devised to limit the capability of SOEs to participate in the markets autonomously. For instance, CFE public electricity supply company can only purchase energy through auctions conducted by the system operator.

De-risking private investment has implications in defining the types of support policies for clean energy promotion, as much as defining which types of decarbonization policies are avoided. Carbon pricing has been part of the policy choices for energy transition in the sector, however it has been too small and narrow to have a systematic impact on the decarbonization of the energy industry (Stevens, 2021; Dibley and Garcia-Miron, 2020). The government has decided not to introduce new "distortions" into markets. Within OECD countries that have officially adopted some form of carbon pricing, such as an emissions cap and trading system (ETS) or a carbon tax, Mexico has adopted the least stringent one, with the lower carbon tax amongst the OECD members. The surcharge covers vehicle fossil fuels and heavy fuel oil, but not natural gas – the second-largest fossil fuel by consumption share and primary energy source for the manufacturing and electricity industries. This has resulted from leaning towards the preferences of incumbent business interests. This logic of investors' support is critical to understanding the first wave of solar and wind expansion between 2009–2013, built on regulatory exceptions that allowed renewable energy associations that resembled bilateral contracts with discounted wheeling fees.

5 The state path: centralizing industrial development

Mexico's waves of liberalization reforms since 1992 have been described as a one-direction process. The turn to the left-wing coalition in 2018 and the calls for increased state intervention in the economy should not be seen as an unexpected turn, since the contestation against liberalization reforms was patent in domestic politics but had not yet gained an electoral majority. But in the 2020s, internationally a growing number of voices embrace the call for a larger state role in the economy to achieve climate goals, for example, in the European New Deal or the US Green New Deal. It is now possible to clearly identify state-capitalism as a form of organizing production through direct state ownership of strategic corporations that can articulate economic activities within and outside borders (Alami et al., 2021).

The 2018–2024 federal government follows a logic of developmental effectiveness as it attempts to revitalize SOEs as the backbone of the energy industry. The preference for industrial coordination through state-owned companies has a long political and institutional history in Mexico. The oil industry was nationalized in 1938, and the electricity industry was progressively brought into state-ownership with a critical inflection point at the 1960 nationalization law. In Mexico, promoters of state-centered energy development consider SOEs as the main tool to limit private (mainly foreign) business power and redirect investment into underdeveloped regions or industrial activities that might have been withering in the last decades. However, industrial development policies have focused chiefly on existing technological platforms, such as the expansion of refining capacity, new fossil fuel power plants, and the renovation of hydropower capacity. These state investment preferences appear inconsistent with domestic and international climate pledges.

The purported advantage of state-owned corporations is their capacity to rapidly change priorities in response to political and societal considerations. However, there is only a limited turn to other renewable energies by the state-owned company, for instance, in developing a 1 GW solar energy project in the Northeast of the country. Instead, the most relevant progress on energy transition has happened on less visible forms of state-ownership, in the transport sector. These examples include expanding electric public transportation systems, from inter-city railways to new cable cars, and the expansion of electricity-based BRT and trams in the capital, most of which happens through existing or new local government owned transport corporations in Mexico City. These developments have not yet reflected a significant legal change but rather major policy revisions by national or local authorities, very slow changes that started in local government over a decade ago (Valenzuela, 2014).

State-managed economic development can address problems that are common to markets, particularly price volatility, and societal externalities and impacts. Having an electricity SOE has been central to the willingness of the state to maintain subsidized electricity rates for final consumers. This has allowed the country to have relatively low electricity prices compared to other OECD countries, with significant public resources that might have a positive development and distributional consequences, even if this represents a burden to public finances. The turbulence of natural gas markets that has affected North America (Texas in particular) and Europe in 2021 and 2022 are important examples of the Mexican state institutions managing what otherwise could have been important disruptions to the supply of energy to final consumers.

In the oil industry, the logic of state-dominated development resulted in important contestation to existing legal mandates. In 2018, the government stopped the leasing programs to limit the expansion of exploration and production by private players. The tension created by the halt of leasing might result in a historical opportunity to consider the progressive and managed decline of fossil fuel production. Actions like the electricity SOE investment in one of the largest solar power plants on the continent, and the decision to halt new leases on hydrocarbons are not articulated within an explicit policy of deep decarbonization but could potentially contribute to that purpose.

6 Mexico's challenges: just transition, local appropriateness and inclusive industrial policy

The "just transition" is a tool for balancing decarbonization with human right protection, accelerating climate action in a governance framework that considers all the actors involved. In turn, the decarbonization of the industry offers an opportunity to redirect economic activities towards sustainability, by reducing environmental damages, enabling local development, and creating industrial jobs.

Only through a just transition approach to decarbonization will these benefits be equitably shared and accessible. The energy matrix should stop using coal and heavy fuel oil for power generation, which cause serious negative environmental, climatic, and health impacts. The current policy sees natural gas in open and combined cycles as serving this purpose. But we claim that faster expansion of renewable energy is desirable, given the existing overcapacity of natural gas power plants able to complement these variable generation technologies.

Decentralization is the other route to respond to the energy needs of the population, making the most of local resources through community/traditional knowledge and ability to use energy systems by and for the population. This option is oriented towards self-production and the sharing of resources, energy efficiency, and consumption reduction.

Finally, in contrast with other, larger industrialized economies, is the lack of domestic industrial manufacturing policies. In the UK, the auctions served to kick-start a domestic offshore wind manufacturing industry, while Brazil achieved it through obligations imposed as part of loans from development banks (Kern et al., 2014; Hochstetler, 2020). The more local high skilled jobs, the more inclusive the transition. The location of production capacity immediately creates further support for the expansion of renewable energy given the growth of skilled employment dedicated to supply the emerging industries (Nahm, 2017). The absence of any such policies in Mexico is noteworthy, given the deployment of centrally coordinated mechanisms like auctions, but also the significant role of development banks in providing funding to winners of long-term auctions.

The implementation of climate policy in Mexico must reflect the ambition of long-term mitigation goals, including actions and objectives for the short-term and long-term, with differentiated roadmaps among GHG sources and sectors. The energy matrix must be expanded to take advantage of all the resource opportunities that the country has, with a view to reaching local and rural areas, where the requirements are diverse.

Although the legal and institutional framework exists to carry out the energy transition in the country, the López Obrador government has placed emphasis on rescuing the oil & gas sector and strengthening the productive state companies (PEMEX and CFE); a decision that, in addition to generating legal uncertainty for investors, makes it clear that decarbonizing the economy and advancing in the just energy transition is not a national priority of the current government (Anglés-Hernández, 2020). The previous government (2013–2018) devised new mechanisms to de-risk private investment in renewable energy, but at the same time locked fossil fuels further into the energy system through a legal framework to expand oil production and transform the state-owned utility into the largest gas trader in Mexico, with long-term liabilities to import gas from the United States (Valenzuela and Buira, 2021).

The government over-committed the country to natural gas imports for the electricity sector due to concern over reliability of the supply of natural gas after critical shortages in 2010–2013. And in 2018, the government paradigm changed to focus on energy sovereignty as equivalent to reducing the exposure to potential influence from foreign private actors and governments in control of assets and supply for fuels. The very recent turn to strengthen state-ownership, curtail the expansion of private investment in oil and gas, and revise the marginalist market model all have domestic political origin. However, they have parallelisms to concerns that have become internationally patent after the Russian invasion of Ukraine. The invasion takes place in the context of a European continent that is highly dependent on Russian fossil fuel supply. But it also takes place after decades of marginalist market reforms in Europe and with national energy markets severely hit by the increase in the price of natural gas – already at historic highs before the invasion.

Certainly, the European experience provides evidence of the significance of understanding energy security beyond a mere timely access to international energy markets in normal times – which is a stance in the 2018–2024 administration to revise liberalization reforms. But the strong calls to expand energy efficiency and the supply of renewable energy to reduce dependence of fossil fuel from Russia, shed light onto the untapped potential for Mexico to search for energy sovereignty in clean energy.

Table 4: Timeline.

	Pre-liberalization (1992–)	First liberalization (1992–2007)	Energy transition appears in the agenda (2008–2012)	Second liberalization (2013–2018)	Contestation to liberalization (2019–2022)
Electricity	**1960**: Nationalization of the electricity industry	**1992**: Law on the Public Service of Electricity **2004**: Regulation on preferential access and wheeling subsidies for renewabe energy	**2009**: Law for the Use Renewable Energy and Financing the Energy Transition	**2013**: Constitutional reform for wholesale market **2014**: Implementing legislation for wholesale market	**2018**: Suspension of long-term auctons **2020**: Electricity legislation reforms (partially struck down by the judiciary **2021**: New proposal for Constitutional Reform
Hydrocarbons	**1938**: Expropriation of oil industry	**1992**: Pemex Law and partial opening of the sector	**2008**: Creation of Sustainable Energy Science and Technology Fund from hydrocarbon rent	**2013**: Constitutonal reform for opening to competition all markets	**2019**: Suspension of all new oil and gas leases
Energy transition	**1988**: General Law on Ecology and Environmental Protection		**2009**: Law for the Sustaintable Use of Energy **2010**: First non-fossil fuel target (35% in 2024, 50% in 2050). **2012**: General Law on Climate Change	**2015**: First and second long-term auctions **2015**: INDC to the Paris Agreement **2015**: Energy Transition Law enacted	**2021**: Revised NDC (without changes on mitigation)

References

Alami, I. Dixon, A.D. and Mawdsley, E., 2021. State Capitalism and the New Global D/development Regime. *Antipode,* 53(5), pp. 1294–1318.

Allan, J.I., Roger, C.B., Hale, T.N. et al., 2021. Making the Paris Agreement: Historical Processes and the Drivers of Institutional Design. *Political Studies*, OnlineFirst, 6 October, pp. 1-21.

Anglés-Hernández, M., 2020. La transición energética en México: un objetivo de largo plazo. In: H.J. Guanipa, M.L. Leal, F. Huber and L.R. Barroso, eds., 2020. *Crisis climática, transición energética y derechos humanos*. Colombia: Fundación Heinrich Böll-Heidelberg Center para América Latina, pp. 395–408.

Anglés-Hernández, M. and Montserrat, R.O., 2019. Mexico. In: E. Lees and J.E. Viñuales, eds., 2019. *The Oxford handbook of comparative environmental law*. Oxford: Oxford University Press, pp. 278–296.

Buira, D. and Tovilla, J., 2015. *Pathways to deep decarbonization in Mexico*. IDDRI-SDSN.

Buira, D., Tovilla, J., Farbes, J. et al., 2021. A whole-economy deep decarbonization pathway for Mexico. *Energy Strategy Reviews*, 33, 100578.

Carreón-Rodríguez, V., Jiménez, A. and Rosellón, J., 2006. The Mexican electricity sector: economic, legal and political issues. In: D.G. Victor and T.C. Heller, eds., 2006. *The political economy of power sector reform*. New York: Cambridge University Press, pp. 175–214.

Dafermos, Y., Gabor, D. and Michell, J., 2021. The Wall Street consensus in pandemic times: what does it mean for climate-aligned development? *Canadian Journal of Development Studies*, 42(1-2), pp. 238–251.

Demôro, L., Maia, S. and Aminoff, F., 2021. *Climatescope 2021*. Energy transition factbook. London: Bloomberg NEF.

Dibley, A. and Garcia-Miron, R., 2020. Can money buy you (climate) happiness? Economic co-benefits and the implementation of effective carbon pricing policies in Mexico. *Energy Research & Social Science*, 70, 101659.

Ekwurzel, B., Boneham, J., Dalton, M. W. et al., 2017. The rise in global atmospheric CO_2, surface temperature, and sea level from emissions traced to major carbon producers. *Climatic Change*, 144(4), pp. 579–90.

Elizondo, A., Pérez-Cirera, V., Strapasson, A. et al., 2017. Mexico's low carbon futures: an integrated assessment for energy planning and climate change mitigation by 2050. *Futures*, 93, pp. 14–26.

Gabor, D., 2021. The Wall Street consensus. *Development and Change*, 52(3), pp. 429–59.

García Alcocer, G.I., 2019. La transición energética hacia las tecnologías limpias: Un motor para el desarrollo de México. In: M. Anglés-Hernández and M. Palomino-Guerrero, eds., 2019. *Aportes sobre la configuración del derecho energético en México*. México: UNAM, IIJ-CRE, pp. 101–118.

Gobierno de México, 2018. *Sexto Informe de Gobierno, pp. 128–134.*.

Hernández Ochoa, C.E., 2018. *Reforma Energética: Electricidad. México.* FCE.

Hochstetler, K., 2020. *Political economies of energy transition: wind and solar power in Brazil and South Africa*. Cambridge: Cambridge University Press.

Howarth, R.W., Santoro, R. and Ingraffea, A., 2011. Methane and the greenhouse-gas footprint of natural gas from shale formations: A letter. *Climatic Change*, 106, pp. 679–690.

Ibarra-Yunez, A., 2015. Energy reform in Mexico: imperfect unbundling in the electricity sector. *Utilities Policy*, 35, pp. 19–27.

IEA. 2017. *Mexico: energy policies beyond IEA countries*. Paris: OECD/IEA.

IEA, 2021. *World Energy Statistics and Balances*. Paris: OECD/IEA. Available at https://www.iea.org/data-and-statistics/data-product/world-energy-statistics-and-balances.

Kern, F., Smith, A., Shaw, C., Raven, R. and Verhees, B., 2014. From laggard to leader: explaining offshore wind developments in the UK. *Energy Policy*, 69, pp. 635–46.

Martinez, A.I., 2022. Shell to hand over deer park refinery to Pemex next week. Reuters, January 14, 2022. https://www.reuters.com/business/energy/shell-hand-over-deer-park-refinery-pemex-next-week-sources-2022-01-13/.

Murray-Tortarolo, G.N., 2021. Seven decades of climate change across Mexico. *Atmósfera*, 34(2), pp. 217–226.

Nahm, J., 2017. Renewable futures and industrial legacies: wind and solar sectors in China, Germany, and the United States. *Business and Politics*, 19(1), pp. 68–106.

OECD, 2018. *Green finance and investment. Energy sector SOEs: you have the power*. Paris: OECD.

Pacheco-Vega, R., 2021. La Gobernanza policéntrica de mitigación y adaptación al cambio climático en México en el contexto de la arquitectura global de política climática. In: I. Solorio Sandoval, ed., 2021. *México ante la encrucijada de La gobernanza climática*. Ciudad de México: UNAM, pp. 43–66.

Reuters, 2020. OPEC+ outlines oil cut deal, but Mexico holds up final agreement. Reuters, April 10, 2020. https://www.reuters.com/article/global-oil-opec-mexico-idUSD5N2AZ01M.

Rodríguez Padilla, V., 2018. *Seguridad energética. Análisis y evaluación del caso de México.* Estudios y Perspectivas 179. CEPAL, available at: https://www.cepal.org/es/publicaciones/44366-seguridad-energetica-analisis-evaluacion-caso-mexico.

Sabel, C.F. and Victor, D.G., 2017. Governing global problems under uncertainty: making bottom-up climate policy work. *Climatic Change*, 144, pp. 15–27.

SENER. 2016. *Estrategia de transición para promover el uso de tecnologías y combustibles más limpios.* México: Secretaría de Energía, available at: https://www.gob.mx/cms/uploads/attachment/file/182202/20161110_1300h_Estrategia_CCTE-1.pdf.

SENER. 2018. *Prospectiva Del Sector Eléctrico 2018–2032.* México: Secretaría de Energía, available at: http://base.energia.gob.mx/Prospectivas18-32/PSE_18_32_F.pdf

Sierra Brozon, L., Jano Ito, M.A., Tinoco, F.O., Ruiz Vilar, A. and Islas Cortés, I., 2020. *National carbon budget for Mexico and 2030 decarbonisation pathways.* Mexico City. United Kingdom: UK Pact Programme.

Stevens, D., 2021. Institutions and agency in the making of carbon pricing policies: evidence from Mexico and directions for comparative analyses in Latin America. *Journal of Comparative Policy Analysis: Research and Practice*, 23(4), pp. 485–504.

Valenzuela, J.M. and Buira, D., 2021. Mexico climate ambition since the Paris Agreement. In: IDDRI Deep Decarbonization Pathways., ed., 2021. *Climate ambition beyond emission numbers: taking stock of progress by looking inside countries and sectors.*

Valenzuela, J.M. and Studer, I., 2017. Climate change policy and power sector reform in Mexico under the Golden Age of Gas. In: D. Arent, C. Arndt, M. Miller et al., eds, 2017. *The political economy of clean energy transitions.* Oxford: Oxford University Press, pp. 410–429.

Valenzuela, J.M., 2014. Climate change agenda at subnational level in Mexico: policy coordination or policy competition?.*Environmental Policy and Governance*, 24(3), pp. 188–203.

Veysey, J., Octaviano, C., Calvin, K. et al., 2016. Pathways to Mexico's climate change mitigation targets: a multi-model analysis. *Energy Economics*, 56, pp. 587–99.

Victor, D.G. and Heller, T.C., eds, 2006. *The political economy of power sector reform.* New York, NY: Cambridge University Press.

Von Lüpke, H. and Well, M., 2020. Analyzing climate and energy policy integration: the case of the Mexican energy transition. *Climate Policy*, 20(7), pp. 832–45.

Wood, D., 2018. Mexico's new energy reform. Wilson Center Mexico Institute.

Mariusz Swora

Polish Pathway to Just Transition: Energy Law and Policy Trapped Between Sustainability and Security of Supply

Abstract: The main characteristic of the Polish energy sector is that, unlike most of the EU countries, it is based on coal-fired power plants, which account for ca. 80% of total energy generation (March 2021) and which are considered to be the main guarantee of security of supply. According to the new Polish Energy Policy (PEP2040), this coal-dependence is to be significantly reduced in forthcoming years to between 37% and 56% in 2030 and to between 11% and 28% in 2040 of Polish energy mix. Along with a declining share of coal in its energy mix, Poland actively seeks its chances to develop nuclear and natural gas power stations, allowing it to assure a stable base for energy supply and backup power for dynamically growing number of RES and planned offshore windfarms. The main problem with successful completion of secure and sustainable energy mix is the timeline, considering that the EU law sets ambitious goals and timeframes within its climate policy that may not be compatible with the need for secure replacement of coal-based generation. The chapter will focus on legal instruments aiming at realization of target scenario of Polish energy mix, the case law that may accelerate changes, and sector specific legislation and co-regulation rules aimed at smoothing transition in the coal and energy sectors. Energy transition in Poland may be accelerated by the CJEU and national courts (for example, a recent ruling of Supreme Court of the Republic of Poland recognizing a right to clean air or Shell case). While accelerating transition, judicial activism in the area of climate law may cross the thin line between law and policymaking.

1 Introduction

There are two main features of energy transition in Poland. First and foremost, Poland as an EU Member State is obliged to implement EU laws and policies related to energy transition. On the other hand, the energy transition in Poland has to take into account individual factors, related to the country's economy and historical dependence on fossil fuels. These two main factors influence Polish legislation and energy policy. Their interplay is the most important feature characterising the Polish path-

Mariusz Swora is Senior Partner at the Law Office of dr hab. Mariusz Swora, Poland and former full member of the EU ACER Board of Appeal.

https://doi.org/10.1515/9783110752403-036

way to energy transition. That is also the main reason for characterising Polish energy policy in terms of 'just transition', which emphasises the need for taking into account the social and economic impact of the energy transition.

The general perception of Poland in the EU has been misguided: the country was presented for many years as *enfant terrible* of European energy transition. It is sometimes too easy to label a country without prior in-depth examination of the technological and economic historical determinants of its industry. In the case of Poland, it needs to be stressed that those historical determinants still have an impact on energy policy but in general they do not block just transition as the country dynamically expands the share of renewables in its energy mix, actively seeks ways for new opportunities for usage of hydrogen, diversifies routes of supply of natural gas (Poland has also actively advocated for such diversification by the EU, warning about threats related to treating energy as a weapon by the Russian Federation) and is determined to develop nuclear power plants as clean sources of energy. Since the beginning of economic transition (1989), Poland has made unprecedented efforts in the reduction of greenhouse gases. In the period 1989 – 2016, Polish GDP has doubled, while greenhouse gas emissions decreased by more than 30%. In other words, the emissivity of GDP fell by over 60%. In the period 2004–2011, Poland has achieved a 40% increase in GDP while accomplishing an 80% reduction in the weighted indicator of environmental impacts. This places Poland in the leading position in the EU in terms of decoupling (Kampas et al., 2021). On the other hand, Poland is still ranked amongst the 5 biggest GHG emitters in Europe, with Germany ranked as the biggest.

Investments in new and cleaner energy sources and necessary infrastructure cannot happen within a day. In order to assure security of supply, and this is probably the main reason for some controversies within the EU, Poland as a country has to assure profitability of the energy generation sector which is still based on fossil fuels. The country seems to be determined to decarbonize its power sector, but it needs some more time. This results in divergences with the ever-more accelerating EU climate agenda. Within the frames of EU energy transition, a common background for moderating these divergences should be sought on the basis of the classically defined EU principle of solidarity (S. Andoura, 2013), which may be interpreted through the lenses of various important individual factors of a social, economic or technical nature, determining individual pathways of different countries, pursuing common climate goals.

In order to analyse legal aspects of just transition in Poland, it is necessary to present institutional aspects and shed some light on regulations which cover main areas of transition which are related to electricity, natural gas, renewables, district heating, energy efficiency and nuclear power. The analysis will be focused on crucial aspects determining the Polish pathway to energy transition, covering institutional, technological and market aspects of the legal pathways approach.

2 Institutions

In order to better understand the Polish pathway to just transition, it is necessary to consider institutional aspects covering the competences of the main architects of policies and legislation. On the institutional level, the main role in energy transition is played by the government, ministries, agencies and energy regulator.

Draft legislation (primary and secondary) and draft policies to be later adopted by government are prepared by the ministry responsible for energy and climate issues. Due to various factors related to organisation of work and tasks within central government, that ministry used to have different names in the past. Now it is named Ministry of Climate and Environment (hereinafter MCE). The role of that ministry is enhanced by the fact that it supervises the main source of funds assigned on energy transformation, which is administered by the National Fund for Environmental Protection and Water Management. An important tool in the hands of MCE is policymaking. According to Article 13 of Energy law, MCE is obliged to formulate of the most important government policy document i.e. draft of general energy policy, which is subsequently adopted by the council of ministers (currently Polish Energy Policy 2040, hereinafter PEP 2040). The goal of the state's energy policy, according to abovementioned article, is to ensure the country's energy security, increase the competitiveness of the economy and its energy efficiency, as well as protect the environment, including the climate. Interesting as it is, the national energy climate plan, adopted according to Regulation 2018/1999, has not been prepared by MCE, but by an intergovernmental task force chaired by the Minister of State Assets (MSA). Policies adopted by the government bind internally, i.e. they bind only administrative bodies subjugated to the government but they do not take effect in external relations. By designing policies of various administrative bodies, government policies influence the energy sector through regulatory and financial tools to achieve the declared goals.

The fact that the largest Polish energy companies are state-owned has traditionally enhanced the role of MSA, which is responsible for exercising ownership. In practice, energy and climate draft legislation is most often an outcome of interplay between MCE and MSA. The institutional landscape on that interplay is complemented by the Plenipotentiary of the Government for Strategic Energy Infrastructure (PGSEI), who amongst all, holds ownership rights of electricity and gas TSOs as well as PERN S.A. (Article 12a of the Energy Law). PGSEI has been responsible for the development of the most important infrastructure projects and the development of the Polish nuclear program.

The scope of Polish government and parliamentary powers in designing energy laws and policies is constantly narrowing, due to gradual expansion of the secondary law of the EU. Apart from the Directives, the EU body of energy law has significantly expanded mainly through adopting directly applicable Regulations and numerous network codes which are replacing domestic laws, regulations and grid codes. It is characteristic that the EU laws penetrate even deeper into the energy sector, shaping the legal framework not only for TSOs and large market players, but also for DSOs, energy communities and prosumers.

Powerful quasi legal instruments of considerable legal impact *in statu nascendi* are also milestones and targets hidden in annexes accompanying National Recovery Plans (NRPs), which are in practice legislative and policy actions a country has to take in order to get the money from the post-Covid financial instrument, i.e. the Recovery and Resilience Facility (RRF). When preparing NRPs, countries have to meet criteria set out in the RRF Regulation and negotiate their plans with the EC, which decides about fulfilment of the milestones before disbursements under the RRF are made. NRPs are in fact rather instruments assuring effective realisation of EU goals than obligations to implement EU law. Analysis of the milestones and targets in Polish NRP shows that they may create requirements going beyond EU law (e.g. provisions on 10H rule, point 5.5.). As regards the energy and climate, Polish NRP could contribute to the implementation of energy transition targets, especially during the hard times of energy crises. The European Commission estimates that the plan devotes 42.7% of its total allocation (35.4 billion Euro) to measures that support climate objectives, although at the time of writing this chapter, the status of payment of these resources is uncertain. Of course, these resources do not cover all the investments needed to transform the Polish energy system towards a carbon neutral one. While the NRPs *prima facie* may be regarded as a powerful tool to ensure the effectiveness of the energy transition, the broad margins of discretion in the assessment of the milestones suggest it is too early to make final judgments.

Apart from government structures formulating policies, drafting laws and exercising ownership rights over energy sector companies, the success of energy transformation depends pretty much on the energy regulator (President of Energy Regulatory Office, hereinafter: PERO), whose role – according to Article 23(1) of Energy Law – is to regulate the activities of energy enterprises in accordance with that Act and the state energy policy, aiming to balance the interests of energy enterprises and fuel and energy end users. Other articles of Energy Law do not explicitly refer to any climate goals to be pursued by PERO but to sustainable development and protection of the environment as general goals of Energy Law (Article 1(2)). Lack of such referrals is not decisive in any way, considering the vast array of energy and climate legislation administered by PERO and the concrete norms of these acts. PERO is of course bound with EU energy and climate laws.

PERO does not have any special competences within the legislative process, but in practice it is consulted on legal acts concerning energy and climate. PERO does not have rulemaking powers, and its main competence is to execute major legislative acts in the area of energy and climate through individual decisions, as the Polish Constitution does not foresee any forms of other administrative acts of general character to be issued by regulators. In practice, PERO issues also other acts which have a general character, like communications or statements, but they are considered non-binding, except in very rare situations identified by courts (Swora, 2013; Swora et al., 2016).

Core tasks and competences of PERO are included in Energy Law, but its jurisdiction is extended over numerous other areas like administering RES and energy efficiency support schemes and the capacity market (examined in subsequent paragraphs of this chapter). What is characteristic about tasks performed by PERO is that the vast majority of them are determined by EU law or executed on the basis of directly applicable EU laws (e.g. network codes). Under Energy Law and other acts, PERO exercises its competences over electricity, natural gas, RES, district heating and oil sectors, deciding about market entry through licensing and financial shape of companies through tariff setting. The obligation to approve tariffs exists in Poland in the case of network operators which are natural monopolies and in the commodity retail market in the case of households (electricity, gas, district heating). Another important competence in the hands of PERO is consulting development plans of network companies which are then translated into tariffs approved by the regulator. Through consultation of development plans, PERO has an impact on directions of investments of network operators towards the just transition. As a result of such transition, apart from incumbent large network companies, PERO also regulates growing small entities mushrooming on the last mile of the energy networks, where the intensity of regulation is considerably lower.

Given the distinctive role PERO plays in all areas mentioned above, it is worthwhile to refer also to official views of this body on energy transition. For the Polish energy regulator, the participation in energy transition, apart from new tasks, also implies revaluation of tasks and duties already granted and exercised within administrative discretion. PERO underlines the necessity of assuring social acceptance of energy transition and focusing on investments, where it intends to introduce a qualitative dimension into regulatory policy. According to the PERO, 'the key in this process is to ensure balance between the benefits of "greening" the energy sector and the costs resulting from the cooperation of these sources with the energy system, including their contribution to the security of system operation' (PERO National Report, 2021).

The role of Polish self-government in energy transition is limited if compared with government administration, energy regulation and state-owned companies. Energy law stipulates the legal basis for self-government energy planning on the lowest level, i.e. local communities, in Article 16(1), which covers planning and organisation of heat, electricity and gaseous fuels supply. In practice, delivery of energy, heat and natural gas is carried out by big energy companies and only in small towns are owned by local communities, delivering heat to its inhabitants. Energy planning by local self-governments covers planning and financing of lighting, planning and organisation of activities aimed at rationalisation of energy consumption and promotion of solutions reducing energy consumption and assessment of the potential of electricity generation in high-efficient cogeneration and energy-efficient heating or cooling systems in the commune. Apart from energy planning, it is also necessary to underline the role of local authorities in spatial planning, which is particularly important in the case of investments in RES. Local governments have also played a very important role in the area of thermal modernization of buildings. Although the current position of local authorities may not seem impressive at the first glance, their tasks are evolving. Local communities are more and more involved in various clean air initiatives and also in clean transport. Furthermore, the role of local communities in the planning of district heating will expand, especially considering the new approach to the planning of heating in new regulations of the EU.

3 Electricity

3.1 Electricity generation sector dependency on coal

Polish electricity generation has been historically dependent on hard coal and lignite, though the development of RES and gas-fired power stations lessened this dependency through the last decade. The share of electricity generated from coal (hard coal and lignite) dropped from 86.6% in 2010 to 68.2% in 2020 (ARE, 2021). Coal-based generation is still an important component of the Polish energy system, considering the role of this type of generation in delivering electricity in the baseload. Due to a mix of reasons, Poland has not historically developed any other significant types of power plants offering stable deliveries or backup power offsetting fluctuation of intermittent sources. Polish coal-dependence is enhanced by the fact that Poland has had rich coal stocks located mostly in the southern region of Silesia and Lubelskie Coal Basin as well as stocks of lignite in various other locations (Swora et al., 2016). Resignation from coal and lignite as a primary energy source has also been difficult for economic reasons, given that mining has always been an important part of the overall industry in coal regions. The high position of coal has been strongly defended by trade unions and politicians. In the case of trade unions, their position has been enhanced by social agreements negotiated with governments. All these factors cannot be overcome quickly, due to the lack of alternatives in baseload generation, which cannot be substituted by import. The social agreement signed in 2021 by trade unions and MSA set the date of full coal phase-out in 2049. Apart from the financial aspects, parties also agreed on the development of clean coal technologies and utilisation of methane from coal mines. Energy crisis and the war in Ukraine have entailed at least partial revision of the phase-out schedule, due to uncertainties concerning natural gas as a transition fuel, in terms of price and stability of supply. On the other hand, the embargo on import of coal from the Russian Federation means that in order to avoid shortage of supply, Poland has to import coal from other countries, resulting in higher prices both for electricity and heat generation sectors and individual households using fossil fuels to heat homes.

Between 2030 – 2040, the coal-based generation is going to be partially replaced by large scale nuclear power plants and SMRs (Small Modular Reactors). This type of energy sources will enable the achievement of the climate neutrality objective in compliance with the provisions of the Paris Agreement and should have a positive effect on the economy through lowering the price of purchase of CO_2 emission allowances (Gierszewski et al., 2021). In the meantime, it is also planned to gradually replace older generation units with gas-fired power plants and/or using old 200 MWe coal based generators after retrofit. Thus, despite forecasted deterioration of long-term profitability of coal mining and coal-based power plants, they cannot be easily replaced on a short notice, as it would result in considerable deterioration in security of supply. Considering this and taking into account the attitude of financial institutions to financing fossil fuels, MSA as the owner of large energy companies actively seeks ways to maintain their profitability and enable them to participate in energy transition, through development of RES. In order to do that, Poland plans a merger of coal-based assets in a separate entity, namely the National Energy Security Agency, though at the time of writing this chapter, the status of this concept is still under discussion.

Defending coal-based generation put Poland on a collision course with the EU, strongly advocating for decarbonization within its climate policy. Apart from lack of agreement on various legislative proposals aiming at phasing-out coal (e.g. Fit for 55: see Penttinen, in this volume), it is also necessary to mention court cases, and especially the Turow case (C-121/21). Controversies related to this case occurred after issuing a precedential interim measure by the Vice-President of the CJEU, ordering ceasing, immediately and pending delivery of the judgement, lignite mining activities at the Turów mine. Poland argued that it was expected that the power plant at Turów (using lignite from a controversial mine) would cover approximately 4.5% of Poland's electricity demand in 2021. The closure of that plant would threaten the security of the electricity supply to some 3.7 million households. Ceasing the mine, resulting in subsequent closing of a neighbouring power plant, could also pose threats to security of supply. The case was finally terminated after reaching an agreement between the governments of the Czech Republic and Poland. But such harsh and far reaching interim measures still pose questions about the borders of judicial powers in the EU. Single-handed interim decision resulting in closing a huge power plant in the middle of the energy crisis in Europe, without detailed dispute including opinions of experts, may raise well-founded doubts about its legitimacy. What also needs to be stressed is that the CJEU issued such interim measure for the first time in a rare inter-state type of court case (based on Article 259 TFEU). Inter-state cases are regarded sometimes as political by their nature. It is reasonable to expect far reaching caution from judges in future cases, in order not to put at risk the authority of the court and create unnecessary tensions between EU Member States. Disagreements should be resolved through the means of political dialogue, especially in cases related to environment and energy security.

3.2 Capacity market

In order to ensure stable supply of electricity, Poland introduced a capacity market in the Act of 7 December 2017 on capacity market (hereinafter ACM). It defines the organisation of the capacity market and the principles pursuant to which the service of maintaining readiness to deliver electrical capacity to the electric power system, as well as of delivering that capacity to the system whenever the system faces stress events, is rendered. According to Article 1(2) ACM, the Act aims is to assure mid- and long-term security of the supply of electricity to final customers in a way that is cost-effective, non-discriminating and in compliance with the principles of sustainable development. Main reasons for introducing this specific mechanism were presented in the decision of the European Commission granting State aid. The Commission agreed that the Polish electricity market will face substantial mothballing and phasing-out of old inefficient power units by 2020. Hence, the electricity market will not be able to meet peak demand. As those concerns were unlikely to be solved by market forces, Poland adopted ACM and received State aid clearance (European Commission, 2018). Under ACM, Polskie Sieci Elektronergetyczne S.A. (Polish TSO) is entrusted with organising auctions to procure the level of capacity required to ensure generation adequacy. Auctions are not open only to existing and new generators (mostly coal- or gas- fired), but – what is crucial from the point of view of the energy transition – also to demand side response (DSR) and storage operators, located in Poland or in the control area of neighbouring EU TSOs. Successful bidders are receiving payments under the capacity agreement in return for a commitment to deliver capacity at times of system stress called on by the TSO. In the case of DSR, participation in the capacity market is not the only opportunity to assure a reduction of consumption. The Polish TSO also offers intervention bid reduction of power consumption by consumers (IRP), which consists in a voluntary and temporary reduction of power consumption by consumers or postponing consumption at the request of the TSO, in exchange for remuneration. It is rightly assumed in the legal literature that 'even when supported by capacity mechanisms, new coal-fired plants could be unable to stay on the market if they face competition from natural gas, renewable energy and nuclear energy' (Bellantuono, 2019). It is even more true if we add another important factor, namely rising costs of CO_2 emissions. Such mix of negative factors, temporarily tempered as a consequence of energy crisis and War in Ukraine (where coal generation, due to market design, benefits extra profits), can hit hard the Polish generation sector right after termination of the capacity market mechanism (end of 2025), unless new forms of State aid are introduced. It is hard to predict that enough clean or cleaner baseload sources will be ready till the end of 2025. Commission of nuclear power plants is planned for 2033. This can result in a capacity gap beyond 2025, seriously threatening security of supply. It is also questionable whether this gap can be filled by import, considering especially German plans related to the phase-out of clean nuclear generation, which may impact not only Germany itself but also the EU Core region.

3.3 Electricity grids

Expansion and modernization of electricity grids, especially at distribution level, is a crucial factor of success from the point of view of the energy transition. The key problem Poland faces in this regard is connected with the historical structure of grids. They have been adjusted to the structure of energy generation and the accompanying "copper plate" approach, i.e. that the physical capacity of electric power transmission is unlimited. In this context, it is worth highlighting that Poland actively promotes on the EU level the concurrent model of nodal pricing, which better reflects the realities of the energy transition with a growing number of distributed generation resources (Simon, 2019). The nodal model enables active participation of consumers because the nodal price can be used as a stimulus signal to transfer power load to a different time when prices are lower (Borowski, 2020). The expansion of the electricity grid depends on the internal capabilities of TSO and DSOs on the one hand and PERO on the other, which organises consultations on their development plans and approves tariffs. There are one TSO and five large DSOs in the Polish electricity market. Due to unbundling rules, DSOs are obliged to separate the distribution activities from other activities. In addition, at the end of 2020, there were 178 companies designated as DSOs operating within vertically integrated companies that are not subject to unbundling (National Report, 2021). The growing number of those small distribution entities, competing with large DSOs on the last mile, seems to be a characteristic feature of the ongoing energy transformation.

Growing inefficiency of Polish electricity grids is first and foremost the result of revolutionary growth in the number of PV installations, accelerated by the support scheme for such sources, which, especially in the first phase of its development, was highly beneficial to prosumers (see sec. 5.4). According to energy experts, 'the increase in investments in PV micro-installations impacts the stability and management of the national power system, as the energy introduced by them into the system cannot be regulated or stored' (Zdonek et al., 2022). Such growth requires flexible reserve sources, adequate number of energy storage and digitalization of the grid. In the case of the latter, much is expected from the new Central Energy Market Information System (CEMIS), which will collect and process energy market data necessary for the administration of electricity market processes, such as switching energy suppliers or making settlements for electricity sale and supply. CEMIS was introduced in one the biggest amendments to Energy Law in 2021, which implemented Directive 2019/944. The amendment assumes that by 31 December 2028 at least 80% of consumers are to have smart meters installed. Digitalization of the electricity grid is a condition *sine qua non* for the development of flexibility services enabling smooth absorption of distributed generation and electric vehicles as well as development of the market for aggregators and DSR.

4 Policy and legal framework related to natural gas and hydrogen

4.1 Polish pathway towards diversification in natural gas

For the last two decades, the EU approach to natural gas has been inconsistent, creating confusion about the role of this fuel in the process of just energy transition. On one hand, the 3rd energy package provided a relatively stable legal environment aimed at the development of a common European energy market. Those market rules were complemented by regulations enhancing security of supply and the regulations ensuring financial support for projects of common interest (PCIs). On the other hand, climate regulations, and especially Fit for 55 proposals, including taxonomy, have caused substantial instability for investments in natural gas-based generation. The role of natural gas is even more unclear, considering past and current threats related to the EU's dependence on the Russian Federation as energy supplier in the context of the war in Ukraine and numerous other historical crises caused by Eastern suppliers. To be sure, natural gas has not been a significant part of the energy mix in Poland, at least until 2022. But it has been rightly perceived as a fuel that facilitates replacement of coal-based power plants and supports development of intermittent RES. One important area of potential usage of natural gas is district heating, where gas-powered CHP plants can replace old coal-fired generation.

4.2 Natural gas infrastructure

Unlike neighbouring Germany, Poland has been developing sound policy aiming at diversification of supply routes. This same approach has been presented by Poland on the EU level, where the country strongly advocated for diversification and opposed Nord Stream 1 and 2. Historically, Poland depended on only one route of supply, i.e. the Russian Federation, through the Transit Gas Pipeline System (TGPS) which is part of the Yamal pipeline, running from Russia through Belarus and Poland to Western Europe. In May 2022, due to Russian sanctions, transit through the pipeline from the East was stopped. The Polish part of Yamal pipeline, owned by EuRoPol GAZ S.A. (hereinafter EuRoPol), is operated by Polish TSO – Gaz-System S.A.. Historically, mixed (Polish and Russian) ownership of EuRoPol became a source of serious legal problems, as the Russian part of the management board boycotted efforts towards implementation of effective operatorship, based on the Independent System Operator model prescribed in Directive 2009/73. Problems concerning relations between the operator and the owner of infrastructure have been solved by adopting in 2019 an amendment to Energy law, which empowered PERO to issue decisions substituting agreements between the owner and operator (so called *entrusting decisions*) in the case of lack of agreement between parties. Especially in view of the Russian decision to cut off natural gas supplies to Poland (but also according to prior plans), the Polish part of the Yamal pipeline will become a part of the national transmission system, serving internal purposes. In November 2022 the Polish government took over Gazprom's stake in EuRoPol Gaz, due to sanctions on Moscow.

Polish energy policy, aiming at diversification of sources and directions of supply, resulted in the development of several projects, which have the status of Projects of Common Interest (PCI) under EU law. These projects contribute to the development of 3 main European gas corridors (NSI West Gas, BEMIP, NSI East Gas). All of them are operated and owned by the Polish TSO (in the case of FSRU, ownership status is not decided yet). LNG is imported to Poland through an LNG terminal in Swinoujscie with initial capacity of 5 BCM p/a, to be increased after modernization to 7.5 BCM p/a. Another important project is Baltic Pipe, a transmission line connecting the Polish transmission system with gas fields in Norway with 10 BCM offshore gas pipeline capacity. There are also plans to install FSRU in Gdansk till 2025, which will additionally increase LNG importing capacity (at least 6.1 to 12 BCM p/a in various scenarios). Poland is also well connected with Lithuania (GIPL pipeline) and Slovakia (Strachocina – Veľké Kapušany interconnection). Building interconnectors also implies huge investments in expansion of the internal network of transmission pipelines. In the context of the energy transition, one must not underestimate the importance of expansion of natural gas distribution networks. Expansion of these networks is crucial from the point of view of the process of switching from coal to cleaner fuels in the case of small and medium CHP generation and individual customers previously heating their homes with coal or other fossil/solid fuels. In the latter case, the future scenario is uncertain, given the tendency to switch rather to heat pumps. It is worth noticing that only in the 1st half of 2022, due to generous financial support, sale of heat pumps almost doubled in comparison with the whole record year 2021, which makes Poland a leader in the number of installations p/c of such devices in Europe (Birnbaum, 2022).

Although Poland seems to be relatively well prepared in terms of diversified and steady gas supplies, considering the EU energy crunch 2021–2022 and the impact of War in Ukraine on the natural gas market, the role of natural gas in Polish energy mix foresaw in PEP 2040 may be revised. At least part of planned gas-fired power plants may be substituted by retrofitted old coal-based 200 MWe class units.

4.3 Legal framework

As regards the legal framework, operation of transmission and distribution gas networks is governed by general norms of Energy Law, which provides for duties of distribution and transmission systems operators as well as powers of PERO related to approving tariffs and development plans. What is interesting from the point of view of the wholesale market participants is that in 2013 Poland introduced special provisions obliging gas suppliers to sell 55% of their gas portfolio through energy exchanges (Article 49b of Energy Law). This obligation concerned first and foremost Polish natural gas incumbent Polskie Górnictwo Naftowe i Gazownictwo (PGNIG S.A.), which is currently under merger procedure with multi-energy concern PKN Orlen S.A. and its main purpose was to make the wholesale market more transparent. A similar obligation had been introduced in 2010 on the Polish wholesale electricity market (Swora and Kamiński, 2017) but later taken away in November 2022, which will potentially result in lowering transparency and liquidity of the energy market. Another important piece of natural gas legislation, namely Act of 16 February 2007 on Reserves of Oil, Oil Products, Natural Gas and on Procedures in Case of Emergency in Security of Fuel Supply and Disturbance on Oil Market, concerns obligatory gas storage for gas shippers. The obligation to maintain reserves for importers had been contested by the European Commission (Mordwa, 2011), but it proved its operability and reliability during the 2021–2022 supply crisis, when Poland was able to secure gas supplies, despite aggressive shortage of supply from Gazprom. There are plans to radically change the legal framework for gas stocks in Poland. According to these plans, in order to ensure gas supplies, in particular to protected customers, the Government Agency for Strategic Reserves will create and maintain strategic reserves of natural gas. The new regulations will enter into force from October 2023.

In the case of investments, rules aiming at lessening administrative burdens were enacted in a special legal provision, namely the Act of 24 April 2009 On Investments In The Liquefied Natural Gas Regasification Terminal In Świnoujście. This dedicated act initially concerned investment in LNG terminal. Later on it was expanded to other types of network investments. Similar provisions can be found in the German act on acceleration of investments in LNG (Gesetz LNG 2022).

4.4 Hydrogen and biogas

Although there is no special legal framework related to hydrogen, the government issued the Polish Hydrogen Strategy until 2030 with an outlook until 2040 (PHS). It sets out the main objectives for the hydrogen economy development in Poland and the actions needed to achieve them. According to the PHS, Poland holds the 3rd position among European hydrogen producers, with an annual production of approx. 1.3 million tons, but only a marginal share of hydrogen comes from renewable sources. One of the objectives is the creation of a long-standing regulatory environment which removes barriers to the development of the hydrogen market and encourages a gradual increase in the use of RES for electrolysis. Poland has not developed the legal framework necessary to assist the development of the hydrogen market and the necessary infrastructure (Suski, 2020). The main reason is probably the ongoing process of revision of the Gas Directive, which also includes amendments related to hydrogen.

According to PEP 2040, biogas may play a principal role in district heating as a renewable source of energy for combined generation of electricity, heat and gaseous fuels. Furthermore, due to its storage potentials, this source of energy might prove useful as a means for regulation and self-balancing of energy clusters and/or cooperatives. Biogas is also to play a noteworthy role in transport, development of energy storage (e.g. as a source of rapid response to the electricity system needs) and as an alternative supply to local island gas networks. Its supplementary significance stems from economic treatment of harmful waste from agriculture or food processing. The potential of biogas in Poland has been poorly utilised so far, especially if compared with rapid development of other RES. According to experts, the main barriers to development of the agricultural biogas industry were unstable level and changing forms of public support as well as complicated formal and legal conditions. As a result, the development of the agricultural biogas industry in Poland has been practically halted in recent years (Ignaciuk and Sulewski, 2021). The situation should change as a consequence of implementation of the European Green Deal and the NRP.

5 Renewable energy penetration

5.1 Renewable energy policy in Poland

The role and significance of renewable energy sources (RES) in the Polish energy mix is the product of several factors. First is the need for the diversification of the sources of electricity generation, which should also reduce dependence on fuel imports and improve energy security. Second, increasing the share of RES in the overall energy consumption is one of the key targets of EU's climate and energy policy, as well as of global efforts to fight climate change.

According to PEP 2040, Poland aims at reaching at least 23% share of RES in gross final energy consumption in 2030. This is a very ambitious target: according to Eurostat, in 2020 the RES share was 16%. It is to be obtained through the development of new types of RES sources, especially offshore wind farms, and further expansion of distributed generation, onshore wind farms, biomass, biogas and geothermal energy in district heating and heat pumps, as well as expansion of advanced biofuels and electricity in transport.

Significant changes in legal and policy frameworks related to RES are foreseen in the NRP. The main objective of component B of the plan is to shift the Polish energy mix towards low-carbon technologies by facilitating the deployment of renewables and increasing the use of alternative energy sources such as hydrogen and biogas. The NRP contains many concrete measures that should translate into a proposal accelerating the development of RES and increasing energy efficiency.

5.2 Law on RES

The key legal framework concerning generation of electricity from RES is included in the Act of 20 February 2015 on Renewable Energy Sources (hereinafter RES Act). This law was to ensure a gradual switch from the previous support system based on the green certificates to a more competitive and market friendly scheme centred around the auctions for the sale of electricity generated from RES. Nevertheless, the RES Act was subsequently and frequently modified and adjusted to ever changing market and technological developments. Consequently, the legal background of the support mechanisms for RES electricity generation is currently much more complex and nuanced. Apart from regulating the support mechanism, the RES Act also deals with other, closely related issues: activities involving RES, guarantees of origin of electricity and procedures on international cooperation.

The regulatory toll relating to generation of energy from RES is strictly associated with the size of the generation unit. All units of up to 50 kW of installed electricity power are not subject to any particular regulatory conditions (so called *microinstallations*). On the other hand, the units between 50 kW and 1 MW (so called *small installations*), come under the obligation of entry in the register. Finally, operating any RES generation installation with installed electricity power of 1MW and more requires a licence, granted by the regulatory authority (PERO).

Guarantees of origin of electricity generated from RES (introduced by EU Law, particularly Directive 2018/2001) show to a final customer that a given share or quantity of energy was produced from renewable sources. It is a separate tool from the (green) certificate of origin. Guarantees of origin may be transferred separately from the electricity to which they relate, but they may be assigned to the final customer only once.

5.3 Support schemes and promotion mechanisms

5.3.1 Green Certificates

The green certificates (certificates of origin) confirm that the electricity has been generated from RES. This mechanism was introduced in 2005 and is still applicable according to the RES Act, though currently only to older RES generation installations, e.g. those which began generating electricity before July 1, 2016 (*existing installations*). Furthermore, this support mechanism is restricted in time to 15 years from the day the installation first generated and fed electricity into the grid. The mechanism is based on the obligation of companies supplying electricity to end users and certain other types of market players (e.g. large end users) to present the green certificates to the regulatory authority (PERO) in order to redeem them, or alternatively pay a substitution fee. Property rights resulting from these certificates can be traded both OTC and on the Polish Power Exchange (TGE).

Additionally, existing installations below 500 kW benefit from the mandatory purchase obligation of electricity by a so-called *obliged supplier* entity designated annually by the regulatory authority. This mandatory purchase is effected at a price indicated in the REC Act – average wholesale market price from the previous calendar quarter, calculated and published also by PERO.

5.3.2 Auctions

Auctions for the sale of electricity generated from RES installation are held by PERO, at least once a year. Auctions are organised separately for groups of RES installations (so-called *auction baskets*), according to following criteria:

1) technology:
   - biogas from landfills and sewage treatment plants, thermal waste treatments and biomass
   - hydro, geothermal, and bioliquids
   - agricultural biogas
   - PV and onshore wind
   - Hybrid
2) existing (which were in operation before entry to force of the RES Act) vs new installations (e.g. which will generate electricity for the first time after winning the given auction);
3) installed electricity power: up to 1MW and above 1MW.

The winners of the auction are selected based on a single criterion, namely the selling price. Those who bid the lowest price are granted the contracts, up until the volume of electricity generated from RES installations that can be sold in a given auction has been attained. Additionally, new installations are obliged to conclude a prequalification procedure, effected by PERO.

The price of the auction is paid to the RES installation operator by the above mentioned *obliged supplier*, which has the obligation to conclude the contract with the auction winners. The *obliged supplier* is reimbursed by the state-owned special entity (*Zarządca Rozliczeń*). This mechanism is financed by the RES fee, which is paid by all end users of electricity.

5.3.3 FiT/FiP systems

The feed-in tariff mechanism (FiT) is applicable to relatively small biogas, biomass and hydro installations (up to 500 kW of installed capacity). Electricity is purchased by the *obliged supplier*, at the reference price – which is essentially a maximum price (set by government) at which electricity generated by installations using the same technology might be purchased at the auction. The contracts are concluded for a maximum period of 15 years. Analogously to the case of the auction, the obliged supplier is subsequently reimbursed by the special entity – Zarządca Rozliczeń S.A.

The feed-in premium scheme (FiP) is dedicated to the installations using the same technology as in FiT mechanism, but with installed capacity from 500 kW up to 2,5MW (for biogas and hydro installations) and 1MW (for biomass installations). Operators of these installations sell the electricity on the market, but are paid the premium (difference between guaranteed price – set again on the basis of respective reference price – and the actual price paid by the purchaser). The premium is paid by the Zarządca Rozliczeń S.A. and the duration of the support is limited to 15 years. Both mechanisms are financed through the RES fee.

5.3.4 Energy prosumers

Prosumers are essentially end users (*electricity consumers*) who operate microinstallations – small RES systems (mostly PV, up to 50 kW of installed capacity) (see the chapter by Lavrijssen et al., in this volume). They are connected to the grid through a very simplified procedure in the same point of connection which is used by this user to withdraw electricity from the grid. Prosumers use the electricity generated by their microinstallations mostly to cover their own needs. Only the surplus of electricity generated in microinstallation is fed into the distribution grid. According to PEP 2040, Poland should reach the target of 1 mln prosumers in 2030, but it was in fact reached already in 2022 – two years after adoption of PEP 2040. Such a revolutionary growth resulted in serious concerns for DSOs, which are responsible for maintenance and operation of LV networks.

The support system for prosumers is based on the mechanism of settling the amount of the electricity taken by prosumer from the grid and the amount of the electricity generated in the microinstallation and exported by the prosumer to the grid (net-metering). The relation of energy taken from and fed into the grid is 1 to 0,8 or 0,7 (1 unit of electricity fed into the grid covers 0,8 or 0,7 unit of electricity taken from the grid). The rest of the electricity fed into the grid (or rather the value of that electricity) is used to cover distribution fees relating to the electricity fed into the grid by the prosumer (who is not obliged to pay distribution fees concerning electricity generated by microinstallation and exported to the grid).

This system has been in force until the end of June 2022. Beginning from 1 of July 2022, the settlement mechanism based on the volume of electricity was replaced by the mechanism in which electricity taken from and fed into the grid is cleared according to its value, using market prices to calculate the worth of electricity fed into the grid by prosumer (net-billing).

5.4 Offshore wind farms as a strategic project

Implementation of offshore wind energy will be one of the crucial elements of decarbonisation of the energy sector in Poland, nuclear energy being the second one. According to PEP 2040, the installed capacity of this particular source of energy should reach 5,9 GW in 2030 and 11 GW in 2040. Development of offshore wind energy is described as a strategic project, with building competence in this field being an important facilitator for overall economic growth. In December 2020, the Parliament adopted dedicated legislation – Offshore Wind Act – concerning promotion of offshore wind energy, since neither RES Act nor Energy Law envisage any special treatment for this sort of electricity generation. A key aspect of integrating offshore wind farms to the national power system (NPS) is the extension and modernization of grid infrastructure in northern Poland, which is currently significantly lagging behind the rest of the country.

The dedicated support mechanism for offshore wind energy, approved by European Commission in 2021, is based on a two-way contract for difference (CfD): the premium paid to installation operator will be the positive difference between the reference price (calculated in relation to costs of generation electricity offshore) and the market price of electricity. If the abovementioned difference is negative (market price higher than the reference price), the operator will be obliged to pay to the settlement body (State controlled counterparty of CfD) the excess over the strike price.

5.5 Rapid development of PV

Since the introduction of RES Act and the net-metering mechanism applicable to prosumers, the installation of PV electricity sources, especially in household and small/micro businesses, is booming. This growth is largely driven by favourable support schemes and subsidies foresaw in the government program 'My electricity' (Zdonek et al., 2022). The numbers describing the growth of installed capacity of PV installations since 2018 are quite impressive (ARE):

- 2018: 565,56 MW
- 2019: 1550,85 MW
- 2020: 3969,76 MW
- 2022 (January): 8 146,5 MW.

However, with the introduction of a less favourable mechanism of net-billing (settling according to value of electricity instead of simple volume thereof), this spectacular growth may actually slow down. On the other hand, one should not downplay the impact of new possibilities for PV installations, which were introduced lately or will be introduced in the near future: collective prosumer (which will make much easier to operate PV installations in condominiums), virtual prosumer (from 2024: it will enable consumers to assign electricity generated by PV owned by someone else) and expected proliferation of energy cooperatives.

5.6 Onshore wind farms – distance restrictions

Growth of this technology has been much less remarkable than PV installations: at the end of 2018 the installed capacity was 5839,92 MW, while in January 2022 it was 7118,4 MW (ARE). According to PEP 2040, the main reason is the much smaller level of social acceptance. This sentiment is exemplified in the 10H rule introduced in the spatial law relating to investments in onshore wind farms: wind turbines cannot be built within the distance from the nearest residential building that is less than ten times the height of the entire turbine. There are plans to lessen this regulatory burden and introduce the absolute minimum distance, not related to the size of wind turbine. The other factor that is perceived as a facilitator of investment in onshore wind farms is the expected propagation of PPA agreements concerning RES-generated electricity (due to anticipated further rise of electricity prices). Some scholars argue that distance regulation, excluding ca. 99% of the territory of Poland for new onshore wind installations, may in fact act in favour of offshore options (Pronińska and Księżopolski, 2021). Prioritising offshore over onshore has been officially pushed in Great Britain since 2015, when the government ended subsidies and introduced stricter planning regulations. This approach has not changed in the new energy strategy adopted in response to the energy crisis and War in Ukraine (British Energy Security Strategy, 2022). In principle, the prioritisation of offshore over onshore or the opposite is a strategic and sovereign decision of the government undertaken within its energy policy. While respecting this principle in general, the Polish NRP provides that the possibility of deviations from the 10H principle shall be enabled and that more power to determine the location of wind farms shall be given to individual municipalities as part of the local planning procedure (NRP, point B23G). Following NRP, respective amendments to the RES Act have been proposed in November 2022 aiming at removing barriers to investments in onshore wind projects.

5.7 Transport

According to its EU obligations, by 2030 Poland should achieve 14% share of RES in the transport sector, of which at least 3.5% should come from advanced (non-food) biofuels (PEP 2040). The main measure to reach this target will undoubtedly be the rapid growth of electromobility, which is also one of the Strategic Projects in PEP 2040 and sectoral policies. Particularly important will be development of electricity storage technologies and other infrastructure, like charging stations. On the other hand, expansion and modernization of the distribution grid is the indispensable condition for successful electrification of transport, with an important role played by new technologies and business models, such as demand side management (Vehicle to Grid), cyber security and last but not least, smart grids. The development of PV infrastructure is the subject of a separate legal act, namely the Act of 11 January 2018 on Electromobility and Alternative Fuels.

6 District heating

Poland has the second largest centralised district heating market in Europe. There are approximately 400 district heating networks with ca 16,5 million residents being supplied with heat, and the dependence on hard coal as far as the heat generation is concerned is still on 80% level (RES DHC, 2021). Conversion of the district heating sector towards renewable energy sources thanks to investment in both individual and system installations is crucial for one of three goals of energy transition, namely good air quality. One of the key elements of PEP 2040 is covering the heating needs of all households by district heating and zero- or low-emission individual sources by the year 2040, with a particular emphasis on developing efficient district heating systems (4–fold increase in number by 2030).

According to PEP 2040, particular measures to achieve the abovementioned goals include:

- priority to district heating systems wherever technical conditions for the supply of heat from an energy-efficient district heating system exist (unless the consumer is able to use a “greener” individual solution to provide heat to his household);
- development of a new market model in order to enable acceptable prices for consumers together with a return on the capital invested;
- 2030 target of meeting the criteria of an energy-efficient district heating system by at least 85% of heating or cooling systems with a contracted capacity exceeding 5 MW;
- development of high-efficiency cogeneration and converting power plants to CHP plants through continuation of support system for electricity generated in high-efficiency cogeneration;
- increasing the use of RES (local renewable energy resources, such as biomass, biogas, geothermal and solar energy) and waste in district heating;
- upgrading and expansion of the heat and cold distribution systems: particularly taking into account poor thermal insulation of existing heat grid and streamlining the investment process for construction of new installations;
- promoting heat storage (e.g. allowing for the use of electricity generated by non-controllable renewable sources, like wind power plants, photovoltaic panels) and

smart grids (enabling optimal heat management, reduction of transmission losses, fault detection and rationalising of maintenance operations);
- Individual heating installations should use low carbon intense sources (heat pumps, electricity, natural gas) with the simultaneous implementation of the efficient monitoring measures of the pollution generated by the single-family houses; use of solid fuels in individual heating installations will be gradually reduced.

The final outcome should be the gradual abandonment of coal in the heating sector: by 2030 in cities and by 2040 in rural areas.

Supplying the heat to customers is organised on the local level, hence the importance of the local/communal and regional energy planning taking into account local potential. Such energy planning should aim at balanced use of energy resources, efficient operation of the existing infrastructure, promotion of low-emission energy sources and finally – upgrading of air quality. Propagation of energy efficiency measures leads to steady decrease of total demand for heat, though the number of district heating consumers is projected to rise.

7 Nuclear energy

7.1 State of play

Preparation works, concerning implementation of nuclear energy in Poland have been ongoing since 2009, when the Council of Ministers decided to initiate the Polish Nuclear Power Program. Crucial tasks relating to realisation of abovementioned Program were allocated to State owned company: Polskie Elektrownie Jądrowe sp. z o.o (PEJ). Opening stages of this enormous investment project comprised of site investigation and environmental assessment for the selection of a preferred site of the Nuclear Power Plant (NPP). In December 2021, final decision concerning location of NPP has been made by indicating the site named "Lubiatowo–Kopalino" situated in northern Pomerania region of Poland, close to the Baltic Sea. According to the results of the site investigation and environmental surveys, this location meets all the environmental and safety requirements set out for NPP. In the following phase, PEJ will be applying for necessary administrative decisions and licences. According to current estimates, the construction works for the first nuclear unit should start in 2026. In November 2022, Polish government chose American AP 1000 technology for the construction of 3750 MWe power plant. There are also plans to develop nuclear projects in two other locations. One of these locations is dedicated to Korean APR 1400 technology, which is to supplement governmental plans, while the third location and technology is still uncertain.

7.2 Regulatory framework

The Act of 29 November 2000 (Nuclear Law) sets the rules and requirements for the whole course of using nuclear energy: beginning with the preparation works and ending with the closing of the NPP and its decommissioning. Specific provisions embrace:

- prerequisites on nuclear safety and radiological security including supervision and control;
- conditions for the approval of the construction and commissioning of a NPP and also decommissioning of nuclear installations;
- rules on public information concerning use of nuclear energy;
- conditions for spent fuel management and nuclear wastes;
- restrictions concerning nuclear technologies and materials, including transport of these;
- radiation incidents procedures;
- liability for nuclear damages;
- promotion of nuclear energy (including Nuclear Power Program);
- principles for the fulfilment of international commitments: on nuclear safety, protection against ionising radiation, security of nuclear materials and nuclear technology controls;
- responsibilities and competences of the President of National Atomic Energy Agency, which is a national authority regarding nuclear safety and radiological security in Poland.

The Act of 29 June 2011 on Preparing for and Performing Investments Involving Nuclear Power Facilities and Accompanying Investments deals with administrative requirements such as issuing a Location Permit or conditions for obtaining the title to the site where the NPP is to be built. This Act also sets the rules concerning distribution of revenues (mainly from property taxes) between community where the NPP is located and the neighbouring communities. Moreover, it regulates procurements concerning building NPP and safety requirements during the whole construction process.

7.3 Nuclear energy in PEP 2040

Implementation of nuclear energy is enclosed in PEP 2040 as one of its specific objectives. NPPs are described in this document as predictable energy sources with zero emissions of air pollutants and also as an important factor of diversification of the structure of energy generation.

Moreover, PEP 2040 indicates the following benefits of functioning of nuclear energy in Poland:
- achievement of climate and energy policy commitments;
- reduction of emissions from the power generation sector;
- diversification of supply of primary energy carriers;
- modernization of the whole electricity generation sector;
- reliable energy supply at reasonable cost;
- economic stimulus for regional development;
- expansion of domestic industries and new specialisations and technologies in the supply chain of components and products;
- creation of sustainable businesses.

The prospect of exploiting the advantages of a potential zero–emission heat source for industry, namely high temperature reactors (HTRs) is also a significant aspect in development of nuclear energy usage according to PEP 2040. Although the Policy does not refer to SMRs, there is a growing interest in Polish industry towards development of this type of reactor. The research undertakings concerning this issue are executed by National Centre for Nuclear Research (NCNR) and the results thereof seem to be promising.

8 Energy efficiency

Polish targets related to energy efficiency correspond with EU climate ambitions. Specifically, in PEP 2040 Poland declared a national target for energy efficiency improvement by 2030 at the level of 23% with respect to primary energy consumption forecasts developed by the European Commission in 2007 (118.6 Mtoe), which matches primary energy consumption of 91.3 Mtoe in 2030. Considering targets stemming from EED, Poland declared savings of at least 0.8% of annual final energy consumption in each year of the 2021–2030 period. Poland's organised efforts towards improving energy efficiency date back to the beginning of the transition of the Polish economy after the collapse of the centrally planned economy and concerned both the residential building sector and industry. Although a lot has been done in the case of buildings, the houses in Poland are still heating-dominated, and the building stock is not well thermally insulated. It is estimated that more than 70% of detached single-family houses in Poland (3.6 million) have no, or inadequate, thermal insulation (S. Attia et al., 2022). Thermal modernization of buildings is the subject of specific legislation, i.e. the Act of 21 November 2008 on supporting thermo-modernization and renovation and on the central register of emissivity of buildings. Specific measures related to energy performance of buildings are enshrined in various acts of Building law, including secondary legislation. Acts providing a legal basis for improvement of old and newly built houses are a part of a wider framework of energy efficiency regulations.

One of the most important pieces in the energy efficiency toolbox is the system of white certificates enacted in the Act of 20 May 2016 on Energy Efficiency. The white certificates scheme was introduced in 2011 and initially based on auctioning. In 2016, the new Energy Efficiency Act redesigned the system by removing the auctioning system. Under new regulations, continuous and permanent calls for energy saving investments were introduced and since then white certificates are granted to everyone who implements energy efficiency measures. Energy traders are obliged to secure a sufficient number of white certificates by acquiring them on the energy exchange in order to meet annual targets. The system is administered by PERO. This is problematic, as PERO is specialised rather in regulatory matters and its ability to assess energy efficiency gains are limited. Critics pointed out the lack of clarity on the accuracy of the verification regime by PERO, with self-declared energy savings incentivizing unrealistic energy savings (Rosenow et al., 2020, p. 11).

The Energy Efficiency Act also obliges large enterprises to conduct an energy audit every 4 years. According to Article 37 of that Act, the energy audit is a procedure aimed at carrying out detailed and confirmed calculations for projects to improve energy efficiency and deliver information on the potential energy savings achieved. In the context of energy efficiency, it is also necessary to underline that, implementing Directive 2019/944, the Polish Energy law adopted norms regulating roll out of smart meters and other measures enabling consumers to individually reduce their energy consumption.

Energy efficiency milestones included in the Polish NRP should result in further amendments to the Energy Efficiency Act. In particular, milestones link energy efficiency and low and lowest income households, which has been to a large extent a grey zone of energy efficiency so far.

9 Conclusions

Analysis of Polish energy legislative acts proves that the country has developed the legal framework necessary to assist policy efforts towards a just transition. Implementing energy directives of the EU, Poland adopted a legal framework supporting RES and energy efficiency. In 2021, the biggest ever amendment to Energy Law introduced instruments enabling digitalization of the energy sector, a necessary condition for the flexibility of energy markets. In the RES sector, support schemes resulted especially in dynamic growth of photovoltaics. Another milestone was introduced by legislation supporting development of offshore wind farms. At the same time, expansion of onshore windfarms is limited due to provisions on distance restrictions effectively blocking new investments. Despite growing interest in utilisation of hydrogen, there are no specific acts regulating the hydrogen market and infrastructure. At the time of writing this chapter, such regulation is not adopted also by the EU. Further significant acceleration in adopting laws and policies related to the energy transition may result from the implementation of milestones and targets included in the National Recovery Plan.

Historically, the Polish energy sector supported big, largely coal – fired energy generation. This is especially the case for capacity market regulation, assuring a good financial stance of energy generation for security of supply reasons. This might probably be also the case of consolidation of coal-based assets within the National Energy Security Agency (if it happens). Another specific feature of the Polish energy sector is the existence of one of the largest district heating sectors, mostly based on coal- or gas- fired power plants and regulated by PERO. The sector will face major challenges connected with switching to green fuels and implementation of RED II. Having diversified supply routes, Poland also plans to invest in natural gas as a transition fuel which will allow further development of RES. Considering plans related to expansion of the hydrogen economy, the system of pipelines should also allow carrying hydrogen in the future.

At the time of writing this chapter, another important legislative act, fully implementing RED II, is the subject of public consultations. Considering the legal framework and the energy policy, the energy transition is well grounded in Polish energy law acts and regulations. The Polish pathway to a just transition may be characterised in terms of the interplay between these new legal and policy frameworks and regulations aiming at securing stability of supply, which is still based mainly on coal-based power plants.

References

Act of 16 February 2007 on Reserves of Oil, Oil Products, Natural Gas and on Procedures in Case of Emergency in Security of Fuel Supply and Disturbance on Oil Market, (consolidated text in Journal of Laws 2021, pos. 2249 as amended).

Act of 21 November 2008 on supporting thermo-modernization and renovation and on the central register of emissivity of buildings (consolidated text in Journal of Laws 2022, pos. 438).

Act of 24 April 2009 On Investments In The Liquefied Natural Gas Regasification Terminal in Świnoujście (consolidated text in Journal of Laws 2021, pos. 1836 as amended.

Act of 29 June 2011 on Preparing for and Performing Investments Involving Nuclear Power (Journal of Laws 2011, No 135, pos. 789 as amended).

ACM: Act of 7 December 2017 on capacity market (Journal of Laws, 2021, pos. 1854 as amended).

Act of 11 January 2018 on Electromobility and Alternative Fuels (Journal of Laws 2018, pos. 317 as amended).

Amdoura, S., Energy Solidarity in Europe: from Independence to Interdependence, Jacques Delors Institute Studies and Reports, July 2013.

Annexes to the Proposal for a Council Implementing Decision on the approval of the assessment of the recovery and resilience plan for Poland {SWD(2022) 161 final}, Brussels, 1.6.2022 COM(2022) 268 final.

ARE, 2021. *Statystyka rynku energii 2020.* Warszawa: Agencja Rynku Energii.

Attia, S. et al., 2022. Energy efficiency in the Polish residential building stock: a literature review. *Journal of Building Engineering*, 45, 103461.

AWB: Außenwirtschaftsgesetz vom 6. Juni 2013 (BGBl. I S. 1482).

Bellantuono, G., 2019. Legal pathways of decarbonisation in the EU: the case of coal phase-out. *Oil, Gas and Energy Law Intelligence*, 17(3). Available at SSRN: https://ssrn.com/abstract=3411986 or http://dx.doi.org/10.2139/ssrn.3411986

Birnbaum, M., 2022, Heat pumps take off in coal-loving Poland amid Ukraine war, Washington Post, 6 September 2022.

Borowski, P., 2020. Zonal and nodal models of energy market in European Union. *Energies*, 13, 4182.

Directive 2009/73/EC of the European Parliament and of the Council of 13 July 2009 concerning common rules for the internal market in natural gas and repealing Directive 2003/55/EC. OJ L 211/55, 14.8.2019.

Directive 2018/2001 of the European Parliament and of the Council of 11 December 2018 on the promotion of the use of energy from renewable sources. OJ L328/82, 21.12.2018.

Directive (EU) 2019/944 of the European Parliament and of the Council of 5 June 2019 on common rules for the internal market for electricity and amending Directive 2012/27/EU. OJ L158/125, 14.6.2019.

Directive 2012/27/EU of the European Parliament and of the Council of 25 October 2012 on energy efficiency. OJ L315/1, 14.11.2012.

Energy Efficiency Act: Act of 20 May 2016 on Energy Efficiency (Journal of Laws 2016, pos. 831 as amended).

Energy law: Act of 10 April 1997 Energy law (Journal of Laws, 2021, pos. 1716 as amended).

European Commission, 2018. *State aid No. SA.46100 (2017/N) – Poland – Planned Polish capacity mechanism.*

European Commission, 2021. *State Aid SA.55940 (2021/N) – Poland Offshore Wind scheme.*

European Commission, 'Fit for 55': delivering the EU's 2030 Climate Target on the way to climate neutrality, COM(2021)550 final.

Eurostat, EU statistic data concerning energy, https://ec.europa.eu/eurostat/web/energy/data/shares .

Gesetz LNG 2022: Gesetz zur Beschleunigung des Einsatzes verflüssigten Erdgases (LNG-Beschleunigungsgesetz – LNGG), BGBl I Nr. 18 (31.05.2022).

Gierszewski, J., Młynarkiewicz, Ł., Nowacki, T.R. and Dworzecki, J., 2021. Nuclear power in Poland's energy transition. *Energies*, 14, 3626.

Ignaciuk, W. and Sulewski P., 2021. Conditions of development of the agricultural biogas industry in Poland in the context of historical experiences and challenges of the European Green Deal. *Problems of Agricultural Economics*, 3(368), pp. 55–77.

Kampas, A., Rozakis, S., Faber A. and Mamica, Ł, 2021. Assessing the Green Growth trajectory through resource and impact decoupling indices: the case of Poland. *Pol. J. Environ. Stud.*, 30(3), pp. 2573–2587.

Mordwa, M., 2011. The obligation of strategic gas storage introduced in Poland as an example of a public service obligation relating to supply security: a question of compliance with European law. *Yearbook of Antitrust and Regulatory Studies*, 4(4), pp. 57–82.

Nuclear Law: Act of 29 November 2000 Nuclear Law (Journal of Laws, 2021, pos. 1941).

Offshore Wind Act: The Act of December 17, 2020 on promoting the generation of the electrical energy in offshore wind farms (Journal of Laws, 2021, pos. 234 as amended).

PEP 2040: Energy Policy of Poland until 2040, https://www.gov.pl/web/climate/energy-policy-of-poland-until-2040-epp2040 .

President of Energy Regulatory Office, National Report 2021, https://ure.gov.pl/en/about-us/reports/67, Reports.html .

Pronińska, K. and Księżopolski, K., 2021. Baltic offshore wind energy development – Poland's public policy tools analysis and the geostrategic implications. *Energies*, 2021, 14, 4883.

Regulation (EU) 2018/1999 of the European Parliament and of the Council of 11 December 2018 on the Governance of the Energy Union and Climate Action. OJ L328/1, 21.12.2018

Regulation (EU) 2021/241 of the European Parliament and of The Council of 12 February 2021 establishing the Recovery and Resilience Facility, OJ L57/17, 18.2.2021

RES Act: Act of 20 February 2015 on Renewable Energy Sources (Journal of Laws, 2021, pos. 610).

RES DHC 2021: New support scheme for decarbonising district heating in Poland. https://www.res-dhc.com/de/2021/01/26/new-support-scheme-for-decarbonising-district-heating-in-poland/.

Rosenow J. et. al, 2020. Evaluating the Polish white certificate scheme. *Energy Policy*, 144, 111689.

Social Agreement of 28 May 2019 concerning the transformation of the hard coal mining sector and selected transformation processes in the Śląskie Voivodeship, https://www.gov.pl/web/aktywa-panstwowe/umowa-spoleczna .

Simon, F., 2019. 100% renewable power requires radical EU market fix, Poles argue, https://www.euractiv.com/section/electricity/news/wed-ready-100-renewable-power-requires-radical-eu-market-fix-poles-argue/ (17 July).

Suski, P., 2021. Kierunki rozwoju regulacji dotyczących infrastruktury do transportu wodoru (Future regulation of hydrogen transport infrastructure). *Nowa Energia*, nr. 2.

Swora, M., *Organy właściwe w energetyce (charakter, zadania i kompetencje)*. In: J. Grabowski, L. Kieres and A. Walaszek-Pyzioł, eds., 2013. *System prawa gospodarczego. Publiczne prawo gospodarcze*. Beck: Warszawa.

Swora, M., Siedlik, K. and Blach, K., 2016. Energy law in Poland. In: M.M. Roggenkamp, C. Redgwell, A. Ronne and I. del Guayo, eds., 2016. *Energy law in Europe: national, EU and international regulation*. 3rd ed. Oxford: Oxford University Press, pp. 885–971.

Swora M. and Kamiński J., 2017. Bringing in liquidity and transparency when the power sector is consolidated: the duty to trade on the power exchange. *Review of Economics and Institutions*, 8(1), Article 3.

Turów Case: Chech Republic v. Poland (C-121/21). ECLI:EU:C:2021:420.

United Kingdom, British energy security strategy, updated 7 April 2022. https://www.gov.uk/government/publications/british-energy-security-strategy/british-energy-security-strategy

Zdonek, I., Tokarski, S., Mularczyk, A. and Turek, M., 2022. Evaluation of the program subsidizing prosumer photovoltaic sources in Poland. *Energies*, 15, 846.

Part V: **Local Experiences**

Editorial introduction

The global energy transition to a low-carbon future epitomizes a shift toward a more sustainable, inclusive, and just energy market. In this process, the importance of local experiences cannot be gainsaid. Participation at the local level is key to facilitating the energy transition and improving resilience. Hence, it is at the local level that the democratic quality of the transition process can be noticed and evaluated. Moreover, it is at this level that much of the necessary coordination between the key sectors of water, energy, waste, and housing must occur: many of the functions within these sectors fall within the remit of local governments or communities.

For implementing the energy transition, the international community increasingly relies on processes and actors at the local level. Recent years have witnessed definite attention being turned to the opportunities brought about by the energy transition at the local level and the barriers experienced at that level. Unfortunately, institutional fragmentation may be a real challenge at the local level. Problems may be exacerbated where there is not a good fit between the implementing institutions and the actors involved. This section explores the impact of the global drive towards a low-carbon future at the local level through four contributions.

In one contribution to this section, Lavrijssen, Reins, and ten Caten draw attention to a major development: the traditional electricity market model is changing. Producing electricity is no longer the sole prerogative of big corporations. At the receiving end, electricity consumers are no longer passive. There have been fundamental behavioral shifts at the individual and market levels. These changes behoove further changes: the legal framework is an obvious terrain to revisit.

Necessarily, a fundamental shift in ways of thinking about energy and its generation will bring about similar shifts in the understanding of energy regulation. Decentralization has been a dominant theme on either side of the Atlantic Ocean, and law and policy reform is its main accompaniment. The result is the emergence of the energy community as a concept.

Savaresi and Outka's contribution demonstrates how individuals (citizens) are being turned into actors in the energy transition by becoming the generators of energy. This shift results from laws and policies that decentralize renewable energy generation and ownership of the means of energy production. Decentralization forces the spotlight onto every community's relationship with their energy sources. This may make for more visibility of the infrastructure and the policy needed for such energy facilities. These shifts bring about a fundamental reconceptualization of the energy community and its parameters. As Savaresi and Outka show, the transition hinges on a dance between contexts, processes, and outcomes.

Several of the other contributions in this section allude to the same phenomenon. Klass and Cerny demonstrate by comparing three US localities' experiences with the uptake of electric vehicles (EVs) in the market. By doing so, they show the importance of context and strategic approaches, both for local governments and private actors,

https://doi.org/10.1515/9783110752403-037

in encouraging EV uptake. They highlight the importance of local-level regulation and governance in countries that may be internally diverse and even oppositional when it comes to politics, climate, and level of urbanization. Interestingly, vehicle preference is what makes these differences tangible.

In some contexts, peer-to-peer transfer has become an important feature of such shifts in the conceptualization of energy accessibility. At the same time, it presents itself as an interesting driver of further change, as Lavrijssen, Reins, and ten Caten illustrate. When consumers who generate more electricity than they consume start trading with other consumers a new type of actor emerges in the energy market: the producer-consumer (or "prosumer" for short). The shift occurring here is one away from a relationship in which a mammoth state-supplier of energy caters to a passive user-base. The 'prosumer' is an empowered, active, and energized consumer *and* producer of energy.

As concerns local governance, du Plessis and Moyo demonstrate clearly with their case studies of Kampala, Cape Town, and Rabat, how important cities have become as actors in global climate governance and low-carbon transition. It is at this level where "doing things differently" for the sake of the transition to a low-carbon future will have a real effect on the lives of people: the basic services to which they have access, the extent to which they are exposed to socio-economic challenges, such as energy poverty, and the attendant effects on economic and social well-being and environmental protection. The scholarship on which they base their study link higher levels of municipal control and/or ownership of certain economic sectors with flexibility in models of governance and multiple applications of such governance models. However, the better-resourced and better-capacitated cities of the global North cannot offer a model that the cities from the global South, so often contending with scarcity, can necessarily emulate. Furthermore, the quality and nature of political processes at the national level may influence how heavily a system can and will rely on local implementation of the energy transition's goals.

du Plessis and Moyo point out that the local governments in their study experience constraints relating to resource scarcity and even disinterest at the law/policy level when attempting to implement a transition to a low-carbon future. They advise for a much stronger focus on knowledge sharing. Especially the development of knowledge related to financial or technical expertise must be encouraged to strengthen local actors and governments. They make a strong case for "supportive and well-targeted national policies, standards and realistic and flexible international and regional initiatives directed at life and governance in cities." Their concern is not only with the central government or the international community. They also point out the immense potential for better collaboration at the intragovernmental level. Then, they acknowledge the role of the private sector, city-to-city peer learning platforms, and organizations can provide such support

All of these contributions show that national laws and policies will continue to drive the transition. Still, the levels of success with implementing those policies at the local level are what will ultimately give the energy transition its substance.

Annalisa Savaresi, Uma Outka

Energy Communities: Comparative Perspectives from the EU and the US

Abstract: This chapter reflects on the emerging phenomenon of energy communities as a tool to support the transition from fossil fuel-based energy generation. While millions of people worldwide already produce renewable energy in their homes, offices, and businesses, including via models of communal electricity generation, the expanding number of small-scale distributed energy sources challenges extant governance and market arrangements. The mainstreaming of community energy requires significant structural adjustment to governance and regulatory systems built around large-scale energy production and distribution. To make sense of this complexity, we first look at how the European Union (EU) has, in recent years for the first time, regulated communities generating renewable energy across its Member States. Then we analyse developments in the US, from long-standing public and cooperative models to new initiatives launched under the Biden Administration and across US states. We contrast the EU and US approaches, reflecting upon lessons that may be learned from these experiences, as global energy systems are reconceived around communities that host energy infrastructure and develop energy resources. We draw some general inferences about the implications of this reorientation for energy law and policy, as well as the benefits and obstacles to integrating energy communities meaningfully into energy systems.

1 Introduction

The expanding number of small energy units challenges extant governance and market arrangements (Lowitzsch, 2019, p. 14). In recent years, law- and policy-makers worldwide have increasingly adopted measures to stimulate and regulate decentralised renewable energy generation, thus turning citizens into prominent actors in the energy transition away from fossil fuels.

The term 'energy community' is commonly used with various phraseologies in policy and scholarly parlance to identify situations in which groups of citizens are

---

Annalisa Savaresi is Associate Professor at the Centre for Climate Change, Energy and Environmental Law, University of Eastern Finland. This author's contribution to this chapter builds on her earlier published works (Savaresi, 2019; 2020).
Uma Outka is William R. Scott Law Professor at the University of Kansas, School of Law, United States. This author's contribution builds upon related published works (Outka 2012; 2015; 2016; 2018; 2021).

https://doi.org/10.1515/9783110752403-038

collectively involved in producing renewable energy, regardless of the technology deployed. One of the most widely cited scholarly papers on the topic distinguishes between *process* (who a given project is owned and managed by) and *outcome* (who benefits from the project) (Walker and Devine-Wright, 2008, p. 498). A community may hence own a renewable energy generation plant and benefit from it. Vice versa, a community may not own the plant but still benefit from it. This definition emphasises, on the one hand, a degree of community agency, and on the other, an element of community recipience of advantages from projects in which they are not necessarily actively engaged. The literature often portrays energy communities as a means to engender greater legitimacy and democratisation in energy governance (Becker and Kunze, 2014; van der Schoor and Scholtens, 2015; Burke and Stephens, 2017), to tackle energy poverty (Saunders, Gross and Wade, 2012), and to achieve greater 'energy justice' (Jenkins *et al.*, 2016, p. 177).

These conceptualisations have greatly influenced law and policy developments in recent years. As this chapter explains, law and policy developments in the European Union (EU) focus on process, rather than outcome, and define energy communities as those that own, in full or in part, energy generation plants (Savaresi, 2019). In the US, the concept of energy communities has a less fixed meaning, with varying emphasis on process and outcome depending on the context.

The mainstreaming of community energy requires significant structural adjustment to governance and regulatory systems built around large-scale energy production and distribution. To make sense of this complexity, this chapter reflects on how the EU has in recent years, for the first time, regulated communities generating renewable energy across its Member States. Then we analyse developments in the US, from long-standing public and cooperative models to new initiatives launched under the Biden Administration and across US states. We contrast the EU and US approaches to reflect upon lessons that may be learned from these experiences, as global energy systems are reconceived around communities that host energy infrastructure and develop energy resources. We conclude with some general inferences about the implications of this reorientation for energy law and policy, as well as the benefits and obstacles to integrating energy communities meaningfully into energy systems.

2 Energy Communities in the EU

In the EU millions of people produce renewable energy in their homes, offices, and factories and share electricity (European Commission, 2020). Community energy generation has a long-standing history in some EU Member States – like Denmark and Germany – with strong cooperative traditions and sizeable renewable energy industries (Bauwens et al., 2016; Süsser et al., 2017; Wagner and Berlo, 2017; Crook *et al.*, 2018; Kooij *et al.*, 2018; Gorroño-Albizu et al., 2019).

With its 'Clean Energy for All Europeans' package, the EU has for the first time mandated the mainstreaming of community energy generation across its Member States. The package is a set of legislative acts on the energy performance of buildings, renewable energy, energy efficiency, governance and electricity market design, for the 2020–2030 decade. Its objective is to contribute to the EU's gradual transition from fossil fuels to a carbon-neutral economy.

The 2018 Directive on the promotion of the use of energy from renewable sources (henceforth 'Renewables Directive') and the 2019 Directive on Common Rules for the Electricity Market (henceforth 'Electricity Directive') have introduced the obligation for Member States to adopt enabling regulatory frameworks for certain categories of energy initiatives in EU legislation. As a result, the European Commission (2016) estimates that by 2030, energy communities could own 17% of installed wind and 21% of solar capacity in the EU.

EU law generally treats energy communities as non-commercial entities that engage in economic activity but whose primary purpose is to provide environmental, economic or social community benefits, as opposed to profit. Energy communities are identified on the basis of specific criteria and activities to ensure they operate without distorting competition and without foregoing rights and obligations applicable to other market parties.

Specifically, the Electricity Directive enables citizens' participation – individually or through so-called 'citizen energy communities' – in all electricity markets, either by generating, consuming, sharing or selling electricity, or by providing flexibility services through demand-response and storage. The Directive aims to improve the uptake of citizen energy communities which are described as legal entities that:

(a) are based on voluntary and open participation and is effectively controlled by members or shareholders that are natural persons, local authorities, including municipalities, or small enterprises;
(b) have, as their primary purpose, the provision of environmental, economic or social community benefits to its members or shareholders or to the local areas where they operate rather than financial profits; and
(c) may engage in generation, including from renewable sources, distribution, supply, consumption, aggregation, storage, efficiency services or charging services for electric vehicles or provide other services to members or shareholders;

Importantly, citizen energy communities are technology-neutral and can therefore also be fossil-fuel based.

Instead, the 2018 Renewable Energy Directive provides more specific measures to stimulate the formation of 'renewable energy communities'. These are defined as 'legal entities' that:

(a) in accordance with the applicable national law, are based on open and voluntary participation, autonomous, and effectively *controlled* by shareholders or members that are located in the proximity of the renewable energy projects owned and developed by that legal entity;
(b) whose shareholders or members are *natural persons, Small and Medium Enterprises* or *local authorities,* including municipalities;
(c) whose primary *purpose* is to provide environmental, economic or social community benefits for shareholders or members or the local areas where they operate, rather than financial profits' (Renewables Directive, Article 2.16).

The criteria to identify renewable energy communities revolve around the nature of shareholders, governance and purpose of the endeavour.

On shareholders, the Directive says that they can be natural persons, local authorities, including municipalities, or Small and Medium Enterprises (Renewables Directive, Article 2.16). It requires that participation in projects be open and voluntary, autonomous, and effectively controlled by shareholders or members *located in the proximity* of the renewable energy projects owned and developed by that community (ibid.). This requirement prioritises those that live on or near a project site, vis-à-vis those that may have an interest in getting involved. However, no definition of proximity is provided, and the Renewables Directive leaves it to Member States to identify the relevant criteria. The notion of community is also rather open-ended and encompasses subjects other than natural persons, such as local authorities, municipalities, and SMEs (ibid.) The Directive however says that participation in projects should be open to 'all consumers, including those in low-income or vulnerable households' (ibid., Article 22.4.f).

On governance, the Renewables Directive specifies that decision-making powers should be limited to those members or shareholders not engaged in large-scale commercial activity and for which the energy sector does not constitute a primary area or economic activity. What meaning will be attached to the expression 'effective control' in practice remains to be seen. Different criteria – including, for example, a 51% community ownership requirement – were considered and discarded during the Directive's drafting process.[1] No criterion was ultimately enshrined in the Directive, which merely specifies how, for private undertakings, participation in community projects should not constitute their primary commercial or professional activity (Renewables Directive, Article 22.1).

On purpose, the Directive says that energy communities should 'provide environmental, economic or social community benefits for its members or the local areas where it operates rather than financial profits' (ibid, Article 2.16.c). This requirement

1 See the criteria listed in EU Commission, *Proposal for a Directive on the promotion of the use of energy from renewable sources*, COM/2016/767 (2016), Article 22.

seemingly expects projects to deliver more than just electricity and financial returns. Yet the Directive does not specify how such benefits ought to be defined, measured or reported.

The Directive distinguishes the notion of renewable energy community from that of 'self-consumer', which it defines as:

> a final customer operating within its premises located within confined boundaries or, where permitted by a Member State, within other premises, who generates renewable electricity for its own consumption, and who may store or sell self-generated renewable electricity, provided that, for nonhousehold renewable self-consumers, those activities do not constitute their primary commercial or professional activity (Renewables Directive, Article 2.14).

The notion of self-consumer, too, encompasses diverse scenarios, such as, for example, residents fitting solar panels on their roofs, or a farmer installing a windmill to cater for the energy needs of his/her farm. The Directive also contemplates the possibility that self-consumers act in groups (ibid., Article 2.15) and that third parties manage their installations (ibid., Article 21.1.5).

The distinguishing features of the notion of renewable energy community vis-à-vis that of self-consumer are the type of agency involved and the size and purpose of projects. On agency, the notion of self-consumer does not necessarily entail collective action, but that of energy community does.

On size, the Directive allows Member States to provide preferential treatment only to self-consumers producing renewable energy below a certain threshold (ibid., Article 21.3.c). In contrast, no such limitation is provided for renewable energy communities. This, in turn, suggests that community projects may generate larger amounts of energy and entail a greater degree of professionalisation.

Finally, self-consumers' main objective is to produce energy for themselves and sell only the excess to the grid. By contrast, community energy projects are expected to provide 'environmental, economic or social community benefits' for members, or the local areas where they operate, 'rather than financial profits' (ibid., Article 2.15.).

Member States must adopt 'enabling frameworks to promote and facilitate' renewable energy communities and self-consumption, by removing unjustified regulatory and administrative barriers (ibid., Articles 21.6 and 22.4). These frameworks should ensure the removal of unjustified regulatory and administrative barriers, access to finance and information, and regulatory and capacity-building support. Member States must report the main elements of these enabling frameworks and the related implementation measures in the periodical updates of their integrated national energy and climate plans (ibid., Articles 21.6 and 22.5). In this connection, the Renewables Directive endows the EU with new powers of scrutiny, the exercise and implications of which remain to be seen.

Renewable energy communities must be subjected to fair, proportionate and transparent procedures and cost-reflective network charges (Ibid., Articles 15 and 22). EU Member States are expected to ensure that communities can participate in available support schemes on equal footing with other market participants. The objective is to empower communities to produce, consume, store and sell renewable energy, advance energy efficiency in households, support the use of renewable energy and contribute to fighting energy poverty through optimising energy consumption and reducing energy bills.

With the measures above, the EU has placed energy communities at the centre of the energy transition. It has, however, largely left it to Member States to resolve the numerous regulatory complexities associated with renewable energy communities (Savaresi, 2019). For example, as noted above, EU law expects renewable energy communities to provide societal benefits. Still, it does not elaborate on how these benefits should be defined, quantified, monitored or distributed. The Directives do, however, point to a set of factors – such as capacity-building, access to information, finance, and markets – that should guide Member States with the mainstreaming of community energy. On governance models in the transition generally, see the chapter 3 in this volume.

The EU has therefore become a living lab to test regulatory reforms to turn energy communities 'from grassroots to mainstream' (Savaresi, 2019) and thus fundamentally restructure energy systems built around centralised large-scale generation. Some studies have painted a picture of the *status quo* before the implementation of EU law concerning renewable energy communities (Ferrari *et al.*, 2020). Others have pointed to the challenges associated with implementing of EU law and strategies (Diestelmeier, 2021; Hoicka *et al.*, 2021).

Evidence emerging from some Member States suggests that mainstreaming renewable energy communities is a complex endeavour with a risk of perverse outcomes. For example, crucial questions arise concerning distributional outcomes for those who do not participate in community projects, and do not have access to the energy or income provided (Creamer *et al.*, 2019: p. 5). Law and policy are important in answering complex, layered, justice questions such as these.

The answers to these questions in the EU Member States vary, depending on the different locations' political, economic and social characteristics. The implementation of the Clean Energy Package will reveal how EU Member States will accommodate renewable energy communities in their energy systems, the right financial support they will provide, and how access to the electricity grid will be regulated.

Simply transplanting solutions from one place to another is unlikely to work. It will take time to identify the regulatory and contractual conditions that make mainstreaming community energy possible. Adjustments in energy governance arrangements require time and a trial-and-error process that has only just begun. What seems clear is that with the Clean Energy Package, the EU has embarked on a journey that may revolutionise energy generation and governance across its Member States.

3 Energy Communities in the US

There is no fixed definition of energy communities in the US with universalized legal import as in the EU. However, the concept of energy communities has long-standing and evolving significance in the US, which might best be described as multifaceted and multi-contextual.

Although investor-owned utilities (IOUs) supply most electricity to end consumers in the US, local non-profit ownership of electric-power generation has a long history in the US, in two primary forms. The first are those entities that comprise what is commonly referred to in the US as "public power." This refers to municipal utilities (or "munis"), which, under a typical arrangement, purchase electricity wholesale or under a long-term contract for IOUs or independent power generators to serve residents' needs, operating essentially as distribution-only utilities. However, a minority of munis own a generating facility outright. Across the nation, there are over 2,000 municipally-owned utilities, far exceeding the number of IOUs. Still, most are owned by small cities and towns, so while more numerous, they serve a smaller percentage of ultimate consumers in the US – 15 percent compared to IOUs' roughly 50 percent (American Public Power Association, 2021, p. 10, 12). They range in size to serve population centres from 1.4 million at the high end (Puerto Rico Electric Power Authority and the Los Angeles Department of Water & Power are the two largest) to much smaller communities (those in the range of 35,000 served, for example, are still in the top 100 largest in the category) (American Public Power Association, 2021, pp. 14–15).

The second long-standing localized energy structure in the US is the rural electric power cooperative. In areas served by "co-ops," as these are often called, local residents have access to electricity typically generated by a power plant that consumers technically own under a cooperative ownership structure. Electric cooperatives developed in the early 20th century, driven partly by the Rural Electrification Act of 1936, which sought to help expand electricity access to rural areas of the US, which were not well served by IOUs (7 U.S.C. §§ 901–950bb-1; Kwoka, 2016). Today, there are approximately 850 cooperatives providing electricity to 12 percent of ultimate consumers in the US (American Public Power Association, 2021, p. 10, 12). Although the percentage of total national population served by cooperatives is lower than IOUs and even municipally-owned utilities, co-ops' service areas cover over half the US land mass, including over 90 percent of the nation's "persistent poverty counties" (National Rural Electric Cooperative Association, 2022).

The emergence of both these forms of locally-based non-profit electricity service models, particularly in the early part of the 20th century, was integrally tied to tensions and policy themes that continue to resonate today. How should the contours of public and private interests be drawn when providing a fundamental service such as electric power? What balance of regulatory control and markets will best assure universal energy access at reasonable rates? A key difference between then and now, however, is the central concern over the climate impacts of energy production. The municipal utility and electric cooperative developed as service models. Existing munis and co-ops were established within their communities long before the now unquestionable imperative to shift from fossil fuels to increased renewable energy. Indeed, differential legal treatment in the US, at both the federal and state level, allows them to lag behind IOUs in transitioning their portfolios to cleaner resources.

For example, modern state renewable energy standards – adopted in most US states requiring IOUs to sell a certain, typically increasing, percentage of electricity from renewable energy sources – typically do not apply to municipal utilities or cooperatives (DSIRE, 2020). These measures have been a driving force for the significant increase in renewable energy development in the US over the last 10–15 years. The validity of differential regulation for publicly-owned versus shareholder-owned utilities was validated by the US Supreme Court over 100 years ago.[2] On the one hand, less regulatory oversight allows munis and cooperatives more autonomy and, in theory, more flexibility to adjust their approach to electricity generation and be responsive to the communities they serve. However, because they operate on a smaller scale, in general, compared to their private shareholder-owned IOU counterparts, and may be bound by long-term contracts, their ability to pivot away from fossil energy assets is often more constrained (*e.g.,* Chan et al., 2019, discussing constraints on that state's munis and co-ops in the shift to clean distributed energy resources). As Miriam Fischlein, Elizabeth Wilson, and others have noted, this has insulated munis and cooperatives from "the same pressures as investor-owned utilities" to develop renewable energy (Fischlein *et al.*, 2009, p. 788). That is not to say that their portfolios, categorically, have not begun to shift to renewable resources, because they have. However, because they generally formed well before the need for renewable energy was widely acknowledged, many munis and cooperatives face significant challenges in reorienting their operations away from fossil fuels.

Municipal utilities and rural electric cooperatives operate in ways that function, to an extent, to define an energy community of sorts. However, the concept of energy communities in modern parlance is evolving along different lines, anchored more commonly to communities that host energy infrastructure and energy extraction, irrespective of the entity delivering their electricity. As noted above, at this point, there is not a universally accepted definition of energy communities in the US. The term is understood in ways aligned with the long-standing concern for environmental justice communities, specifically those closely connected to the energy sector, and concern

2 See, Springfield Gas & Elec. Co. v. City of Springfield, 257 U.S. 66 (1921) (holding state laws treating city utility and IOU differently was constitutional because "whatever its public duties," an IOU "is organized for private ends," in contrast with a municipal corporation, explaining that any gain from the sale of electricity "is a gain to a public body and must be used for public ends." *Id.* at 70).

for communities in economic decline due to changes in the energy sector.[3] The term evokes fenceline communities near a polluting power plant.[4] Often, such communities have long been economically disadvantaged. They have often raised environmental and energy justice issues and emphasised the need to reduce local pollution. The term is also frequently used to reference communities that have long depended on fossil fuel extraction or production industries, such as those now facing economic hardship with coal's declining share of the electricity sector – a key focus within the just transition literature (Eisenberg, 2019; McGinley, 2013).[5] For more on meanings of energy justice, see Bhullar, in this volume.

A presidential executive order has now formally recognized these dimensions of the energy community concept. In 2021, President Joseph R. Biden's Executive Order 14008, one of the first of his presidency, outlined measures to address the climate crisis (for summary see White House Fact Sheet, Jan. 27, 2021). The Executive Order states the goal of "Empowering Workers Through Revitalizing Energy Communities," directing federal agencies to "coordinate investments and other efforts to assist coal, oil and natural gas, and power plant communities" (sec. 217). The Order established an Interagency Working Group on Coal and Power Plant Communities (sec. 218). The Working Group's initial report addressed energy communities as a "set of communities across the country hard-hit by coal mine and coal power plant closures" (Interagency Working Group on Coal and Power Plant Communities and Economic Revitalization, 2021). The Working Group also recognized "a broader set of energy impacted-impacted communities," including "fenceline communities and other communities impacted by environmental and health effects of fossil energy generation." The Executive Order (sec. 217) acknowledges that "[m]ining and power plant workers drove the industrial revolution and the economic growth that followed, and have been essential to the growth of the United States."

At the same time, the Executive Order prioritized environmental and economic justice for "disadvantaged communities" by explicitly seeking to ensure that they benefit from economic opportunities expected with the clean energy transition (sec. 219). To that end, the Order established the Justice40 Initiative, setting a goal of delivering "40 percent of the overall benefits" of federal climate investments "to dis-

3 For a discussion of how the environmental justice movement and concept connects to modern notions of energy justice, see Outka (2017).

4 See, e.g., NAACP (2016) (studying how coal-fired power plants across the US are disproportionately located in close proximity to economically disadvantaged communities of color); NAACP (2017) (assessing harms from oil and gas facilities, including those that supply gas-fired power plants). See also US Envtl. Prot. Agency, Power Plants and Neighboring Communities (last visited Feb. 2022). On community benefits agreements that can be used to acknowledge community scale impacts in the context of new energy infrastructure, see US Dep't of Energy (2017).

5 See, also Center for a New Energy Economy, Energy Communities in Transition (providing resources related to coal communities).

advantaged communities," with a focus on "clean energy and energy efficiency"; "clean transit"; "remediation and reduction of legacy pollution" (sec. 223). As directed by the Executive Order, the White House Council on Environmental Quality is (at the time of this writing) developing recommendations and implementation tools for the Justice40 Initiative, including a Climate and Economic Justice Screening Tool to assist with identifying disadvantaged communities within the meaning of the Order.[6] If effective implementation can be achieved, the Justice40 Initiative has the potential to advance renewable energy and reduce the household energy burden in disadvantaged communities (e.g. Ross et al., 2018).

Importantly, the energy communities concept is also understood in the forward-looking context of renewable energy development, referring to communities that host new energy facilities, such as a community that approves a wind farm (sometimes called "host communities"). Professor Ann Eisenberg (2022) describes energy communities as both those "losing their role as energy producers and [] those who are becoming new energy producers" as hosts to utility-scale renewable energy facilities. For example, the state of New York has established a "Clean Energy Communities" program to assist localities in advancing the renewable energy transition at a community scale with a range of strategies grounded in local government authority.[7] However, tensions with and benefits for host communities of utility-scale renewable energy projects should be considered (Outka, 2021).

Community-centred approaches to decentralizing the electric grid come in other forms worthy of mention, adding further texture and nuance to the concept of energy communities in the US at this point in the energy transition. These include, for example:

- *Local government power purchase agreements (PPAs) for renewable energy.* PPAs are increasingly providing a way for local governments that do not operate a municipal utility to buy electricity output from a wind or solar facility, often aligned with local climate plans. According to RMI, a renewable energy think-tank, around 200 US cities and counties had, by the end of 2021, committed to 100 percent renewable energy, with most utilizing large-scale PPAs for off-site renewable energy to reach that goal (Shea and Abbott, 2020, p. 6).
- *Community choice aggregation (CCA).* In certain parts of the US, community choice aggregation is available as a means for local governments and related entities to aggregate community demand for electricity and procure it in an aggregated purchase on behalf of retail electricity customers (O'Shaughnessy *et al.*, 2020). When this model first emerged in the 1990s, the primary goal of local gov-

6 See, Council on Environmental Quality, Climate and Economic Justice Screening Tool (beta), at: https://screeningtool.geoplatform.gov/en/ (last visited Feb. 2022).

7 See, New York State Energy Res. and Dev. Authority, Clean Energy Communities Program, at: https://www.nyserda.ny.gov/cec (last visited Feb. 2022).

ernments was to obtain lower electricity rates for their residents. However, it is nowadays possible in some parts of the US for a CCA to facilitate a community's goal of shifting to renewable energy, perhaps faster than the incumbent IOU in the area may be doing.

- *Municipalization.* In some communities, the prospect of divorcing their IOU in favour of a public power model holds real appeal as a means to control the energy portfolio locally to align with community values and climate goals. There are high barriers to local governments shifting from being served by an IOU to operating their municipal utility – again, a model that is not new, but which some communities are considering from new perspectives, as US law does provide an avenue for local governments to acquire the infrastructure serving their communities for this purpose. At a minimum, even where municipalization has not proved economically feasible, some localities have been able to leverage their consideration of the possibility of pushing their IOUs to reorient their holdings more rapidly toward renewables (Outka, 2016; Welton, 2017).
- *Community solar/shared renewables projects.* In the US, some so-called community solar projects are small-scale solar arrays owned by the dominant service provider in the area, whether IOU (the majority), municipal utility or electric cooperative (Heeter et al., 2020). The output from these systems is offered to customers on a subscription basis. As state law allows, other community solar projects can be owned by an entity other than an IOU. Among the benefits of community solar is the opportunity it provides for access to solar power for people who are not in a position to install solar panels for home use themselves, either due to financial barriers or renter status. Community solar projects can be tailored specifically to alleviate the energy burden for low-income households (DenHereder et al., 2020).

As this overview demonstrates, the community-based energy models are long-standing but still very much evolving in the US, with state law varying widely in how well it supports local and grassroots innovation. For more on the role of cities in the low-carbon transition, with a focus on African cities, see Ch. 30.

4 Looking Forward: Comparative Perspectives on Energy Communities

The emergence of a regulatory notion of renewable energy communities in the EU, and the evolving energy communities concept in the US, underscores an important theme of the current energy transition that is equally relevant on both sides of the Atlantic: the energy system is increasingly decentralized to accommodate renewable energy technologies. As law and policy are reformed to accelerate this energy transition, communities are affected in wide-ranging, often significant ways. Under a highly centralized energy system, only select communities would be in view, if even aware, of their energy sources. In contrast, the proliferation of decentralized energy facilities, from small to utility-scale, makes energy infrastructure much more visible, and the policy questions presented by these changes more salient, and, at times, controversial.

Municipal utilities and rural electric cooperatives clearly have similarities with renewable energy communities in the EU. However, a key difference is that long-standing community energy efforts in the EU are being reoriented to a modern energy future. This will not be an easy reorientation. While the EU approach was developed with a specific renewable energy transition in mind and a recognition that community engagement and benefit from this transition must be well integrated, it remains to be tested. Nonetheless, with a regulatory framework to advance renewable energy at the community level, the EU is expected, over time, to refine and improve its regulatory framework as experience reveals unanticipated challenges.

This purposeful approach to defining and reinforcing energy communities to advance energy transition goals has no clear parallel in the US. The concept of energy communities in the US is less fixed. As a result, it may also be more inclusive of the wide-ranging ways that energy affects communities. Such effects may be from economic losses and gains due to market and policy shifts affecting the energy sector, new infrastructure development, and aesthetic and health impacts associated with energy production. As more local governments in the US define new ways to pursue renewable energy for their communities, they exert influence on the electric grid more broadly by helping to drive higher levels of renewable electric power into regional systems. At the same time, with President Biden's Executive Order and the Inflation Reduction Act of 2022, alongside simultaneous law-making at the state level related to the energy transition, the concept of energy communities seems likely to retain multiple meanings across varied contexts. There is a growing concern for energy justice and the environmental impacts of energy on host communities and for just transitions in communities that developed around now-outmoded energy industries. These concerns centre the notion of energy communities in the lived experiences of people in those communities.

With the implementation of the EU directives still in the early stages, it is too soon to draw definitive conclusions about the efficacy of energy communities as conceived by those reforms. However, key aspects of the EU approach seem to hold useful lessons for the US. For example, the lack of dedicated provisions on energy communities' "environmental, economic or social community benefits" in the US undoubtedly contributes to the frequent opposition to new proposed renewable energy projects from host community residents who are not benefiting from land leases – they see harm to their local landscape, for example, without seeing any clear benefits. The result can sometimes be time-consuming litigation, stalling a project indefinitely. When rapidly accelerating renewable energy is essential, mechanisms for bolstering support for new energy infrastructure are as needed in the US as in the EU.

Thus, as the implementation of the EU directives continues, the degree to which it proves successful in some respects and possibly falters in others will serve to inform both the EU and the US on the prospects for energy communities as drivers of the global energy transition.

References

American Public Power Association. 2021. *Public Power Statistical Report*. Available at:< https://www.publicpower.org/resource/public-power-statistical-report> [Accessed 2 May 2022].

Bauwens, T., Gotchev, B. and Holstenkamp, L., 2016. What drives the development of community energy in Europe? The case of wind power cooperatives. *Energy Research & Social Science*, 13, pp. 136–147.

Becker, S. and Kunze, C., 2014. Transcending community energy: collective and politically motivated projects in renewable energy (CPE) across Europe. *People Place and Policy*, 8(3), pp. 180–191.

Burke, M.J. and Stephens, J.C., 2017. Energy democracy: Goals and policy instruments for sociotechnical transitions. *Energy Research & Social Science*, 33, pp. 35–48.

Chan, G. et al., 2019. Barriers and Opportunities for Distributed Energy Resources in Minnesota's Municipal Utilities and Electric Cooperatives.

Creamer, E. *et al.*, 2019. Community renewable energy: What does it do? Walker and Devine-Wright (2008) ten years on. *Energy Research & Social Science*, 57, 101223.

Crook, N. *et al.*, 2018. *Models of local energy ownership and the role of local energy communities in energy transition in Europe.* Available at: <http://publications.europa.eu/publication/manifestation_identifier/PUB_QG0118933ENN>[Accessed 14 October 2019].

DenHereder, T. et al. /Inst. For Local Self-Reliance, *Equitable Community Solar: Policy and Program Guidance for Community Solar Programs that Promote Racial and Economic Equity* (Feb. 2020).

Diestelmeier, L., 2021. Citizen energy communities as a vehicle for a just energy transition in the EU – Challenges for the transposition, *Oil, Gas & Energy Law*, 19(1). Available through: <https://www.ogel.org/article.asp?key=3945> [Accessed 6 September 2021].

Directive 2018/2001 of the European Parliament and of the Council on the promotion of the use of energy from renewable sources, [2018] OJ L328/82.

Directive 2019/944 on Common Rules for the Internal Market for Electricity and Amending Directive 2012/27/EU, [2019] OJ L158/125.

Directorate-General for Energy (European Commission) *et al.*, 2020. *Energy Communities in the Clean Energy Package: Best Practices and Recommendations for Implementation*. LU: Publications Office of the European Union. Available at: <https://data.europa.eu/doi/10.2833/51076> [Accessed 7 September 2021].

DSIRE, Clean and Renewable Energy Standards Summary Map (last updated Sept. 2020).

Eisenberg, A.M., 2019. Just transitions. *S. Cal. L. Rev.*, 92, pp 273–330.

Eisenberg, A.M., 2022. Transitions in energy communities. *George Wash. U. J. of Energy & Envtl. L.*, 12, pp. 103–112.

European Commission, Staff Working Document Impact Assessment Accompanying the Document Proposal for a Directive of the European Parliament and of the Council on the Promotion of the Use of Energy from Renewable Sources (Recast), SWD(2016)418.

Executive Order 14008, *Tackling the Climate Crisis at Home and Abroad,* 86 Fed. Reg. 7619 (Feb. 1, 2021).

Ferrari, A. *et al.*, 2020. *The Future of Renewable Energy Communities in the Eu: An Investigation at the Time of the Clean Energy Package*. European University Institute. Available at: <https://data.europa.eu/doi/10.2870/754736> [Accessed 6 September 2021].

Fischlein et al., 2009. Carbon emissions and management scenarios for consumer-owned utilities. *Environmental Science & Policy*, 12, pp. 778–788.

Gorroño-Albizu, L., Sperling, K. and Djørup, S., 2019. The past, present and uncertain future of community energy in Denmark: Critically reviewing and conceptualising citizen ownership. *Energy Research & Social Science*, 57, 101231.

Heeter, J. et al./Nat'l Renewable Energy Lab., Sharing the Sun: Understanding Community Solar Deployment and Subscriptions (Webinar) (Apr. 28, 2020).

Hoicka, C.E. *et al.*, 2021.Implementing a just renewable energy transition: Policy advice for transposing the new European rules for renewable energy communities. *Energy Policy*, 156, 112435.

Inflation Reduction Act of 2022, Public Law No. 117–169, sec. 13101(g) (117th Cong. 2021-22).

International Renewable Energy Agency (IRENA), 2019. *Renewable Energy Statistics 2019*, IRENA. p. 398. Available at: <https://www.irena.org/publications/2019/Jul/Renewable-energy-statistics-2019> [Accessed Dec. 2022].

Interagency Working Group on Coal and Power Plant Communities and Economic Revitalization, 2021. *Initial Report to the President on Empowering Workers Through Revitalizing Energy Communities*. [pdf] Available at: <https://netl.doe.gov/sites/default/files/2021-04/Initial%20Report%20on%20Energy%20Communities_Apr2021.pdf> [Accessed Dec. 2022].

Jenkins, K. *et al.*, 2016. Energy justice: A conceptual review. *Energy Research & Social Science*, 11, pp. 174–182.

Kooij, H.-J. *et al.*, 2018. Between grassroots and treetops: Community power and institutional dependence in the renewable energy sector in Denmark, Sweden and the Netherlands. *Energy Research & Social Science*, 37, pp. 52–64.

Kwoka, J.E., Jr., 1996. *Power structure: ownership, integration, and competition in the US electricity industry*. Cham: Springer.

Lowitzsch, J., 2019. Introduction: The challenge of achieving the energy transition. In: J. Lowitzsch, ed., 2019. *Energy transition. Financing consumer co-ownership in renewables*. Cham: Palgrave Macmillan, pp. 1–26.

McGinley, P., 2013. Collateral damage: Turning a blind eye to environmental and social injustice in the coalfields. *J. Envtl. & Sust. L.*, 19, pp. 304–425.

NAACP, Coal Blooded: Putting Profits Before People (2016).

NAACP, Fumes Across the Fence-Line: The Health Impacts of Air Pollution from Oil & Gas Facilities on African American Communities (2017).

National Rural Electric Cooperative Association. NRECA (2022). Co-op Facts & Figures. Available at: <https://www.electric.coop/electric-cooperative-fact-sheet> [Accessed: February 2022].

O'Shaughnessy et al./National Renewable Energy Lab, 2019. Community Choice Aggregation: Challenges, Opportunities, and Impacts on Renewable Energy Markets (Thech. Rep. NREL/TP-6A20-72195). Available at: https://www.nrel.gov/docs/fy19osti/72195.pdf [Accessed Dec. 2022]

Outka, U., 2012. Environmental justice in the renewable energy transition. *J. Env. & Sust. Law*, 19, pp. 60–122.

Outka, U., 2015. Prospects for public power and distributed renewable energy. *Env. L. Rep.*, 45, pp. 10537–10541.

Outka, U., 2016. Cities and the low-carbon grid. *Env. L.*, 46, pp. 105–156.

Outka, U., 2017. Fairness in the low-carbon shift: Learning from environmental justice. *Brooklyn L. Rev.*, 82, pp. 789–824.

Outka, U., 2018. Fairness in the low-carbon shift: Learning from environmental justice, In: C. Gonzalez, R. Salter & E. Kronk Warner, eds., 2018. *Energy justice: US and international perspectives*. Cheltenham: Edward Elgar, pp. 12–40.

Outka, U., 2021. Renewable energy siting in the critical decade. *Kansas L. Rev.*, 69, pp. 857–888.

Ross, L. et al., The High Cost of Energy in Rural America: Household Energy Burdens and Opportunities for Energy Efficiency, Am. Council for an Energy-Efficient Economy (July 2018)

Saunders, R.W., Gross, R.J.K. and Wade, J, 2012. Can premium tariffs for micro-generation and small scale renewable heat help the fuel poor, and if so, how? Case studies of innovative finance for community energy schemes in the UK. *Energy Policy*, (42). pp. 78–88.

Savaresi, A., 2019. The rise of community energy from grassroots to mainstream: The role of law and policy. *J. Env. L.*, 31(3). pp. 487–510.

Savaresi, A., 2020. Community Energy and a Just Energy Transition: What We Know, and What We Still Need to Find Out. In: Guayo, I. del et al., eds., 2020. *Energy Justice and Energy Law*. Oxford, New York: Oxford University Press.

van der Schoor, T. and Scholtens, B., 2015. Power to the people: Local community initiatives and the transition to sustainable energy. *Renewable and Sustainable Energy Reviews*, (43). pp. 666–675.

Shea, R. and Abbott, S., 2020. *A Local Government's Guide to Off-Site Renewable PPA Risk Mitigation*, Rocky Mountain Institute. Available at: <https://rmi.org/insight/a-local-governments-guide-to-off-site-renewable-ppa-risk-mitigation/>[Accessed Dec. 2022]

Süsser, D., Döring, M. and Ratter, B.M.W., 2017. Harvesting energy: Place and local entrepreneurship in community-based renewable energy transition. *Energy Policy*, 101, pp. 332–341.

U.S. Dep't of Energy, Off. of Minority Bus. & Econ. Dev., Guide to Advancing Opportunities for Community Benefits Through Energy Project Development (2017).

US Envtl. Prot. Agency, Power Plants and Neighboring Communities (last visited Feb. 2022).

Walker, G. and Devine-Wright, P., 2008. Community renewable energy: What should it mean? *Energy Policy*, 36(2), pp. 497–500.

Wagner, O. and Berlo, K.V., 2017. Remunicipalisation and foundation of municipal utilities in the German energy sector: details about newly established enterprises. *Journal of Sustainable Development of Energy, Water and Environment Systems*, 5(3), pp. 396–407.

Welton, S., 2017. Public energy. *N.Y. U. L. Rev.*, 92, pp. 267–349.

Saskia Lavrijssen, Leonie Reins, Thijs ten Caten

Realizing Peer-to-Peer Trading in the Electricity Market in the EU and its Member States

Abstract: In order to realise the energy transition towards a more sustainable, inclusive and just energy market, the traditional model of the electricity market, with big corporations producing electricity and passive consumers at the receiving end, is changing. These changes also require the adaptation of the existing legal framework to new market realities. In this regard, peer-to-peer (P2P) electricity trading has emerged as one mode to enable this transition. The International Renewable Energy Agency has defined the P2P model as "creat[ing] an online marketplace where prosumers and consumers can trade electricity, without an intermediary, at their agreed price". This new innovation poses technical challenges to the market and also requires changes in the underlying regulatory framework of these markets. More concretely, the fields of consumer (protection) law, contract law, platform liability, data law, competition, and property law need to be revised in order to facilitate the innovation. The purpose of this contribution is to examine which legal obstacles P2P trading encounters. The article will start with some general reflections on these hurdles, followed by a specific focus on energy law in two Member States, Germany and the Netherlands.

1 Introduction

The energy transition is largely driven by innovative technological developments (Khorasany et al., 2020, p. 223711). These technological developments, such as smart meters, create opportunities for consumers to become more active in the energy market (Khorasany et al., 2020, p. 223711) and become active consumers (better known as prosumers) (Lavrijssen et al., 2022, p. 4–5). The term 'prosumer' most often denotes consumers who both produce and consume electricity (European Parliament, 2016, p. 2), but EU legislation often uses other terms such as 'renewable self-consumers'

Saskia Lavrijssen is Full Professor of Economic Regulation and Market Governance of Network Industries at the Law School of Tilburg University, The Netherlands and director of the Tilburg Institute of Law, Technology and Society (TILT).
Leonie Reins is Professor of Public Law and Sustainability at Erasmus School of Law, The Netherlands.
Thijs ten Caten is Student Assistant at Tilburg Institute for Law, Technology, and Society (TILT), Tilburg University, The Netherlands.

https://doi.org/10.1515/9783110752403-039

(Article 2(14) and 21(1 and 2(a)) of the Renewable Energy Directive II) or 'active consumers' (Article 2(8) of the Recast Electricity Directive). The legal framework relating to prosumers at the European Union level is formed in particular by the Recast Electricity Directive, the Energy Efficiency Directive, the Renewable Energy Directive and Guidelines on State Aid (European Parliament, 2016, p. 2).

As consumers can generate their own electricity, for example by using solar panels, it is not inconceivable that they will have more electricity left over than they consume (Lavrijssen et al., 2022, p. 5) and generate an electricity surplus. In the classic market model, they feed this surplus electricity back into the grid via an energy supplier (Lavrijssen et al., 2022, p. 5). However, interesting in this context is the situation where consumers but start trading it with other consumers (Lavrijssen et al., 2022, p. 5). This is called P2P trading (Zang et al., 2017, p. 2563). P2P trading has a number of characteristic features. First of all, P2P trading is possible without the intervention of a third party (Georgarakis et al., 2021). It is therefore a decentralised system (Georgarakis et al., 2021). Secondly, the system focuses on supply and demand (Georgarakis et al., 2021). Finally, P2P trading is practised through an online platform, within which prosumers can be connected to each other (IRENA, 2020, p. 6). In this context, one can think of a blockchain platform (Lavrijssen et al., 2022, p. 5). In other words, P2P trading can be seen as an online marketplace where prosumers can sell their energy surpluses to each other (IRENA, 2020, p. 6).

The P2P trading model consists of a virtual and a physical layer (Tushar et al., 2020, p. 3186). The virtual layer makes it possible to connect prosumers with each other so that transactions can take place (Tushar et al., 2020, p. 3186). The physical layer makes it possible to move the traded electricity from the seller (the supplier) to the buyer (the demander) (Tushar et al., 2020, p. 3186). It is important to emphasize that, before P2P trading can be applied, a number of conditions must be met (Thukral, 2021, p. 115–116; Lavrijssen et al., 2022, p. 16). Firstly, there must be sufficient prosumers who wish to participate to make P2P trading possible (Mengelkamp et al., 2018, p. 873). Secondly, there must continue to be a link with the traditional energy market, because in addition to P2P trading, prosumers must also be able to trade in this market (Mengelkamp et al., 2018, p. 873). It is impossible to guarantee that the whole demand is exclusively satisfied through platform trading. In other words: a 'plan B' is always needed. Thirdly, the use of data must be properly organised and, fourthly, a bidding and pricing system must be developed to enable trading between peers (Mengelkamp et al., 2018, p. 874–875). Finally, this system must also be able to provide an overview of the existing supply and demand (Mengelkamp et al., 2018, p. 874–875).

Three types of P2P markets can be distinguished (Tushar et al., 2020, p. 3188). The first type of market is the *fully decentralised market,* in which exists a bilateral relationship between prosumers who trade directly on the basis of contracts (Tushar et al., 2020, p. 3188). Secondly, *community-based markets* can be highlighted (Tushar et al., 2020, p. 3188). These are markets that are smaller in size, because they are communities with the same interests, (Tushar et al., 2020, p. 3188) such as small microgrids or neighbourhoods. In such a market, a community manager acts as supervisor (Tushar et al., 2020, p. 3188). The third type of market concerns *composite markets*, in which individual prosumers can trade within communities without a supervisor (Tushar et al., 2020, p. 3188). These markets are a mixture of the above two.

At the European Union level, P2P trading in the context of the energy transition has been the focus of attention earlier. Already in 2018, the Renewable Energy Directive II included a definition for P2P trading: "the sale of renewable energy between market participants by means of a contract with predefined conditions for the automated execution and settlement of the transaction, either directly between market participants or indirectly through a certified third-party operator, such as an aggregator" (Article 2(18) of the Renewable Energy Directive II).

An important question in this context is whether the current (national) legal frameworks can facilitate P2P trading. Moreover, it is important to consider what obstacles there are to the widespread introduction of P2P trading in the electricity sector. For this contribution we will therefore examine the situations in two EU Member States: The Netherlands and Germany. The Netherlands is interesting to examine in this context because the government is in the process of adopting a new Energy Act to replace the current Gas and Electricity Acts (Rijksoverheid.nl, 2022). This new act should make P2P trading possible (Section 2.3 of the Dutch Draft Energy Act). Moreover, Germany is important because it has a very progressive attitude towards the energy transition (Rechseinter, 2021, p. 306–307), without however regulating P2P trading directly.

The aim of this contribution is to outline existing legal challenges relating to the facilitation of P2P trading with a particular focus on energy law. Thereto the contribution outlines the existing legal challenges applicable to P2P trading in the European Union, as well as the manner in which the legislation is implemented in the Netherlands and Germany. The contribution will conclude with some reflections on the existing regulatory frameworks in the EU and its Member States and the challenges that still exist and need to be overcome to facilitate P2P electricity trading. After having provided an introduction to P2P trading in the electricity sector, the following section outlines the existing legal challenges applicable to P2P trading in the European Union, as well as the manner in which the legislation is implemented in the Netherlands and Germany. The contribution will conclude with some reflections on the existing regulatory frameworks in the EU and its Member States and the challenges that still exist and need to be overcome to facilitate P2P electricity trading.

2 The legal framework applicable to P2P Trading in the EU

P2P trading is subject to regulatory provisions from various fields of law, most importantly energy law, consumer (protection) law, contract law, platform liability, data law, competition, and property law (De Almeida et al., 2021, p. 9–12). A literature review carried out by De Almeida et al has discussed these issues extensively and we will at this stage only summarize the most important challenges per field of law (De Almeida et al., 2021, p. 9–12).

Accordingly, in the area of **consumer law,** the most important legal issue is the definition of the status of a prosumer as a consumer or a business (De Almeida et al., 2021, p. 14–18). The classical definition of a consumer, as a "natural person who is acting for purposes that are outside his trade, business, craft, or profession" (De Almeida et al., 2021, p. 14) and hence is very much in line with the definition of a prosumer as included in Article 2 (14) RED II and Article 2 (8) IMED, namely that household prosumers are allowed to generate and sell self-generated renewable electricity, "provided that those activities do not constitute the primary commercial or professional activity". The "gradual openness" (De Almeida et al., 2021, p. 14–15) is also confirmed by the case law on the definition of the consumer by the European Court of Justice (*Condominio di Milano, via Meda v Eurothermo SpA*, [2020]; *Maximilian Schrems v Facebook Ireland Limited*, [2018]) and the European institutions (De Almeida et al., 2021, p. 15).

From the perspective of **energy law**, grid and market access are the most important legal hurdles that P2P traders faced (De Almeida et al., 2021, p. 11–12) which has been addressed in the Clean Energy Package. Regarding grid access, non-discriminatory Third-Party Access (TPA) to the energy grid for P2P traders is guaranteed by Article 6(1) of the Internal Market Directive, which states that "the implementation of a system of third-party access to the transmission and distribution systems [shall be] based on published tariffs, applicable to all customers and applied objectively and without discrimination between system users". Here it is important to mention that the ECJ explained the background and the meaning of the non-discrimination principle in the context of the electricity directive in the VEMW and others case from 7 June 2005 (*VEMW,* [2005]). The ECJ considered "... it should be borne in mind that the provisions of the Directive, which require that the action of the system operator and that of the State in creating access to the system should not be discriminatory, are specific expressions of the general principle of equality". "The prohibition of discrimination, which is one of the fundamental principles of Community law, requires that comparable situations are not treated differently unless such difference in treatment is objectively justified". However, an unanswered legal question is how to apply this principle in practice. Should P2P traders be subject to the same network charges that are applied to standard electricity consumption, or can they be treated differently based on objectively justified differences (Universiteit Utrecht, 2022, p. 44)? For instance, when P2P trading is done locally, this could mean that the network is used more efficiently and that less transportation costs are being caused to the system. This justifies that local P2P trading can benefit from lower transportation tariffs which could also act as an incentive for P2P trading (De Almeida et al., 2021, p. 11; Universiteit Utrecht, 2022, p. 44)). Additional outstanding legal issues remain and relate to the question on how to address imbalances in the electricity grid and about access to and reliance on modern communication technologies. In addition, there is still legal uncertainty regarding the question how P2P traders can access retail and wholesale and flexibility markets and the controversial role of DSOs in P2P trading (De Almeida et al., 2021, p. 11–12).

P2P trading marks a fundamental change with the traditional electricity market in the sense that **contracts** are no longer made on a "bilateral" basis between a consumer, buyer, producer, and seller. Rather, in a community of "prosumers", a fundamental re-think of the contractual relationships between the different participants is necessary. In this regard, the most pressing questions and issues pertain to the automated nature of transactions and the decentralized market design of P2P trading platforms. Smart contracts based on blockchain technology offer a promising solution enabling owners of PV-installations to directly sell their excess electricity to neighbors (De Almeida et al., 2021, p. 18). Still, many questions remain, such as those relating to (i) the non-performance of contracts and issues of liability, (ii) the interaction with Article 10 of the IMED, (iii) questions of applicable law in situations where the P2P electricity trading occurs across national borders.

P2P electricity platforms have been described as collaborative **platforms**, raising the question whether they can be classified as providers of information society services within the meaning of Directive 2000/31/EC (the E-Commerce Directive). De Almeida et al. (2021, p. 18) have suggested that qualifying them as such, whilst simultaneously considering them as electricity suppliers under the Electricity Directive would be the most suitable solution. In this regard, it is important to be mindful of the fact that, as explained by Smale and Kloppenburg (2020, p. 14),

> [h]ow energy platforms members intend to employ their renewable energy to achieve which energy and climate goals, and what type of relationships they wish to form with fellow platform members and non-members, and with actors in the wider grid, has important implications for the transition towards decarbonised, decentralised, and digitised energy systems.

Indeed, the different forms that P2P electricity trading can adopt requires a comprehensive reconsideration of the manner in which the legal framework regulates such trading. It is to note that these platforms also fall under the provisions of the Digital Services and Digital Markets Act (European Commission, 2022a). These acts are complementary to sector-specific laws and regulations and therefore do not replace them (European Commission, 2022b).

The availability of and access to large amounts of **data** is critical to the successful functioning of P2P electricity trading. Automation and the use of a so-called digital platform environment are considered as indispensable elements to make P2P trading successful in practice. The key legal instrument in this regard is the EU's General Data Protection Regulation ("GDPR") which imposes constraints on the manner in which P2P electricity trading systems can be designed as it seeks to safeguard privacy (De Almeida et al. 2021: p. 18). The GDPR also imposes constraints on the use of blockchain-based smart contracts, particularly in terms of the right to be forgotten which is enshrined in Article 17 of the GDPR (De Almeida et al., 2021: p. 18). Further questions arise as a result of the use of smart meters which, inevitably, and by design, collect significant amounts of individualized data (Lavrijssen and Carrillo, 2017, p. 4–5). The key challenges identified in existing literature are the design of privacy friendly (i) optimal bidding strategies; and (ii) market operation (Abidin et al., 2020).

From a **competition law** perspective, the main "concern" is the potential market dominance of electronic platform intermediaries. At present, however, the academic consensus is that P2P electricity trading platforms are far from achieving a dominant market position within the meaning of Article 102 of the TFEU (Mischau, 2020, p. 233). Moreover, the general consensus is that the existing competition law framework is sufficiently flexible and accommodating to address the challenges posed by new business models in the electricity market. In addition, specifically with regard to Blockchain, it has been argued that blockchain and competition law strive for the same objective, namely decentralization, meaning that they should work in tandem (Schrepel and Buterin, 2020).

Property law also plays an important role in facilitating the practical implementation of P2P electricity trading platforms to the extent that there is an inherent tension between the role of tenants and that of landlords. The former has an interest in the assets, i.e. PV installations, but they are not in a position to influence whether such installations will be installed. In this regard, legislative changes may be required so as to entice or induce landlords to install smart and distributed energy systems whenever tenants request this. A separate issue is the public-private connection, whereby ownership is often still key to participation in a P2P agreement.

On 30 June 2022, the Council and the European Parliament reached an agreement on the markets in **crypto-assets** (MiCA) proposal, which covers issuers of unbacked crypto-assets, and so-called "stable coins", as well as the trading venues and the wallets where crypto-assets are held. The new MiCA may be highly relevant for P2P electricity in case of using blockchain technologies and paying with crypto currencies. P2P trading will then be made possible via smart contracts (Thukral, 2021, p. 105; Wongthongtham et al., 2021, p. 6). In this case, direct trading between peers without intermediation of third parties can take place within microgrids (Thukral, 2021, p. 105; Zheng et al., 2013). However, this raises questions, and perhaps obstacles, in relation to the GDPR, for example, because data subjects can only invoke their rights to a limited extent (Lavrijssen et al., 2022, p. 21). In addition, it can be considered that the use of blockchain requires a lot of electricity, which raises questions in the context of the energy transition as this technology may be fed by electricity that is not CO_2 neutral (Monrat et al., 2019, p. 117146). Compared to, for example, transactions via the VISA system, blockchain transactions emit much more (Monrat et al., 2019, p. 117146). It has hence been considered that blockchain technology is therefore an unsustainable way of enabling P2P trading (Monrat et al., 2019, p. 117146). This does not fit well with the desired transition to the generation and use of sustainable energy.

The foregoing shows that a critical literature on the platformization of (P2P) energy services is emerging. However, the regulatory framework that applies to these services is still far from focused. As observed by Montero and Finger, to the extent that energy services are increasingly important to meet energy security needs, and considering that, accordingly, it is part of an industry that is

> of general interest for the well- being of citizens and society, necessary for trade and even a precondition for democratic participation, the regulation of the new network industries cannot be further delayed (Montero and Finger, 2021).

Indeed, various fields of regulation are relevant for P2P energy services and the novelty of the technology raises systemic questions about the applicability of traditional legal concepts such as liability, ownership, and market dominance. Some fields of law, notably competition law, appear flexible enough to accommodate the novel legal challenges brought about by the emergence of P2P energy services, whereas for others a deeper reflection on the applicability of the aforementioned traditional legal concepts to new types of technology and market developments will be required. It will now be examined whether some of these issues are addressed by national legislation.

3 Implementation of the EU legal framework in The Netherlands and Germany

3.1 The Netherlands

In the Netherlands, the Dutch government is currently in the process of adopting a new Energy Act, which provided for specific provisions on P2P trading or the facilitation of P2P trading (Rijksoverheid, 2022). This new Energy Act will replace the current, outdated, Gas Act and Electricity Act (Rijksoverheid, 2022). This new Energy Act must reform the legal field of energy law in order to facilitate the digitization of the energy sector, the energy transition and to implement the Clean Energy Package (Rijksoverheid, 2022).

In the draft Energy Act, P2P trading regularly receives attention. In the Explanatory Memorandum to the Energy Act, the following definition is used for P2P trading:

> Peer-to-peer trading involves the automated handling of the supply of electricity between a final customer that feeds electricity into the grid and a final customer that wants to buy this electricity, either directly, or through the market participant that realises the automated execution and settlement. (Ministerie van Economische Zaken en Klimaat, 2022, p. 26).

This definition shows that there are two options: either direct trade between final customers, or trade through a 'market participant'. This market participant is the actor who facilitates P2P trade by matching supply and demand and providing administrative processing (Ministerie van Economische Zaken en Klimaat, 2022, p. 30–31). One could think of, for example, a supplier or an aggregator (Ministerie van Economische Zaken en Klimaat, 2022, p. 44). Because of this definition, the economic operator can also be considered a P2P trader (Ministerie van Economische Zaken en Klimaat, 2022, p. 30–31). This concerns an implementation of the Renewable Energy Directive (Ministerie van Economische Zaken en Klimaat, 2022, p. 30–31). The definition used for P2P trading in the Dutch Energy Act therefore hardly differs from that in the Renewable Energy Directive (Renewable Energy Directive II, Article 2(18)). Very complicated, however, is that if a producer or active costumer trades in electricity without the intervention of a market participant, it is itself considered a market participant, creating additional legal duties as will be discussed below (Ministerie van Economische Zaken en Klimaat, 2022, p. 44).

Despite the good intentions of the new modern Energy Act which intends to facilitate technological innovations such as P2P trading, there are still a number of legal hurdles and obstacles to be discovered that may hinder energy consumers and energy communities engaging in P2P trading.

The identified hurdles and obstacles can be divided in three groups: obligations, tariffs and triangular relations. These three groups will therefore be discussed.

3.1.1 Obligations

Firstly, the Explanatory Memorandum of the Energy Act makes it clear that a final customer only receives the protection and rights as an active customer if the generation of electricity is not the main economic activity of this customer (Ministerie van Economische Zaken en Klimaat, 2022, p. 30–31). This seems to suggest that inactive costumers cannot participate in P2P trading. If generation becomes the main economic activity, the consumer will be qualified as a supplier creating additional responsibilities and legal duties. This creates uncertainties to what extent a consumer can benefit from the rights to engage in P2P trade with other consumers. For instance, for a certain period an active consumer could generate a big surplus of energy and sell it to other consumers. This raises the question from which moment on this consumer does not qualify as an active consumer anymore. This is for example the case if a person is no longer working, i.e. does not carry out any, or hardly any, economic activities. In such a case, the generation of electricity will soon be considered as the only economic activity of the consumer. This situation can lead to legal inequality, because these persons can relatively easily fall outside the protection of an active consumer.

In addition, there is an obstacle in the new Energy Act with regard to the requirement to obtain a supply license for supplying energy to end customers with a small connection, but also to the *facilitation* of P2P trading for this end costumer with a small connection (Dutch Energy Act, Article 2.19(1)). This is a considerable hurdle, since a licensee must meet stringent requirements in terms of financial, administrative and technical qualities, sufficient expertise and a licensee must be affiliated with an out-of-court dispute resolution body (Dutch Energy Act, Article 2.20(1)). However, an active consumer does not have to meet the obligation to obtain a supply license in the case of P2P trading, provided that a number of conditions are met to grant an exception.

A first exception is supply to final customers with a small connection who are members or shareholders of an energy community (Dutch Energy Act, Article 2.19(2 (a)). According to the new Energy Act, an energy community is a legal entity that carries out activities on the energy market for its members, associates or shareholders and whose main objective is to provide environmental, economic or social benefits to its members, associates or shareholders or to the local areas in which it operates, and which does not aim to make profits (Dutch Energy Act, Article 1.1). This exception is logical, given the fact that members of an energy community also carry out P2P trading among themselves.

As a second exception, an active customer with a small connection may supply electricity without a license if, over a period of one year, he does not supply more electricity than he feeds into the system (Dutch Energy Act, Article 2.19(2(b))). In other words, a person may not supply more than he has delivered to the grid in a period of a year. However, the scope of this exception is not clear. After all, it is uncertain whether 'feeding into the system' refers to energy the customer generates himself (via solar panels, for example) or whether it also refers to energy that is purchased and stored in a battery. 'Feeding into the system' is not defined by the Dutch legislator, which makes this exception unclear.

A third problem arises with regard to the balancing obligations. This balancing obligation implies that there should be a balance between supply and demand in the energy network and that sufficient reserves should be available for this purpose (Regulation (EU) 2019/943, Article 2(10); Directive (EU) 2019/944, Article 17(3(d)). The balancing responsibility lies with all market participants that cause imbalances in the electricity system (Regulation (EU) 2019/943, Article 5(1); Directive 2019/944, Article 17 (3)(d)). As discussed earlier, this can be an entity that facilitates P2P trading, but also an active buyer or producer itself if it acts without the intervention of a market participant (Ministerie van Economische Zaken en Klimaat, 2022, p. 44). A market participant may also take responsibility for any imbalances that may be caused by other market participants, such as active consumers (Regulation (EU) 2019/943, Article 5(1)). In principle an energy community of citizens or an active consumer are financially responsible for possible imbalances they cause; to the extent they are balance responsible or have delegated this responsibility to another party (Directive 2019/944, Article 15(2)(f) and Article 16(3)(d)). In the case of P2P trading, this would therefore mean that the individual participating households could be responsible for balancing and the financial consequences of unbalances (Universiteit Utrecht, 2022: p. 38–39). The question of whether households are capable of taking care of balance responsibility is a legitimate question in this regard. In any case, the new Dutch Energy Act confirms the line of Article 5 of Regulation 2019/943: if there is no market participant (i.e. directly) active on their allocation point taking care of the balance responsibility, the producer or active customer is responsible for balancing electricity (Dutch Energy Act, Article 2.41(2)). This obligation might be far too demanding for small consumers who want to participate in P2P trading, frustrating their willingness and possibilities to engage in P2P trading.

With this, the Energy Act is very short on the implications of balancing responsibility for active consumers in the case of P2P trading. This can lead to legal uncertainty, especially for the active customer. In the explanatory memorandum accompanying the draft Energy Act, it is considered that the balancing task is limited in content, but that the task must be carried out in accordance with the EU Regulation and that this task must be further specified by the Dutch regulator, the ACM (Ministerie van Economische Zaken en Klimaat, 2022, p. 17). As this has not yet happened, this situation leads to a great deal of legal uncertainty for individuals who want to participate in P2P trading. In this context, actively informing balancing responsible parties could be of great importance. Furthermore, the provision of information to balancing responsible parties and to active consumers regarding the principle of balance responsibility, the financial consequences and the possibility of the delegation of balance responsibility, is therefore of utmost importance.

3.1.2 Tariffs

A relevant question that needs to be solved is what type of network tariffs will be applied to stimulate P2P trading. Currently, consumers in the Netherlands pay a transport tariff based on the capacity tariff, which means that the tariff depends on the maximum capacity of the connection of the consumer (Werkgroep "tarieven", 2018, p. 15).

This tariff structure does not incentivize energy users to make a more efficient use of their energy and the available network capacity, for instance by using less energy or supplying energy to the grid in times of high demand and capacity restrictions. Under these circumstances P2P trading can also facilitate a more efficient (local) supply and use of energy in certain areas, however active customers are not (yet) incentivized to change their behavior via the network tariffs. New, more flexible, tariff structures have to be developed which can also stimulate network users to engage in P2P trading if this contributes to a more efficient use of network capacity (Universiteit Utrecht, 2022, p. 30–31). However, there is not a clear vision by the regulator what types of tariffs can facilitate a more efficient network use by the network users and how these tariffs relate to the EU law principles of tariff regulation, including the principles of transparency and non-discrimination (Universiteit Utrecht, 2022, p. 30–32).

Furthermore, the digitalization of the energy sector may raise broader social concerns. After all, P2P trade requires a certain base of online skills and skills to understand electricity prices. People who do not have these skills cannot benefit from the lower costs of P2P trade compared to the higher prices and tariffs in the traditional electricity market.

It is unfortunate that the Energy Act does not address this broader social concern. After all, in principle all energy consumers should be able to benefit from the energy transition. The provision of transparent information as well as digital skill trainings could make the necessary skills more accessible for a larger group of energy consumers.

3.1.3 Triangular relations

Another problem arises with regard to the use of platforms to enable P2P trading. The Dutch Ministry of Economic Affairs and Climate government pays attention to platforms in the explanatory memorandum of the new Energy Act. After all, a market participant must link parties together if they wish to trade (Ministerie van Economische Zaken en Klimaat, 2022, p. 40). The government explicitly sees a role for platforms in the improved provision of information, the rise of the platform economy and digitalization (Ministerie van Economische Zaken en Klimaat, 2022, p. 40). This means that a three-party relationship is created: the providers, consumers and the platforms (Mak, 2021, p. 8).

However, no concrete legislation has been enacted to standardise the use of platforms for enabling P2P trading. In fact, most of the rules are set by the online platforms themselves, which is why they are also called 'private legislators' (Mak, 2021, p. 20). Dutch legislation and regulations are therefore lacking in this respect.

For years, Dutch legislation has been geared towards the classic idea of Business to Consumer relationships, and the aim here is to provide a high level of consumer protection (Mak, 2022, p. 1978). With current developments, such as the encouragement to make sustainable choices and the development of the platform economy, this classic idea is outdated (Mak, 2022, p. 1978–1979). Moreover, the prosumer does not easily fit into this classic idea, because in case of a prosumer, a person is both a consumer and a producer (Mak, 2022, p. 1981). It all depends on how P2P trading via platforms can be qualified (Mak, 2022, p. 1981). If a business-to-consumer relationship is assumed, then the obligations under consumer law may be too heavy for prosumers to meet (Mak, 2022, p. 1981). If, however, a consumer-to-consumer relationship is assumed, it is primarily contract law that applies, so that consumer protection law takes a back seat (Mak, 2022, p. 1981). In conclusion, P2P trading via platforms does not fit into one of these two boxes, but the applicable law should be recalibrated (Mak, 2022, p. 1981).

New legislation regarding prosumers in the platform economy therefore seems necessary. To this end, Mak calls for legislation to regulate the triangular relationships (Mak, 2022, p. 1982). This seems a good step to remove, or at least reduce, this hurdle for prosumers and platforms in the future Dutch electricity market.

3.2 Germany

In Germany, currently not enough investment incentives exist for companies to invest in technologies and models for P2P trading (Rijkers-Defrasne et al., 2021, p. 4). It is to be expected that government policy will encourage and support P2P trading in the coming years (Rijkers-Defrasne et al., 2021, p. 11) and first steps are already taken with the Act on immediate measures for accelerated expansion of renewable energies and further measures in the electricity sector (Deutscher Bundestag, 2022).

However, for the large-scale implementation of P2P trading, it is concluded that a reform of the current market model with a new regulatory framework may be required (Rijkers-Defrasne et al., 2021, p. 4). The Act has amended amongst others the Renewable Energy Act (EEG). The new EEG will enter into force in January 2023. Whether it holds up to the expectations of being a "reform of the current market model" remains to be seen. However, it can already be derived from the justification for the Act on immediate measures for accelerated expansion of renewable energies and further measures in the electricity sector that "energy sharing" generally and "small rooftop PV systems in the private sector", as well as "Small-scale solar plants ("balcony PV")" are considered an important building block in order to realise the energy transition, without however explicitly regulating P2P activities (Deutscher Bundestag, 2022). Hence "the use of small-scale solar installations should be as simple as possible" (Deutscher Bundestag, 2022). At the same time, it is noted that "many citizens shy away from the bureaucratic effort involved" (Deutscher Bundestag, 2022), as further discussed below. The Parliament also recognizes the need to optimize self-consumption by "intelligent solutions", including "fixed storage facilities on the electricity market, intelligent control of the grids and an attractive pricing mechanism that discounts electricity when supply is high" (Deutscher Bundestag, 2022).

At the same time, the Parliament calls on the Federal Government to submit a proposal for an expansion of the definition of self-consumption in the Renewable Energy Sources Act (EEG) that would "enable electricity consumers to purchase electricity generated on, at or in the structural facilities of the residential building or where suitable within their respective neighborhoods by way of self-consumption, while at the same time preserving the right to free choice of supplier" (Deutscher Bundestag, 2022). It further calls to create an incentive to "activate local electricity consumption, especially at times when a lot of renewable electricity is generated locally, which can increase the elasticity of electricity demand and also have a relieving effect on the electricity distribution grids" (Deutscher Bundestag, 2022).

Currently, in Germany P2P trading is especially interesting for generating plants that do not benefit from a fixed feed-in tariff and which have to generate revenue on the market. These are usually renewable energy plants that are already selling their electricity on the exchange market or via direct marketers – mostly as part of "subsidized direct marketing with a market premium" scheme (geförderten Direktvermarktung mit Marktprämie) under the Renewable Energy Act (EEG) (Rijkers-Defrasne et al., 2021, p. 17). However, direct marketing is already being chosen today only by larger plants above a certain threshold and is technically permitted (Rijkers-Defrasne et al., 2021, p. 4). Smaller plants make use of alternative revenue models, such as maximized self-consumption or direct delivery in the immediate vicinity, in addition to the declining EEG remuneration (Rijkers-Defrasne et al., 2021, p. 17). P2P hence becomes interesting for all generating plants, such as wind and solar plants for example, once their support period under the EEG has stopped; as well as new plants which do not profit from the EEG as it has been abolished (further discussed below).

However, in addition to the Netherlands, there are also obstacles and hurdles in the case of Germany with regard to the introduction of P2P trading into the electricity market. Several regulatory challenges and/or uncertainties for the successful implementation of P2P trading in Germany have already been identified in a report by Fietze et al. (2020).

3.2.1 Prohibition of double marketing and mandatory labeling

Accordingly, one of the key hurdles or uncertainties was the prohibition of double marketing and mandatory labeling for electricity generated from renewable energy and subject to the EEG levy (Doppelvermarktungsgebot, Art. 80 EEG; Kennzeichnugspflicht, Art. 78f EEG). Germany made use of the option not to issue a certificate to a producer who receives financial support from a support scheme, as in included in Article 19 of the Renewable Energy Directive relating to the guarantees of origin. The reasoning behind this rule was that consumers already paid for the "green characteristic" of the electricity through the EEG levy and hence the issuing of such a certificate would constitute a double marketing. Whereas this problem did not apply to unsubsizised P2P suppliers, for suppliers who had received a subsidy, it was advised to not identify subsidized renewable electricity as green electricity to consumers and to refrain from providing information about the producer (Fietze et al., 2020). Something that is add odds with the original idea of P2P trading (see also section 1).

The same problem applies in relation to the marketing of the regional characteristics of the electricity (Fietze et al., 2020). It is to note however, that the Act on immediate measures for accelerated expansion of renewable energies and further measures in the electricity sector (Deutscher Bundestag, 2022) which amends the current EEG permanently abolished the EEG levy on own consumption and direct supply downstream of the grid interconnection point and hence addressed this issue. This reduces bureaucracy and increases the business case also for P2P trading. This will also benefit tenant electricity and storage projects, as in addition, the annual limit on subsidized tenant electricity projects in the Renewable Energy Sources Act will be lifted. The lifting of the ban on self-supply in the tenders also contributes to this (Deutscher Bundestag, 2022). Nevertheless, the justification of the Act recognizes that the implementation of energy sharing (without explicitly referring to P2P trading) still remains complex, mainly due to "unresolved definitional issues regarding the design of energy sharing" and the need for a reform of the grid charges (Deutscher Bundestag, 2022)).

3.2.2 Obligations

Similar to Dutch legislation, the German system further does not foresee a lot of exceptions to supplier obligations for "small" producers. If a prosumer wants to sell its self-generated electricity directly to end consumers via a platform, they are treated as "normal" suppliers and the general obligations under energy law and (electricity) tax law are applicable (Fietze et al., 2020). These relate for example to the notification of energy supply according to Article 5 EnWG and the change of supplier requirements according to the Business Processes for the Supply of Electricity to Customers (GPKE), but also the fact that they have to pay the entire EEG surcharge (until March 2022), the grid fee and electricity tax with no or only very narrowly defined exemptions (Fietze et al., 2020); and the fact that once a system reaches the 10 kWp, the system operator is legally obligated to claim his income for income and trade tax purposes and becomes an entrepreneur in the sense of the Value Added Tax Act (Deutscher Bundestag, 2022).

A solution for the first issue is to take recourse to external service providers to fulfill these supplier obligations, but details should first be clarified with the Federal Network Agency. "Any use of the grid for the purpose of fulfilling a power purchase agreement concluded on a regional energy market must, moreover, be covered by a grid usage agreement" (Fietze et al., 2020). These requirements are arguably not very consumer friendly and may constitute a hurdle for consumers to engage in the P2P business. As regarding the taxation problem, the Parliament as called upon the government to "raising the threshold from 10 to 30 kWp and simplifying income and trade taxation" and to investigate and address another other tax law barriers but does not formally address these issues as yet (Deutscher Bundestag, 2022).

In addition to this, according to Fietze et al. regional energy platforms can be classified as critical infrastructures if they are "systems for active bundling of electrical power or control of generation plants and the platforms have access – at least temporarily – to generation plants with a net installed capacity of at least 420 MW" (Fietze et al., 2020). Following from this, if the threshold is met, P2P traders are subject to extensive requirements from the EnWG, the BSIG and the IT security catalog of the Federal Network Agency (Fietze et al., 2020).

3.2.3 Digital skills

In addition to these legal requirements, from a socio-economical perspective, P2P trading in Germany requires, next to the development of business models, the acquisition and development of digital skills and securing qualified professionals (Rijkers-Defrasne et al., 2021, p. 4). It hence can be concluded for Germany that the legislator recognizes the challenges but has not addressed these fully in its recent regulatory reform.

4 Conclusion: The way forward – issues that need to be addressed in order to facilitate P2P Trading

The goal of facilitating P2P trading in the electricity market is in line with the goals of the electricity market to empower energy consumers to be active in the energy market. The idea of P2P trading is that consumers who generate more electricity than they consume can start trading with other consumers. This possibility is created by large-scale technical developments and innovations.

However, P2P trading also requires large-scale legal changes. These changes are accompanied by current legal barriers. Even though P2P trading is now stimulated by important European Directives the regulation of P2P trading is still fragmented and generates further legal uncertainties and questions on EU level. The fragmented nature of the legal framework governing P2P electricity trading and energy services is further exemplified by the different ways in which EU Member States have implemented the relevant EU directives impacting such services. The differences in implementation show that there is a way to go before we can speak of a harmonized legal framework for P2P electricity trading in the EU. The question can be raised whether, given the "local" nature of P2P energy services, EU harmonization is desirable or even required. However, given that such services may also be traded across the borders of EU Member States, (limited) harmonization would be worthwhile to consider. In this regard, it is necessary to assess to what extent the manner in which the legal framework has been implemented in different EU Member States actually diverges and is likely to cause difficulties in cross-border P2P trading in energy services.

Both in Germany and the Netherland legislators are facing challenges in facilitating P2P trade in energy law. This contribution identified several legal obstacles which may hamper active consumers to engage in P2P trading. First of all, the question is whether certain obligations are not too demanding for active consumers. Uncertainties regarding whether or not consumers fall within the definition of active consumers, an unclearly defined licensing obligation and uncertainties regarding the possible exceptions pose a legal burden on consumers and may discourage P2P trading.

It may be considered whether these obligations actually comply with Article 15 of the Recast Electricity Directive, requiring that:

> Member States shall ensure that final customers are entitled to act as active customers without being subject to disproportionate or discriminatory technical requirements, administrative requirements, procedures and charges, and to network charges that are not cost-reflective. (Recast Electricity Directive, Article 15).

Moreover, the obligations regarding balancing responsibility are very complex and there are still uncertainties and unclarities in this regard what the implications are for active consumers. In addition, network tariffs have to be redesigned to facilitate a more efficient use of the energy network and to stimulate P2P trading. The regulator in the Netherlands have and Germany have not yet provided clarity how more flexible tariffs relate to other regulatory principles, including the principle of non-discrimination. Also, the Dutch and German government should make sure that the energy transition is inclusive and that all consumers will have access to the relevant digital skills to engage in P2P trading. Finally, new regulation is necessary to regulate new emerging triangular relationships in the platform economy.

In general, it may be observed, that studying the role of regulation in facilitating P2P trading is a new field. New implementing laws and regulations should leave sufficient leeway to allow regulators and market participants experiment with new approaches on to adjust them on the basis of experiences with what works and what does not.

Funding Announcement

This research was funded by the Dutch Research Council (NWO) as part of the MegaMind Program, nr P19–25.

References

Abidin, A., Callaerts, R., Deconinck, G. et al., 2020. 'POSTER: SNIPPET – Secure and privacy-friendly peer-to-peer electricity trading', Network and distributed system security symposium (NDSS). San Diego: Internet Society.

Condominio di Milano, via Meda v Eurothermo SpA [2020], European Court of Justice, C-329/19. ECLI:EU:C:2020:263.

De Almeida, L., Cappelli, V., Klausmann, N., and Van Soest, H., 2021. *Peer-to-Peer trading and energy community in the electricity market – Analysing the literature on law and regulation and looking ahead to future challenges. EU Working Paper RSC 2021/35* . Available at: https://fsr.eui.eu/publications/?handle=1814/70457 (Accessed: 27 July 2022).

Deutscher Bundestag, 2022. *Gesetz zu Sofortmaßnahmen für einen beschleunigten Ausbau der erneuerbaren Energien und weiteren Maßnahmen im Stromsektor. 20. Wahlperiode*. Available at: https://dserver.bundestag.de/btd/20/025/2002580.pdf (Accessed: 22 August 2022).

European Commission, 2022a. *The Digital Services Act package*. Available at: https://digital-strategy.ec.europa.eu/en/policies/digital-services-act-package (Accessed: 2 August 2022).

European Commission, 2022b. *Questions and Answers: Digital Services Act*. Available at: https://ec.europa.eu/commission/presscorner/detail/en/QANDA_20_2348 (Accessed 22 August 2022).

European Parliament, 2016. *Briefing. Electricity 'prosumers'*. Available at: https://www.europarl.europa.eu/RegData/etudes/BRIE/2016/593518/EPRS_BRI(2016)593518_EN.pdf. (Accessed: 22 August 2022).

Fietze, D., Papke, A., Wimmer, M., Antoni, O. and Hilpert, J., 2020. *Der Rechtsrahmen für regionale Peer to Peer-Energieplattformen unter Einbindung von Blockchains. Würzburger Studien zum Umweltenergierecht Nr. 16, September 2020*. Available at: https://stiftung-umweltenergierecht.de/wp-content/uploads/2020/09/Stiftung_Umweltenergierecht_WueStudien_16_Rechtsrahmen_Energieplattformen_pebbles.pdf (Accessed: 27 July 2022).

Georgarakis, E., Bauwens, T., Pronk, A. and Al Skaif, T., 2021. 'Keep it green, simple and socially fair: A choice experiment on prosumers preferences for peer-to-peer electricity trading in the Netherlands', *Energy Policy*, 159, 112615.

International Renewable Energy Agency (IRENA), 2020. *Peer-to-peer electricity trading. Innovation landscape brief*. Available at: https://irena.org/-/media/Files/IRENA/Agency/Publication/2020/Jul/IRENA_Peer-to-peer_trading_2020.pdf (Accessed: 20 July 2022).

Khorasany, M., Razzaghi, R., Dorri, A., Jurdak, R., and Siano, P., 2020. Paving the path for two-sided energy markets: an overview of different approaches. *IEEE Access*, 8, pp. 223708–223722.

Lavrijssen S., Espinosa Apráez, B. and ten Caten, T., 2022. The legal complexities of processing and protecting personal data in the electricity sector. *Energies*, 15, 1088.

Lavrijssen, S., 2016. The right to participation for consumers in the energy transition. *European Energy and Environmental Law Review*, 25(5), pp. 152–171.

Lavrijssen, S. and Carrillo Parra, A., 2017. Radical prosumer innovations in the electricity sector and the impact on prosumer regulation. *Sustainability*, 9, 1207.

Mak, V., 2022. De 'prosument' in de platformeconomie: Startpunt voor herijking van het privaatrecht. *Nederlands Juristenblad*, 97(25), pp. 1978–1984.

Mak, V., 2021. De prosument en de digitale economie: een verkenning van het privaatrecht van de toekomst, oratie. Leiden: Universiteit Leiden, pp. 1–26.

Maximilian Schrems v Facebook Ireland Limited [2018], European Court of Justice, C-498/16. ECLI:EU:C:2018:37.

Mengelkamp, E., Gärttner, J., Rock, K., Kessler, S., Orsini, L. and Wheihardt, C., 2018. Designing microgrid energy markets: A case study: The Brooklyn Microgrid. *Applied Energy*, 210, pp. 870–880.

Ministerie van Economische Zaken en Klimaat, 2022. *Memorie van Toelichting wetsvoorstel Energiewet – versie RvS*. Available at: https://wetgevingskalender.overheid.nl/Regeling/WGK010483/Download/16e16d6f-7087-4734-b65a-f063e54ad831_1.pdf (Accessed: 18 July 2022).

Ministerie van Economische Zaken en Klimaat, 2022. *Wetsvoorstel Energiewet – versie RvS*. Available at: https://wetgevingskalender.overheid.nl/Regeling/WGK010483/Download/d9938a6a-04de-45d9-b9ee-e6ff1f0d62fb_1.pdf (Accessed: 27 August 2022).

Mischau, L., 2020. Market power assessment in digital markets – A German perspective, *Gewerblicher Rechtsschuts under Urheberrecht International*, 69(3), pp. 233–248.

Monrat, A.A., Schelén, O. and Andersson, K., 2019. A survey of blockchain from the perspectives of applications, challenges, and opportunities. *IEEE Access*, 7, pp. 117134–117151.

Montero, J. and Finger, M., 2021. *The Rise of the new network industries. Regulating digital platforms*. Oxfordshire: Taylor & Francis Ltd.

Overheid.nl, 2022. *Energiewet*. Available at: https://www.internetconsultatie.nl/energiewet (Accessed: 17 July 2022).

Rechsteiner, R., 2021. German energy transition (Energiewende) and what politicians can learn for environmental and climate policy. *Clean Technologies and Environmental Policy*, 23, pp. 305–342.

Rijkers-Defrasne, S., von Versen, T. and Malanowski, N., 2021. *Herausforderung Peer-to-Peer-Energiehandel in Deutschland: Potenziale, Herausforderungen und Ausblick. Working Paper Forschungsförderung, No. 209*. Available at: https://www.econstor.eu/bitstream/10419/232573/1/1752706498.pdf (Accessed: 27 July 2022).

Rijksoverheid, 2022. *Nieuwe Energiewet wordt fundament van de energietransitie*. Available at: https://www.rijksoverheid.nl/actueel/nieuws/2022/07/01/nieuwe-energiewet-wordt-fundament-van-de-energietransitie (Accessed 18 July 2022).

Schrepel, T. and Buterin, V., 2020. Blockchain code as antitrust. *Berkeley Technology Law Journal*. Available at: https://papers.ssrn.com/sol3/Delivery.cfm/SSRN_ID3781441_code2189629.pdf?abstractid=3597399&mirid=1&type=2 (Accessed: 22 August 2022).

Smale, R. and Kloppenburg, S., 2020. Platforms in power: householder perspectives on the social, environmental and economic challenges of energy platforms. *Sustainability*, 12, 692.

Thukral, M.K., 2021. Emergence of blockchain-technology application in peer-to-peer electrical-energy trading: A review. *Clean Energy*, 5(1), pp. 104–123.

Tushar, W., Saha, T.K., Yuen, C., Smith, D. and Poor, H.V., 2020. Peer-to-Peer trading in electricity networks: an overview. *IEEE Transactions on Smart Grid*, 11(4), pp. 3185–3200.

Universiteit Utrecht, 2022. *Power to the people: Een onderzoek naar alternatieven voor de huidige balansonverantwoordelijkheid van kleinverbruikers*. Available at: https://www.uu.nl/sites/default/files/rebo-Power-to-the-People-rapport-TKi-2021.pdf (Accessed: 18 July 2022).

Vereniging voor Energie, Milieu en Water and others v Directeur van de Dienst uitvoering en toezicht energie [2005], European Court of Justice, C-17/03. ECLI:EU:C:2005:362.

Werkgroep "tarieven", 2018. *Belemmeringen in nettarieven. Overlegtafel Energievoorziening*. Available at: https://www.netbeheernederland.nl/_upload/Files/OTE_Rapport_Belemmeringen_in_nettarieven_127.pdf (Accessed: 2 August 2022).

Wongthongtham, P., Marrable, D., Abu-Salih, B., Liu, X. and Morrison, G., 2021. Blockchain-enabled peer-to-peer energy trading. *Computers and Electrical Engineering*, 94, 107299.

Zhang, C., Wu, J., Long, C., and Cheng, M., 2017. Review of existing peer-to-peer energy trading projects. *Elsevier Energy Procedia*, 105, pp. 2563–2568.

Zheng, J., Lin, L. and Gao, D.W., 2013. *Smart Meters in Smart Grid: An Overview*. Proceedings of the 2013 IEEE Green Technologies Conference (GreenTech), Denver, CO, USA, 4–5 April 2013, pp. 57–64.

Alexandra B. Klass, Christopher Cerny

Subnational Policies Driving Low-Carbon Mobility in the United States

Abstract: This Chapter examines subnational policies in the United States to electrify transportation and otherwise transition to low-carbon mobility. While many countries have developed comprehensive national legislation to decarbonize the transportation sector, the bulk of US policies to date have occurred at the state and local levels. This Chapter explores some of the key factors that result in vastly different subnational policies regarding low-carbon mobility. These factors include the urban-rural divide; the political orientation of sub-national governments; and local electric utilities' economic interests in supporting investments in transportation electrification.

The Chapter begins by highlighting existing and proposed federal policies that support low carbon mobility in the United States. It then addresses the example of California – an early adopter and aggressive promoter of vehicle electrification – as an outlier in the low-carbon mobility transition by highlighting the unique and forward-thinking actions of the state's legislature and regulatory bodies. The Chapter then looks to three subnational case studies in different parts of the United States – Minnesota, North Carolina, and Wyoming – to explore the range of policies supporting and resisting passenger vehicle and public transit electrification and to demonstrate how local geographies, economies, and politics shape low-carbon mobility policies separate and apart from any existing federal policies.

1 Introduction

In the United States, electrification of the transportation sector is critical to the nation's efforts to reduce domestic greenhouse gas (GHG) emissions. As of 2020, the US transportation sector was responsible for the largest share of the nation's CO_2 emissions, constituting 27% of the total emissions. This compares with 25% from the electric power sector, 24% percent from the industrial sector, 13% from the commercial and residential sector, and 11% from the agricultural sector (EPA, n.d.(b); Larson *et al.*, 2021, p. 1). Important to note is that there was a 13% decrease in transportation-related emissions due to the COVID-19 pandemic in 2020 (EPA, n.d.(a)). Despite this decrease, the sector remained the top contributor of CO_2 emissions.

Alexandra B. Klass is the James G. Degnan Professor of Law at the University of Michigan Law School.
Christopher Cerny is an Attorney at Winthrop & Weinstine, Minneapolis, United States.

https://doi.org/10.1515/9783110752403-040

As the GHG emissions associated with other energy-related sectors have decreased over time, particularly in the electric power sector, transportation-related emissions have remained relatively unchanged despite increases in fuel economy. This is due to consumer preferences for larger vehicles and an increase in vehicle miles traveled (EIA, 2022a, p. 207–-209). Between 1990 and 2020, vehicle miles traveled increased by 30%, even taking into account the dramatic decline in travel in 2020 due to the COVID-19 pandemic (EPA, n.d.). With regard to vehicle size, in 2021, approximately 78% of total vehicle sales in the United States were trucks and sport utility vehicles, up from 52% in 2013 (Shilling, 2022).

In light of these trends, widespread adoption of electric public transportation and a massive shift in consumer preference for plug-in electric vehicle (PEV or EV) technology in the United States is the primary development that could effectively reduce vehicle emissions. (This Chapter uses the abbreviation "EV" solely in reference to plug-in electric vehicles and excludes hybrid, plug-in hybrid, and fuel cell electric vehicles). But the United States has not yet embraced aggressive national legislation and programs to decarbonize the transportation sector as have been undertaken in other countries. Further, outside of major metropolitan areas in the northeastern United States, there is a substantial preference for personal, automotive transportation over the widespread use of public transportation for both daily commutes and long-distance trips. This trend not only complicates the effectiveness of greater electrification of public transportation, but further compounds the problem of slow adoption of EV technology in the personal automotive space.

Notably, some subnational US governments have had some success in creating policies, laws, and incentives to encourage consumer adoption of EVs. Private actors have also developed programs and incentives to foster EVs. This chapter evaluates three US states in different geographic regions of the country to demonstrate the different tactics and approaches both subnational governments and private actors have adopted to encourage EV uptake in their respective localities.

2 National EV Policies in the United States

There are limited examples of federal efforts to encourage EV adoption in the United States over the last twenty years. One of the first, and arguably the most effective, federal initiatives was the Energy Improvement and Extension Act of 2008. The Act created a tax credit for purchases of new EVs, including both battery electric vehicles (BEVs) and plug-in hybrid electric vehicles (PHEVs) (*Energy Improvement and Extension Act 2008*). This passenger vehicle tax credit, ranging from $2,500 to $7,500 depending on battery capacity, was designed to phase out for each manufacturer once that manufacturer sells 200,000 qualifying EVs in the United States (ibid.; AFDC, n.d. (c)). Critics of using tax credits to incentivize EV adoption argue that, although the credit ostensibly provides up to $7,500, consumers may not realize the full value of the incentive (Siry, 2009). The full benefit is not realized if a purchaser owes less federal tax than the eligible credit (Yang *et al.*, 2016, p. 22). Despite efforts of the Obama administration in 2011 to transition to a rebate program to address this criticism, the federal incentive structure remains tax credit based and was largely unchanged since its passage in 2008 until the enactment of the Inflation Reduction Act of 2022.

Under the Obama administration, the United States enacted the first major attempts at what could be considered a national EV policy (Egbue et al., 2017, p. 1928). The American Recovery and Reinvestment Act – legislation crafted to provide government stimulus funding following the Great Recession – included $2.1 billion in subsidies to support EV development, including battery manufacturing, production facilities, and demonstrations of EV technologies (Carley et al, 2013, p. 39). In his 2011 State of the Union address, President Obama announced a goal of one million EVs on the road by 2015, an average of just 1.7% of light-duty vehicle sales (DOE, 2011, p. 2). Despite this call for action, the United States only reached 557,000 EVs sold by the end of 2015, well below the intended target (Egbue et al., 2017, p. 1928).

The Trump administration took a markedly different approach that was more antagonistic to EV adoption. Late in his tenure, President Trump stated he wanted to end all EV subsidies and also end the US Department of Energy loan program that helped vehicle manufacturers develop and build EV, internal combustion, and alternative powered vehicle models with improved fuel efficiency (Shepardson, 2019). Ultimately, Congress rejected these efforts but the dramatic differences between the Obama and Trump administrations' approaches to EVs and vehicle emissions illustrate the lack of consensus and partisan divide in the United States when it comes to the benefits and desirability of EVs.

President Biden began his presidency with aggressive goals to foster EV adoption. Since he was elected, President Biden has issued Executive Orders establishing a goal to make half of all new vehicles sold in the United States in 2030 zero-emissions, directing federal agencies to develop policies for state and local governments to follow when deploying charging infrastructure, and directing the federal government to procure only zero-emissions vehicles by 2035 (White House, 2021a,b,c). In 2021, Congress enacted the Infrastructure Investment and Jobs Act which, among other things, appropriated $5 billion to provide states with up to 80% of the cost of installing EV charging infrastructure along designated Alternative Fueling Corridors; appropriated $5 billion to cover up to 100% of the cost of replacing school buses with clean certified or zero-emission replacements; and directed states to consider measures that would promote the electrification of the transportation sector (*Infrastructure Investment and Jobs Act 2021*).

In 2022, the US Department of Transportation and other federal agencies had begun soliciting comments as part of the rulemaking process to implement the law's provisions (DOT, 2022). Also in 2022, Congress enacted the Inflation Reduction Act, which revised the passenger vehicle tax credit program by providing a tax credit of

$4,000 for the purchase of a used electric vehicle; extended tax credits of up to $7,500 until 2032 for purchases of new EVs that were assembled in the United States; eliminated the provision that phased out the credit when a manufacturer sold 200,000 qualifying vehicles; expanded the EV tax credit to commercial vehicles for the first time for up to 30% of the vehicle's sales price; and appropriated $1 billion to states, municipalities, and Indian tribes for up to 100% of the cost of transitioning to medium- and heavy-duty commercial electric vehicles, including costs of charging infrastructure and workforce training (*Inflation Reduction Act 2022*).

However, as explained below, subnational governmental policies may be more important in the short term in encouraging EV adoption in the United States based on the vast differences in politics, climate, vehicle preference, and urbanization in different parts of the country. States and local governments can use the federal funding and programs described above to tailor regulatory approaches to EV adoption that are best suited to their citizens.

3 Factors Impacting EV Adoption in the United States

Studies show that laws and regulations at both the national and subnational level can encourage EV adoption through financial and non-financial incentives, and with consumer outreach programs (Yang et al., 2016, p. 22). Looking at communities with high adoption rates, it is possible to identify factors that influence the rate of EV adoption. These factors include the legislative and regulatory landscape designed to encourage adoption, vehicle model availability, access to a developed charging infrastructure, incentive structures, whether owners live in urban or rural regions, and political affiliation. (Bui et al., 2020, p. 11; Viswanath, 2021, pp. 6 & 10). The wide range of these factors demonstrates the difficulty of crafting a national EV policy to encourage adoption in a country with disparate geographies, urban densities, climate, and politics. Thus, subnational governments and local actors can play a significant role in encouraging EV adoption to address the unique conditions in their regions.

3.1 Laws, Regulations, and Incentives

The US federal government primarily utilizes financial incentives to encourage EV adoption, both through tax credits to reduce the overall cost of purchasing an EV and through infrastructure project subsidies to increase the nation's EV charging capacity. Subnational governments, public utilities, and rural electric cooperatives have adopted a wider range of incentives.

In a 2018 study, Jenn et al. (2018, pp. 351–352) evaluated EV-related incentives offered in the United States. The authors identified the most common incentive structures offered by subnational governments and utility-level actors. These include individual consumer credits, fleet credits, EV charger subsidies, high-occupancy vehicle (HOV) lane access, emissions inspection exemptions, registration fee reductions, and time-of-use rates (ibid.). These incentives include a mix of legislative, regulatory, and private action.

"Individual consumer credits" is a broad category that includes both tax credits and rebates (ibid.) The study found that credit amounts and program methodology varied widely between subnational programs (ibid.). For example, methodologies implemented by various subnational governments condition credits on the type of EV technology, battery size, the manufacturer's suggested retail price, and the model type of the vehicle, or do not condition the credit at all (ibid.). At the state level, as of 2022, Colorado offered the highest valued tax credits at $2,500 for the purchase of a light-duty passenger EV and $3,500 for the purchase of a light-duty electric truck (Co. DOR, 2019, p. 2). At the local level, the San Joaquin Valley Air Pollution Control District, a regional environmental regulatory agency in California, offered the highest valued rebate in 2022 of $3,000 to purchase an EV (San Joaquin Valley Air Pollution Control District, n.d.). Individual consumer credits are not limited to subnational programs. Many electricity providers, such as private, investor-owned utilities and rural electric cooperatives, have recognized the benefit of selling more electricity to power the transportation sector. They thus offer rebates to their customers who purchase qualifying EVs.

Fleet credits function much like the individual credits, except they are available to businesses, governments, and other large entities (Jenn et al., 2018, pp. 351) The study found that subnational programs frequently limit the number of vehicles an entity can purchase and were much more limited in the types of vehicles that met the program requirements (ibid.). Subnational governments and electricity providers also offer rebates and loans to customers who install EV chargers, also known as electric vehicle supply equipment (EVSE), in their homes, businesses, or public areas (ibid. at 352).

Unique to subnational governments are three incentive program types that do not offer a pure fiscal incentive. These include HOV lane access stickers that permit EV drivers to use highway and freeway lanes reserved for passenger vehicles with minimum occupancy requirements, colloquially known as carpool lanes, without the required minimum number of passengers (ibid. at 351.) Others exempt EV owners from emissions inspections (ibid.). A limited number of programs reduce or eliminate vehicle registration fees, but at least thirty states impose additional fees to register an EV (ibid. at 352; Hartman and Shields, 2021a). This reflects the fact that most states utilize taxes on fuel to fund road and highway projects. Without being able to recover those taxes from EV owners, some subnational governments instead impose an upfront additional registration fee. The cost of that fee varies from region to region with those governments that seek to incentivize EV adoption commonly imposing much lower fees. For example, Colorado only imposes an additional $50 annual fee, while Georgia and Wyoming impose an annual fee of $200 on EV owners. Finally, dedicated time-of-use or off-peak charging rates are reduced rates designed to encourage EV charging during non-peak hours, mostly overnight, to limit strain on the electric grid and offer customers cost savings to charge at these specific times (ibid.). Some legislatures and many public utility commissions in the United States mandate that at least some electricity providers offer time-of-use or off-peak rates to consumers.

3.2 Vehicle Model Availability

Vehicle model availability, both in terms of model and vehicle type, appears to have a major impact on EV adoption rates. Model variety is an important predictor of EV adoption. Manufacturers have offered a total of eighty-six EV models in the United States since 2008, and there were twenty-eight models of EVs available for sale in 2022. However, model availability varies considerably from locality to locality (Schoettle and Sivak, 2017b, pp. 4; Bui et al., 2020, p. 11; Wallach, 2022). In states or regions with greater variety, adoption rates trend higher. For example, areas with over 4% EV adoption rates – a relatively high adoption rate in the US – have at least twenty-five available EV models (Bui et al., 2020, p. 12) The top five metropolitan areas by EV sales volume in the US – San Jose, San Francisco, San Diego, Los Angeles, and Sacramento; all cities in California – also represented the five markets with the most model availability (ibid.; Viswanath, 2021, p. 6). These five markets represented 41% of new EV purchases in 2019 and were more than double the national average for EV adoption (Bui et al., 2020, p. 12). In contrast, more than half of the population of the United States lives in markets with twelve EV models or fewer (ibid.)

Beyond model variety, vehicle type appears to be a significant factor for EV uptake in the US market. A 2017 study from the University of Michigan found a nationwide trend of consumers choosing to purchase light trucks, a market segment that includes pick-ups, sports utility vehicles (SUVs), vans, and minivans (Schoettle and Sivak, 2017a, p. 2). With the introduction of the Rivian R1 and the Hummer EV to market in 2021; the Ford F-150 Lightning to market in 2022; and the announcements of EV light truck models from Tesla, Chevrolet, Toyota, Lordstown Motors, and Canoo, manufacturers are beginning a major push into the EV light truck market. However, to date most EV models are passenger vehicles, such as sedans, coupes, hatchbacks, and crossovers. States and regions with a higher percentage of light truck purchasers are unlikely to have a higher percentage of EV adopters until the number of EV light truck options increase (Archsmith et al., 2022, p. 78).

For this reason, the Ford F-150 Lightning represents a massive shift in the potential for widespread EV adoption in the United States. Ford presented the F-150 Lightning to the public in May 2021 (Ford, 2021). It is the first EV truck from a major US automotive manufacturer with established name recognition in the light truck market. The F-150 was the bestselling truck for the last forty-four years in the United States and was the bestselling model of any vehicle model, not just light trucks, in thirty states (Valdes-Dapena, 2021; Viswanath, 2021, p. 12). The F-150 Lightning, by utilizing the name recognition of the F-150, shows that Ford recognizes the potential value of expanding into the relatively untapped EV light truck market as the technology becomes more efficient and widely accepted. Further, almost 15% of one study's respondents indicated that they would be willing to consider purchasing an all-electric version of their current light truck model (Schoettle and Sivak, 2017a, p. 19). Given the F-150's sales history, this is a strong indication that Ford may be able to convert a significant portion of current F-150 owners to an electric model. Early signs are positive, as the company sold out of all variations of the 2022 model year F-150 Lightning by April of 2022 and was hoping to build 150,000 EV trucks annually going forward.

3.3 Access to Charging Infrastructure

Studies indicate that range anxiety, the general fear that an EV battery will run out of charge before reaching a destination or the next charger, is a major impediment to more widespread EV adoption. (Klass, 2019, p. 561). As of 2021, the United States had roughly 48,000 charging locations encompassing 122,000 charging ports (Skibell, 2021). Studies indicate that areas with greater public charging availability have greater numbers of EV registrations. A 2020 study by Bui et al. (2020) found there was a positive relationship between areas with higher rates of EV adoption and access to public charging infrastructure. The five localities with the highest adoption rates also had between 2.5 to 6.5 times more public EV chargers than the national average. (ibid., p. 10) Thirteen of the fifteen localities with greater than 5% EV adoption rates for new cars sold had twice the national average of public EV chargers (ibid.).

The Infrastructure Investment and Jobs Act included $7.5 billion to promote less carbon-intensive transportation. Of that, $5 billion is to be distributed to the states to create a nationwide network of over 500,000 EV charging stations (Behr, 2021; Skibell, 2021; DOT, 2022). The Inflation Reduction Act included authorization to spend a portion of the $1 billion set aside for medium- and heavy-duty electrification on charging infrastructure. The Inflation Reduction Act also revised a tax credit that provided individual consumers 30% of the cost of hardware and installation of household chargers for private use. This may be vital, as The International Council on Clean Transportation estimates that the United States will need up to 17 million residential chargers to meet President Biden's goal of 50% EV sales share by 2030 (Bauer *et al.*, 2021, p. 17). This amounts to roughly eleven times the number of residential chargers deployed in 2020 and would require a 27% annual increase in the number of residential charger installations (ibid.).

3.4 The Urban/Rural Divide

The rural United States comprises 97% of the landmass but only contains 19.3% of the population. Urban centers, conversely, occupy a small fraction of the physical land but are home to 80% of the population (Ratcliffe *et al.*, 2016, p. 4). Rural regions are defined as having less than 2,500 people by population and less than 1,000 people per square mile. (Baatar et al., 2019, p. 8). Because this is a function of both population and population density, large states do not necessarily contain large rural populations. California, for example, is the third largest US state but has the lowest rural population with less than 5% of the population living in rural areas. In comparison, Vermont is the sixth smallest US state but has the second highest rural populations, with 61% of residents living in rural areas (US Census Bureau, n.d.(a)). High rural populations can result in a disparity when it comes to factors that impact EV adoption, such as vehicle miles traveled per trip and frequency of trips (ibid.) This is compounded by the general lack of EV infrastructure in rural areas, resulting in "charging deserts" (Byington, 2022). Income disparity between rural and urban areas also imposes an impediment to EV adoption. The median household income of rural US households was 4% less than that of urban households, according to 2015 figures (Baatar et al., 2019, p. 10). Roughly 13.3% of the rural population lives below the poverty line (ibid.) EVs, on average, cost between $9,000 and $13,000 more than internal combustion engine vehicles (ibid.). Further disincentivizing EV adoption, the rural population shows a greater preference for trucks. The five most-owned vehicle models in the rural United States are trucks, with the top four spots held by light-duty pick-ups (ibid., p. 11). These factors help explain, in large part, why EV adoption in rural areas lags that of its urban counterparts (ibid., p. 9).

Electrifying public transit such as city buses also faces barriers in the rural United States. Roughly 40% of the rural population does not have access to any form of public transit (ibid., p. 11). In the areas with some form of public transit, trips take an average of 87% longer than those in urban locales (ibid.). On the other hand, school bus transportation is readily available and often necessary in rural areas. This has led subnational governments in rural regions to begin experimenting with electrifying parts of their school bus fleet by replacing older, more inefficient diesel school buses with electric school buses. There are currently almost 500,000 school buses in the US, 95% of which run on diesel fuel (Lazer and Freehafer, 2021). Fewer than 1% of school buses, on the other hand, are electric (ibid.).

Subnational governments can support these efforts through funds from the Volkswagen Diesel Emissions Environmental Mitigation Trust. The Trust was created by court decree as a settlement with Volkswagen AG, its partners, and its subsidiaries after it was discovered Volkswagen intentionally installed software in its "clean diesel" vehicles that cheated emissions inspections (*Volkswagen Diesel Emissions Environmental Mitigation Trust*). The Volkswagen Mitigation Trust names the fifty states, the District of Columbia, and Puerto Rico as beneficiaries, and those states and territories are permitted to finance certain eligible projects, including the conversion of diesel school buses to EVs, with trust funds if the projects are designed to reduce emissions of nitrogen oxides (ibid.; Klass, 2020, p. 623)

3.5 Political Party Affiliation

The partisan, two-party system of government in the United States is also a major factor in EV adoption. Identification with a political party is often indicative of willingness to adopt EVs. A 2020 study evaluating the willingness of non-EV owners to consider a future EV purchase found that self-identifying Democrats were significantly more willing than self-identifying Republicans (Sintov et al., 2020, p. 8). That study hypothesized that this disparity in willingness to consider an EV is likely due to factors of self- and social-identity that are often more important to one political party than the other (ibid., p. 2). The study demonstrated through regression modeling that EVs have likely become associated with these “symbolic attitudes,” such as environmentalism, technological innovation, and social responsibility (ibid., p. 8). The study found that Democrats were more likely than Republicans to identify positively with labels such as “environmentally concerned,” “technological-innovator,” and “socially concerned” (ibid.).

4 California – The Early Adopter

California is the major outlier in any evaluation of EV adoption in the United States. Between the end of 2010 and the third quarter of 2022, California consumers purchased 1,304,581 zero-emission vehicles (ZEVs), inclusive of BEVs, PHEVs, and fuel cell electric vehicles. (California Energy Commission, n.d.). This accounts for a remarkable 39% of the nation’s total (Veloz, 2022). The state saw roughly 256,000 EV registrations in 2018, nearly equal to the approximately 286,000 registered in all other states combined (Electric Vehicle Council, 2021, p. 14). Although the gap is closing, California still outpaced the rest of the United States with 563,070 EV registrations in 2021, over a third of the 1,454,480 registrations nationally. (AFDC, (2022); Doll, 2021). EV sales accounted for 5.16% of the state’s total vehicle sales in 2019, compared to the national average of 1.54% for the same year (EVAdoption, n.d.). Governor Gavin Newsom issued an executive order in 2020, requiring all new light-duty cars and trucks sold by 2035 to be zero emission and for all medium- and heavy-duty trucks to reach that goal by 2045 (Office of Gov. Gavin Newsom, 2020). In 2022, the California Air Resources Board (CARB) unanimously voted to adopt Gov. Newsom’s mandate, finalizing a rule upholding the 100% electric vehicle sales requirement by 2035 (CARB, 2022; Mitchell, 2022). The success of California’s aggressive push for ZEV adoption is due to a wide range of factors and a nearly two-decade-long effort to cultivate EV and ZEV acceptance. These factors include the adoption of air quality standards stricter than those of the national Clean Air Act, a requirement that automotive manufacturers sell an increasing percentage of hybrids and ZEVs in the state each year, and a program of incentives to consumers who purchase ZEVs.

In addition to these state actions, there are factors inherent to the population that may make Californians more predisposed to adopting EVs. Demographic data from 2019 shows that EV owners tend to be middle-aged white men that earn over $100,000 per year, have an undergraduate degree or higher, and live in a household with at least one other vehicle (Electric Vehicle Council, 2021, p. 1). As discussed, EV purchasers tend to be more politically liberal and concerned about climate change (ibid., p. 13). The population of California, broadly speaking, is relatively wealthy, liberal, and demonstrates a heightened concern about climate change and its impacts (Archsmith et al., 2022, p. 77). Californians also show a slight preference for sedans, which currently represent by far the largest share of fleet options of EVs (ibid.).

4.1 California Clean Air Standards

The California Legislature enacted Assembly Bill 1493 in 2002. AB1493 – now more commonly known as the Pavley Law, named after the lawmaker who introduced it – is a landmark piece of legislation recognizing the impact of vehicle emissions on global warming (McCarthy, 2002). The law required CARB to promulgate regulations by January 1, 2005 that reduce emissions while considering the technical feasibility of the measures implemented and the impact they would have on the state's economy (ibid.). Importantly, the law's language grants CARB significant regulatory authority, prohibiting only the agency's imposition of additional fees and taxes, the banning of vehicle types, and the requirements of reducing weight, speed limits, or miles traveled (ibid.). Pursuant to Section 209 of the Clean Air Act, CARB applied for a waiver from the US EPA to adopt more stringent standards for vehicle emissions in 2005 to satisfy the mandate of the Pavley Law (AB 1493) (CARB, n.d(c)). The Bush administration EPA initially denied the waiver in 2008, but after the California Air Resources Board and other state actors worked with several automakers and the federal government to resolve concerns, the Obama administration EPA granted the waiver in 2009 (ibid.).

CARB promulgated regulations to achieve the goals of the Pavley Law and meet the more stringent vehicle emissions standards it adopted, the most recent version of which is known as the Advanced Clean Cars Program. The program works by addressing GHG emissions from two directions. It sets limits on smog-causing criteria pollutants through vehicle emission standards and emissions inspections, known as the Low-Emissions Vehicle (LEV) regulations, while simultaneously promoting ZEV adoption through automotive manufacturer ZEV production mandates (CARB, n.d.(b);

CARB, n.d.(e)). The ZEV program requires auto manufacturers that sell vehicles in the state to make a growing percentage of their fleet ZEVs, tracked through the issuance of "credits" for the manufacture of ZEVs (ibid.; Klass, 2020, p. 622). Large volume manufacturers were required to produce 9.5% of their total average production of all light-duty vehicles that were delivered for sale in California as ZEVs in 2020, and the percentage quickly scales upwards each year, with 22% required by 2025 (CARB, n.d.(a); CARB, n.d.(b)). As of early 2022, 16 states had adopted California's LEV regulations and 13 of those states have also adopted California's ZEV program (CARB, n.d.(d)).

4.2 Incentives

California adopted and still utilizes an aggressive incentive structure as a supplement to the federal tax credit to "close the upfront cost gap between electric and conventional vehicles" (Archsmith et al., 2022, p. 77). California offers a rebate to drivers purchasing a new ZEV, most often $2,000 but it can range up to $7,000 depending on model and "fuel" technology (Bui et al., 2020, p. 12; CVRP, n.d.). Further supplementing the cost of EV purchases, California electricity providers – such as investor-owned public utilities, municipal power companies, and rural electric cooperatives – also offer rebates, ranging from $600 to $1,000 for the purchase of an EV (Bui et al, 2020, p. 12). One of the most effective and creative measures in California was the creation of the Clean Air Vehicle decal program. The purchase of a qualifying vehicle that meets established emissions standards and other criteria allows the consumer to use HOV lanes even if the driver is the only occupant (CA DMV, n.d.). A 2014 study examined the program and determined the value of the sticker was approximately $5,800 over its lifetime.

4.3 Infrastructure

California also leads the nation in public chargers with 14,240 charging stations encompassing 37,143 EVSE ports as of June 2022 (AFDC, n.d.(a)). Inclusion of shared chargers in the count, such as those in common parking areas of apartment complexes, brings the number of EVSE ports to over 70,000, and the California Public Utilities Commission plans to install an additional 123,000 more to hit the state's goal of 250,000 chargers by 2025 (Plautz, 2021). This aggressive stance on infrastructure is likely a major factor in California's success encouraging EV adoption. A study published in 2017 evaluated, among other things, the effect public charging stations per capita had on the rate of EV adoption in California (Javid and Nejat, 2017, p. 36). Utilizing datasets from a survey that collected information from all counties in the state, the study determined that the likelihood of EV adoption increased 1.9% for each additional charging station per 10,000 capita (ibid.) But despite the significant number of charging stations already built and the significant number on the way, a recent California Energy Commission analysis indicates that the state will need even more (Mulkern, 2021). The agency predicts that the state requires at least 1.2 million total chargers to have an infrastructure sufficient to meet Governor Newsom's executive order mandating exclusively ZEV sales by 2035 (ibid.).

5 Case Studies

As demonstrated by the California example discussed above, subnational government policies can be significant drivers of EV adoption. But regional differences pose challenges unique to each subnational government in the United States. For example, rates of adoption in states with higher rural populations are lower than in states with higher urban populations, with a large majority of non-urbanized areas capturing EV registration rates between 0%–0.5% (Archsmith et al., 2022, p. 77; Tolbert, 2021). These rural states also tend to have substantially less EV charging infrastructure, with most rural areas having no chargers. In contrast, major metropolitan areas average between 500 to 1,000 public outlets per 25 square miles (ibid.). Adoption is more prevalent in coastal states than in the interior of the United States (Archsmith et al., 2022, p. 88). As discussed above, states with populations that prefer light trucks over sedans have lower adoption rates given the overrepresentation of sedans in the EV market (ibid., pp. 89–90). Regional politics also influence EV adoption. However, as described in this Section, a range of subnational governments, along with private entities, particularly electric utilities, have adopted measures to increase EV adoption, even in more rural and politically conservative states.

5.1 Minnesota

Minnesota exemplifies the local experience where subnational governments are making a concerted effort to drive EV adoption and reduce carbon emissions through a statutory and regulatory approach. As of the end of 2021, the US Department of Energy's Alternative Fuels Data Center showed that Minnesota ranked twenty-first among the states in market share of EVs registered in the United States with 15,000 annual registrations, representing 1.03% of national electric vehicle sales (AFDC, (2022); Doll, 2021).

At the time of this publication, the Democratic Farm Labor Party had single-party control of the state government, occupying the governorship, the office of the secretary of state, the attorney general's office, and control of both the state House of Representatives and state Senate. (Ballotpedia, n.d.). However, over the last decade, Minnesota has had a divided government for all but three years (ibid.). Although this divide often made legislative action to increase EV adoption challenging, control of the executive branch of state government provided regulatory opportunities. For this reason, executive orders by Democratic Governor Tim Waltz, as well as state agency regulations and programs, were, until recently, the more effective means of creating a statewide EV policy. Minnesota's recent history of divided government and the state's reliance on more traditional means of legislative and regulatory actions to encourage adoption is likely a major factor for the slower uptake in Minnesota, despite its reputation as an environmentally conscious state and a Democratic stronghold in the otherwise Republican-leaning Midwest. In 2021, however, the Minnesota Pollution Control Agency (MPCA), the state's environmental regulatory arm, adopted the California LEV and ZEV Standards as part of its "Clean Cars Minnesota rule" under the direction of Gov. Tim Waltz (Office of Gov. Tim Walz, 2019; *In the Matter of the Proposed Rules of the Minn. Pollution Control. Agency Adopting Vehicle Greenhouse Gas Emissions Standards* 2021; MPCA, n.d.(a)). It was the first Midwestern state to do so. Another state regulatory agency, the Minnesota Department of Transportation (MNDOT), also experimented with incentivizing EV adoption through a pilot program to test another of California's successful initiatives – the HOV pass. MNDOT provided a one-time credit of $250 for EVs and $125 for PHEVs to consumers who purchased or leased eligible vehicles between November 2019 and the end of October 2022 for use towards the state's toll-road service that meters HOV lane access (MNDOT, n.d.).

Yet, a strictly regulatory approach is not the only method by which subnational governments in Minnesota have attempted to encourage adoption. Demonstrative of a combined legislative and regulatory approach, the Minnesota legislature enacted multiple statutes to drive a transition to low-carbon transportation by directing regulatory agencies to promulgate plans and rules that will speed the transition. One such statute, Minn. Stat. § 473.3927, governs zero-emission and electric transit vehicles and requires the Metropolitan Council – a policy-making body and planning agency for the Minneapolis-St. Paul metropolitan region – to develop a Zero-Emission Bus Transition Plan (MetroTransit, n.d.). The plan, designed to be revised every five years, is required to look to short-, medium-, and long-term strategies to transition the Twin Cities metropolitan transit service towards zero-emissions technologies (ibid.).

The Minnesota legislature also enacted Minn. Stat. § 216B.1614, a law requiring investor-owned electric utilities operating in the state to offer time-of-use or off-peak charging rates, as well as the option to create outreach programs to educate consumers about the benefits of EVs. Following the enactment of this statute, the Minnesota Public Utilities Commission (MPUC) initiated an inquiry in 2017 to evaluate the benefits and barriers to greater EV adoption in the state (*In the Matter of a Commission Inquiry into Electric Vehicle Charging and Infrastructure*, 2019, pp. 1–3). The inquiry led the Commission to conclude that transportation electrification was in the public interest and that utilities have an important role in furthering this goal (ibid., p. 10). At the conclusion of its inquiry, the MPUC adopted a plan that requires Minnesota's three investor-owned utilities – Xcel Energy, Minnesota Power, and Otter Tail Power

– to file annual EV reports that summarize the utilities' available programs and efforts to encourage EV adoption as well as proposals for infrastructure plans, EV proposals, and a Transportation Electrification Plan (ibid., p. 9). There are limits, however, to the MPUC's ability to approve programs under the current grants of authority from the state legislature. For example, Xcel Energy proposed a rebate program for up to $150 million to incentivize EV purchases in the state. In 2022, the MPUC unanimously voted against the program on the grounds that state law does not permit the agency to approve an EV rebate program funded by Xcel's ratepayers (*In the Matter of Xcel Energy's Petition for Approval of Electric Vehicle Programs as part of its COVID-19 Pandemic Economic Recovery Investments*, 2022, p. 10).

Although EV registrations are on the rise, with year-over-year growth of 44.51% between 2020 and 2021, Minnesota's charging infrastructure will require additional build-out to accelerate further growth to reach the state's goal of 20% EVs by 2030. (Doll, 2022; Minnesota Climate Change Subcabinet, 2022, p. 26). Increased charging capacity will be necessary to capture consumers without home charging capabilities, with long commutes, or who reside in rural areas, all factors that lead to range anxiety. Minnesota's current charging infrastructure reflects a state in transition from one reliant on market forces developing EV infrastructure to one that encourages growth through more direct governmental actions. Minnesota ranks twenty-second in the nation with 561 charger stations for a total of 1,388 EVSE ports (AFDC, n.d.(a)). This lack of substantial EV infrastructure is at the heart of a new endeavor between Minnesota and four other Midwest states. In 2021, Minnesota joined Illinois, Indiana, Michigan, and Wisconsin in a Memorandum of Understanding to develop a regional partnership with the goal of collectively positioning the upper Midwest for federal funding opportunities offered through the Infrastructure Investment and Jobs Act (Regional Electric Vehicle Midwest Coalition, 2021, p. 1; Ebert, 2021). The multistate partnership aims to coordinate the siting of future charging stations to alleviate range anxiety and make travel and commuting in EVs easier (Ebert, 2021).

Minnesota regulatory agencies are also taking action to develop a statewide EV charging network. The MPCA earmarked $3.525 million of the state's share of the Volkswagen settlement to develop EV corridors through the state, including in many rural counties. The initiative will spend 10% of the funds to create charging stations in public areas, such as around workplaces or near multi-unit housing, and the remaining 90% will be used to develop fast-charging stations on highways to expand the state's EV charging network by over 2,500 miles (MPCA, 2020). Similarly, Minnesota utilities are also working to build out greater charging infrastructure outside of governmental mandates and programs. Xcel Energy and Otter Tail Power joined the National Electric Highway Coalition (NEHC), a collaboration between electric utilities to develop EV charging infrastructure along major US travel corridors (NEHC, 2021). The NEHC's members have invested $3 billion to date through customer programs and infrastructure projects and the Coalition aims to facilitate build-out on the identified travel corridors by 2023 (NEHC, 2021).

Investment in rural EV charging infrastructure beyond highway corridors will also likely be necessary. Roughly 1.26 million of Minnesota's residents are rural: 22% of a population of 5.71 million. As of 2021, there were 14 counties in Minnesota categorized as entirely rural with another 35 categorized as rural/town mixed (Asche, 2021, p. 3). Consistent with national trends, those entirely rural counties had only 79 of the 23,748 registered EVs in Minnesota, according to the MPUC's 2021 year-end figures (MPUC, n.d.). As expected, counties that are split town/rural see increased adoption with 950 registered EVs, but still pale in comparison to urban counties (ibid.). These 49 rural and rural/town counties only account for 4.3% of EV registrations, but state and local electric utilities are attempting to incentivize greater adoption. Many of these rural and split rural/town counties are serviced by rural electric cooperatives that avoid much of the regulation imposed on investor-owned utilities, such as the requirements under Minn. Stat. § 216B.1614. Despite this, four Minnesota cooperatives offer time-of-use or off-peak charging rates and offer rebates for EVSE equipment purchased by their customers. In addition to adopting the Clean Cars Minnesota rule and building out the EV charging infrastructure, the MPCA was investing $4.7 million of Minnesota's share of the Volkswagen settlement funds in electric school buses (MPCA, n.d.(c)). In the most recent round of grant funding in 2020, five grant recipients received funds that will deliver four electric school buses to rural areas and four to school districts in the metropolitan area (MPCA, n.d.(b)).

Minnesota exemplifies a model in which subnational governments drive the low-carbon transportation transition. Although many of these laws, regulations, and initiatives are in early stages, the process by which Minnesota governmental units – including the legislature, state agencies, and the Office of the Governor – coordinate demonstrates a concerted effort by subnational government to be aggressive after reliance on consumer behavior and market forces have failed to spur widespread demand for EVs.

5.2 North Carolina

North Carolina is an exemplar of both governmental and non-governmental actors encouraging EV adoption, with a particular emphasis on driving growth in rural localities. Democratic Governor Roy Cooper issued Executive Order No. 80 in 2018 that established statewide goals to transition to a clean energy economy – including the goal of having 80,000 registered ZEVs by 2025 – and issued Executive Order No. 246 in 2022 establishing the goal that EVs will comprise at least half of all in-state vehicle sales by 2030. North Carolina had the sixteenth largest market share of EVs registered in the United States by the end of 2021, with 25,190 registered vehicles representing 1.73% of all electric vehicles sold nationwide (Alternative Fuels Data Center, 2021; Doll, 2021). North Carolina also claims the seventh largest number of electric transit buses in the nation (Smith, 2021, p. 2).

North Carolina's charging infrastructure is indicative of a state attempting to develop a more robust charging network to alleviate range concerns. North Carolina ranks fifteenth in the nation with 1,036 public charging stations with 2,662 EVSE ports; however, the state ranks only thirty-seventh in the nation in the number of DC fast charging ports per person (AFDC, n.d.(a); Smith, 2021, p. 2). Demonstrative of the state-level government's efforts to encourage greater development of public EVSE infrastructure, in 2019 the North Carolina's Department of Environmental Quality (NCDEQ) allocated about $3.45 million of the state's portion of the Volkswagen Mitigation Trust to build ZEV DC fast chargers (NCDEQ, 2019, p. 3). The NCDEQ accepted applications from nonprofits, school districts, municipal, state, and tribal governments, municipal and rural planning organizations, and businesses to receive funding to install and host DC fast chargers (ibid.). The NCDEQ ultimately awarded the $3.4 million to a variety of proposed plans that include the addition of 19 DC fast charger ports in 15 rural locations, 13 DC fast charger ports in 9 suburban locations, and 13 DC fast charger ports in 7 urban locations (NCDEQ, n.d.).

Although North Carolina does not incentivize the purchase of EVs with a tax credit or rebate, the state encourages adoption through other means. Plug-in electric vehicles and fuel cell electric vehicles are exempt from state emissions inspection requirements (N.C. Gen. Stat. §20-1832.2(b)(9–10)). North Carolina also permits EV drivers to use HOV lanes, even if the vehicle has only a single occupant (N.C. Gen. Stat. §146.2(a)(4–6)). However, registering an EV in North Carolina requires an additional annual fee of $130, which is in the mid-to-upper range of EV-specific fees among the states that impose them (N.C. Gen. Stat. § 20-87(13); Hartman and Shields, 2021a). The state government is also utilizing other mandates to reach the goal of 80,000 EVs. Among those mandates is an evaluation of the feasibility of replacing vehicles in the state's fleet with zero-emissions vehicles (NC DOA, 2019, p. 7). The North Carolina Department of Administration's initial feasibility study evaluated 2,417 vehicles. It determined that 572 could be replaced with EVs, utilizing current charging infrastructure, and that it would save taxpayers over $3.8 million over the vehicles' lifetimes (ibid., p. 7 & 9). Further, these efforts would reduce gasoline consumption by at least 2.7 million gallons and cut GHG emissions by 22,000 metric tons (ibid., p. 9). A subsequent study conducted by Sawatch Labs in partnership with the National Renewable Energy Laboratory between February 2018 and January 2020 identified 3,049 vehicles suitable for EV replacement over time, and projected a potential gasoline reduction of 8.2 million gallons and GHG emissions reductions of nearly 70,000 metric tons (NC DOA, 2021, pp. 4–5). As of October of 2021, North Carolina had procured a few EVs and ordered 510 hybrid vehicles for fiscal year 2021–2022 (ibid., 2021, pp. 6–8).

One factor that typically weighs against EV adoption is a higher proportion of rural population. Despite this, North Carolina has demonstrated a relatively high rate of EV registrations despite a rural population of 34% (Tippett, 2015). This may be, in part, due to efforts of rural electric cooperatives. These member-owned electricity providers are uniquely situated to develop and implement programs that can incentivize their customers to purchase and use electric vehicles, independent of the region's subnational governments. Rural electric cooperatives are typically smaller in terms of customers served, have more governance flexibility, and are subject to less state regulation than larger investor-owned utilities. Because of these factors, they can innovate and adopt creative programs to develop infrastructure and entice customers to purchase EVs. In turn, this creates more demand for electricity and benefits the cooperative, which by being customer owned, returns profits to the customers.

These rural electric cooperatives are helping the state develop public EV infrastructure. As of year-end 2020, they had invested more than $1 million and built out over 30 charging stations in rural locales (Smith, 2021, p. 19). Rural cooperatives are using incentives to encourage customer adoption of EVs. As of 2022, five rural electric cooperatives in the state were utilizing time-of-use rates to encourage EV charging at off-peak and low-volume times, such as from midnight to 4 AM (AFDC, n.d.(b)). Two cooperatives offered EVSE rebates of either $100 or $500. (ibid.) One cooperative even offered a rebate of $500 to customers who purchased an EV, and NC Electric Cooperatives, the state industry association, offered $3,500 towards the purchase of a Nissan Leaf (Surry-Yadkin, n.d.; Smith, 2021, p. 19). One rural cooperative, Roanoke Electric Cooperative, partnered with Fermata Energy for a pilot program to determine the feasibility of vehicle-to-grid technology (Brodd, 2020). The program utilized a Nissan Leaf, one of the most prevalent EV models in the US market, to test a bidirectional charger that would deliver power back to the grid in emergencies or peak demand conditions (ibid.) If technologically and fiscally feasible, this would allow customers to sell power to the cooperative as distributed energy resources.

Duke Energy, the largest investor-owned electric utility in North Carolina, is also heavily engaged in expanding EV adoption. Duke proposed a pilot program in 2019 to assess the charging load profiles from residential, fleet, and transit bus EVs, and DC fast charging stations in the state (*In the Matter of Application for Approval of Proposed Electric Transportation Pilot*, 2019, p. 7). Approved in part by the North Carolina Public Utilities Commission in late 2020, the pilot was aimed at achieving the goals of Gov. Cooper's Executive Order (ibid., p. 4). Approved portions of the pilot include providing up to $215,000 in funding to school districts per EV school bus to investigate the potential for utilizing the buses as battery storage with bidirectional chargers, and installing 160 "Level 2" charging stations and up to 40 DC fast charger stations within Duke's service territory with an additional 80 "Level 2" charging stations located at multifamily dwellings in the service area (*In the Matter of Application for Approval of Proposed Electric Transportation Pilot*, 2020, pp. 16–19). Duke proceeded to file a request to proceed with Phase II in 2021, aiming to provide funding for an addition 60 school buses by offsetting the difference between the purchase price of a tradition internal combustion engine bus and an EV model (*In the Matter of Application for Approval of Proposed Electric Transportation Pilot*, 2021, p. 19). Duke's Phase II application is yet to be approved by the North Carolina Public Utilities Commission. Duke planned to use load profile information from the approved charging infrastructure to better understand EV charging behavior, the effect of multiple charging types on EV usage, and create procedures to integrate EV charging loads on the utility's grid.

These private incentives and programs offered by Duke, Roanoke, and others require little to no dependence on the actions of a national or subnational government. The programs are indicative of non-state actors' efforts to incentivize EV adoption, and offer an alternative to relying on state action to drive EV growth at the local and regional level.

5.3 Wyoming

Wyoming exemplifies historically high resistance to EV adoption in subnational government policy. As of the end of 2021, Wyoming had the second lowest market share of EVs registered in the United States with 510 registered vehicles, representing only 0.04% of national electric vehicle sales (AFDC, 2022; Doll, 2021). In stark contrast to Minnesota and North Carolina, subnational governments in Wyoming are reluctant to utilize incentives, mandates, or laws that have been shown to increase EV purchases and registrations. Surprisingly, even electricity providers in Wyoming offer little in the way of incentives, despite the clear financial interest many investor-owned utilities and rural electric cooperatives have in growing electricity consumption in their service areas. Multiple reasons may explain Wyoming's reluctance to commit to more aggressive EV adoption policies. Wyoming shows a strong preference for light trucks over cars, is politically conservative, is heavily rural, and is the least populous state. Further, Wyoming's economy is based heavily on oil and natural gas extraction, and thus the widespread adoption of EVs poses a direct threat to the state's economy.

Wyoming nears the bottom of the list of states when it comes to EV charging stations, ranking forty-ninth in the nation when counting the District of Columbia (AFDC, n.d.(a)). Only South Dakota and Alaska have less (ibid.). As of December 2022, Wyoming had only 74 public charging stations, totaling 199 EVSE ports in the state. (ibid.). This lack of EV charging infrastructure is likely due to both a lack of incentivization and lack of interest. As of 2022, the only infrastructure incentive available in Wyoming was a $5,000 rebate towards the purchase of EVSE, offered by Yellowstone-Teton Clean Cities to business and municipalities surrounding Yellowstone and Grand Teton National Parks (Hartman and Shields, 2021b). Further compounding these infrastructure issues, the population of Wyoming appears to have very little interest in supporting an EV charging network or hosting charging stations. A state survey conducted in 2021 by the Wyoming Department of Transportation found that only about 15% of respondents had an interest in owning or operating EV charging stations, with only half of that 15% willing to invest in the necessary infrastructure (Wy. DOT, 2021, p. 8). The Department of Transportation also determined that Wyoming does not have the regulatory environment needed to foster EV infrastructure development (ibid., p. 9).

There are some signs that the Wyoming government's traditional reluctance to support EV infrastructure may be changing. In 2017, Wyoming entered into a non-binding agreement with seven other states in the Intermountain West region of the United States to create a network of EV chargers, known as the Regional Electric Vehicle Plan (REV Plan) for the West (2019). The REV Plan aimed to encourage tourism and recreation in the rural areas of those eight states by improving the EV infrastructure along major highways (ibid.). The state also created the Zero Emissions Working Group in 2021 to consolidate planning efforts previously divided among the Department of Transportation, Wyoming Energy Authority, and Wyoming Department of Environmental Quality, and created a zero-emissions vehicle strategy to address the infrastructure shortcomings and prepare for the Infrastructure Investment and Jobs Act funding disbursement (State of Wyoming, 2022, pp. 1–23). Wyoming identified strategic goals, such as updating statutes and regulations to remove hinderances and support EV infrastructure development, and build-out beyond the highway corridors into off-corridor and rural communities (ibid., p. 13–15).

Despite this recent focus on EV infrastructure development, the state continues to be reluctant to encourage greater EV adoption by its residents. The state does not have individual or fleet consumer credits, either as a tax credit or a rebate. The state also imposes one of the highest costs to register an EV, requiring the yearly purchase of a decal for $200 (Wy. Stat. §31-3-102). Unlike the HOV decal offered in California and other states to incentivize the EV purchase in exchange for a benefit, this decal is required as a component of registration in excess of the base cost of registering a vehicle and functions as a surcharge for ownership of an EV. Given the wealth of research that shows costs of ownership as one of the main barriers to EV adoption, the lack of financial incentives and imposition of additional costs is certainly a continuing factor in the low rates of EV uptake in Wyoming.

Another factor that may explain the low adoption rate of EVs in Wyoming is its highly rural population with very few urbanized areas. According to the 2020 census, Wyoming is the least populous state in the United States (US Census Bureau, n.d.(b)). Wyoming's rural population represents 35.2% of the state's total (US Census Bureau, 2012, p. 2). Seventeen of the state's twenty-three counties have fewer than six people per square mile, and the state averages only 5.9 people per square mile (Wy. DOH, n.d.). The state only has two metropolitan centers with a population of over 50,000 residents – Casper and Cheyenne (US Census Bureau, n.d.(b)). The remaining urban population is spread among urban clusters with populations of less than 50,000 residents. The high rural population, combined with most of the urban population living in urban clusters and not urbanized areas, follows the trends expected in areas with low density. Moreover, Wyoming residents show a strong preference for light trucks over cars, with trucks making up roughly 80% of the market share in the state (Archsmith et al., 2022, p. 97). Regarding public transportation, a 2018 study showed that only 51% of Wyoming residents had access to intercity bus services, with the western and northern parts of the state having little to no service at all (Chaudhari et al., 2016, p. 1). As discussed earlier, these factors weigh heavily against EV adoption. Compounding the issues of truck preference is likely the income gap between urban and rural populations. In a comparison between the state of Colorado and Wyoming, both demonstrating a strong preference for light trucks, Colorado showed a much higher rate of EV adoption (Archsmith et al., 2022, p. 90 & 97). The study presenting this data hypothesized this was likely due to Colorado's higher income and politically progressive population (ibid., p. 20).

6 Concluding Remarks

This examination of subnational policies serves to demonstrate the effect of local geographies, economics, and politics on the low carbon mobility transition. The ongoing development of national policies will certainly have an impact on driving the transition toward lower-carbon mobility, but the implementation of those policies at the subnational level will likely continue to differ significantly based on regional geography. The examples in this chapter help highlight the gaps in implementation and show where national policies can best be utilized to fill regional gaps and develop more effective transitional programs.

References

Alternative Fuels Data Center (AFDC), 2022. *Maps and Data – Electric Vehicle Registrations by State*. Available at: https://afdc.energy.gov/data/10962. (Accessed: 9 December 2022).

Alternative Fuels Data Center (AFDC), n.d.(a). *Alternative Fueling Station Counts by State*. Available at: https://afdc.energy.gov/stations/states (Accessed: 4 December 2021).

Alternative Fuels Data Center (AFDC), n.d.(b). *North Carolina Laws and Incentives*. Available at: https://afdc.energy.gov/laws/state_summary?state=nc (Accessed: 4 December 2021).

Alternative Fuels Data Center (AFDC), n.d.(c). *Qualified Plug-In Electric Vehicle (PEV) Tax Credit*. Available at: https://afdc.energy.gov/laws/409 (Accessed: 3 December 2021).

Archsmith, J., Muehlegger, E. and Rapson, D.S., 2022. Future paths of electric vehicle adoption in the United States: predictable determinants, obstacles, and opportunities. *Environmental and Energy Policy and the Economy*, 3, pp. 71–110.

Asche, K., 2021. *The State of Rural Minnesota*. Center for Rural Policy and Development, June, pp. 1–35.

Baatar, B., Heckmann, K., Hoang, T. Et al., 2019. *Preparing Rural America for the Electric Vehicle Revolution*. University of California, Davis, Environmental Policy and Management Program, pp. 1–27. Available at: https://epm.ucdavis.edu/sites/g/files/dgvnsk296/files/inline-files/Preparing%20Rural%20America%20for%20the%20Electric%20Vehicle%20Revolution.pdf.

Ballotpedia, n.d. *Party control of Minnesota state government*. Available at: https://ballotpedia.org/Party_control_of_Minnesota_state_government (Accessed: 9 December 2021).

Bauer, G., Hsu, C.-W., Nicholas, M. And Lutsey, N., 2021. *Charging Up America: Assessing the Growing Need for U.S. Charging Infrastructure through 2030*. International Council on Clean Transportation, pp. 1–45. Available at: https://theicct.org/sites/default/files/publications/charging-up-america-jul2021.pdf.

Behr, P., 2021. Missing from Biden EV plan: State support for charging. *E&E News*. 2 Dec. Available at: https://subscriber.politicopro.com/article/eenews/2021/12/02/missing-from-biden-ev-plan-state-support-for-charging-283312?/.

Brodd, K., 2020. Roanoke Electric Cooperative to Pilot Cutting-Edge Vehicle-to-Grid Technology. *Clean Technica*. Available at: https://cleantechnica.com/2020/12/01/roanoke-electric-cooperative-to-pilot-cutting-edge-vehicle-to-grid-technology/.

Bui, A. *et al.*, 2020. *Update on electric vehicle adoption across U.S. cities*, International Council on Clean Transportation, pp. 1–18. Available at: https://theicct.org/sites/default/files/publications/EV-cities-update-aug2020.pdf (Accessed: 5 December 2021).

Build Back Better Act 2021 (H.R.).

Byington, L., 2022. 'Charging Deserts' Challenge Electric Car Growth in Rural Areas. *Bloomberg Government*. 12 Jan. Available at: https://about.bgov.com/news/charging-deserts-challenge-electric-car-growth-in-rural-areas/.

California Air Resources Board (CARB), 2022. *Public Hearing to Consider the Proposed Advanced Clean Cars II Regulations Staff Report: Initial Statement of Reasons*. Available at: https://ww2.arb.ca.gov/sites/default/files/barcu/regact/2022/accii/isor.pdf .

California Air Resources Board (CARB), n.d.(a). *2020 Zero-Emission Vehicle Credits.* Available at: https://ww2.arb.ca.gov/sites/default/files/2021-12/2020_zev_credit_annual_disclosure_ac.pdf (Accessed: 7 January 2022).

California Air Resources Board (CARB), n.d.(b). *Advanced Clean Cars Program*. Available at: https://ww2.arb.ca.gov/our-work/programs/advanced-clean-cars-program/about (Accessed: 4 December 2021).

California Air Resources Board (CARB), n.d.(c). *California's Greenhouse Gas Vehicle Emission Standards under Assembly Bill 1493 of 2002 (Pavley)*. Available at: https://ww2.arb.ca.gov/californias-greenhouse-gas-vehicle-emission-standards-under-assembly-bill-1493-2002-pavley (Accessed: 4 December 2021).

California Air Resources Board (CARB), n.d.(d). *States that have Adopted California's Vehicle Standards under Section 177 of the Federal Clean Air Act.* Available at: https://ww2.arb.ca.gov/sites/default/files/2022-01/177_states_12062021_nada_sales.pdf (Accessed: 7 January 2022).

California Air Resources Board (CARB), n.d.(e). *Zero-Emission Vehicle Program*. Available at: https://ww2.arb.ca.gov/our-work/programs/zero-emission-vehicle-program/about (Accessed: 4 December 2021).

California Clean Vehicle Rebate Project (CVRP), n.d. *CVRP Eligible Vehicles*. Available at: https://cleanvehiclerebate.org/eng/eligible-vehicles (Accessed: 4 December 2021).

California Department of Motor Vehicles (CA DMV), n.d. *Clean Air Vehicle Decals for Using Carpools and HOV Lanes*. Available at: https://www.dmv.ca.gov/portal/vehicle-registration/license-plates-decals-and-placards/clean-air-vehicle-decals-for-using-carpool-lanes/ (Accessed: 4 December 2021).

California Energy Commission, n.d. *New ZEV Sales in California*. Available at: https://www.energy.ca.gov/data-reports/energy-almanac/zero-emission-vehicle-and-infrastructure-statistics/new-zev-sales (Accessed: 8 December 2022).

Carley, S., Krause, R.M., Lane, B.W. and Graham, J.D., 2013. Intent to purchase a plug-in electric vehicle: a survey of early impressions in large US cites. *Transportation Research Part D: Transport and Environment*, 8, pp. 39–45.

Chaudhari, J., Kack, D. and Vasquez, A., 2016. *Wyoming Intercity Bus Study*, pp. 1–104.

Colorado Department of Revenue (Co. DOR), 2019. *Income 69: Innovative Motor Vehicle and Innovative Truck Credits*, pp. 1–5. Available at: https://tax.colorado.gov/sites/tax/files/Income%2069.pdf (Accessed: 12 January 2022).

Doll, S. 2021. *Current EV registrations in the US: How does your state stack up?* Electrek (24 Aug.). Available at: https://electrek.co/2021/08/24/current-ev-registrations-in-the-us-how-does-your-state-stack-up/.

Ebert, A., 2021. Midwest States Ink EV Charging Pact to Draw More Funding. *Bloomberg Law News* (30 Sep.). Available at: https://news.bloomberglaw.com/environment-and-energy/midwest-states-ink-ev-charge-pact-as-infrastructure-fate-unclear.

Egbue, O. et al., 2017. Mass deployment of sustainable transportation: evaluation of factors that influence electric vehicle adoption. *Clean Technologies and Environmental Policy*, 19(7), pp. 1927–1939.

Electric Vehicle Council, 2016. *EV Consumer Behavior*. Fuels Institute, pp. 1–65.

Energy Improvement and Extension Act 2008.

Energy Information Administration (EIA), 2022(a). *July 2022 Monthly Energy Review*, pp. 1–267. Available at: https://www.eia.gov/totalenergy/data/monthly/pdf/flow/CO2-spaghettichart-2021.pdf.

Energy Information Administration (EIA), 2022(b). *U.S. CO_2 emissions from energy consumption by source and sector, 2021*, pp. 1–2. Available at: https://www.eia.gov/totalenergy/data/monthly/pdf/flow/CO2-spaghettichart-2021.pdf.

Environmental Protection Agency (EPA), n.d.(a). *Inventory of U.S. Greenhouse Gas Emissions and Sinks*. United States Environmental Protection Agency. Available at: https://www.epa.gov/ghgemissions/inventory-us-greenhouse-gas-emissions-and-sinks (Accessed: 26 August 2022).

Environmental Protection Agency (EPA), n.d.(b). *Sources of greenhouse gas emissions*. United States Environmental Protection Agency. Available at: https://www.epa.gov/ghgemissions/sources-greenhouse-gas-emissions (Accessed: 26 August 2022).

EVAdoption, n.d. *EV Market Share by State*. Available at: https://evadoption.com/ev-market-share/ev-market-share-state/ (Accessed: 8 December 2022).

Ford, 2021. *Ford to Reveal All-Electric F-150 Lightning May 19 with Livestreamed Event at Ford HQ*. 10 May. Available at: https://media.ford.com/content/fordmedia/fna/us/en/news/2021/05/10/ford-to-reveal-all-electric-f-150-lightning.html.

Hartman, K. and Shields, L., 2021a. Special Fees on Hybrid and Electric Vehicles. *National Conference of State Legislatures* (12 Oct.). Available at: https://www.ncsl.org/research/energy/new-fees-on-hybrid-and-electric-vehicles.aspx (Accessed: 6 December 2021).

Hartman, K. and Shields, L. 2021b. State Policies Promoting Hybrid and Electric Vehicles. *National Conference of State Legislatures* (20 Aug.). Available at: https://www.ncsl.org/research/energy/state-electric-vehicle-incentives-state-chart.aspx (Accessed: 6 December 2021).

Hughlett, M., 2022. State regulators nix Xcel plan for ratepayer-funded electric vehicle rebates. *Star Tribune* (24 Mar.). Available at: https://www.startribune.com/state-regulators-nix-xcel-plan-for-ratepayer-funded-electric-vehicle-rebates/600159117/?refresh=true.

In the Matter of a Commission Inquiry into Electric Vehicle Charging and Infrastructure, (2019) Docket No. E-999/CI-17-879.

In the Matter of Application for Approval of Proposed Electric Transportation Pilot, (2021) Docket Nos. E-2, Sub 1197 and E-7, Sub 1195, Joint Request by Duke Energy Carolinas, LLC, and Duke Energy Progress, LLC for Approval of Phase II Electric Transportation Pilot Programs.

In the Matter of Application for Approval of Proposed Electric Transportation Pilot, (2019) Docket Nos. E-2, Sub 1197 and E-7, Sub 1195, Application for Approval of Proposed Electric Transportation Pilot.

In the Matter of Application for Approval of Proposed Electric Transportation Pilot, (2020) Docket Nos. E-2, Sub 1197 and E-2, Sub 1195, Order Approving Electric Transportation Pilot, in Part.

In the Matter of the Proposed Rules of the Minn. Pollution Control. Agency Adopting Vehicle Greenhouse Gas Emissions Standards, (2021) OAH No. 71-9003-36416.

In the Matter of Xcel Energy's Petition for Approval of Electric Vehicle Programs as part of its COVID-19 Pandemic Economic Recovery Investments, (2022) Docket Nos. E-002/M-20-745, E, G-999/M-20-492, Order Approving Public Charging Stations Proposal.

Inflation Reduction Act of 2022, Public Law 117-169 (August 16, 2022).

Infrastructure Investment and Jobs Act 2021, Public Law 117-58 (November 15, 2021).

International Energy Agency (IEA), 2021. *Fuel economy in the United States*. Available at: https://www.iea.org/articles/fuel-economy-in-the-united-states.

Javid, R. and Nejat, A., 2017. A comprehensive model of regional electric vehicle adoption and penetration. *Transport Policy*, 54, pp. 30–42.

Jenn, A., Springel, K. and Gopal, A.R., 2018. Effectiveness of electric vehicle incentives in the United States. *Energy Policy*, 119, pp. 349–356.

Klass, A., 2020. Regulating the Energy Free Riders. *Boston University Law Review*, 100, pp. 581–649.

Klass, A., 2019. Public Utilities and Transportation Electrification. *Iowa Law Review*, 104, pp. 545–617.

Lazer, L. and Freehafer, L., 2021. *The State of Electric School Bus Adoption in the US*. World Resources Institute. Available at: https://www.wri.org/insights/where-electric-school-buses-us.

McCarthy, K., 2002. *California Global Warming Legislation*. Office of Legislative Research, Connecticut General Assembly. Available at: https://www.cga.ct.gov/2002/rpt/2002-R-0652.htm.

MetroTransit, n.d. *Electric Buses*. Available at: https://www.metrotransit.org/electric-buses. (Accessed: 7 January 2022).

Minnesota Climate Change Subcabinet, n.d. *Minnesota's Climate Action Framework*. Available at: https://climate.state.mn.us/sites/climate-action/files/Climate%20Action%20Framework.pdf. (Accessed: 9 December 2022).

Minnesota Department of Transportation (MNDOT), n.d. *E-Zpass Minnesota electric vehicle incentive*. Available at: https://www.dot.state.mn.us/ezpassmn/news.html (Accessed: 7 January 2022).

Minnesota Pollution Control Agency (MPCA), 2020. *Phase 2 (2020–2023)*. Available at: https://www.pca.state.mn.us/sites/default/files/aq-mvp2-36.pdf.

Minnesota Pollution Control Agency (MPCA), n.d.(a). *Clean Cars Minnesota*. Available at: https://www.pca.state.mn.us/air/clean-cars-minnesota (Accessed: 13 January 2022).

Minnesota Pollution Control Agency (MPCA), n.d.(b). *Electric school bus pilot project*. Available at: https://www.pca.state.mn.us/air/electric-school-bus-pilot-project (Accessed: 7 January 2022).

Minnesota Pollution Control Agency (MPCA), n.d.(c). *Minnesota's Plan*. Available at: https://www.pca.state.mn.us/air/minnesotas-plan (Accessed: 7 January 2022).

Mitchell, R., 2022. California Bans Sales of New Gas-Powered Cars by 2035. Now the Real Work Begins. *Los Angeles Times* (25 Aug.). Available at: https://www.latimes.com/business/story/2022-08-25/california-ban-gasoline-mandate-zero-emission-2035 .

Mulkern, A. 2021. California looks to electric vehicles for grid stability. *E&E News* (23 Mar.). Available at: https://subscriber.politicopro.com/article/eenews/1063728061 .

National Electric Highway Coalition (NEHC), 2021. *Electric Companies Join Together to Form National Electric Highway Coalition* (7 Dec.). Available at: https://www.eei.org/News/news/All/electric-companies-join-together-to-form-national-electric-highway-coalition (Accessed 7 January 2022).

North Carolina Department of Administration (NC DOA), 2021. *Motor Fleet ZEV Plan Update*, pp. 1–20. Available at: https://ncadmin.nc.gov/media/8134/download .

North Carolina Department of Administration (NC DOA), 2019. *Motor Fleet ZEV Plan EO80*. pp. 1–22. Available at: https://files.nc.gov/ncdeq/climate-change/interagency-council/EO-80-DOA-MF-ZEV-PLan–Final-.pdf .

North Carolina Department of Environmental Quality (NCDEQ), 2019. *VW Settlement Phase 1 – DC Fact Charge Program Request for Proposals*, pp. 1–30. Available at: https://deq.nc.gov/media/13914/open.

North Carolina Department of Environmental Quality (NCDEQ), n.d. *Phase 1 Zero Emission Vehicle Infrastructure Program*. Available at: https://files.nc.gov/ncdeq/Air%20Quality/motor/volkswagen/DCFAST-AWARDEES–New.pdf (Accessed: 4 December 2021).

Office of Gov. Gavin Newsom, 2020. *Governor Newsom Announces California Will Phase Out Gasoline-Powered Cars & Drastically Reduce Demand for Fossil Fuel in California's Fight Against Climate Change* (23 Sept.). Available at: https://www.gov.ca.gov/2020/09/23/governor-newsom-announces-california-will-phase-out-gasoline-powered-cars-drastically-reduce-demand-for-fossil-fuel-in-californias-fight-against-climate-change/ (Accessed: 4 December 2021).

Office of Gov. Tim Walz, 2019. *Governor Tim Walz Announces Clean Cars Standards in Minnesota* (25 Sept.). Available at: https://mn.gov/governor/news/?id=1055-403887 (Accessed: 7 January 2022).

Plautz, J., 2021. California PUC proposes rules to accelerate near-term EV charger deployment. *UtilityDive*, 3 Jun. Available at: https://www.utilitydive.com/news/california-puc-proposes-rules-to-accelerate-near-term-ev-charger-deployment/601189/.

Ratcliffe, M., Burd, C., Holder, K. and Fields, A., 2016. *Defining Rural at the U.S. Census Bureau: American Community Survey and Geography Brief*. U.S. Census Bureau, pp. 1–8. Available at: https://www.census.gov/content/dam/Census/library/publications/2016/acs/acsgeo-1.pdf.

Regional Electric Vehicle Midwest Coalition, 2021. *Memorandum of Understanding Between Illinois, Indiana, Michigan, Minnesota, and Wisconsin*.

Regional Electric Vehicle Plan (REV) for the West, 2019. *Memorandum of Understanding Between Arizona, Colorado, Idaho, Montana, Nevada, New Mexico, Utah, and Wyoming*.

San Joaquin Valley Air Pollution Control District, n.d. *Drive Clean in the San Joaquin | Rebate*. Available at: http://valleyair.org/drivecleaninthesanjoaquin/rebate/ (Accessed: 12 January 2022).

Schilling, E., 2022. *Trucks and SUVs are Now Over 80 Percent of New Car Sales in the U.S.* Jalopnik. Available at: https://jalopnik.com/trucks-and-suvs-are-now-over-80-percent-of-new-car-sale-1848427797 .

Schoettle, B. and Sivak, M., 2017a. *Consumer Preferences and Motivations for Owning Light Trucks versus Passenger Cars*. University of Michigan Transportation Research Institute, pp. 1–62. Available at: http://websites.umich.edu/~umtriswt/PDF/SWT-2017-7.pdf .

Schoettle, B. and Sivak, M., 2017b. *Electric Vehicles in the U.S.: Progress Toward Broader Acceptance*. University of Michigan Transportation Research Institute, pp. 1–45. Available at: http://websites.umich.edu/~umtriswt/PDF/SWT-2017-9.pdf.

Shepardson, D., 2019. Trump budget proposes ending electric vehicle tax credit, *Reuters* (11 Mar.). Available at: https://www.reuters.com/article/usa-trump-budget-autonomous/trump-budget-proposes-ending-electric-vehicle-tax-credit-idUSL1N20Y0W2 (Accessed: 4 December 2021).

Sintov, N.D., Abou-Ghalioum, V. and White, L.V., 2020. The partisan politics of low-carbon transport: why democrats are more likely to adopt electric vehicles than Republicans in the United States. *Energy Research & Social Science*, 68, 101576.

Siry, D., 2009. Federal EV Tax Credit Must Be Changed. *WIRED*, 13 Oct. Available at: https://www.wired.com/2009/10/ev-tax-credit/ (Accessed: 3 December 2021).

Skibell, A., 2021. Biden to put down payment on 500,000 EV chargers. *E&E News*, 30 Nov. Available at: https://subscriber.politicopro.com/article/eenews/2021/11/30/biden-to-put-down-payment-on-pledge-to-build-500-000-ev-chargers-283695?/.

Smith, C., 2021. *Transportation Electrification in North Carolina*. Atlas Public Policy and Southern Alliance for Clean Energy, pp. 1–46. Available at: https://cleanenergy.org/wp-content/uploads/Transportation-Electrification-in-North-Carolina.pdf.

State of Wyoming, 2022. *Zero Emission Vehicle Strategy*, pp. 1–23. Available at: https://www.dot.state.wy.us/files/live/sites/wydot/files/shared/Planning/Electric%20Vehicles/State%20of%20Wyoming%20Zero%20Emission%20Vehicle%20Strategy%20%20final.pdf .

Surry-Yadkin Electric Membership Corporation, n.d. *Member Rates*. Available at: https://www.syemc.com/content/member-rebates (Accessed: 4 December 2021).

Tippett, R., 2015. Urbanization Trends. *Carolina Demography*. Available at: https://www.ncdemography.org/2015/01/05/urbanization-trends/.

Tolbert, J., 2021. *Beyond cities: breaking through barriers to rural electric vehicle adoption*. Environmental and Energy Study Institute, 22 Oct. Available at: https://www.eesi.org/articles/view/beyond-cities-breaking-through-barriers-to-rural-electric-vehicle-adoption.

U.S. Census Bureau, 2012. *Wyoming: 2010 – Population and Housing Unit Counts*. pp. 1–55

U.S. Census Bureau, n.d.(a). *Rural America*. Available at: https://mtgis-portal.geo.census.gov/arcgis/apps/MapSeries/index.html?appid=49cd4bc9c8eb444ab51218c1d5001ef6 (Accessed: 7 January 2022).

U.S. Census Bureau, n.d.(b). *Quick Facts: Wyoming*. Available at: https://www.census.gov/ .

U.S. Department of Energy (DOE), 2011. *One Million Electric Vehicles by 2015*. pp. 1–11. Available at: https://www.energy.gov/sites/prod/files/edg/news/documents/1_Million_Electric_Vehicle_Report_Final.pdf.

U.S. Department of Transportation (DOT), 2022. National Electric Vehicle Infrastructure Formula Program Notice of Proposed Rulemaking. 23 CFR Part 680. Available at: https://www.fhwa.dot.gov/environment/alternative_fuel_corridors/resources/nprm_evcharging_unofficial.pdf .

Valdes-Dapena, P., 2021. Ford is the undisputed king of trucks. Here's how it got there. *CNN Business* (25 May). Available at: https://www.cnn.com/2021/05/25/success/ford-pickup-trucks-lightning-american-history/index.html.

Veloz, 2022. *Electric Vehicle Sales in California and the U.S.* Available at: https://www.veloz.org/wp-content/uploads/2022/10/Q3-2022_EV-Sales-in-California-and-the-U.S._Final.png.

Viswanath, T., 2021. *Co-op Evolution – Bridging the Rural-Urban Divide on EV Adoption*. CoBank, pp. 1–16. Available at: https://www.cobank.com/documents/7714906/7715341/Electric-Vehicles-June2021.pdf/f36a0724-62da-97f4-1615-002b893e68b0?t=1643240393660 (Accessed: 6 December 2021).

Wallach, O., 2022. *Visualizing All Electric Car Models Available in the U.S.* Visual Capitalist Available at: https://www.visualcapitalist.com/visualizing-all-electric-car-models-available-in-the-us/ .

White House, 2021a. *FACT SHEET: President Biden Announces Steps to Drive American Leadership Forward on Clean Cars and Trucks* (5 Aug.). Available at: https://www.whitehouse.gov/briefing-room/statements-releases/2021/08/05/fact-sheet-president-biden-announces-steps-to-drive-american-leadership-forward-on-clean-cars-and-trucks/ (Accessed: 5 December 2021).

White House, 2021b. *FACT SHEET: President Biden Signs Executive Order Catalyzing America's Clean Energy Economy Through Federal Sustainability* (8 Dec.). Available at: https://www.whitehouse.gov/briefing-room/statements-releases/2021/12/08/fact-sheet-president-biden-signs-executive-order-catalyzing-americas-clean-energy-economy-through-federal-sustainability/ (Accessed: 7 January 2022).

White House, 2021c. *FACT SHEET: The Biden-Harris Electric Vehicle Charging Action Plan* (13 Dec.). Available at: https://www.whitehouse.gov/briefing-room/statements-releases/2021/12/13/fact-sheet-the-biden-harris-electric-vehicle-charging-action-plan/ (Accessed: 7 January 2022).

Wyoming Department of Health (Wy. DOH), n.d. *What is Rural*. Available at: https://health.wyo.gov/publichealth/rural/officeofruralhealth/what-is-rural/ (Accessed: 4 December 2021).

Wyoming Department of Transportation (Wy. DOT), 2021. *Zero Emission Vehicle Working Group Briefing*, pp. 1–14. Available at: https://wyoleg.gov/InterimCommittee/2021/08-2021081719-01WYDOTZeroEmissionsPresentation.pdf .

Yang, Z. *et al.*, 2016. *Principles for effective electric vehicle incentive design*. International Council on Clean Transportation, pp. 1–43. Available at: https://theicct.org/sites/default/files/publications/ICCT_IZEV-incentives-comp_201606.pdf (Accessed: 5 December 2021).

Anél du Plessis, Chantelle G Moyo

The Role of Cities in Low(er)-Carbon Transition

Abstract: The point of departure of this chapter is that cities are deemed key sites for climate action and that city authorities have in recent years become important actors in global climate governance and low-carbon transition. The Paris Agreement acknowledges the role of sub-national authorities in climate action. At the same time, Sustainable Development Goal 11 (SDG 11) makes explicit reference to cities in the pursuit of urban safety, sustainability, inclusivity, and resilience. The United Nations New Urban Agenda (NUA) projects the same message. A few targets in SDG 11 and the ideals in the NUA speak to issues of climate resilience, mitigation and adaptation as relevant to the urban context. In parallel, the work of global city networks relative to issues of climate justice, climate governance, energy security and the water-food-energy (WEF) nexus is fast proliferating.

This chapter is set against the backdrop of the above. It focuses on the role of the city in the low(er)-carbon transition from the perspective of international urban and climate change law and policy in general. The chapter further critically considers this role on the basis of concrete examples of local law and policy action from Africa as one of the fastest urbanising continents in the world, that simultaneously faces a critical need to address energy poverty. This chapter focuses specifically on Southern and Northern Africa (South Africa, Uganda and Morocco).

1 Introduction

We stand witness to the urban turn in global governance in the sense that today's global growth is very much urban. Cities of different sizes serve as contemporary conduits for the unstoppable transnational movement of people, things, ideas and danger. The so-called "planetary urbanisation" is blamed for many of the calamities around the anthropocene (Kotzé, 2021, pp. 354–367). Urban processes are said to cause

Note: The research for this chapter was conducted with the financial support of the National Research Foundation of South Africa (NRF) (Grant Nr: 115581). All views and errors are the authors' own and do not represent the views of the NRF.

Anél du Plessis is Professor of Law and the South African Research Chair in Cities, Law and Environmental Sustainability, North-West University, South Africa.

Chantelle Moyo is PhD candidate at the South African Research Chair in Cities, Law and Environmental Sustainability, North-West University, South Africa.

https://doi.org/10.1515/9783110752403-041

much of global climate change (UNEP and UN-Habitat, 2021, p. 10). It is further widely accepted that the success and failure of urban governance – the creation, design and use of space, the erection and maintenance of infrastructures, the deliberate yet diplomatic regulation of people, human (and non-human) conduct and processes as well as the close involvement of local peoples – will help determine the future success or failure of global climate governance. It was predicted a decade ago that: "(c)ities will shape the way the dual industrial and socio-ecological transitions unfold over the next 20 to 30 years as they shape the dynamic of the next long-term development cycle" (Swilling and Annecke, 2012, p. 129).

It makes sense, therefore, that cities feature on the global low-carbon transition agenda, an agenda in essence aimed at the multi-level changes needed to move from a mixed use of high carbon and low-carbon energy to just using low-carbon energy such as solar power, wind and hydropower to reduce the total emissions causing global climate change. Globally over 50 per cent of all people reside in cities, and more than 50 per cent of all economic output is generated there (UNEP and UN-Habitat, 2021, p. 22–24). Furthermore, it is estimated that between 40 to 70 per cent of anthropogenic greenhouse gas (GHG) emissions are generated from activities in cities (Energy Cities, 2014; Bulkeley, 2019). While cities are considered catalysts of increased GHG emissions, they can also be perceived as potential drivers of low-carbon energy transitions (Fuhr, 2018; Haase *et al.*, 2017; Sullivan, Gouldson and Webber, 2013, p. 514). City-level authorities are uniquely placed to help drive emissions reductions through local policies, programmes and bylaws speaking to building regulations, municipal transport systems and service delivery costs, for example (Vaughter and Pham, 2021, p. 30; Calderon and Calderon, 2021; Bizikova, Robinson and Cohen, 2007). Most importantly, the proximity between local authorities and others (e.g. local public and private sectors and the community) places them in a strategically meaningful position to inform and influence innovative action for low-carbon transitions (Nishida and Hua, 2011).

The Paris Agreement (article 7(2)) acknowledges the role of sub-national authorities in climate action. At the same time Sustainable Development Goal 11 (SDG 11) makes explicit reference to cities in the pursuit of urban safety, sustainability, inclusivity and resilience. The United Nations New Urban Agenda (NUA) projects a similar message. Several of the targets in SDG 11 and the ideals in the NUA speak to issues of climate resilience, mitigation and adaptation as relevant to the urban context. In parallel, the work of global city networks around issues of climate justice, climate governance, energy security and the water-food-energy (WEF) nexus is fast proliferating (see, e.g., Aust and Du Plessis, 2019; and the relevant topics in Aust and Nijman, 2021).

This chapter is set against the backdrop of the above. It focuses on the role of the city in low(er)-carbon transitions from the perspective of international urban and climate change law and policy in general. The chapter further critically reflects on this role on the basis of examples of local law and policy action from Africa (South Africa, Uganda and Morocco) as one of the fastest urbanising continents that simultaneously faces a critical need to address energy poverty and the impacts of climate change on human and ecological systems. While work of this kind has been done in the context of European cities (see e.g. Bulkeley, 2019), the literature coming from the global South and Africa specifically remains limited.

2 Low(er)-carbon transition as an imperative of international urban policy and global city networks

The link between climate change, cities and the changing global environmental governance landscape lies therein that urbanisation is deeply rooted in everyday life (and its processes contributing to climate change) as well as in the quality of urban space, which involves a complex constellation of material, social, institutional, environmental and other transformations (UNEP and UN-Habitat, 2021, pp. 44–45; Brenner and Schmid, 2018, p. 57). The quality of urban space is being increasingly affected by climate change as well as the mitigative and adaptive measures required to address it. The reciprocal relationship between cities and climate change speaks to how cities and urban processes contribute to climate change (e.g. carbon-intensive urban development) as well as to the present and future impacts that climate change will have on the health and well-being of urban dwellers, city infrastructures and the ability to predictively plan urban development. Scientific reports indicate that urban areas are a major source of CO_2 emissions, contributing to greenhouse gas-forced climate change, and that associated waste heat released to the environment in cities is a driver of urban micro-climates (see e.g. WMO, 1996; UNEP and UN-Habitat, 2021, p. 46). Cities thus have a meaningful role to play in low(er)-carbon transition planning, for example. At the same time, as the Covid-19 pandemic has shown, cities are dense areas of people, economic activity and infrastructure that are heavily impacted when health or environmental risks materialise in their areas. For this reason, cities and the socio-ecological systems they support must be resilient and part of the global process of transformation towards climate change adaptation and the much-needed low-carbon transition.

The body of knowledge on cities and global climate governance has developed rapidly over the past two decades. Some of the key understandings include that:

Firstly, cities intensify human-induced warming locally (IPCC, 2021, ch.12). They are sites of high energy consumption and waste production and in general local authorities have control over these processes with functional powers in relation to land-use planning, urban transport, energy supply and management and building regulations. In principle, many municipalities thus influence processes that are critical for emissions reduction and a smaller carbon footprint (IPCC, 2014, ch. 12).

Secondly, cities are home to vulnerability – of human beings and socio-ecological systems – and may be best placed to facilitate the inclusive articulation and formulation of short- and longer-term adaptation and transformation needs. Here the emphasis is on inclusiveness, responsiveness, and accountability as key features of democratic local governance (De Sherbinin, Schiller and Pulsipher, 2007).

Thirdly, many cities are democratic institutions that can foster partnerships, engage stakeholders, facilitate public participation and lobby national (federal) governments in efforts to transition to low(er) carbon as part of the response to climate change (Barber, 2013).

Fourthly, many cities have joined one or more global or transnational cities networks. This "ecosystem of city networks" such as ICLEI (Local Government for Sustainability, 2022), C40 (C40 Cities, 2022) and UCLG (United Cities and Local Government, 2022) creates a global forum for information sharing and experimental local governance that is meaningful for individual municipalities devoted to environmental sustainability and for innovative climate change response action (Acuto and Leffel, 2020; Aust, 2019).

Fifthly, cities play a nuanced yet increasingly visible role in transnational climate change law and policy-making (Lin, 2018). While international agreement and consensus on climate response action often falter due to nationalistic sentiments, fears and the protection of domestic interests, cities have been bold in making commitments on emission reduction targets, for example (see e.g. C40 Cities, no date). At the World Summit of Local and Regional Leaders held in Durban in 2019, city leaders formally announced that they would promote a shift in production and consumption patterns. They would also work to ensure clean city transport and aim to curb urban sprawl to the extent that "(l)ocal governments of all sizes will have a key role to play in the transition from a productive to a creative society by rethinking the complexity of the global supply chain, as well as shorter and natural circuits in cities." They further asserted that cities "will need to enhance the use of renewable energies and consider the lifespan of greenhouse gas emissions …" (UCLG, 2019, para. 17).

Bulkeley's research on environmental and energy transitions in cities has revealed that the specific capacities and levers that city authorities (municipalities) have at their disposal to effect urban transitions vary (Bulkeley, 2019). She has further found that where municipalities have either direct ownership or a high degree of control with respect to key sectors (e.g. energy and waste), one can witness

> the use of modes of governing that seek to directly intervene to regulate for sustainability transitions (e.g. in terms of the building standards for energy efficiency). Municipal governments operating under such conditions or with a high level of autonomy can also seek to govern through provision of key services, technologies or incentives – for example providing free bike schemes, supporting domestic installation of solar panels, or providing subsidies for public transport. Research has also identified the dominance of enabling modes of governing, which seek to govern through harnessing the capacities of other agents (individuals, communities, civil society groups,

> corporations) towards particular ends. Most often, efforts to effect environmental and energy transitions contain a 'governance mix', utilising different modes … in combination as the situation demands (Bulkeley, 2019, p. 14).

There are, however, also critiques of the statement that cities are global climate change actors co-responsible for the low-carbon transition agenda. The critics warn, and justifiably so, that there are localities that have been "left behind" and that representativity in the global arena leans towards the major, well-resourced and well-capacitated cities mostly situated in the global North (Bansard, Pattberg and Wilderberg, 2017, pp. 233–235, 242). They further warn that a focus on cities and urban localities in making sense of the "local" in "global" climate governance signals a level of ignorance about critical rural-urban linkages and the interdependence of life-supporting systems embedded in ecosystems, water systems and micro-climates within and beyond city borders (IPCC, 2014, ch.9). Of further concern should be the kind of role played by cities in countries where democratic processes are undermined. Critique has further been levelled against the tangible overall impact that city-level climate actions have (Bulkeley, 2019). Another limitation lies in the institutional fragmentation that cities cannot escape. Bulkeley (2019, p. 24) states for example that:

> Whilst multilevel governance conditions shape the overall capacities and effectiveness of efforts to govern environmental and energy transitions, they are particularly acute at the urban level where institutional fragmentation may be particularly high and where the 'fit' between the remit of urban institutions and actors and the issues to be tackled is often poor. In large metropolitan areas, municipal authorities can exist at regional and local levels, with a poor level of co-ordination in relation to key sectors such as water, energy, waste and housing.

These concerns caution against sweeping generalisations and romanticising an absolute role for cities in the global low-carbon transition. It is true, though, that those responsible for urban governance have no choice but to question if and how global climate change demands that things be done differently. Doing so must bear in mind the impact of carbon-intensive operations and economies on the present and future generations and how they affect the core functions of local authorities such as the delivery of basic services and addressing socio-economic problems such as energy poverty (Leck and Roberts, 2015).

In the remaining sections of this paper we turn to cities in Southern and Northern Africa in an attempt to elucidate the potential and role of cities in low(er)-carbon transitions albeit with the realities surrounding energy poverty as an add-on issue in several developing countries, in mind.

3 The nexus between energy poverty and low(er)-carbon transition in the urban context

Many cities in the global South find themselves addressing inequality ranging from unequal access to housing and services and spatial injustice to city-level income inequalities (UN-Habitat, 2020, p.xvii). The fear exists that the drive for low-carbon transitions at all levels may further entrench pre-existing inequalities or give rise to new forms. This fear stems from the understanding that low-carbon transitions have implications for short-term local economic development, constrained municipal budgets and established resource consumption patterns and procurement chains in cities and towns.

As stated earlier, Africa is one of the fastest urbanising continents with no projections pointing to a significant decline in such urbanisation any time soon (UN-Habitat, 2020, p. 12). The continent's rapid urbanisation is driven mainly by the natural increase in the population, rural-urban migration, the spatial expansion of urban settlements and the reclassification of rural areas (UN-Habitat, 2020, p. 12). This understandably puts pressure on any low-carbon vision or plans for economic transition for the continent as well as on attempts to strengthen socio-ecological climate resilience (Mahumane and Mulder, 2021, p. 12). At this juncture we briefly dwell on the nexus between energy poverty and the possibilities for a low(er)-carbon transition in Africa's fast-growing urban areas.[1] At the same time, we reflect on the issue of low-carbon transition justice.[2] In real terms, this nexus also casts light on some of the limitations and possibilities for a low-carbon transition in at least some cities of the world.

There are many definitions of energy poverty and ways of measuring it. Energy poverty is notoriously difficult to define in as far as it denotes living conditions which cannot be reduced to numerical data (Chipango, 2022, p. 3). What is known, though, is that the concept of energy poverty essentially evolved from that of fuel poverty (Boardman, 2020). As against fuel poverty, energy poverty is defined as the lack of the electricity required to service basic household needs, including modern cooking facilities (Parajuli, 2011, p. 2299; IEA, 2010, p. 5). Energy poverty generally refers to the lack of access to the modern energy services necessary for human development, including (but not limited to) electricity for cooking, heating, and lighting (Vermaak, Kohler and Rhodes, 2009, pp. 165–166). This definition is similar to that proposed by the International Energy Agency (IEA), which considers energy poverty as the signifi-

1 Interestingly enough, as indicated by Mahumane and Mulder, energy poverty and urbanisation are often studied as separate phenomena.

2 Low-carbon transition justice is understood to refer to equitable distribution and access to resources and technologies as well as participation in decision-making and equal capabilities in the process of transitioning away from fossil fuel-based energy.

cant absence of modern services (IEA, 2010, p. 5). In addition, the United Nations Development Programme (UNDP) defines energy poverty as the absence of choice in energy services in terms of quality, reliability, and environmental protection, leading to the social and economic under-development of individuals and families (UNDP, 2018, pp. 1–2). It is clear from this definition that energy poverty translates into the inability of households to acquire the necessary energy services required to live a healthy and decent life (Middlemiss and Gillard, 2015, pp. 146–147).

The above definitions reflect an absence of choice for clean sources of energy. Sen argues that the very notion of development involves various options that enable citizens to choose and obtain a specific lifestyle (Sen, 2001, p. 5). This means that limited options in energy access threaten development. Therefore, constrained access or a complete lack of access to energy means that one is deprived of essential services such as heating and cooking. It also extends to other aspects of individual and collective development such as access to information, health services, education, and even the ability to participate in decision-making processes (González-Eguino, 2015, p. 380).

Secondly, the definitions emphasise the need to meet the demand for energy services (UNDP, 2018, pp. 2–3). The goal is not limited to energy consumption but extends to energy services from various sources. This focus exemplifies the context specificity and subjective nature of energy poverty (Bhattacharyya, 2012, pp. 260–261). This means that people from different regions, countries, and urban settings need different amounts of energy to meet their basic needs and what constitutes a need will vary (Bhattacharyya, 2012, pp. 260–261). For instance, low-income urban households might not need the same amount of energy as medium-high income households due to the lack of luxury appliances that consume a great deal of energy, such as washing machines and dishwashers.

Thirdly, the focus on a reliable energy supply suggests the level of technological investment and sustained maintenance required in the sector (González-Eguino, 2015, p. 380). Well-maintained energy infrastructure will ideally not be subject to breakdowns, safety concerns or operational health hazards. Also embedded in the definitions provided is the proviso that energy technologies should not be detrimental to the environment. It is pertinent for technological solutions intended to reduce energy poverty to consider their environmental impacts. Furthermore, since the use of energy merely *supports* economic and human development, the availability of energy as a resource does not guarantee in any absolute sense that there will be development (González-Eguino, 2015, p. 381).

In this context it has been held that energy poverty cannot be delinked from the broader, more complex problem of poverty in general, and that access to energy infrastructure could help advance development (González-Eguino, 2015, p. 378). The flip side is that energy poverty alleviation in developing nations and the provision of universal access to modern energy could increase energy demand and therefore CO_2 emissions – especially in cities. The potential impact of low(er)-carbon transitions in countries where fossil fuel is cheap and accessible is self-evident. It follows that energy poverty inevitably triggers questions about energy vulnerability and energy (in) justice, from which a successful low(er)-carbon transition project at city level cannot escape. Chipango's research, for example, explains with reference to the Zimbabwean context that the electricity grid and access to electricity "are embedded in institutional and policy contexts that favour certain outcomes, geographies and social groups" (Chipango, 2022, p. 2).

We are of the view that systemic change in what has been called "a city's energy metabolism" requires a series of initiatives if dramatic reductions are to be achieved in the demand for energy inputs to meet the present and future human and economic needs. This means, for example, that a systemic transformation of city transport would have to involve more than the electrification of vehicles, the increased use of shared mobility (transit services) or cycling. It would also require a shift in the need for mobility to provide access to parts of the city in addition to changes in the energy sources needed to power the different modes of transportation. It would typically also need an enabling local law and policy framework that directs city planning (spatial and strategic) and provides for financial incentives and disincentives towards low(er)-carbon activities and development trajectories.

4 Law and policy perspectives on cities for low-carbon transition in the sub-Saharan and North African contexts

Considering the internationally celebrated (potential) role of sub-national authorities in global climate governance and the low-carbon transition, on the one hand, and the opportunities and limitations created by energy poverty, on the other, what is the status in law? To the extent that the law regulates the behaviour of all people and industries existing and operating in cities, it is important to question if and how the law is directed at city-level involvement in low-carbon transitions. For the purposes of this chapter, we confine ourselves to the dictates of the African regional and domestic legal systems applicable to South Africa, Uganda, and Morocco.

In terms of continent-wide policy, the Convention of the African Energy Commission entered into force in 2006. Although this was more than 15 years ago, the Commission acknowledged at the time that Africa was experiencing energy poverty and that this was constraining the industrial development of the continent despite the extensive potential for developing both conventional and renewable energy sources (preamble of the Convention). In June 2022, the African Union adopted the African Union Climate Change and Resilient Development Strategy and Action Plan 2022–2032 with a prominent vision for 'energy justice' and energy security with specific emphasis on decarbonising and detoxifying existing energy systems and low-carbon industrialisation across the continent.

In 2015, the Heads of State and Governments of the African Union adopted Agenda 2063. It sets out a vision for "an integrated, prosperous and peaceful Africa, driven by its own citizens and representing a dynamic force in the international arena". In connection with the low-carbon transition, Agenda 2063 for example emphasises the implementation of the Grand Inga Dam Project as a key development priority and a means to support regional power pools and help transform the continent from traditional to modern sources of energy (African Union Commission, 2015).[3] For an in-depth discussion on the legal and policy framework governing Africa's energy transition, refer to the chapter by Addaney and Kengni, in this volume.

In terms of the commitment to environmental protection we know from the African regional legal order that the protection of the environment has been an essential part of African social, cultural and religious life for many generations (for a detailed chronological analysis of the recognition and development of environmental rights, see Addaney et al., 2020). It is also an essential part of human rights protection in Africa. As observed by the African Commission on Human and Peoples' Rights "collective rights, environmental rights, and economic and social rights are essential elements of human rights in Africa" (*SERAC v Nigeria* Comm No. 155/96 (2001), para. 68). It is of significance that environmental rights are explicitly recognised at the African regional level. For instance, the African Charter on Human and Peoples' Rights proclaims the right of African peoples to "a general satisfactory environment favourable to their development" (article 24 of the African Charter on Human and Peoples' Rights, 1981). Regionally, the Southern African Development Community launched its Climate Change Strategy and Action Plan in 2015 (SADC, 2015). According to this Plan, there is a need for harmonised and coordinated regional and national action to address and respond to the impacts of climate change, in line with global and continental objectives (SADC, 2015, p. 12).[4] In North Africa the Arab Maghreb Union (AMU) does not have specific treaties or conventions that speak specifically to environmental rights (AMU, 2022) but the Constitutive Treaty of the AMU recognises the need for effective cooperation in political, economic and cultural spheres and a continuous

---

3 The Grand Inga Dam Project forms part of the Flagship Projects of Agenda 2063. It is a project to be implemented under the so-called Transport, Infrastructure and Energy Initiatives. The project seeks to support current regional power pools and their combined service to transform Africa from traditional to modern sources of energy and ensure access of all people in Africa to clean and affordable electricity.

4 This is in line with Article 12 of the provisions of the Protocol on Environmental Management for Sustainable Development, the SADC Region is mandated to develop legislative and administrative measures to enhance adaptation to the impacts of climate change, bearing in mind the diverse and gender differentiated levels of vulnerabilities and to take appropriate voluntary climate change mitigation measures.

complementarity in various fields, including those of natural and strategic resources (AMU, 2022).[5]

When one considers the African Charter on the Values and Principles of Decentralisation, Local Governance and Local Development (2014) it becomes evident that the African Union is committed to the decentralisation and devolution of power. The Charter seeks to promote the values and principles of decentralisation, local governance and local development in Africa to improve the livelihoods of all peoples on the continent (preamble of the Charter). This places local government at the centre of developmental efforts. As such, countries in sub-Saharan and North Africa have experienced meaningful state reform to enable local governments to play an active role in development, especially in the energy sector. For example, in South Africa and Uganda we see cities taking the initiative in the uptake of renewable energy programmes.[6] Although the decentralised gains of the North African region have been described as incomplete, partial and limited by concerns related to regime security and patronage, Morocco has seen significant success in the decentralisation of energy governance (for a full discussion of decentralisation efforts in the Middle East and North Africa region, see Carter, Payne and Springborg, 2020, p. 2).[7]

In terms of environmental and other constitutional rights, the need to address climate change, and the process of energy and local government law reform in the countries mentioned, we know for example that all three countries are signatories of international agreements that promote a low-carbon energy transition. All three countries have also taken steps to domesticate these international commitments – an elaborate discussion that falls beyond the purview of this chapter.

Based on the above, it is possible to argue that, in principle, the existing regional, sub-regional and national law frameworks promote a low-carbon energy transition in the sub-Saharan and North African regions. The following section considers specific city-level legal responses and institutional factors that currently help facilitate the low-carbon energy transition. This is done with specific reference to the cities of Kampala (Uganda), Cape Town (South Africa) and Rabat (Morocco).

5 Similarly, the Charter of the League of Arab States also does not explicitly mention environmental management as a priority area. It could be argued that since the Charter was adopted in 1945, many environmental concerns might not have been at the forefront of their developmental agenda. See the Charter of the League of Arab States (1945).

6 In some instances, such as in the case of the City of Cape Town, cities are seen to be taking initiative and having better developed strategies for low-carbon energy transition than those of national government. See discussion under 5.2 below.

7 See, discussion under 5.3 below.

5 City-level law, policy responses and institutional factors in Kampala, Cape Town and Rabat

As suggested earlier, globally, sub-national governments are increasingly adopting a leading role in climate change mitigation and adaptation, including attempts to decarbonise urban electricity generation and use (Webb *et al.*, 2020: pp. 7–8). For instance, Renewable Energy Now (REN21) reported that in 2020 at least 834 cities in 72 countries had targets (through city-level policies and strategic documents) to achieve 100 per cent renewable energy in heat, electricity and transport (REN 21, 2021). While some cities have the financial capability to invest in infrastructure to purchase renewable energy, others (especially in Africa) do not (IRENA, 2016). As such, African cities, through the city authorities, are involved in decarbonisation processes in various ways, including through experimenting in and piloting new electricity service models, through municipal utilities or bulk-buying electricity for redistribution in cities (Bulkeley, McGuirk and Dowling, 2016).

In what follows, we briefly consider city-level law, policy responses and institutional factors for a low-carbon energy transition in Cape Town, Kampala and Rabat. These city-specific discussions are based on research that has been conducted through desktop research to show only how a few cities in the sub-Saharan and North African region are taking the initiative in achieving a low-carbon energy transition. While an extensive research project that investigates every single country and city from these regions would be necessary to arrive at conclusive findings, our research on the three selected cities, yielded interesting insights for the purposes of this chapter.

5.1 Kampala

Kampala, Uganda's capital city (and largest urban centre), has approximately 1.7 million inhabitants (Uganda Bureau of Statistics, 2017). Kampala is also the country's economic hub, which accounts for 80 per cent of Uganda's commercial and industrial activities. It generates approximately 65 per cent of the national GDP a year (Uganda Bureau of Statistics, 2017). This means that Kampala has considerable energy needs to grow the economy. In keeping up with its commitments under the Paris Agreement, the city unveiled the Kampala Climate Change Action Strategy in 2016 (KCCA, 2016). The Strategy was developed through a transversal and participatory approach involving all stakeholders (KCCA, 2016). This Strategy includes a target of 50MW of renewable energy generation in the city. This is a significant amount, considering that it is several times higher than Uganda's total small-scale decentralised renewable generation capacity (KCCA, 2016). Moreover, provision is being made to achieve a broader energy transition through the electrification of the transport system (Webb *et al.*, 2020, p. 25).

The Kampala city operations fall under the Kampala Capital City Authority (KCCA) (REN21, 2021, p. 143). The KCCA is one of the pioneer signatories to the Covenant of Mayors in sub-Saharan Africa (having joined in 2015). The city developed its first energy and climate action plan in 2016 (KCCA, 2016). This plan frames KCCA's efforts to further the deployment of renewables through assessing the local renewable energy potential, promoting the implementation of a feed-in tariff system, supporting the city's green economy and reducing the use of individual motorised transport in favour of non-motorised mobility and green and public transport (KCCA, 2016). The KCCA's energy strategy is consistent with the Draft National Energy Policy of 2019, which promotes non-hydro power renewable generation sources to diversify the energy mix (Ministry of Energy and Mineral Development, 2019). This objective of diversifying the energy mix in Uganda is to mitigate the country's over-reliance on hydropower, which accounted for approximately 90.5 per cent of the national energy supply in 2018–2019 (Ministry of Energy and Mineral Development, 2019). Kampala does not have any specific by-laws that regulate or promote renewable energy but seems to be using the KCCA in conjunction with the Draft National Energy Policy to do so.

5.2 Cape Town

Cape Town is South Africa's second-largest economic hub and contributes an average of 9.8 per cent of the national economic output (Western Cape Government, 2017).[8] The city has significant energy needs and has adopted an active leadership role in renewable energy deployment. The City values technology change, robust energy governance systems and engagement with all the relevant stakeholders (including the national government, the private sector and civil society) in contributing to the energy transition (SEA, 2020, pp. 49, 142). The City's long history of working towards providing renewable energy includes forming the energy and climate change unit in 2006.[9] This unit grew to be a fully staffed Energy and Climate Change Unit over the next ten years and has been given further impetus by the inclusion of energy and climate goals in the City's Integrated Development Plan from 2008 (SEA, 2020).

South Africa had no national standards for solar PV on buildings by 2013. Still, during that period, the City of Cape Town published guidelines for the legal installation of distributed renewable energy use in commercial and residential buildings (City of Cape Town, 2018b). This led to the City of Cape Town reportedly having the

8 The largest economic hub in South Africa is Johannesburg, contributing 17 per cent of the country's GDP.

9 Cape Town's local sustainable energy approach mirrored that of the National White Paper on Energy of 1998, with a strong emphasis on energy poverty, environmental protection, including climate mitigation and adaptation.

country's highest number of registered rooftop solar PV systems by 2019 (SALGA, 2020, p. 13). Between 2011 and 2020 Cape Town approved the installation of approximately 42 MW of rooftop solar PV and 0.6 MW of city buildings (SALGA, 2020, p. 13). The significance of this programme is that the installed capacity fed into the local electricity network and significantly reduced overreliance on coal-fired electricity from the national grid (SEA, 2020, pp. 67–69).

The City of Cape Town developed the Cape Town Energy 2040 Vision in 2015. This strategic document was developed through an extensive process of stakeholder engagement and set city-wide targets for improving energy access, promoting energy efficiency and reducing GHG emissions (City of Cape Town, 2015a). The Energy 2040 Vision is significant in several ways. Firstly, it will achieve 500 MW of renewable energy capacity by 2040 (City of Cape Town, 2015a). Secondly, to effect this target the City restructured its institutional organogram and combined the energy and climate division with the electricity generation and distribution division (City of Cape Town, 2015a). The combination of these divisions established the Energy and Climate Change Directorate (City of Cape Town, 2015b). Finally, these changes signalled the City's intention to expand its role in electricity supply, resulting in a court case in which the City challenged the National Energy Regulator of South Africa (NERSA) to enable it to purchase its electricity from independent power producers without having first to obtain a ministerial determination to this effect (*City of Cape Town v NERSA and Minister of Energy* unreported case number 51765/17 of 11 August 2020). Although the judgement was not in favour of the City, the attempt to take such a step displayed an advanced level of readiness and commitment to transition to low(er)-carbon energy (for a complete analysis of this case, see Moyo, 2021).

In terms of local legislation, the City of Cape Town has an Electricity Supply By-law of 2010 (City of Cape Town, 2010) and the Electricity Supply Amendment By-law of 2017 (City of Cape Town, 2017). The Electricity Supply By-law makes provision for the supply of electricity from licenced entities but does not provide for the sources from where it must be generated (section 20 of the Electricity Supply By-law of 2010). The same applies to the Electricity Supply Amendment By-law of 2017. It also makes provision for matters related to the electricity supply but still perceives the City of Cape Town as a reseller of electricity only. Neither of the two by-laws refers to renewable energy or its use.

The City of Cape Town also honours its international commitments to climate action. It is a signatory to the Mexico City Pact, the Carbon Climate Registry, the Covenant of Mayors in sub-Saharan Africa and the C40 Cities Leadership Programme (City of Cape Town, 2020), for example. Furthermore, the City has boldly committed to achieving carbon neutrality by 2050. These commitments are further translated into a policy vision through the City of Cape Town's Integrated Development Plan for

2017–2022 (City of Cape Town, 2018a).[10] It would seem that over the past couple of years, the City has put in place strategic plans and strengthened its institutional capacity to transition to low-carbon pathways.

5.3 Rabat

Alongside Cairo, Rabat is the leader in energy transition in North Africa (for a detailed discussion of the energy transition in Morocco, see Choukri, Naddami and Hayani, 2017; Schinke and Klawitter, 2017; Carafa, Frisari and Auktor, 2016; Komendantova *et al.*, 2012; Schinko and Komendantova, 2016). Rabat leads the region in transitioning to low-carbon pathways in terms of installed capacity from renewable energy sources and in advocating a clean-energy transition in and outside Morocco (Liga, 2021, p. 67). Although Rabat does not have a specific by-law on renewable energy, its progressive action can be traced to 2009 when the city adopted its National Energy Strategy and projected 42 per cent of installed power capacity from renewable energy by 2020 (Ministry of Energy, Mines, Water and Environment in Morocco, 2010). Currently, 31 per cent of Rabat's electricity comes from renewable energy. This is one of the highest percentages of renewable energy among the countries in the entire MENA region (Liga, 2021, p. 68).

Morocco has reaffirmed its commitment to the Paris Agreement by presenting a revision of its nationally determined contributions (NDCs) to reduce greenhouse gas emissions by 45.5 per cent by 2030. This essentially supports targets and programmes designed by Rabat to reduce GHGs and to promote the transition to renewable energy. Furthermore, there has been strong institutional support from the Moroccan Agency for Solar Energy (MASEN), now the Moroccan Agency for Sustainable Energy, the National Electricity Regulatory Authority of Morocco (ANRE), the Institute for Research on Solar Energy and New Energies (IRESEN), and the Moroccan Agency for Energy Efficiency (AMEE) to facilitate the promotion of clean energy resources (Liga, 2021, pp. 79–80). IRESEN, a leading research organisation in renewable energy, has been vital to the growth of the renewable energy transition in Rabat. Beyond Rabat, IRESEN has also reinforced innovation in renewable energy across Morocco by developing the first innovation network on the African continent, called the FARABI Network (IRESEN, 2021). The network is built around regional platforms for testing and research and training in renewable energy. Furthermore, this territorial network is linked with universities and educational institutions which aid in developing mechanisms for transferring knowledge to local industries (IRESEN, 2021). It is promising

10 The IDP is further broken down in sectoral plans such as the Comprehensive Integrated Transport Plan, the Cape Town Metropolitan Spatial Development Framework, and the Cape Town Energy and Climate Change Strategy, among others.

that with the support of these institutions, Rabat continues to be capacitated to transition to low-carbon pathways through the use of renewable energy.

6 Way forward in support of African cities for the low-carbon transition

There is evidence of mounting international reliance on city-level authorities around the world to actively assist in global climate governance and the accompanying transitions to be made; including the low-carbon transition. The three case studies from Southern and Northern Africa highlight that at least some cities are taking the initiative to help champion the low-carbon energy transition through local planning and experimentation. We glean from this that cities are potentially valuable actors in energy governance and that some are progressively exploring ways to transition towards low(er)-carbon pathways. In Africa in particular, this is being done in the face of serious levels of energy poverty and the knock-on effects it has on social development and efforts to better protect the environment.

Implicitly this chapter focused on the strength of local level (sub-national) law and policy – a power (local governance authority) that cannot be taken for granted as it sits entrenched in varying systems of domestic law. It is our view that when it gets to the legally entrenched powers that city authorities have in relation to energy governance, one should be mindful of constitutional, resource and other constraints that local governments often experience. There is accordingly much reason to be excited about the local initiatives towards a low(er)-carbon energy transition in the African countries that were considered.

It would seem that some of the areas where cities (at least cities in Africa) may most evidently need support to ensure a just and fair low(er)-carbon transition in the short to medium term (in terms of access, availability and affordability) are financial and technical expertise in combination with good intergovernmental relations. Such support is arguably to be provided by other organs of state (e.g. the central authorities), the private sector, international development agencies, city-to-city peer learning platforms and organisations etc. In our view, room exists for supportive and well targeted national policies, standards and realistic and flexible international and regional initiatives directed at life and governance in cities. While it has not been explored in-depth, the consistent work of global city networks in this area is commendable.

Many of the aspects of the urbanisation-energy transition-development nexus could not be covered in this chapter, especially those aspects that fall beyond the purview of the law and policy frameworks. It is suggested that future research in this field may explore the following in greater detail:

- The manner(s) in which international urban policy, multilevel energy law and international climate change law seem to converge in terms of ambition and envisioned future outcomes;
- The importance of redesigning urban landscapes and areas rich in urban ecosystems along the lines of energy performance indicators and environmental criteria to achieve the minimisation of city-level energy consumption at no or lower cost e.g. in the built environment;
- The role and cost of renewables – especially in fast-growing medium-sized towns as opposed to large metropolitan areas; and
- The need for climate finance, urban infrastructure investment and revised supply-chain management standards in the clockwork and financing of local governance.

References

Acuto, M. and Leffel, B., 2020. Understanding the global ecosystem of city networks. *Urban Studies*, 58(9), pp. 1–17.

Addaney, M., Moyo, C.G. and Ramakhula, T., 2020. Human rights, regional law and the environment in africa: legal and conceptual foundations. In: M. Addaney and A.O. Jegede, eds., 2020. *Human rights and the environment under African Union law.* Cham: Palgrave Macmillan, pp. 3–24.

African Union Commission, 2015. *Flagship projects of Agenda 2063*. Available at: https://au.int/agenda2063/flagship-projects (Accessed 25 February 2022).

AMU (Arab Maghreb Union), 2022. *Home page*. Available at: https://maghrebarabe.org/ (Accessed 25 February 2022).

Aust, H.P., 2019. The shifting role of cities in the global climate change regime: from Paris to Pittsburgh and back?. *RECIEL*, 28(1), pp. 57–66.

Aust, H.P. and Du Plessis, A., eds., 2019. *The globalisation of urban governance: legal perspectives on Sustainable Development Goal 11.* London and New York, NY: Routledge.

Aust, H.P. and Nijman, J.E., eds., 2021. *Research handbook on international law and cities.* Cheltenham: Edward Elgar Publishing.

Bansard, J.S., Pattberg, P.H. and Wilderberg, O., 2017. Cities to the rescue? Assessing the performance of transnational municipal networks in global climate governance. *International Environmental Agreements: Politics, Law and Economics*, 17, pp. 229–246.

Barber, B., 2013. *Democracy and climate change: how cities can do what states can't*. Available at: https://www.humansandnature.org/democracy-benjamin-barber [Accessed 10 February 2022].

Bhattacharyya, S.C., 2012. Energy access programmes and sustainable development: a critical review and analysis. *Energy for Sustainable Development*, 16(3), pp. 260–271.

Bizikova, L., Robinson, J.B. and Cohen, S., 2007. Linking climate change and sustainable development at the local level. *Climate Policy*, 7(4), pp. 271–277.

Boardman B., 2010. Liberalisation and fuel poverty. In: I. Rutledge and P. Wright, eds., 2010. *UK energy policy and the end of market fundamentalism*. Oxford: Oxford University Press, pp. 355–380.

Brenner, N. and Schmid, C., 2018. Elements for a new epistemology of the urban. In: S. Hall and R. Burdett, eds., 2018. *The SAGE handbook of the 21st century city.* London: SAGE, pp. 47–68.
Bulkeley, H., 2019. *Managing environmental and energy transitions in cities: state of the art and emerging perspectives (Background paper for an OECD/EC workshop on 7 June 2019 within the workshop series 'Managing environmental and energy transitions for regions and cities', Paris).* Available at: https://www.oecd.org/cfe/regionaldevelopment/Bulkeley-2019-Managing-Transition-Cities.pdf (Accessed on 17 February 2022).
Bulkeley, H., McGuirk, P. and Dowling, R., 2016. Making a smart city for the smart grid? Urban material politics of actualising smart electricity networks. *Environment and Planning A: Economy and Space*, 48(9), pp. 1709–1726.
C40 Cities (no date) *Working together: global aggregation of city climate commitments.* Available at: https://c40-production-images.s3.amazonaws.com/researches/images/24_Working_Together_Global_Aggregation.original.pdf?1411483385 [Accessed 21 February 2022].
C40 Cities (2022) *About C40.* Available at: https://www.c40.org/about-c40/ (Accessed on 18 January 2022).
Calderon, C. and Calderon, J.K., 2012. Modelling frameworks for delivering low-carbon cities: advocating a normalized practice. *Building Research and Information*, 40(4), pp. 504–517.
Carafa, L., Frisari, G. and Auktor, G.V., 2016. Electricity transition in the Middle East and North Africa: a de-risking governance approach. *Journal of Cleaner Production*, 128, pp. 34–47.
Carter, L., Payne, R. and Springborg, R., 2020. *Comparative analysis of MENA subnational governance: governance integration for stabilization and resilience in the Middle East and North Africa (GISR MENA).* Available at: https://pdf.usaid.gov/pdf_docs/PA00X83Z.pdf (Accessed 27 February 2022).
Chipango, E.F., 2022. Political ecologies of energy poverty in Zimbabwe. *GeoJournal*, (January).
Choukri, K., Naddami, A. and Hayani, S., 2017. Renewable energy in emergent countries: lessons from energy transition in Morocco. *Energy, Sustainabilty and Society*, 7(25), pp. 1–11.
City of Cape Town, 2010. *Electricity supply by-law of 2010.* Available at: https://resource.capetown.gov.za/documentcentre/Documents/Bylaws%20and%20policies/Electricity%20Supply%20By-law.pdf (Accessed 3 March 2022).
City of Cape Town, 2015a. *Cape Town Energy 2040 Vision and associated energy and carbon targets.* Available at: https://resource.capetown.gov.za/documentcentre/Documents/Graphics%20and%20educational%20material/Cape_Town_Energy2040_Vision_pres_2015-09.pdf (Accessed 23 February 2022).
City of Cape Town, 2015b. *Cape Town State of Energy 2015 Report.* Available at: https://africancityenergy.org/uploads/resource_22.pdf (Accessed 23 February 2022).
City of Cape Town, 2017. *Electricity supply amendment by-law of 2017* . Available at: https://resource.capetown.gov.za/documentcentre/Documents/Bylaws%20and%20policies/Electricity%20Supply%20Amendment%20By-law.pdf (Accessed 3 March 2022).
City of Cape Town, 2018a. *Comprehensive Integrated Transport Plan 2018-2023.* Available at: https://tdacontenthubstore.blob.core.windows.net/resources/fd3ddc0d-b459-4d26-bb01-7f689d7a36eb.pdf (Accessed 23 February 2022).
City of Cape Town, 2018b. *Rooftop PV: guidelines for safe and legal installations in Cape Town.* Available at: https://www.westerncape.gov.za/energy-security-game-changer/files/atoms/files/Energy-PV-Brochure.pdf (Accessed 23 February 2022).
City of Cape Town, 2020. *Draft City of Cape Town Climate Change Strategy.* Available at: http://www.capetown.gov.za/councilonline/_layouts/OpenDocument/OpenDocument.aspx?DocumentId=509d02cf-c744-4aba-b913-6fc05e2dfeea (Accessed 23 February 2022).
De Sherbinin, A., Schiller, A. and Pulsipher, A., 2007. The vulnerability of global cities to climate hazards. *Environment and Urbanisation*, 19(1), pp. 39–64.
Energy Cities, 2014. *30 cities' proposals for the energy transition of cities and towns.* Available at: https://energy-cities.eu/publication/30-energy-cities-proposals-for-the-energy-transition-of-cities-and-towns/ (Accessed 23 February 2022).

Fuhr, H.H., 2018. The role of cities in multi-level climate governance: local climate policies and the 1.5 C target. *Current Opinion in Environmental Sustainability*, 30, pp. 1–6.

González-Eguino, M., 2015. Energy poverty: an overview. *Renewable and Sustainable Energy Reviews*, 47, pp. 377–385.

Haase, D. *et al*., 2017. Greening cities – to be socially inclusive? About the alleged paradox of society and ecology in cities. *Habitat International*, 64, pp. 41–48.

IEA (International Energy Agency), 2010. *Energy poverty: how to make modern energy access universal?* Paris: OECD.

IPCC (Intergovernmental Panel on Climate Change), 2014. *5th Assessment Report*. Geneva: IPCC.

IPCC (Intergovernmental Panel on Climate Change), 2021. *6th Assessment Report*. Geneva: IPCC.

IRENA (International Renewable Energy Agency), 2016. *Renewable energy in cities*. Abu Dhabi: International Renewable Energy Agency.

IRESEN (Institute for Research on Solar Energy and New Energies), 2021. *Green InnoBoost 2.0*. Available at: https://www.iresen.org/ (Accessed 23 February 2022).

KCCA (Kampala Capital City Authority), 2016. *Energy and climate profile*. Available at: https://www.kcca.go.ug/uDocs/Energy%20and%20Climate%20Profile.pdf (Accessed 27 February 2022).

Komendantova, N. *et al*., 2012. Perception of risks in renewable energy projects: the case of concentrated solar power in North Africa', *Energy Policy*, 40, pp. 103–109.

Kotzé, L.J., 2021. Cities, the Anthropocene and earth system law. In: H.P. Aust and J.E. Nijman, eds., 2021. *Research handbook on international law and cities*. Cheltenham: Edward Elgar, pp. 354–367.

Leck, H. and Roberts, D., 2015. What lies beneath: understanding the invisible aspects of municipal climate change governance', *Environmental Sustainability*, 13, pp. 61–67.

Liga, A., 2021. Managing climate change and mapping an energy transition in North Africa. In: K. Mezran and A. Sanguini, eds., 2021. *North Africa 2030: what the future holds for the region*. Milan: Italian Institute for International Political Studies, pp. 65–80.

Lin, J., 2018. *Governing climate change: global cities and transnational lawmaking*. Cambridge: Cambridge University Press.

Local Governments for Sustainability, 2022. *Home page* [Online]. https://www.iclei.org/ (Accessed on 18 January 2022).

Mahumane, G. and Mulder, P., 2021. Urbanisation of urban poverty? The case of Mozambique. *Renewable and Sustainable Energy Reviews*, 159, pp. 1–37.

Middlemiss, L. and Gillard, R., 2015. Fuel poverty from the bottom-up: characterising household energy vulnerability through the lived experience of the fuel poor. *Energy Research and Social Science*, 6, pp. 146–154.

Ministry of Energy and Mineral Development, 2019. *Draft National Energy Policy*. Available at: https://www.energyandminerals.go.ug/site/assets/files/1081/draft_revised_energy_policy_-_11_10_2019-1_1.pdf (Accessed 27 February 2022).

Ministry of Energy, Mines, Water and Environment in Morocco, 2010. *Law No. 13-09 on Renewable Energy* [Online]. Available at: http://www.mem.gov.ma/SiteAssets/PdfDocumentation/LoiEnergiesRenouvelables.pdf (Accessed 23 February 2022).

Moyo, C.G., 2021. Strained relations in the provision of electricity services: *City of Cape Town v National Energy Regulator of South Africa and Minister of Energy. Southern African Public Law*, 36(2), pp1–9.

Nishida, Y. and Hua, Y., 2011. Motivating stakeholders to deliver change: Tokyo's cap-and-trade program. *Building Research and Information*, 39(5), pp. 518–533.

Parajuli, R., 2011. Access to energy in Mid/Far west region-Nepal from the perspective of energy poverty. *Renewable Energy*, 36(9), pp. 2299–2304.

REN21 (Renewable Energy Now), 2021. *Renewables in cities: 2021 global status report*. Paris: REN21 Secretariat.

Schinke, B. and Klawitter, J., 2017. *Energy for the future-evaluating different electricity generation technologies against selected performance characteristics and stakeholder preferences: insights from the case study*

Morocco. Available at: https://germanwatch.org/sites/default/files/publication/18876.pdf (Accessed 23 February 2022).

Schinko, T. and Komendantova, N., 2016. De-risking investment into concentrated solar power in North Africa: impacts on the costs of electricity generation. *Renewable Energy*, 92(C), pp. 262–272.

Sen, A.K., 2001. *Development as freedom*. Oxford: Oxford University Press.

SADC (Southern African Development Community), 2015. *SADC Climate Change Strategy and Action Plan*. Available at: https://www.sadc.int/files/5615/9126/1263/SADC_Climate_Change_Strategy_and_Action_Plan-English.pdf (Accessed 25 February 2022).

SALGA (South African Local Government Association), 2020. *Status of small scale embedded generation in South African municipalities*. Available at: https://www.sseg.org.za/status-of-sseg-2020 (Accessed 23 February 2022).

SEA (Sustainable Energy Africa), 2020. *State of energy in South African cities*. Available at: https://www.sustainable.org.za/uploads/resources/resource_84.pdf (Accessed 27 February 2022).

Sullivan, R., Gouldson, A. and Webber, P., 2013. Funding low carbon cities: local perspectives on opportunities and risks. *Climate Policy*, 13(4), pp. 514–529.

Swilling, M. and Annecke, E., 2012. *Just transitions: explorations of sustainability in an unfair world.* Claremont: UCT Press.

Uganda Bureau of Statistics, 2017. *The national population and housing census 2014 – area specific profile series*. Available at: https://www.ubos.org/wp-content/uploads/publications/2014CensusProfiles/KAMPALA-KCCA.pdf (Accessed 27 February 2022).

UCLG (United Cities and Local Governments), 2019. *The Durban Political Declaration issued at the UCLG World Summit of Local and Regional Leaders*. Available at: https://www.durban2019.uclg.org/sites/default/files/2019-11/UCLG_TheDurbanPoliticalDeclaration_EN_.pdf (Accessed 21 February 2022).

UCLG (United Cities and Local Government), 2022. *Home page* [Online]. Available at: https://www.uclg.org/ (Accessed 18 January 2022).

UN-Habitat, 2020. *World Cities Report 2020: the value of sustainable urbanization*. Nairobi: UN-Habitat.

UNDP (United Nations Development Program), 2018. *Policy Brief #8: Interlinkages among energy, poverty and inequalities*. New York: United Nations.

UNEP (United Nations Environment Programme) and UN-Habitat, 2021. *Global environmental outlook for cities: towards green and just cities report*. Nairobi: UNEP.

Vaughter, P. and Pham, N., eds., 2021. *Tackling climate action at the local level: education for sustainable development projects*. Tokyo: UNU-IAS.

Vermaak, C., Kohler, M. and Rhodes DB., 2009. Developing energy-based poverty indicators for South Africa', *Journal of Interdisciplinary Economics*, 21(2), pp. 163–195.

Webb, M. *et al*., 2020. *Urban energy and the climate emergency: achieving decarbonisation via decentralisation and digitalization*. Available at: https://urbantransitions.global/wp-content/uploads/2020/03/Urban_Energy_and_the_Climate_Emergency_web_FINAL.pdf (Accessed 23 February 2022).

Western Cape Government, 2017. *Socio-economic profile: City of Cape Town*. Available at: https://www.westerncape.gov.za/assets/departments/treasury/Documents/Socio-economic-profiles/2017/city_of_cape_town_2017_socioeconomic_profile_sep-lg_-_26_january_2018.pdf (Accessed 27 February 2022).

WMO (World Meteorological Organization), 1996. *Climate and Urban Development*. Geneva: World Meteorological Organization.

Giuseppe Bellantuono, Lee Godden, Hanri Mostert, Hannah Wiseman, Hao Zhang

Conclusion: Legal Knowledge for the Low-Carbon Transition

Abstract: The chapters of the Handbook confirm that decarbonization is a context-dependent process. Goals, institutions, and tools are selected through decision-making processes that reflect the architectures of each legal system. As discussed in the Introduction, the legal feasibility of the low-carbon transition entails focusing on reforms that exploit existing complementarities and harness the capabilities of each institutional level. In this concluding chapter, we summarize the insights offered by the Handbook on both perspectives. They are arranged according to six broad areas. At the macro level, we ask how meaningful it is to distinguish the legal pathways in developed and developing countries and which signs of incremental or radical legal change can be detected. We then move to the meso level to discuss the allocation of competencies and the regulation of cross-border and decentralized infrastructures. Finally, we focus on the micro level with the analysis of legal tools. We conclude with some reflections on the meanings of energy justice, an issue that cuts across the other areas.

1 Context first (and quantification later)

The latest assessment by the IPCC (2022: p. 3–22) shows that keeping the global temperature within safe limits is possible only if steep reductions in GHG emissions are undertaken by 2030. In 2010, the required emission cuts were, on average, 2% per year up to 2030. From 2020, the required cuts rose to more than 7% per year for the 1.5°C target (Höhne et al., 2020). The world lost many decades: global emissions kept rising, and only a few countries (mostly in the Global North) were able to reduce

Giuseppe Bellantuono is Professor of Comparative Law at the University of Trento, Faculty of Law, Italy.
Lee Godden formerly was Professor at the Centre for Resources, Energy and Environmental Law, Melbourne Law School, The University of Melbourne, Australia.
Hanri Mostert is the DST/NRF SARChI Research Chair for Mineral Law in Africa and Professor of Law at the University of Cape Town, South Africa.
Hannah J. Wiseman is a Professor of Law, Professor and Wilson Faculty Fellow in the College of Earth and Mineral Sciences, and Institutes of Energy and the Environment Co-funded Faculty Member, Penn-State Law, United States.
Hao Zhang is Associate Professor at the Faculty of Law, The Chinese University of Hong Kong.

https://doi.org/10.1515/9783110752403-042

them, although not in all sectors (Roelfsema et al., 2020; Stoddard et al., 2021; Minx et al., 2021; Lamb et al., 2022). Multiple causes prevented energy systems from moving toward new equilibria with lower shares of fossil fuels and lower demand for energy services. One such cause has been the inability to enact and implement regulatory frameworks that foster the low-carbon transition. The most urgent question is how those frameworks can be quickly introduced. This Handbook was grounded on the hypothesis that the legal pathways of decarbonization are highly varied across countries and regions. Reasons for such variety must be understood as shifting investments toward low-carbon technologies and redressing the old and new injustices of energy systems.

The chapters of the Handbook confirm that decarbonization is a context-dependent process. Goals, institutions, and tools are selected through decision-making processes that reflect the architectures of each legal system. As discussed in the Introduction, the legal feasibility of the low-carbon transition entails focusing on reforms that exploit existing complementarities and harness the capabilities of each institutional level. This means that the only chance for an accelerated transition is an almost perfect match between institutional contexts and climate policies. Establishing a new climate institution, creating a new coordination mechanism, or choosing a specific policy instrument may or may not advance the transition, depending on how good the match is. Not surprisingly, the social science literature depicts governance mechanisms, policies, and institutions as triggers, drivers, or barriers (Moore et al., 2021). Each of these roles is influenced by the many institutional interconnections shaping climate policy effectiveness. Of course, legal factors do not work in isolation. The institutional context maintains a two-way relationship with technological, economic, and social changes. Such interplay can foster additional variety in decarbonization pathways. We argue that both an internal and an external perspective are needed. The former allows us to reflect on how legal systems react to the climate change challenge. The latter allows us to connect legal knowledge to results and methods in other disciplines.

In this concluding chapter, we summarize the insights offered by the Handbook on both perspectives. They are arranged according to six broad areas (Table 5). The factors we underline are not the ones usually referred to by the social science literature. And they might not be easily amenable to quantification. Given the unsatisfactory outcomes of decarbonization strategies so far, they should not be dismissed as legalistic details. We hope they help readers see the many avenues for future research on the institutional contexts of the low-carbon transition. We start from the macro level and ask how meaningful it is to distinguish the legal pathways in developed and developing countries and which signs of incremental or radical legal change can be detected. We then move to the meso level to discuss the allocation of competencies and the regulation of cross-border and decentralized infrastructures. Finally, we focus on the micro level with the analysis of legal tools. We conclude with some reflections on the meanings of energy justice, an issue that cuts across the other areas.

Table 5: The variety of legal pathways of decarbonisation.

Level of analysis	Areas	Variety of legal pathways	Interplay with non-legal factors
Macro	Developed-developing countries	Exploit supranational institutions to fill gaps in national regulatory frameworks Ensure RES support is compatible with partially deregulated market structures Ensure market-driven innovation is compatible with environmental protection	Political commitments on climate policies Electricity market design Economic profitability of clean technologies
	Incremental-radical change	Understand which components of the legal system change Consider reasons for legal incrementalism Integrate taxonomies of technological and legal change	Transition theories
Meso	Institutional levels	Balance cooperation and enforcement across levels Focus on opportunities and constraints at each level in each legal system	Multi-level governance
	Infrastructures	Establish a future-proof planning process	Technological and economic factors for infrastructure planning
Micro	Tools	Identify the factors affecting the selection, design and implementation of policy tools in each legal system	Economic theories of policy tools Policy studies on sequencing, feedbacks, and mixes
	Energy justice	Two-step analysis for the legal feasibility of energy justice	Interdisciplinary studies on energy justice

2 Developed and developing countries

Since the first industrial revolution, developed countries have contributed about 57% of historical cumulative emissions. Least developed countries only contributed about 0.4% (IPCC, 2022b: p. 2–26). Since 1990, historical trends were reversed: developed countries stabilized their emissions, and emergent economies increased theirs (IPCC, 2022b: pp. 2–25 f.). By 2050, two-thirds of the world's energy consumption will be in the Global South (Apfel et al., 2021). At the same time, regions where basic services and resources are unavailable will be more vulnerable to climatic hazards (IPCC, 2022a: pp. 1193–1213). Accelerating the low-carbon transition in developing countries is, first of all, an ethical imperative. It is also the only way to ensure that the Paris climate targets are met. The question, though, is which legal pathways are feasible.

Two mistaken assumptions should be avoided: that developing countries should mirror the legal pathways of developed countries and that the same legal pathways are feasible in all developing countries. In light of the sheer variety of institutional contexts in developing countries, both assumptions are untenable. These observations resonate with the studies of comparative environmental politics, suggesting that simply pointing to what developing countries usually have in common (weak institutions and lack of resources) does not help identify decarbonization strategies (Hochstetler, 2021). A contextual analysis is needed, to show how developing countries can manage the trade-offs between environmental protection and development, how their regulatory choices are influenced by international organizations and the international donor community, and what kind of innovative solutions they can put in place by exploiting the peculiar nature of the relationships between the public sector, the private sector, and local communities.

Several chapters of the Handbook offer suggestions on what legal pathways could look like in emerging economies and developing countries. In Africa, the exploitation of the huge renewable potential is hampered by the lack of regulatory frameworks, a dearth of financial resources, and limited political commitment at the country level. Pan-continental and sub-regional initiatives strive to overcome these barriers (Addaney and Kengni, in this volume). They fill gaps in national regulatory frameworks by making it possible to organize power pools that foster cross-border electricity trade and support large shares of renewable energy. This process is also fuelled by the African states, which have already stepped up their climate ambitions and adopted ambitious climate policies at the national level. The African Continental Free Trade Area Agreement is another legal framework that could help African states to implement policies aimed at developing clean technologies without creating barriers to regional integration (with regard to hydrogen, see Chege, in this volume). Analogies to the integration process fostered by the EU's Energy Union strategy are visible. A crucial difference is that the African continental or sub-regional regulatory frameworks are often put in place before national ones. In the low-carbon transition, sequencing is of the essence (see sec. 6). Without suitable regulatory choices at the country level, the effectiveness of the supranational frameworks in promoting the transition could be seriously curtailed.

Brazil provides an example of an emerging economy that has been slow to embrace the transition despite significant renewable potential. Strong political resistance to the phase-out of fossil fuels on the grounds of economic development and energy security persisted under different presidential administrations. Participation in the international climate regime could provide external pressure to ease the domestic shift. The international commitments proved too weak to jumpstart the transition, however (Leal and Miranda, in this volume). Unlike African countries, no support came from cross-border initiatives in the Latin American region (Landa et al., in this volume).

The dilemma for developing countries with abundant fossil-fuel resources is how to avoid being locked into high-carbon energy systems without compromising development goals. In Africa, investments in fossil-fuel projects are still significant (Geuskens and Butijn, 2022; Climate Action Tracker, 2022). They could be further increased due to the EU countries' diversification needs after the start of the Russia-Ukraine war. A leapfrogging strategy, which makes it immediately profitable to invest in renewables and displaces fossil fuels, has clear benefits (Cilliers, 2020: pp. 221 ff.). Two examples of legal factors determining the feasibility of this strategy can be identified.

The first example has to do with the integration of renewable sources in market structures. In China, the partial deregulation of the electricity sector makes such integration more difficult (Wu, in this volume). Adequate remuneration for renewable generators cannot be provided either with wholesale prices, still partially regulated, or with capacity remuneration mechanisms, the design of which depends heavily on transparent and competitive wholesale electricity markets. The goal of controlling wholesale prices can also distort the choice between price-based or quantity-based support schemes for renewables. Moreover, how wholesale prices reflect the carbon prices of the Chinese ETS depends on the selection of dispatching rules.

The second example concerns the technological capabilities required to leapfrog to a low-carbon energy system. Investments in hydrogen-based generation technologies could appeal to emerging economies to reduce their dependence on fossil fuels. But national innovation policies should consider the transition's cost for different sectors, from industry to transport. Moreover, national hydrogen strategies should avoid a new form of technological dependence on foreign patents (Goldthau et al., 2020). This problem was flagged for India (Shankar and Basu, in this volume). The decision to postpone carbon neutrality to 2070 can be read as an attempt to create room for domestic innovation. The problem is that such innovation could come at the expense of more stringent regulation of the environmental impacts of new technologies. South Africa is trying to avoid this problem by linking its hydrogen strategy to incentives for research (Chege, in this volume). However, partnerships between South Africa, other African countries, and developed countries clearly show that international standards will strongly influence the African regulatory frameworks for the hydrogen economy.

Investments in nuclear energy, too, could be made by developing countries both to foster economic and technological development and to reduce dependence on fossil fuels or hydro-electric resources. The comparison between the divergent experiences of Kenya and Zambia (Chisanga, this volume) clearly shows that uncertainty about the financial sustainability of nuclear power plants and their environmental risks cannot be completely dispelled. While Kenya was able to introduce legislation fully complying with international standards and moved on with its nuclear program, Zambia slowed down the implementation of its nuclear strategy. The analogy with the investments in the hydrogen sector is that the technological choices of developing countries are largely dependent on a mixture of domestic and international conditions.

The overall indication is that the meanings of the low-carbon transition differ in the Global North and the Global South because of the relevance granted to competing paradigms. With energy access still precluded to hundreds of millions of people in the foreseeable future (World Bank et al., 2022), and impelling development goals, it can be expected that legal pathways will reflect each country's perception of the legitimate roles of markets and states in managing these priorities. The crucial research question is how to identify the climate policies that better reflect such perceptions and, simultaneously, push forward the transition. From this perspective, aiming for convergence with the Global North should be seen as the wrong approach (Höffken et al., 2021). Rather, comparative research (both of the North-South and of the South-South type) and interdisciplinary dialogue should enrich our understanding of the variety of institutional innovations prompted by the transition.

3 Incremental or radical legal change

The low-carbon transition is a systemic transformation that requires changes to all components of energy systems and the interactions among them. It is a non-linear process open to many possible outcomes. Despite the urgency of the climate change challenge, the transition is likely to happen through a mixture of incremental and radical innovations (Geels and Turnheim, 2022: p. 30). This observation has been made with regard to socio-technical and policy innovations (Geels and Turnheim, 2022: pp. 309–315). When discussing the latter type of innovations, transition theories rely on the concepts and analytical frameworks provided by institutional economics and historical institutionalism (e.g., Andrews-Speed, 2016; Lockwood et al., 2017). Adding a legal perspective on transition-induced change is useful for two reasons. First, social science concepts do not automatically map onto legal ones. Each discipline deems some components of the institutional context more relevant and puts aside other ones. A legal perspective helps extend the analysis to contextual factors which could play an instrumental role in hindering or fostering the transition. Second, transition theories tend to assume that legal change follows from technological innovation or political choices. Of course, these external factors are of crucial importance. But legal change often occurs according to the internal dynamics of each legal system. Without assuming that the domain of law is completely independent from other domains, it should be acknowledged that it is not fully shaped by them, either. A legal perspective helps determine where the line between external and internal influences should be drawn. Moreover, such a line is not identical in all legal systems.

Starting from the premise of a semi-autonomous legal domain, three contributions to transition theories can be envisaged: first, which components of the legal system do change; second, whether legal change is incremental or radical; and third, to what extent patterns of legal change can be connected to patterns of socio-technical change.

Regarding the first issue, we can go back to the distinction between the two domains proposed in the Introduction: legal change can happen either in the broader institutional context or in the tools and institutions directly dealing with climate change. The mutual influences between the two domains suggest that both types of changes should be attended to. Climate litigation is the channel through which legal change becomes more visible. At the same time, it is also the most fragmentary approach to legal change because of the dependence of adjudication on the nature of the legal disputes submitted by the parties. As a matter of first approximation, the interactions between the two domains suggest two types of changes (Fisher et al., 2017): first, changes in legal concepts and interpretative practices that happen in the broader institutional context as a reaction to climate change issues; and second, legal changes brought by the application of climate policies.

The first type of change has to produce a displacement of traditional approaches that identify the boundaries between state intervention and individual freedoms. Two examples discussed in this Handbook can be mentioned. In Latin America, foreign investments in the low-carbon transition require a stable regulatory framework that prevents abrupt changes (Landa et al., in this volume). This constraint cannot become too rigid: governments and regulators must adapt climate policies to changing circumstances. A new equilibrium has to be found between business interests and the collective interest in the effectiveness of climate law. The Modernization of the Energy Charter Treaty, still under discussion in early 2023, aspires to represent a global standard for such a new equilibrium. It will offer new opportunities to states that want to phase out investment protection for fossil fuels. But difficult calls will still be required on the breadth of the right to regulate. In global chains, a trend toward binding obligations to reduce GHG emissions is visible (Mitdikis, in this volume). Here, too, the question is to what extent such obligations usefully complement voluntary private governance initiatives or lead to a reorganization of global chains, which reduces the effectiveness of climate policies. Australia is a striking example of the disjunction between domestic decarbonization policies and high-carbon, export-oriented global chains (Godden, in this volume).

The second type of change has to locate a new body of rules within the existing institutional context. Two options are available: to define a whole set of new concepts specifically tailored to climate policies or try to establish strong links with existing concepts. Consider, for example, the legal nature of emissions rights in ETS: are they equivalent to property rights or administrative entitlements, or are they a third category of legal entitlements (Guo, in this volume, for the Chinese ETS; Ballesteros et al., 2019 and Holligan, 2020 for the EU ETS)? Relying on existing concepts has the advantage of providing certainty of the applicable rules but needs strong assumptions about their fitness for the new carbon markets. Similar observations can be made for the regulation of platforms organizing P2P energy trading (Lavrijssen et al., in this volume). Is general consumer law enough for the protection of platform users? Or are new rules needed for these markets to become viable?

When the alternative between radical and incremental change is considered, the focus is on the depth of the transformations and their speed. The debate is ongoing on the technological and economic feasibility of accelerated low-carbon transitions (see the overview in IPCC, 2022b: pp. 2–56 ff., 13–76 ff.). What about the legal feasibility of accelerated transitions? If we consider macro-level legal changes, so-called 'legal revolutions' are long-term historical processes spanning decades, if not centuries (e.g., Halperin, 2014; Samuel, 2017; Worthington et al., 2020). For many reasons, the law tends to change slowly. Legal reasoning evolves through the stratification of concepts and interpretations, none of which are ever entirely replaced by new ones. A web of connections among legal concepts and institutions supports their daily operation and cannot be easily supplanted.

Furthermore, within each legal system, there often are veto points that institutions or agents interested in changing the status quo cannot overcome. Closer to the field of climate law, we have to acknowledge that the legal change supporting the low-carbon transition affects the diffusion of clean technologies and the workings of energy markets directly. In both cases, we can expect reciprocal feedbacks, with legal interventions fostering change and at the same time reacting to changes in technologies and markets (see, for an example related to renewable energy, Davies and Allen, 2014). It is difficult to believe that transformations involving so many legal and non-legal interactions can take place on short notice (Powers et al., 2017). Complexity is further compounded when significant distributive impacts on different groups have to be considered, an issue discussed in sec. 7. Of course, policymakers sometimes copy solutions from other legal systems to accelerate change. But comparative legal studies alert us to the complexities of legal transplants (for a discussion in the field of climate change see Pozzo, 2021; Pozzo and Jacometti, 2021; as well as references in the Introduction).

Does legal incrementalism dash any hopes for an accelerated low-carbon transition? Not necessarily. What is needed is a clearer understanding of the interplay between legal and non-legal change. If both types of changes can be managed simultaneously, there could be better chances of finding decarbonization pathways tailored to each context. One useful step in this direction could be the development of taxonomies of transformations that link socio-technical reconfigurations to legal changes. For example, Geels and Turnheim (2022: pp. 32 f.) distinguish between changes that affect the components and the architecture of energy systems. The former entail more limited reconfigurations, the latter deeper ones. It is likely that both modular and architectural reconfigurations need specific types of legal change. From a legal pathway perspective, the question becomes which options are available in each legal system to prompt the needed modular or architectural reconfiguration.

4 Multi-level governance

The low-carbon transition should be supported simultaneously by all institutional levels. This ideal condition is rare. Often, multi-level governance systems face huge coordination problems in climate decision-making. Depending on legal traditions, centralized, decentralized, or hybrid arrangements can be implemented (H. Wiseman, in this volume). None of them ensures the effectiveness of climate policies. Still, each legal system has at its disposal solutions that can move forward with the transition. From the chapters in the Handbook, we pick up two examples of top-down approaches and two examples of bottom-up approaches.

In the Indian federal system, the federal legislator could exploit its concurrent powers on electricity to introduce a legal framework for renewable sources (Shankar and Basu, in this volume). The obligations imposed on private companies to buy a minimum share of renewable energy were backed by the Indian Supreme Court, which linked such obligations to the right to life in Article 21 of the Indian Constitution. Still, enforcement mechanisms for such obligations are missing. Therefore, any progress on renewable investments crucially depends on the cooperation between the central and the state levels.

In China, the move from the pilot ETSs at the provincial level to the national ETS was premised on a strong degree of collaboration between the central and the decentralized government structures (Guo, in this volume). The collaboration extended to crucial components of the national ETS, from target setting to emission monitoring. The EU's experiment with a decentralized governance structure of its ETS was a failure and forced it to adopt a more centralized structure (Woerdman et al., 2021). It is unclear whether the Chinese governance structure will fare better. But it looks like an attempt to devise a hybrid solution that keeps development and decarbonization goals together.

Turning to bottom-up approaches, energy communities and urban climate policies are two of the most promising avenues. The comparison between the EU and US legal frameworks supporting the decentralization of energy systems shows a variety of possible approaches with regard to tasks, governance, goals, and criteria for sharing benefits. The common trend toward decentralization in the two legal systems does not mean that energy communities will play the same role. From a multi-level perspective, the crucial factor is the relationship with other public and private players in the energy sector. Broadening the inquiry to energy communities in developing countries confirms that their role is shaped by social relationships, local customs, and the organization of the national energy system (e.g., Holstenkamp, 2019; Sharma, 2020; Ambole et al., 2021; Nuru et al., 2022). With regard to urban climate policies, the chapter by du Plessis and Moyo shows that mitigation and adaptation efforts in African cities depend crucially on a significant number of institutional conditions: framework legislation at the national level, a good degree of autonomy in managing and regulating the activities more directly related to GHG emissions, support from regional and global networks, and the ability to address energy poverty issues.

Climate governance needs both top-down and bottom-up approaches. The risk of uncoordinated action is real, but much less worrisome than the risk of inaction and regulatory gaps. A legal perspective on multi-level governance suggests that the search for the optimal level of intervention should be dismissed in favour of more detailed analyses focused on the opportunities and the constraints available at each level.

5 Infrastructures

Legal pathways of decarbonization have to deal with the twin goals of phasing out high-carbon infrastructures and fostering investments in low-carbon ones. In countries that liberalized the energy sector, more or less advanced versions of network unbundling determine how the costs of dismissing high-carbon infrastructure are shared (J. Wiseman, in this volume) and how strong the incentives to innovate are (Kallies, in this volume). Sometimes the competition and the climate change frames converge in supporting investments that increase network efficiency and reduce emissions. This is usually the case for smart grid technologies. Though, regulatory frameworks must be ready to deal with trade-offs. Integrating increasing shares of renewables means changing network access rules and market designs (Kallies, in this volume; Wu, in this volume). Also, promoting the deployment of new energy carriers like hydrogen and low-carbon fuels means planning for tighter integration of electricity, natural gas, thermal, and transport infrastructures (Chyong et al., 2021; Arent et al., 2021; Ramsebner et al., 2021). No less relevant are the trade-offs related to the reliability and resilience of the grids. With the spread of intermittent renewable sources and decentralized energy resources, reliability takes on new meanings and leads to new obligations. Resilience is an aspect of adaptation policies and could become the guiding principle in infrastructure planning processes (Banet et al., 2022).

The low-carbon transition does not exclusively impact domestic regulatory frameworks. It also enhances the centrality of cross-border regulatory frameworks. One reason for this shift of perspective is the difference between fossil fuels trading and renewables trading. The former is unidirectional and requires connecting a few extraction sites to many consumption markets. The latter is multidirectional and requires connecting many producing sites to a large number of consumption markets. Harmonized legal frameworks across national boundaries and continental-wide areas are a necessary condition for renewables trading, to a much larger extent than is the case for fossil fuels trading. Cross-border trading of hydrogen is likely to require a higher degree of regulatory convergence, due to the integration of many energy systems and markets.

Several chapters in this Handbook show that regulatory frameworks for cross-border energy infrastructures face several hurdles. The first one is that they have to accommodate conflicting goals. In Central Asia, geopolitical factors are a major determinant of infrastructure investments (Chykanayev, in this volume). In North America, oil, gas, and electricity transmission infrastructures face opposition at different institutional levels. Such opposition can be due to environmental concerns or different political priorities. No special continental regime for low-carbon infrastructures is available (Coleman, in this volume; also see Mildenberger and Stokes, 2021). In Africa, the African Union's Programme for Infrastructure Development (PIDA) promotes cross-border energy infrastructures specifically aimed at fostering the deployment of renewable sources. Still, its success depends on the availability of supporting national regulatory frameworks (Addaney and Kengni, in this volume). In the Asia-Pacific region, plans for cross-border connectivity are still at an early stage (Zhang, in this volume).

The EU is at a more advanced stage of creating a pan-continental framework for decarbonized infrastructures. Regulation 2022/869 introduced a mandatory sustainability assessment for Projects of Common Interest, to be carried out with reference to the integration of renewable energy. To support the EU Strategy on Offshore Renewable Energy (EC, 2020), the Regulation introduced integrated development plans within each sea basin. Compliance with guidance on climate proofing is also a requirement for EU-funded projects (EC, 2021). These examples have similar elements to discussions of energy regionalism in the political science literature (Hancock et al., 2021; Johnson and VanDeveer, 2021; Herman and Ariel, 2021): infrastructure connections can be supported by a vast array of formal agreements and informal collaborations. It is simplistic to assume that all regions will converge towards EU-style integration. Not all cases of regional governance lead to the avoidance of conflicts. Nor is regional governance necessarily supportive of low-carbon initiatives. But comparatively assessing the legal dimensions of energy regionalisms provides useful insights into the factors which could ease the transition.

Another hurdle is the uncertainty surrounding the profitability of long-term investments, which depend on the unfolding of the low-carbon transition. For example, which transport infrastructures will play a central role in future mobility systems? Can multistate partnerships foster cross-border investments in new infrastructures (Klass and Cerny, in this volume)? Which digital platforms will attract a critical mass of consumers and prosumers (Lavrijssen et al., in this volume)? And is the digitalization of the energy sector another leapfrogging strategy for developing countries (Nwaiwu, 2021)?

This topic is rife with opportunities for interdisciplinary dialogues. The technological and economic aspects should not be considered in isolation. Infrastructures lock in investments for decades and are one of the main causes of path dependency in energy systems. Administrative procedures allowing consideration of the broadest possible range of interests, including those of future generations, should be the key component of a future-proof infrastructure planning process.

6 Tools

What is the legal feasibility of each policy tool in a specific legal system? And how feasible are policy mixes? There is a rich literature, reviewed by Richards in this Handbook, on taxonomies of climate tools. Unfortunately, much of this literature does not adopt a comparative approach. It does not focus on the components of the institutional context, which ease or hinder the uptake of specific tools and packages. Several chapters in this Handbook start to fill this gap. A few legal factors can be highlighted.

First, the design of policy tools is shaped by competing goals. In India, the preventive controls of environmental impact assessments were reduced to speed up investments in green infrastructures (Shankar and Basu, in this volume). In China, the choice of a variable intensity-based cap instead of an absolute cap in the national ETS is driven by the goal of making room for larger emissions during favourable economic cycles (Guo, in this volume). In Japan, climate change goals cannot be prioritized with respect to security of energy supply (Kurokawa, in this volume). If different goals cannot be addressed with different tools, a lower impact of each tool should be factored in.

Second, enforcement mechanisms are deeply rooted in legal traditions and cannot be overhauled in the short term. The selection of policy tools should be made with the strengths and weaknesses of enforcement mechanisms in mind. For example, in China, the national ETS suffers from weak enforcement of emissions caps because monitoring bodies lack independence from political bodies at the provincial level (Guo, in this volume). In the EU and the US, different ways to coordinate the enforcement of anti-manipulation rules for energy markets and energy-related financial products depend on the allocation of competencies both vertically and horizontally across institutional levels (Hiemstra, in this volume).

Third, there usually is more than one way to pursue the same goal. The point of least resistance to climate policies in each legal system should be sought. Climate litigation in unfavourable political settings is a good example. In Brazil, the unwillingness of the Bolsonaro administration to ratchet up international climate commitments might have prompted a broad reading of climate obligations by the Federal Supreme Court (Lehmen, 2021; Setzer and de Carvalho, 2021; Leal and Miranda, in this volume). In Australia, the lack of a federal framework for climate legislation sparked intense (and sometimes successful) litigation (Benjamin and McCallum, J. Wiseman, Godden, all in this volume). In China, the slow pace of the transition might be connected to tort cases against companies infringing air pollution limits and administrative law cases challenging the application of legislation on environmental impact assessments (Benjamin and McCallum, in this volume).

Fourth, several chapters of the Handbook show how context matters in implementing policy tools. Transition theories argue that the required transformations depend on the right sequence (e.g., Jordan and Moore, 2020; Béland et al., 2022) and the right mix of policy tools (e.g., Kern et al., 2019; Edmondson et al., 2019; Sewerin et al., 2022). Yet, neither is always available everywhere. Quantitative analyses suggest that, even when the number of climate measures increases, they do not necessarily ensure an emission trajectory compatible with the Paris Agreement targets. Furthermore, mixes remain stable over time and do not include all useful options (see, concerning the EU, Schoenefeld et al., 2021; Moore et al., 2021; Jordan and Moore, 2022; beyond the EU borders, see Schmidt and Sewerin, 2019; Nascimento et al., 2022; Schaub et al., 2022). Political factors could play a big role: for example, it has been suggested that electoral systems, interest intermediation, the structure of financial institutions, and the forms of community organization could explain weaker or stronger support for renewable sources (Fernández-i-Marín et al., 2021; Lockwood, 2022). It is plausible that political factors interact with legal factors. The latter could affect the initial design choice, scope, and interactions with other tools. The argument could be made that legal factors are more proximate causes of tool choices than political institutions. Consider the following examples:

1. Japan started to support renewables with Renewable Portfolio Standards, then moved to Feed-In Tariffs and finally to Feed-In Premia. Meanwhile, carbon taxes, carbon prices (at the local level), and the non-fossil-fuel value certificate were enacted (Kurokawa, in this volume).
2. Poland moved from green certificates to auctions, while simultaneously implementing two-way contracts for difference for offshore wind and specific support measures for prosumers and efficient district heating (Swora, in this volume).
3. Mexico relied on long-term power purchase agreements for both renewables and natural gas, while at the same time reducing the role of the wholesale electricity

market and implementing a carbon tax with a limited scope (Anglés-Hernández and Valenzuela, in this volume).

4. Countries of the Asia-Pacific region relied heavily on Feed-In Tariffs, then reduced or discontinued them and introduced auctions with different design features. At the same time, curtailment policies for renewables dampened the effectiveness of support schemes (Zhang, in this volume).

In each of these cases, sequences and mixes of policy tools, as well as the positive or negative feedbacks they generated, can be explained by political factors. However, several legal factors could equally bear on sequencing, mixing, and feedbacks: allocation of competencies within the executive, regulatory powers of energy authorities, state ownership of energy infrastructures, cross-border agreements with regional neighbours, and the availability of public and private organizational forms for decentralized resources. A richer understanding of energy transitions would come from explanations focusing on the interplay between political and legal factors. Depending on institutional contexts, the latter could be less, more, or equally relevant than political factors. Disentangling the different influences could go a long way toward improving long-term energy planning.

7 Energy justice

Energy justice should be the dominant paradigm of the low-carbon society. So far, no energy system has managed to jettison old and new injustices. Bhullar (in this volume) reviews the plurality of meanings the concept of energy justice takes in the academic debate and its (partial) translation into climate policies. On a positive note, the plurality of meanings increases the chances that policymakers pay attention to energy justice dimensions. On a more negative note, the risk cannot be excluded, that only the dimensions requiring limited changes are picked up. Accelerated low-carbon transitions could marginalize some vulnerable groups (Skjølsvold and Coenen, 2021; Newell et al., 2022). The paradox of energy justice is that it could be perceived as too radical and face strong resistance. An opposite narrative is equally plausible: current inequalities in energy systems represent the largest barriers to the transition. Hence, the radicality of energy justice could be the best catalyser for an accelerated transition.

Amidst the variety of context-dependent and geography-bound definitions of energy justice, significant advancements could be possible by assessing feasibility conditions. It has been observed that such assessment should be integrated into decarbonization scenarios and draw on deliberative processes to identify desirable futures (Lenzi and Kowarsch, 2021). Progress has been made on identifying metrics that allow for consideration of different types of inequalities and distributive impacts (Emmerling and Tavoni, 2021; Jafino et al., 2021). Still lacking is the acknowledgement of alternative worldviews, for example, those held by Indigenous cultures (McGregor et al., 2020). Additionally, identifying inequalities leads to questions about the feasibility of policies aimed at redressing them. For example, Lamb et al. (2020) argue that low-carbon goals are compatible with more equitable, cohesive, and fairer societies and cultures. The necessary condition is well-functioning institutions supporting policies that directly address equity and procedural justice. Rephrased according to the approach we are using in this Handbook, the question becomes: how can the legal feasibility of energy justice be assessed?

In line with our definition of legal pathways, energy justice concepts should be assessed both from the point of view of the broader institutional context and of climate institutions and tools. The theoretical frameworks reviewed by Bhullar (in this volume) should be seen as useful starting points, but none of them should be superimposed on a specific legal system. A two-step analysis for the legal feasibility of energy justice can be proposed: the first step should identify energy justice concepts compatible with national or local cultures; the second step should be devoted to a detailed evaluation of the institutions and legal rules promoting or hindering the selected meaning of energy justice. This two-step analysis would transform the discussion of energy justice into one necessary dimension of the broader assessment of legal feasibility (for a similar proposal, but about the concept of energy policy failure, see Sokolowski and Heffron, 2022). One significant advantage would be clarifying the institutional conditions that allow moving from incremental to radical change. To pick up one example among many, the two-step analysis could be applied to energy communities (Outka and Savaresi, in this volume). In the first step, different concepts of energy justice compatible with the institutional contexts of developed and developing countries should be identified. In the second step, the institutional conditions for implementing energy justice through activities of energy communities should be evaluated. If in an early phase only non-binding guidance could be provided, for example, with regard to the inclusion of vulnerable consumers in energy communities, at a later stage, more radical proposals could be made, and the possibility for energy communities to become the vehicles for universal basic services (Gough, 2019; Vogel et al., 2021; Button and Coate, 2021) should be explored.

References

Ambole, A., Koranteng, K., Njoroge, P. and Luhangala, D.L., 2021. A review of energy communities in Sub-Saharan Africa as a transition pathway to energy democracy. *Sustainability*, 13, 2128.

Andrews-Speed, P., 2016. Applying institutional theory to the low-carbon energy transition. *Energy Research & Social Science*, 13, pp. 216–225.

Arent, D.J., Barrows, C., Davis, S. et al., 2021. Integration of energy systems. *MRS Bulletin*, 46, pp. 1139–1152.

Ballesteros, M., Wemaere, M., Reins, L. et al., 2019. *Legal nature of EU ETS allowances*. Luxembourg: Publications Office of the European Union.

Banet, C., Mostert, H., Paddock, L. et al., eds., 2022. *Resilience in energy, infrastructure and natural resources law*. Oxford: Oxford University Press.

Béland, D., Campbell, A.L. and Wever, R.K., 2022. *Policy feedback: how policies shape politics*. Cambridge: Cambridge University Press.

Button, D. and Coote, A., 2021. *A social guarantee: the case for universal services*. New Economics Foundation, September.

Chyong, C.K., Pollitt, M., Reiner, D. et al., 2021. *Electricity and gas coupling in a decarbonised economy*. Brussels: Centre on Regulation in Europe.

Cilliers, J., 2021. *The future of Africa: challenges and opportunities*. Cham: Palgrave Macmillan.

Climate Action Tracker, 2022. *Natural gas in Africa: why fossil fuels cannot sustainably meet the continent's growing energy demand*.

Davies, L.L. and Allen, K., 2014. Feed-in tariffs in turmoil. *West Virginia Law Review*, 116, pp. 937–1005.

Edmondson, D.L., Kern, F. and Rogge, K.S., 2019. The co-evolution of policy mixes and socio-technical systems: towards a conceptual framework of policy mix feedback in sustainability transitions. *Research Policy*, 48, 103555.

Emmerling, J. and Tavoni, M., 2021. Representing inequalities in integrated assessment modelling of climate change. *One Earth*, 4(2), pp. 177–180.

European Commission, 2020. *An EU strategy to harness the potential of offshore renewable energy for a climate neutral future*, COM(2020)741.

European Commission, 2021. *Technical guidance on the climate proofing of infrastructure in the period 2021–2027*, 2021/C 373/01.

Fernández-i-Marín, X., Knill, C. and Steinebach, Y., 2021. Studying policy design quality in comparative perspective. *American Political Science Review*, 115(3), pp. 931–947.

Fisher, E., Scotford, E. and Barritt, E., 2017. The legally disruptive nature of climate change. *Modern Law Review*, 80(2), pp. 173–201.

Geels, F.W. and Turnheim, B., 2022. *The great reconfiguration: a socio-technical analysis of low-carbon transitions in UK electricity, heat and mobility systems*. Cambridge: Cambridge University Press.

Geuskens, I. and Butijn, H., 2022. *Locked out of a just transition. Fossil fuel financing in Africa*. BankTrack, Milieudefensie and Oil Change International.

Goldthau, A., Eicke, L. and Weko, S., 2020. The global energy transition and the Global South. In: M. Hafner and S. Tagliapietra, eds., 2020. *The geopolitics of the energy transition*. Cham: Springer, pp. 319–339.

Gough, I., 2019. Universal basic services: a theoretical and moral framework. *The Political Quarterly*, 90(3), pp. 534–542.

Halpérin, J.-L., 2014. *Five legal revolutions since the 17th century: an analysis of a global legal history*. Cham: Springer.

Hancock, K.J., Palestini, S. and Szulecki, K., 2021. The politics of energy regionalism. In: K.J. Hancock and J.E. Allison, eds., 2021. *The Oxford handbook of energy politics*. Oxford: Oxford University Press, pp. 173–195.

Herman, L. and Ariel, J., 2021. Comparative energy regionalism: North American and the European Energy Community, *Review of Policy Research*, Early View 12 March.

Hochstetler, K., 2021. Environment and development: crossing the divide between Global South and Global North. In: J. Sowers, S.D. VanDeveer and E. Weinthal, eds., 2021. *The Oxford handbook of comparative environmental politics*. Oxford: Oxford University Press.

Höffken, J., Pols, A. and Kumar, A., 2021. Energy transitions in the global South: towards just urgency and urgent justice. In: A. Kumar, J. Höffken and A. Pols, eds., 2021. *Dilemmas of energy transitions in the global South: balancing urgency and justice* pp. 154–162.

Höhne, N., den Elzen, M., Rogelj, J. et al., 2020. Emissions: world has four times the work or one-third of the time. *Nature*, 579, pp. 25–28.

Holligan, B., 2020. Commodity or propriety? Unauthorized transfer of intangible entitlements in the EU emissions trading system. *Modern Law Review*, 83(5), pp. 979–1007.

Holstenkamp, L., 2019. What do we know about cooperative sustainable electrification in the Global South? A synthesis of the literature and refined social-ecological systems framework. *Renewable and Sustainable Energy Reviews*, 109, pp. 307–320.

IPCC, 2022a. *Climate change 2022: Impacts, adaptation and vulnerability. Contribution of Working Group II to the Sixth Assessment Report.*

IPCC, 2022b. *Climate change 2022: Mitigation of climate change. Contribution of Working Group III to the Sixth Assessment Report.*

Jafino, B.A., Kwakkel, J.H. and Taebi, B., 2021. Enabling assessment of distributive justice through models for climate change planning: a review of recent advances and a research agenda. *WIREs Climate Change*, 12, e721.

Johnson, C. and VanDeveer, S.D., 2021. Energy regionalisms in theory and practice. *Review of Policy Research*, Early View 21 March.

Jordan, A.J. and Moore, B., 2020. *Durable by design? Policy feedback in a changing climate*. Cambridge: Cambridge University Press.

Jordan, A.J. and Moore, B., 2022. The durability-flexibility dialectic: the evolution of decarbonization policies in the European Union. *Journal of European Public Policy*, online 6 March.

Kern, F., Rogge, K.S. and Howlett, M., 2019. Policy mixes for sustainability transitions: new approaches and insights through bridging innovation and policy studies. *Research Policy*, 48, 103832.

Lamb, W.F., Antal, M., Bohnenberger, K. et al., 2020. What are the social outcomes of climate policies? A systematic map and review of the ex-post literature. *Environmental Research Letters*, 15, 113006.

Lamb, W.F., Grubb, M., Diluiso, F. and Minx, J.C., 2022. Countries with sustained greenhouse gas emissions reductions: an analysis of trends and progress by sector. *Climate Policy*, 22(1), pp. 1–17.

Lehmen, A., 2021. Advancing strategic climate litigation in Brazil. *German Law Journal*, 22, pp. 1471–1483.

Lenzi, D. and Kowarsch, M., 2021. Integrating justice in climate policy assessments: towards a deliberative transformation of feasibility. In: S. Kenehan and C. Katz, eds., 2021. *Principles of Justice and real-world Climate Politics*. Lanham, MD: Rowman & Littlefield, pp. 15–34.

Lockwood, M., 2022. Policy feedback and institutional context in energy transitions. *Policy Sciences*, 55, pp. 487–507.

Lockwood, M., Kuzemko, C., Mitchell, C. and Hoggett, R., 2017. Historical institutionalism and the politics of sustainable energy transitions: a research agenda. *Environment and Planning C: Politics and Space*, 35(2), pp. 312–333.

McGregor, D., Whitaker, S. and Sritharan, M., 2020. Indigenous environmental justice and sustainability. *Current Opinion in Environmental Sustainability*, 43, pp. 35–40.

Mildenberger, M., and Stokes, L.C., 2021. The energy politics of North America. In: K.J. Hancock and J.E. Allison, eds., 2021. *The Oxford handbook of energy politics.* Oxford: Oxford University Press, pp. 407–428.

Minx, J.C., Lamb, W.F., Andrew, R.M. et al., 2021. A comprehensive and synthetic dataset for global, regional, and national greenhouse gas emissions by sector 1970–2018 with an extension to 2019. *Earth System Science Data*, 13, pp. 5213–5252.

Moore, B., Benson, D., Jordan, A. et al., 2021. Governing with multiple policy Instruments? In: A. Jordan and V. Gravey, eds., 2021. *Environmental policy in the EU: actors, institutions and processes.* 4th ed. London and New York, NY: Routledge, pp. 299–316.

Moore, B., Verfuerth, C. and Minas, A.M. et al., 2021. Transformations for climate change mitigation: a systematic review of terminology, concepts, and characteristics. *WIREs Climate Change*, 12, e738.

Nascimento, L., Kuramochi, T., Iacobuta, G. et al., 2022. Twenty years of climate policy: G20 coverage and gaps. *Climate Policy*, 22(2), pp. 158–174.

Newell, P.J., Geels, F.W. and Sovacool, B.K., 2022. Navigating tensions between rapid and just low-carbon transitions. *Environmental Research Letters*, 17, 041006.

Nuru, J.T., Rhoades, J.L. and Sovacool, B.K., 2022. Virtue or vice? Solar micro-grids and the dualistic nature of low-carbon energy transitions in rural Ghana. *Energy Research & Social Science*, 83, 102352.

Nwaiwu, F., 2021. Digitalisation and sustainable energy transitions in Africa: assessing the impact of policy and regulatory environments on the energy sector in Nigeria and South Africa. *Energy, Sustainability and Society*, 11(48).

Pozzo, B., 2021. Climate change litigation in a comparative law perspective. In: F. Sindico and M.M. Mbengue, eds., 2021. *Comparative climate change litigation: beyond the usual suspects*. Cham: Springer, pp. 593–619.

Pozzo, B. and Jacometti, V., eds., 2021. *Environmental loss and damage in a comparative law perspective*. Cambridge et al.: Intersentia.

Powers, M., Jewell, E. and Sliger, J., 2017. Quick fixes or real remedies: the benefits and limitations of climate and energy fast policy. *San Diego Journal of Climate & Energy Law*, 8, pp. 67–127.

Ramseber, J., Haas, R., Ajanovic, A. and Wietschel, M., 2021. The sector coupling concept: a critical review. *WIREs Energy and Environment*, 10, e396.

Roelfsema, M., van Soest, H.L., Harmsen, M. et al., 2020. Taking stock of national climate policies to evaluate implementation of the Paris Agreement. *Nature Communications*, 11, 2096.

Samuel, G., 2017. Have there been scientific revolutions in law? *Journal of Comparative Law*, 11(2), pp. 186–213.

Schaub, S., Tosun, J., Jordan, A. and Enguer, J., 2022. Climate policy ambition: exploring a policy density perspective. *Politics and Governance*, 10(3), pp. 226-238.

Schmidt, T.S. and Sewerin, S., 2019. Measuring the temporal dynamics of policy mixes – An empirical analysis of renewable energy policy mixes' balance and design features in nine countries. *Research Policy*, 48, 103557.

Schoenefeld, J.J., Schulze, K., Hildén, M. and Jordan, A.J., 2021. The challenging paths to net-zero emissions: insights from the monitoring of national policy mixes. *The International Spectator*, 56(3), pp. 24–40.

Setzer, J. and de Carvalho, D.W., 2021. Climate litigation to protect the Brazilian Amazon: establishing a constitutional right to a stable climate. *Review of European, Comparative & International Environmental Law*, 30, pp. 197–206.

Sewerin, S., Cashore, B. and Howlett, M., 2022. New pathways to paradigm change in public policy: combining insights from policy design, mix and feedback. *Policy and Politics*, Early View 23 June.

Sharma, A., 2020. 'We do not want fake energy': the social shaping of a solar micro-grid in rural India. *Science, Technology and Society*, 25(2), pp. 308–324.

Skjølsvold, T.M. and Coenen, L., 2021. Are rapid and inclusive energy and climate transitions oxymorons? Towards principles of responsible acceleration. *Energy Research & Social Science*, 79, 102164.

Sokolowski, M.M. and Heffron, R.J., 2022. Defining and conceptualising energy policy failure: the when, where, why and how. *Energy Policy*, 161, 112745.

Stoddard, I., Anderson, K., Capstick, S. et al., 2021. Three decades of climate mitigation: why haven't we bent the global emissions curve? *Annual Review of Environment and Resources*, 46, pp. 653–689.

Vogel, J., Steinberger, J.K., O'Neill, D.W. et al., 2021. Socio-economic conditions for satisfying human needs at low energy use: an international analysis of social provisioning. *Global Environmental Change*, 69, 102287.

Woerdman, E., Roggenkamp, M.M. and Holwerda, M., 2021. EU emissions trading system. In: E. Woerdman, M.M. Roggenkamp and M. Holwerda. *Essential EU climate law*. 2nd ed. Cheltenham: Elgar Publishing, pp. 44–73.

World Bank, IEA, IRENA, United Nations and World Health Organization, 2022. *The energy progress report 2022*. Washington, DC: The World Bank.

Worthington, S., Robertson, A. and Virgo, G., eds., 2020. *Revolution and evolution in private law*. Oxford and Portland, OR: Hart Publishing.

Index

https://doi.org/10.1515/9783110752403-043

www.ingramcontent.com/pod-product-compliance
Lightning Source LLC
Chambersburg PA
CBHW080930240926
51849CB00003BA/426
* 9 7 8 3 1 1 0 7 5 2 3 3 5 *